ANNUAL REVIEW OF ANTHROPOLOGY

ANNUAL REVIEW OF ANTHROPOLOGY

BERNARD J. SIEGEL, *Editor*
Stanford University

ALAN R. BEALS, *Associate Editor*
University of California, Riverside

STEPHEN A. TYLER, *Associate Editor*
Rice University

VOLUME 8

1979

ANNUAL REVIEWS INC.   4139 EL CAMINO WAY   PALO ALTO, CALIFORNIA 94306

ANNUAL REVIEWS INC.
Palo Alto, California, USA

International Standard Serial Number: 0084-6570
International Standard Book Number: 0-8243-1908-7
Library of Congress Catalog Card Number: 72-82136

Annual Reviews Inc. and the Editors of its publications assume no responsibility for the statements expressed by the contributors to this Review.

PRINTED AND BOUND IN THE UNITED STATES OF AMERICA

PREFACE

In discussing Volume 6 (1977) of our series for the *American Anthropologist,* one reviewer made two specific suggestions. One was that a preface to each volume explain the principles which served as the basis for the selection of chapters and the subject matter to be covered. The other was that authors be requested to introduce their chapters with a brief section that would inform nonspecialist readers, in clearly written nontechnical language, about the substance of the topic under review. To take the latter suggestion first, we did initiate the policy of requesting chapter introductions about two years ago. Some authors have succeeded better than others, but we shall continue to try to improve the overall performance.

The principles of chapter selection were laid out in prefaces to previous volumes, commencing with the first in this series in 1972. We especially draw attention to Volumes 1, 2, 3, and 5. To recapitulate, we seek first to obtain critical reviews of published research on those topics in all branches of anthropology that have received special attention within a relatively short span of years prior to the annual meeting of the Editorial Committee. From time to time we also discuss projections over a three- to five-year period and make modifications as necessary. In view of increasing specialization in the discipline, coverage will usually consist of certain dimensions of a field such as social organization, or even of a subfield such as political or economic anthropology, culture change, or human evolution. Depending on the advice of contributors and others, the Editorial Committee members also make decisions about the frequency with which a topic should be reviewed. By scheduling subjects for review at varying intervals, we seek over the years to keep abreast of development in the discipline as a whole.

When special circumstances suggest it, we try to include chapters on problems that we anticipate will be of interest to our readers. The chapter dealing with the Sahel and the implications of the recent drought there (Volume 6) is a case in point. We are also concerned with providing some kind of balance between specialized reviews and essays of more general theoretical interest. We have not succeeded in doing this to our satisfaction, but we will continue to attend to the problem.

Conventional geographic areas are reviewed as research contributes significant new understandings about them. An effort is made to provide, on a systematic basis, current "state of the art" evaluation of work in given regions within as many of the subfields of the discipline as possible, either in a single volume or in successive ones. This year, for example, we have been very fortunate to obtain reviews in all major areas (including physical anthropology, prehistory, linguistics, and ethnology) of current research among the Australian Aborigines. In the next volume, we shall devote several chapters in a similar fashion to the American sub-Arctic.

Additionally, we have invited and received recommendations from readers of topics they consider to merit review. A number of these have been anticipated by the Committee; some have not. We are most grateful for these suggestions as a means of broadening the bases provided by colleagues consulted in the critical task of topic selection. On a number of occasions we have not only received advice but also volunteered manuscripts. Some of these have been accepted for publication, usually with revision, but we cannot guarantee to do so. To be considered for publication, papers must (*a*) conform to the composition of planned volumes, which ultimately is the responsibility of the Editorial Committee, and (*b*) be consistent with the aim of the enterprise. Several papers that have been submitted were more suitable for publication in other scientific journals because of their more narrow and specialized concerns.

A tight publishing schedule and the unpredictability of receipt of manuscripts by the production editor make it virtually impossible to arrange chapters in the most logical sequence—linguistic chapters in one section, prehistory chapters in another, area chapters consecutively, and so forth. For the convenience of the reader, however, we do provide at the end of each volume cumulative indexes of contributing authors and chapter titles arranged by more conventional headings and subheadings.

The EDITORS

Annual Review of Anthropology
Volume 8, 1979

CONTENTS

CONTENTS (*continued*)

ARTICLES IN OTHER *ANNUAL REVIEWS* OF INTEREST
TO ANTHROPOLOGISTS

From the *Annual Review of Psychology,* Volume 30 (1979):

What's Cultural About Cross-Cultural Cognitive Psychology?
Laboratory of Comparative Human Cognition

Organizational Behavior, Terence R. Mitchell

Social and Cultural Influences on Psychopathology, John S. Strauss

From the *Annual Review of Sociology,* Volume 5 (1979):

Revitalizing the Culture Concept, Richard A. Peterson

Reality Construction in Interaction, Arthur W. Frank, III

Sociology of Later Life, George L. Maddox

Black Identity and Self-Esteem, Judith R. Porter and Robert E.
Washington

Ascribed and Achieved Bases of Stratification, Anne Foner

Sociology of Mental Health and Illness, Michael S. Goldstein

Sociology of Contemporary Religious Movements, Thomas Robbins
and Dick Anthony

Methods for Temporal Analysis, Michael T. Hannan and Nancy
Brandon Tuma

Sociology of South Africa, A. Paul Hare and Michael Savage

From the *Annual Review of Earth and Planetary Sciences,* Volume 7
(1979):

Influences of Mankind on Climate, William W. Kellogg

From the *Annual Review of Ecology and Systematics,* Volume 10
(1979):

Origins of Some Cultivated Plants of the New World, Charles B.
Heiser, Jr.

Annual Reviews are published in the following sciences: Anthropology, Astronomy and Astrophysics, Biochemistry, Biophysics and Bioengineering, Earth and Planetary Sciences, Ecology and Systematics, Energy, Entomology, Fluid Mechanics, Genetics, Materials Science, Medicine, Microbiology, Neuroscience, Nuclear and Particle Science, Pharmacology and Toxicology, Physical Chemistry, Physiology, Phytopathology, Plant Physiology, Psychology, and Sociology. The *Annual Review of Public Health* will begin publication in 1980. In addition, four special volumes have been published by Annual Reviews Inc.: *History of Entomology* (1973), *The Excitement and Fascination of Science* (1965), *The Excitement and Fascination of Science, Volume Two* (1978), and *Annual Reviews Reprints: Cell Membranes, 1975–1977* (published 1978). For the convenience of readers, a detachable order form/envelope is bound into the back of this volume.

Photograph by B. Gaye

Grahame Clark

Ann. Rev. Anthropol. 1979. 8:1–20

ARCHAEOLOGY AND HUMAN DIVERSITY

♦9624

Grahame Clark

Emeritus Professor of Archaeology, Cambridge University, The Master's Lodge, Peterhouse, Cambridge CB2 1QY, England

An invitation to contribute an essay to the *Annual Review of Anthropology* is flattering to the self-esteem of anyone engaged in the profession of Anthropology. Nevertheless, I intend to resist the tempation to reminisce or recapitulate. Instead, I intend to step out from my narrow corner and examine what experience of prehistoric archaeology leads me to think about the way we have all been heading since the Industrial Revolution. In particular, I would draw attention to the nature of the threats posed to some of the attributes which distinguish the archaeological from the merely palaeontological record, above all those epitomized in the cultural diversity of man. I would suggest that danger threatens not merely from the homogenizing pressures of natural science and mass production, but also and perhaps even more from an ideology that seeks to justify the destruction not merely of our heritage but of our very humanity in the name of economics and an ostensibly liberal political philosophy.

The esteem which archaeology has always enjoyed, particularly in the Old World, has derived in the main from its ability to dignify and validate the status quo by investing it with the sanction of antiquity, at the same time as providing the visual images needed to attract and sustain the adherence of the common man. The patronage traditionally accorded to archaeology by heads of state related not merely to the material symbols of their own sovereignty, but even more significantly to establishing, validating, and displaying the identity of peoples and their attachment to their native lands. Archaeology has been harnessed equally to ideologies distinct from, and in the long run inconsistent with, the maintenance of national identity. Much

1

0084-6570/79/1015-0001$01.00

of the impetus behind the rapid development of archaeology during the nineteenth century came from the objective support it appeared to give to the idea of progress. Conversely, the dominance of this idea itself helped to determine the preoccupation of archaeologists with establishing an overall sequence of development from rude beginnings to the complexity and sophistication of modern industry, as first comprehensively displayed in the Great Exhibition of 1851. The idea of progress which archaeology appeared to validate not merely obscured or compensated for some of the less pleasing aspects of industrial society, but it also made possible and in a sense inevitable the conscription of nonindustrialized peoples both in Europe and overseas. Archaeology has been no less esteemed by protagonists of another by-product of the Industrial Revolution. It has been accorded favored treatment and systematically cultivated by the Institutes of the History of Material Culture maintained by the several academies of the USSR and its satellites in the simple faith that excavation, by recovering the material products of former states of society, automatically validates the central doctrine of Marxism.

According to the English summary of *Historical Relics Unearthed in New China* (Peking, 1972):

> The remarkable achievements in the excavation of historical relics since the founding of New China have been due mainly to the emphasis the Party and government have laid on this work. At the same time, the active support and participation in the work by the masses of workers, peasants and soldiers has been very important. The broad masses of people fully understand that these priceless historical relics represent in essence the ancient working people's wisdom, their sweat and blood. They recognise these as the best teaching material in knowing their own history and creative power, *as well as in studying dialectical and historical materialism* (my italics).

In a sense this expectation is self-fulfilling. At the very least, the muteness of archaeological evidence ensures that it is hardly in a position to be contradicted.

It follows from the privileged position of their subject that archaeologists have tended to conform to the canons of the societies in which they operate. Protest in anthropology on such topics as racism or imperialism has issued exclusively from physical and social anthropologists. One of the main purposes of this essay is to suggest that archaeologists may also have something to say, not indeed on overtly political problems, but on matters of arguably greater importance bearing on the very quality of human life. Archaeologists base their claim to speak with professional authority on such key issues primarily on the unique perspective opened up by their subject. Archaeology not only ranges over the whole earth but spans the entire period of man's existence. The artefacts that provide its basic documents form a continuous network. They encompass and indeed provide the most reliable diagnostic evidence for the earliest manifestations of human culture, and they document progressive advances in man's ability to exploit and shape his environment in accordance with his desires up to and including the phase of literacy during which he has become increasingly aware of himself and his context in time and space. The mere fact that archaeology spans the gap between biology and recorded history, between primate behavior and that of civilized man, helps to account for its ambiguous position in the hierarchy of knowledge. In the final resort, archaeology—and prehistoric archaeology in particular—is concerned with nothing less than the identity of man. The converse is also true. The way an archaeologist approaches his data, the view he takes of his subject in the hierarchy of knowledge, depends ultimately on the view he takes of man.

From one point of view, archaeology can be held not merely to document and validate the materialist interpretation of history, but to extend the range of this over the entire prehistory of man (4). It is true enough that, barring local vicissitudes, the archaeological record reveals a progressive growth in the complexity of material culture, that is, in the apparatus by which men supplement their limbs in manipulating and shaping their environment, from the most primitive stone industries to the most advanced products of modern science-based technology. To anyone satisfied to regard man as a mere animal, as a biological species that fulfills its highest destiny by utilizing its environment with ever greater efficiency in competition with other species, the archaeological record and the future of mankind can be contemplated with an equal measure of equanimity. It is only if he prefers to concern himself with the quality of life that an archaeologist may feel impelled to question the wisdom of succumbing unreservedly to the ideology and way of life envisaged by modern industrial society.

The position taken in this essay is humanist only in the sense that it accepts that the unique interest of man resides in the degree to which he diverges from the other primates and the rest of the animal world. Artefacts, as animal behaviorists are never tired of reminding us, are not entirely unique to man. Nor is man the only species whose behavior is influenced by cultural patterns acquired by belonging to social groupings constituted by sharing common histories, rather than being transmitted by genetic inheritance. The uniqueness of man resides in the degree to which his behavior is conditioned by culture and in particular in the way his artefacts have until quite recently displayed an ever greater increase in diversity as well as mere complexity. From this point of view the main interest of prehistory is the scope it offers for tracing the process of humanization. The artefacts which provide the basic archaeological record embody and exemplify the very attributes that enable us to recognize men as beings distinct from apes or monkeys.

There is no intention, on the other hand, of falling into the basic fallacy of liberal humanism and forgetting the animal nature of man. The zoological classification of modern man as *Homo sapiens sapiens* expresses more an aspiration than a commonly accomplished fact. When Teilhard de Chardin (8) spoke of the noosphere he merely hypothesized a new dimension that man is uniquely capable of inhabiting, surely not one that men automatically inherit by the mere fact of belonging to this species. From a palaeontological point of view, distinctions between fossils of *Australopithecus* and *Homo* and again between successive stages in the evolution of *Homo* are sufficiently blurred to occasion serious differences of view on matters of classification and nomenclature (12). The fact that the fossils in effect form continuous series should be enough to remind us that men, even of the most advanced culture, remain animals and inherit genes that issue from far up the stream of life. Without strong evidence to the contrary, it can hardly be supposed that the basic appetites of men are any more widely separated from those of his primate forebears than is his bodily structure. On the contrary, we must accept the fact that the basic drives and appetites of men are likely to resemble those of their closest relatives and are not likely to differ widely from those activating even lowlier organisms. It is at this level and only at this level that the findings of animal behaviorists are directly relevant to the study of man.

The Hebrews of old were so appalled by what they saw as the wickedness of man that they could only suppose him to have fallen from a former state of grace. Darwin and his followers have shown that the evidence suggests a more economical explanation. The hypothesis of biological evolution ought to have prepared us for the almost unimaginable horrors perpetrated by the Nazis or the masters of the Kremlin during the second quarter of the twentieth century, not to mention the atrocities still being practiced in and by societies equipped with advanced technologies. Pain or at least surprise can only stem from ignoring the continuing role of our animal natures. Paradoxically, the converse also applies. If we sin, it is not because we are still animals, but because we are men with the faculty of self-awareness. As our own times so grimly emphasize, the mere elaboration of the cultural apparatus by no means ensures that human values prevail in our affairs. On the contrary, it may even amplify the scope and intensify the destructiveness of our animal appetites. The idea of automatic progress at any other than a material level is surely one of the silliest as well as among the most pernicious illusions of our time.

The case for culture is not that it can make us better unless indirectly by making us more acutely aware of the beastliness, in its most literal sense, of our uncontrolled natural appetites. It is rather that it is capable of making life fuller, richer, and more human in the sense of diverging increasingly from the primate prototype. Because archaeology depends for its main source on the material embodiments of cultures in the form of artefacts, it ought to be capable of assessing rather precisely the degree to which they embody human values. In this sense archaeology allows objective assessments to be made about whether at any particular juncture conditions are favorable or unfavorable to the further enrichment of human life in the sense of making it more or less possible to enjoy experiences accessible to men alone, whether in a word they enhance or impair the quality of life.

Archaeology shows very plainly that we have achieved our humanity only to the extent that we have constrained our animal natures by means of artificial conventions acquired in the course of history and incorporated in cultural traditions. The most palpable index of progression from mere animality is provided not merely by the increasing complexity but still more by the cultural diversity of the artefacts which constitute the archaeological record of human history down to quite modern times. If a main part of this essay is given to an examination of the process of cultural enrichment, this should not be taken to endorse the idea of progress as this has commonly been understood, still less the complacent doctrines of liberal humanism. On the contrary, it is offered as a reminder of the heritage that mankind stands in imminent danger of losing in the name of science and social justice. From this standpoint archaeology by no means stops short at validating contemporary trends and goals. Instead it poses questions more radical than those commonly asked by political science or sociology because they are framed in an ampler perspective.

The most palpable and also the most pervasive attribute of man featured in the archaeological record is his capacity to make artefacts. These artefacts owe part of their importance to the mere fact that certain of them, notably those made of stone, constitute a continuous network extending over the last two million years. Moreover, artefacts and the technology that informs them illuminate not only the way man has adapted to and manipulated his environment but also his ideology and social life. They preserve an unrivaled record of the way human culture has increased in complexity and diversity.

It is worthy of note that the earliest material equipment, that of *Homo erectus,* was not merely elementary and uniform but also remarkably static. The first significant change came in the Middle Pleistocene with the addition of bifacially flaked hand axes (mode 2) to the earlier repertoire of elementary flake and core tools (mode 1). These hand axes were so uniform in style over their entire territory that, short of recognizing local materials, an archaeologist might have difficulty in deciding whether individual specimens came from England, the Cape, or Madras. As Desmond Clark, our leading authority on this phase of prehistory, has so well expressed it:

One of the most striking things ... about the broad cultural pattern of the Middle Pleistocene is its general "sameness" within the limits imposed by the stone industries ... Handaxes from Europe, South Africa, or peninsular India are all basically similar tools, and this is also true for the rest of the heavy duty and the light duty elements (7, p. 45).

Yet the appearance of these hand axes introduced for the first time an element of industrial diversity, since they never reached as far as East Asia. The inhabitants of Chou-kou-tien near Pekin, while capable hunters and well accustomed to the use of fire, continued to shape their stone tools in an earlier mode.

The first substantial signs of cultural dynamism and diversity appeared in conjunction with the earliest large-brained men of *Homo sapiens* type. Although the stone industries of Neanderthal man and his cousins north and south of the Sahara shared the same prepared core technique (mode 3), they displayed a wide range of regional differentiation and a more perceptible rate of change. To some extent this reflects a closer adaptation to ecological circumstances than had existed when generalized equipment was used over the total range of environments exploited by man. The grasslands and savannah of sub-Saharan Africa continued to support men equipped with Acheulian-type stone industries, but the colonization of forest zones in that territory elicited the adaptations displayed in the Sangoan and ultimately Lupemban traditions. Similarly, when in northern Eurasia Neanderthal man colonized periglacial territories as far north as the Lower Pechora basin close to the Arctic zone, ecological adaptation once again promoted distinctive changes in the industrial apparatus and so furthered cultural diversity.

The increase in cultural responsiveness evinced by the first sapient men was significant more for what it presaged than for what it achieved. The acceleration in cultural dynamism that found its ultimate expression in the rich diversity of the great historic civilizations of mankind was accomplished after all by the men of modern type who emerged as *Homo sapiens sapiens* only 40,000 years or so ago. The complexity, diversity, and sheer richness of cultural patterns were the achievement and peculiar glory of our own species.[1] The artefacts that archaeologists are privileged to study, and above all those least subject to the constraints of the physical world, such as works of art, insignia of social hierarchy, and symbols of religious cult and observance, are very embodiments and measures of our humanity.

There was scope for diversity even at the basic levels of subsistence and technology. The archaeological record shows an overall trend from a gener-

[1]That is why I dedicated the illustrated third edition of *World Prehistory* to "the diversity of men" (6).

alized to a more specialized and therefore more diverse quest for food. This can be discerned at the level of relatively advanced catching and foraging economies, as well as more notably in those based on different forms of farming. A large measure of diversity can be observed in the game and the hunting and catching gear used by the Upper Palaeolithic and Mesolithic communities of Eurasia and neighboring parts of north Africa and, again, by the Paleo-Indian and Archaic inhabitants of different parts of the Americas. The adoption during the last 10,000 years of sedentary economies based on the cultivation of crops and the keeping of livestock lent a further strong impetus to the process of diversification. The mere fact of adopting settled life intensified adjustments to local conditions. Of greater importance is the fact that the great civilizations of mankind have grown up on wealth based ultimately on the cultivation of a variety of highly diverse crops. The raising, harvesting, and preparation of plants as various as rice, maize, beans, manioc, potato, wheat, or barley would alone have served to promote diversity, not merely in subsistence and technology, but also in settlement and social organization. Even within the cereal zone of Europe, widely differing regimes adjusted to regional ecosystems are reflected in the archaeological record of early peasant communities. One has only to contrast, for example, the dry farming regime of the Mediterranean zone, complemented by the cultivation of vines, almonds, figs, and olives, with the mixed farming based on year-round rainfall in the deciduous zone of Temperate Europe or again with the hybrid economies of the northern territories where the growing season was too short for the cereals available in prehistoric times to play more than a marginal role in relation to catching and foraging.

The adoption of settled life based primarily on farming also served to promote hierarchy in the organization both of settlement and of society. The increased yield of cultivated over wild crops and the fact that these could be stored in some cases over appreciable periods of time made it safe for substantial numbers of people to enjoy the benefits of urban life. For their part, the inhabitants of villages, hamlets, and farmsteads in the surrounding territories that supplied the city dwellers with food were able to secure not merely the products of specialized crafts but also such important services as protection against enemies, insurance against death through access to central granaries and, not least, the possibility of sharing in the intensified religious rites celebrated in the urban temples. Again the adoption of permanent settlement made it practicable to construct buildings more elaborate than mere shelters, as well as to accumulate movable property in the form of artefacts beyond what could readily be carried on the person. In this way, sedentary life made practicable the material embodiments of the varying status of individuals occupying different ranks in the emerging hierarchy.

Every advance in technology that allowed a more effective manipulation of natural resources conferred competitive advantages on those adopting it. Progress at a material level was therefore cumulative for ongoing communities (5). One sign of material progress was that artefacts served for progressively more specialized ends. So long as production was organized on a local preindustrial basis, increased specialization resulted in the use of a wider range of materials and the application of novel techniques, as well as in the development of artefacts calculated to attain better results for a smaller input of energy.

For almost the whole of his history, man's most effective tools were made from flint, stone, and wood. The utilization of an ever-wider range of raw materials necessarily made for greater diversity. The Upper Palaeolithic and Mesolithic hunter-fishers of Eurasia were distinguished in the archaeological record by their sophisticated use of animal skeletal material for a wide range of specialized gear. The adoption of fired clay pottery for receptacles, as well as serving to distinguish pottery making from aceramic communities, provided a medium peculiarly well adapted to a variety of modeling and ornamentation.

Another craft frequently taken up by settled peoples was weaving, and this also assumed a diversity of forms corresponding in part to the materials used in different territories, notably wool of different kinds, flax, cotton, and silk. Metal working also served to distinguish those who adapted it, as well as providing a number of variants according to the kinds of metals and the techniques used in working them. And so it was with every new material, including some such as amber, jade, or jet, occurring only in restricted localities, and others, like faience, manufactured by special processes.

Although it was variation in subsistence and technology that was most readily documented in the archaeological record, the increasing diversity of artefacts was the outcome in reality more of social than of merely economic factors. Economic ones like the adoption of particular patterns of subsistence or the multiplication of crafts stemming from specialization and the use of an ever-widening range of materials implied a subdivision of labor far beyond that of age groups and sexes. On the other hand, purely social forces were also important. The larger and more complex communities became, the more insistent was the need to promote identity and cohesion. Conversely, there was the need to emphasize definition from neighbors, something that became more pressing with every increase in the permanence of settlement and the accumulation of wealth that accompanied successive improvements in farming. It is significant that when Gordon Childe first tried to define the frontiers of the early peasant communities of prehistoric Europe in his *Dawn of European Civilization* (3), he sought to do so by mapping cultures. These he defined by conformities in the whole range of social activities reflected in the archaeological record, notably subsistence patterns, productive techniques, tool and weapon forms, defensive systems, personal ornaments, art styles, religious observances, and funerary practices, stressing in each case abstentions as well as affirmative choices. In a word, his method depended on the extent to which the various communities of Europe had already developed richly divergent cultural expressions between the fifth and the second millennia B.C. This diversity was indeed sufficiently pronounced to make it reasonable to require a first-year undergraduate to assign assemblages of artefacts from this phase of European prehistory to their correct geographical provenance. And the same would go for any territory that supported peasant communities during early times.

Whereas the hunting bands and peasant kin groups described by Childe in *The Dawn* (3) were homogeneous and within the primary divisions of age and sex made up of individuals of equal status, the societies that experienced the explosive increase in diversity documented in the finest exhibits displayed in the great museums of the world were invariably of a more complex order. The climax of cultural achievement coincided in various parts of the world with the replacement of segmented by vertically structured societies. It is not my purpose here to examine the forms taken by vertical structuring, still less to propose a typology from chiefdoms and kingdoms to empires. I merely wish to emphasize that in every traditional society known to history, hierarchy and inequality, whatever forms these took in particular cases, were the invariable accompaniment, indeed the formative factor, behind the emergence of high cultures. And by high cultures I mean those most widely separated from the behavioral patterns of animals whose fossils in fact appeared at lower levels in the palaeontological record. In terms of archaeology, high cultures were represented by artefacts farthest removed from the sticks and stones of *Homo erectus* and far transcending the homely products of Gordon Childe's egalitarian peasants of prehistoric Europe. The material embodiments of high culture invariably appeared as a matter of stratigraphic fact in the context of hierarchically organized societies. Conversely, the archaeology of lower levels in stratified societies incapsulates earlier stages in cultural history. Whereas the peaks of cultural attainment, the finest products of human craft, were exclusively associated with and indeed helped to define and signal the highest levels in the social hierarchy, the objects and structures used by the mass of the population, including the very craftsmen who made the noblest insignia and built the most symbolic monuments, often compared with those made by their remote forebears.

In terms of early Britain, one might recall that the plainer pottery of the Celtic peoples, who created in the metal insignia of their chiefly class (1) one of the outstanding manifestations of decorative art known to man, hardly differs in appearance from that made by stone age peasants two or three thousand years previously in the same territory. Again, if the jewelry from the Sutton Hoo burial (2) or even some of the richest Kentish graves of the pagan Anglo-Saxon period (11) would tax the finest craftsmen of the present age, undecorated pottery of this archaeological phase has on occasion been assigned to the pre-Roman Iron Age or even to the Neolithic. Even more striking comparisons might be made by reference to the material equipment of the peasants who supported the elaborate structures of pharaonic Egypt or from recent times of princely India or Tsarist Russia.

It is no contradiction that the overall cultural patterns displayed by hierarchical societies should have been so much richer and more sharply defined than those of the humbler segmented societies from which they developed. Archaeology documents that, whereas in segmented societies settlements tend to be of approximately the same size and to comprise structures of more or less homogeneous form and scale, stratified societies are often marked by a hierarchy of settlement with major centers ministering to and drawing upon a number of lesser ones distributed over dependent territories and themselves sometimes of more than one order of importance. The precise role of such major centers varied in different societies. They might be primarily foci of religious observance, combining with this social functions and often playing a role in the redistribution of commodities. Alternatively, they might be cities containing rulers and their courts and bureaucracies, temples and their priests, specialized craftsmen and merchants, in fact everyone and everything that rendered specialized services of whatever kind to the communities of which the cities were capitals and foci. The frequent presence at such centers of granaries or other storage facilities reminds us of the redistributive functions implicit in hierarchy. Town dwellers who produced no food depended on rations derived ultimately from the surrounding countryside. Conversely, cities had responsibilities to their dependent realms in times of death. Temple stores were not, as some Marxists have implied, symbols of priestly exploitation so much as prototypes of banks and mutual assurance corporations, mechanisms of social well-being.

A counterpart to the concentration of wealth that more than anything distinguished stratified from segmented societies was a preoccupation with armament and defensive works. In the archaeological record it is a matter of observation that whereas it was exceptional for peasant communities to erect defensive works, this was normal practice among hierarchically structured groups more richly endowed with movable wealth. Moreover, the scale of defenses matched the status of particular sites. Central sites housing leaders and the focus of specialized activities were more likely to be defended strongly than less important ones. Again, the finest personal arma-ment, weapons, helmets, and body armor were concentrated on leaders and their immediate associates, and the same applies over much of Eurasia to equipment concerned with personal mobility. Mycenaean princes, Celtic chieftains, and Shang knights were conveyed to and from the thick of battle on splendidly accoutred chariots, just as the kings of Ur and the nomad leaders of the Altai were brought to burial in horse-drawn wagons for reasons of status as well as of convenience.

The archaeological record shows that in stratified societies the most specialized craftsmen worked primarily for the uppermost stratum. Fore-most among the objects which denoted and enhanced status were personal weapons, helmets and shields and body armor, harness and chariot gear, personal jewelry and ornaments, not to mention mirrors and utensils relat-ing to feasting and drinking. As well as displaying the highest technical expertise available, such things were frequently made of materials inher-ently precious or valuable because they were only obtainable from a distance and sometimes, as in the case of jade, also extremely expensive to work. Since they were thus precious in all measurable respects, they provided ideal media for conspicuous consumption and display. Exotic artefacts, particu-larly those originating in more advanced and prestigious cultures, provided another medium through and by which the higher ranks in stratified soci-eties advertised their status. Appropriation of such attributes was not left as in a modern society to individual initiative, but, to judge from usage in historically known situations, was assigned to people occupying particular ranks by custom if not by explicit sumptuary laws. Although the prime purpose of this was undoubtedly to define and validate the hierarchic struc-ture of stratified societies, it also played a significant part in cultural dynam-ics. Thus the use of exotic artefacts and materials as insignia of status was a potent factor in promoting change in communities marginal to the main foci of cultural development. Within societies, therefore, the degree to which the most skilled craftsmen were specialized and concentrated on the fabrication of the richest objects for comparatively few people acted like a forcing house of innovation and enrichment, not merely for the upper ranks but for all those to whom new types of artefact or decorative motif were in time devolved from above. The myth that the average man was likely to display cultural creativity or contribute to rapid innovation if only given the opportunity is much less dangerous but no less mistaken than the assump-tion that he would be good if only he were free from the constraints of social hierarchy.

Both the persistence of the myth and its falsity may be illustrated in the attitude towards the finest products of early civilizations adopted by mod-ern communist states. Exhibits from the Han dynasty shown in the recent exhibition of Chinese archaeology on either side of the Atlantic were held, for example, to "glaringly expose the luxury and decadence of the feudal ruling class." In particular the funeral garments made up of jade plates linked by gold wire that formed a focus of the exhibition were singled out as exposing "the feudal class's luxury and depravity at the expense of the labouring people." The same could have been written of the jade vessels, the silks, porcelains, fine metal work, lacquers, and paintings of this and later periods of Chinese history or, indeed, the luxury products of any age. The fact is that such things, if not made for superiors in social hierarchies, would never have been made at all. If the ruling classes had not been luxurious and sophisticated and if they had not been in a position to enlist the skill of the artificers, these things which define and illustrate the essential qualities of Chinese art would never have existed. And the same applies to the treasures of Tutankhamen's tomb or the Sutton Hoo ship. Without a hierarchic structure, without a marked degree of inequality in consumption, the astonishing diversity of Chinese, Egyptian, or Anglo-Saxon culture would never have developed. This is not a matter of speculation. We know what the culture of China, Egypt, or Britain was like before class societies developed in these lands. Archaeology tells us much about their prehistoric peasant populations. They were egalitarian. They were illiterate. And their material products by comparison with the fine things produced in the ambience of class societies were as dull and boring as those used by the lower classes in Shang China, Pharaonic Egypt, or Anglo-Saxon England. Archaeology shows unequivocally that the finest artefacts made by man, the most superb and diverse embodiments of his humanity, were made to celebrate and render more effective the operation of social systems in which craftsmen exercised their most refined skills on the most precious materials in the service of the highest levels of social hierarchies.

In his slim but pregnant volume, *The Birth of Civilization in the Near East,* Henri Frankfort (10) strongly attacked the notion that the early civilizations of Egypt and southwest Asia—and by implication those of Europe, south and east Asia, and the New World—can be adequately appraised as mere representatives of a stage in social evolution. Instead he insisted on the autonomy of cultural manifestations. Each civilization, he believed, had its own peculiar genius and identity. In each, he wrote, we can recognize "a certain coherence . . . a certain consistency in its orientation, a certain cultural 'style' which shapes its political and its judicial institutions, its art as well as its literature, its religion as well as its morals" (10, p. 16). This elusive identity, which was nevertheless embodied in the material products available to archaeology, was termed by Frankfort its form. It was this form that "is never destroyed though it changes in the course of time." Although more clearly defined in the more advanced cultures of stratified socieites, it needs to be emphasized that even the humblest cultures of *Homo sapiens sapiens* were marked by this precious quality of unique identity. It is cultural form that gives meaning and savor to human life, a savor only men can perceive and without which they revert to the status of the primates from which they evolved in the course of prehistory.

Much has been made in this essay of the contributions to cultural diversity and enrichment made by economic and social factors. It is important not to overlook ideology. As Henri Frankfort so clearly recognized, religion and the ideological attitudes associated with religious beliefs have played a role of great importance both in validating individual cultural systems and in promoting their distinctiveness. Ideology is important both because it motivates men over a wide range of their activities and still more, historically speaking, because of its key role in perpetuating and indeed deepening the coherence of social traditions. Religion and the ideas associated with it have not only been leading factors in promoting diversity among men. They also provide keys to defining this diversity since, though by nature incorporeal, they are nevertheless impressed on a wide range of archaeological data including shrines and temples, utensils used in ritual observance, and elements in the iconography of graphic art. Again, the diversity of literate societies is nowhere more beautifully exemplified than in the scripts used to communicate and perpetuate liturgies, histories, and laws (9).

What Frankfort discerned in the civilizations of antiquity available only from their archaeological and epigraphic remains, civilizations which included the Harappan, the Maya, and the Shang no less than the Egyptian or Sumerian, was present also in the cultural traditions known to us from the much fuller sources of recent history, those for instance of Ch'ing China, the France of Versailles, Georgian England, or Tsarist Russia. Anyone traveling through a territory as restricted as Europe as recently even as 1914 could have savored a diversity not merely of material products but of social and political styles transcending that available today in the entire world. The texture of life was so immeasurably richer then that to experience even an inkling of it today people have to resort as they do in their millions to monuments, museums, illustrated books, or the theater.

It is not difficult to see why an archaeologist should view the trends and some of the tenets of modern industrial society with a certain ambivalence or even disenchantment, nor is it surprising that this attitude should be widely shared by laymen. Whereas his studies have documented the attainment of humanity through the gradual emergence of hierarchically structured societies distinguished by patterns of ever-increasing distinctiveness and diversity, the archaeologist finds himself confronted in his daily life by an increasingly rapid reversion toward the intraspecies homogeneity of a prehuman situation. The brutal rapidity at which this process of cultural impoverishment has unfolded in the face of science and technology and the economic systems stemming from them explains why men everywhere are registering their dismay. In trying to understand his situation the ordinary person has received little help from the intelligentsia. Indeed, by a supreme irony the undermining of human values has been furthered rather than diagnosed, still less arrested, by those who like to see themselves as leaders of opinion. The quality of human life is threatened not by some supreme cataclysm of nature or untoward social catastrophe so much as by the proponents of self-styled progressive philosophies.

An immediate cause of the homogenization of culture has been the incorporation of traditional societies within the nexus of a world-wide market in the products of machine industry. Whereas in preindustrial societies of the kind most commonly encountered in archaeology the elaboration of hierarchy and the enrichment and diversification of culture were adaptive and for that reason selected not merely for survival but for enhancement, in the case of industrial society the precise opposite applies. Standardized products of the kind most readily manufactured by machines, because of their greater cheapness, have a built-in advantage over handmade ones reflecting local skills and the styles of diverse cultural traditions. Economic forces left to themselves increasingly ensure that handmade products displaying regional diversity become too costly for daily use. Outside museums they can only survive as luxuries, but luxuries imply disparities in consumption which industrial societies serve to reduce. The trend toward uniformity applies not merely to different societies but to classes within them. Articles that deviate from the standard become too expensive to buy in the very societies in which it pays to spend the maximum amount in promoting the consumption of standard ones by means of advertising and persuasion in a variety of media.

The price mechanism is powerfully reinforced in this regard by ideology. The "enlightenment" which generated natural science and in due course modern industrial economies itself seeks to promote equality as a desirable aim of society. Egalitarian notions affect patterns of consumption directly through the impact of steeply progressive taxation, but also indirectly through psychological constraints. Even the very rich are increasingly inhibited from consuming luxuries they can still afford for fear of appearing conspicuous. In striking contrast to their behavior in hierarchically structured societies in which status is in a measure defined by conspicuous consumption, in industrial societies they strive to remain inconspicuous and so to avoid even heavier fiscal penalties for their success. Economic, social, political, and psychological forces thus combine to maximize the production and consumption of common things while penalizing that of uncommon ones. Indeed, the degree to which the common man dominates consumption has come to be accepted by capitalists and Marxists alike as an index of progress. Societies in which the production of exceptional things is matched by marked inequality in consumption have even come to be accepted as backward. The richer in economic and the more "progressive" in political terms the world becomes the more relentlessly it is impoverished with respect to the very attributes that mark the emergence and cultural enrichment of mankind.

Another powerful force making for cultural homogenization has been the dramatic advance in systems of communication in the industrial world. Railways, motor vehicles, and aircraft have shrunk the world so that formerly remote territories have been brought within effective reach of a single market dominated by a comparatively few states which share a common technology and modes of thought powerfully influenced by the concepts of natural science. The installations and mechanisms that now girdle the earth not merely conform in all essentials to universal patterns but for the most part are themselves manufactured at a few centers. They bear no more relationship to modes of transport traditional in most parts of the world than they do to local ecological systems.

Even more important as a factor in the process of homogenization than the movement of men and goods is the communication of ideas. Printing and the electronic transmission of texts and the spoken word have brought the peoples of the world within range not merely of a single technology and market but even more significantly of concepts linked with the pursuit of economic profit, scientific comprehension, and notions of social justice. Again, the new facilities have conferred decisive advantages on those able to communicate directly with representatives of the dominant Western culture. Just as mass production involved the standardization of goods, so improvements in communication have promoted the domination of progressively fewer languages. Again, as modern business soon appreciated, television is an unrivaled medium for manipulating, standardizing, and so making more profitable the satisfaction of consumer tastes. More than that, its effect must be to undermine traditional modes of thought and values. The impact of electronics has been further amplified by computers, which by sorting data from the whole range of science and the humanities has helped still further to break down conceptual barriers while at the same time giving rise to a jargon common to all cultures and disciplines. Inevitably, modern media for the transmission of ideas operate to favor universal as opposed to local patterns of behavior. In this way they serve to reinforce uniformity at the expense of diversity both within and between communities.

The process of impoverishment by homogenization, which has already done much to destroy the diversity and richness of the artefacts used in the physical activities of daily life, poses an even more lethal threat to the more spiritual dimensions of human experience. In the traditional cultures recovered by archeology, the products of graphic and sculptural art and architecture mirror cultural diversity with all the greater sensitivity that they are relatively freer from the constraints of utility than the generality of artefacts. The converse is no less true. The graphic and sculptural products of modern society reflect with startling clarity the degree to which the human spirit has already been impoverished by abstraction. In painting the process has taken two main forms but the outcome is essentially the same. At one extreme the artist resorts to elementary geometric forms or covers the whole of his picture with a single color, as with Malevich's famous white on white series or Rodchenko's riposte in black on black. At the other extreme he depicts natural forms of artefacts with a fidelity that rivals the camera. The effect in either case is to deprive the work of cultural content. Geometry and photography operate, like the laws of natural science or the processes of modern technology, irrespective of cultural endowments. Furthermore, the practitioners of modern abstract art, while striving for originality as innovators as though they were scientists, often seek to eliminate personal as well as cultural diversity, if necessary by using spray guns or applying natural or ready-made materials.

Sculptors have equally sought to evade cultural affiliations or even personal identity. This has sometimes been achieved, as with Paolozzi, by combining parts of machines or, as with Vantangerloo or Caro, by using wire or standard products of machine industry. An alternative has been to adopt and improve upon natural forms such as Brancusi's eggs or Moore's animal bones. In architecture it is much the same. Modern structures recalling factory products betray their indifference to ecology by obtruding alike from Brazilian rain forests or Arabian deserts and display their contempt for man and his traditions by overshadowing without prejudice oriental mosques and pagodas or the classical, gothic, and neogothic structures of the Western world. As eloquent as the nature of its products in some respects is the fact that the very term "architecture" has been abandoned by some progressives as in itself anachronistic because of discriminating in respect of quality. The substitute term "built form" serves the dual purpose of advertising the divorce of building from culture and the devaluation of that very discrimination by which men emerged from the other primates and diverse civilizations developed in the course of ages from the base of primitive communism.

A similar process of homogenization deforms the ideas and concepts that once inspired and embodied the identities of the several civilizations of mankind. This is true most notably of the religions that more than anything inform the arts and enshrine the beliefs of these civilizations. The positivist temper until recently prevalent in natural science undermined traditional beliefs in whatever sphere primarily on the ground that their validity was incapable of proof. Religion of whatever description was regarded as incredible, irrational, and superfluous because all phenomena that were real were held to be susceptible to explanation by natural science. Religious belief indeed could even be condemned on the ground that it impeded the progress of natural science and was therefore not merely obscurantist but positively harmful to the prospects of mankind. If rationalism was hostile to religion in general, it was still more opposed to the notion of diversity of belief. It is of the nature of scientific laws to be universal in their application, whereas beliefs, codes of social behavior, or artistic conventions are by their mere origin particular to historically constituted communities. The universalizing character of natural science has so conditioned modes of thought that even those who retain religious faith find themselves increasingly unable to tolerate religious differences. So far from proclaiming belief in the rightness of their own particular creed, religious leaders proclaim the need for ecumenical thought, not merely as a practical necessity but as desirable on its own account. Religions when not flatly repudiated are increasingly being homogenized not by their enemies but by their friends.

In many ways the most revealing manifestation of popular feeling in societies of collapsed hierarchy is the cult of what Karl Popper aptly termed "biological naturalism," manifested in diet, the immitigable growth of hair, nudism, sexual permissiveness, and even bestiality. It is encouraging to a prehistorian whose profession leads him to trace the emergence of man from a state of nature, whose subject rests on the assumption that men become human to the extent that they elaborate cultural modes of behavior, to find the following appreciation of the implications of this vulgar heresy set out by this eminent philosopher, more especially since he finds himself unable to accept so much else of his message:

> ... it must be admitted that certain forms of behaviour may be described as more "natural" than other forms; for instance going native or eating only raw food; and some people think that this in itself justifies the choice of these forms. But in this sense it is not natural to interest oneself in art, or science, or even in arguments in favour of naturalism. The choice of conformity with "nature" as a supreme standard leads to consequences which few will be prepared to face; it does not lead to a more natural form of civilization, but to beastliness (13, p. 70).

As Popper wrote later on in the same work, emphasizing his meaning by italicizing the sentence: *"There is no return to a harmonious state of nature. If we turn back, then we must go the whole way—we must return to the beasts"* (13, p. 200). Indeed, the position of lapsed men is in many ways worse, since they have lost the instinctive guides to behavior on which other animals are able to depend.

The course of history has been shaped less by popular heresies than by the original thinking of outstanding men. This is particularly true when the insights of successive pioneers are incorporated in an organized body of codified thought like that presented by the natural sciences. The importance of the sciences far transcends their contribution to advancing the technology of production, distribution, and communication. Of greater significance in the long run is their role in promoting abstract and universal modes of categorizing experience. Whereas cultural traditions by their very nature reflect the diversity of their parent cultures and favor historical modes of thought, scientific laws are abstract and necessarily universal if they are true. As modes of thought proper to the natural sciences spread over the world they served to promote and intensify the process of homogenization exhibited in tangible form in the products of machine industry.

If the natural sciences operated to lessen diversity and impose homogeneity among different societies, another product of increasing human awareness, that of concern for others and specifically for the weak and unsuccessful, not only promoted a greater degree of equality and hence of homogeneity within societies, but made their attainment a talisman of philosophic and indeed political morality. In Karl Popper's rhetoric, the attainment of "open" societies of the kind that stemmed from the experience of Classical Greece was held to be a self-evident aim in contrast with "closed" societies of tribal character which were by the same token considered to be outmoded. What was regarded as particularly reprehensible about "closed" societies is that they were hierarchically ordered and informed by traditional values invested with the sanction of history and even of the supernatural. By contrast, open societies, to the attainment of which all the previous experience of mankind was thought of as a mere preliminary, were held to be rational rather than magical, abstract rather than organic, equalitarian rather than hierarchical, and universal rather than tribal. It is paradoxical that Popper, who saw with such clarity of vision the fallacy of naturalism, should have failed to appreciate the contradiction implicit in the very notion of an "open" society. The artificial values that constrain human behavior and make it so distinct from that of the nonhuman primates are neither abstract nor necessarily rational. They are the product not of logic but of history, not the generalized history of mankind, but that of particular societies. To speak of abstract culture is a contradiction in terms. A society truly open would soon enough revert to a state of nature with all that that implies. Conversely, culture can only exist by constraining or at least moulding individual men, the sole way of ensuring the viability of traditional patterns and values.

The object of this essay is by no means to advocate reaction. On the contrary, the last thing archaeology should encourage is any disposition to believe that the historical process can safely be ignored. It would be suicidal as well as futile to dream of returning to a golden age before the "enlightenment" spawned the natural science, machine technology, and egalitarian philosophies that between them threaten those diverse expressions of the human spirit that we term civilizations. The extended view of history made possible by archaeology is valuable above all for the improved perspective from which it allows us to view the present and indeed the future. If the past is embalmed in history, the future lies open before us. As we peer ahead, our knowledge of the past should nevertheless stand us in good stead by defining perils and reminding us of what we stand to lose if we ignore them.

It has been a main contention of this essay that whereas for long ages the course of social evolution was benign, in that it promoted diversity and so enriched mankind, we are now in a new phase of world history, one in which prevailing trends are malignant and even threaten to terminate the adventure chronicled by archaeology. Our future has been in peril since during our own times the concepts and techniques of modern science have engulfed the world. Unless we can hold fast to the values defined by our history, we shall be reduced not to a pristine and therefore still hopeful state, not to a prehuman so much as a subhuman condition. If our common aim is to enhance our lives, our guiding light must surely be quality rather than quantity, hierarchy rather than equality, and diversity rather than homogeneity. By the same token, we should not be afraid to count archaeology as a humane study. Since men necessarily derive their humanity by virtue of belonging to and sharing the heritage of social groups, it follows that archaeologists must concern themselves with, and where appropriate use methods developed by, the social sciences. Equally, since man is an animal and his societies can only exist in the context of nature, his history can only be fully understood by applying the insights and techniques of the biological and physical sciences. This is not to say that the natural and social sciences are to be worshipped, revered, or even mimicked. They are merely there to be used in order to promote understanding. The objective of archaeology is to elucidate the manner in which in the course of ages we have become human and in this way define what we mean when we declare ourselves to be men. By the same token, a prime objective of social policy ought surely to be not to undermine but to conserve and promote the values by which in the course of their long history men have managed to distance themselves from their primate relatives.

Literature Cited

1. Brailsford, J. 1975. *Early Celtic Masterpieces from Britain in the British Museum.* London: British Museum Publ.
2. Bruce-Mitford, R. 1972. *The Sutton Hoo Ship-Burial: A Handbook.* London: British Museum Publ.
3. Childe, V. G. 1925. *Dawn of European Civilization.* Sixth and last edition published in 1957. London: Routledge & Kegan Paul
4. Childe, V. G. 1942. *What Happened in History.* London: Pelican Books
5. Clark, G. 1970. *Aspects of Prehistory,* Chap. 2. Berkeley: Univ. California Press
6. Clark, G. 1977. Dedication. *World Prehistory in New Perspective.* Cambridge: Cambridge Univ. Press. 3rd ed.
7. Clark, J. D. 1976. African origins of man the toolmaker. In *Human Origins: Louis Leakey and the East African Evidence,* ed. G. L. Isaac, E. R. McCown. California: Benjamin
8. de Chardin, T. 1959. *The Phenomenon of Man.* London: Collins
9. Diringer, D. 1962. *Writing.* London: Thames & Hudson
10. Frankfort, H. 1951. *The Birth of Civilization in the Near East.* London: Williams & Norgate
11. Jessup, R. 1950. *Anglo-Saxon Jewelry.* London: Methuen
12. Le Gros Clark, W. E. 1955. *The Fossil Evidence for Human Evolution,* Chap. 1. Chicago: Univ. Chicago Press
13. Popper, K. R. 1966. *The Open Society and its Enemies,* Vol. 1. London: Routledge & Kegan Paul. 5th ed.

Ann. Rev. Anthropol. 1979. 8:21–43

WHAT IS LOWER CENTRAL AMERICAN ARCHAEOLOGY?

♦9625

Olga F. Linares

Smithsonian Tropical Research Institute, Box 2072, Balboa,
Panama Canal Zone

INTRODUCTION

The archaeology of Lower Central America is just beginning to emerge from decades of scientific neglect and antiquated research. Large tracts of hinterland between eastern Honduras and eastern Panama still remain unexplored. Much of the literature has been concerned almost exclusively with ceramic sequences, tribal ascriptions, influences from nuclear America, and impressionistic site surveys. The assumption that Lower Central America served only as a corridor through which ideas, objects, and even people moved back and forth between Mesoamerica and the Andean region colors much of the writing. So much so that one is justified in asking if Lower Central America will ever constitute a viable study unit. Is it an area with historic depth, where groups sharing common roots underwent similar adaptive processes? Are there important problems to be studied here?

By shifting research priorities from the definition of culture areas to the investigation of cultural processes, younger colleagues are just beginning to find affirmative answers to these questions. But this is a very recent development. If I am forced by the nature of much of the previous literature to be somewhat critical, it is with the hope of moving the field toward more scientific methodologies and broader theoretical considerations. For the new generation I hope this essay provides further encouragement and possibly some new insights.

21

0084-6570/79/1015-0021$01.00

ARE FRONTIERS NECESSARILY UNSTABLE?

The Lower Central American archaeological area has been defined negatively as the region below and beyond the boundaries of the Mesoamerican culture area to the north. Much confusion still remains as to where Mesoamerican cultures leave off and Lower Central America begins. (For location of places mentioned in the text, see Figure 1.)

The Southeastern Mesoamerican Frontier

No less than in the past, Mayanists are still puzzling over the problem of how far south the Maya wandered from their presumed homeland. One of the first to take up this problem seriously was Lothrop (94), who placed the farthest limit of Maya settlement in Honduras, east of Lake Ulua-Yojoa, and in El Salvador along the Lempa river. Because so little was known of the time-depth of Maya developments, his approach was essentially ahistorical, linking sixteenth century accounts of Maya peoples with what he conceived of as Maya pottery. While taking Lothrop to task for making these connections, Longyear (91) accepted the equally doubtful proposition that linguistic groups formed distinct archaeological cultures. Arguing that there is very little that was Maya in the Ulua-Yojoa archaeological complexes, he put the Maya frontier during Classic times further to the west in Honduras, roughly where the Maya met the Lencan peoples.

Other archaeologists have generally accepted the Lenca line as the Maya frontier, but not without making assumptions of their own concerning the linguistic affiliations of this now extinct group: that the Lenca were not Maya though they were definitely Mesoamerican (129); that they were neither Mayan nor Mesoamerican but South American (139); that the proto-Lencas were macro-Mayanas who in Late Preclassic times brought Usulután pottery to eastern Salvador and Honduras (2, 3). In all these arguments a strange logic prevails. While it is considered speculative to infer shifts in social organization from marked changes in community patterns at a site (3), archaeologists show little hesitation when it comes to tieing in ceramic traditions with specific languages 3000 years ago. And whereas great ethnic and linguistic complexity is accepted for Spanish contact times (139), the tendency has been to simplify the prehistoric picture.

Not surprisingly, recent efforts by qualified linguists to define language groupings in the southeastern Maya frontier (14, 16, 54, 59, 90) reveals a situation every bit as complex as indicated by both the archaeology and the ethnohistory. As Holt & Bright (54) point out, at least six genetically different language families co-existed in the Hondurean, Salvadorean region alone. These families fall into two broad phonological clusters—the Mayoid

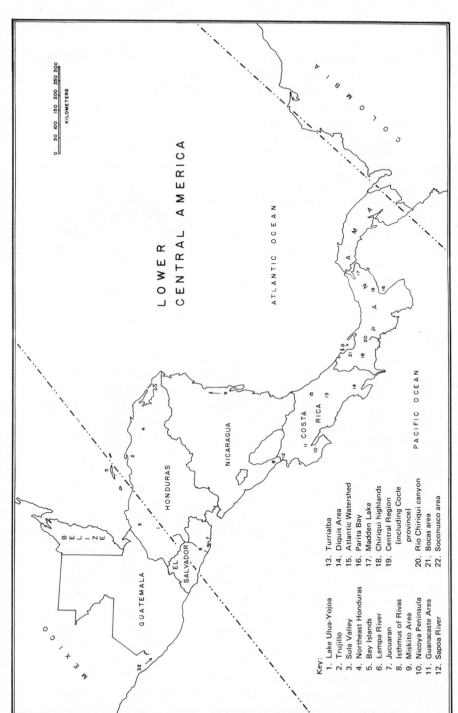

Key:

1. Lake Ulua-Yojoa
2. Trujillo
3. Sula Valley
4. Northeast Honduras
5. Bay Islands
6. Lempa River
7. Jucuaran
8. Isthmus of Rivas
9. Miskito Area
10. Nicoya Peninsula
11. Guanacaste Area
12. Sapoa River
13. Turrialba
14. Diquis Area
15. Atlantic Watershed
16. Parita Bay
17. Madden Lake
18. Chiriqui highlands
19. Central Region (including Cocle province)
20. Rio Chiriqui canyon
21. Bocas area
22. Soconusco area

Figure 1 Map of Lower Central America showing location of places mentioned in text.

versus the Central American cluster—with the line between them extending from Trujillo in Honduras to Jucuarán on the Pacific coast of El Salvador. The same authors are careful to point out that several languages, among them Jicaque and Lenca, exhibit traits of both clusters, which they interpret as evidence for a gradual transition from one cluster to the other. There are further disagreements among specialists. Thus, while Longacre (90) puts the Chorotega-Mangue of the Nicoya peninsula in Costa Rica in the Mesoamerican camp, Holt & Bright (54) put them in the Central American camp; and while Campbell (15) lists Lenca not as one but two languages and refers to them as non-Maya, Holt & Bright (54) rather hesitantly align Lenca with the Mayoid group, and Kaufman (58, 60) points out that the connection of Xincan-Lencan with any other group, Mayan, Chibchan or Uto-Aztecan, has not been demonstrated. Finally, while Campbell (14) favors putting the Misumalpan languages (Cacaopera, Matagalpa, Misquito, and Sumu), which once occupied parts of Salvador and Nicaragua, with the Macro-Chibchan group of Central and South America, Kaufman (59) places them with the Mesoamerican languages.

Leaving the question of possible Olmec linguistic affiliations to specialists (17), archaeologists have paid more attention to other problems: how to recognize Olmec influences (93), when in the Preclassic were these influences felt in the southeastern peripheries (143), and what social factors were behind the spread of the Olmec style. Answers to the last question have been diverse. It has been suggested that Olmec objects were disseminated by itinerant male sculptors (93); that trade was facilitated by contact between elites for the acquisition of prestige goods (31); that the Olmec set up trade control stations among autochthonous groups (117, 118), and so forth. While inferences of this kind seem perfectly justified and necessary, in some instances they have been carried too far. Culture-historical schemes have been built upon an insufficient data base by using concepts such as acculturation, diffusions, migrations, and trade (117, 118) as if their meanings were generally agreed upon among ethnographers.

Fortunately, some of the traditional criteria used to define the southeastern Mesoamerican frontiers are now being queried by recent scholars. Emphasizing the fact that a great deal of ethnic complexity underlies all culture-contact situations, Henderson (51–53) and other members of the Cornell University project in western Honduras have begun to investigate synchronic variation within a region. They point out that it may be impossible to define external relations at a site such as Naco (an important Postclassic center) without first determining its economic and political role within the Valley (51). Their conception of frontiers as multiethnic situations, where resident groups and foreign enclaves maintained symbiotic relations grounded on ecological differences and economic necessities, seems well taken. Lange (68, 71) has also emphasized that frontiers are dynamic, changing through time. Although the emphasis on ceramic similarities has not been abandoned, it is now a commonplace that they may mean different things, not just a common ethnic origin or a common language (53). Incidentally, some of the old monographs (133) are much more sophisticated on this score than more recent ones (128).

Given present realities, an awareness of the need to understand how a site functioned before assessing its external relations may have come too late. Whereas archaeologists in the past wasted unique opportunities to study sites while they were still accessible and relatively undisturbed, the present generation has to make do with partial salvage programs (119).

The Outlying Areas: Gran Nicoya and Eastern Honduras

There is no doubt that most of western Honduras (7, 92) and western Salvador (117, 118) were part of real Mesoamerica. Pacific coastal Nicaragua and Costa Rica, the so-called Gran Nicoya (4, 6, 9, 19, 20, 102, 144), was also supposed to have been strongly influenced by Mesoamerica. More recent workers, however, are arguing for more southerly influences, in Nicoya and even eastern Honduras.

In the Sula Valley of Honduras, N. C. Kennedy (61) sees ties between the famous Playa de los Muertos and South American complexes during the Early and Middle Formative periods. In the Bay Islands of Honduras, several investigators (29, 140) note connections with Lower Central America after A.D. 1000, a position not unlike that taken earlier (28, 132). Disagreeing with earlier conclusions (20), Sweeney (136, 137) argues for the total exclusion of the Guanacaste section of Gran Nicoya from the Mesoamerican sphere of influence. Finally, in two overlapping publications, Lange (64, 65) suggests that the societies of Gran Nicoya, and perhaps even the Maya themselves, were Circum-Caribbean in type. He argues that Maya subsistence and social organization were closer to those of Circum-Caribbean chiefdoms than to those of the central Mexican highland states. To this reviewer his idea that the Maya did not develop complex civilizations, however loosely this term is defined, seems, to say the least, to overstate the case. Nevertheless, Lange (65) does provide a healthy reminder that the Maya economy, with a great deal of dependence among the Yucatecan Maya on marine resources (66), was more diversified than had been previously assumed. Freidel (36) has documented the same point more extensively.

Frontiers and Outliers Reconsidered

Actually it may be misleading to place too much emphasis on outside connections and foreign influences. Frontiers may be stable or unstable according to circumstances. Within the Mesoamerican frontier area, a great deal of linguistic diversity probably antedated 1500 B.C., by which time most of the important language families had long been in the region (58). We are reminded by Kaufman (58) that the distribution of most languages suggests few large-scale migrations of peoples, and that cultural patterns and complexes move more often than nations, though individuals may move about as contact men. The obvious exception in the area under consideration may have been the Uto-Aztecans, represented by the Pipil latecomers, who by the time the Spanish arrived had taken over western Salvador and penetrated into Honduras (91). It seems likely, in fact, that most artifacts from Middle America found here and there within the frontier area (33, 47, 67, 148) may be attributed to individual traders or perhaps to trading enclaves (51). The rest of the population by and large probably stayed put most of the time.

In my opinion, the difficulty that linguists have in deciding whether to place the Chorotega-Mangue and Misumalpan languages in the Mesoamerican or Central American camps may reflect a long-term stability and coherence of the northern frontier. Since Salvador and Honduras probably were settled as early as the Maya area, the local populations may have made many innovations on their own. At any rate, there is little justification for conceiving of these groups as "poor relations" (7), even though some of their pottery was at times under heavy Mayan or Mesoamerican influences. In reality, the groups in the so-called Mesoamerican frontier exhibited a gradual, in situ, and successful adaptation to coastal conditions for at least 3000 years.

Beyond the frontier, a single language phylum, Macro-Chibchan, dominates the area from Nicaragua through Panama to coastal Colombia and Venezuela and onto northern Ecuador (135, 141). It may be useful to consider how far this whole enormous region, the so-called Intermediate area, can be considered to be divided into separate cultural subregions. We can begin by reviewing the latest literature on the Lower Central American section.

UPDATING PREVIOUS SYNTHESES

Within this decade we have seen the publication of two different summary volumes (7, 130). I have already commented upon them elsewhere (79, 80); they are very different in organization, conception, and even content. Baudez is strict in his coverage of the area. Stone, on the other hand, includes long sections on Chiapas, Guatemala, and central Mexico. Well-known sites in the Maya heartland are discussed at some length, and many Maya objects are included for illustration. Middle American groups are seen as penetrating, influencing, overriding, or otherwise making their presence felt everywhere except for the Panamanian Isthmus. How much can be gained from this kind of approach is a matter for conjecture. In any case, such things as "influences," even if they were subject to proof, do not take us very far in thinking about developments in an area. Neither does the strictly chronological approach (7), but it is preferable. By presenting a sketch for each subarea in terms of five periods (see also 5), Baudez allows us to follow with ease the regional chronologies. His presentation is, however, marred by his division of Lower Central America into a zone of Mesoamerican and a zone of South American tradition. In keeping with Baudez's own interests, the first zone is covered in 30 pages, the latter in about 14. This makes for a thin and sketchy manual, but I found it useful as a starting point for this review of the post-1970 literature.

Special Works

Much new work has appeared on the northern sector which can only be mentioned here: reports on western Salvador (117, 118), eastern Salvador (1), central Honduras (8), northwest Honduras including the upper Sula Valley (45), the Bay Islands (29), the Naco Valley (51, 52), and the site of Travesía (119, 120). In addition, Healey (48, 49) has done research on the long-neglected area of northeast Honduras (see section below on coastal adaptations).

For the southern sector of Gran Nicoya, three new dissertations have substantially changed our views of developments in this area. Two of them, both still unpublished (46, 136), use second-hand materials that were left largely unanalyzed by the original excavators. The other work (64) summarizes the author's own investigations and presents an excellent description of the Nicoya macroecology (see also 67, 69). Lange's reporting of the Sapoa River survey and ceramic analysis are particularly useful, as he manages to reduce Baudez's (6) 41 pottery types to 21—a service to mankind. In a more speculative section, he suggests that maize agriculture was very late in the Sapoa River, an idea that has not gone without comments (89) and counterclarifications (70). His general conclusions, repeated elsewhere (65), raise important queries as to the presumed Mesoamericanization of the Nicoya area.

Sweeney's work on the archaeology of the Guanacaste part of Nicoya (136) presents the full material collected by Coe (20). She offers an exhaustive pottery classification, backed up by a number of consistent radiocarbon dates (134), and discusses trading networks during the last centuries of the Zoned Bichrome period. The area may have been too poorly endowed in natural resources to participate in the later trading spheres of developing civilizations further north. But to the south, the local people were in contact with the Panamanian groups of Parita Bay, and possibly with those of Ecuador in the Santa Elena Peninsula. The supposed Nicoya-Ecuadorean connections are perhaps debatable. Since there does not seem to have been much reciprocal trade between areas within Nicoya itself, according to both Lange and Sweeney, I find it difficult to believe in significant exchanges with very distant groups. Be that as it may, Sweeney's remark that Nicoya never divorced itself from its Chibchan origin, and never became part of Greater Mesoamerica, seems well supported by the settlement pattern and linguistic evidence.

Healey's (46) analysis of the materials collected by Norweb and Willey in 1959-1961 in the Nicaraguan Nicoya, on the Isthmus of Rivas, includes excellent summaries of the ecology, ethnohistory, and archeology of this area, but it is essentially another ceramic report, with the emphasis placed on the time-space ordering of the data. Referring to the connections between Rivas and the Nicoya peninsula itself *(sensu stricto)*, Healey suggests that ties between the two areas were closer during the earlier periods than during Late Polychrome times (A.D. 1200). His inclusion of the Rivas area in the Mesoamerican camp may have been influenced by Longacre's (90) classification of the Chorotega languages (see above). Of course, if influences are to be deduced mostly from ceramics, then it may be appropriate to include Rivas in the Mesoamerican sphere. If other aspects such as ecological adaptations are considered, an inclusion within the Circum-Caribbean or Intermediate Area seems more justified.

Proceeding to the south and east, i.e. to Baudez's supposed zone of South American tradition, and to the earlier of the five periods he proposes, we learn that new Paleo-Indian points have been reported from Turrialba in Costa Rica (125) and from Madden Lake in Panama (12, 13). Although the points were found on the surface, they contribute to our understanding of the arrival of early man in South America. Since the technique of pressure flaking was discontinued by 5000 B.C. (13), the points must be earlier. Much of the extinct Panamanian megafauna (39) was South American in origin; hence it is not surprising to learn that the Madden Lake points resemble those from Fell's cave in Chile, where they were found associated with extinct sloth and the native horse at a radiocarbon age of 11,000 years (10).

In the next preceramic period, Baudez (7) lists only the site of Cerro Mangote in Parita Bay (100). Since 1970, however, six more preceramic sites have been found in Panama, in noncoastal locations. The significance of these sites was touched upon in the Puerto Rican symposium by me (81) and by Ranere (108); I will also discuss them later. Here it may be sufficient to note that these new preceramic sites indicate a greater variety of subsistence adaptations than the presumed shellfish-gathering pattern ascribed to Cerro Mangote.

With respect to developments during the first half of the first millenium B.C., there is still a gap in our knowledge. The archaeological complexes which may belong to this period (41, 64, 123) have not been securely dated.

After 300 B.C. to A.D. 500, corresponding to Baudez's (5, 7) periods III and IV, we have new information from the highlands of Chiriquí in Panama (87–89). The colonization of these cold and wet highlands seems to have been late because they were unsuitable for both hunting-gathering and root crop agriculture. They were finally occupied only as a result of demographic pressures subsequent to the introduction of expansive seed culture in the plains (88).

The innovative research of Cooke (22–24) is essential to the understanding of the prehistory of the Central Region of Panama. His work has demonstrated the unity of this area and the uselessness of previously recognized subdivisions (95, 96). His studies of human adaptations in the provinces bordering Parita Bay have transformed a bare ceramic chronology (63) into a real developmental cultural-ecological sequence. This work has provided the basis for a reinterpretation (84) of the function and iconography of the art objects of the famous Sitio Conte site.

General Works

Recent syntheses of the archaeology of the whole of Lower Central America have not taken into account any of the new approaches mentioned above. They still tend to emphasize comparisons within one country only, or within one aspect of the prehistoric record, usually ceramics, or within spatiotemporal correlations. The narrow focus of these works contrasts with Willey's (142, 144) broad perspectives on developments in the whole of the Intermediate Area.

If we ignore some passages in purple prose, and misleading simplifications, the book on Costa Rica by Stone (131) is useful in providing a clear and orderly discussion of each of the three areas into which Costa Rican archaeology is usually divided, namely Nicoya, Diquís, and the Atlantic watershed. This work is easier to consult than her more general volume (130), and it is a beautifully produced guide to museum collections. But it suffers from the lack of any sense of problem, or of the need for methodology. Ferrero's revised edition (30) provides a more basic understanding of men-environment interactions, and a more up-to-date account of archaeological work in Costa Rica. He is also one of the editors of *Vínculos,* a new bilingual journal which publishes articles on any part of Central America. A special issue of this journal [Volume 2(1), 1976] considers ceramic sequences in 11 different areas, from Lake Yojoa in Honduras to central Panama. Seven out of the 11 articles report the conclusions of unpublished dissertations. The rest discuss work in progress or old work that was never fully published.

The subject of ceramic sequences seems to absorb much of the Central American synthesizer's time. Haberland's article (41) on the chronologies of Lower Central America is a case in point. Although published only very recently, it was written in 1973 and never revised. It is, therefore, seriously out of date, as the bulk of publications has increased dramatically in the last 5 years. His efforts are not without merit, for he presents an excellent resumé of the history of archaeological work and does much to reconcile disparities in Greater Nicoya, central Costa Rica, and greater Chiriquí. But he is a firm believer in having chronological and distributional problems settled first, before turning to "fancy questions" about settlement patterns, ecological adaptations, the nature of culture contact, and the like. There is, of course, an obvious reason why chronological and ecological interpretations have not been more closely associated, to their mutual enrichment. Because of the preoccupation with ceramics, little attention is paid to the recovery of organic remains, the reconstruction of utility areas, the functional study of lithic artifacts, and so forth. The result is what I call diachronic ecology: deducing broad shifts in adaptations, between periods of many centuries, without adequate quantitative data. The unconscious assumption that spatiotemporal correlations are prior to, and not simultaneous with, the study of cultural processes has produced pottery descriptions, including some of my own (78), of unjustified length. Ecological interpretations, based on skimpy evidence, poorly recovered, and incompletely analyzed, are still being appended to these descriptive works without any prior hypothesis. To say that these chronological works are "essentially factual and narrowly historic" (145, p. 513) seems a gentle comment indeed.

SUBSISTENCE AND SETTLEMENT SYSTEMS DURING THE PRECERAMIC AND FORMATIVE PERIODS

The new generation of archaeologists working in Lower Central America are beginning to seek answers to such problems as the nature of preceramic hunting-gathering adaptations, the transition from vegeculture to seed culture, marine versus riverine lifeways along both coasts, and the basis for chiefdom formation. Their work is going in the direction of broader theories and more fundamental processes. Thus, they are following in the footsteps of Willey and Reichel-Dolmatoff, while sharing the same concerns of Flannery, Harris, Lathrap, and others.

Adaptive Variability During the Preceramic and Formative Periods (5000 B.C. to 500 B.C.)

The assumption that the hunting-gathering way of life in the tropics was fairly uniform finds little support in recent work in Panama. Not only were preagricultural peoples of the interior different from those of the coast, but even the coastal groups differed among themselves.

The inhabitants of Cerro Mangote (4800 B.C.), the first preceramic site reported in Central America, were thought to have been shellfish gatherers (100). A similar adaptation was attributed to the pottery-using peoples of the nearby Monagrillo site at 2100 B.C. (146). New radiocarbon dates (A. J. Ranere, personal communication) have apparently extended the history of Monagrillo back to the middle of the fourth millenium B.C. If correct, these dates would make Monagrillo pottery among the oldest in the New World. The first groups intermittently camped at the site when it was still an active beach. Reexcavation of the site using fine-screening techniques (110) point to a heavy reliance upon fish and crustaceans as well as shellfish.

Two additional types of adaptations have recently been documented in the plains and interior lands away from the Parita Bay shoreline. At the Aguadulce shelter, about 18 kilometers from the present coastline, a preceramic broad-spectrum plant-collecting and hunting pattern, with some emphasis on fishing and catching freshwater turtles, lasted from the fifth millenium B.C. to the middle of the third millenium B.C. (110, 111). Further inland, in the foothills of the continental divide in the province of Coclé, at an altitude of 400 meters above sea level, a pure hunting camp was discovered at Cueva de los Ladrones (11). Even more recently, Cooke (personal communication) has found another preceramic site which is neither a rockshelter nor a cave, but a small open camp in the Chiriquí highlands.

In the early 1970s, Ranere's (106) pioneering excavations of four preceramic rockshelters and one open campsite in the canyon of the Río Chiriquí, at elevations between 600 and 900 meters, produced thousands of flakes and stone tools which he analyzed using experimental procedures (107). By combining replication experiments with wear-pattern analysis, he concludes that during the Talamancan phase (4800 B.C. to 2300 B.C.) most chipped stone tools were used as grinding, pounding, or mashing instruments to process wild plants or to work wood. In a subsequent paper (109), he proposes the intriguing idea that the simplicity of tropical forest lithic assemblages may be due to the fact that these were tools to make tools; that is, that stone tools were manufactured, not as ends in themselves, but probably as instruments in the production of more sophisticated implements of wood such as projectile points. Incidentally, this may mark the beginning of man's alteration of the tropical forest. By removing trees for his use, for tools as well as shelter, man must have changed the species composition and structure of the forest, opening it to accelerated invasion by sun-loving herbaceous plants. Among these were probably the ancestors of many cultivated species. By hunting, he also affected predator-prey interactions, removing animals such as the agouti (*Dasyprocta punctata*) on which several tree species are dependent for the dispersal of their seeds (122). Modifications of tropical environments at the hunting-gathering stage must be seen in terms of subtle processes such as these and not only in the dramatic use of fire in the hunt (43).

Ranere's suggestion that the pounding-mashing tools he recovered from the Río Chiriquí shelters were used to process wild plant foods finds support in the carbonized plant remains he recovered. These have been identified by Smith (121) as belonging to two species of seasonally flowering trees (*Hymenaea courbaril* and *Byrsonima* sp.) and two species of nut-bearing palms (*Acrocomia vinifera* and *Scheelea zonensis*). The predominance of trees is suggestive. Lathrap's argument (76) about the antiquity of the bottle gourd in the New World should be interpreted as pointing to the importance of aboriculture in the tropics. Harris (43) proposes that the harvesting of nuts, as among the ancient California Indians, was one of the specialized systems of food procurement that did *not* lead to agriculture. He points out that trees are cross-pollinated and take a long time to yield, while herbs are fast growing and tend to be self-pollinating, which facilitates selection by man. "As a system of food procurement tree nut harvesting is an efficient use of available wild resources, but in terms of the development of food production it is a cul de sac" (43, p. 208). As Harris and many others have pointed out, this is especially true if the collection of patchily distributed forest resources involves maximum movement, which in itself discourages population growth, retards sedentarization, and delays agriculture.

To sum up, the total number of excavated preceramic sites in the western half of the Isthmus of Panama is seven. They show a variety of slightly different settlement-subsistence patterns: a woodworking, forest adaptation in the rockshelters and open sites at midaltitudes in the Chiriquí highlands; a hunting and plant-gathering inland adaptation in the coastal savannas of the central provinces; a shoreline adaptation of fishing and collecting crustaceans and shellfish in Parita Bay; a pure hunting camp in the foothills of the central provinces. This variability in the preceramic record has been attributed (84, 110) to a probable pattern of movement by peoples with a plant-gathering base in search of protein resources.

From Hunting-Gathering to Root Crop Cultivation

Whether plants were domesticated in a single (18, 75) or in multiple centers (32, 105, 127) in the New World, most scholars would agree that Lower Central America is not likely to have been one of the earliest hearths. Incipient cultivation began in Mesoamerica and South America by at least 7000 B.C.–5000 B.C. (112). Manioc agriculture was intensive in the eastern Amazonian lowlands by 3000 B.C. (76) and in northwest Colombia and Venezuela by 2500 B.C. (35, 116) (see also 114). Lower Central America seems to have been late all along the line.

Ranere (106) suggests that the first important shift in subsistence patterns in Chiriquí occurred around 2300 B.C. The sudden appearance of such implements as adzes, chisels, and a stone axe indicate increased clearance of the forest, probably for extensive (as opposed to intensive) manioc cultivation. Snarskis (126) has found *budares* or clay griddles perhaps associated with manioc (see below) in Costa Rica at 1500 B.C. In the Soconusco area of coastal Chiapas and Guatemala (97) during the Early Formative Barras phase (1500 B.C.), the presence of manioc is inferred from thousands of obsidian chips shown by replication experiments (25) to have been used in processing a soft substance.

None of the archaeological evidence for manioc cultivation is conclusive, however. In an exhaustive comparison of the artifacts classified in museums as manioc griddles (*budares*) or as maize-cooking griddles (*comales*), De Boer (26) concludes that it is not possible to distinguish between these two categories on any criteria such as shape, size, or form. Such differences as there are seem to be purely geographical. If the objects were found in Mesoamerica, they have been called *comales;* if in South America, *budares.* De Boer also mentions a study by Barricklo to the effect that manioc grater teeth used ethnographically were much smaller than those ascribed to the same purpose in archeological deposits in Colombia (114). We should keep in mind that griddles can be used to cook other products besides manioc, and that grater teeth can be made of many products besides stone. Because the soft parts of tubers do not preserve well, final proof of manioc cultivation in early times is going to have to rest on the analysis of pollen and phytoliths. And even if and when these are found in datable deposits, it would not settle the problem of one vs several independent centers of manioc domestication. Not only the archaeologists, but also the botanists have different thoughts on this matter. While Spath (127) suggests at least four centers of domestication for the varities now subsumed under *Manihot esculenta* Crantz, other experts favor the idea of only one wild progenitor, the Colombian *M. cartagenensis.* On archaeological grounds I tend to favor the idea of several centers of domestication, including Mesoamerica (where more than 100 species of *Manihot* are found at the present time).

While on the subject of manioc, I would suggest that the great phenotypic variation in this plant (127) made it possible for man to select against, as well as for, the more toxic strains. Lathrap (73) has emphasized human selection in favor of the "bitter" (i.e. poisonous) forms which store better and are richer in starch. He argues that in the eastern South American lowlands the nontoxic, less productive strains were the earlier forms. Toxicity itself is an antipredator device in many "wild" plants (56). Thus, it is quite conceivable that many of the ancestral forms were highly toxic. They may have become less so under cultivation in areas where population densities were low and there was comparatively little premium on maximum starch production with maximum effort. The use of "sweet" manioc as a pot vegetable, in association with many other crops, may have been characteristic of past as it is of present groups in Lower Central America.

In the interior valleys of the Panamanian Isthmus, where the fishing potential of most rivers was reduced by their rapid and rocky course, a pattern based on the cultivation of root crops and the hunting of terrestrial mammals may have lasted well into the first millenium B.C., until the introduction of maize (89). As Harris (42) has convincingly argued, root-crop or vegeculture is a stable system in contrast to seed-crop agriculture which tends to cause ecological degradation and to force people to expand into new areas.

Early Maize in Lower Central America

In the levels of the Aguadulce shelter containing Monagrillo-like ceramics and dated to slightly after 1680 ± 95 B.C., Piperno (personal communication) has recently isolated cross-shaped phytoliths [silica structures in the epidermal cells of some plants (104)] of a grass that may in fact be maize. She used the same techniques as Pearsall (104) did in identifying phytoliths of maize at 2450 B.C. from Real Alto, a Valdivia-phase site in the Santa Elena peninsula of coastal Ecuador (77, 99). In neither case, however, is this data relevant to the origins of maize domestication, which go back in Mesoamerica to much earlier periods (112; see also above). As Galinat (37) points out, the oldest maize cobs found in the Tehuacán valley of south central Mexico at about 7000 B.C. are in the early cultivated rather than in the wild category. According to Pickersgill & Heiser (105), the absence of a suitable ancestor for *Zea mays* in South America and the fact that the earliest maize dates only to 3000 B.C. in the Peruvian highlands and to 2500 B.C. in the Peruvian coast rules out, at least for the moment, a possible hearth of *Zea* domestication in South America. These same authors also suggest that a Nal-Tel-like race of maize spread from Mexico to Peru between 5000 B.C. and 3000 B.C. Two very distinct races—a large-kernel, eight-rowed corn, and a smaller-kernel popcorn—occur in the Valdivia deposits (150). These Ecuadorean strains may represent the first movement south of the cultivar. The later Monagrillo-phase maize could have come to Panama from either north or south.

There has been some confusion surrounding the status of the so-called *Pollo* race of maize of presumed Colombian derivation and its diffusion to Lower Central America. Snarskis (123, 124) mentions the possibility that the one corncob of this race found in highland Costa Rica at the time (more have been found since) should be interpreted as evidence of connections with Colombia. The same corncob has been cited elsewhere (70) as suggesting a possible South American origin for maize farming in the Nicoya peninsula. Dunn (27) warns against the overinterpretation of a single specimen, especially of a cultivar which is botanically so ill defined (see also 32). Recently we have found more than 40 or so cobs of a *Pollo*-like maize on living floors and hearths in the Chiriquí highlands where they have been dated by numerous radiocarbon dates to A.D. 300–A.D. 600 (87). Galinat (38), who has analyzed this collection, suggests that the characteristics of smallness and hardness in the *Pollo* race may be an adaptation to wet and cold conditions and not necessarily a proof of primitiveness or of great antiquity.

Formative Period Interaction Spheres

The idea that during the Formative period (3000 B.C. to 300 B.C.) a whole series of material traits and religious ideas were transmitted from Middle America to the Andean area has a long history in New World studies and will not be reviewed here (see 34). Debate still continues as to whether these presumed contacts took place directly by sea, bypassing southern Central America, or whether they took place by land, through the Isthmian area. In one instance, an earlier argument for direct sea contacts has been revived (103) long after the original proponent has begun to have his doubts (21).

The whole concept of two centers of New World civilization, Mesoamerica and Andean South America, from which everything else was derived, has been questioned recently by Myers (101). Following Lathrap (74), he emphasizes the role played by the tropics in early Formative period developments, and suggests that contacts between the centers of civilization took place by land, through the Intermediate area, and was in the hands of traders. His argument rests on ceramic similarities. I have always been skeptical (81) of the use of simple ceramics in tracing connections at this time level. Peoples living in similar coastal environments would have at their disposal similar "tools" (reeds, shell, spines) to decorate their pottery, and would need the same simple vessel shapes to fulfill their everyday needs. In any case, Myers's conclusion that long-distance sea-contacts need not be invoked to account for widespread similarities in material culture anywhere in the New World tropics is well taken. This caution applies to the spread of plants as well as pots. If Spath (127) is correct in suggesting several centers of manioc domestication in the Americas, then it may not be necessary to call upon ceramic connections as corollary proof for the early diffusion of manioc cultivation directly from coastal Ecuador to coastal Guatemala (25, 40, 97). Incidentally, sea contacts must be high on the list of things that are not subject to proof.

Even if I doubt that simple ceramics can be used to document long-distance trade or significant movements, this does not mean that such contacts did not take place and could not have been important. Lathrap's essay (74) is highly relevant. He shows that existing trade networks in the eastern South American lowlands cover thousands of miles. This trade includes perishable materials such as manioc flour.

On several occasions I have expressed misgivings as to the explanatory value of terms such as diffusion, contact, influence, and so forth. These concepts are diversionary and may discourage us from searching for interaction models of greater generality and resolving power. For instance, "gravity models" of several kinds may be useful (57). Another promising line of investigation might be the role played by trade in the growth of regional centers (149). Much of the trade among tropical forest groups in South America seems to have been subsistence related, or related to the communal ceremonial life, and to have been relatively "democratic." By contrast, much of the Mesoamerican or Andean South American trade may have been status related and controlled by elites in regional centers (31). The growth of comparable centers in lowland tropical South America and the Intermediate area may have been discouraged by the widespread dispersion of the resources traded and by the relatively slow demographic increase. Models that take into account the size and proximity of resource areas, the methods of exploiting and distributing these resources, the uses to which they were put, and their possible effects on demographic increase are likely to be more satisfactory than unicausal explanations.

What I believe should be stressed is that small group size, dispersion of populations, flexibility in resource use, and so forth, is a pan-tropical strategy of great adaptive value.

COASTAL VERSUS INLAND ADAPTATIONS

If any single factor characterizes the ecology of Lower Central America, it is the relative amount of land that is coastal rather than inland. Not surprisingly, coastal adaptations were diverse and important. The mountains of Lower Central America are also relatively narrow, with only small valleys and poorly developed river systems. Nowhere in the region do we find the wide expanses of fertile soils of such areas as the Cauca in Colombia or Oaxaca in southern Mexico. Neither do we encounter floodplains on the immense scale of the Orinoco and Magdalena, not to mention the Amazon. The contrast between highlands and lowlands may also be less pronounced in southern Central America than elsewhere (71). Such as they are, the highlands may be considered first.

Sites with extensive mound complexes, carved monuments, elaborate pottery and the like were described from moderately high elevations in Costa Rica at the beginning of this century (44). They would seem to have been produced by minimally ranked societies, roughly equivalent to the "chiefdoms" of Colombia (113, 115). Recent research confirms the initial impression that these complexes were late in the archaeological record, dating from a few centuries before the Christian era (72) to a few centuries after (62). It may be a general rule that wet and cold highland environments were colonized late, after the introduction of maize (see above). A complete survey of all the sites occurring in two highland valleys of Chirquí in Panama has revealed a site distributional pattern which relates both to natural and to social factors (89). The larger and apparently more ranked villages occurred in the drier, more seasonal of the two valleys. Despite the availability of good cultivable land, the area between the two valleys was sparsely settled, a phenomenon we have attributed to territorial boundary maintenance rather than to environmental causes.

All the other areas of Lower Central America that have been studied in recent years are on or near the coast. Within this decade, three studies have pointed out the great diversity of prehistoric adaptations on the Atlantic coast. Healey (48–50), working on northeast Honduras with a quantifiable faunal collection, provides an excellent discussion of the prehistoric use by one group of three different ecological zones: a freshwater lagoon, the mangrove coast, and the lowland forest. The prosperous groups he describes are very different from the societies of the Bocas area on the Atlantic coast of Panama. This area was a backwater because of its wet, nonseasonal climate and distance from any river. The local peoples had to relie on certain particular techniques. I have applied the term "garden-hunting" to a technique for taking animals from cultivated plots (82). This strategy in effect increased the numbers and biomass of terrestrial mammals, permitting the cropping of the animals as well as of the plants. In a more recent article, Wing (147) has emphasized that this technique was complementary to the use of marine resources.

Magnus (98) has developed an interesting model for the Miskito area of coastal Nicaragua, comparing archaeological remains with modern ethnographic data. In the prehistoric past, there were inland permanent villages and coastal fishing camps; the reverse situation holds today. This is a good reminder of the fact that very different adaptations can coexist within relatively small areas, and that drastic changes can occur, especially in the tropics where many settlement alternatives are possible.

Two studies of Gran Nicoya have an ecological bias. Lange (70) gives a general summary of subsistence through 3000 years. Sweeney's discussion (138) of the Guanacaste area is based on an actual but incomplete faunal sample that includes marine and terrestrial forms. Her reconstruction of hunting and fishing practices is convincing, despite the deficiencies in the materials left to her.

We have attempted controlled comparisons of cultural developments on both coasts of Panama (83, 86, 147) and between different parts of the Pacific coast (85). These comparisons seem to indicate that systems based on high species diversity but low biomass tend to stay generalized and stable for longer periods of time than systems based on more abundant but less diverse resources permitting intensive cropping. The most populated area, where the more "developed" chiefdoms appeared, was the central region of Panama bordering on Parita Bay (22, 23, 55). This is the area of most abundant resources, and it has the longest record of changes in subsistence patterns. I have also discussed the process of chiefdom formation in the central Panamanian provinces using published evidence from archaeology, ecology, ethnohistory, and iconography (84). My suggestion that the so-called Conte style of pottery and gold decoration reflected a ranked society is being tested further by P. Briggs (personal communication).

It is not enough to ask when or where the Circum-Caribbean type chiefdoms arose in Lower Central America (62). It is more important to consider how and why they did so. A proper approach to these problems should combine a knowledge of ecology with an appreciation for the dynamics of social and religious organization.

CONCLUSIONS

The archaeology of Lower Central America so far has not produced many interesting ideas or novel approaches. There has been too much miscellaneous description and not enough analytic thought. Too often the ancient peoples of the region have been regarded as "backward," pale country cousins of their more "civilized" Mesoamerican contemporaries. As any anthropologist should know, these are meaningless labels. Lower Central American societies evolved their own successful and complex systems. The resources of the region supported peoples in considerable abundance. Future work will need to be focused carefully on testable hypotheses of some real theoretical import. There are already encouraging signs of progress in this direction.

The whole stretch from El Salvador to Panama resembles northwest South America. Similar ecological adaptations and a single language family, Macro-Chibchan, were dominant throughout. Other common features were: an ancient coastal-inland symbiosis, combined root and seed crop systems, developed ceramic and metallurgical crafts, small nonhereditary chiefs whose power was ritual and consensual rather than "coercive," and contingent political alliances. It would seem best to abandon parochial distinctions and talk about the Intermediate Area as a whole. (I hope this is the last paper to treat Lower Central America per se).

The real interest of the Intermediate Area is that it illustrates a whole series of ecological and cultural adaptations within a well-defined range. If anything is worth studying, it is the development of local variations and their correlated social forms. It is only by understanding the particular that useful general theory can emerge.

ACKNOWLEDGMENTS

I am grateful to the staff of the Tozzer Library, and to the Peabody Museum, Harvard University, for providing me with facilities and assistance during the research for this paper. The Smithsonian Tropical Research Institute gave encouragement and financial support. I am indebted to M. H. Moynihan for reassurance and his editorial scissors.

This paper would have never been completed had I not been trapped in a hotel room in Mahaballipuram, India, by the northeast monsoon. I must thank whoever was responsible.

Literature Cited

1. Andrews V., E. W. 1971. *The Archeology of Quelepa, El Salvador.* New Orleans: Middle Am. Res. Inst. 199 pp.
2. Andrews V., E. W. 1972. Correspondencias fonológicas entre el Lenca y una lengua mayence. *Estud. Cult. Maya* 8: 341–87
3. Andrews V., E. W. 1977. The southeastern periphery of Mesoamerica: a view from eastern El Salvador. In *Social Process in Maya Prehistory: Studies in Honour of Sir Eric Thompson,* ed. N. Hammond, Chap. 7, pp. 113–34. New York: Academic
4. Baudez, C. F. 1962. Rapport préliminaire sur les recherches archéologiques enterprises dans la vallée de Tempisque, Guanacaste, Costa Rica. *Akt. Int. Amerikanistenkongr., 34th, Wien,* pp. 344–57
5. Baudez, C. F. 1963. Cultural development in Lower Central America. In *Aboriginal Cultural Development in Latin America: an Interpretative Review,* ed. B. J. Meggers, C. Evans. *Smithson. Misc. Collect.* 146(1):45–54
6. Baudez, C. F. 1967. *Recherches archéologiques dans la vallée du Tempisque, Guanacaste, Costa Rica.* PhD thesis. Fac. Lett. et Sci. Hum., Univ. Paris
7. Baudez, C. F. 1970. *Central America.* Geneva: Nagel. 256 pp.
8. Baudez, C. F., Becquelin, P. 1973. Archéologie de Los Naranjos, Honduras. *Etudes Mésoaméricaines,* Vol. 2.
9. Baudez, C. F., Coe, M. D. 1962. Archeological sequences in northwestern Costa Rica. See Ref. 4, pp. 366–73
10. Bird, J. B. 1969. A comparison of south Chilean and Ecuadorean "fishtail" projectile points. *Kroeber Anthropol. Soc. Pap. 40,* pp. 52–71
11. Bird, J. B., Cooke, R. G. 1974. *Excavaciones en la Cueva de los Ladrones, distrito de La Pintada, Provincia de Coclé, Rep. de Panamá.* Informe prelim. Inst. Nac. de Cult., Panama
12. Bird, J. B., Cooke, R. G. 1977. Los artefactos más antiguos de Panamá. *Rev. Nac. Cult.* 6:7–31
13. Bird, J. B., Cooke, R. G. 1977. The occurrence in Panama of two types of Paleo-Indian projectile points. In *Early Man in America from a Circum-Pacific Perspective,* ed. A. L. Bryan. Dep. Anthropol. Univ. Alberta Occas. Pap. 1, pp. 263–72
14. Campbell, L. 1975. Cacaopera. *Anthropol. Ling.* 17(4):146–53
15. Campbell, L. 1976. The last Lenca. *Int. J. Am. Ling.* 42(1):73–78
16. Campbell, L. 1977. Quichean linguistic prehistory. *Univ. Calif. Publ. Ling.* 81. 132 pp.
17. Campbell, L., Kaufman, T. 1976. A linguistic look at the Olmecs. *Am. Antiq.* 41(1):80–89
18. Carter, G. F. 1977. A hypothesis suggesting a single origin of agriculture. In *Origins of Agriculture,* ed. C. A. Reed, pp. 89–133. The Hague: Mouton
19. Coe, M. D. 1962. Costa Rican archeology and Mesoamerica. *Southwest. J. Anthropol.* 18(2):170–83
20. Coe, M. D. 1962. Preliminary report on archeological investigations in coastal Guanacaste, Costa Rica. See Ref. 4, pp. 358–65
21. Coe, M. D. 1977. Discussion. In *The Sea in the Pre-Columbian World; A Conference at Dumbarton Oaks, 1974,* ed. E. P. Benson, pp. 163–66. Washington DC: Dumbarton Oaks
22. Cooke, R. G. 1972. *The Archaeology of Western Coclé Province, Panama.* PhD thesis. Univ. London, England
23. Cooke, R. G. 1976. El hombre y la tierra en el Panamá prehistórico. *Rev. Nac. Cult.* 2:17–38

24. Cooke, R. G. 1976. Panamá: región Central. *Vínculos* 2(1):122–41

25. Davis, D. D. 1975. Patterns of early Formative subsistence in southern Mesoamerica 1500–1100 B.C. *Man* (N.S.) 10:41–59

26. De Boer, W. R. 1975. The archaeological evidence for Manioc cultivation: a cautionary note. *Am. Antiq.* 40(4): 419–33

27. Dunn, M. E. 1978. Suggestions for evaluating archaeological maize. *Am. Antiq.* 43(1):97–99

28. Epstein, J. F. 1959. Dating the Ulua Polychrome Complex. *Am. Antiq.* 25(1):125–29

29. Epstein, J. F., Véliz, V. 1977. Reconocimiento arqueológico en la Isla de Roatán, Honduras. *Yaxkin* 2(1):28–39

30. Ferrero, M. 1978. *Costa Rica Precolombina.* San José: Editorial Costa Rica

31. Flannery, K. V. 1968. The Olmec and the Valley of Oaxaca: A model for interregional interaction in Formative times. In *Dumbarton Oaks Conference on the Olmec,* ed. E. P. Benson, pp. 79–110. Washington DC: Dumbarton Oaks

32. Flannery, K. V. 1973. The origins of agriculture. *Ann. Rev. Anthropol.* 2: 271–310

33. Fonseca, Z. O., Richardson, J. B. III. 1978. South American and Mayan cultural contacts at Las Huacas site, Costa Rica. *Ann. Carnegie Mus.* 47(13):299–317

34. Ford, J. 1969. A comparison of the Formative cultures in the Americas. *Smithson. Contrib. Anthropol.* Vol. 11

35. Foster, D. W., Lathrap, D. W. 1973. Further evidence of a well-developed tropical forest culture on the north coast of Colombia during the first and second millenium B. C. *J. Steward Anthropol. Soc.* 4(2):160–99

36. Freidel, D. A. 1978. Maritime adaptation and the rise of Maya civilization: the view from Cerros, Belize. In *Prehistoric Coastal Adaptations: the Economy and Ecology of Maritime Middle America,* ed. B. L. Stark, B. Voorhies, chap. 11, pp. 179–243. New York: Academic

37. Galinat, W. C. 1977. The origin of corn. In *Corn and Corn Improvement,* ed. G. F. Sprague, pp. 1–47. Madison: Am. Soc. Agron.

38. Galinat, W. C. 1979. The archaeological maize remains from Volcan, Panama—a comparative perspective. See Ref. 87

39. Gazin, C. L. 1957. Explorations for the remains of giant ground sloths in Pan-

ama. *Smithson. Inst. Ann. Rep. 1956,* pp. 341–54. Washington DC

40. Green, D. F., Lowe, G. W. 1967. Altamira and Padre Piedra, early Preclassic sites in Chiapas, Mexico. *New World Archeol. Found. Pap.* 20(15). 133 pp.

41. Haberland, W. 1978. Lower Central America. In *Chronologies in New World Archaeology,* ed. R. E. Taylor, C. W. Meighan, pp. 398–430. New York: Academic

42. Harris, D. R. 1973. The prehistory of tropical agriculture: an ethnoecological model. In *The Explanation of Culture Change,* ed. C. E. Renfrew, pp. 391–417. London: Duckworth

43. Harris, D. R. 1977. Alternative pathways toward agriculture. See Ref. 18, pp. 179–243

44. Hartman, C. V. 1901. *Archaeological Researches in Costa Rica.* Stockholm: Royal Ethnogr. Mus.

45. Hasemann, G., Véliz, V., Van Gerpen, L. 1978. *Informe preliminar, Currusté: Fase 1.* Honduras: San Pedro Sula (Mimeo). 78 pp.

46. Healey, P. F. 1974. *Archaeological survey of the Rivas region, Nicaragua.* PhD thesis. Harvard Univ., Cambridge, Mass. 567 pp.

47. Healey, P. F. 1974. The Cuyamel Caves: Preclassic sites in northeast Honduras. *Am. Antiq.* 39(3):435–47

48. Healey, P. F. 1975. H-CN-4 (Williams Ranch Site): Preliminary report on a Selin period site in the Department of Colon, northeast Honduras. *Vínculos* 1(2): 61–71

49. Healey, P. F. 1978. Excavations at Río Claro, northeast Honduras: preliminary report. *J. Field Archaeol.* 5:16–28

50. Healey, P. F. 1978. *Preliminary report on the paleoecology of the Selin Farm Site (H-CN-5), Department of Colon, Honduras.* Presented at Ann. Meet. Soc. Am. Archaeol., 43d, Tucson

51. Henderson, J. S. 1976. Pre-columbian trade networks in northwestern Honduras. *J. Field Archaeol.* 3:342–46

52. Henderson, J. S. 1976. Vínculos comerciales precolombinos en el noroeste de Honduras. *Yaxkin* 1(3):14–20

53. Henderson, J. S. 1977. *Northwestern Honduras and the eastern Maya frontier.* Presented at Ann. Meet. Soc. Am. Archaeol., 42nd, New Orleans

54. Holt, D., Bright, W. 1976. La lengua Paya y las fronteras lingüísticas de Mesoamérica. *Yaxkin* 1(2):35–42

55. Ichon, A. 1974. *Archéologie du sud de la Péninsule d'Azuero, Panama.* PhD the-

sis. Univ. Paris. Lille: Serv. Reprod. Thèses

56. Janzen, D. H. 1973. Tropical agroecosystems. *Science* 182:1212–19

57. Johnson, G. A. 1977. Aspects of regional analysis in archaeology. *Ann. Rev. Anthropol.* 6:479–508

58. Kaufman, T. 1973. Areal linguistics and Middle America. In *Current Trends in Linguistics,* ed. T. Sebeok, 2:459–83. The Hague: Mouton

59. Kaufman, T. 1974. Meso-american Indian languages. *Encyclopedia Britannica* 11:952–63. 15th ed.

60. Kaufman, T. 1976. Archaeological and linguistic correlations in Maya-land and associated areas of Meso-america. *World Archaeol.* 8(1):101–18

61. Kennedy, N. C. 1977. On the frontier of Playa de los Muertos, Honduras. Presented at Ann. Meet. Soc. Am. Archaeol., 42nd, New Orleans

62. Kennedy, W. J. 1974. The appearance of the chiefdom and its environmental setting in the Raventazón River area, Costa Rica. *Proc. Int. Congr. Americanists, 41st, Mexico,* 1:560–67

63. Ladd, J. 1964. Archaeological investigations in the Parita and Santa Maria zones of Panama. *Bur. Am. Ethnol. Bull. 193*

64. Lange, F. W. 1971. Cultural history of the Sapoa River Valley, Costa Rica. *Logan Mus. Anthropol. Occas. Pap. 4*

65. Lange, F. W. 1971. Northwestern Costa Rica: Pre-Columbian Circum-Caribbean affiliations. *Folk* 13:43–64

66. Lange, F. W. 1971. Marine resources: a viable subsistence alternative for the prehistoric lowland Maya. *Am. Anthropol.* 73(3):619–39

67. Lange, F. W. 1972. The salvage archaeology of a Zoned Bichrome cemetery, Costa Rica. *Am. Antiq.* 37(2):240–45

68. Lange, F. W. 1976. The northern Central American buffer: a current perspective. *Lat. Am. Res. Rev.* 11:177–83

69. Lange, F. W. 1977. Estudios arqueológicos en el Valle de Nosara, Guanacaste, Costa Rica. *Vínculos* 2(1–2):27–36

70. Lange, F. W. 1978. Coastal settlements in northwestern Costa Rica. See Ref. 36, Chap. 6, pp. 101–19

71. Lange, F. W. 1979. Theoretical and descriptive aspects of frontier studies. *Lat. Am. Res. Rev.* 14(1):221–25

72. Lange, F. W., Murray, T. A. 1972. The archaeology of San Dimas Valley, Costa Rica. *Katunob* 7:50–91

73. Lathrap, D. W. 1970. *The Upper Amazon.* New York: Praeger

74. Lathrap, D. W. 1973. The antiquity and importance of long-distance trade relationships in the moist tropics of Pre-Columbian South America. *World Archaeol.* 5(2):170–86

75. Lathrap, D. W. 1975. *Ancient Ecuador: Culture, Clay and Creativity.* Chicago: Field Mus. Nat. Hist.

76. Lathrap, D. W. 1977. Our father the cayman, our mother the gourd: Spinden revisted, or a unitary model for the emergence of agriculture in the New World. See Ref. 18, pp. 713–51

77. Lathrap, D. W., Marcos, J. G., Zeidler, J. A. 1977. Real Alto: an ancient ceremonial center. *Archaeology* 30(1):3–13

78. Linares, O. F. 1968. Cultural chronology in the Gulf of Chiriquí, Panama. *Smithson. Contrib. Anthropol.* Vol. 8

79. Linares, O. F. 1971. Review of *Central America* by C. F. Baudez. *Am. Anthropol.* 73(6):1413–14

80. Linares, O. F. 1973. Review of *Pre-Columbian Man Finds Central America* by D. Stone. *Am. J. Archaeol.* 77(3):361–62

81. Linares, O. F. 1976. From the Late Preceramic to the Early Formative in the Intermediate Area: some issues and methodologies. In *Proc. Puerto Rican Symp. Archaeol., 1st, San Juan, 1974,* ed. L. S. Robinson, pp. 65–77

82. Linares, O. F. 1976. "Garden hunting" in the American tropics. *Hum. Ecol.* 4(4):331–49

83. Linares, O. F. 1977. Adaptive strategies in western Panama. *World Archaeol.* 8(3):304–19

84. Linares, O. F. 1977. Ecology and the Arts in Ancient Panama. *Studies in Pre-Columbian Art and Archaeology,* 17. Washington DC: Dumbarton Oaks

85. Linares, O. F., Cooke, R. G. 1975. *Differential exploitation of lagoon-estuary systems in Panama.* Presented at Ann. Meet. Soc. Am. Archaeol., 40th, Dallas

86. Linares, O. F., Ranere, A. J. 1971. Human adaptations to the tropical forests of western Panama. *Archaeology* 24(4):346–55

87. Linares, O. F., Ranere, A. J., eds. 1979. *Adaptive Radiations in Western Panama.* Peabody Mus. Monogr. Ser. 5. In press

88. Linares, O. F., Sheets, P. D. 1979. Highland agricultural villages in the Volcan Baru region. See Ref. 87

89. Linares, O. F., Sheets, P. D., Rosenthal, E. J. 1975. Prehistoric agriculture in tropical highlands. *Science* 187:137–45

90. Longacre, R. 1974. Systemic comparison and reconstruction. In *Handbook of Middle American Indians, Vol. 5: Linguistics*, ed. N. McQuown, pp. 117–59. Austin: Univ. Texas Press

91. Longyear, J. M. III. 1947. Cultures and peoples of the southeastern Maya frontier. *Theoretical Approaches to Problems.* Carnegie Inst. No. 3 (Mimeo)

92. Longyear, J. M. III. 1966. Archaeological survey of El Salvador. In *Handbook of Middle American Indians, Vol. 4: Archaeological Frontiers and External Connections*, ed. G. Ekholm, G. R. Willey, Chap. 7, pp. 132–56. Austin: Univ. Texas Press

93. Longyear, J. M. III. 1969. The problem of Olmec influences in the pottery of western Honduras. *Proc. Int. Congr. Americanists, 38th, Stuttgart* 1:491–97

94. Lothrop, S. K. 1939. The southeastern frontier of the Maya. *Am. Anthropol.* 41(1):42–54

95. Lothrop, S. K. 1948. The archaeology of Panama. In *Handbook of South American Indians*, ed. J. Steward, 4:143–67

96. Lothrop, S. K. 1959. The archaeological picture in southern Central America. *Proc. Int. Congr. Americanists, 33rd, San José,* 1:165–72

97. Lowe, G. W. 1975. The early Preclassic Barra Phase of Altamira, Chiapas: a review with new data. *Pap. New World Archaeol. Found.* 38:1–39

98. Magnus, R. W. 1978. The prehistoric and modern subsistence patterns of the Atlantic coast of Nicaragua: a comparison. See Ref. 36, pp. 61–80

99. Marcos, J. G., Lathrap, D. W., Zeidler, J. A. 1976. Ancient Ecuador revisited. *Bull. Field Mus. Nat. Hist.* 47(6):3–8

100. McGimsey, C. R. III. 1956. Cerro Mangote: a preceramic site in Panama. *Am. Antiq.* 22(2):151–61

101. Myers, T. P. 1978. Formative-period interaction spheres in the Intermediate Area: archaeology of Central America and adjacent South America. In *Advances in Andean Archaeology*, ed. D. L. Browman, pp. 203–34. The Hague: Mouton

102. Norweb, H. A. 1964. Ceramic stratigraphy in southeastern Nicaragua. *Proc. Int. Congr. Americanists, 35th, Mexico,* pp. 551–61

103. Paulsen, A. C. 1977. Patterns of maritime trade between south coastal Ecuador and western Mesoamerica, 1500 B.C.-A.D. 600. See Ref. 21, pp. 141–60

104. Pearsall, D. 1978. Phytolith analysis of archaeological soils: evidence for maize cultivation in Formative Ecuador. *Science* 199:177–78

105. Pickersgill, B., Heiser, C. B. Jr. 1977. Origins and distribution of plants domesticated in the New World tropics. See Ref. 18, pp. 803–35

106. Ranere, A. J. 1972. *Early human adaptations to the New World tropical forest.* PhD thesis. Univ. California, Davis, Calif.

107. Ranere, A. J. 1975. Toolmaking and tool use among Preceramic peoples of Panama. In *Lithic Technology: Making and Using Stone Tools*, ed. E. Swanson, pp. 173–209. The Hague: Mouton

108. Ranere, A. J. 1976. The Preceramic of Panama: the view from the Interior. See Ref. 81, pp. 103–37

109. Ranere, A. J. 1979. Preceramic shelters in the Talamancan Range (5000 B.C. to 300 B.C.) See Ref. 87

110. Ranere, A. J., Hansell, P. 1978. Early subsistence along the Pacific coast of Panama. See Ref. 36, pp. 43–59

111. Ranere, A. J., McCarty, R. 1976. Informe preliminar sobre la excavación de un sitio precerámico en Panamá. *Actas IV Simp. Nac. Antropol., Arqueol. Etnohist. Panamá, 1973, Panama* 483–93

112. Reed, C. A. 1977. Origins of agriculture: discussion and some conclusions. See Ref. 18, pp. 879–953

113. Reichel-Dolmatoff, G. 1953. *Colombia: Período Indígena.* Mexico: Inst. Panam. Geog. e Hist.

114. Reichel-Dolmatoff, G. 1957. Momíl, a Formative sequence from the Sinú Valley, Colombia. *Am. Antiq.* 22:226–34

115. Reichel-Dolmatoff, G. 1961. The agricultural basis of the sub-Andean chiefdoms of Colombia. In *The Evolution of Horticultural Systems in Native South America, Causes and Consequences*, ed. J. Wilbert, pp. 83–100, Caracas: La Salle

116. Roosevelt, A. 1977. *La Gruta: an early tropical forest community in the middle Orinoco basin.* Presented at Ann. Meet. Am. Anthropol. Assoc., 76th, Houston

117. Sharer, R. J. 1974. The prehistory of the Southeastern Maya periphery. *Curr. Anthropol.* 15(2):165–87

118. Sharer, R. J. 1978. Pottery and conclusions. In *The Prehistory of Chalchuapa, El Salvador*, ed. R. J. Sharer, 3:209. Philadelphia: Univ. Pennsylvania Press

119. Sheehy, J. J. 1976. Direcciones temáticas en los estudios de las poblaciones mayas. *Yaxkin* 1(3):42–54

120. Sheehy, J. J. 1976. *Excavations at Travesía: a preliminary report.* Pre-

sented at Ann. Meet. Soc. Am. Archaeol., 42nd, New Orleans

121. Smith, C. E. 1979. Plant remains from the Chiriqui sites and ancient vegetational patterns. See Ref. 87

122. Smythe, N. E. 1978. *The Natural History of the Central American Agouti* (*Dasyprocta punctata*). Smithson. Contrib. Zool. 257. 52 pp.

123. Snarskis, M. J. 1975. Excavaciones estratigráficas en la vertiente Atlántica de Costa Rica. *Vínculos* 1(1):2–17

124. Snarskis, M. J. 1976. Stratigraphic excavations in the eastern lowlands of Costa Rica. *Am. Antiq.* 41(3):342–53

125. Snarskis, M. J. 1977. Turrialba (9-FG-T), un sitio Paleoindio en el este de Costa Rica. *Vínculos* 3(1–2):13–25

126. Snarskis, M. J. 1978. *The earliest ceramics from Costa Rica: La Montaña, a middle Formative site on the Atlantic watershed.* Presented at Ann. Meet. Soc. Am. Archaeol., 43rd, Tucson

127. Spath, C. D. 1973. Plant domestication: the case of *Manihot esculenta. J. Steward Anthropol. Soc.* 5(1):45–67

128. Stone, D. 1957. The archaeology of central and southern Honduras. *Pap. Peabody Mus. Archaeol. Ethnol, Harvard,* 49(3)

129. Stone, D. 1959. The eastern frontier of Mesoamerica. *Mitteilungen aus dem* 25:118–21. Hamburg: Mus. Volkerkunde

130. Stone, D. 1972. *Pre-Columbian Man Finds Central America.* Cambridge: Peabody Mus. Press. 231 pp.

131. Stone, D. 1977. *Pre-Columbian Man in Costa Rica.* Cambridge: Peabody Mus. Press

132. Strong, W. D. 1935. Archaeological investigations in the Bay Islands, Spanish Honduras. *Smithson. Misc. Collect.* 92(14). 176 pp.

133. Strong, W. D., Kidder, A. II, Paul, A. J. D. Jr. 1938. Preliminary report of the Smithsonian Institution—Harvard University expedition to northwestern Honduras, 1936. *Smithson. Misc. Collect.* 97(1):1–29

134. Struiver, M., ed. 1977. *Radiocarbon,* p. 219

135. Suárez, J. A. 1974. South American Indian languages. *Encyclopedia Britannica* 17:105–12. 15th ed.

136. Sweeney, J. W. 1975. *Guanacaste, Costa Rica: an Analysis of Precolumbian Ceramics from the Northwest Coast.* PhD thesis. Univ. Pennsylvania, Philadelphia, Pa.

137. Sweeney, J. W. 1976. Ceramic analysis from three sites in northwest coastal Guanacaste. *Vínculos* 2(1):37–44

138. Sweeney, J. W. 1976. *Subsistence in three villages in Precolumbian coastal Guanacaste.* Presented at Ann. Meet. Soc. Am. Archaeol., 42nd, New Orleans

139. Thompson, J. E. S. 1970. *Maya History and Religion.* Norman: Univ. Oklahoma Press

140. Véliz, V., Willey, G. R., Healey, P. F. 1977. Clasificación descriptiva preliminar de la cerámica de Roatán. *Yaxkin* 2(1):7–18

141. Wheeler, A. 1972. Proto-Chibchan. In *Comparative Studies in American Languages,* ed. E. Mattron et al, pp. 93–108. The Hague: Mouton

142. Willey, G. R. 1959. The "Intermediate Area" of nuclear America; its prehistoric relationships to Middle America and Peru. See Ref. 96, pp. 184–94

143. Willey, G. R. 1969. The mesoamericanization of the Honduran-Salvadorean periphery: a symposium commentary. See Ref. 93, pp. 537–42

144. Willey, G. R. 1971. *An Introduction to American Archaeology, Vol. 2, South America.* Englewood Cliffs, NJ: Prentice Hall

145. Willey, G. R. 1978. A summary scan. See Ref. 41, pp. 513–63

146. Willey, G. R., McGimsey, C. R. III. 1954. The Monagrillo culture of Panama. *Pap. Peabody Mus. Archaeol. Ethnol.* 49(2)

147. Wing, E. 1979. Aquatic fauna and reptiles from the Atlantic and Pacific sites. See Ref. 87

148. Wyckoff, L. L. 1974. The Nicaragua archaeological survey, a preliminary report. *Indian Notes* 10(4):99–107

149. Zeitlin, R. N. 1978. Long-distance exchange and the growth of a regional center; an example from the southern Isthmus of Tehuantepec. See Ref. 36, pp. 183–210

150. Zevallos, C. M., Galinat, W. C., Lathrap, D. W., Leng, E. R., Marcos, J. G., Klumpp, K. M. 1977. The San Pablo corn kernel and its friends. *Science* 196:385–89

Ann. Rev. Anthropol. 1979. 8:45-69

MESOAMERICAN COMMUNITY STUDIES: THE PAST DECADE

♦9626

Erve J. Chambers

Department of Anthropology, University of South Florida,
Tampa, Florida 33620

Philip D. Young

Department of Anthropology, University of Oregon, Eugene, Oregon 97403

INTRODUCTION

For more than 50 years, Mesoamerica[1] has provided the field for an impressive amount of anthropological research. The overwhelming bulk of the work has been reported in the form of community studies. To date, there are more than 100 published book-length studies of Mexican and Guatemalan communities; more than half of these have appeared during the past decade.

Our concern in this essay is to review the work published in book form within the decade 1967–1977. The sheer quantity of available material evidences the discipline's continued interest in the peoples of Mesoamerica. In spite of the number of studies cited in this essay, the actual amount of work that has been done over the past 10 years is underrepresented. Only a few studies by European scholars are discussed here; we have ignored almost totally the wealth of journal articles; we have made no attempt to trace the numerous relevant dissertations;[2] and we have only touched on the

[1]We use "Mesoamerica" to mean Mexico and Guatemala. More traditional usage (80) specifies the boundaries of Mesoamerica as coinciding with the area of prehispanic high culture. Our usage, we trust, generates no great confusion, does no great violence to convention, and is certainly less clumsy than the constant repetition of "Mexico and Guatemala."

[2]See the recent compilation by Deal (39). This source lists only dissertations published by University Microfilms International, yet since 1967 there are at least 120 that deal with Mesoamerica as we define it and that would qualify as community studies.

45

0084-6570/79/1015-0045$01.00

contributions of disciplines other than anthropology. Despite our omissions, we believe we have sampled widely enough to provide a broad view of current research trends.

Notwithstanding the considerable and continuing interest in conducting Mesoamerican community studies, there have been few serious attempts to review or critique recent research. The last attempt at a comprehensive overview of work of this nature was Cline's (31) review of Mexican community studies, which appeared in 1952 in the context of an extended review of Lewis's restudy of Tepoztlan (83). Tax's (129) *Heritage of Conquest,* based on a Viking Fund Seminar devoted to summarizing existent knowledge of Middle American ethnology, was published in the same year. Surveys of Mesoamerican Indian groups based extensively on community study research have appeared in three volumes of the *Handbook of Middle American Indians* (97, 138, 139) and in Benítez's (16) *Los Indios de Mexico,* all published in the late 1960s. With the exception of Beals (13), most commentary since that time has appeared either in the community studies themselves or in review essays of limited scope (14, 25, 28, 41, 45, 55, 59, 131, 132).

We have chosen the study of change and persistence as a central focus for this essay. It was not a difficult choice, because the great part of the literature we have reviewed is directed to these two complementary themes. It should be noted that adoption of this theme has led us to emphasize some studies and pay less attention to others, not entirely on the basis of the overall merits of each contribution.

For the sake of avoiding later confusion, a few terms should be clarified. In this essay, *Indian* populations are those which identify at least in part with an indigenous past and which generally accept the appellation. *Mestizo* (for most of Mexico) and *Ladino* (Guatemala) populations are those of mixed Spanish and Indian heritage. Both Indian and Mestizo or Ladino populations can and often do reside in the same community and, in many instances, the terms have become virtually meaningless as accurate markers of ethnic boundaries. The term *peasant* has been used loosely in the literature, and is often applied to communities which rely very little on agricultural production. We prefer the usage *rural peoples.* The term *community study* is also subject to misunderstanding. In our sense, a *community* is a group of people living in close proximity, most often in a place with recognized geographical or political boundaries. A community study may be the result of research devoted to a single such place, or to a part of a community (as, for example, in the study of an Indian group within a larger community), or to the comparison of a number of recognized and bounded communities.

APPROACHES TO THE COMMUNITY

Historically, Mesoamerican ethnographic research may be divided into four stages, each with the fuzzy boundaries that characteristically result from efforts to divide local developmental stages chronologically. The first stage, by far the longest temporally, includes the work of enthusiastic but amateur ethnographers—explorers, churchmen, local historians, and the like—carried out during and immediately after the colonial period. These individuals left us detailed if somewhat spotty accounts of rural life in Mexico and Guatemala. Among the most remarkable is John Lloyd Stevens's (127) justly famous *Incidents of Travel in Central America, Chiapas, and Yucatan.*

The beginning of stage two coincides with both the mid-nineteenth century publication of Stevens's work and with the beginnings of professional anthropology. Area studies, offered both by European and American anthropologists, are the notable contributions of this stage. Much of the work is of a survey nature, clearly marked by the aims of culture history, and almost completely devoted to the study of Indian "tribal" groups. LaFarge & Byers' (81) research in northwest Guatemala is a good example.

Robert Redfield's (110) study of Tepoztlan marks the beginning of a third stage of Mesoamerican research. It is the first clear example of a detailed study focused on a single community. A significant number of the contemporary community studies discussed in this essay do not depart appreciably from the standards and presumptions of research laid out during the two decades of study beginning with Redfield's work and culminating in Oscar Lewis's (83) restudy of the same village. This stage is discussed in Cline's (31) review of Mexican community studies and in Carmack's (25) briefer discussion of Guatemalan community studies.

For the most part, our essay is concerned with a fourth stage. It is represented by numerous contributions which prove virtually impossible to typify. If anything, the period might be described as one of challenge and response. It is a time in which the genre of community study and its specific applications to Latin America have managed to survive serious criticism (2, 82, 102, 148), giving rise to a considerable amount of innovation and experimentation in the process.

Traditions of Community Study: Mexico and the United States

After a brief period of relative inactivity following the methodological controversies focused on the community study approach in general, the past decade has seen an unprecedented proliferation of Mesoamerican community studies. In anthropology, some of this expansion can be attributed to the growth of the profession and to increased opportunities for publication. For United States and Mexican researchers alike, recent difficulties in obtaining funding for overseas research have no doubt also contributed to the popularity of research sites nearer to home. But we doubt that these factors alone can fully account for the unprecedented amount of attention currently being focused on this region of the world, not only by anthropologists but by colleagues in other social science disciplines as well.

In the United States, the community study approach since the 1930s has been closely linked with an interest in the peoples of Mexico and Guatemala. The earlier studies (cf 11, 19, 21, 40, 51, 83, 104, 110) tended to be holistic—sometimes to the point of exhaustion—and focused on the single community as an isolated unit. Little attention was paid to links between the community and wider spheres of influence, and this tendency became fuel for much of the later criticism of the method.

Recent studies contributed by researchers from the United States have generally been more problem oriented than holistic. In Arensberg's (5) terms, the community has become more a convenient "object" for testing hypotheses and assumptions about a variety of human characteristics than a "sample" from which to make broad and general pronouncements about the rural peoples of Mesoamerica. Perhaps because of their problem orientation, recent studies tend to be less bulky than their predecessors. All in all, they treat a wide variety of the current concerns of anthropology.

Given the number of community studies published during the past decade, we are surprised to see that researchers in the United States have done little serious follow-up on the earlier critiques of the community study method. Neither have there been any attempts to utilize systematically the wealth of community study materials in any kind of comparative effort directed toward a broader statement concerning the rural peoples of Mesoamerica.

Our view of community studies contributed by Mexicans working in their own country is quite different. There is no comparable recent record of interest in the community study on the part of Guatemalan anthropologists. As was true in earlier decades, there are isolated instances of studies emanating from European researchers (cf 50, 72, 123, 137), and French regional geographers (10) have shown a decided interest in contemporary Mexico. As for Mexican anthropologists, Beals (13) notes that more often than not they have gone directly into government employment in development related projects and, until recently, have not pursued basic research in the same way as have their more academically oriented colleagues in the United States. It is only during the past decade that any substantial number of community studies have emerged from Mexico. The more notable of these have been the series of ethnographies published by the Instituto Nacional Indigenista (INI) and a recent series originating from the Instituto Nacional de Antropología e Historia (INAH).

The applied focus has been evident in most of the community studies contributed by Mexican anthropologists. Controversies related to philosophies of development have provided fuel for considerable debate over the intent of the community study and over the anthropologist's view of rural life in Mexico (3, 4, 18, 27, 50, 86, 103, 121, 124, 126, 142, 143). There is a vitality in these arguments which seems lacking in most of the material currently being published in the United States. The work of the INI, an agency of the Mexican government, generally takes a more moderate (i.e. capitalistic) view of rural development, while most recent contributions from the INAH clearly present a Marxist perspective.

Topical Interests

Policy-oriented and applied studies have grown in importance, owing partly to the emphasis given them by Mexican anthropologists. Particular attention has been paid to agrarian reform, economic development, and education. Topics related to identity and ethnic awareness and to urbanization have also grown in importance. Some areas of long interest, such as world view and religion, continue to be represented. Other areas which have never seemed to be of great interest to Mesoamericanists, such as social organization, are still underrepresented in the community study literature.

Regions of Study

Eighty-six community studies were reviewed for this essay. Of these, 74 are devoted to Mexican communities. The regional distribution of recent community studies in Mexico is put off balance by several team research efforts of long duration which have yielded a number of separate studies. The most notable are the Harvard Chiapas Project, directed by Evon Vogt, and joint research in the state of Morelos, directed by Arturo Warman. Even so, the studies are more widely distributed than they were 20 years ago (31). Nearly two-thirds of the states of Mexico are represented by at least one recent community study. The favored state regions are much as they were for previous decades: Chiapas, 13 studies: Oaxaca, 11; Michoacan 9; Mexico, 8; Puebla, 5; Morelos, 5. Among the studies devoted to Mexican Indian groups, more than half concentrate on Maya and Zapotec peoples.

As in earlier decades, Guatemalan community studies continue to be concentrated in rural highland areas north of the capital.

Methods and Boundaries

Most of the recent innovations in community study methods can be attributed to earlier criticisms which saw the approach trapped in time and space. In response to the synchronism of most earlier studies, there have been several new contributions which make considerable use of archival sources. These often combine this material with research based on participant observation (29, 33, 56, 59, 88, 117, 130, 144–146). Also, Mexican historians have sometimes managed convincingly to combine current observations with local histories (cf 61), and an interesting perspective has been gained from the still rare approach of community restudy (47, 69).

There have been several kinds of responses to the spatial boundedness of past community studies. Group and team research approaches (cf 9, 12, 32, 36, 49, 57, 90, 140, 144, 145) have become increasingly popular and serve to expand the microcosmic view so often associated with the lone ethnographer working among a select and necessarily small population. Much the same effect has been gained from the increased use of quantifiable survey research (cf 44, 90, 99, 114, 133, 145, 146) and other expansive methods such as network analysis (3, 69, 133, 144). Still, participant observation and intensive interviewing have remained the mainstays of community study in Mesoamerica. This influence is further evidenced by the extent to which these methods have been adopted by researchers from other disciplines (49, 57, 61, 117, 147).

While still attending to a single community, some studies have included data from neighboring communities (cf 69, 137); others have paid considerable attention to influences from outside the community (cf 15, 54, 76, 107).

A number of studies have included several communities within a particular region (cf 46, 91, 105). Still others have focused on tribal rather than community boundaries (cf 8, 30, 62, 112, 134). A few studies have viewed communities in their relationship to a central place, such as an urban market or industrial employer (cf 12, 35, 90). Others have focused on the *ejido* (communal land allotments) as a collectivity of communities (cf 58, 117, 147).

Many recent community studies have taken the political unit of the municipality as the research parameter rather than the single community. This trend is exemplified in most of the work of the Harvard Chiapas Project as well as numerous other studies (cf 26, 73, 88, 99). Some studies have included regions even larger than the municipality (cf 24, 32, 48, 144, 145). There are also instances of comparison of communities in different regions (7, 100).

In all, the experimentation in regional focus which has emerged during the last decade (not, we note, without some precedents in earlier years) stands as one of the greatest contributions of recent Mesoamerican community studies.

FOCUS ON CHANGE

There are no more prevalent issues developed in recent Mesoamerican community studies than those pertaining to social, economic, and political change. These are all subsumed in the concern for development or the lack of it in rural settings. This interest is hardly surprising in view of the rapid and uneven development Mexico and Guatemala are currently experiencing. Nor is it surprising in view of the political and economic controversies of our time. Many of these peaked during the late 1960s, roughly the beginning of the period of community study described in this essay.

Obstacles to Change: Three Views

THE COMMUNITY AS OBSTACLE   A number of recent community studies (e.g. 14, 76, 79, 95, 137) have tended to view the community itself as a major obstacle to change and development. Influenced both by Foster's (52) concept of the "Image of Limited Good" and by Lewis's (84) approach to the "Culture of Poverty," community studies in this vein support the hypothesis that the values of rural peoples, especially those at the bottom of the rural stratification system, hinder their ability to respond to opportunities for change.

It is a view which describes the rural environment as fundamentally conservative. Foster's (53) own study depicts a community situation where attitudes of envy and distrust prevail and where sustained intergroup cooperation seems virtually impossible. Similar conclusions are arrived at by two of Foster's students. Nelson (98) focuses on community responses to planned social innovation sponsored by the United Nations' Center for Fundamental Education in Latin America (CREFAL). In describing the community's response to actual development opportunities, Nelson suggests that the villagers' inability to work for a "common good" or to adopt a view favorable to capital accumulation has effectively sabotaged most development goals. Diaz (42), working in a town near Guadalajara, finds that most of the opportunities available in this rapidly urbanizing center are seized by the established middle class and outsiders. Lower class townspeople, she asserts, appear to maintain a lifestyle and value system that is antithetic to full participation in the town's economic growth.

Belshaw (15), Kearney (76), and van Zantwijk (137) arrive at nearly identical conclusions. It has become fashionable to be highly critical of such studies because of their tendency to lay the blame for underdevelopment on the least powerful members of society, but they are nonetheless worth our attention. The fact that most of the studies are devoted to Tarascan communities and that several of the investigators (53, 98, 137) were associated with the CREFAL project suggests that their conclusions might be bound to a particular set of circumstances. Van Zantwijk (137) goes the furthest in suggesting that there might be some special meaning to be gleaned from Tarascan social character and the disappointing results of the CREFAL project.

REGIONS OF REFUGE   The Tarascan studies as well as the Tarahumara study of Kennedy (79) represent the case for Aguirre Beltrán's (3, 71) notion of the "region of refuge," an area physically and culturally isolated from mainstream Mexican society. In Aguirre Beltrán's view, Spanish activities in such areas during colonial times led to the development of "dominical" mechanisms of control which enabled Spanish settlers to dominate the Indian peoples of the regions. These mechanisms were not significantly different from those adopted in less marginal parts of Mexico, but they have endured longer. This has forced the Indian populations in these regions into ever greater socioeconomic marginality.

The influence of the regions-of-refuge model can be seen in many of the recent activities and publications of the INI (cf 8, 70, 112), a not altogether surprising development considering that Aguirre Beltrán has long served as director of the Institute. The model's influence is also seen in Collier's (33) study of land utilization in Chiapas, Margolies's (88) study of the municipality of San Felipe del Progreso, and Favre's (50) work with the Maya.

One advantage of the model is that it has encouraged anthropologists to attend to history and to think in terms of regions rather than single communities. Its developmental implications, which call for the immediate integration of marginal Indian populations into the national society, have generated considerable debate among Mexican anthropologists and stimulated an increase in productive research.

CAPITALISM AS AN OBSTACLE   Contrasting with both the "regions of refuge" model of Aguirre Beltrán and the community resistance model is a third view, clearly influenced by Marxist doctrine, which places the onus of rural underdevelopment more squarely on recent capitalistic patterns of exploitation and downplays as causes both internal community resistance and colonial patterns of domination. This view is particularly evident in the contributions of Stavenhagen (125, 126) and Warman and his colleagues (144, 145).

It is only very recently that community study data have been offered to substantiate this latter view. Stavenhagen's (126) most recent contribution includes six Mexican case studies. Warman and his colleagues (144, 145) have offered an impressive series of research reports devoted to describing patterns of capitalistic exploitation in the Mexican state of Morelos. Glantz's (58) study of an *ejido* and Molina's (92) work in a provincial city lay further stress on the importance of understanding the processes by which political and economic power, since the Mexican revolution of 1910, increasingly have been wrested from local control and invested in central governmental authority. All of these studies were published under the sponsorship of the INAH. In contrast to the research inspired by the "regions of refuge" model, these studies tend to conclude that cultural pluralism is a positive force in rural development.

Durand (44), a French Canadian Marxist anthropologist, indicates similar findings in his study of a Totonac community. Deriving from a different tradition but leading us to similar conclusions are two studies of the indigenous market system conducted under the direction of Beals (12, 35). While identifying the indigenous system as sharing elements of capitalistic structure with the national marketing system alongside which it operates, these studies tend to emphasize the importance of the indigenous system for the entire regional economy and to decry efforts to incorporate it into the national system.

Most of these studies relate to what Gunder Frank has called "the metropolis-satellite structure of the capitalist system" (64, p. vii). It is therefore curious that many of them appear to be advocating economic and cultural pluralism as a solution to problems of underdevelopment.

Positive Responses to Change

Most of the studies mentioned above emphasize the negative aspects of change and development. They focus on resistance to change and the failure of development efforts. Another substantial body of recent research, continuing in the tradition of Tax (128) and Redfield (111), emphasizes the positive and apparently successful changes that have occurred at the community level, or at least tries to identify those conditions under which positive responses to development opportunities are most likely to occur.

A number of these studies of successful change focus on single communities rather than regions. Interestingly enough, all of them incorporate an historical focus. Of the single community studies, several focus on towns with established occupational opportunities other than agriculture. This is true, for example, of Hinshaw's (69) restudy of Panajachel, the Guatemalan town that served as a source for Tax's (128) *Penny Capitalism.* The "thirty-year perspective" between Hinshaw's and Tax's research provides ample evidence of successful adaptation to opportunities for change on the part of Panajachel's Indian population. At the same time, in a brief comparison with nearby villages, Hinshaw does suggest that the favorable location of

Panajachel as a Lake Atitlán tourist center may make the community a special case.

Still, Hinshaw's study provides an example of peoples' receptivity to change in the face of opportunity. Similar cases are found in Thompson (133), Press (107), Pi-Sunyer (106), Cancian (22), Iszaevich (73), Carter (26), and in Elmendorf's (47) study of Chan Kom. It is worth noting that most of these studies deal with Mayan Indian populations in the Mexican states of Yucatan and Chiapas. Once again, we ought to consider the possibility of regional traits and value orientations which may not be fully applicable to other parts of Mexico and Guatemala. There are, however, two reasonably firm exceptions even to the idea of regionally bounded orientations. One is Iszaevich's study of a Zapotec community in Oaxaca, which contrasts sharply with that of Kearney (76). The two communities are of nearly identical size, almost equidistant from the urban center of Oaxaca, and not more than 25 kilometers distant from each other. The other is Acheson's (1) research on the response to economic opportunity in a Tarascan community. It is a cogent challenge of Foster's (52) view.

Most of the above research has offered historical perspective of short duration in demonstration of the reality of social change and economic development in the contemporary communities studied. Other recent anthropological studies have turned away from the present almost entirely in order to seek out new responses to the unraveling of the Mesoamerican past (29, 75, 118, 130, 146). Of these, the regional histories of colonial Oaxaca by Chance (29) and Taylor (130) stand out. They challenge our usual view of the Mexican colonial period as one dominated by a land-owning class of Spanish descent which systematically exploited the indigenous peoples. While evidence for exploitation is present in both studies, Chance and Taylor agree that the Indians of Oaxaca were quick to adapt to social and economic changes wrought by Spanish colonialists. *Hacienda* type patterns of land use never dominated the region, the Indians managed to retain most of their land, and the urban inhabitants of Oaxaca were forced to rely on independently produced and marketed Indian foodstuffs throughout most of the colonial period.

In addressing other controversies, Chance (29) also argues that the colonial system in Oaxaca was essentially capitalistic (this in contrast to those views which have seen capitalism as emerging only with industrialization). The rural producers, he implies, were willing and vital participants in this incipient capitalism.

A Sense of Loss

The tradition of community study in Mesoamerica has always included a few contributions which poignantly suggest that neither the vagaries of change and development nor the quality of life can be measured simply as a result of higher per capita incomes, increased employment opportunities, or improved nutrition. The current decade is no exception. In a portrait of the town of his birth, González (60) sums up the gains and losses of the community's recent history with a final tally calculated to leave us all in doubt as to the merits of progress. Elmendorf (47) and Reck (109) both draw compelling portraits of something that might be described as an Indian way of life and generously allow their emotions and doubts to intrude as they attempt to grapple with the certainty of change and with what must certainly be lost in the process.

NATIONAL POLICY AND THE COMMUNITY

A promising new emphasis for community research in Mesoamerica is in the investigation of local responses to explicit national policies. In the past, most community research dealing with social and economic change only touched on such issues. Scholars preferred to discuss community development issues in terms of generalities rather than carefully tracing the roots of these issues to the influence of national policy (or, conversely, identifying changes in national policy as resulting from unexpected responses on the community level). It is only within the past decade that we see a number of researchers taking a closer look at the relationships between national development policy and local events (cf 119). Their focus is on two principal issues: agrarian reform and education.

Agrarian Reform in Mexico

We would be hard pressed to find a better policy issue linking the central government of Mexico to the rural community than that of agrarian reform, the promise of the Mexican Revolution of 1910. In this vein, Friedrich (56) has contributed a study of the revolutionary impetus for agrarian reform in a community in the state of Michoacan. The Mexican Revolution is seen as a regional as well as a national event. Other studies make it clear that subsequent responses to agrarian reform must also be understood on a regional basis. This viewpoint is apparent, for example, in the interdisciplinary study conducted by Restrepo Fernández & Sánchez Cortés (114), detailing the differing impacts of agrarian reform policies in four major areas of Mexico.

Closer looks at individual *ejidos* established after the Revolution lead to similar conclusions. Ronfeldt (117) describes an *ejido* in the state of Matamoros and its failure, which he attributes to co-option at the national level. On the basis of two periods of research, one in 1953 and the other in 1967, Wilkie (147) finds factionalism and economic decline threatening the stability of an *ejido* which he had originally selected for study because it had been one of the most prosperous in the region. In an impressive historical study, Glantz (58) describes how changing features of life in an *ejido* in the state of Morelos are closely linked to the agrarian policies of four successive presidents of Mexico.

Carlos (24) approaches the problem from the opposite direction. He makes a good case for detailed regional analysis. His research includes 34 *ejido* communities in the state of Sinoloa, where he finds considerable variation in the rate of community development. This is based on factors such as political traditions and the availability of resources which are specific to the communities. Similar conclusions, though not involved solely with the issue of agrarian reform, are arrived at by Pérez Lizuar (105) in an ecological study of four communities in the state of Morelos.

National Education Policy and the Indian Community

Mexico has devoted considerable effort to education for indigenous peoples (4), and Modiano's (91) study of the national education programs in three Indian communities in Chiapas attempts to evaluate some of these efforts. In line with the policies of the INI, these programs are conscious attempts to bring Indian populations into the national mainstream through their schools. As advocates of this goal, Modiano finds that the schools' teachers are often in direct conflict with the wishes of many of the children's parents.

Addressing similar concerns in Guatemala, Moore (93) views education as a lifelong process and describes several efforts of the Guatemalan government to incorporate adult as well as youth training in a rural education program in a Guatemalan highland community. The success of the program, however, remains limited by the presence of three distinct models of education in the community: Indian, Ladino, and national. Similar results are obtained by Sexton (122) in his quantitative analysis of the success of national education programs in another Guatemalan community.

SOCIAL STRUCTURE

Problems in social structure have received little attention in recent Mesoamerican community studies. Many studies merely allude to social structure. A number of the more holistically oriented ethnographies (cf 8, 78, 79, 134) devote considerable attention to descriptions of indigenous social structure and family life, and a few others, like Haviland's (66) study of gossip in Zinacantan and Méndez-Dominguez's (89) study of social stratification in a Guatemalan Ladino community, treat social structure in a specially delimited context. But very few studies have dealt with community social structure and kinship in an analytic fashion.

A clear exception is Nutini's (99) study of a Tlaxcalan municipality and a later collection of papers edited by Nutini, Carrasco & Taggart (100) dealing comparatively with kinship and the family in a number of Mexican communities.

Nutini's study of San Bernardino Contla is without a doubt the most detailed account available in English of indigenous kinship patterns in a Mexican community. The study is also atypical in its attempt to look beyond parochial issues in the context of Mesoamerica. Nutini moves from a detailed analysis of a specific case to a more general discussion of kinship models. Perhaps he was forced to take this direction by the lack of comparable analyses in the Mesoamerican literature, but we would prefer to think that it was a deliberate attempt which could profitably be emulated by researchers interested in other aspects of rural life in Mexico and Guatemala.

Neither Nutini's community study (99) nor the collection of brief studies to which he contributed (100) treat change at any length. This omission is acknowledged in the introduction to the latter book, along with the observation that material for both long and short-term studies of change in Mexican kinship is readily available.

A more recent contribution, Arizpe's (6) study of a community in the Mexican state of Puebla, deals with the relative importance of kinship in determining the patterns of community life. Noting that most Mexican anthropologists, as a result of their interest in Marxian analysis, have emphasized economic considerations as the prime determinants of rural life in Mexico, Arizpe argues that social organization merits at least equal recognition. Her emphasis on kinship as a major determinant of social and economic patterns deserves attention because it provides us with one of the few recent examples of what a community study that does *not* emphasize economic determinants might look like. Cancian (22) does much the same thing with his focus on social stratification.

BELIEF, BEHAVIOR, AND THE COMMUNITY

The study of indigenous value systems, community ethos, and their relation to community and individual behavior has been an enduring concern of anthropologists interested in Mesoamerica. The presumed force of community-sanctioned value systems has figured prominently in arguments which view the community itself as a major obstacle to change, as well as in some discussions which see community values as providing an impetus to positive responses to development opportunities. The focus on change that we have seen in other aspects of Mesoamerican community research is also evident in the studies considered in this section, even though they concentrate on those facets of community life which tend to be the most enduring.

Belief Systems and Change

Because most traditional belief systems are not easily separable into familiar ethnographic categories like "religion," "politics," or "economics," it seems virtually unimaginable that changes in one aspect of life would not be recorded in all other aspects. Still, the single most notable finding of recent studies focusing on indigenous belief systems in Mesoamerica is the persistence of many aspects of these belief systems. In some communities, as Vogt (140) has suggested, it actually seems that some features of the traditional belief systems are strengthened by major changes in other parts of community life.

Recent studies, devoted more directly to problems in economic change and development, have pointed to the existence of dual value systems with respect to political and economic institutions within a national setting. Studies centrally concerned with change and persistence in community ethos often reveal the presence of dual belief systems within the community itself. The meaning of these dual systems is interpreted variously by a number of researchers. Nash (96), working in a Mayan community, describes a clear break between traditional beliefs and modern behaviors. She identifies the incongruity as a symptom of societal disequilibrium. Still, she sees the survival of indigenous belief systems as cushioning the impact of rapid change. Dow (43) views the phenomenon in a similar fashion.

In one of the few studies of this persuasion devoted exclusively to a mestizo population, Olivera de Vásquez (101) sees changes in religious practice as primarily a function of age. Younger members of the community avoid or abstain from many traditional religious practices. In contrast, Reina (113), working in a Guatemalan Indian community, sees little discrepancy between an innovative response to community changes and adherence to traditional religious beliefs. Iwanska's (74) study of a Mazahua Indian village in Mexico reports a high level of acceptance of national educational goals. The trappings of modern society exist alongside a belief system which encourages community members to maintain a separate spiritual and emotional identity.

Two recent studies focus on specific aspects of belief systems. Hermitte (67) describes the not uncommon coexistence of two structures of social sanction in a Maya Indian community. Explicit governing functions are maintained by local mestizos, while most Indians continue to be ruled also by beliefs in the sanctioning powers of supernatural guardians. In their study of medical beliefs in a Guatemalan town, Woods & Graves (149) conclude that contacts with the outside world and the ability to innovate do not in themselves provide sufficient impetus for changes in traditional belief systems. They suggest that changes in medical practices are rapid when the opportunity to change (in this case the availability of Western medicine) is real.

The Rituals of Belief

Several recent Mexican community studies have concentrated on the rituals associated with indigenous belief systems. With one exception (37), this work has centered on the Maya Indians of Chiapas. Vogt (140, 141) sees Zinacantan ritual as both a communication and meaning system, with direct relationships to the Zinacanteco view of the world. Interestingly, he finds little change in Zinacanteco ritual and its meanings, either from a long view or within the 15 year history of the Harvard Chiapas Project. While he acknowledges that the Zinacantecos have been quick to take material advantage of their contacts with the outside world, he also suggests that these very contacts have served to reinforce rather than alter the Zinacanteco world view.

Bricker (20) comes to a similar conclusion in her description of ritual humor among the Zinacantecos. She portrays humor as a basic part of the Indians' ceremonial life, and suggests that it functions as a direct expression of their morality and solidarity. It is no accident, she maintains, that outsiders and community deviants are so often the targets of ritual jokes.

Gossen (63) deals with a broad range of myth and other oral traditions in an outstanding effort to develop a perspective on the Chamulas' sense of cosmic order. The persistence of traditional ideas relating to social order is seen as being a direct result of oral traditions through which the ancient Mayan cosmology continues to be transmitted.

In addition to the above, recent studies of the ritual use of peyote among the Huichol Indians of northwestern Mexico (17, 94, 95) argue for the persistence of indigenous rituals and associated beliefs in the face of centuries of contact and active efforts directed toward their eradication.

Personality and Change

Personality tests and intensive psychoanalytic interviews serve as the basis for an interesting study of rural Mexican character by Fromm & Maccoby (57). They identify a number of personality types. The dominance of any one, they suggest, is due to the particular historical and socioeconomic forces which define village life in the twentieth century. Different backgrounds (hacienda, free village, and capitalistic) lead to and in turn are reinforced by different social character types. The ultimate result is varied ideologies and values.

While Fromm and Maccoby feel that a particular receptive-passive manifestation of social character predominates in the village they studied, an important aspect of their work is the recognition of a deep-rooted heterogeneity of character traits in the village. In this respect, the study offers a profile relevant to many of the individual and group differences in community beliefs noted in other studies.

Romanucci-Ross (116) worked with Fromm and Maccoby to provide an ethnographic component to their research. Her book provides an interesting contrast to the other in her search for a general moral code which links community values with manifestations of conflict and violence. Romanucci-Ross's presentation of an essentially homogeneous value system contrasts so sharply with Fromm and Maccoby's view of heterogeneity in the value system that it is difficult to believe that the two studies were drawn from the same community.

Norms and Deviance

Studies of the relation between personality and community life in Mesoamerica have not been limited to a psychological approach. Selby (120) introduces his study of deviant behavior in an isolated Zapotec community with a discussion of psychological and interactionist theories of deviance. The "new" interactionist approach, which he favors, is more concerned with the social environment in which deviance is defined than with measuring the incidence of deviant acts or searching for psychological clues to deviant behavior. Much of Selby's discussion of Zapotec deviance is devoted to demonstrating the utility of an interactionist approach, particularly in areas of sexual deviance and witchcraft.

The Zapotec themselves, he says, do not view deviance in terms of individual symptomology. Their concern, like that of the interactionist sociologist, is with the social situation in which deviance occurs.

There is, of course, the possibility that Selby's enthusiasm for interactionist sociology has led him to see it everywhere he looks. But the suggestion that the Zapotec have traditionally viewed deviance (and hence probably most kinds of social behavior) in terms of a social environment rather than a psychological process is certainly intriguing and worthy of further exploration.

Collier (34) examines conflict management in Zinacantan within the context of the legal system. Her view that Zinacantecos are concerned with resolving conflict by means of compromise to restore harmony, rather than with crimes per se and their legally indicated punishments, makes it appear that the people of Zinacantan are no less concerned with social context than Selby's Zapotec and thus just as interactionist.

Cancian's (23) study of norms in Zinacantan, in which she rejects her earlier Parsonian socialized actor hypothesis in favor of a social construction-of-reality model, also does not appear to differ markedly from Selby's (120) interactionist model in terms of the importance accorded to social context.

THE POLITICS OF IDENTITY

In the briefest of terms, a concern for the politics of identity can be understood as an interest in who is calling whom what, and for what reason. Anthropologists (and some sociologists) working in Mesoamerica have long shown a concern with categories of ethnic identity, and this involvement has not abated in recent years. Another aspect of the politics of identity, that of women's roles, has come to receive significant attention in Mesoamerica (as well as elsewhere) during the past decade.

Ethnic Identity

Whether isolated in "refuge regions" or residing in loose enclaves within the mainstream of society, the large numbers of indigenous peoples in Mesoamerica have always been a special concern of anthropologists. The degree to which these peoples identify themselves as Indian or as belonging to a particular indigenous tradition has been the subject of considerable debate. As in other matters discussed in this essay, the possibility of regional variations has not been addressed adequately. Most of the arguments center on a rather crude distinction between "Indian" peoples and all others.

A recent classic in the field of Mesoamerican ethnic research is Colby & van den Berghe's (32) study of Indian and Ladino relations in the highlands of northern Guatemala. In applying the concept of plural societies to the situation in Guatemala, Colby and van den Berghe are careful to point out that the principal support for maintaining a distinction between the two groups comes from the economically and politically powerful Ladino minority. They also note that the Indian view includes many more (and, in this context, important) distinctions among Indian groups.

The use of the concept of pluralism in describing ethnic identity has come under attack in two recent studies. Both support the claim that "Indian" groups are considerably more the victims of other peoples' self-serving categorizations than willing participants in an indigenous way of life. Friedlander (54) makes this case in reference to misguided attempts to define an Indian way of life by representatives of the Mexican national culture. Margolies (88) describes a similar situation in another Mexican community, although her focus is on social and economic relations at the local level.

On the other hand, the persistence of ethnic tradition has been described by several anthropologists working in Mesoamerica. Evidence that some indigenous groups have become the willing progenitors of their own ethnic tradition has been provided by van Zantwijk (137) in his portrayal of Tarascan ethnic identity, by Crumrine (38) in his description of Mayo revivalism, and by Collier (33) in his brief account of how the Zinacantecos have accepted the Mexican national concept of Indianism and thereby managed to create for themselves a fairly effective bloc through which they are able to participate (albeit on a limited basis) in the institutions of Mexican society.

It is certain that a clearer understanding of the "politics" of identity (i.e. who is identifying whom, and for what reasons) must await a greater understanding of regional and historical variations within Mexico and Guatemala. Erasmus (48) has achieved this to some extent for Indian communities in northwestern Mexico. Ebel's (46) comparative study of modernization in three Indian communities offers a similar case for Guatemala. Both studies demonstrate considerable differences in the strength and rationale of ethnic identity even within these fairly circumscribed regions.

Women's Roles

While there are notable exceptions, such as studies by Parsons (104) and Bunzel (21), most of the early Mesoamerican community studies were written by men. This circumstance has left us, as has been noted in regard to anthropological research in many areas of the world, not only with sparse information, but frequently with misconceptions about how women lead their lives in rural areas. However, during the last decade of research, approximately 30 percent of the anthropologically oriented community studies have been written by women. Some of these deserve special mention for their emphasis on women's roles.

Chiñas (30) notes that there is a clear distinction between male and female roles in the community life of the Isthmus Zapotecs. She also suggests that the Zapotec rank high in the amount of recognition and prestige they accord to women's roles. This observation also seems true in the case of Friedlander's (54) detailed portrait of a single Hueyapan woman, and is certainly the case in Elmendorf's (47) restudy of Chan Kom which centers upon the lives of nine women.

Some researchers (cf 69) have suggested that rural women appear to be more resistant than males to opportunities for change and modernization. Recent studies focusing on women's place in the community do not seem to substantiate this claim. Evidence exists for seeing resistance due to perceived differences in prestige between indigenous roles for women and those accorded women in mestizo and ladino society. The contrast between the above mentioned studies of Indian communities and some of those based on mestizo communities (e.g. 53, 57, 116) is instructive.

URBANIZATION AND URBAN LIFE

Although the discipline's interest in Mesoamerica has remained predominantly with rural peoples, the last decade has seen a significant increase in urban studies. Even many of the recent rural studies are located in occupationally diversified towns and municipal centers which are distinct from the predominantly agricultural villages most often investigated in earlier decades.

Two of the recent studies describe the processes of urban decline in small Mexican cities. Diaz (42) studied the decline of Tonalá, attributing it to a gradual merging of patterns of influence emanating from the much larger city of Guadalajara and the beginning of engulfment by the urban sprawl of Guadalajara. Molina (92), in another of the INAH studies, describes the decline of San Bartholomé de los Llanos as a result of political and economic decisions made at national and state levels of government.

Several of the recent urban studies deal with the situation of rural migrants in major Mexican and Guatemalan cities. Unfortunately, few of the rural based studies devote much attention to migration as a reaction to change. Kemper (77), following migrants from Tzintzuntzan (the community studied earlier by Foster) to Mexico City, finds their adaptation to city life more positive than not. His is the most optimistic of the collection.

Like Kemper's, most of the other migration studies focus on social and economic strategies which permit migrants to survive in a marginal urban environment. Three of these (6, 36, 87) focus on Mexico City, one (115) on Guatemala City, and one on the Mexican border city of Ciudad Juarez (136).

Less concerned with the problems of recent migrants, Higgins (68) offers a detailed study of a poor urban neighborhood and its relationship to the larger political and economic environment of Oaxaca. Lewis (85) provides a brief follow-up study based on the poor urban family he first studied during the late 1950s.

While most urban anthropologists working in Mexico and Guatemala appear to be concentrating either on the poor or the plight of the recent migrant, there are a few recent examples of alternative approaches. Price (108) attempts an overview of urban growth and development in Tijuana. Miller (90) describes the impact of a new industrial town established by the Mexican government in a declining rural area.

Other studies, though not by anthropologists, suggest interesting directions for future research. These include a study of social mobility in the Mexican city of Monterrey (9) and two participant observation studies of provincial politics (49, 135) contributed by political scientists.

At present, our view of urban processes in Mesoamerica and their effects on neighborhood and community life is limited by the reluctance of anthropologists to depart from their interest in studying marginal populations. Perhaps this reluctance exists simply because our interest in the urban situation is so recent. After all, it took some time and a lot of groundwork for most anthropologists working in rural settings to come to the conclusion that they had to extend their research to other sectors of the society.

CONCLUSIONS

The tradition of Mesoamerican community studies remains one of the most impressive contributions of anthropological literature. The past 10 years have seen a florescence of this tradition, with more studies published than in any previous decade. It has been a period of innovation and experimentation.

Within the general "change and persistence" orientation of most studies, two major trends are evident. First, there is clearly a greater focus than in the past on particular problems and themes and fewer attempts to provide holistic descriptions of community life. Second, there is a healthy and growing emphasis on viewing communities in the broader context of region and nation. This trend may be a natural consequence of the influence of exogenous factors on culture change at the community level. We now seem to realize that to understand what goes on within a community we must examine what goes on beyond a community's boundaries. The broader cultural milieu is crucial.

From our point of view, perhaps the greatest need in the tradition of Mesoamerican studies is for comprehensive, analytic studies of the available literature. Scholars of Mesoamerica seem to prefer doing new community studies rather than attempting to grapple in any systematic manner with the material that is already available.

The importance of developing a comprehensive view can be illustrated from the themes of change and persistence. It should be apparent from this essay that there is considerable disagreement with regard to both the causes and directions of change in rural Mesoamerica. Similarly, the persistence of cultural traits and social identities has been treated in strikingly different ways. These differences can be attributed to a number of factors, including the unique characteristics of some communities and regions, the methods of research employed, and even the ideological commitments of the researchers—but nowhere in the literature are any of the differences adequately accounted for.

In the face of so much diversity of findings, we assume that there is a little truth in each approach. That is perhaps an inevitable response for the moment, but it will not get us far in the long run. If community studies are to realize their potential, our thinking about them must continue to progress. The following recommendations are made in this light.

1. We need analytic studies of the genre of community study and of the results of community study research in Mesoamerica. What is required is not simply a compendium, but careful analyses which account for the diversity of findings. These analyses should include study of the available literature and an assessment of the methods and traditions of scholarship

employed. To what extent can the diversity be attributed to ethnic, regional, and historic variations? To what extent is it a result of the ideological commitments of the researcher?

2. Community studies should continue, but researchers ought to consider the advances made during the last 10 years in planning for additional work. Regional, comparative, and team research ought to be encouraged. Quantitative research, coupled with participant observation, has proved well worth the effort, particularly in approaching problems related to change and development.

3. More interchange and cooperation between researchers on both sides of the border are clearly in order. Community researchers are not taking maximum advantage of work already done. One of the most regrettable aspects of this tendency has been for researchers from the United States to ignore almost totally the excellent studies being conducted by Mexican anthropologists.

4. More attention should be paid to community heterogeneity. Many anthropologists continue to search for a sense of community that will somehow permit them to view the community as a unified, integrated whole —an approach which often seriously distorts the reality of most Mesoameri-can communities. There are a number of recent community studies which provide ample evidence for the merits of an approach which sees the community as composed of many parts and containing separate ideologies.

5. Mesoamerican researchers should expand their work to a more general level of discourse. In terms of theory building, most Mesoamerican scholars appear to be parochial. They prefer to essay their theoretical concerns strictly in terms of the Mesoamerican experience. This tendency is especially disappointing coming from a region which, relatively speaking, has been so well studied and has a considerable amount to contribute to our general understanding of human adaptation and control.

Literature Cited

1. Acheson, J. M. 1972. Limited good or limited goods? Response to economic opportunity in a Tarascan pueblo. *Am. Anthropol.* 74:1152–69
2. Adams, R. N. 1970. *Crucifixion by Power: Essays on Guatemalan National Social Structure, 1944–1966.* Austin: Univ. Texas Press. 553 pp.
3. Aguirre Beltrán, G. 1967. *Regiones de Refugio: El Desarrollo de la Comunidad y el Proceso Dominical en Mestizo América.* Mexico: Inst. Indig. Interam. 366 pp.
4. Aguirre Beltrán, G. 1973. *Teoría y Práctica de la Educación Indígena.* Mexico: SepSetentas. 282 pp.

5. Arensberg, C. A. 1961. The community as object and as sample. *Am. Anthropol.* 63:246–64
6. Arizpe, L. 1975. *Indígenas en la Ciudad de Mexico: El Caso de las "Marias."* Mexico: SepSetentas. 157 pp.
7. Avila, M. 1969. *Tradition and Growth: A Study of Four Mexican Villages.* Chicago: Univ. Chicago Press. 219 pp.
8. Báez-Jorge, F. 1973. *Los Zoque-Popolucas: Estructura Social.* Mexico: Inst. Nac. Indig. 245 pp.
9. Balán, J., Browning, H. L., Jelin, E. 1973. *Men in a Developing Society: Geographic and Social Mobility in Monter-*

rey, Mexico. Austin: Univ. Texas Press. 384 pp.
10. Bataillon, C. 1976. Estudios Regionales sobre México en Francia: Evolución desde 1965. In *Contemporary Mexico,* ed. J. W. Wilkie, M. C. Meyer, E. M. de Wilkie, pp. 769–74. Berkeley: Univ. California Press. 858 pp.
11. Beals, R. L. 1946. *Cheran: A Sierra Tarascan Village.* Smithson. Inst., Inst. Soc. Anthropol. Publ. No. 2. Washington DC: GPO. 225 pp.
12. Beals, R. L. 1975. *The Peasant Marketing System of Oaxaca, Mexico.* Berkeley: Univ. California Press. 419 pp.
13. Beals, R. L. 1976. Anthropology in contemporary Mexico. See Ref. 10, pp. 753–68
14. Beaucage, P. 1973. Anthropologie Economique des Communantes Indigenes de la Sierra Norte de Puebla (Mexique). *Can. Rev. Sociol. Anthropol.* 10:114–33
15. Belshaw, M. 1967. *A Village Economy: Land and People of Huecorio.* New York: Columbia Univ. Press. 421 pp.
16. Benítez, F. 1968. *Los Indios de Mexico.* Mexico: Biblioteca Era. 2 vols.
17. Benítez, F. 1975. *In the Magic Land of Peyote.* Austin: Univ. Texas Press. 198 pp.
18. Bonfil Batalla, G. 1966. Conservative thought in applied anthropology: A critique. *Hum. Organ.* 25:89–92
19. Brand, D. D. 1951. *Quiroga: A Mexican Municipio.* Smithson. Inst., Inst. Soc. Anthropol. Publ. No. 11. Washington DC: GPO. 242 pp.
20. Bricker, V. R. 1973. *Ritual Humor in Highland Chiapas.* Austin: Univ. Texas Press. 257 pp.
21. Bunzel, R. 1959. *Chichicastenango: A Guatemalan Village.* Seattle: Univ. Washington Press. 438 pp.
22. Cancian, F. 1972. *Change and Uncertainty in a Peasant Economy: The Maya Corn Farmers of Zinacantan.* Stanford: Stanford Univ. Press. 208 pp.
23. Cancian, F. M. 1975. *What are Norms? A Study of Beliefs and Action in a Maya Community.* London: Cambridge Univ. Press. 212 pp.
24. Carlos, M. L. 1974. *Politics and Development in Rural Mexico: A Study of Socio-Economic Modernization.* New York: Praeger
25. Carmack, R. M. 1973. *Quichean Civilization: The Ethnohistoric,Ethnographic, and Archaeological Sources.* Berkeley: Univ. California Press
26. Carter, W. E. 1969. *New Lands and Old Traditions: Kekchi Cultivators in the*

Guatemalan Lowlands. Gainesville: Univ. Florida Press. 153 pp.
27. Caso, A. 1971. *La Comunidad Indigena.* Mexico: SepSetentas
28. Chambers, E. J. 1977. Modern Mesoamerica; The Politics of Identity. *Am. Anthropol.* 79:92–97
29. Chance, J. K. 1978. *Race and Class in Colonial Oaxaca.* Stanford: Stanford Univ. Press
30. Chiñas, B. L. 1973. *The Isthmus Zapotecs: Women's Roles in Cultural Context.* New York: Holt, Rinehart & Winston. 122 pp.
31. Cline, H. 1952. Mexican community studies. *Hisp. Am. Hist. Rev.* 32:212–42
32. Colby, B. N., van den Berghe, P. L. 1969. *Ixil Country: A Plural Society in Highland Guatemala.* Berkeley: Univ. California Press. 218 pp.
33. Collier, G. A. 1975. *Fields of the Tzotzil: The Ecological Bases of Tradition in Highland Chiapas.* Austin: Univ. Texas Press. 255 pp.
34. Collier, J. F. 1973. *Law and Social Change in Zinacantan.* Stanford: Stanford Univ. Press. 281 pp.
35. Cook, S., Diskin, M., eds. 1976. *Markets in Oaxaca.* Austin: Univ. Texas Press. 329 pp.
36. Cornelius, W. A. 1975. *Politics and the Migrant Poor in Mexico City.* Stanford: Stanford Univ. Press. 319 pp.
37. Cortés Ruiz, E. 1972. *San Simón de la Laguna: La Organización Familiar y lo Mágico-Religioso en el Culto al Oratorio.* Mexico: Inst. Nac. Indig. 177 pp.
38. Crumrine, N. R. 1977. *The Mayo Indians of Sonora.* Tucson: Univ. Arizona Press. 167 pp.
39. Deal, C. 1978. *Latin America and the Caribbean: A Dissertation Bibliography.* Ann Arbor: Univ. Microfilms Int. 164 pp.
40. de la Fuente, J. 1949. *Yalalag: Una Villa Zapoteca Serrana.* Mexico: Mus. Nac. Antropol.
41. DeWalt, B. R. 1976. Recent anthropological studies in Mesoamerica. *Latin Am. Res. Rev.* 2:169–76
42. Diaz, M. N. 1966. *Tonalá: Conservatism, Responsibility, and Authority in a Mexican Town.* Berkeley: Univ. California Press. 234 pp.
43. Dow, J. 1974. *Santos y Supervivencias: Funciones de la Religión en una Comunidad Otomí, México.* Mexico: Inst. Nac. Indig.
44. Durand, P. 1975. *Nanacatlan: Société Paysanne el Lutte des Classes au Mexique.* Montreal: Univ. Montreal Press

45. Early, D. K. 1977. Mexican peasants and the unfulfilled revolution: Recent publications from La Casa Chata. *Anthropol. Q.* 50:151–54
46. Ebel, R. H. 1969. *Political Modernization in Three Guatemalan Indian Communities.* New Orleans: Tulane Univ. Press
47. Elmendorf, M. L. 1976. *Nine Mayan Women: A Village Faces Change.* New York: Schenkman
48. Erasmus, C. J. 1967. Culture change in northwest Mexico. In *Contemporary Change in Traditional Societies,* ed. J. H. Steward, 3:1–131. Urbana: Univ. Illinois Press. 3 vols.
49. Fagen, R. R., Tuohy, W. S. 1972. *Politics and Privilege in a Mexican City.* Stanford: Stanford Univ. Press
50. Favre, H. 1974. *Cambio y Continuidad entre los Mayas de México.* Mexico: Editorial Siglo XXI. 392 pp.
51. Foster, G. M. 1948. *Empire's Children: The People of Tzintzuntzan.* Smithson. Inst., Inst. Soc. Anthropol. Publ. No. 6. Mexico: Imprenta Nuevo Mundo, S. A. 297 pp.
52. Foster, G. M. 1965. Peasant society and the image of limited good. *Am. Anthropol.* 67:293–315
53. Foster, G. M. 1967. *Tzintzuntzan: Mexican Peasants in a Changing World.* Boston: Little, Brown. 372 pp.
54. Friedlander, J. 1975. *Being Indian in Hueyapan: A Study of Forced Identity in Contemporary Mexico.* New York: St. Martin's. 205 pp.
55. Friedlander, J. 1976. The social scientist and the Indian. *Latin Am. Res. Rev.* 2:184–90
56. Friedrich, P. 1970. *Agrarian Revolt in a Mexican Village.* Englewood Cliffs: Prentice-Hall. 158 pp.
57. Fromm, E., Maccoby, M. 1970. *Social Character in a Mexican Village.* Englewood Cliffs: Prentice-Hall. 303 pp.
58. Glantz, S. 1974. *El Ejido Colectivo de Nueva Italia.* Mexico: Inst. Nac. Antropol. Hist. 212 pp.
59. Gold, G. L. 1977. The Indian as subject and object of Mexican ethnography. *Rev. Anthropol.* 4:176–89
60. González, L. 1973. *Invitación a la Microhistoria.* Mexico: SepSetentas. 187 pp.
61. González, L. 1974. *San José de Gracia: Mexican Village in Transition.* Transl. J. Upton. Austin: Univ. Texas Press. 362 pp.
62. González Ramos, G. 1972. *Los Coras.* Mexico: Inst. Nac. Indig. 179 pp.

63. Gossen, G. H. 1974. *Chamulas in the World of the Sun: Time and Space in a Maya Oral Tradition.* Cambridge: Harvard Univ. Press. 382 pp.
64. Gunder Frank, A. 1967. *Capitalism and Underdevelopment in Latin America.* New York: Monthly Rev. Press. 298 pp.
65. Deleted in proof
66. Haviland, J. B. 1977. *Gossip, Reputation, and Knowledge in Zinacantan.* Chicago: Univ. Chicago Press. 260 pp.
67. Hermitte, M. E. 1970. *Poder Sobrenatural y Control Social en un Pueblo Maya Contemporáneo.* Mexico: Inst. Indig. Interam.
68. Higgins, M. J. 1974. *Somos Gente Humilde: Etnografía de una Colonia Urbana Pobre de Oaxaca.* Mexico: Inst. Nac. Indig.
69. Hinshaw, R. E. 1975. *Panajachel: A Guatemalan Town in Thirty-Year Perspective.* Pittsburgh: Univ. Pittsburgh Press
70. Hinton, T. B., compiler. 1972. *Coras, Huicholes y Tepehuanes.* Mexico: Inst. Nac. Indig. 177 pp.
71. Hunt, R. C. 1969. Review of G. Aguirre Beltrán (see Ref. 3). *Am. Anthropol.* 71:545–52
72. Ichon, A. 1969. *La Religion des Totonoques de la Sierra.* Paris: Cent. Nac. Rech. Sci.
73. Iszaevich, A. 1973. *Modernización de una Comunidad Oaxaqueña del Valle.* Mexico: SepSetentas. 182 pp.
74. Iwanska, A. 1971. *Purgatory and Utopia: A Mazahua Indian Village of Mexico.* Cambridge, Mass: Schenkman. 214 pp.
75. Jones, G. D., ed. 1977. *Anthropology and History in Yucatan.* Austin: Univ. Texas Press. 344 pp.
76. Kearney, M. 1972. *The Winds of Ixtepeji: World View and Society in a Zapotec Town.* New York: Holt, Rinehart & Winston. 140 pp.
77. Kemper, R. V. 1977. *Migration and Adaptation: Tzintzuntzan Peasants in Mexico City.* Beverly Hills: Sage
78. Kennedy, J. G. 1970. *Inápuchi: Una Comunidad Tarahumara Gentil.* Mexico: Inst. Indig. Interam.
79. Kennedy, J. G. 1978. *Tarahumara of the Sierra Madre: Beer, Ecology, and Social Organization.* Arlington Heights: AHM. 245 pp.
80. Kirchhoff, P. 1952. Mesoamerica: Its geographic limits, ethnic composition and cultural characteristics. See Ref. 129, pp. 17–30
81. LaFarge, O., Byers, D. 1931. *The Year Bearer's People.* Middle Am. Res. Ser.

No. 3. New Orleans: Tulane Univ.
Press. 379 pp.

82. Leeds, A. 1974. Brazilian careers and
social structure: A case history and
model. In *Contemporary Cultures and
Societies of Latin America*, ed. D. B.
Heath, pp. 285–307. New York: Random House. 572 pp. 2nd ed.

83. Lewis, O. 1951. *Life in a Mexican Village: Tepoztlan Restudied.* Urbana:
Univ. Illinois Press. 512 pp.

84. Lewis, O. 1966. Introduction. In *La
Vida*, pp. xi-lix. New York: Random
House. 669 pp.

85. Lewis, O. 1969. *A Death in the Sanchez
Family.* New York: Random House.
119 pp.

86. Lombardo Toledano, V. 1973. *El Problema del Indio.* Mexico: SepSetentas.
207 pp.

87. Lomnitz, L. A. 1977. *Networks and
Marginality: Life in a Mexican Shantytown.* New York: Academic

88. Margolies, B. L. 1975. *Princes of the
Earth: Subcultural Diversity in a Mexican Municipality.* Washington DC:
Am. Anthropol. Assoc. 179 pp.

89. Méndez-Dominguez, A. 1967. *Zaragoza: La Estratificación Social de una
Comunidad Ladina Guatemalteca.*
Guatemala: Ministerio Educ. Publica

90. Miller, F. C. 1973. *Old Villages and a
New Town: Industrialization in Mexico.*
Menlo Park: Cummings. 161 pp.

91. Modiano, N. 1973. *Indian Education in
the Chiapas Highlands.* New York:
Holt, Rinehart & Winston. 150 pp.

92. Molina, V. 1976. *San Bartolomé de los
Llanos: Una Urbanización Frenada.*
Mexico: Inst. Nac. Antropol. Hist.

93. Moore, A. 1973. *Life Cycles in Atchalán: The Diverse Careers of Certain
Guatemalans.* New York: Teachers
College Press. 220 pp.

94. Myerhoff, B. G. 1974. *Peyote Hunt: The
Sacred Journey of the Huichol Indians.*
Ithaca: Cornell Univ. Press. 285 pp.

95. Nahmad Sittón, S., ed. 1972. *El Peyote
y Los Huicholes.* Mexico: SepSetentas.
196 pp.

96. Nash, J. 1970. *In the Eyes of the Ancestors: Belief and Behavior in a Mayan
Community.* New Haven: Yale Univ.
Press. 368 pp.

97. Nash, M., ed. 1967. *Handbook of Middle American Indians, Soc. Anthropol.*
Vol. 6. Austin: Univ. Texas Press

98. Nelson, C. 1971. *The Waiting Village:
Social Change in Rural Mexico.* Boston:
Little, Brown

99. Nutini, H. G. 1968. *San Bernardino
Contla: Marriage and Family Structure
in a Tlaxcalan Municipio.* Pittsburgh:
Univ. Pittsburgh Press. 420 pp.

100. Nutini, H. G., Carrasco, P., Taggart,
J. M., eds. 1976. *Essays on Mexican
Kinship.* Pittsburgh: Univ. Pittsburgh
Press. 256 pp.

101. Olivera de Vázquez, M. 1967. *Tlaxalancingo.* Mexico: Inst. Nac. Antropol. Hist.

102. Olivera de Vázquez, M. 1970. Algunos
Problemas de la Investigación Antropológica Actual. See Ref. 142, pp.
94–118

103. Palerm, A. 1969. La Investigación Social: Problemas y Posibilidades. In *Los
Recursos Humanos y el Desarrollo
Agrícola*, ed. O. Méndez Nápoles, pp.
63–186. Mexico: Ediciones Productividad

104. Parsons, E. C. 1936. *Mitla, Town of the
Souls.* Chicago: Univ. Chicago Press.
590 pp.

105. Pérez Lizaur, M. 1975. *Población y
Sociedad: Cuatro Comunidades del
Acolhuacan.* Mexico: Cent. Invest. Super., Inst. Nac. Antropol. Hist.

106. Pi-Sunyer, O. 1973. *Zamora: Change
and Continuity in a Mexican Town.*
New York: Holt, Rinehart & Winston

107. Press, I. 1975. *Tradition and Adaptation: Life in a Modern Yucatan Maya
Village.* Westport: Greenwood. 224 pp.

108. Price, J. A. 1973. *Tijuana: Urbanization
in a Border Culture.* Notre Dame:
Univ. Notre Dame Press. 195 pp.

109. Reck, G. C. 1978. *In the Shadow of Tlaloc: Life in a Mexican Village.* New
York: Penguin

110. Redfield, R. 1930. *Tepoztlan: A Mexican Village.* Chicago: Univ. Chicago
Press. 247 pp.

111. Redfield, R. 1950. *A Village that Chose
Progress: Chan Kom Revisited.*
Chicago: Univ. Chicago Press. 187 pp.

112. Reed, K. B. 1972. *El INI y los Huicholes.* Mexico: Inst. Nac. Indig.
176 pp.

113. Reina, R. E. 1966. *The Law of the
Saints: A Pokomam Pueblo and Its
Community Culture.* Indianapolis:
Bobbs-Merrill. 338 pp.

114. Restrepo Fernández, I., Sánchez
Cortés, J. 1972. *La Reforma Agraria en
Cuatro Regiones: El Bajío, Michoacán,
La Laguna y Tlaxcala.* Mexico: SepSetentas. 177 pp.

115. Roberts, B. R. 1973. *Organizing Strangers: Poor Families in Guatemala City.*
Austin: Univ. Texas Press. 300 pp.

116. Romanucci-Ross, L. 1973. *Conflict, Violence and Morality in a Mexican Village.* Palo Alto: Natl. Press. 202 pp.

117. Ronfeldt, D. 1973. *Atencingo: The Politics of Agrarian Struggle in a Mexican Ejido.* Stanford: Stanford Univ. Press. 283 pp.
118. Scholes, F. V., Roys, R. L. 1968. *The Maya Chontal Indians of Acalan-Tixchel: A Contribution to the History and Ethnography of the Yucatan Peninsula.* Norman: Univ. Oklahoma Press. 565 pp.
119. Schwartz, N. B. 1978. Community development and cultural change in Latin America. *Ann. Rev. Anthropol.* 7: 235–61
120. Selby, H. A. 1974. *Zapotec Deviance: The Convergence of Folk and Modern Sociology.* Austin: Univ. Texas Press. 166 pp.
121. SepSetentas. 1971. *Ha Fracasado el Indigenismo? Reportaje de una Controversia.* Mexico: SepSetentas
122. Sexton, J. D. 1972. *Education and Innovation in a Guatemalan Community: San Juan la Laguna.* Los Angeles: Latin Am. Cent., Univ. California. 72 pp.
123. Siverts, H. 1969. *Oxchuc: Una Tribu Maya de México.* Mexico: Inst. Indig. Interam. 214 pp.
124. Spicer, E. H. 1966. The process of cultural enclavement in Middle America. In *Actas y Memorias, 36th Congr. Int. Americanistas, España,* 1964, 3:267–79. Sevilla: Editorial Católica Española, S. A. 4 vols.
125. Stavenhagen, R. 1969. *Las Clases Sociales en las Sociedades Agrarias.* Mexico: Siglo Veintiuno Editores
126. Stavenhagen, R., ed. 1976. *Capitalismo y Campesinado en Mexico: Estudios de la Realidad Campesina.* Mexico: Inst. Nac. Antropol. Hist. 246 pp.
127. Stevens, J. L. 1841. *Incidents of Travel in Central America, Chiapas and Yucatan.* New York: Harper
128. Tax, S. 1953. *Penny Capitalism: A Guatemalan Indian Economy.* Smithson. Inst., Inst. Soc. Anthropol., Publ. 16. Washington DC: GPO. 230 pp.
129. Tax, S., ed. 1952. *Heritage of Conquest: The Ethnology of Middle America.* Glencoe: Free Press. 312 pp.
130. Taylor, W. B. 1972. *Landlord and Peasant in Colonial Oaxaca.* Stanford: Stanford Univ. Press. 287 pp.
131. Taylor, W. B. 1975. Time and community studies: Four books on rural societies in contemporary Mexico. *Peasant Stud. Newsl.* 4:13–17
132. Taylor, W. B. 1976. Revolution and tradition in rural Mexico. *Peasant Stud. Newsl.* 5:31–37
133. Thompson, R. A. 1974. *The Winds of Tomorrow: Social Change in a Maya Town.* Chicago: Univ. Chicago Press. 182 pp.
134. Turner, P. R. 1972. *The Highland Chontal.* New York: Holt, Rinehart & Winston. 96 pp.
135. Ugalde, A. 1970. *Power and Conflict in a Mexican Community: A Study of Political Integration.* Albuquerque: Univ. New Mexico Press. 193 pp.
136. Ugalde, A. 1974. *The Urbanization Process of a Poor Mexican Neighborhood.* Austin: Univ. Texas Press
137. van Zantwijk, R. A. M. 1967. *Servants of the Saints: The Social and Cultural Identity of a Tarascan Community in Mexico.* Atlantic Highlands: Humanities Press
138. Vogt, E. Z., ed. 1969. *Handbook of Middle American Indians, Ethnology: Part One,* Vol. 7. Austin: Univ. Texas Press
139. Vogt, E. Z., ed. 1969. *Handbook of Middle American Indians, Ethnology: Part Two,* Vol. 8. Austin: Univ. Texas Press
140. Vogt, E. Z. 1969. *Zinacantan: A Maya Community in the Highlands of Chiapas.* Cambridge: Harvard Univ. Press. 733 pp.
141. Vogt, E. Z. 1976. *Tortillas for the Gods: A Symbolic Analysis of Zinacanteco Rituals.* Cambridge: Harvard Univ. Press. 234 pp.
142. Warman, A., ed. 1970. *De Eso que Llaman Antropología Mexicana.* Mexico: Editorial Nuestro Tiempo
143. Warman, A. 1972. *Los Campesinos: Hijos Predilectos del Regimen.* Mexico: Editorial Nuestro Tiempo. 138 pp.
144. Warman, A., ed. 1974. *Los Campesinos de la Tierra de Zapata.* Mexico: Cent. Investig. Super., Inst. Nac. Antropol. Hist. 3 vols.
145. Warman, A. 1976. *... y Venimos a Contradecir.* Mexico: Inst. Nac. Antropol. Hist.
146. Whitecotton, J. W. 1977. *The Zapotecs: Princes, Priests, and Peasants.* Norman: Univ. Oklahoma Press
147. Wilkie, R. 1971. *San Miguel: A Mexican Collective Ejido.* Stanford: Stanford Univ. Press. 190 pp.
148. Wolf, E. 1956. Aspects of group relations in a complex society: Mexico. *Am. Anthropol.* 58:1065–78
149. Woods, C. M., Graves, T. D. 1973. *The Process of Medical Change in a Highland Guatemalan Town.* Los Angeles: Latin Am. Cent., Univ. California. 61 pp.

Ann. Rev. Anthropol. 1979. 8:71-85

HOMINID EVOLUTION IN EASTERN AFRICA DURING THE PLIOCENE AND EARLY PLEISTOCENE

♦9627

Noel T. Boaz

Department of Anthropology, New York University, New York, NY 10003

INTRODUCTION

Eastern Africa has for several years been an important area for investigations into early hominid evolution. Depositional factors related to the subsiding Rift Valley system have provided favorable situations for fossils to be preserved, and subsequent erosion has caused fossiliferous sediments to become exposed for surface collection and excavation. Intercalations of potassium-rich volcanic ash layers or tuffs have allowed an unprecedented chronological documentation by potassium-argon dating techniques, and in recent years paleomagnetic dating has been a valuable adjunct to these results. Thus, not only have early hominid fossils been preserved and discovered in eastern Africa, but geological circumstances have facilitated their accurate dating.

Eastern Africa has also seen the flowering of an empirical paleoanthropology, i.e. one which is supported by data collected in such a way that questions relating to early hominid evolution, paleobiology, and paleoecology can be answered. In addition to the elucidation of hominid phylogenesis, the documentation of early hominid behavior is a primary focus of research. Better dating techniques, paleoecological investigations, and multidisciplinary approaches have all contributed to this research.

Some of the major recent advances in early hominid studies in eastern Africa are discussed here. The time period treated extends from approximately 4 to 1 million years before the present (my BP).

The multidisciplinary research project has profoundly affected paleoanthropological research in eastern Africa, and has now spread to other areas

71

0084-6570/79/1015-0071$01.00

and time periods, eg. the Siwaliks (53). The development of this approach in eastern Africa can be seen clearly in looking at two examples, that of Olduvai Gorge, Tanzania, and that of the lower Omo Valley, Ethiopia. Louis Leakey and a small group of associates first began (primarily archaeological) research at Olduvai in 1931 (40). Leakey's initial and partially inadequate attempts at describing all aspects of the project (19; 30, p. 2) eventually gave way to involving a number of specialists in geology and paleontology (30, 43).

Camille Arambourg first traveled to Omo with a small group in 1932 and 1933 for paleontological collection. After a hiatus of 34 years, the first modern multidisciplinary project, the Omo Research Expedition, was organized by Arambourg, F. C. Howell, Y. Coppens, and L. Leakey in 1966 (see 22, pp. v-vi). It initiated a rigorous collection and excavation method based on mapping of localities on large-scale aerial photographs, a program of detailed stratigraphic work prior to and during paleontological and archaeological investigations, and concerted paleobotanical (palynological and fossil wood) researches. For the first time all of these data were computerized, thus allowing efficient synthesis and analysis.

The East Lake Turkana (formerly Rudolf) and Hadar projects have largely followed in this multidisciplinary approach. The former project first added the dimension of taphonomic analyses and underlined its importance as a step in paleoecological reconstruction.

The fruits of this multidisciplinary approach have not yet fully accrued to paleoanthropology, but as data are synthesized and analyses are completed, it will be apparent that early hominid studies have been taken in new directions and set on new courses of investigation.

CHRONOLOGY OF EVENTS IN EARLY HOMINID EVOLUTION IN EASTERN AFRICA

Eastern Africa is noted for its continuing discoveries of "earliest" documents in the hominid fossil record, many of which are initially claimed to totally revise current thinking about man's past. Highly publicized first remarks are many times qualified or disproved later, thus causing confusion in the lay public as well as in anthropologists with a general interest in hominid evolution. A review of some of the more important evidence as it now stands, beginning with a chronological discussion, is offered below.

The longest and best-dated fossiliferous sequence in eastern Africa consists of the Omo Beds, encompassing the Shungura, Usno, and Mursi Formations. Omo has yielded some 236 fossil hominid specimens, many of them individual teeth, from 3.4 to 1.0 my BP (Upper Member A to Member L). It is thus the only eastern African site documenting the interstitial period between gracile *Australopithecus* and *Homo* (Figure 1).

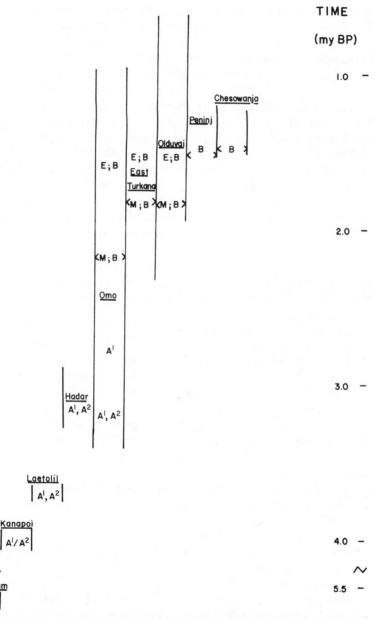

Figure 1. Temporal relationships of sites yielding remains of early hominids in eastern Africa. First or only occurrence of stone artifacts are indicated by: < >. Hominid taxa are indicated by: A¹ = *Australopithecus africanus;* A² = *Australopithecus afarensis;* M = *Homo modjokertensis* (= *habilis*); E = *Homo erectus;* B = *Australopithecus boisei.* Symbols used are the following: ";" = both present; "," = one or both present; "/" = either present.

The Omo Beds are dated by a series of potassium-argon determinations (12, 13) complemented by stratigraphically closely spaced paleomagnetic results (14, 15). In addition to these absolute dating methods, the plethora of faunal remains has allowed a number of biostratigraphic studies (see 22) as well as a statistical biostratigraphic overview (55).

Research begun in 1968 as an adjunct of the Omo Research Expedition resulted in the discovery of important early hominids in an area of low topographic relief east of Lake Turkana (then Rudolf). The lack of vertical sedimentary exposures made the initial attempts at stratigraphy difficult (10, 58). Lateral correlations of sedimentary units under these conditions were difficult or impossible and, not surprisingly, later studies have shown the earlier stratigraphic work inadequate (16, 27). Compounding these stratigraphic problems were absolute dates on some Koobi Fora tuffs that have now been shown to be spuriously old assessments of the true ages of the tuffs (16, 24). Of primary interest was the ^{40}Ar-^{39}Ar date of 2.6 ± .26 my BP by Fitch & Miller (28, 29) on the "KBS Tuff." Paleomagnetic studies at East Turkana (11) proved of little utility in initially solving the problem of the age of the "KBS Tuff," primarily because of stratigraphic problems, but also perhaps because there was too great a stratigraphic distance between collected samples.

The "KBS Tuff" is of considerable importance and interest because of its relation to hominid (e.g. KNM-ER 1470) and other vertebrate fossils from the Lower Member of the Koobi Fora Formation (of which it is the overlying delimiter) and its relation to the so-called first hominid tools (35).

H. B. S. Cooke (20) first published observations from faunal (suid) studies that showed a disagreement between 2.5 to 3.0 million-year-old sediments from Omo and sediments of that supposed age (below the "KBS Tuff") from East Turkana. Cooke suggested that the ^{40}Ar-^{39}Ar date of the "KBS Tuff" was perhaps too old. The same conclusions were reached by White & Harris (65; see also 21).

Curtis et al (24) redated the "KBS Tuff" and found two clusters of dates, around 1.8 my BP and 1.6 my BP, respectively. This implied that more than one tuff was being sampled. Cerling et al (16) have now demonstrated on mineralogical grounds that the "KBS Tuff" in Area 131 (where KNM-ER 1470 was found) and in part of Area 105 (where the KBS archaeological occurrence was discovered) is the same tuff as Tuff H2 in the Shungura Formation of the Omo (1.8 my BP). The "KBS Tuff" in the eastern portion of Area 105 was demonstrated by these authors to be identical to Tuff H4 of Omo, and they therefore redesignated the East Turkana tuff as "Tuff H4." This work by Cerling et al (16) effectively silences support for an older ^{40}Ar-^{39}Ar date by Fitch and Miller and a fission-track determination of 2.4 my BP by Hurford, Gleadow & Naeser (34). Wagner (64) showed that the latter authors used a generally unaccepted decay constant in calculating this age. Stratigraphic correlations between Omo and East Turkana are summarized in Figure 2.

Eastern Africa is unique in preserving an abundance of potassium-rich volcanic tuffs, lavas, and basalts for potassium-argon (or ^{40}Ar-^{39}Ar) dating. Determinations at a number of sites allow the arrangement of a chronologi-

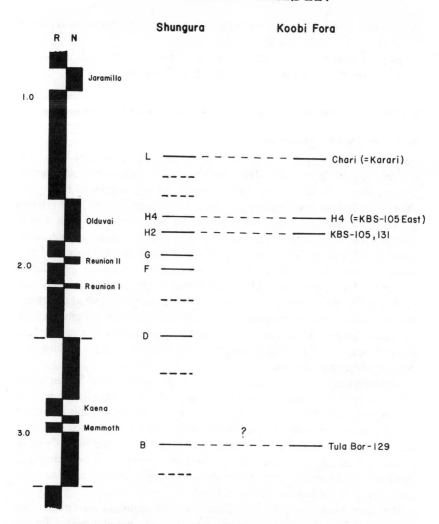

Figure 2. Geological correlations between tuffs within the Lake Turkana basin (Ethiopia and Kenya), based on results reported by Cerling et al (16). Paleomagnetic time scale is from Brown, Shuey & Croes (15) for Omo Shungura sediments.

cal sequence of sites (Figure 1) which is consistent with biostratigraphic evidence (e.g. 65). This arrangement of sites, along with anatomical and archaeological considerations (see next sections), allows several generalizations to be set forth:

1. Only gracile hominid (australopithecine) species are present early, prior to approximately 2.1 to 2.2 my BP.
2. Hominid specimens attributable to the genus *Homo* first occur at slightly over 2.0 my BP.
3. The first identifiable remains of the robust australopithecine also appear at about 2.1 to 2.2 my BP.
4. Stone artifacts of hominid manufacture are first known from in situ occurrences at 2.2 my BP [Member E of Omo (see 18)].

HOMINID MORPHOTYPES AND TAXONOMY

Gracile Australopithecines

Australopithecus africanus is a relatively small-brained hominid (probable cranial capacity from under 400 to over 600 cm^3) with a characteristically "dished face," i.e. an area around the nasal opening depressed relative to the rest of the face. Its anterior teeth, incisors and canines, are large relative to its premolars and molars. Certain traits ally the taxon with robust australopithecines, such as dished face, small cranial capacity, postorbital constriction, and molars with intricate crenulations on their occlusal surfaces. These, with other more detailed criteria, account for the inclusion in the genus *Australopithecus*. Other traits relate *A. africanus* to (later) *Homo*, such as a smooth cranial contour, large anterior teeth compared to premolars and molars, and nonmolariform premolars. *A. africanus* is morphologically more primitive than *Homo* in its relatively long premolars and molars, its tendancy for a "V-shaped" mandible, its smaller cranial capacity, and certain postcranial features.

Remains attributable to *Australopithecus africanus,* found first in South Africa in 1924, were not recognized in eastern Africa until a hemimandible was discovered in 1967 at Lothagam, Kenya (52). Since then this taxon has been stated to be present at a number of eastern African localities, including Omo, Hadar, Laetolil, East Turkana, and Olduvai. The presence of gracile australopithecines seems unlikely at the latter two sites, when ranges of morphological variability and presently known ages of the hominid samples are taken into consideration (see below).

It seemed likely from the initial finds that the hominid specimens from Hadar and Laetolil respectively comprised single populations of gracile australopithecines (5), although they were in the main referred to *Homo* sp.

indet. [(37, 38) for Hadar; (45) for Laetolil]. Johanson & Taieb (37) also suggested the co-occurrence of *A. boisei* and *A. africanus* with *Homo* sp. at Hadar. All specimens, however, from these two sites were recently reassigned to a new taxon, *Australopithecus afarensis* (39). While this new taxon may eventually prove to be warranted, several problems prevent its immediate acceptance.

The morphological range of variation of *A. africanus* is still incompletely known. For example, only one relatively complete adult cranium (from South Africa) exists (Sts 5). No complete crania have been recovered of the newly proposed taxon. It is thus difficult to assess whether or not the morphology of the Hadar and Laetolil specimens can be subsumed under the nomen *A. africanus.* Johanson, White & Coppens (39) also note that their diagnosis includes body parts not known for *A. africanus,* which with future discoveries could closely resemble those reported for *A. afarensis.*

Even though *A. afarensis* is suggested to be a more primitive australopithecine species, Hadar (dating from 3.3 to 2.9 my BP) overlaps in time with available age estimates of *A. africanus* from South Africa [ca 3 my BP (62, 63)]. This fact, coupled with close morphological similarities with *A. africanus,* brings into question the appropriateness of the new taxonomic name.

Nevertheless, some of the morphology seen in the referred specimens of *A. afarensis* is indeed apparently primitive, such as large canines which expose a line of enamel along their distal borders in wear, obliquely set lower third premolars, and a mandible with a small anterior region for incisors which tend to be somewhat procumbent. A relatively high degree of observed size variation may be attributable to sexual dimorphism. Howell (32) has also suggested the presence of a separate species of gracile australopithecine in the Laetolil and Hadar sequences which he referred to as "Hominidae gen. et sp. indet. (B)." Further discoveries in this time range and in even earlier Late Miocene sediments will help to clarify the nature of *A. afarensis.*

Homo

Morphologically *Homo* is characterized by a lightly constructed cranium with little postorbital constriction and a relatively prominent midfacial region compared to australopithecines. The probable population range for cranial capacity is at least from under 600 to over 800 cm^3. There is a "harmonious" relationship between anterior and posterior teeth, as in *A. africanus.* Postcanine teeth tend to be shorter than in gracile australopithecines, and molars tend to lack complicated crenulations on their surface.

There now seem to be no grounds for proclaiming the appearance of the genus *Homo* prior to 2.0 to 2.2 my BP. First occurrences are in Member

E (Omo, Shungura), Lower Member of the Koobi Fora Formation, and Bed I of Olduvai. The near coincidence of first and last appearances of *Homo* and *A. africanus,* respectively, in the Omo sequence and the similarities in morphology in the two taxa (5, 32) imply an ancestor-descendent relationship. An ancient separate *Homo* lineage coevolving with gracile *Australopithecus* species (46, 47; see Figure 3C) is improbable based on recent redating of *Homo* specimens from East Turkana and on the recent recognition of the Hadar and Laetolil samples as australopithecine (39). Nevertheless, the morphological (and cultural) definition of the genus *Homo* is still a difficult problem and remains to be resolved (7, 51).

The first species of the genus *Homo* recognized in eastern Africa was named *Homo habilis* by L. Leakey, Tobias & Napier (44), based on a hominid sample from Olduvai Beds I and II, dated at 1.7 to 1.8 my BP (30). Soon after the initial description, Tobias & von Koenigswald (57) noted the close similarities between Olduvai *Homo habilis* and specimens from the Djetis fauna of Java, to which the taxonomic names *H. modjokertensis* (59) and *Meganthropus palaeojavanicus* (60) had been applied. Only two or three specimens have been ascribed to the latter taxon (49, 60), and these are morphologically comparable to the *H. modjokertensis* sample, though slightly larger in size. Their robusticity can be matched in the gracile East African early hominid sample from Omo (e.g. Omo 222-73-2744) and East Turkana (e.g. KNM-ER 1506). *H. dubius* (60, 61) is also within the range of variability of this population.

Jacob & Curtis (36) provided a relatively imprecise potassium-argon date (because of small amounts of available potassium) of 1.9 ± 0.4 my BP on Djetis-level pumice. Recently Ninkovich & Burckle (50), correlating marine diatoms with paleomagnetic and oxygen isotope records, showed that the base of the Putjangan Beds, yielding the Djetis fauna and hominids, dated to between 1.9 and 2.1 my BP. This age is similar to Omo Shungura Members E and F, Olduvai Bed I, and the Lower Member of the Koobi Fora Formation.

Based on morphological similarities and the similarity in ages, Boaz & Howell (7) suggested that *H. modjokertensis* (59) and *H. habilis* (44) might be taxonomically synonomous. The former nomen thus has taxonomic priority. Recent redating confirms that these two samples of pre-*erectus Homo,* in sub-Saharan Africa and in southeastern Asia, are contemporaneous and should probably be referred to the same species, *H. modjokertensis.*

Robust Australopithecines

The robust australopithecines are an aberrant yet interesting group of hominids not lineally related to Homininae and characterized by their own peculiar adaptations. They possess massive crania with sagittal crests and

robust zygomatic arches and very large mandibles, as well as other morphological traits related to their adaptation for heavy mastication. The incisors
and canines are insignificant in relation to the large molars and molariform
premolars. Although body size (extrapolated from postcranial remains) is
somewhat larger, cranial capacity is in the same range as that of the gracile
australopithecines, i.e. around 400 to over 600 cm^3.

The eastern African robust australopithecine was first recognized at Olduvai in 1959 and named *Zinjanthropus boisei* (41). It is generally considered to be within the genus *Australopithecus*, but the species name has been
in the main retained as distinct from the South African *A. robustus*, probably primarily due to Tobias's (56) excellent monograph on the Olduvai
specimen (Old. Hom. 5). The robust early hominid is recognized from Omo
Shungura Members E,F,G,H, and perhaps L, Lower and Upper Members
of the Koobi Fora Formation, Beds I and II of Olduvai, Peninj (Natron)
and Chesowanja in eastern Africa. Its temporal range is from 2.1 or 2.2 my
BP to 1.5 my BP, and perhaps up to 1.0 my BP (Shungura Member L,
Figure 1).

HOMINID PHYLOGENETIC RELATIONSHIPS

Figure 3 diagrams some of the possible interpretations of early hominid
evolution, based on the evidence from eastern Africa as well as southern
Africa.

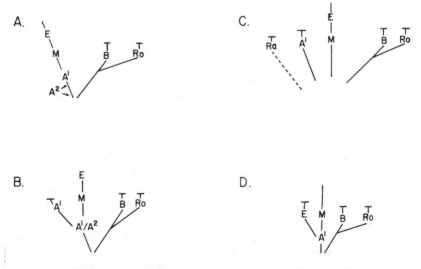

Figure 3.   Phylogenetic interpretations of Plio–Pleistocene Hominidae, as discussed in the
text. Phylogeny A is considered here the most probable. Abbreviations are as in Figure 1, with
the addition of: Ro = *Australopithecus robustus* (= *crassidens*); Ra = *Ramapithecus*.

For reasons discussed above, phylogeny A seems the most conservative hypothesis. B (33) differs only in proposing a late-surviving *A. africanus* population, difficult to demonstrate empirically on the basis of present fossil material. There are strong arguments now against phylogeny C (47), based on dates showing that *Homo* is much later in time than classical *A. africanus.* C also fails to take into account adequate population variability as regards cranial capacity, mandible contour, or tooth size. Hypothesis D (42), in which *H. erectus* is relegated to an extinct side-branch, is rendered improbable by recent findings, particularly at East Turkana (e.g. KNM-ER 1813 and 3733), which morphologically bridge the gap between the earlier *H. modjokertensis* (*habilis*) and later *H. erectus.* Other phylogenetic hypotheses are possible, but much more data and analysis (with the emphasis on the former) would be necessary to displace phylogeny A as the most probable.

PALEOECOLOGY

Hominid paleoecology is the study of the environmental conditions, the associated vertebrate and invertebrate fauna, the flora, the paleodemography, the diet, and the ecological relations of fossil Hominidae. Paleoecological investigations are necessary in order to understand the nature of hominid adaptations which evolve within environmental and ecological nexes. With the further realization that primate social behavior is profoundly affected by ecological conditions (23), the study of hominid paleoecology takes on much more significance in investigating human evolution.

The techniques of paleoecological research are many and varied and are still being developed. The attribution of animals, whose bones have been discovered at a site, to particular habitats is one of the oldest and still most common investigative techniques. Two problems attendant to these faunal paleoenvironmental reconstructions are that (*a*) depending on the species under consideration, the animal may move with greater or lesser ease from one habitat to another (a frequently cited problem in attributing specific habitats to adaptable large mammals); and (*b*) even if the animals under consideration are known to have had specific habitat affinities, their fossil bones may or may not have been deposited in that habitat, i.e. they may have been transported to a depositional site in a habitat different from that in which the animal died. The first problem is partially solved by viewing fossil animal species as occupying a range of habitats (similar to their modern analogs), by looking at numerous taxa from one site and by employing in analyses species with more specific environmental requirements, such as micromammals or amphibians. The second problem is (at least partially) dealt with by a study of the sedimentology and paleontology of the depositional site and its contained bone assemblage, a synthetic field now known as taphonomy. The aim of taphonomy is the discovery of the relation of fossil bones at a site to the actual past animal communities from which they derived [for eastern African taphonomy see (1, 2, 6, 31, 54)].

Paleobotany has been an important addition to hominid paleoecology in eastern Africa. Bonnefille (8) recovered pollen profiles from Omo, East Turkana, Olduvai, and Hadar, analyses of which are as yet incomplete. Macrobotanical remains at Omo in the rare finds of fossil fruit (9) and the more abundant fossil wood, analyzed by Dechamps (25), supplement this record, particularly as regards plants with rare environmental pollen, e.g. those species which are insect pollinated.

Geological work on paleoenvironment, including stratigraphy, sedimentology, and mineralogy, has been most rigorously carried out by Hay (30) at Olduvai. Related studies at East Turkana (17, 27), at Omo (26), Laetolil (see 30, p. 187), and at several central Kenyan sites (3, 4) have also been carried out.

Successful paleoecological research requires a multidisciplinary, rigorous, and coordinated research effort, as has only recently come about in eastern Africa. Nevertheless, at no single locality have all possible areas of potential paleoecological data been investigated and much remains to be done.

Figure 4 diagrams the sites in eastern Africa on axes of time and general habitat, the latter based on available faunal, floral, and geological evidence [see (5) for a more detailed review]. Hominid taxa, as discussed previously, are also represented. Gracile australopithecines (*A. africanus* and perhaps *A. afarensis*) appear to have been adaptable to a range of habitats. They occur not only in well-watered savanna woodland sites such as Hadar and early Omo, but also in drier more open savanna conditions at Laetolil. Robust australopithecines, on the other hand, occur generally during drier conditions at Omo (Members E and F show drier climate and increased areas of savanna) and are the only hominids present in the sites of Peninj and Chesowanja, both low-lying sites on the margins of saline lakes (with associated habitats of probably treeless to scrub savanna). *Homo* is also present at Omo, East Turkana, and Olduvai with *A. boisei,* and was likely adaptable to a relatively wide range of environments. The niche specializations of *Homo* and *A. boisei,* i.e. in what manner these two species spatially, temporally, and dietarily partitioned their common environment, is as yet unknown and is an important area of continuing investigation.

CONCLUSION AND FURTHER PROBLEMS

Some of the main events in early hominid evolution have now been better documented and dated in eastern Africa, but a number of problems remain. Although the "single species hypothesis," at least as regards eastern African

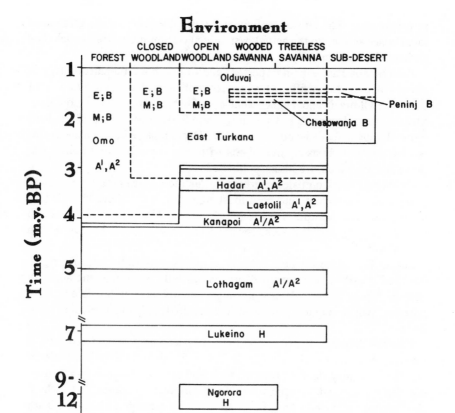

Figure 4.   Diagrammatic representation of paleoenvironments at eastern African early hominid sites (see 5). The horizontal axis ranges from forested closed conditions on the left to more open grassland conditions on the right. Abbreviations are as in Figure 1, with the addition of: H = Hominidae indet.

early hominids, has been shown morphologically to be unlikely (48), the theoretical and paleoecological reasons are still far from clear.

Stone tools have been found in sites which have yielded both *Homo* and robust australopithecines, and in some cases with the latter and without the former (e.g. 4). How did the various species of Plio-Pleistocene hominids utilize tools and what were their cultural capabilities?

Many new and frequently conflicting models of early hominid behavior have been proposed using primate behavioral analogies and social carnivore analogies. The development of research methodologies to test these hypotheses empirically is a challenge to paleoanthropology.

There are many phylogenetic questions regarding the origin of the australopithecines, the place and time of differentiation and the causes for the eventual extinction of the robust forms, and the first appearance of the genus *Homo.* The eastern African Plio-Pleistocene can be expected to provide some of the answers to these questions, with continued paleontological and paleoecological research, but in other cases answers will lie in earlier time periods, in the Upper Miocene.

Literature Cited

1. Behrensmeyer, A. K. 1975. The taphonomy and paleoecology of Plio-Pleistocene vertebrate assemblages east of Lake Rudolf, Kenya. *Bull. Mus. Comp. Zool.* 146 (10):473–578
2. Behrensmeyer, A. K. 1978. The habitat of Plio-Pleistocene hominids in East Africa: Taphonomic and microstratigraphic evidence. In *Early Hominids of Africa,* ed. C. J. Jolly, pp. 165–89. London: Duckworth
3. Bishop, W. W., Pickford, M. H. 1975. Geology, fauna and palaeoenvironments of the Ngorora Formation, Kenya Rift Valley. *Nature* 254:185–92
4. Bishop, W. W., Pickford, M. H., Hill, A. 1975. New evidence regarding the Quaternary geology, archaeology and hominids of Chesowanja, Kenya. *Nature* 258:204–8
5. Boaz, N. T. 1977. Paleoecology of early Hominidae in Africa. *Kroeber Anthropol. Soc. Pap.* 50:37–62
6. Boaz, N. T., Behrensmeyer, A. K. 1976. Hominid taphonomy: Transport of human skeletal parts in an artificial fluviatile environment. *Am. J. Phys. Anthropol.* 45:53–60
7. Boaz., N. T., Howell, F. C. 1977. A gracile hominid cranium from upper Member G of the Shungura Formation, Ethiopia. *Am. J. Phys. Anthropol.* 46:93–108
8. Bonnefille, R. 1976. Palynological evidence for an important change in the vegetation of the Omo basin between 2.5 and 2 million years. See Ref. 22, pp. 421–31
9. Bonnefille, R., Letouzey, R. 1976. Fruits fossiles d'*Antrocaryon* dans la vallée de l'Omo. *Adansonia* 16:65–82
10. Bowen, B. E., Vondra, C. F. 1973. Stratigraphic relationships of the Plio-Pleistocene deposits, East Rudolf, Kenya. *Nature* 242:391–93
11. Brock, A., Isaac, G. Ll. 1976. Reversal stratigraphy and its application at East Rudolf. See Ref. 22, pp. 148–62
12. Brown, F. H. 1972. Radiometric dating of sedimentary formations in the lower Omo valley, Ethiopia. In *Calibration of Hominoid Evolution,* ed. W. W. Bishop,

J. A. Miller, pp. 272–87. Edinburgh: Scottish Acad. Press
13. Brown, F. H., Lajoie, K. R. 1971. Radiometric age determinations on Pliocene/Pleistocene formations in the Lower Omo Basin, southern Ethiopia. *Nature* 229:483–85
14. Brown, F. H., Shuey, R. T. 1976. Magnetostratigraphy of the Shungura and Usno Formations, lower Omo basin, Ethiopia. See Ref. 22, pp. 64–78
15. Brown, F. H., Shuey, R. T., Croes, M. K. 1978. Magnetostratigraphy of the Shungura and Usno Formations, southwestern Ethiopia: New data and comprehensive re-analysis. *Geophys. J. R. Astron. Soc.* 54:519–38
16. Cerling, T. E., Brown, F. H., Cerling, B. W., Curtis, G. H., Drake, R. E. 1979. Preliminary correlations between the Koobi Fora and Shungura Formations, East Africa. *Nature.* In press
17. Cerling, T. E., Hay, R., O'Neil, J. R. 1977. Isotopic evidence for dramatic climatic changes in East Africa during the Pleistocene. *Nature* 267:137–38
18. Chavaillon, J. 1976. Evidence for the technical practices of early Pleistocene hominids, Shungura Formation, lower Omo Valley, Ethiopia. See Ref. 22, pp. 565–73
19. Cole, S. 1975. *Leakey's Luck: The Life of Louis Seymour Bazett Leakey, 1903–1972.* London: Collins
20. Cooke, H. B. S. 1976. Suidae from Plio-Pleistocene successions of the Rudolf basin. See Ref. 22, pp. 251–63
21. Cooke, H. B. S. 1978. Suid evolution and correlation of African hominid localities: An alternative taxonomy. *Science* 201:460–63
22. Coppens, Y., Howell, F. C., Isaac, G. Ll., Leakey, R. E. F., eds. 1976. Earliest man and environments in the Lake Rudolf basin. Chicago: Univ. Chicago Press. 615 pp.
23. Crook, J. H. 1970. The socio-ecology of primates. In *Social Behavior of Birds and Mammals,* ed J. H. Crook. New York: Academic
24. Curtis, G. H., Drake, R., Cerling, T. E., Hampel, J. 1975. Age of the KBS Tuff

in the Koobi Fora Formation, East Rudolf, Kenya. *Nature* 258:395–98

25. Dechamps, R. 1979. Résultats préliminaires de l'étude des bois fossiles de la basse vallée de l'Omo. *Ann. Mus. R. Afr. Cent.,* Tervuren, *Sci. Geol.* In press

26. de Heinzelin, J., ed. 1979. Sedimentary formations of Pliocene and early Pleistocene age in the Omo basin, Ethiopia. *Ann. Mus. R. Afr. Cent., Tervuren, Sci. Geol.* In press

27. Findlater, I. C. 1976. *Stratigraphic analysis and palaeoenvironmental interpretation of a Plio-Pleistocene sedimentary basin east of Lake Turkana.* PhD thesis. Univ. London, London, England

28. Fitch, F. J., Miller, J. A. 1970. Radioisotopic age determinations of Lake Rudolf artefact site. *Nature* 226:226–28

29. Fitch, F. J., Miller, J. A. 1976. Conventional potassium-argon and argon-40/argon-39 dating of volcanic rocks from East Rudolf. See Ref. 22, pp. 123–47

30. Hay, R. L. 1976. *Geology of the Olduvai Gorge.* Berkeley: Univ. California Press. 203 pp.

31. Hill, A. 1975. *Taphonomy of contemporary and late Cenozoic East African vertebrates.* PhD thesis. Univ. London, London, England

32. Howell, F. C. 1978. Hominidae. In *Evolution of African Mammals,* ed. V. Maglio, H. B. S. Cooke, pp. 154–248. Cambridge: Harvard Univ. Press

33. Howell, F. C., Coppens, Y. 1976. An overview of Hominidae from the Omo succession, Ethiopia. See Ref. 22, pp. 522–32

34. Hurford, A. J., Gleadow, A. J. W., Naeser, C. W. 1976. Fission-track dating of pumice from the KBS Tuff, East Rudolf, Kenya. *Nature* 263:738–40

35. Isaac, G. Ll., Leakey, R. E. F., Behrensmeyer, A. K. 1971. Archaeological traces of early hominid activities east of Lake Rudolf, Kenya. *Science* 173:1129–34

36. Jacob, T., Curtis, G. H. 1971. Preliminary potassium-argon dating of early man in Java. *Contrib. Univ. Calif. Archaeol. Res. Fac.* 12:50

37. Johanson, D. C., Taieb, M. 1976. Pleistocene hominid discoveries in Hadar, Ethiopia. *Nature* 260:293–97

38. Johanson, D. C., Taieb, M., Gray, B. T., Coppens, Y. 1978. Geological framework of the Pliocene Hadar Formation (Afar, Ethiopia) and notes on paleontology, including hominids. In *Geological Background to Fossil Man,* ed. W.

W. Bishop, pp. 549–64. Edinburgh: Scottish Acad. Press

39. Johanson, D. C., White, T. D., Coppens, Y. 1978. A new species of the genus *Australopithecus* (Primates: Hominidae) from the Pliocene of eastern Africa. *Kirtlandia* 28:1–14

40. Leakey, L. S. B. 1937. *White African.* Cambridge, Mass: Schenkman

41. Leakey, L. S. B. 1959. A new fossil skull from Olduvai. *Nature* 184:491–93

42. Leakey, L. S. B. 1963. East African fossil Hominoidea and the classification within this super-family. In *Classification and Human Evolution,* ed. S. L. Washburn, pp. 32–49. Chicago: Aldine

43. Leakey, L. S. B. 1967. *Olduvai Gorge, 1951–61. Vol. 1. A Preliminary Report on the Geology and Fauna.* Cambridge: Cambridge Univ. Press

44. Leakey, L. S. B., Tobias, P. V., Napier, J. R. 1964. A new species of the genus *Homo* from Olduvai Gorge. *Nature* 202:7–9

45. Leakey, M. D., Hay, R. L., Curtis, G. H., Drake, R. E., Jackes, M. K., White, T. D. 1976. Fossil hominids from the Laetolil Beds. *Nature* 262:460–66

46. Leakey, R. E. F. 1976. An overview of the Hominidae from East Rudolf, Kenya. See Ref. 22, pp. 476–83

47. Leakey, R. E. F. 1977. Hominids in Africa. *Am. Sci.* 64:174–78

48. Leakey, R. E. F., Walker, A. C. 1976. *Australopithecus, Homo erectus* and the single species hypothesis. *Nature* 261:572–74

49. Marks, P. 1952. Preliminary note on the discovery of a new jaw of *Meganthropus* von Koenigswald in the lower Middle Pleistocene of Sangiran, central Java. *Indonesian J. Nat. Hist.* 109:26–33

50. Ninkovich, D., Burckle, L. H. 1978. Absolute age of the base of the hominid-bearing beds in eastern Java. *Nature* 275:306–8

51. Olson, T. R. 1978. Hominid phylogenetics and the existence of *Homo* in Member I of the Swartkrans Formation, South Africa. *J. Hum. Evol.* 7:159–78

52. Patterson, B., Behrensmeyer, A. K., Sill, W. D. 1970. Geology and fauna of a new Pliocene locality in northwestern Kenya. *Nature* 226:918–21

53. Pilbeam, D., Meyer, G. E., Badgley, C., Rose, M. D., Pickford, M. H., Behrensmeyer, A. K., Shah, S. M. I. 1977. New hominoid primates from the Siwaliks of Pakistan and their bearing on hominoid evolution. *Nature* 270:689–95

54. Shipman, P. L. 1977. *Paleoecology, taphonomic history, and population dynamics of the vertebrate fossil assemblage from the Middle Miocene deposits exposed at Fort Ternan, Kenya.* PhD thesis. Dep. Anthropol., New York Univ., New York, NY

55. Shuey, R. T., Brown, F. H., Eck, G. G., Howell, F. C. 1978. A statistical approach to temporal biostratigraphy. See Ref. 38, pp. 103–24

56. Tobias, P. V. 1967. *The Cranium and Maxillary Dentition of Australopithecus (Zinjanthropus) boisei.* Cambridge: Cambridge Univ. Press

57. Tobias, P. V., von Koenigswald, G. H. R. 1964. A comparison between the Olduvai hominines and those of Java and some implications for hominid phylogeny. *Nature* 204:515–18

58. Vondra, C. F., Johnson, G. D., Behrensmeyer, A. K., Bowen, B. E. 1971. Preliminary stratigraphic studies of the East Rudolf basin. *Nature* 231:245–48

59. von Koenigswald, G. H. R. 1936. Ein fossiler Hominide aus dem Altpleistocän Ostjavas. *Ing. Ned.–Indie* 8:149–57

60. von Koenigswald, G. H. R. 1950. Fossil hominids from the lower Pleistocene of southern China. *Proc. Int. Geol. Congr.* 9:59–66

61. von Koenigswald, G. H. R. 1970. Java: Prae–Trinil man. *Proc. 8th Int. Congr. Anthropol. Ethnol. Sci.* 1:104–5

62. Vrba, E. S. 1974. Chronological and ecological implications of the fossil Bovidae at the Sterkfontein australopithecine site. *Nature* 250:19–23

63. Vrba, E. S. 1975. Some evidence of chronology and palaeoecology of Sterkfontein, Swartkrans and Kromdraai from the fossil Bovidae. *Nature* 254:301–4

64. Wagner, G. A. 1977. Fission–track dating of pumice from the KBS Tuff, East Rudolf, Kenya. *Nature* 267:649

65. White, T. D., Harris, J. M. 1977. Suid evolution and correlation of African hominid localities. *Science* 198:13–21

Ann. Rev. Anthropol. 1979. 8:87-113

POLITICAL SYMBOLISM[1]   ♦9628

Abner Cohen

Department of Anthropology, School of Oriental and African Studies,
University of London, London WC1E 7HP, England

Much of the recent literature that bears directly on political symbolism has
already been surveyed for the *Annual Review of Anthropology* in two excellent papers, the one on "Symbolic Studies" by Turner (65), the other on
"Political Anthropology" by Vincent (67). In this paper I explore a number
of key conceptual, analytical, and methodological issues that are involved
in this topic, covering some of the more recent publications, including
relevant Marxian literature. A good deal of the discussion will be concerned
with unfolding the political implications of cultural symbols. This is because
many, indeed most, of the symbols that are politically significant are overtly
nonpolitical. Often, the less obviously political in form symbols are, the
more efficacious politically they prove to be. The greatest contribution of
sociocultural anthropology to the study of politics has been the analysis of
the political functions of symbolic, nonpolitical institutions like kinship and
religion.

It is the very essence and potency of symbols that they are ambiguous,
referring to different meanings, and are not given to precise definition. The
most dominant symbols are essentially bivocal, being rooted, on the one
hand, in the human condition, in what may be called "selfhood," and on
the other in the relations of power. Forms that are clearly and formally
political tend to be signs, not symbols; they lack ambiguity and are thus
unidimensional. Some of them do in time become efficacious, but only when
they acquire nonpolitical, existentialist meanings in addition to their formal
connotation.

[1]This paper was written while I was a Fellow at the Center for Advanced Study in the
Behavioral Sciences, Stanford California, 1978–1979. I am grateful to the staff of the Center
for their untiring assistance and for the financial support provided by the National Science
Foundation, Grant No. BNS 76–22943 A02.

EXTENSIVE DEFINITIONS

These are categorical statements which make a number of basic assumptions that are highly controversial. First among these is the statement that politics refers to the distribution, maintenance, exercise of, and struggle for power within a social unit. Power is analytically conceived as an aspect of nearly all social relationships. Even such primary relationships as those between husband and wife, father and son, or friend and friend have their own power element and thus form part of the political system in any society.

Some political scientists would object to this extensive definition of politics, principally because it makes the study of politics coextensive with the study of all society. This objection is methodological rather than theoretical and is met by most social anthropologists by focusing their studies on one small area of political life at a time. Besides, the more restricted definition of politics, which covers only activities related to state institutions, is inapplicable to the study of the political organization of those tribal, preindustrial societies that are acephalous and non-centralized. In such societies law and order are generally maintained by a balance of power between segments of groupings of equal order, sometimes assisted by the mediation of formally nonpolitical, ritual men.

The term "power" is an abstraction referring simply to relations of domination and subordination. These are either economic relations, arising in the course of production, exchange, and distribution, or "purely political," deriving ultimately from command over organized physical force. These two types of relations, though distinct in many respects, are interrelated and in many situations inseparable. Nearly everywhere in small-scale preindustrial societies the system of land tenure, client-patron relationships, exchange, and the distribution of goods are inseparable parts of the political order. In many centralized tribal societies, the chief holds the land in trust and allocates it to his people; in exchange he is given allegiance and part of the produce, which he then redistributes. In many uncentralized societies, mythologies of kinship that are often articulated in the form of elaborate genealogies regulate the distribution of land and define political groupings at one and the same time. Similarly, in the advanced industrial societies the relationships between property owner and user, employer and employee, producer and consumer, and a host of similar relationships are maintained and regulated by the laws of the state. Economic and political interests interpenetrate each other and react on one another. They continually exert pressure on the state and the state continually exerts pressure on them.

Some Marxists would object to these formulations on the ground that all relationships of power derive from the relations of production and that the state itself is but an instrument used by the economically dominant class to develop and protect its interests and maintain the relations of production by organized coercion. Thus in their celebrated metaphor of the superstructure and infrastructure, Marx & Engels (50) placed politics and law in the superstructure, not in the economic base. This view of the state and of politics was no doubt greatly affected by the conditions prevailing in industrializing European societies during the nineteenth century. But the state is now almost everywhere, in capitalist as in communist societies, a power in its own right, regulating the increasingly complex public services, running industries, and becoming to a large extent autonomous, and it is not simply the agent of one class or another. There is no evidence that it is "withering away" in communist countries.

On the other hand, as Anderson (6, pp. 46–48) points out:

> the aftermath of the Second World War also saw the establishment, for the first time in the history of bourgeois rule, of representative democracy based on universal suffrage as the normal and stable structure of the State in all the main capitalist countries—West Germany, Japan, France, USA, England, Italy.

These are conditions unaccounted for by classical Marxism. It is probably a reflection of these developments that Althusser (4, 5) has modified the Marxian metaphor, giving a relative autonomy to politics and law which is separate from the superstructure (see also 52, p. 51). This is not to deny that the state, while attending to universalistic functions for the society as a whole, both internally and externally, is at the same time and to a larger or lesser extent also particularistic, serving the interests of one power group or another.

The two types of power, the economic and the political, are of course distinguishable in many respects. But for heuristic purposes most social anthropologists have concentrated on the common denominator between them, namely power relations. When anthropologists study economic activity, their ultimate aim is to discover the relations of power that are involved in production, exchange, and distribution.

Power relations are objectified, developed, maintained, expressed, or camouflaged by means of symbolic forms and patterns of symbolic action, both of which are referred to here as "symbolism." In most of the systems that anthropologists have studied, kinship and ritual have been the main form of symbolism; they are deployed alternatively, or combined together as articulating principles that are dialectically related to power relations. There are of course other symbolic forms that are similarly related to power. Indeed the whole of normative culture is involved here. "Culture," writes Raymond Williams (70, p. 76), "is one of the two or three most complicated words in the English language." It is a highly ambiguous term which is extensively used in many different senses and is thus too wide in its various connotations to be useful in sociological analysis. What is astonishing is that anthropologists who specialize in the analysis of culture should continue to use this term in the global, ragbag definition formulated by nineteenth century writers. In its current usage in social anthropology, the word often covers both utilitarian and normative traits, both objective and subjective phenomena.

Marxist writers use the term "ideology" as a substitute. Indeed, as Anderson (6) points out, Western Marxists since the end of the First World War have been principally concerned with the analysis of ideology or superstructure. Literally hundreds of books and articles have recently been published on the subject, mostly attempting to define what ideology is and what Marx and his followers have said about it. The most systematic comprehensive analysis in this respect to date is that of Althusser (3–5). But what is clear from reading Marxist literature is a complete lack of consensus about what ideology is and what functions it plays in society. What makes the subject more confusing is that Marx himself and even Althusser changed their views about ideology in the course of their careers. The result is that the concept is now as confused, if not more so, as that of culture. Ideology has been conceived as an epistemological concept, as the way men know their world; as a systematic body of values, norms, and beliefs; as synonymous with all culture, including ritual and ceremonial beliefs and practices. It has been described as "false consciousness" (47), inspired by the ruling classes to mystify people and prevent them from uncovering exploitation, and as such it exists only in class societies (50). Althusser (3, pp. 231–36), on the other hand, emphasized that ideology is an organic part of every social identity, that it is indispensable in any society, communist or capitalist. Some writers conceive ideology as expressive of, or determined by, the relations of production; others—including Althusser—regard it as relatively autonomous and as instrumental in recreating the relations of production.

One way of overcoming some of the difficulties and ambiguities involved is to apprehend culture or ideology in their manifestations in symbolic performances that are objective and collective and hence observable and verifiable, indicating normative patterns of action, in sharp contrast with utilitarian and technical patterns.

It is obvious that there is a great deal of oversimplification here, for there are significant differences between symbolic forms such as those between kinship and ritual. But symbols are highly complex sociocultural phenomena and can therefore be classified according to a variety of criteria, depending on the purpose of the classification, which in turn depends on the theoretical problem that is being investigated and the variables that are considered in the study. In political symbolism various types of symbols are analyzed in their involvement in the relations of power, and this would call for a type of classification which is often at variance with that provided by the cultural traditions of which they are a part. It would often entail lifting a ceremonial performance out of its ordinary phenomenological sequence to examine it in relation to political functions such as authority or the boundaries of groups.

Power relations and symbolism are present in all social relationships. This broad conception of political symbolism led me to conclude a paper on "Political Anthropology: The Analysis of the Symbolism of Power Relations" (12) by the statement that "political anthropology is nothing other than social anthropology brought up to a high degree of abstraction." This view drew sharp criticism from some colleagues, and it will be instructive to discuss some of the arguments involved, as they will highlight the central theoretical issues in the study of political symbolism.

Firth (25, pp. 205–6) describes this approach as "autologic to a considerable degree." He states:

> Cohen goes so far as to say that in social anthropology we are interested in symbols mainly in so far as they affect and are affected by power relations. I think this is a reductionist argument—that a great range of expressive symbols at life crises, for instance, are not power symbols; and that status symbols, which are equally a concern of the anthropologist, should not be merely equated with power symbols.

Turner (66) makes a similar criticism and suggests that I should pay as much attention to "action semiotics" as to "power relationships."

POLITICS AND THE SYMBOLISM OF LIFE CRISES

It will be important in many ways here to take Firth's example of the symbols of life crises and to inquire whether they are in any sense politically significant. For here we seem to be dealing with purely individual psychological and existential problems which are formally remote from politics.

If we consider the crisis of death, we shall immediately be struck by its universality and pervasiveness. "Why are we born and why do we die?" is a problem that has confronted all people in all societies at all times. It is a perennial problem in the sense that it can have no scientific solution. There have been, in fact, almost as many "solutions" as there have been cultures, and no one can tell which solution is more scientific than which. Everywhere the crisis is marked by symbolic patterns of action. The crisis is thus and to that extent irreducible; it is universal and is probably the most crucial factor in the human condition generally.

But if the symbolism of death is purely expressive of a universal, perennial human problem, we would expect it to be ceremonialized *in equal intensity* (although allowing for differences in symbolic forms) throughout humanity.

A quick comparative survey of the literature, however, will immediately show considerable variations in the degree of ceremonialization. In some societies, or groups within large societies, death ceremonials are simple and brief; in others they are highly elaborate and extensive. In some cases death is considered terminal and the dead are thought to be gone forever; in other cases death is regarded as a phase in the biography of persons, after which the dead resume existence as spirits which interact with the living and affect their life in a variety of ways. In this latter case the dead, or some of the dead, are revered and feared, and extensive recurring rituals are performed for them.

A comparison between different groups will also indicate that the intensity of the ceremonials of death and of the dead is not related to the level of education or to so-called civilization. Even my own very limited ethnographic field studies demonstrate this clearly. Neither Middle East peasants nor indigenous African traders nor West Indian proletariat in London show a fraction of the elaborate cult of the dead which is practiced among the highly educated and sophisticated Creoles of Sierra Leone. Indeed, among these the cult has been considerably intensified during the last three decades as more and more Creoles acquired higher education and joined the professional elite of the country.

This is not the place to give a detailed discussion of the variety of cults related to death and to the dead. What is evident from the ethnographic literature is that the intensity of the ceremonialization of this motif is closely related to fundamental politico-economic factors. The ancestors' cult reported for numerous societies, including the Chinese (2, 32), the Tallensi (26), and the Lugbara (51), has been shown to be instrumentally related to the structure of the lineage system, to political alignments, territorial divisions, and the organization of authority. Among the Creoles of Sierra Leone (17), the intensification of the cult in the last three decades is related to the political cleavage that has developed between them and the provincials over political power and public employment, but more particularly over control of vast freehold land and housing estates in the Freetown peninsula. Comprising less than 2 percent of the population of the country, yet dominating the civil service and the professions, they believe that as long as they maintain their control over land in the most politically and economically strategic part of the country, they can maintain their privileged position. But Creole landlords are under constant pressure and sometimes temptation to sell housing and land at ever mounting prices. The only force stopping them from doing so is their fear of the dead who bequeathed to them most of this property, where the spirits of the dead continue to dwell.

In all these cases, the cult of the dead is a collective representation which constrains individuals—sometimes against their conscious wills and private interests—and its symbolism is charged with political significance. Thus the question of "why are we born and why do we die" is embedded in the very core of human nature, but the symbolic beliefs and practices that are developed to deal with it are rarely individual constructions; they are often collective and always loaded with meanings and functions that develop and maintain the interests of the group.

There is no reductionism here. On the contrary, the problem of death is such a deep-rooted and powerful human issue that power groups everywhere seize on it and exploit it for their ends. This is true of all societies, including the modern, officially secular communist societies. The cult of Lenin is an eloquent example. Lenin's body was embalmed, mummified, and put on display in a special mausoleum in Red Square, which is the center of all major national political gatherings. Millions of people from all over the Soviet Union go on pilgrimage to the shrine, queuing up for hours in long rows, silently watching the change of the guard, then file up to view the body in awe and respect. It was of course initially a *consciously* institutionalized cult aiming at commemorating and glorifying "the Father of the Revolution" and unifying his people behind the party that he founded. The authors of the cult might have been highly rational men who planned "scientifically" the whole procedure. But such innovators are few in number and for the millions of ordinary people, young and old, the cult is powerful principally because it is also mystically related to something rooted in their very human nature. For the leaders, the body might have been a political "sign" with specifically defined meaning, but for the masses of people it is a symbol with different connotations, some of which touch some of their innermost thoughts and feelings.

The political significance of this kind of cult can be seen even more dramatically in the development in our time of a similar practice surrounding Mao Tse Tung in China. For about three decades the communist authorities have waged a relentless war against the traditional Chinese lineage which had been the basis of regional political organization, often competing and sometimes challenging the authority of the central government. This meant an attack on the ancestors' cult which expressed and maintained the corporateness and the organizing principle of the lineage. However, the sentiment relating to the dead is not itself suppressed, but is now partly channeled to what may well become the most massive cult of the dead in history, as the communist authorities have planned and actually set up a mausoleum for Mao which would dwarf that of Lenin.

This manipulation of dead corpses to serve as dominant political symbols is successful, not for purely rational considerations. For if that were the case, a memorial picture or statue, or any monument to the dead, rather than a decaying corpse, would have been sufficient. But the sight of the corpse by the masses of visitors, amidst strictly observed silence and solemnity, the association of the mausoleum with supreme state power, the guards of honor, reverence and admiration for the deceased, all these combine significantly with the enigmatic problem of life and death to conjure up in the minds of the pilgrims a complex psychic experience which can add further to what political philosophers call "political obligation."

Other societies or groups, though, do not neglect the motif of death, but seize on other life crises to infuse power into the symbolism of political authority. Significant among these crises is the initiation of the young to adulthood. In many small-scale preindustrial societies, initiation is dramatic in the sense that it transforms, within a brief period, children into adults. It is also collective in that a whole group of children go through the process at one time. Thus almost overnight, a new generation of men or women comes into being and begins to compete with the established adults over authority and control of resources, in effect threatening to and eventually succeeding in supplanting their parents' generation. The crisis of initiation is thus essentially not individual but social. This is why it is highly ritualized and why its symbolism is of such great political potential. In some societies the crisis serves as a perpetual basis for the organization of political authority and for politicking generally. Thus in Sierra Leone and Liberia alone, there are numerous tribal societies where the initiates become incorporated as permanent members within a secret society: the Poro for men, the Sande for women. Indeed, the importance of the Poro is so pronounced that one anthropologist, d'Azevado (18), has labeled the whole region as "the Poro Belt."

The political significance of this cult can be seen from the way the cult is practiced among the Mende of Sierra Leone (44–46). Here, Poro initiation is the rite of passage from boyhood to manhood. It takes place in the "secret bush," where the boys are taken and placed under the custody of Poro officials. Rituals are performed to signify the death and subsequent rebirth of the initiates, who in the process undergo physical pain and become imbued with the fear of the horrors that may be inflicted on wrongdoers by the masked spirits of the society. At the same time, the novices are instructed about sex and the procreation of children, duties to one's tribe and obedience to its elders, and the meaning of life and death. In this way the anxieties caused by passage to adulthood, physical pain, dramatic rituals, and the horrors behind the masks combine to leave in the initiates a deep psychic experience which remains a source of emotional and sentimental agitation that can be triggered and kept alive by the repetitive display of the symbols of the society and the performance of its rituals.

In the process, a powerful bond of loyalty is created in the initiates toward their Poro masters, who are thus loved, revered, feared, and obeyed.

While most of the initiates remain ordinary members of the Poro all their lives, a small minority continues to pursue a ritual career by undergoing further courses of instruction and being subsequently initiated into higher ritual degrees within the order. To achieve this they have to pay high fees and costs, and this means that only the wealthy and influential will rise up in the hierarchy of leadership, at the apex of which stands the "inner circle," whose members are in effect the arbiters of chiefly authority, supporting it and sometimes checking its excesses even to the extent of deposing the incumbent. Little (45, 46) says that among the Mende, the Poro provides the mystical element to the otherwise purely secular authority of the chief. The two hierarchies, the ritual and the secular, are in fact overlapping in roles and in personnel. The powerful men in the one tend to be the powerful men in the other.

This makes the Poro into a significant weapon in the hands of chiefly families who use it in some situations, particularly when their own interests are threatened. Such use has actually occurred on a number of occasions during the colonial and postcolonial periods (9, 40, 62). Thus, Poro organization and loyalties were manipulated in the planning and conduct of the Hut Tax War in 1898 against the British and in the organization of the riots of 1955–56. When the British established the franchise and the country gained independence, Poro institutions were used to mobilize votes in elections. Sierra Leone political parties at the time were loose coalitions without any kind of organization in the provinces and thus relied on the provincial chiefs for the mobilization of votes for them.

A similar organization is based on the initiation of females into the Sande secret society, though because political power in the area is mainly in the hands of men, its political significance is less pronounced. [For some details see MacCormack (48).] Poro and Sande cults are also found extensively in Liberia (18, 37, 38, 43). Many other societies in other parts of Africa and elsewhere seize on the crisis of initiation and politicize it in the service of one interest or another.

In industrial and postindustrial societies, initiation is gradual and diffused, though it is no less politicized. Here the rising, maturing young men and women are on the one hand socialized and trained in the dominant culture of the established order and on the other radicalized by the counter-cultures of discontented groups. When they finally graduate, they begin to compete with the more senior cohorts over employment, control of resources, and political power generally. Tension is particularly high in societies increasing in population, where more men and women reach adulthood than retire or die.

Another type of life crisis that is intensely politicized is that of sudden unpredictable misfortune resulting from accident, illness, loss, and calamities of all sorts. A whole system of symbolic beliefs and practices is developed to diagnose, explain, and compensate for the misfortune. This system is concerned not with the *how* but with the *why* of the singularities of misfortune. The Azande (22), for example, know the natural process by which a man is killed when a tree trunk falls on him; their concern, however, is not with the immediate natural cause but with the power that brought about such a unique combination of factors and circumstances that led this particular man to pass through that particular spot near that particular trunk at that particular moment, and so on. In many societies this singularity of misfortune is explained not as an accident but as the mystical work of witches, and no redress can be realized until they are discovered and brought to justice. Divination is called for and the witch, often a person innocent of the particular crime in question, is eventually punished. In the not so remote past, witches in Europe, North America, and Africa were even put to death.

Studies of witchcraft in a number of societies have shown that the *incidence* of accusations—i.e. who accuses whom—is not haphazard but occurs mostly between certain related categories of persons. Thus in some matrilineal systems (see 49, 55) accusations are often made by a man against his mother's brother, from whom he would eventually inherit property and whom he would replace politically. This relationship is always fraught with tension and quarrel. When the total incidence is considered throughout the extent of the society, it will emerge as the manifestation of a struggle for power between one generation and another.

In some patrilineal societies like the Zulu (see 35), most accusations are directed against married women by their in-laws. The Zulu tend to live in extended families consisting of father, mother, and married sons. When the father dies the sons continue to live within the same household. However, as time passes by and the families of the sons expand, the division of the household becomes inevitable. But because of brothers' solidarity, no one would dare suggest such a division. When a member of the household becomes ill, one of the wives (who because of exogamy are strangers from outside the lineage of the husbands) is accused of exercising witchcraft, and this enables her husband to claim that in order to save his brothers from her wickedness he would move with her to live in a separate household; the other brothers seize the opportunity and hive off, each to establish his own separate household.

There are many other variations in the pattern of the incidence of witchcraft accusations. In some tribal systems the chief is endowed with, among many other mystical powers, witchcraft in order to enhance further his authority. In some changing social systems, the ideology of witchcraft serves as a basis for the formation of political factions that are mobilized as *antiwitchcraft movements* whose purported aim is to combat the evil designs of witches, who are in fact their political enemies (see 57).

In some systems the emphasis is not on redressing but on averting misfortune. This is the case, for example, among a Hausa community based on long-distance trade in Nigeria (11). This trade is full of pitfalls and perils because of numerous factors and circumstances whose combination cannot be predicted by the trader. As a result, almost every trade expedition hovers between success and disaster. In the absence of insurance, banking, modern means of communication, swift and effective procedures of adjudication and hence security of contract, an effort is made to divine the likely outcome of every enterprise. Thus every trader has his own malam, a ritual specialist, whom he regularly consults. Consultation is not exclusively about the prospects of trade but also about every affliction or important stage in life. For example, when a new baby is born the parents consult the malam about the most propitious name to give to it. Malams thus have a strong hold on their clients. They form an order of their own, with a ritual hierarchy which is almost parallel to the political hierarchy, largely made up of the landlords of the trade, of the chief of the community, and of his advisors. All landlords and senior malams have the title *hajji,* gained after pilgrimage to Mecca. They regularly meet with the chief to deal with problems affecting the community as a whole. In these meetings decisions are conveyed to the more junior malams, who duly translate them and pass them on as ritual advice imparted to their clients. Thus the ritual activities of the malams uphold the authority of the chief and ensure the compliance of his subjects to his decisions.

Other crises of life are similarly dramatized and politicized in differing degrees of intensity. Marriage is everywhere related to the distribution of power between groups, and every marriage is thus a political event of the first order whose elements are symbolized in the ceremonials. In some systems its symbolism serves as an articulating principle of social organization, such as in the caste system or in lineage systems of different sorts (see 14, pp. 110–18). Even the birth of first son is an occasion for both rejoicing and anxiety for the father, and in many systems there are elaborate customs of avoidance between the two throughout life in order to relieve tension and inhibit violence (29). Among the Hausa, almost invariably a relative of the parents would by custom take the first born to raise in her or his own home. The conflict between father and first born son is caused by the potential competition between the growing son and the father over property and authority. Fortes (29) emphasized that in addition to these causes—in fact underlying them—there is a more fundamental source of anxiety felt by the father after the birth of his son. The latter transforms him into a parent and this, while being cause for rejoicing, is also a sign that a biological replacement of him now exists.

All crises of life are interrelated and form the basis of the human condition. In all societies nearly all crises are ceremonialized, but often unequally. In some societies one crisis is emphasized and made to serve as an articulating idiom of political organization; in others two or more are equally emphasized. In the same society an affliction can be attributed to different mystical causes such as the anger of the dead or the wicked activities of witches, and it is the insight of the diviner that decides which is the relevant cause in each particular case.

THE OBLIGATORY IN SYMBOLISM

Why is the symbolism of life crises so universally manipulated in politics? First, it deals with perennial problems that are not amenable to scientific solutions and is therefore essentially ambiguous, not given to immediate searching scrutiny. This is why it is often said that one cannot argue with a ritual. For the same reasons, symbolic forms and practices are highly manipulable. The employment of dramaturgical techniques such as music, dancing, poetry, costuming, and alcohol drinking at most life crises ceremonies plays on the sentiments of the participants and sways their belief and action in this direction or that. Often in these circumstances it is not belief that gives rise to ceremonial but ceremonial that conjures up and gives definite form and structure to belief. It is reported that the Prophet Muhammad once said that what concerned him was that a Muslim should pray five times a day; as to what went on in the mind of the worshipper, it was between him and Allah.

All this points out that the frequent and repetitive performance of ceremonials related to a crisis of life within a group would raise and enhance the consciousness of its members about the existential problem involved. For example, in a society where for some reasons death is not intensively and extensively ceremonialized, the reality of death is for most of the time absent from the minds of its members. In contrast, where death and the dead are heavily celebrated, as among the Creoles of Sierra Leone, the problem of existence is frequently on people's minds. For this reason it is difficult if not futile to look for basic common psychological denominators across cultures, because the intensity of feeling is itself a variable. The symbolism of life crises is like a rectangle which by definition has two dimensions, one existential, the other political. Both dimensions are to some extent manipulable. But if one dimension is reduced to nil, the shape will cease to be a rectangle and the whole reality of culture will disappear, which means that the phenomenon one is investigating would slip away. All normative culture is two-dimensional and is thus irreducible to either politics or psychology.

The second reason why the symbolism of life crises is so universally politicized is its intrinsic potential for becoming an impelling force, a valence, a categorical imperative, an "ought" that can move women and men to action spontaneously "from the inside," without the immediate incentives of reward or the threats of punishment from the outside. This feature of symbolism stands in sharp contrast with patterns of action that are contractual, utilitarian, and rational, and are implicit in purely political relations, though both types of action, the symbolic and the political, are interrelated. When a political group cannot coordinate its collective action by means of a formal association, it resorts to an informal type of organization that relies for the compliance of its members on the obligatory instead of the contractual. The obligatory, whether moral or ritual, pervades all social life. Even the most formal associations rely, in one organizational function or another, on some forms of obligation. The difference between formal and informal, between the associational and the communal, is a matter of degree. Thus, social order in a modern society, whose framework is maintained by state institutions like the police, courts, laws, and the ultimate threat of physical coercion, is largely effected in day-to-day living by moral and ritual obligations that are developed, objectified, and maintained through symbolic forms and symbolic action.

To probe deeper into the nature and the dynamics of political symbolism, it is therefore essential to explore the source of the obligatory in symbolic action. Why does political man—shrewd, calculating, utilitarian—also have to be symbolist man—idealist, altruistic, nonrational? How are purely political interests transformed to the most intimate moral and ritual obligations that impel man to action without exterior constraints? This is a problem with which I have dealt in a paper (15) from which I give here a few points.

The nature of obligation has been the subject of extensive discussion and controversy among philosophers over the centuries. Two schools of thought have been evident in the continual debate: the intuitionists, who uphold the uniqueness and irreducibility of obligation, and the utilitarians, who deny this uniqueness and explain it away in terms of egoistic calculations of consequences aimed at maximizing benefit. In social anthropology the controversy has appeared in a number of theoretical issues. For example, is kinship an irreducible principle of social organization, as Fortes (27) maintained, or is it only an idiom standing for political and economic interests, as Worsley (71) and others have argued? Is society a natural system that can be studied scientifically, as Radcliffe-Brown (59, 60) and Fortes (28) have contended, or is it a moral system whose study can therefore never be scientific, as Evans-Pritchard (23, 24) and others have argued. More recently, the utilitarian stand has received powerful support from some orthodox Marxists who interpret all normative culture as the ideology or the mystification of a dominant class, and from the anthropologists of the transactionalist school who reduce moral action to egocentric strategies directed toward the maximization of personal benefit.

But the majority of social anthropologists remain essentially two-dimensional in their orientation regarding the obligatory and the contractual as different variables intimately involved in all social relationships. Kinship relationships, for example, have both moral and utilitarian strands, and the main task of the anthropological inquiry is to isolate the one variable from the other and to show the nature of the causal or dialectical relation between them. Thus, within the main paradigm of social anthropology, the obligatory in symbolism is a phenomenon *sui generis,* having its own impelling force which, though always interrelated with the political constraints of the collective, remains essentially irreducible.

One attempt to identify and define the source of the valence, the impelling force, in symbolism is implicit in Turner's (64) well-known distinction between the sensory and the ideological poles within the structure of the ritual symbol. In the course of ritual, the symbol effects an interchange of qualities between the two poles. Norms and values become saturated with emotion, while the gross and basic emotions aroused by the sensory pole become ennobled through contact with values. The irksomeness of moral constraint is transformed into the love of goodness. Ritual symbolism is thus a mechanism which periodically converts the obligatory into the desirable.

This is a very illuminating analysis of the manner in which symbols operate. But it is mainly concerned with the working of symbolic techniques such as color, music, dancing, and the use of the human body, and not the obligatory in symbols. What is more, not all symbols have material representation, and some of those that do are not particularly pleasing or desirable.

Another formulation is provided by Moore & Myerhoff (54), who, in a discussion of secular ritual, suggest that the hold of ceremony on participants derives from its "traditionalizing effect"—a phrase they borrowed from Apter (7)—from its potentiality for making new material traditional as well as perpetuating old traditions. Ceremony does this by employing some formal properties that mimic its message. These properties include repetition, acting, stylization, order, evocative style, and the presentation of a social message by its very occurrence. They go on to explain (54, p. 8):

> In the repetition and order, ritual imitates the rhythmic imperatives of the biological and physical universe, thus suggesting a link with the perpetual processes of the cosmos. It thereby implies permanence and legitimacy of what are actually evanescent cultural constructs. In the acting, stylization and presentational staging, ritual is attention-commanding and deflects questioning at the time. All these formal properties make it an ideal vehicle for the conveying of messages in an authenticating and arresting manner. . . . Even if it is performed once, for the first and only time, its stylistic rigidities, and its internal repetitions of form or content make it tradition-like.

Again, this sheds further light on the way symbolism operates by indicating the dynamic nature of the symbolic process, though it does not deal with the inner source of obligation, with the uniqueness of "ought." The formulation may be sufficient for the practical purposes of field study and of sociological analysis, and it may be that any further search may only lead to sheer speculative discussion. However, because the issue is so crucial for social anthropology, the inquiry is worth pursuing, as it may affect further advance in our discipline, particularly as we seek to understand *how* our two major variables are interrelated and how a change in the one affects the other.

In an attempt to probe further in this rather meta-anthropological direction, I have focused on the dynamics of selfhood (15) in relation to power and symbolism. Selfhood, the "I," the oneness of an integrated psyche, is not innate in man, but is achieved in the course of interaction with significant other human beings and of developing a body of symbolic beliefs and practices, forming a world view. Almost by definition, symbolic action involves the totality of the self and not a segment or a role within it. We achieve selfhood through continual participation in patterns of symbolic activities. These are for most people provided by the interest group to which they are affiliated: the lineage, tribe, ethnic group, caste, class. When for some reasons groups cannot organize themselves as formal associations based on contract, they attempt to organize informally through the mobilization and manipulation of the obligatory, moral or ritual, in conduct. To that extent, the pursuit of the group's aims will be ensured, not by contractual mechanisms that operate on the individual from the outside through reward and punishment, but by moral and ritual obligations, by "oughts," operating from the inside and involving the total self. The self reacts to this in a variety of ways, including the creation of new symbolic patterns that are free from utilitarian interests. In time the new patterns are exploited by new or old interests and the search for new patterns can be resumed.

A PARADIGM FOR ANALYSIS

What the above discussion indicates is that much of the traditionalizing effect of ceremonial and of the symbolic process generally derives from some basic existential and political imperatives. In all societies people are involved in networks of primary interpersonal relationships: parenthood, marriage and affinity, friendship, brotherhood, ritual kinship, cousinhood. These relationships are developed and maintained by a complex body of symbolic beliefs and practices. People also engage in symbolic activities purporting to deal with the perennial problems of the human condition. These symbolic activities may have different forms and employ different techniques of dramatization in different social groups, or in the same group at different historical periods, but the basic themes are the same, though the intensity of involvement may vary from case to case.

At the same time, the same people are the members of interest groups with some basic organizational needs such as distinctiveness and authority. These groups may differ in size, composition, and aims, but they tend to have the same organizational requirements which, when for some reasons they cannot be met by means of formal associations, are met by some basic symbolic constructions.

Thus, despite drastic changes in power relationships and the almost endless variety of cultural traditions, there are basic symbolic forms that tend to recur in different sociocultural systems and at different historical periods within the same system. The symbolic repertoire of culture is therefore not unlimited. Furthermore, both sets of basic requirements, the existential and the organizational, tend to be met by the same set of symbols. For example, the symbolism of an exclusive cult would articulate the various organizational functions of the group, provide the members with solutions to basic existential problems, and express and maintain their interpersonal relationships. Again, kinship relationships would provide members with primary, affective, moral links with other members and would thus be instrumental in the creation of their selfhoods. At the same time, the relationships may be instrumental in articulating organizational functions such as the definition of the boundaries of the group or the provision of channels for the communication of group messages.

This is indeed the very essence of normative symbols, that they cater at one and the same time to the two types of requirement. Normative symbols are thus essentially *bivocal,* satisfying both existential and political ends. This bivocality is the very basis of the "mystery" in symbolism. A man performing a ritual or participating in a ceremonial is simply unclear, mystified, as to whether his symbolic activities express and cater to his own inner needs or the organizational needs of the group to which he belongs.

At times he may be inclined this way, at others that, but often he is unaware of the issue altogether. And it is this ambiguity in their meaning that forges symbols into such powerful instruments in the hands of leaders and of groups in mystifying people for particularistic or universalistic or both purposes.

There is thus a high degree of continuity of symbolic forms, even amid substantial changes in the disposition of power. But their functions within the new political context may be different. This change in function is usually effected through changes in their recombination within a new ideology. In the process they will undergo change in their weighting, when the significance of some forms will be heightened and exaggerated and that of others deemphasized. It is through these subtle changes in symbolic forms, in their restructuring within new ideologies, that a great deal of organizational change is effected, though a few new forms may appear here or there. Thus a great deal of organizational change is often effected through continuity of old forms.

On the basis of the foregoing discussion, it is possible to develop a tentative outline of a paradigm for the study of political symbolism. In such a paradigm, normative culture, as expressed in symbols, is considered in its relation to political organization on different levels. To simplify the discussion, a model of an interest group, such as a power elite in a contemporary state, can be taken as an example (16, 17). The members of such an elite perform functions that are both *particularistic,* pertaining to their own sectional interests, and *universalistic,* pertaining to the public interest. Both types of interests are developed and maintained by means of an *organization,* which is usually complex in its structure, being partly *associational,* based on formal contractual lines, and partly *communalistic,* based on informal primary relationships [for these terms see Weber (69, pp. 136–39)]. The associational part is clearly visible and its observation and study pose no methodological or analytical problem. It is the communalistic part that poses a challenge to the sociological imagination.

To deal with this part methodically and empirically, we can study it in its manifestations in symbolic patterns. These can be analyzed in terms of *symbolic functions, symbolic forms,* and *techniques of symbolization.* A symbolic function, such as the achievement of communion between disparate individuals or groups, can be achieved by means of different symbolic forms, such as a church service, the celebration of the memory of an ancestor, or the staging of extensive ceremonials among overlapping groupings within the elite. Similarly, a ritual performance can employ different techniques of symbolization, such as poetry, music, dancing, commensality. Different organizational functions such as distinctiveness and communication can be achieved by the same symbolic form such as kinship. On the other hand, the same organizational function such as authority can be achieved through a combination of different symbolic forms, such as kinship and ritual, as in the power of elders derived simultaneously from their genealogical position and from their monopoly of intercession with the dead on behalf of their offspring.

Such a paradigm can be significant for further meaningful research in two main directions. First, it facilitates comparative analysis across cultures and subcultures. It makes it possible to see how different symbolic forms and techniques of symbolization can be developed to achieve the same symbolic functions, and how different symbolic forms, functions, and techniques achieve the same organizational functions.

Second, it is probably a most promising device for the fruitful study of the dynamics of politico-cultural change and hence of the nature of politico-cultural causation. For although power relations and symbolic patterns of action are intimately interconnected, they differ sharply in their process of change. Marxists would refer to this as "the principle of uneven development." Changes in the relationships of power are often effected by means of symbolic continuities, not by means of new symbolic forms. An example is the manipulation of the local traditional Poro symbolic beliefs and practices in modern national election campaigns in Sierra Leone. Similar use has been made in modern contexts of such traditional forms as lineages (10, 39), castes, and ethnicity. On the other hand, a change in symbolic forms need not indicate a change in power relations. Thus, under some new political circumstances, interest groups that in the past articulated their organizational functions in terms of ethnicity may now resort to religious symbolism as a substitute to articulate the same functions. Again, some apparent change in symbolic forms may be due only to change in techniques of symbolization. For example, facial and bodily markings to indicate sex, age, and status differences may give way under new circumstances to the adoption of different types of dress to indicate the same lines of differentiation without necessarily indicating any fundamental changes in the distribution of power or in symbolic functions.

The comparative study of such situations and developments will make it possible to probe deeper into the analysis of politico-cultural causation. Analysis in social anthropology generally has so far tended to be in terms of sociocultural correlations. We often juxtapose the social and the cultural and state that the two are interdependent without going deeper into the nature of mediation between them. But two processes may operate together epiphenomenally without any necessary direct causal connection between them. It is thus essential to attempt to show how the two variables act and react on one another.

One way of doing this is to explore the dramatic process underlying the rituals, ceremonials, and other types of symbolic activities in social life. For it is mainly in the course of such key dramatic performances that the symbolic order and the power order interpenetrate one another, so to speak, to produce, and repetitively reproduce, the bivocality and hence the mystificatory nature of the major symbolic forms. In these performances, selfhood is recreated in terms of the symbolic forms that articulate the changing organizational needs of the group; and organizational needs are thereby transformed into categorical imperatives that impel the individual to action through the inner dynamics of selfhood. In this way, the study of sociocultural causation and change becomes the analysis of the creation or transformation of dramatic forms, their production, direction, authentication, the techniques they employ, the process of acting them out, living them through, and the transformation they bring about in the relationships between the men and women involved in them.

The sociological importance of the analysis of the dramas of ritual and ceremonial has been stressed within social anthropology by a number of writers, among them Gluckman (33, 34, 36), Turner (63), Peters (58), Mitchell (53), and Frankenberg (30, 31). Turner in particular has developed dramatic analysis into an effective method for the study of the dialectical relations between politics and ritual action. It is possible that further advance can be made in this direction through a more systematic isolation and definition of the variables involved and through the application of the method to the study of symbolic action generally. This will also have the effect of rendering the vexing controversy about the difference between ritual and secular ceremonial irrelevant.

A drama is a limited sequence of symbolic action, defined in space and time, which is formally set aside from the ordinary flow of purposeful social action. In this sense the drama is not an imitation of life but a symbolic construction. It is also in a sense timeless. Ordinary social life consists of complex processes of events involving a multiplicity of actors, themes, variables, issues, and purposes in a never-ending sequence. In contrast, the drama selects a few elements that are not obviously related in ordinary life, indeed that are often contradictory, and integrates them within a unity of action and of form, a *gestalt,* that temporarily structures the psyches of the actors and transforms their relationships.

This usage of the term drama is thus narrower than the metaphorical sense in which "all the world's a stage" and the ordinary phenomenological flow of ongoing social life and social crises are treated as "theatrical" events. Turner's (63, p. 19) "social drama" encompasses both a series of actual events occurring over a long period of time and involving a number of people in their daily quarrels and alliances, and the performance of ritual dramas in the narrower sense of the term, within an overall analytical framework for which Gluckman (36) coined the term "extended case method." I am here using the term in its more restricted sense in order to highlight a number of issues involved in the analysis of sociocultural causation. The two senses of the term "drama" are of course not opposed to one another but mark differences in emphasis. For even a "pure," formalized, highly conventional drama like a church service or a wedding reception or a ball is always interpenetrated in its procedure by nondramatic events that are not formally designed as parts of the original dramaturgical script.

Politico-cultural causation operates in a continual series of dramatic performances on different levels of social organization. These performances objectify norms, values, and beliefs; interpret the private in terms of the collective, the abstract in terms of the concrete; confirm or modify relationships, temporarily resolving contradictions; and always recreate the belief, the conviction of the actors in the validity of their roles in society.

The work of the anthropologist in such analysis is akin to that of the dramatist in the Brechtian tradition (see 3, pp. 129–51; see also 41) whose play would take a familiar, everyday event out of its ordinary ideological sequence and "throw it into crisis" by placing it in the context of a power struggle in society. In a recent study (17) I attempt to do this by demonstrating how ordinary symbolic performances—a dancing ball, a university graduation ceremony, a funeral service, a wedding festivity—repetitively reproduce or modify power relationships and how they combine in a culture which functions instrumentally in transforming a category of senior civil servants and professionals to an interacting, cooperating, and cohesive power elite. In a more recent study I focus on a West Indian annual carnival in London, showing how in the course of about 14 years a cultural performance originally staged by a few hundred people has evolved into a massive politico-symbolic drama, mobilizing in its preparation and staging hundreds of thousands of black unemployed and semiemployed for political action.

The analysis of cultural performances as dramas is only the last stage of a long, sustained, and demanding research procedure. This is because the paradigm requires a *holistic coverage* of the social and cultural life of the group one would be studying. In order to discover the relations of power, one has to study economic and political institutions and to analyze the interconnections between them; and in order to discover the symbolic order, one has to study the major symbolic institutions because these are often complementary and interchangeable. It is only after identifying the two major variables that a final analysis and presentation of dramatic performances can be made, although a more preliminary analysis of them would have to be made in the process before this stage is reached.

This holistic coverage of both the total culture and the total power structure of a collectivity distinguishes social anthropology from other social sciences like economics and political science, each of which tends to be concerned mainly with one institution which is abstracted from the total social reality. In this respect it is not open to the charge, often made by Marxian writers against "the bourgeois sciences," of compartmentalizing knowledge and of thus preventing the student from comprehending and apprehending sociocultural totalities.

But because the method is so demanding, social anthropologists are forced to confine themselves to a small area of social life at a time, though without losing sight of the fact that that area is a part of ever-encompassing social units that form a total structure. How to delineate such a small area of social life, and within which total structure to consider it, are methodological problems that have been hotly debated in the literature. One systematic attempt to deal with them within social anthropology can be found in Devons & Gluckman (19).

A more elaborate discussion of the issue is given in recent Marxist literature, including formulations by some of those Marxists who still regard themselves as anthropologists. On the whole, these writers are opposed to the study of such social units as status groups, ethnic groups, religious groups, elite groups, neighborhoods, and villages, on the ground that by concentrating on these the anthropologist would wittingly or unwittingly reify them, present them as given "in the nature of things," and thereby in effect legitimize the capitalist system which has created them. Since a true Marxist is a person whose theoretical work is related to the *praxis* of struggling against world capitalism, nothing would be valid short of the study of the total structure of world capitalism, which is supranational, cutting across all boundaries. However, some of these writers would concede that a smaller unit must be delineated, and the current tendency by many Marxists is to study a "social formation," a unit defined in terms of both mode of production and the ideological institutions that are related to it. But the application of the concept is far from easy and clearcut, and writers have been using it in a rather loose fashion, sometimes applying it to a small-scale area of social life, sometimes to a whole complex nation-state, and sometimes even to the whole world (see 56, pp. 367–68). Some Marxists even use the term "ideological formation" [see, for example, Adlam et al (1, p. 27)] for a discipline like psychology. A more pragmatic approach has been to recognize the present nation-state as a meaningful unit (see 68) in such studies. This is particularly so as even those societies that have a "communist mode of production" today form separate nation-states which are sometimes even in conflict with one another, like the Soviet Union and China, indicating that often national interests override class interests.

In my own work (10, 11, 13, 16, 17), I have dealt with communal groups within the framework of nation-states and advocated this explicitly as a research strategy. To operationalize this for anthropological research one can adopt, *as a heuristic device* at least, a pluralistic view of the nation-state as consisting of a multiplicity of power groups based on economic and political interests, including groups organized on the bases of age, sex, ethnicity, religion, occupation, locality. This concentration on the study of sociocultural groupings need not entail, as some Marxists fear, a subscription to pluralism as a political ideology, although the communist parties of Western Europe have now publicly declared their abandonment of the principle of the dictatorship of the proletariat and their intention to uphold the pluralistic nature of their societies. Even Marx conceived of classes as each consisting of a plurality of different interest groups, not as simple overarching global entities. It was in this sense that I once stated (14, p. 17) that classes are a figment of the imagination of sociologists, a statement which predictably drew some caustic remarks from some commentators.

The study of the total structure of world history must certainly be the goal of all social science. But if this study is not to be merely an ideological doctrine imposed by a monolithic political party in the name of *praxis,* it will unavoidably have to depend all the time on the cumulative findings of numerous studies of various formations, aspects, and levels by different people with different interests, experience, knowledge, and training. World society today is a colossal and complex system and its study cannot possibly be accomplished by jacks-of-all-trades. Thus the study of international capitalist corporations will require knowledge of extensive bodies of facts and figures as well as methodological skills that can be acquired only after long training. The same applies to the study of law and the judicial process or to the study of international relations. The student in such studies may not have the interest, the training, and the time for the comparative study of the forms and workings of ideologies of cultural performances. The argument by some Marxists in anthropology (see 20) that such specializations are only mystificatory bourgeois strategies cannot really be taken seriously. One can do *original* research in only a limited field at a time, but the findings can be systematically related to the cumulative findings of others. All true development of knowledge proceeds from the parts to the whole and from the whole to the parts.

In the study of political symbolism, the anthropologist can thus apply microsociological techniques to the holistic study of a relatively small area of social life, which is systematically considered within the framework of the nation-state, relying on the findings of other students for knowledge about the economic, political, social, and cultural institutions of the wider system.

TOWARD A UNIVERSAL DISCIPLINE
OF SOCIOCULTURAL ANTHROPOLOGY

What is clear from the foregoing discussion is that the symbols of normative culture are almost by definition bivocal, being simultaneously both political and existential. They are not politically neutral. One result of this for the anthropological enterprise is the difficulty of establishing a science of cultural symbols, a symbolic anthropology, which seeks to study pure "symbolic systems" by discovering regular relations between symbols without systematic reference to the dynamics of power relations.

Some serious attempts to overcome this difficulty have been made by a number of anthropologists whose findings have been reviewed recently by Turner (65). A few of these schools of thought explain the symbols of culture in terms of a system of logic which is ultimately rooted in the structure of the mind or of language. A survey of their literature will so far yield only a few, rather axiomatic, general formulations. For example, numerous studies in this field seek to demonstrate the truisms of binary or complementary oppositions: right-left, white-black, and so on. A good example can be found in a recent book, *The Reversible World*, edited by Babcock (8), containing a collection of studies arguing the universality of symbolic inversion in all human activities, including literature, art, religion, play, relations between the sexes, systems of classification, the marking of group boundaries. The idea of inversion is also brought to bear on political action by some of the contributors. Thus Rosaldo (61) shows how colonizers sought to enhance or justify their control of the Ilongots by attributing to them traits that are the inversion or negation of what they regarded as their own traits. The individual papers in the collection are interesting and important, each in itself, but the general argument does not add much to what was said earlier by many other writers.

A different orientation in developing a science of symbols is represented by the formulations made by Dolgin, Kemnitzer & Schneider (21) in their lengthy introduction to a recent volume of readings. The collection contains 28 papers by different writers, including C. Geertz, D. H. Hymes, H. Marcuse, K. Marx, M. Sahlins, D. M. Schneider, and V. Turner. Many of the works are well-known masterpieces on different topics; all deal with issues involving symbolism. But the introduction seeks to develop an analysis of the common denominator between the papers, namely symbols and their meanings as considered on their own, and to offer a definition and outline of "Symbolic Anthropology." The result is a series of astonishingly obscure and mystifying formulations that in many places defy understanding, purporting to show in the end that symbolic action can be understood only in terms of other symbolic action. The confusion is not so much a reflection on the editors as on the nature of the enterprise. This is perhaps symbolized in the title of the Introduction: "As people express their lives, so they are . . ."—an out-of-context quote of a half statement made by Marx in *The German Ideology* (50, p. 42), in effect inverting the founder of dialectical materialism into a tautologous idealist!

The endeavor to develop a science of symbols and meanings has attracted some of the most brilliant, original, and imaginative minds in anthropology. This has been its strength and also its limitation. Its strength stems from the *individual* creativity displayed in works of contemplation and vision, covering topics from art, literature, logic, linguistics, philosophy, theology, and psychology, marshalling stimulating quotations and apt illustrations, making witty statements and observations, and conjecturing meanings for symbols. Leach (42, p. xvii) once said that Lévi-Strauss inspires him even when he does not understand what Lévi-Strauss is saying. In a similar fashion different readers find different points of interest and inspiration in the works of these symbologists. But when one finishes reading a work in this genre, one begins to wonder where the exposition would lead and how the inquiry could be developed further from there. So far, the different individual contributions in this field do not seem to add up to a *discipline* —a discipline in the sense of the recognition of a clearly defined problematic, a clear methodology, and a clear procedure for cumulative effort —discipline in the sense that students can acquire the knowledge and the skills that will enable them to make their own original contributions to the collective enterprise. There are of course those who argue that the study of human society generally cannot lead to the development of a discipline of this kind. But many others believe that it can, or at least postulate such a possibility as a guide for systematic research.

Power and symbolism are the two major variables that pervade all social life, and social anthropology already has the possibilities for developing the study of the relations between them into a promisingly cumulative discipline with a working paradigm to guide a fairly open-ended research. What it needs further as a discipline is to be truly comparative, covering the study of urban as well as rural, industrial as well as preindustrial, communist as well as capitalist systems, demystifying in the process ideologies of all sorts, particularistic and universalistic, rendering conscious what is essentially nonconscious, and thereby throwing new light on the nature of man, society, and culture.

There are Marxists who deny the possibility of objectivity in such research [see for example(20)]. They are of course right in that all students of society bring to their intellectual activity, knowingly or unknowingly, their own sectional interests, prejudices, sentiments, and ideologies. But the remedy is not to abdicate from our intellectual effort and surrender our reason to the dictates of a monolithic ideology in the name of *praxis*. The remedy is in a never-ending, constructive criticism directed at our findings, in classes, seminars, conferences, journals, papers, and books. The potentialities for such a permanent, institutionalized tradition of criticism already exists in many centers of sociocultural research. In these centers the training of a social anthropologist involves continuous, rigorous, and relentless criticism, often made by students and teachers and general readers who hail from different social, cultural, and ideological backgrounds, including Marxism. Indeed, as Anderson (6) points out, Marxism itself, as a living critique of society and of thought, exists today principally in Western or Western-oriented universities; in the Soviet Union it was eradicated soon after the death of Lenin, when Stalinism took over. I would go further and say that as a discipline that aims at the analysis of political symbolism in all the various aspects discussed here, social anthropology is essentially the child of Marxism, for it was Marx who initiated the systematic analysis of culture in relation to the power structure.

Literature Cited

1. Adlam, D., Henriques, J., Rose, N., Salfield, A., Venn, C., Walkerdine, V. 1977. Psychology, ideology and the human subject. *Ideology and Consciousness*, No. 1, pp. 5–56
2. Ahern, E. M. 1973. *The Cult of the Dead in a Chinese Village.* Stanford: Stanford Univ. Press
3. Althusser, L. 1969. *For Marx.* Harmondsworth: Penguin
4. Althusser, L. 1970. *Reading Capital.* London: New Left Books
5. Althusser, L. 1971. *Lenin and Philosophy.* New York: Monthly Rev. Press
6. Anderson, P. 1976. *Considerations on Western Marxism.* London: New Left Books
7. Apter, D. E. 1963. Political religion in the new nations. In *Old Societies and New States,* ed. C. Geertz. Glencoe: Free Press, Collier-Macmillan
8. Babcock, B. A., ed. 1978. *The Reversible World: Symbolic Inversion in Art and Society.* Ithaca & London: Cornell Univ. Press
9. Cartwright, J. R. 1970. *Politics in Sierra Leone 1947–1967.* Toronto: Univ. Press

10. Cohen, A. 1965, 1972. *Arab Border Villages in Israel: A Study of Continuity and Change in Social Organisation.* Manchester: Manchester Univ. Press
11. Cohen, A. 1969. *Custom and Politics in Urban Africa: A Study of Hausa Migrants in Yoruba Towns.* Berkeley & Los Angeles: Univ. California Press
12. Cohen, A. 1969. Political anthropology: the analysis of the symbolism of power relations. *Man* (N.S.) 4:215–35
13. Cohen, A. 1974. Introduction: The lesson of ethnicity. In *Urban Ethnicity,* ed. A. Cohen. ASA Monogr. No. 12, pp. ix–xxiv. London: Tavistock
14. Cohen, A. 1974. *Two-Dimensional Man: An Essay on the Anthropology of Power and Symbolism in Complex Society.* Berkeley & Los Angeles: Univ. California Press
15. Cohen, A. 1977. Symbolic action and the structure of the self. In *Symbols and Sentiments,* ed. I. M. Lewis. London: Academic
16. Cohen, A. 1979. Variables in ethnicity. In *Ethnic Change,* ed. C. F. Keyes. Seattle: Univ. Washington Press. In press

17. Cohen, A. 1980. *The Power Mystique: Explorations in the Dramaturgy of Eliteness in Modern Africa.* In preparation
18. d'Azevedo, W. L. 1973. Mask makers and myth in Western Liberia. In *Primitive Art and Society,* ed. A. Forge. London: Oxford Univ. Press
19. Devons, E., Gluckman, M., eds. 1964. Conclusion. *Closed Systems and Open Minds,* pp. 158–261. Edinburgh: Oliver & Boyd
20. Diamond, S., Scholte, B., Wolf, E. 1975. Anti-Kaplan: Defining the Marxist tradition. *Am. Anthropol.* 77:870–76
21. Dolgin, J. L., Kemnitzer, D. S., Schneider, D. M., eds. 1977. Introduction. *Symbolic Anthropology: A Reader in the Study of Symbols and Meanings,* pp. 3–44. New York: Columbia Univ. Press
22. Evans-Pritchard, E. E. 1937. *Witchcraft, Oracles and Magic among the Azande of the Anglo-Egyptian Sudan.* Cambridge: Cambridge Univ. Press
23. Evans-Pritchard, E. E. 1951. *Social Anthropology.* London: Cohen & West
24. Evans-Pritchard, E. E. 1963. *The Comparative Method in Social Anthropology.* L. T. Hobhouse Memorial Trust Lecture No. 33, Univ. London. London: Athlone
25. Firth, R. 1973. *Symbols: Public and Private.* Ithaca: Cornell Univ. Press
26. Fortes, M. 1945. *The Dynamics of Clanship among the Tallensi.* London: Oxford Univ. Press
27. Fortes, M. 1949. *The Web of Kinship among the Tallensi.* London: Oxford Univ. Press
28. Fortes, M. 1953. *Social Anthropology at Cambridge since 1900,* an inaugural lecture. Cambridge: Cambridge Univ. Press
29. Fortes, M. 1974. The first born. *J. Child Psychol. Psychiatry* 15:81–104
30. Frankenberg, R. 1957. *Village on the Border.* London: Cohen & West
31. Frankenberg, R. 1966. British community studies: Problems of synthesis. In *The Social Anthropology of Complex Societies,* ed. M. Banton. London: Tavistock
32. Freedman, M. 1966. *Chinese Lineage and Society: Fukien and Kwantung.* London: Athlone
33. Gluckman, M. 1942. *Analysis of a Social Situation in Modern Zululand.* Manchester: Manchester Univ. Press
34. Gluckman, M. 1954. *Rituals of Rebellion in South-East Africa.* Manchester: Manchester Univ. Press

35. Gluckman, M. 1956. *Custom and Conflict in Africa.* Oxford: Blackwell
36. Gluckman, M. 1961. Ethnographic data in British social anthropology. *Sociol. Rev.* (N.S.) 9:5–17
37. Harley, G. W. 1941. Notes on the Poro in Liberia. *Peabody Mus. Pap.* 19:(2)
38. Harley, G. W. 1950. Masks as agents of social control. *Peabody Mus. Pap.* 28:(2)
39. Hill, P. 1963. *The Migrant Cocoa Farmers of Southern Ghana. A Study in Rural Capitalism.* Cambridge: Cambridge Univ. Press
40. Kilson, M. 1966. *Political Change in a West African State.* Cambridge, Mass: Harvard Univ. Press
41. Lacey, S. 1976. Brecht. *Cultural Studies* 9, pp. 124–28. Birmingham: Cent. Contemp. Cult. Stud.
42. Leach, E. 1967. *The Structural Study of Myth and Totemism.* London: Tavistock
43. Libenow, J. G. 1969. *Liberia: The Evolution of Privilege.* Ithaca: Cornell Univ. Press
44. Little, K. 1951. *The Mende of Sierra Leone.* London: Routledge & Kegan Paul
45. Little, K. 1965. The political function of the Poro (Part One). *Africa* 35:349–65
46. Little, K. 1966. The political function of the Poro (Part Two). *Africa* 36:62–72
47. Lukács, G. 1971. *History and Class Consciousness.* London: Merlin
48. MacCormack, C. P. 1975. Sande women and political power in Sierra Leone. *West Afr. J. Sociol. Polit. Sci.* 1:42–50
49. Marwick, M. G. 1965. *Sorcery in its Social Setting: A Study of the Northern Rhodesian Cewa.* Manchester: Manchester Univ. Press
50. Marx, K., Engels, F. 1970. *The German Ideology.* London: Lawrence & Wishart
51. Middleton, J. 1960. *Lugbara Religion: Ritual and Authority among an East African People.* London: Oxford Univ. Press
52. Milliband, R. 1974. *The State in Capitalist Society.* London: Quartet Books
53. Mitchell, J. C. 1956. *The Kalela Dance.* Rhodes-Livingstone Pap. 27. Manchester: Manchester Univ. Press
54. Moore, S. F., Myerhoff, B. G. 1977. Introduction: Secular ritual forms and meanings. In *Secular Ritual,* ed. S. F. Moore, B. G. Myerhoff, pp. 3–24. Amsterdam: Van Gorcum
55. Nadel, S. F. 1952. Witchcraft in four African societies: An essay in comparison. *Am. Anthropol.* 54:18–29

56. O'Laughlin, B. 1975. Marxist approaches in anthropology. *Ann. Rev. Anthropol.* 4:341–70

57. Parkin, D. J. 1968. Medicines and men of influence. *Man* (N.S.) 3:424–39

58. Peters, E. L. 1963. Aspects of rank and status among Muslims in a Lebanese village. In *Mediterranean Countrymen,* ed. J. Pitt-Rivers. Paris: Mouton

59. Radcliffe-Brown, A. R. 1952. *Structure and Function in Primitive Society.* Glencoe: Free Press

60. Radcliffe-Brown, A. R. 1957. *A Natural Science of Society,* ed. M. N. Srinivas. Glencoe: Free Press

61. Rosaldo, R. I. 1978. The rhetoric of control: Ilongots viewed as natural bandits and wild Indians. In *The Reversible World,* ed. B. A. Babcock, pp. 240–57

62. Scott, D. J. R. 1960. The Sierra Leone election, May 1957. In *Five Elections In Africa,* ed. W. J. Mackenzie, K. Robinson, pp. 168–280. London: Oxford Univ. Press

63. Turner, V. W. 1957. *Schism and Continuity in an African Society.* Manchester: Manchester Univ. Press

64. Turner, V. W. 1964. Symbols on Ndembu ritual. See Ref. 19, pp. 20–51

65. Turner, V. W. 1975. Symbolic studies. *Ann. Rev. Anthropol.* 4:145–61

66. Turner, V. W. 1975. Book review. *Man* (N.S.) 10:139–40

67. Vincent, J. 1978. Political anthropology: Manipulative strategies. *Ann. Rev. Anthropol.* 7:175–94

68. Wallerstein, I. 1960. Ethnicity and national integration. *Cahiers d'Etudes Africaines,* pp. 129–39

69. Weber, M. 1947. *The Theory of Social and Economic Organization.* New York: Free Press

70. Williams, R. 1976. *Key Words.* Glasgow: Fontana

71. Worsley, P. M. 1956. The kinship system of the Tallensi: a reevaluation. *J. R. Anthropol. Inst.* 86:37–75

Ann. Rev. Anthropol. 1979. 8:115–36
Copyright © 1979 by Annual Reviews Inc. All rights reserved

GRAPH THEORY
AS A STRUCTURAL MODEL
IN CULTURAL ANTHROPOLOGY

♦9629

Per Hage

Department of Anthropology, University of Utah, Salt Lake City, Utah 84112

> If the example is permissible, I would say that we are less concerned with the theoretical consequences of a 10 per cent increase in the population in a country having 50 million inhabitants than with the changes in structure occurring when a 'two-person household' becomes a 'three-person household.'
>
> Lévi-Strauss, "The Mathematics of Man" (64).

The aims of this review are to indicate the diversity of applications and some of the specific and general advantages of graph theory as a structural model in cultural anthropology. The review also considers some problems of application, extensions of the model, and concepts of potential empirical significance. For convenience of exposition the format is based on graph theoretic rather than anthropological topics.

Graph theory is a branch of mathematics concerned with the analysis of structures consisting of points joined by lines. It is related to such fields as matrix theory, set theory, combinatorics, and topology. It has been used as a model in the physical and, much more recently, the social sciences. Anthropological interest stems primarily from social network studies where it has been recommended as a metalanguage for the description of structure (4, 72). There are, however, also applications to such topics as belief systems, semantic and task structures, mythology, and cultural change.

An important advantage of graph theory, which largely accounts for its intuitive appeal, is that it contains a means for the depiction of structure (17).[1] Thus in an early application, Conklin (22) found it helpful to represent land utilization sequences as a directed graph in order to see ideal and

---

[1]Graph theory, in contrast to algebraic models, is in Berge's (11) phrase, "linked with reality."

0084-6570/79/1015-0115$01.00

potential patterns and to interpret actual cases. As a general method, Maranda (e.g. 69) has used directed graphs to represent in exact fashion the relations between elements (dramatis personae) in myths, and Kay (60) and Werner & Fenton (88) have used them to represent the structure of folk taxonomies.

As a mathematical model, the advantages of graph theory for anthropology are those enumerated by Harary, Norman & Cartwright (51) for digraph theory in the social sciences generally. (*a*) It contains a language of structure which provides exact and rich definitions of such concepts as connectedness, balance, mediation, status, and structural transformation. (*b*) It contains techniques for the calculation of quantitative aspects of structure; for example, relative status in political structures, the degree of balance in alliance and sentiment structures, and the degree of connectedness in communication structures. (*c*) It contains theorems which facilitate and extend the analysis of structure: "By specifying properties of digraphs that necessarily follow from given conditions they [the theorems] permit us to draw conclusions about certain properties of a structure from knowledge about other properties" (51, p. 3). As the authors also point out, graph theory is relatively self-contained.

There are a number of mathematical texts on graph theory (10, 48, 74, 91), some with empirical applications (11, 15, 75) and some directed to the social sciences (28, 50, 51). Some anthropological expositions and discussions are contained in (6, 13, 72, 89). This review is based mainly on Harary, Norman & Cartwright's *Structural Models* (51) and on various articles by the first and third authors. It considers in order the following topics: (*a*) the different types of graphs—linear, signed, and directed—;[2] (*b*) graphs and matrices; (*c*) networks; and (*d*) structural duality.

GRAPHS

Graphs (also termed linear, undirected, or simple graphs) represent symmetrical relations. Concepts with anthropological applications include *cycles*[3] and *blocks, articulation points, trees,* and *cliques.*

A graph *G* consists of a finite, nonempty set *V* of *p points* and a finite set *X* of (undirected) *q lines* which join pairs of points, for example the structures in Figure 1. The *degree* of a point is the number of lines incident with it. A *path* is a sequence of distinct points and lines and a *cycle* consists of a path together with a line joining the initial and terminal points. Two points are *reachable* if there is a path joining them. The length of a path

---

[2]In certain places, which should be clear from context, the terms graph and graph theory are used generically.

[3]It is appropriate to begin with cycles since the origin of graph theory is attributed to the eighteenth century mathematician Euler and the Koenigsberg Bridge Problem (48, 75).

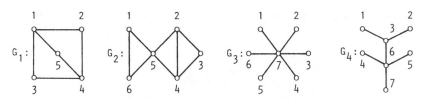

Figure 1 Graphs.

is the number of lines in it and the *distance* between two points is the length of the shortest path which joins them. *G* is *connected* if every pair of points is joined by a path and *complete* if every pair of points is adjacent (joined by a line). An *articulation* or *cut point* is one whose removal disconnects a graph or *component* of a graph (maximal connected subgraph). A connected graph or component with no cut points is a *block* and every graph can be uniquely partitioned into its blocks. In G_2, which is connected but not complete, the degree of 5 is 4; the distance from 5 to 3 is 2; 5 is a cut point; (1, 5, 6) and (2, 3, 4, 5) are blocks; and (15, 56, 61) is a 3-cycle.

An Euler line is a cycle which traverses every line of *G* exactly once,[4] and a Hamilton line is a cycle which passes through every point of *G* exactly once. Schwimmer (79, 80) represents a system of gift exchange between households in a Papuan village as a graph. Exchange partners may make economic and political requests directly, and also indirectly using partners' partners. His analysis shows two structural features: "clusters" of intimate association (maximal complete subgraphs) and "circuits" which unite partners through intermediaries. The latter he notes is ". . . close to what graph theorists call a Hamilton circuit . . . and would be consistent with an almost total absence of stratification" (80, p. 231). While neither of the cycles he isolates is actually Hamiltonian, his remarks about their association with structural unity and an absence of stratification raise a general question about the significance of *cycles* per se in communication structures (41). Although it is difficult in general to determine whether every point lies on a complete cycle of *G* since there is no unique criterion for such a graph (48), it is relatively easy to determine whether every pair of points lies on a common cycle of *G*. The latter is true of any block ($p \geqslant 3$) which may or may not be Hamiltonian and which is therefore more common. In Figure 1, for example, G_1 is a non-Hamiltonian block. In many situations it may be sufficient and useful to simply know this, for if *G* is a block ($p \geqslant 3$), then a number of conclusions can be drawn about the system using the following theorem from Harary (48, pp. 27–28):

[4]*G* is Eulerian if it is connected and the degree of every point is even. A famous anthropological graph which is not Eulerian is the Kula Ring, which means that there is no cycle of exchange that activates every relation.

Theorem 3.3. Let *G* be a connected graph with at least three points. The following statements are equivalent:
1. *G* is a block.
2. Every two points of *G* lie on a common cycle.
3. Every point and line of *G* lie on a common cycle.
4. Every two lines of *G* lie on a common cycle.
5. Given two points and one line of *G*, there is a path joining the points which contains the line.
6. For every three distinct points of *G*, there is a path joining any two of them which contains the third.
7. For every three distinct points of *G*, there is a path joining any two of them which does not contain the third.

Applied to a communication system such as the one Schwimmer describes, this means that there is no individual whose disappearance will disrupt communication within the group (condition 1); that every pair of individuals has (at least) two paths by which to communicate (condition 2); that any particular relation may occur in a mediational chain between any two individuals (condition 5); and that any particular individual may occur in a chain but no particular individual must necessarily occur (conditions 6 and 7). Thus the system is invulnerable and flexible, and it is egalitarian or unstratified to the extent that relative power depends on the ability of any one individual to uniquely control the flow of information between any two others or sets of others.

Blocks may well turn out to be significant units of social structure since they permit communication which is flexible and also redundant (an important consideration in norm enforcement)[5] and since they preserve some of the integrative properties of a complete graph while requiring as few as *p* relations (an important consideration in the case of large or expanding groups).[6]

Conversely, *G* may have as many as $(p-1)(p-2)/2+1$ lines and still not be a block, which illustrates the lack of a close relation between density and structure. Many social network studies are, unfortunately, exclusively concerned with the former. (See also 51, chapter 3, on density and connectedness in directed graphs.)

Articulation or *cut points* join blocks, and it is easy to see that in communication structures such points or "liaison persons" (47) may occupy a privileged or perhaps stressful (54) position. They may also be significant in semantic structures. Fox (31, 32) uses graphs to represent dyadic pairs of categories in a form of ritual language based on semantic parallelism. The phenomenon is best explained by example. In the verse "With what do you marry pig? And with what do you wed civet?" pig and civet occur as a pair.

[5]In a block one may "get it from all sides."
[6]See (51) for blocks in directed graphs. This application was suggested by an example given there.

Fox shows that some elements may combine in multiple dyads. Thus " 'civet' forms dyadic sets with 'cat,' 'pig,' and 'bee,' each signalling an altered significance for its constituent elements" (32, p. 110). The determination of each element's combinatorial possibilities results in a connected graph or network of semantic associations. Cut points unite different clusters of elements, for example an element that links terms for body parts and directional coordinates. These are characterized as the "most general semantic elements" in the core of primary elements (membership in the core being determined by degree size). Fox concludes that in "binary symbolic analysis" it may not be sufficient to simply list dyads in a table, and cites Frake's (33) early emphasis on the importance of interlinkage of semantic domains.

Another interesting use of graphs to study cognitive associations is Dailey's (24) proposal for the analysis of personal documents. Here the points represent autobiographical statements and the lines their judged psychological similarity. Significant points include those of high degree ("the event one keeps coming back to") and cut points ("the turning points in one's life"). The procedure is intended as a middle ground between the clinician's protocols, which eliminate too much data, and the anthropologist's life history, which retains too much.

A *tree* is a connected acyclic graph. In a tree there are p-1 lines, all of the points are articulation or end points (deg = 1), and in contrast to a block every pair of points is joined by a unique path. Trees have figured prominently in the representation of chemical, electrical, and organization structures. In Figure 1, G_3 and G_4 are two of the 11 nonisomorphic trees with seven points.[7]

In anthropology trees are most often used to represent egocentric networks. Barnes (5) uses a graph like G_3 as the basis for his taxonomy of ego- or actor-centered structures in a network, termed "Alpha's primary or first-order star of social relations." Alpha's primary zone includes individuals in his star who are adjacent to each other. Stars and zones may be combined as primary, secondary, and n-ary; they are especially useful in the analysis of the mobilization of support (e.g. 59) and exertion of pressure to conform in social networks.

Crump (23) uses stars to dramatize the centralization of power based on the occupancy of politico-religious offices in two groups in Southern Mexico, and also other types of trees to represent a road network. An interesting feature of Crump's paper is his observation on the correspondence between the anthropologist's and the folk models: "To a very large extent my own reason for seeing these structures as points and lines of a graph is that this

---

[7]Some trees are more beautiful than others (49). In psychology, graphs have been used in studies of cognition and learning.

is substantially how informants have analyzed them for me, often in quite explicit terms" (23, p. 27).

Intuitively a *clique* is a group of people in close association. Graph theory provides a number of alternative definitions: (a) a maximal complete subgraph, (b) a strong component of a digraph (see below), (c) a unilateral component, (d) a subgraph of a certain density, (e) a subgraph of diameter n, n being the most links that join individuals. The first and last definitions are taken up by Seidman & Foster (82, 83) in their developing program of network analysis which "uses graph theory to generalize methods of traditional kinship studies."

In an attempt to find significant subgroups in a large network, they tried to find some way in which the clique concept defined as (a) above could be relaxed or generalized. The result was the *k-plex*, a group in which "each individual is connected [adjacent] to at least n-k others" (83, p. 67). In Figure 1, G_1 is a 3-plex. The k-plex "highlights two fundamental properties of the clique concept"—the shortness of the paths and the number of direct links which join members. It is described as a "robust" structure since "if as many as n-$2k$+1 arbitrary points are removed from a k-plex with n points, the resulting graph will have a diameter of at most two" and "since any subgraph of a k-plex is a k-plex" (83, p. 68). Forthcoming applications, e.g. an analysis of Fortes's notions of "clan" and "fields of clanship," should be interesting. Generally their work illustrates the use of graph theory to elucidate significant but nontraditionally defined social groups, a topic which was part of the original motivation for social network studies (72) and also a felicitous form of collaboration between mathematics and anthropology in which new problems are posed for the former and refined analytical tools gained by the latter [Hoffmann (55)].[8]

SIGNED GRAPHS

A signed graph S is one in which the lines have positive or negative values which represent antithetical relations, e.g. love vs hate, friend vs enemy, intimacy vs restraint. The principal applications use social psychological theories of *structural balance* and *clustering* in the analysis of interpersonal kinship and intergroup alliance structures.

In a cognitive system, if person P likes an other O, he will tend to have the same attitude, positive or negative, toward some object (or person) X as O has. If P dislikes O, he will tend to have the opposite attitude toward X as O has. The same considerations apply for positive and negative relations in general, either symmetric or asymmetric (signed digraphs) in inter-

---

[8]The renaissance of graph theory has been attributed to applications in the physical and social sciences.

personal and societal systems. Situations which conform to these structures are balanced, presumably tension-free and stable; those which do not are unbalanced, presumably tension-filled, unstable, and subject to internal pressure toward change. The theory was first formulated by Heider (53) and subsequently generalized by Cartwright & Harary (18). Theoretical variations and a vast number of social psychological studies are summarized in Taylor (85).

> The sign of a path and of a cycle is the algebraic product of the signs of its lines.
> *Theorem 1.* The following conditions are equivalent for a signed graph *S:*
> 1. *S* is balanced, that is, every cycle is positive.
> 2. For each pair of points *u, v* of *S,* all paths joining *u* and *v* have the same sign.
> 3. There exists a partition of the points *S* into subsets (one of which may be empty) such that every positive line joins two points of the same subset and every negative line joins points from different subsets (21, p. 5).

The degree of balance is defined in terms of the ratio of positive to the total number of cycles in *S* or in the blocks of *S,* or by the number of lines which must be negated or the number of points which must be removed to make *S* balanced (45). Balance may be restricted by considering only cycles of a certain length—*n*-balance, e.g. 3-balance. Figure 2 shows all of the *s*-graphs consisting of a single 3-cycle; the first two are balanced, the second two are not.

An interesting case is the G/wi Bushmen kinship system (37). The G/wi bipartition their kinship universe into binary, antithetical, and symmetric "joking" and "avoidance" relations which signify respectively conventional attitudes of familiarity and intimacy vs respect, restraint, and "fear." The G/wi have a folk model of balance since they say (*a*) that a person should

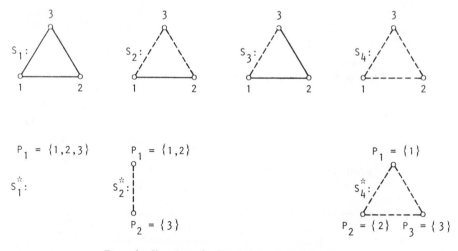

Figure 2   Signed graphs *S* and their condensation *S*.*

joke with the joking relative of his joking relative, (*b*) that a person should avoid the avoidance relative of his joking relative, and (*c*) that it would be "bad" or "embarrassing" for a person to joke with the avoidance relative of his joking relative, situations which would be represented respectively by S_1, S_2, S_3 in Figure 2.

Although the three criteria are formally equivalent, any one of them may be used to characterize balance. Thus in three independent treatments of Lévi-Strauss's "atom of kinship" (66), Flament (28) and Carroll (16) use cycle balance and Abell (1) partition balance. An examination (42) of individual cases shows that any one or some combination of the three criteria may be appropriate: in one system, cycle balance characterizes culturally conceived desirable combinations of positive and negative relations; in a second, partition balance defines a structure of overlapping coalitions of kinsmen; while in a third, path balance shows the alternative paths by which ego exerts the same type of effect on alter.

In Figure 2, S_4 is not balanced. Empirically, however, it may not be a difficult situation for three individuals or groups to be mutual enemies or to avoid each other. Furthermore, it often happens that a group divides into more than two opposing cliques, the consideration of which has led to the concept of *clustering* [Davis (26, p. 181)]:

A clustering of a signed graph S is a partition of the point set $V(S)$ into subsets, P_1, $P_2, \ldots, P_n$ (called plus sets) such that each positive line joins two points in the same subset and each negative line joins two points from different subsets. *Theorem 1.* Let S be any signed graph. Then S has a clustering if and only if S contains no cycle having exactly one negative line.

Additionally and equivalently, "S has no negative line joining two points in the same positive component" (19, p. 5).[9] By this formulation balance is a special case of clustering: S is balanced if it is 2-partitionable and more generally clusterable if it is n-partitionable; e.g. in Figure 2 S_4 is 3-partitionable. S is uniquely clusterable if its condensation S^* into its positive components (plus sets) is complete (i.e. if there is at least one negative line between every pair of positive components). Measures of clusterability are given by Peay (77).

An empirical application emerged from an analysis of an alliance structure in Highland New Guinea (36). An examination of the 3-cycles of an s-graph defined by 16 subtribes joined by traditional friend/enemy relations showed that 91 percent of the unbalance was due to all negative cycles. An application of the clustering concept, however, revealed an almost perfect,

---

[9]There the concept is related to the classic topic of the coloring of graphs. G may be colored by assigning different colors to every pair of adjacent points. An interesting application is suggested by Bateson's (7) principle and geometrical metaphor of "diagonal duality" in Iatmul eidos.

unique 3-clustering which turned out to correspond to three submerged superalliances. It remains an open and interesting problem to determine what conditions produce balance rather than clustering. Two possibilities are coalition formation and communicative consistency (21).

There are two studies of the temporal aspects of balance: an elegant simulation of the evolution of intergroup relations and an undoubtedly rare documentation of shifts in interpersonal relations. Both have important methodological and theoretical implications because they consider the strength as well as the sign of relations and they reveal limitations on the tendency toward consistency.

In order to account for the properties of an alliance structure of a set of Ethiopian towns, Hallpike (43) performs a simulation which consists of a model network of towns initially joined by relative friendship, enmity, or neutrality, in which the relations change as a result of random successive battles between pairs of principal combatants and potential allies. The latter choose between the former in accordance with an ordered set of rules based on their relative evaluations of each other. Each encounter changes the evaluations of all the participants, and the process continues until all rate each other as extreme friends or enemies. The results correspond in remarkable detail to the actual alliance structure: there are similar proportions of nuclear alliances and of n-member alliances, and there are also numerous unbalanced (and unclusterable) substructures. Hallpike observes that the assumptions are realistic (real battles are "gamelike," not based on economic or political considerations) and accord with the facts better than alternative explanations based on "large town magnetism" or migration. The model may well be generalizable, e.g. to certain forms of tribal warfare.

Jongmans (58) describes a political conflict in a Tunisian town. In a dispute between two leading members of different factions, not all relations between members of these groups and those of a third change to unequivocal positive or negative states as balance theory would predict. Instead, some relatively positive bonds based on common residence, descent, and affinity persist. These are "absolutely essential for the smooth running of daily life." In this case positive relations which produce unbalance maintain cohesion within the group. In the G/wi case (37), on the other hand, it is speculated that negative relations which produce a measure of unclusterability maintain alliances between groups. In other cases tendencies toward completeness may override balance and clustering (45).

Two problems which have not been considered are ambivalent and multiple relations. In some systems certain relations may contain both positive and negative components. Beattie (9), for example, describes the mother's brother/sister's son relation (U/S) in Bunyoro as structurally ambivalent since S as a member of another clan is an outsider and thus feared and at the same time S is a "child" and thus loved. One way around this difficulty might be, following a suggestion by Taylor (85), to split S and U into two parts S_1, S_2 and U_1, U_2 as affines and kinsmen of each other. The first relation would be negative, the second positive, and the relations of S and U to themselves positive.[10]

In some systems there may be multiple positive or negative relations, for example, both unit (U) relations which signify possession or identity and evaluative (L) relations which signify attitudes, a distinction in Heider's original formulation. A solution by Cartwright & Harary (18) is to construct an "s-graph of type 2" which includes both sets of relations. Parallel lines between points would count as 2-cycles and would each count independently in the evaluation of S. Graphs of type 2 may be generalized to graphs of type r, $r = 1, 2, \ldots, n$. Such graphs might clarify Mazur's (71) model of balanced and identity consistent structures, which uses the segmentary lineage as an example.

A third problem, but one not inherent in graph theory, is the proper coding of positive and negative relations. In Carroll's (16) study which failed to confirm a prediction of balance in kinship structures, it appears that relations of reciprocity, sentiment, and authority were equated and averaged and treated as a single relation instead of distinguished and treated as separate relations in graphs, s-graphs, and digraphs respectively. The general point was first made by Sweetser (84) and subsequently taken up in Hage (38).

DIGRAPHS

In a digraph D the lines have arrows (the pairs of points are ordered). Thus a point has both an indegree, *id,* and outdegree, *od.* Points are joined by semipaths, "a collection of distinct points, v_1, $v_2 \ldots$, v_n, together with n-1 lines, one from each pair of lines v_1v_2 or v_2v_1, v_2v_3, or v_3v_2, $\ldots$, $v_{n-1}v_n$ or v_nv_{n-1}" (51, p. 31), and more specifically by paths if the lines have a consistent direction and by strict semipaths if they do not. Analogously, points lie on semicycles, cycles, and strict semicycles. Concepts with applications include *connectedness, level assignments, path consistency, trees, unipathic digraphs,* and *implicational digraphs.*

Connectedness refers to relations of joining and reaching. D is weak if every pair of points is joined by a semipath, unilateral if for every pair of points at least one can reach the other and strong if every two points are mutually reachable. The category C_n of D is its highest level of connectedness. The condensation D^* of D is the (unique) partition of D into its strong

---

[10]Cartwright & Harary (20) have proposed a network model to treat ambivalence and also indifference and intensity of relations.

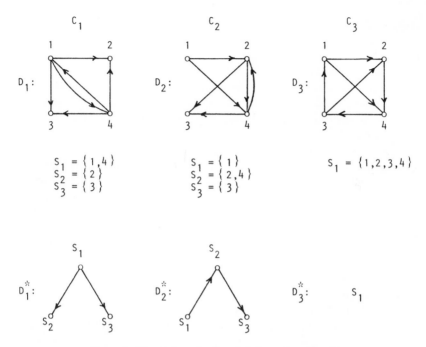

Figure 3   Directed graphs D and their condensation D^*.

components $S_1, S_2, \ldots, S_n$ in which there is a line from S_i to S_j if there is a line in D from some v_i in S_i to some v_j in S_j. Figure 3 shows digraphs which are weak (C_1), unilateral (C_2), and strong (C_3), together with the condensations of each.

Hawkes's (52) analysis of a big man system from New Guinea contains an explicit use of condensation and an implicit use of connectedness category. A digraph defined by adult males and the relation "advises" is shown to consist of one large strong component, which includes precisely those individuals unambiguously regarded as big men, which is adjacent to all of the remaining components, each of which is trivial (consists of a single point) and some of which are adjacent to each other. Her characterization of the system as lacking a "chain of command" is expressed both by the relation of mutual reachability in the large component and by the weak rather than unilateral category of D (since one of the properties of the latter is a complete path in D^* [(51) Theorem 3.10].

Livingstone (67) exploits a number of theorems for tournaments (non-trivial, complete, asymmetric digraphs, D_3 in Figure 3, for example), to characterize the structure of marriage systems. Thus one criterion of a matrilateral connubium is a strong tournament since by Theorem 11.11 (51) every such digraph has a cycle of length p (as well as of 3, 4, ... , p-1). A proposed measure of equilibrium is the number of cyclic triples (the maximum number of which is given in Theorem 11.10 (51).

A transitive tournament and more generally an acyclic digraph has a *level assignment:* "For each point v_i let us denote by n_i the integer assigned to it. A digraph D has an *ascending level assignment,* and the integers are *levels* if for each line $v_i v_j$ of D the corresponding integers satisfy $n_i < n_j$" (51, p. 267).

Figure 4 shows two digraphs of the atom of kinship (a unit chosen for convenience) in which the level assignments represent the relative rank of positions (38). The first is from Tonga, the second from Truk. In both cases status relations are consistent, internally because they are transitive and externally because they reflect the pervasive ordering in the political (and other cultural) structures of the societies. The method would be useful in measuring the rank of different positions within a society and also the elaboration of rank in different societies, for example in proto- as opposed to fully developed chiefdoms. By making rank relations fully explicit in this manner, two interesting questions are posed: out of all the logically possible systems of rank for a given set of positions, which ones actually occur and in what circumstances, and given an array of the latter, how are these related as transformations or permutations of each other [for the example above, see Hage (38)]?

Since every digraph can be made acyclic by condensing it, the method may be extended to any digraph of social structure, i.e. one may obtain a "quasi-level assignment" in which points in the same strong component are given the same level [(51) Theorem 10.3].

Another digraph model of status is Sweetser's (84) *rule of path consistency* of authority relations. Path-consistent triads are those in which, given an authority relation between two positions, the third position has authority

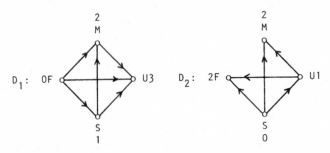

Figure 4   Directed graphs with level assignments. The atom of kinship where F = Fa, M = Mo, S = So, U = MoBr after Flament (28).

over both or over neither.[11] The rationale is that non-path-consistent structures allow conflicts in authority or attempts at subversion or inconsistent images of authority. Supporting evidence comes from two cross-cultural studies, one on the structure of grandparenthood (2) and the other on avuncular superordination (84). There are two qualifications of the model: (*a*) Sweetser's contention that balance is usually an inappropriate tool for kinship analysis is too sweeping; it can be used if authority and sentiment are coordinated to the appropriate type of graph. (*b*) In many kinship situations, authority may be complementary rather than homogeneous, so that if A and B are neutral to each other and superior to C in different spheres, the structure need not be unstable even though formally it is path inconsistent.

Trees may be directed. In an original and interesting article, which appears to be one of the few anthropological applications influenced by Bavelas's (8) independent invention of graph theory, Henry (54) describes two contrastive types of formal organization, "pine trees" and "oak trees." If G_4 in Figure 1 is made a digraph with the lines (13, 23, 36, 46, 56, 67), an oak tree results, that is, an organizational structure of multiple subordination. It contrasts with a pine tree in which each member receives orders from only one source. Although the first is abhorred by organization theorists, it may arise from the task structure of a group. Henry's example is a psychiatric hospital where patient care requires overlapping and therefore possibly contradictory lines of authority. Here the formal organization operates in disregard of the personalities and wishes of the staff and gives rise to compensatory structures. The result is stress for the staff and poor therapy for the patients, e.g. schizophrenics whose divided internal world is reproduced by their external world.

The last point raises a problem of general interest in structural studies where graph theory may be very useful: the coherence or consistency of a culture as manifested in the formal similarities of diverse empirical structures. A recent study (39) along these lines shows how in two cultures of different evolutionary type the mnemonic structures of each contrast and are consistent with social and political structures: in one case all structures are *unipathic digraphs* (those in which every pair of points is joined by a single path), while in the other they are clusters of signed dyads.

White, Burton & Brudner (14, 90) use *implicational digraphs* or "entailograms" to analyze the structure of constraint in the sexual division of labor. The method which derives from Greenberg's (35) essay on implicational

---

[11]Sweetser's general definition can be simplified by saying that a path-consistent triad (which is not totally disconnected) has a unique point of highest od.

universals in grammar consists of taking dichotomized variables, tabulating their frequencies of occurance in 2 X 2 tables, and observing from the pattern of zero entries their implicational structure. For example, female participation in soil preparation entails (→) female participation in harvesting if the single zero entry in the table occurs in the cell showing participation in the former and nonparticipation in the latter. Some of the entailments may be linked into larger structures consisting of chains, convergences, branches, or some combination of these.[12]

Their theory is based on the optimization of effort and the safety of women (given child care constraints) in production tasks. Optimization occurs when the same persons perform adjacent tasks and when women are more removed from the production of raw materials than from their subsequent processing. The first article (90) shows complete entailment digraphs for clusters of related tasks, and the second (14) shows predicted digraphs for specific production sequences. The results in general support the theory or can be accommodated by it. The method is clearly a significant innovation. As they emphasize, it improves on correlational analysis which ignores the direction of relations and on Guttman scaling which does not allow for branchings or convergences (which would be "errors").

D'Andrade (25) uses implicational digraphs to analyze American beliefs about illness. The data consist of a list of elicited disease categories and a list of sentence frames which state properties of some diseases, e.g. "—brings on fever," "—is caused by germs," etc. The substitutability of the diseases in the sentence frames taken two at a time show the implicational relations which exist between the sentence frame properties. The final result is a digraph, or more accurately a network, showing the inclusion and contrast relations among sentence frame properties where all transitive and therefore derivable relations are eliminated.[13] The model has a triple significance with regard to traditional techniques based on the feature model (componential analysis or multidimensional scaling): (a) it shows the logical relations between categories; (b) it is generative (the transitively derivable lines); (c) it considers the connotative rather than the distinctive features of categories (which informants are often unable to state even though they clearly "know" a lot about the diseases). One problem which remains is to determine the specific relations covered by the generic inclusion and contrast relations.

---

[12]In a personal communication, D. R. White cites a forthcoming "generalized statistical method for evaluating tendencies toward perfect implicational relationships (i.e. nonzero cells which are less than their expected value rather than zero cells) and for deciding at what level of exceptions such tendencies depart from statistical independence for a multivariate data set" (see 89a).

[13]As in Atkins & Curtis's (3) set and graph theoretic model of the structure of cultural rules.

GRAPHS AND MATRICES

A graph may be represented as a matrix, which is convenient if p is large, and which permits the application of mechanical procedures for the elucidation of structural properties. Figure 5 shows three associated matrices of D_2 in Figure 3 calculated using Theorems 5.7, 5.19 in *Structural Models*.[14]

The *adjacency matrix* $A(D)$ is a square matrix of order p whose entries are $aij = 1$ if i is adjacent to j and $aij = 0$ if not. $A(D)$ is the basis for calculating the other matrices and is highly useful in the collection and presentation of data (6, 58, 72). A dramatic example is provided by Marriott (70), who finding it impossible to draw intelligible diagrams of a large number of intercaste food transactions, availed himself of adjacency matrices. The result was a complete depiction of all transactions and a ready method of caste ranking based on the difference between the od (giving) and id (receiving) for each caste.[15]

The *reachability matrix* $R(D)$ has the entries $rij = 1$ if i can reach j and $rij = 0$ if not. R may be used to find the connectedness category (51, Theorem 5.14 - 5.16) and the connectedness and distance matrices of D. In one of the numerous independent inventions of graph theory, Lemaitre (63) proposes what amounts to $R \times R'$ (the transpose of R) to find the equivalence classes (strong components) in a digraph of interisland voyaging in Oceania. The resulting condensed digraph provides an immediately interpretable model of the communication possibilities in the entire area. An important modification of $R(D)$ for networks is Doreian's (27), which shows both the existence and the strength of a reachability relation. As an example he uses Kapferer's (59) analysis of the mobilization of support in a factory dispute in which one individual is more effective than another by virtue of the strength (multiplicity) of his direct and indirect ties—the

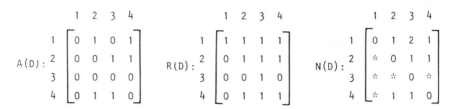

Figure 5   The matrices, A, R, N of D_2 in Figure 3.

---

[14]Two important matrices not shown are connectedness $C(D)$ and condensation $A(D^*)$. A matrix for clustering in s-graphs is given in (34).

[15]The pattern of $A(D)$ may show interesting structural properties, e.g. the matrix of an acyclic digraph is upper triangular (51) and in a citation matrix (93) classics have large ids.

winner is able to draw potential support away from the latter (see also 76).

The *distance matrix N(D)* has the entries $dii = 0$, $dij = 1, 2, \ldots, p\text{-}1$, and $dij = *$ if there is no path from i to j. $N(D)$ has been used directly to measure the relative centrality of places in graphs of trade networks (e.g. 57) and of leaders in an influence structure (52) using the row sum of each point. It has been used indirectly (36) to determine the block structure of a graph using some theorems for articulation points (47). A potential use of $N(D)$ is the measurement of status and its directional dual (see below) contrastatus in an organization, given by the row and column sums respectively (46).

Computer programs for these matrices are easy to write and cheap to use. Various refinements may be added such as provisions for point and line deletions[16] and for finding particular types of subgraphs, e.g. cliques. SO-NET-I (30, 81) is a comprehensive program for the graph theoretic analysis of social networks.

NETWORKS

Many structures of anthropological interest consist of relations which are nonbinary, probabilistic, or multiple. Some of these can be accommodated by an extension of digraphs to networks N in which values are assigned to lines and loops are permitted. Two applications are *Markov chains* and *flows in networks.*

A (discrete, stationary) *Markov chain* is a network in which the points are states and the lines transition probabilities between them, where the probability of movement from state v_i to state v_j is independent of the steps which led to v_i. When the transition matrix M is multiplied by the initial probability vector P_0 (the vector showing the proportions of things in different states at time t_0), the resulting vector P_1 shows the proportions of things in the states at time t_1. Multiplying M^n by P_0 shows the proportions at successive times t_n. An illustration from Hoffmann (56) is given in Figure 6.

Hoffmann uses the model to estimate cultural stability. His example is a Gada age set system in which fathers produce sons for the various age sets, s_1, s_2, s_3, in the next generation. The entries in M say that "There is a probability of 0.154 that the sons of an s_1 father will enter the Gada system in s_1" (56, p. 187) and so on. His analysis shows that contrary to what one might expect, each age set will continue in succeeding generations to have sufficient proportions of members for the system as a whole to remain

---

[16]For example, to find strengthening, weakening, and neutral points and strengthening and neutral lines (51).

$$M$$

$$
\begin{array}{c}
P_0 \\
(0.25, 0.55, 0.20)
\end{array}
\quad
\begin{array}{c}
\\
S_1 \\
S_2 \\
S_3
\end{array}
\begin{array}{ccc}
S_1 & S_2 & S_3 \\
\left[\begin{array}{ccc}
0.154 & 0.384 & 0.462 \\
0.367 & 0.400 & 0.233 \\
0.200 & 0.600 & 0.200
\end{array}\right]
\end{array}
=
\begin{array}{c}
P_1 \\
(0.28, 0.44, 0.28)
\end{array}
$$

Figure 6   A Markov chain.

operative (provided the transition probabilities remain constant). Olnick (73) contains an extended discussion.

A similar application is Thompson's (86) analysis of class mobility in a Yucatec town which predicts the rate and direction of change in the immediate future. He aptly characterizes the method as providing a "sort of structural history of the subsystems of a given culture and society." Elsewhere Thompson (87) also considers the limitations of the model which may arise from ignorance of the regularity of transition rates. A different type of application is Robbins & Robbins' (78) study of the "cumulative adoption of microtechnology." Here the states are numbers of introduced goods owned, and since adoption is cumulative, the process is absorbing rather than ergodic, i.e. there is a receiver in N.

The lines in N may represent channels along which things, e.g. information or goods, flow, the number of a line designating its capacity. A flow goes from a source s to a sink t. A cut is a set of lines separating s from t and the capacity of a cut is the sum of the values of its lines. According to the Ford-Fulkerson theorem (29, p. 11): "For any network the maximal flow from s to t is equal to the minimal cut capacity of all cuts separating s and t." In figure 7 from *Structural Models* (where the source is labeled t, transmitter, and the sink as r, receiver $\{(t, v_1) (t, v_3) (t, v_5)\}$ is a cut whose capacity is 12 and $\{(t, v_1) (v_3, v_4) (v_5, v_4) (v_5, r)\}$ is a cut whose capacity is 7. The latter is the minimal cut capacity.

Zachary (92) uses an undirected network model to study fission in a small voluntaristic group whose communication structure is defined by different levels of information flow between pairs of individuals. His assumption is that the group is most vulnerable at the minimum cut (a kind of "bottleneck"). In a crisis involving two leaders, each considered first as a source and then as a sink, the fission of the group into two separate subgroups is predicted by the minimum cut, that is, the members in each are either on the source or the sink side of the cut. Zachary suggests the general applicability of the model to small groups characterized by unequal flows of information or sentiment and emphasizes its superiority to static, nonprocessual social network models.

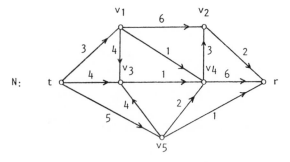

Figure 7   A network *N.*

STRUCTURAL DUALITY

In a rich and provocative article, Harary (44) shows how for each type of graph there is an operation which gives a law of structural duality. The concept is potentially of real significance for structural analysis because it clarifies and enriches one set of meanings of the term "opposite," and because it may be used to show how a given structure is a transformation of another one, for example, how ritual is "normal social life . . . played in reverse" (62) or how one myth is an "inversion" of another.

Existential duality is based on the operation of complementation: "The complement of a graph *G* is that graph *G'* having the same set of points as *G,* but in which two points are adjacent or joined by a line if and only if they are not adjacent in *G*" (44, p. 257). *Antithetical duality* is based on the operation of negation: "The negation S^- of the signed graph *S* is obtained from *S* by changing the sign of each line of *S*" (44, p. 260). *Directional duality* is based on the operation of conversion: "The converse $D^\smile$ of the digraph *D* is that digraph with the same set of points as *D* in which the directed line AB occurs if and only if the line BA is in *D*" (44, pp. 258–59). *Uncontra-duality* combines the first and third and *anticontra-duality* the second and third. (The first and second cannot be combined.) For each type of graph there is an operation which produces its "opposite" graph, as illustrated in Figure 8, and each theorem in graph theory gives another theorem (its dual) upon replacing all of its concepts with their complements, converses, or negations. For example, corresponding to the structure theorem for balance (condition 3 above), there is a structure theorem for antibalance. Either or both might be useful in a particular situation.

Crump (23) uses the complement to define exogamous groups in a graph of marriage exchange. Hage (40) uses the negation and the converse separately and jointly to show the transformational relationships between two versions of Freud's Oedipus myths analyzed along the lines proposed by

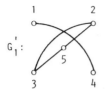 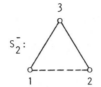 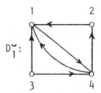

Figure 8   The complement, negation, and converse of G_1 in Figure 1, S_2 in Figure 2, and D_1 in Figure 3.

Lévi-Strauss (65). Thus, for example, sibling rivalry in version one—a negative relation in the junior generation induced by positive relations to the senior generation—is negated by patricide in version two—a positive relation in the junior generation induced by negative relations to the senior generation. Buchler & Selby (12) use the directional dual of a conclusion which follows from Theorem 11.4 on tournaments (51) in the derivation of variants of a myth.

CONCLUSIONS

Graph theory is applicable to a broad range of social and cultural phenomena involving relations of various sorts between such diverse elements as "persons, objects, places, events, and propositions" (51). As a purely abstract model it may be used in a variety of anthropological approaches. It offers a means for the depiction of structure, an exact and rich language of structure, computational techniques, and theorems which state necessary properties of structure.

Aside from tactical, but significant, problems in coordinating graphs to empirical data (38, 42, 61), further work will probably emphasize increased concern with cognitive structures, more exploitation of digraphs which are conceptually richer and broader in application than graphs, more use of network models, the introduction of reduction techniques to make graphs more manageable, and the use of graph theory in conjunction with other models, e.g. group theory. While there are many things graph theory will not do—for example, deal with the interrelations between relations in a network (68)—and while it is not the best model for all occasions—the analysis of myth, for example, may be better served by algebraic models—it is highly suitable and promising for a number of types of structural analysis. The significance of the whole family of models of which graph theory is a member was stated in Lévi-Strauss's early essay on "The Mathematics of Man" (64, p. 586):

> In the past, the great difficulty has arisen from the qualitative nature of our studies. If they were to be treated quantitatively, it was either necessary to do a certain amount of juggling with them or to simplify to an excessive degree. Today, however, there are many

branches of mathematics—set theory, group theory, topology, etc.—which are concerned with establishing exact relationships between classes of individuals distinguished from one another by discontinuous values, and this very discontinuity is one of the essential characteristics of qualitative sets in relation to one another and was the feature in which their alleged 'incommensurability,' 'inexpressibility,' etc., consisted.

ACKNOWLEDGMENTS

I am most grateful to a large number of individuals for their comments on a preliminary version of this chapter. I wish to acknowledge the long-standing interest and help of J. A. Barnes, Hans Hoffmann, and especially Dorwin Cartwright.

Literature Cited

1. Abell, P. 1970. The structural balance of the kinship systems of some primitive peoples. In *Structuralism,* ed. M. Lane, pp. 359–66. New York: Basic Books. 456 pp.
2. Apple, D. 1956. The social structure of grandparenthood. *Am. Anthropol.* 58:656–63
3. Atkins, J. R., Curtis, L. 1969. Game rules and the rules of culture. In *Game Theory in the Behavioral Sciences,* ed. I. R. Buchler, H. G. Nutini, pp. 213–34. Pittsburgh: Univ. Pittsburgh Press. 268 pp.
4. Barnes, J. A. 1969. Graph theory and social networks: a technical comment on connectedness and connectivity. *Sociology* 3:215–32
5. Barnes, J. A. 1969. Networks and political process. See Ref. 72, pp. 51–76
6. Barnes, J. A. 1972. *Social Networks.* Addison-Wesley Module in Anthropology. 29 pp.
7. Bateson, G. 1958. *Naven.* Stanford: Stanford Univ. Press. 312 pp. 2nd ed.
8. Bavelas, A. 1948. A mathematical model for group structure. *Appl. Anthropol.* 7:16–30
9. Beattie, J. 1964. *Bunyoro.* New York: Holt, Rinehart & Winston. 86 pp.
10. Behzad, M., Chartrand, G. 1971. *Introduction to the Theory of Graphs.* Boston: Allyn & Bacon. 271 pp.
11. Berge, C. 1962. *The Theory of Graphs.* New York: Wiley. 247 pp.
12. Buchler, I. R., Selby, H. A. 1968. *A Formal Study of Myth.* Austin: Univ. Texas Center Intercult. Stud. Folklore
13. Buchler, I. R., Selby, H. A. 1968. *Kinship and Social Organization.* New York: Macmillan. 366 pp.
14. Burton, M. L., Brudner, L. A., White, D. R. 1977. A model of the sexual division of labor. *Am. Ethnol.* 4:227–51
15. Busacker, R. G., Saaty, T. L. 1965. *Finite Graphs and Networks: An Introduction with Applications.* New York: McGraw-Hill. 294 pp.
16. Carroll, M. P. 1973. Applying Heider's theory of cognitive balance to Claude Lévi-Strauss. *Sociometry* 36:285–302
17. Cartwright, D. 1959. The potential contribution of graph theory to organization theory. In *Modern Organization Theory,* ed. M. Haire, pp. 254–70. New York: Wiley. 324 pp.
18. Cartwright, D., Harary, F. 1956. Structural balance: a generalization of Heider's theory. *Psychol. Rev.* 63:277–93
19. Cartwright, D., Harary, F. 1968. On the coloring of signed graphs. *Elem. Math.* 23–24:85–89
20. Cartwright, D., Harary, F. 1970. Ambivalence and indifference in generalizations of structural balance. *Behav. Sci.* 15:497–513
21. Cartwright, D. Harary, F. 1975. *Balance and Clusterability: An Overview.* Prepared for Math. Soc. Sci. Board, Conf. Soc. Networks, Hanover, NH
22. Conklin, H. C. 1967. Some aspects of ethnographic research in Ifugao. *Trans. NY Acad. Sci.* Ser. 2. 30:99–121
23. Crump, T. 1979. Trees and stars: graph theory in Southern Mexico. In *Numerical Techniques in Social Anthropology,* ed. J. C. Mitchell. Philadelphia: ISHI. In press
24. Dailey, C. A. 1959. Graph theory in the analysis of personal documents. *Hum. Relat.* 12:65–74
25. D'Andrade, R. G. 1976. A propositional analysis of U.S. American beliefs about illness. In *Meaning in Anthropology,* ed. K. H. Basso, H. A.

Selby, pp. 155–80. Albuquerque: Univ. New Mexico Press. 255 pp.

26. Davis, J. A. 1967. Clustering and structural balance in graphs. *Hum. Relat.* 20:181–87

27. Doreian, P. 1974. On the connectivity of social networks. *J. Math. Sociol.* 3:245–58

28. Flament, C. 1963. *Applications of Graph Theory to Group Structure.* Englewood Cliffs, NJ: Prentice-Hall. 142 pp.

29. Ford, L. R., Fulkerson, D. R. 1962. *Flows in Networks.* Princeton: Princeton Univ. Press. 194 pp.

30. Foster, B., Seidman, S. 1978. *SONET-I: Social Network Analysis and Modelling System. Vol. 1, User's Manual.* Binghamton: NY State Univ. Cent. Soc. Anal. 79 pp.

31. Fox, J. J. 1974. 'Our ancestors spoke in pairs': Rotinese views of language, dialect and code. In *Explorations in the Ethnography of Speaking,* ed. R. Bauman, J. Sherzer, pp. 65–85. Cambridge: Cambridge Univ. Press. 501 pp.

32. Fox, J. J. 1975. On binary categories and primary symbols: some Rotinese perspectives. In *The Interpretation of Symbolism,* ed. R. Willis, pp. 99–132. London: Malaby, 181 pp.

33. Frake, C. 1964. Notes on queries in ethnography. *Am. Anthropol.* 66:132–45

34. Gleason, T. C., Cartwright, D. 1967. A note on a matrix criterion for unique colorability of a signed graph. *Psychometrika* 32:291–96

35. Greenberg, J. H. 1963. Some universals of grammar with particular reference to the order of meaningful elements. In *Universals of Language,* ed. J. H. Greenberg, pp. 73–113. Cambridge: MIT Press. 337 pp.

36. Hage, P. 1973. A graph theoretic approach to alliance structure and local grouping in Highland New Guinea. *Anthropol. Forum* 3:280–94

37. Hage, P. 1976. Structural balance and clustering in signed graphs of Bushmen kinship relations. *Behav. Sci.* 21:36–47

38. Hage, P. 1976. The atom of kinship as a directed graph. *Man* 11:558–68

39. Hage, P. 1978. Speculations on Puluwatese mnemonic structures. *Oceania* 49:81–95

40. Hage, P. 1979. A Viennese autochthonous hero: structural duality in Freud's origin myths. *Soc. Sci. Inf.* In press

41. Hage, P. 1979. A further application of matrix analysis to communication structure in Oceanic anthropology. *Math. Sci. Humaines.* In press

42. Hage, P. 1979. On some empirical considerations in applications of structural balance theory to kinship relations. Unpublished manuscript, Dep. Anthropol., Univ. Utah, Salt Lake City

43. Hallpike, C. R. 1970. The principles of alliance formation between Konso towns. *Man* 5:258–80

44. Harary, F. 1957. Structural duality. *Behav. Sci.* 2:255–65

45. Harary, F. 1959. On the measurement of structural balance. *Behav. Sci.* 4:316–23

46. Harary, F. 1959. Status and contrastatus. *Sociometry* 22:23–43

47. Harary, F. 1959. Graph theoretic methods in the management sciences. *Manage. Sci.* 5:387–403

48. Harary, F. 1969. *Graph Theory.* Reading, Mass: Addison-Wesley. 274 pp.

49. Harary, F. 1971. Aesthetic tree patterns in graph theory. *Leonardo* 4:227–31

50. Harary, F., Norman, R. Z. 1953. *Graph Theory as a Mathematical Model in Social Science.* Univ. Mich. Inst. Soc. Res. 45 pp.

51. Harary, F., Norman, R. Z., Cartwright, D. 1965. *Structural Models: An Introduction to the Theory of Directed Graphs.* New York: Wiley. 415 pp.

52. Hawkes, K. 1977. Big men in Binumarien. *Oceania* 48:161–87

53. Heider, F. 1946. Attitudes and cognitive organization. *J. Psychol.* 21:107–12

54. Henry, J. 1954. The formal social structure of a psychiatric hospital. *Psychiatry* 17:139–51

55. Hoffmann, H. 1970. Mathematical anthropology. *Bien Rev. Anthropol.* 6:41–79

56. Hoffmann, H. 1971. Markov chains in Ethiopia. In *Explorations in Mathematical Anthropology,* ed. P. Kay. pp. 181–90. Cambridge: MIT Press. 286 pp.

57. Irwin, G. 1974. The emergence of a central place in coastal Papuan prehistory: a theoretical approach. *Mankind* 9:268–72

58. Jongmans, D. G. 1973. Politics on the village level. In *Network Analysis: Studies in Human Interaction,* ed. J. Boissevain, J. C. Mitchell, pp. 167–217. The Hague: Mouton. 271 pp.

59. Kapferer, B. 1969. Norms and the manipulation of relationships in a work context. See Ref. 72, pp. 181–244

60. Kay, P. 1975. A model-theoretic approach to folk taxonomy. *Soc. Sci. Inf.* 14:151–66

61. Killworth, P. D., Bernard H. R. 1976. Informant accuracy in social network data. *Hum. Org.* 35:269–86

62. Leach, E. R. 1961. Time and false noses. In *Rethinking Anthropology.* London: Athlone. 143 pp.
63. Lemaitre, Y. 1970. Les relations inter-insulaires traditionelles en Océanie: Tonga. *J. Soc. Océanistes* 27:93–105
64. Lévi-Strauss, C. 1955. The mathematics of man. *Int. Soc. Sci. Bull.* 6:643–53
65. Lévi-Strauss, C. 1963. The structural study of myth. In *Structural Anthropology,* pp. 206–31. New York: Basic Books. 410 pp.
66. Lévi-Strauss, C. 1963. Structural analysis in linguistics and anthropology. See Ref. 65, pp. 31–54
67. Livingstone, F. B. 1969. The applicability of structural models to marriage systems in anthropology. See Ref. 3, pp. 235–51
68. Lorrain, F., White, H. C. 1971. Structural equivalence of individuals in social networks. *J. Math. Sociol.* 1:49–80
69. Maranda, P. 1977. Cartographie semantique et folklore: "le diable beau danseur" a Rimouski. *Rech. Sociographique* 18:247–70
70. Marriott, M. 1968. Caste ranking and food transactions: a matrix analysis. In *Structure and Change in Indian Society,* ed. M. Singer, B. Cohn, pp. 133–71. Chicago: Aldine. 507 pp.
71. Mazur, A. 1968. A non-rational approach to theories of conflict and coalitions. *J. Conflict Resolut.* 12:196–205
72. Mitchell, J. C. 1969. The concept and use of social networks. In *Social Networks in Urban Situations,* ed. J. C. Mitchell, pp. 1–50. Manchester: Manchester Univ. Press. 378 pp.
73. Olnick, M. 1978. *An Introduction to Mathematical Models in the Social and Life Sciences.* Reading, Mass: Addison Wesley. 466 pp.
74. Ore, O. 1962. *Theory of Graphs.* Providence, RI: Am. Math. Soc. 270 pp.
75. Ore, O. 1963. *Graphs and Their Uses.* New York: Random House. 131 pp.
76. Peay, E. R. 1976. A note concerning the connectivity of social networks. *J. Math. Sociol.* 4:319–21
77. Peay, E. R. 1977. Indices for consistency in qualitative and quantitative structures. *Hum. Relat.* 30:343–61
78. Robbins, M. C., Robbins, L. C. 1978. A stochastic model of the adoption of microtechnology in rural Buganda. *Hum. Org.* 37:16–23
79. Schwimmer, E. 1973. *Exchange in the Social Structure of the Orokaiva.* New York: St. Martin's. 244 pp.
80. Schwimmer, E. 1974. Objects of mediation: myth and praxis. In *The Unconscious in Culture,* ed. I. Rossi, pp. 209–37. New York: Dutton. 487 pp.
81. Seidman, S., Foster, B. 1978. *Sonet-I: Social Network Analysis and Modelling System, Vol. 2, Program Listings and Technical Comments.* Binghamton: State Univ. New York, Cent. Soc. Anal. 91 pp.
82. Seidman, S., Foster, B. 1978. A graph theoretic generalization of the clique concept. *J. Math. Sociol.* 6:139–54
83. Seidman, S., Foster, B. 1978. A note on the potential for genuine cross-fertilization between anthropology and mathematics. *Soc. Networks* 1:65–72
84. Sweetser, D. A. 1967. Path consistency in directed graphs of social structure. *Am. J. Sociol.* 73:287–93
85. Taylor, H. 1970. *Balance in Small Groups.* New York: Van Nostrand Reinhold. 321 pp.
86. Thompson, R. A. 1970. Stochastics and structure: cultural change and social mobility in a Yucatec town. *Southwest. J. Anthropol.* 26:354–74
87. Thompson, R. A. 1974. *The Winds of Tomorrow.* Chicago: Univ. Chicago Press. 182 pp.
88. Werner, O., Fenton, J. 1970. Method and theory in ethnoscience or ethnoepistemology. In *A Handbook of Method in Cultural Anthropology,* ed. R. Naroll, R. Cohen, pp. 537–78. New York: Nat. Hist. Press. 1017 pp.
89. White, D. R. 1973. Mathematical anthropology. In *Handbook of Social and Cultural Anthropology,* ed. J. J. Honigmann, pp. 369–446. Chicago: Rand McNally. 1295 pp.
89a. White, D. R. 1979. Multivariate entailment analysis. In *Classifying Social Data,* ed. H. C. Hudson. San Francisco: Jossey-Bass. In press
90. White, D. R., Burton, M. L., Brudner, L. A. 1977. Entailment theory and method: a cross-cultural analysis of the sexual division of labor. *Behav. Sci. Res.* 12:1–24
91. Wilson, R. 1975. *Introduction to Graph Theory.* London: Longman. 168. pp.
92. Zachary, W. W. 1977. An information flow model for conflict and fission in small groups. *J. Anthropol. Res.* 33:452–72
93. Zubrow, E. B. 1972. Environment, subsistence and society: the changing archaeological perspective. *Ann. Rev. Anthropol.* 1:179–206

Ann. Rev. Anthropol. 1979. 8:137–60
Copyright © 1979 by Annual Reviews Inc. All rights reserved

DEMOGRAPHY AND ARCHAEOLOGY

❖9630

Fekri A. Hassan

Department of Anthropology, Washington State University, Pullman, Washington 99164

INTRODUCTION

A consideration of the role of demographic variables in the operation and change of cultural systems is now one of the major currents in contemporary archaeology (14, 33, 36, 37, 69, 112, 115, 121). This review is an attempt to highlight the probable role of these variables in prehistoric subsistence, settlement, technoculture, and social organization (Figure 1).

My aim here is to present demographic variables in a systematic framework and to show the relevance of this approach to explanation in archaeology. The review stresses the structural uniformity of human-cultural interactions with natural environments and thus crosses the boundaries between ecology, ethnology, and archaeology. Many archaeologists have frequently crossed these boundaries with remarkable success. Yellen's (141) recent investigation of the cultural present and the archaeological past of the !Kung is most rewarding, because it attempts to delve beyond descrip-

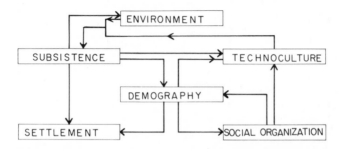

Figure 1 Diagrammatic presentation of the systemic relationships linking environment, subsistence, technoculture, settlements, social organization, and demography.

137

0084-6570/79/1015-0137$01.00

tion and idiographic explanation to a general ecological model of cultural strategy. In a previous work (67), I have examined some general concepts of the population ecology of hunter-gatherers. Such concepts and models of prehistoric cultural systems are critical for archaeological research.

In addition to theoretical models, demographic explanations in archaeology must be based on empirical data. The archaeological methods for reconstructing the demographic past have been the subject of recent reviews (34, 69) and need not be covered here.

PREHISTORIC SUBSISTENCE REGIMES, DEMOGRAPHY, AND SETTLEMENTS

Subsistence regimes, resulting from an interaction between people, culture, and the environment to satisfy dietary needs, are closely linked with population size, density, growth rate, population regulation, and dispersal. Prehistoric peoples subsisted by hunting and gathering throughout the Pleistocene. This mode of subsistence has been pursued by some peoples up to the present. During the early Holocene, agriculture was introduced and adopted by many groups and is today the dominant mode of subsistence for human populations. The basic principles governing the resources-settlement-demographic interactions (Figure 2) apply uniformly to both hunter-gatherers and farmers, but the differences in the potential for economic growth between the two modes of subsistence creates some major differences in cultural patterns and the potential for cultural change.

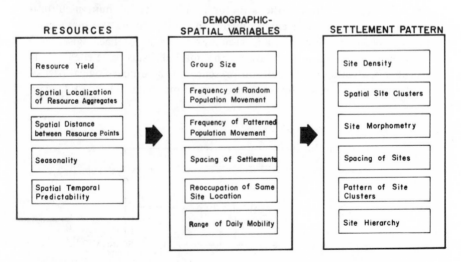

Figure 2 Diagram showing the influence of various attributes of food resources on demographic-spatial variables and settlement patterns.

It would be a grave mistake to model prehistoric hunting-gathering populations after any of the ethnographically known populations because of the variability exhibited both in the past and the present. However, it would be a worse mistake to ignore the structural basis of the population dynamics of hunter-gatherers as revealed by ethnographic cases and archaeological examples. Steward (116), Hallowell (59), and Suttles (120) have examined the structural relationship between resources and population, a topic which forms the basis for the present discussion and which has been the subject of more recent formulations (12, 17, 21, 47, 67, 80, 84, 123, 141–144). Figure 3 is an attempt to single out some of the key variables governing the relationship between subsistence and demography under hunting-gathering conditions. This general model can be extended to agricultural and pastoral food resources (141) and may even be extended to carnivores and other primates (39, 106, 132, 145).

In the case of hunter-gatherers, dependence on wild resources means that the size and mobility of a group are conditioned by the yield available at a given level of extractive efficiency, as well as the spatial distribution, density, and seasonality of the resources. These ecological constraints place an upper limit on the size of the regional population unit that is well below

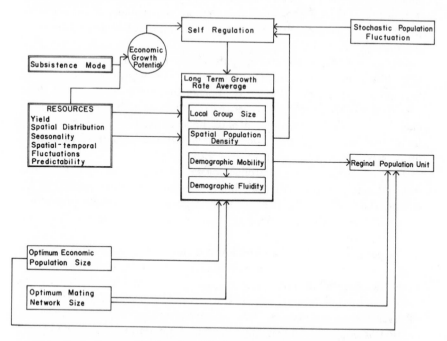

Figure 3   A diagram of a general model of resources, subsistence, and demography.

what is possible under conditions of food production. However, the size of a population unit must be sufficiently large to guarantee efficient exploitation of resources by cooperative endeavors (67) and to maintain reproductive viability (137), especially since small populations are much more vulnerable to random fluctuations than large groups (83). Estimates of 500–1000 persons are often cited for ethnographic hunting-gathering regional population units (16, 136–138) and 20–50 persons for local units.

The archaeological record indicates that such small bands were prevalent during the Palaeolithic, and that by implication the regional units were of the magnitude observed in the ethnographic cases. Isaac (78, 79) estimates 10–20 persons for the group size of the Australopithicenes who occupied Site F1K I at Olduvai. Freeman (51) estimates 25 persons as the possible minimal number commensurate with the pattern of distribution of material during the Acheulian at Torralba in Spain.

During the Middle Palaeolithic, the data by Mellars (87) on the dimension of Mousterian settlements in Southwestern France indicate groups of 31 to 48 persons. Data by Mellars on Upper Palaeolithic sites in the same region indicate that the group size was about 20–50 persons for most of the sites, with an average of 40 persons. In the Ukraine (82) the remains of house foundations provide estimates of 9–11 persons per house in six cases, 4–8 in five, and 2–3 persons in two. Where the remains of houses were preserved, the total number of inhabitants is estimated between 20 and 55 persons.

During the Mesolithic and Epipalaeolithic the areas of archaeological sites show a dramatic increase in many parts of the world. Some of the sites are as large as 10,000 m^2 (87). It appears that settlements during these periods were characterized by repetitive occupations with horizontal expansion. In the Nile Valley, small sites of the same technological tradition as larger sites suggest that the basic residential unit was perhaps no more than 50 persons (65, 72).

The population density of archaeological hunting-gathering populations was very likely as low as that of ethnographic hunter-gatherers (0.01 to 1.0 persons/km^2) (67, 137). Ecological models used to estimate prehistoric population density (28, 29, 65, 80, 110) provide figures usually of less than 1 person/km^2.

The persistence of small groups, low population density, and the slow rate of growth of the Palaeolithic populations is a phenomenon of great interest, given the potential of human populations—even with high mortality rates —for rapid population increase (64, 67, 76, 95). Instead of multiplying to survive, prehistoric peoples seem to have practiced various methods of population control to diffuse the potential of population explosion (43, 74) and to maintain a margin of unrealized fertility (46). Such a margin permits the population to recover from periods of population decline and to expand into new niches when the opportunity arises, thus adding to the adaptive success of human populations in the biological sense.

An explanation of the predominance of relatively small population units, low population density, and depressed rates of population growth during the Pleistocene can be obtained by examining the relationship between exploitation of wild food resources, settlements, and demography (Figures 4 and 5).

In general, the aspects of the resources that seem to affect the demographic-settlement system consist of the productivity of the resources, their seasonality, spacing, aggregation, and spatiotemporal predictability. In any region, a combination of these resource attributes creates a resource pattern which is likely to influence subsistence activities and settlements.

Wilmsen (135) discusses the relationship between population size in response to the aggregation and movement of resources. Scattered, sedentary resources are optimally exploited by small, dispersed groups. If the yield of the resources is low, we would thus expect the regional density of settlements to be low and the exploited or "catchment" territory to be large, i.e. the spacing between sites would be wide. The settlements in an environment

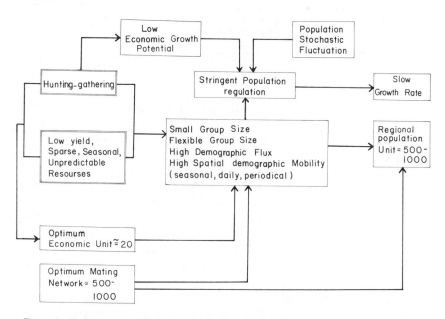

Figure 4 Bushmen type of hunting-gathering and its implications for population size, demographic fluidity, and population regulation. Note importance of limited potential for economic growth and low productivity.

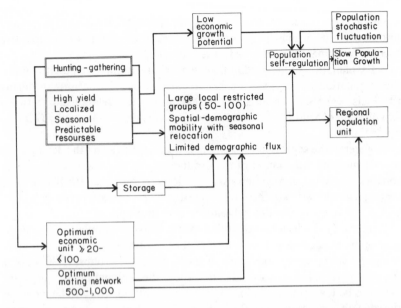

Figure 5   US Northwest Coast type of hunting-gathering and its implications for population size, demographic fluidity, and population regulation. Note the importance of limited potential for economic growth. Although this subsistence type is characterized by high productivity, and is thus different from the Bushmen type, the low potential for economic growth provides limits that are absent in agricultural systems. However, in this respect it is interesting to compare swidden agriculture with agriculture in temperate areas and with irrigation agriculture.

with very low resources would be even more distantly spaced and likely to be occupied for shorter time periods, with a random or rotational movement from one campsite to another.

Yellen (141) provides an example of this pattern. The environment of the !Kung Bushmen consists of a combination of dispersed but patterned low yield and seasonal resources. The seasonal yield, however, is highly variable. Because a minimal cooperative unit of 20–50 is necessary for economic, social, and biological reasons, the territory exploited daily from a base camp must be large in view of the scarcity of the resources. According to Yellen, the boundaries of the daily range is a day's round trip. The scarcity and spatial flux of resources from one year to the next is successfully met by a flexible territorial boundary and a fluid population composition through intergroup shuffle of individuals and families (Figure 4). Seasonal availability also dictates a seasonal round. Because of the frequent relocation, a high site density is obtained. The sites—because of the short duration of occupation—are small and located where a mix of resources is available. It should be noted that factors such as water or shelter can be limiting factors of settlement location. In arid environments, as is the case with the Bushmen, proximity to water is important. This applies to prehistoric occupations in desert regions. By the same token, rock shelters and caves in cold regions seem to have been exceedingly important, as in southwest France during the Middle and Upper Palaeolithic.

Yellen (141) and Yellen & Harpending (142) suggest that the subsistence demographic settlement pattern of the !Kung Bushmen is applicable to the Late Stone Age Wilton populations. The terminal Palaeolithic desert populations in Egypt (68, 70, 71) also seem to have had a similar pattern of man-land relationships.

Thomas (123) has modeled the subsistence-demographic pattern of the prehistoric inhabitants of the Reese River Valley, in the Great Basin. The results compare well with the ethnographic pattern, which consists of exploiting the Upland pinyon ecotone by three to five nuclear families from late fall to early spring, and a dispersal of the population from early spring to early fall exploiting lowland seed and root crops. Bettinger (12) suggests that this is one pattern of subsistence-demographic adaptation in the prehistoric Great Basin. The other pattern consists of relatively stable, sedentary, large population aggregates intensively exploiting the lowland plant resources.

The Northwest Coast area of the United States presents an environment diametrically opposed to that of the Kalahari and the Great Basin. It is characterized by high yield, aggregated and seasonally predictable resources (120). Such an environment presents the opportunity for specialized subsistence activities and permits the aggregation of large population units, high population density, and limited daily and periodic mobility (Figure 5). Seasonal movements for exploiting the salmon runs are characteristic of this system. The settlement pattern reflects this subsistence strategy and demographic profile. Permanent houses, large settlements, and seasonal camps are presented. This settlement-subsistence-demographic pattern is apparently of considerable antiquity (38). It is not unlikely that some of the Mesolithic populations were of the Northwest Coast type.

The exploitation of migratory herds of big game animals may allow the seasonal aggregation of population, and the high yield of meat can be stored and consumed over a long time period. This seems to have been the case during the Upper Palaeolithic in the USSR, where hunting villages with house structures were occupied (88).

The transition to an agricultural mode of production presents a shift toward high-yield, localized resources which encourage large residential units. The storability of cereal crops also permits a reduction in spatial mobility (Figure 6).

The agricultural settlement pattern and its evolution during the Neolithic and subsequent periods can be interpreted in the light of the great economic growth potential of agricultural food production through modifi-

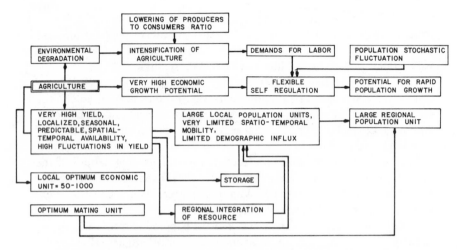

Figure 6 A diagram illustrating the potential influence of agricultural production on demographic conditions. Note that this subsistence mode differs from hunting-gathering mainly in: (*a*) high potential for economic growth, (*b*) high potential for environmental degradation, and (*c*) influence on the ratio of producers to consumers. Some hunting-gathering modes are similar to agriculture in their high productivity, localization of resources, and predictability, but they are invariably characterized by a very limited potential for economic growth since the upper limits for production are set by the yield of wild resources.

cation of land use, irrigation, weeding, improving cultigens, fertilization, etc. The model presented here predicts a progressive enlargement of the size of local settlements, associated with an increase in the regional population density and the differential growth of those settlements where the ratio of consumers to producers is upset by the rise of administrators and craft specialists. The archaeological record shows demographic settlement patterns conforming to this model.

In Mesopotamia, for example (4, 6), there is evidence for a progressive increase in the number of settlements, a deruralization of the countryside beginning with the Early Dynastic I, and a reduction in the spatial distance in the northeastern area during the Early Dynastic II/III. The size of the settlements indicates about a 27-fold increase in population. During the Early Dynastic I (81) the size of settlements indicates a predominance of hamlets and villages ranging from 50 to 1000 persons, with towns and cities of greater than 5000 persons (5).

In Mesoamerica, for another example, the population of the lowland Maya site of Tikal, Guatemala, is estimated between 30,000–35,000 (103), 40,000–49,000 (73) and 64,000 (42). Many estimates of population size and growth trends in other parts of Mesoamerica are available (18, 45, 103, 104, 124).

LIMITS TO GROWTH AND ECONOMIC CHANGE

The probable link between subsistence and population (58) has led many archaeologists to borrow the concept of "carrying capacity" from animal ecology. In many cases, carrying capacity—the number of people who can be supported in a given region under a specific mode of food production—has been employed to estimate probable size of prehistoric populations (10, 25, 28, 34, 37, 80, 110, 146, 147). However, carrying capacity is often invoked as a ceiling to which populations climb, then, faced with food scarcity, are forced to change their subsistence practices in order to lift the ceiling (32, 33, 62, 89, 112). This model has been criticized repeatedly because it discounts the common practice of population controls, the sociology and anthropology of innovation, and the limits to economic growth (11, 22, 35, 36, 66, 126).

For the most part, the utility of "carrying capacity" in archaeology is mainly of theoretical nature because of the methodological problems involved in its estimation (22, 55, 75, 86, 119). For example, all ethnographic accounts indicate that native populations seldom reach the environmental potential of their habitat and are normally well below the carrying capacity (16, 28, 102). This has been attributed in part to Liebig's rule (28, 42, 112), but recent attempts to deal with carrying capacity refer not only to environmental potentials but to the standard of living (acceptable levels of consumption and labor input), cost of food procurement, and the marginal product of labor (55, 71, 93). Changes in population size resulting from stochastic fluctuations (83) or unanticipated changes in the yield or spatiotemporal predictability of resources (75, 111) may alter the benefit/cost ratio of exploited resources. Such alterations are likely to lead to demographic or economic adjustments.

Therefore, carrying capacity as estimated from average resource yield or ethnographic observations in one or two years is a misleading estimate of limits to population growth. Rare but severe fluctuations in the yield of resources must be taken into consideration (75) if the population is to maintain a certain measure of economic stability. The "optimum" level of carrying capacity thus is likely to be well below the level of [maximum] carrying capacity. The existence of such safety margins, either in the form of unexploited species or a hinterland, militates against the kind of food crisis underlying population pressure models (33). Such safety margins, in addition, allow the people to anticipate an impending demographic or environmental change and provide, moreover, the time to undertake some kind of action that may prevent a deterioration of the standard of living. It is only when people live at a critical level close to that of the maximum carrying capacity or when the demographic or environmental change is sudden that severe food shortage and famines arise. It is paradoxial that cultures with the capacity for food production are more likely to experience these conditions, mainly as a result of the sudden and unanticipated ecological disasters associated with the intensive modification of the natural landscape.

Many authors, following Boserup (19), have argued that population pressure resulting from population increase has been a major, if not *the* major, single cause of culture change (33, 34, 112–114), but the use of population pressure in archaeological explanations is not without critics (11, 12, 20, 35, 36, 66, 126). The supposition that population increase is an omnipresent force, central to the argument of population pressure, is difficult to substantiate. World population throughout most of the Pleistocene was very small, perhaps no more than 9 million persons by the close of that period, and the annual growth rate was on the average extremely small. The rate was most probably less than 0.01% and very likely as low as .0007% during the Lower Palaeolithic (69, 95). As I have mentioned earlier, this slow rate was not a result of an intrinsic failure to achieve a rapid rate of population increase, since even with a 4-year child-spacing period, a depressed life expectancy, and a low rate of survivorship to child-bearing age, hunter-gatherers have the potential of rapid population increase (63, 76, 95).

Population increase, it has also been pointed out (35, 36, 66, 69), does not automatically lead to technological innovations. If we assume that a population permits its numbers to grow to the limit of its resources, such a population has several alternatives, including (*a*) dispersal, (*b*) reduction of food consumption, (*c*) intensification of subsistence activities, (*d*) no action, and (*e*) regulation of population size by cultural practices (67, 69). Dispersal is a viable solution as long as there are no physical or cultural barriers and as long as suitable habitats are present. Reduction in food consumption is likely to lead, in the long run, to morbidity, increased mortality, and reduction in labor input which would only tend to aggravate the crisis. The crisis also intensifies if no action is taken or if resources are overexploited. Since the economic growth potential of hunting-gathering is severely limited by the optimum yield to man—which is ultimately determined by the productivity of a resource—the room for economic expansion under that subsistence mode is very limited. It would seem then that other than dispersal, cultural population controls are the most advantageous for group survival and are most likely to have been selected by prehistoric populations. A pattern of periodic population expansion followed by an economic crash, starvation, and death is most disruptive to the continuity and operation of cultural systems. Human populations with this kind of growth pattern do not have a good chance for cultural or biological survival, and could not compete successfully with other groups having a more regulated population regime.

The practice of cultural population control, however, does not imply a state of infinite equilibrium. It only indicates that human populations can be protected by cultural mechanisms from recurrent scarcities and occasional overpopulation over the perceived span of environmental variability.

It is imperative to note here that changes in subsistence can be precipitated by causes that have nothing to do with population growth. Changes in the yield, quality, aggregation, association, seasonal predictability, and spacing of resources as a result of natural or man-made climatic-environmental changes were most likely of greater frequency in the prehistoric past than runaway population increase. The Quaternary record is replete with incidences of macroclimatic changes (23, 24). Of perhaps greater frequency are microclimatic events and small environmental disturbances over tens or hundreds of years, such as those we are all too familiar with in historical times and at present. Environmental changes by man-made fires (85, 92), overgrazing, overkill, salinization, erosion, and soil depletion (3, 48, 125, 131, 133) are not to be underestimated.

Subsistence changes must also be viewed in man's propensity to accept innovations that may better satisfy his needs, lower his subsistence effort, or increase the yield at lower or the same levels of effort.

It is important to note here that the emergence of large sedentary population units must have had a greater impact on the environment. Many of the changes were long-term effects that might not have been initially obvious. Under agricultural conditions these changes might have consisted both of lower agricultural productivity and depletion of wild resources in the catchment territory of the site leading to intensification of labor to maintain the standard of living. The intensification of labor and the changes toward more productive modes of agriculture might have promoted population increase as a source of labor.

This may provide a guideline for understanding terminal Pleistocene–post-Pleistocene adaptations. The terminal Pleistocene-Holocene transition was a period of marked changes in global climatic conditions (23, 24) with frequent fluctuations that might have disrupted the spatial distribution and seasonal availability of food resources under exploitation. The emergence of a generalized subsistence strategy, the broad spectrum adaptation of Flannery (50), and its consequences for population patterns could be a result of an attempt to enhance economic security by diversifying the subsistence base so that the impact of the unpredictability of resources may be minimized. Also, if the abundance of preferred animal game declined, a generalized strategy might have been favored as a result of the rising cost of time and energy expended in search and capture (98). On the other hand emphasis on one or a few species with a shift in the exploitative strategy to increase the yield by keeping in close spatial association with game movements is an alternative solution to the problem.

It is also important in discussing the link between subsistence and demography to introduce the concept of *"optimum economic population size"* as developed by Sauvy (105). For each subsistence mode there is an optimum group size, below and above which the yield per capita is diminished. Under hunting-gathering conditions the optimum size is smaller than that for agricultural groups, where certain key activities, e.g. harvesting, sowing, and food-processing, provide a greater yield per person if a relatively large group is working cooperatively. Thus, the rise of agricultural economy provided an incentive for larger families and local residential units. We may also note here that the potential for economic growth under agricultural conditions is very high through waterworks, weeding, selection of more productive cultigens, land reclamation, fertilization, etc. We have yet to exhaust the economic growth potential of agriculture. The advantages of a large group and the opportunities for economic growth made it possible to relax population control mechanisms, creating an ethic of fertility.

It should also be noted that early agriculture was associated with epidemics, famines, and nutritional deficiencies which may have led to a higher rate of infant mortality, thus encouraging further relaxation of population controls (122).

The emergence of agriculture was soon followed by the development of administrative personnel, craft specialists, soldiers, tradesmen, and other nonfood producing individuals. This demographic segment changed the ratio of "dependents" to producers and necessitated an increase in the total amount of yield required for the population. The demographic consequence was an increase in the number of producers (through higher fertility rates), accompanied by an increase in the workload per producer, as well as greater yield per unit of energy expended through agricultural innovations.

These remarks on prehistoric agriculture and culture change emphasize the reciprocal link between demography and cultural variables and underline the role of economic motives for population increase (e.g. greater payoff with a large economic family and community units, and increasing demands as a result of an increase in the ratio of consumers to producers). Degradation of the environment as a result of the intensive exploitation of a fixed locality by a large group of people would also prompt intensification of labor (through more labor input per producer and more producers) and agricultural economic expansion which may also involve greater labor demands (Figure 6).

In summary, environmental conditions and the mode of subsistence determine the size of local and regional population units, as well as the pattern of demographic flux and spatial shifts of population units or subunits. The population unit, on the other hand, is the basic unit for food production or extraction. The size and age/sex composition of the population unit will thus determine the marginal yield per capita and the ratio of dependents to potential producers.

Because of the high potential for population increase and stochastic fluctuations in population size and the limits to economic growth (especially under hunting-gathering conditions), cultural population controls tend to curb the population size so that an acceptable standard of consumption is realized at a reasonable level of effort. This has the effect of placing the population well below the apparent limits of the carrying capacity. Changes in environmental conditions may alter the yield or the spatiotemporal predictability of resources. Modification of the subsistence mode may follow in order to maintain the preexisting standard of consumption and labor input or to gain a greater amount of yield at no additional labor cost. This may be associated with changes in the size of the population unit, seasonal fusion/fission, or periodic flux.

DEMOGRAPHY AND TECHNOCULTURAL SYSTEMS: REGIONAL DIFFERENTIATION AND CHANGE

Explanation of the continual, gradual, and abrupt changes in prehistoric tool-making methods and artifact styles is a topic of great interest to archaeologists. An understanding of prehistoric demographic processes can provide some significant insights in this area (13, 94). The basic concept in a demographic explanation rests on the assumption that technology is transmitted, among other things, from one generation to the next and through intergroup interaction. Accordingly, a high degree of intergroup demographic flux is likely to facilitate transfer of information, producing regional technocultural homogenization, whereas restrictions on intergroup interaction would tend to inhibit information flow and enhance technocultural differentiation. Yellen & Harpending (142) demonstrated that the fluid pattern of population distribution, as characteristic of the Bushmen today, can explain the regional homogeneity of the Wilton stone tool assemblages of the Late Stone Age Wilton industry. Differences between the assemblages located in different places and assemblages from successive strata in the same site were insignificant. Conservatism and almost pancontinental homogeneity of technoculture in Prehistoric Australia from 30,000 to 18,000 B.C. (57) may also be a reflection of the high mobility of Australian prehistoric population and a pattern of demographic flux as is common among the Bushmen at present.

The demographic fluidity of a group, as suggested in the previous section, can be in part attributed to the scarcity/abundance and spatiotemporal patterning of key resources. In addition, Wobst (139) draws our attention to the role of mating networks in intergroup information transfer. Given low population density, small local group size, and a minimal mating network of 475 persons for maintaining biological viability, a very large area is characterized by multidirectional flow of mates and, by implication, information. At a population density of 0.03 persons/km^2 for desert populations (based on the figures for Australian hunting-gathering populations), a regional mating group would require an area of about 16,000 km^2 or radii of about 70 km. Investigations of the Siwa Oasis region in the Western Desert of Egypt indicate that the terminal Palaeolithic industries do show a regional homogeneity consistent with this model (68, 71). In contrast, in the Nile Valley, where population density was about 0.2–0.8 persons/km^2 or .5 persons/km^2 on the average (65), the mating network would have required an area of 950 km^2, but given the linear pattern of Nilotic resources over a width of less than 1 km in places to 22 km in others, the length of the mating network area along the Nile would have been 195 or 100 km. These figures are based on a width of 5–10 km for the catchment territory of regional groups. The homogeneity of archaeological industries of the final Palaeolithic over such distances, e.g. the Isnan at Dishna and Isna (65), does corroborate an exchange of technocultural information. During the Middle and Lower Palaeolithic, with lower population densities, the lines of communication would be even longer. The homogeneity of Mousterian traditions over the whole length of the Nile Valley from Nubia to the Delta (70) again suggests that Wobst's model of the impact of spatial extent and shape of the mating network (hexagonal vs linear) and regional technocultural homogeneity is critical to our understanding of the variability in lithic artifact assemblages. It should also be noted here that with greater population densities allowing a certain measure of territorial monopoly, the flow of mates and information can be restricted. This can lead to intergroup regional technocultural variability as a result of drift. However, the inevitability of intergroup flow would enhance a short life-span of technocultural traditions. This seems to have been the case in the Nile Valley during the Final Palaeolithic where numerous industries of relatively short duration were recognized (65), compared to that of the Middle and Lower Palaeolithic industries (127, 128). This may also explain the acceleration of technocultural change during the Mesolithic and Epipalaeolithic in many places in the world.

The implications of this model for the regional and temporal pattern of art forms and burial rites are explored by Wobst (136), who cites the case of Pavlovian portable art in Moravia, French and Cantabrian cave-painting, and German Magdalanian ritual sites as obvious examples. The implications for the continuity and survival of sociocultural traditions and subsistence modes should be apparent.

Isaac (79, p. 186) also suggests that "low density networks lacking in mechanisms for preventing the equalization of information content between neighbouring nodes would have great inertia to fundamental changes." This, Isaac argues, explains the persistence of the basic features of Acheulian stone artifact assemblages over large parts of the world surface during approximately a million years. In contrast, tightly knit networks associated with high population density "might engender localized, partial isolates, which, on occasions, might be more prone to the acceptance and exploitation of innovations." This would have characterized Terminal Pleistocene-Holocene populations.

Changes in demographic mobility in the form of intergroup demographic flux and migration/fusion caused by changes in the yield or the spatio temporal pattern of resources may also lead to changes in the magnitude of the flow of mates or technocultural traits. David (40) suggests that the mixing of the Noaillan and Perigordian lithic artifact traditions resulted from migration and demographic fusion. Smith (112) also suggests that a reduction in food resources or an expanding population is responsible for the regional diversity in the late Solutrean of France.

Thus, the duration and regional diversity of technocultural traditions as reflected in artifact assemblages may be, at least in part, amenable to interpretation from a demographic perspective. The demographic variables include population density, the size of the population unit, demographic mobility, and mating network size and spatial pattern. For a long time, archaeologists have been occupied with the classification of artifact assemblages and the formulation of regional and temporal technocultural units. They have failed to explain the regional variability and temporal succession, clinging to the antiquated and empty explanatory framework of "diffusion and evolution." The demographic perspective provides a processual framework for explanation that has been lacking for so long.

DEMOGRAPHY AND SOCIAL ORGANIZATION

Many prehistoric hunting-gathering populations consisted of small local groups to which the label "bands" can be applied. The social organization of band societies is viewed by many scholars from a demographic perspective (1, 16, 31, 53, 94, 101, 108, 114, 117, 118, 134, 135).

Steward (118), in his analysis of the social basis for small band societies, suggests that the low population density and small group size of many hunting-gathering groups, exploiting scarce resources, favors the formation of alliances to avoid conflicts. Postmarital residence, because of male dominance, is patrilocal and the allied groups are partilineal. Service (108) suggests that the exchange of wives as "gifts" for making alliances is another reason for patrilocality (113, 134).

Formation of alliances to avoid conflict may be just one of many mechanisms based on subsistence-demographic patterns. For example, small groups are not biologically viable because shortage of mates is endemic. Exogamous marriage patterns may emerge to guarantee group survival (137).

The frequent fluctuations in small groups are likely to affect not only the size of the group but also the sex ratio. The sex ratio is also often distorted by female infanticide (16). A high frequency of female infanticide during the Pleistocene is suggested by Birdsell (16) and by Harris (63). Schrire & Steiger (107) and Denham (41) are opposed to this view. The high metabolic cost of pregnancy would suggest that other population controls, e.g. those restricting mating, might have been more frequent. Infanticide, however, could be practiced as a last resort population control in times of excessive population increase because of its immediate effect. Female infanticide not only removes a dependent, but also removes a potential mother. Freeman (52) argues that infanticide increases ecosystem stability by regulating population size.

Changes in social organization of band societies resulting from environmental-subsistence changes have been suggested by Sally Binford (15) for early upper Pleistocene hunters in the Levant. She envisions an aggregation of a large number of individuals to take advantage of migratory herds as game became scarce following an increase in aridity during the last part of Early Würm. The population aggregation would have been associated with a concomitant change to a broader exogamous linkage between formerly distant groups.

It may also be noted that in small groups with high mobility the chances for the development of a coresidential kin group is low (7). This is further aggravated by the short life expectancy. Long life expectancy, low dispersal rates, and large population size are prerequisites for a coresidential kin-based social system.

The transition to agriculture is marked by the emergence of large residential units and sedentary large regional population units (4, 6, 18, 30, 77, 100, 103). Carneiro (26) and Naroll (90) provide empirical evidence for an increase in the complexity of social organization from small to large groups. White (130) suggests that maintenance of large population units requires an organization complexity greater than that for the small band societies. Barry (9) examined the relationship between social complexity and population size for 186 societies and concluded that unilinear descent and a large number of levels of political hierarchy are both effective means of maintaining social cohesion for large groups of people. It should be noted that the subsistence regime of mobile hunter-gatherers would not be compatible with strong integrative social organizations, whereas large groups practicing a mode of subsistence as complex as agriculture, requiring a good deal of coordination of communal activities, would benefit from a complex and centralized organization.

The demographic consequences of agriculture are also significant. As a result of the shift to a larger optimum economic group size, there was a change toward large family units and large cooperative local groups. Agricultural economy also fostered the emergence of a large number of nonproducers consisting of administrators, middlemen, and craft specialists. It also led to a rise in the consumption of nonsubsistence goods to be exchanged for subsistence items with neighboring groups. All of these factors had the effect of creating an economic stimulus for labor intensification and agrarian change and further expansion in those three demographic variables (Figure 6). The discussion by White (129) on demand for labor and population growth is relevant here. A feedback loop was thus created leading, among other things, to greater centralization of power and the emergence of rank stratification. The great economic growth potential of agriculture made agricultural intensification possible. The emergence of rank societies begins with early farming communities and can be detected even earlier as in the context of the Natufian villages immediately before agriculture (99). Randsborg (96, 97) provides an excellent analysis of the relationship between population and social stratification under agricultural economy in prehistoric Denmark.

In contrast to agricultural systems, social stratification among hunter-gatherers is absent in most cases, except when the population units are large and there is a payoff for coordinating internal and intergroup social and economic affairs, as among the US Northwest Coast populations. Social distinction among small, mobile population units rests on individual prestige and personal leadership. Prestige can be gained by one's ability to provide needed resources of limited availability and high risk, e.g. meat of scarce, dangerous big game mammals (80).

It is interesting also to note the case of agricultural societies having high population density but lacking a complex social organization. Dumond (44) cites the Ifugao, the Chimbu, and the Ibo. These populations practice swidden agriculture, one aspect of which is periodic spatial mobility. This mobility, which also bestows the label "shifting agriculture" to this subsistence mode, the greater stability of the agriculture system, and the lower potential for economic growth compared to that of dry or irrigation farming in temperate and semiarid lands might have set some limitations on the level of social complexity.

Carneiro (27), Smith & Young (114), Service (109), and Gibson (54) suggest that population increase leading to population pressure is the cause of political centralization [for a favorable review of these models see (8)]. These models do not explain the reasons for population increase and do not take into consideration the economic consequences of the rise of nonfood producers and the emergence of a new economy based on the removal of food outside the subsistence system and the exchange of this food with nonsubsistence goods. The role of population growth as a "prime mover" in the origins of civilization has been rejected by Wright & Johnson (140) as a result of recent archaeological studies in Southwestern Iran, and is objected to by Cowgill (35, 36) and Hassan (66, 69).

Various aspects of demography are important in understanding marriage patterns and kinship among agricultural groups (2, 49, 56, 60, 61, 91), so archaeologists working with problems of social organization may find a demographic perspective of some help.

CONCLUSIONS AND FINAL REMARKS

Archaeologists today are making vigorous strides toward explaining the processes by which cultural systems were maintained and modified in the prehistoric past. A demographic perspective brings significant insights to this area of expanding interest. Prehistoric subsistence, settlements, technology, and social organization cannot be dealt with adequately in a demographic vacuum. Prehistoric societies were made of people. The longevity, sex and age composition, number, demographic mobility, and population growth patterns of those people are inseparable from their cultural behavior.

In the present review an attempt has been made to demonstrate that a general model of the interrelations between subsistence, settlement, and demography promises to serve as a source of tremendous insight into the operation and change of prehistoric cultural systems. The subsistence mode, whether based on the extraction of wild resources or food production, can be characterized in terms of yield, seasonality, spacing, aggregation, and spatiotemporal predictability of the food resources. These in turn influence population size, population density, sedentariness, and demographic-spatial mobility. Hunting-gathering subsistence modes are not identical for populations in habitats of different resource characteristics, and it would be a serious mistake to speak of hunting-gathering as a single mode of subsistence. For example, the bushmen may be contrasted with the Indians of the Northwest Coast in North America. Agriculture is not a single mode of subsistence either. Differences in seasonality, amount of yield, and spacing of arable plots are significant in shaping the demographic conditions and settlement patterns.

One of the major differences between agriculture and hunting-gathering is the remarkable potential for economic growth in agricultural systems. Agricultural yield can be increased manyfold by improving cultigens, irrigation, fertilization, land-clearing, terracing, weeding, and mechanization. It seems that this exceptional capacity for economic growth associated with the practice of agriculture was a necessary condition for the rapid rise in world population since the Neolithic. This increase did not take place because the potential was there, but rather because economic and political conditions associated with agricultural production provided a motive for a large labor force. Large coresidential units and large families were advantageous under that system of production. Two major economic factors have emerged since the Neolithic: (*a*) a progressive increase in the number of nonproducers, e.g. administrators, craft-specialists, tradesmen; (*b*) a progressive increase in the econommic demand for nonfood goods for prestige or utilitarian purposes. Environmental degradation by sedentary populations as a result of repeated or uninterrupted exploitation of local wild resources and perhaps from poor agricultural practices could also have been a motivating factor for agrarian changes or intensification of labor input. The occasional impact of severe losses of agricultural yield on large, sedentary populations might also have prompted an increase in productivity coupled with regional integration of agricultural produce. Many scholars underscore the role of food shortage resulting from excessive population increase as the major force behind cultural evolution. It is not unlikely that population pressure could have stimulated change in some cases, but there are too many substantive and theoretical weaknesses in that hypothesis, so it should be handled with extreme care.

The general model of the relationships between subsistence, demography, and settlements also promises to shed light on two major spheres of archaeological concern, namely the regional distribution and life span of technoculture traditions, and social organization. Demographic-spatial mobility and the size of residential population units seem to be two important factors in information flow and hence the dissemination of artifacts or manufactural/stylistic practices.

The complexity of social organization is correlated with population size, and certain kinship patterns might be a function of the size of the residential population unit and the magnitude of demographic-spatial flux. It may be noted here that in addition to the influence of subsistence modes on these two demographic parameters, the quest for [reproductive] mates is also equally influential.

I hope that in this review I have contributed, by culling from the contemporary works on demographic archaeology, a glimpse into the exciting potential of demographic studies in archaeology. In spite of the vast literature of which only a sample is presented here, the field is still underdeveloped. A great deal of work concerns the methods of reconstructing the demographic past, but literature on serious demographic explanations is patchy and in many instances marred by a limited view of population dynamics.

Literature Cited

1. Aberle, D. F. 1961. Matrilineal descent in cross-cultural perspective. In *Matrilineal Kinship*, ed. D. M. Schneider, K. Gough, pp. 655–727. Berkeley: Univ. California
2. Adams, J. W., Kasakoff, A. B. 1975. Factors underlying endogamous group size. In *Population and Social Organization*, ed. M. Nag, pp. 147–73. The Hague: Mouton
3. Adams, R. McC. 1960. Early civilizations, subsistence, and environment. In *City Invincible*, ed. C. H. Kraeling, R. McC. Adams, pp. 269–95. Chicago: Univ. Chicago Press
4. Adams, R. McC. 1965. *Land Behind Baghdad: A History of Settlement on the Diyala Plains*. Chicago: Univ. Chicago Press
5. Adams, R. McC. 1972. Demography and the urban revolution in lowland Mesopotamia. See Ref. 115, pp. 60–63
6. Adams, R. McC., Nissen, H. J. 1972. *The Uruk Countryside: The Natural Setting of Urban Societies*. Chicago: Univ. Chicago Press
7. Altman, S. A., Altman, J. 1978. *Demographic Constraints on Behavior and Social Organization*. Presented at Hudson Symp. Biosoc. Mech. Popul. Regul., April 13–15, 1978, State Univ. New York, Plattsburgh
8. Baker, P. T., Sanders, W. T. 1972. Demographic studies in anthropology. *Ann. Rev. Anthropol.* 1:151–78
9. Barry, H. III. 1973. *Interrelationships among population size, kinship and societal complexity*. Presented at Ann. Meet. Am. Anthropol. Assoc., 72nd, New Orleans
10. Bayliss-Smith, T. 1974. Constraints on population growth: the case of the Polynesian Outlier Attols in the precontact period. *Hum. Ecol.* 2:259–95
11. Bender, B. 1978. Review of M. N. Cohen: the food crisis in prehistory. *Antiquity* 52:77–78
12. Bettinger, R. L. 1978. Alternative adaptive strategies in the prehistoric Great Basin. *J. Anthropol. Res.* 34:27–46
13. Binford, L. R. 1963. 'Red ocher' caches from the Michigan area: a possible case of cultural drift. *Southwest. J. Anthropol.* 19:89–108
14. Binford, L. R. 1968. Post-Pleistocene adaptations. In *New Perspectives in Archeology*, ed. S. R. Binford, L. R. Binford, pp. 313–41. Chicago: Aldine
15. Binford, S. R. 1968. Early Upper Pleistocene adaptations in the Levant. *Am. Anthropol.* 70:707–17
16. Birdsell, J. G. 1968. Some predictions for the Pleistocene based on equilibrium systems among recent hunter-gatherers. In *Man the Hunter*, ed. R. B. Lee, I. DeVore, pp. 229–40. Chicago: Aldine
17. Bishop, C. A. 1972. Demography, ecology, and trade among the northern Ojibwa and Swampy Cree. *West. Can. J. Anthropol.* 3:58–71
18. Blanton, R. E. 1972. Prehispanic adaptation in the Ixtapalapa Region, Mexico. *Science* 175:1317–26
19. Boserup, E. 1975. *The Conditions of Agricultural Growth*. Chicago: Aldine
20. Bronson, B. 1975. The earliest farming: demography as cause and consequence. In *Population, Ecology and Social Evolution*, ed. S. Polgar, pp. 53–78. The Hague: Mouton
21. Brown, P., Podolefsky, A. 1976. Population density, agricultural intensity, land tenure, and group size in the New Guinea Highlands. *Ethnology* 15:211–38

22. Brush, S. B. 1975. The concept of carrying capacity for systems of shifting cultivation. *Am. Anthropol.* 77:799–811
23. Butzer, K. W. 1971. *Environment and Archaeology.* Chicago: Aldine. 2nd ed.
24. Butzer, K. W. 1977. Environment, culture, and human evolution. *Am. Sci.* 65:572–84
25. Carneiro, R. L. 1960. Slash-and-burn agriculture: a closer look at its implications for settlement patterns. In *Men and Cultures. Selected Pap. 5th Int. Congr. Anthropol. Ethnol. Sci.,* Sept., 1956, ed. A. F. C. Wallace, pp. 131–45. Philadelphia: Univ. Pennsylvania Press
26. Carneiro, R. L. 1967. On the relationship between size of population and complexity of social organization. *Southwest. J. Anthropol.* 23:234–43
27. Carneiro, R. L. 1970. A theory of the origin of the state. *Science* 169:733–38
28. Casteel, R. W. 1972. Two static maximum population-density models for hunter-gatherers: a first approximation. *World Archaeol.* 4:19–40
29. Casteel, R. W. 1973. *The Relationship Between Population Size and Carrying Capacity in a Sample of North American Hunter-gatherers.* Presented at 9th Int. Congr. Anthropol. Ethnol. Sci., Chicago
30. Chang, K. C. 1958. Study of the Neolithic social groupings: samples from the New World. *Am. Anthropol.* 60: 298–334
31. Childe, V. G. 1936. *Man Makes Himself.* New York: New American Library. 1951 rev. ed.
32. Cohen, M. N. 1975. Population pressure and the origins of agriculture: an archaeological example from the Coast of Peru. See Ref. 20, pp. 79–121
33. Cohen, M. N. 1977. *The Food Crisis in Prehistory.* New Haven: Yale Univ. Press
34. Cook, S. F. 1972. Prehistoric demography. *McCaleb Module in Anthropology.* Reading, Mass: Addison-Wesley
35. Cowgill, G. L. 1975. Population pressure as a non-explanation. See Ref. 121, pp. 127–31
36. Cowgill, G. L. 1975. On causes and consequences of ancient and modern population changes. *Am. Anthropol.* 77: 505–25
37. Cowgill, U. M. 1962. An agricultural study of the southern Maya lowlands. *Am. Anthropol.* 64:273–86
38. Croes, D. R. 1977. *Basketry from the Ozette Village archaeological site: a technological, functional, and compara-tive study.* PhD thesis. Washington State Univ., Pullman, Wash.
39. Crook, J. H. 1972. Sexual selection, dimorphism and social organization. In *Sexual Selection and the Descent of Man: 1871–1971,* ed. B. Campbell, pp. 255–72. Chicago: Aldine
40. David, N. 1973. On Upper Palaeolithic society, ecology, and technological change: the Noaillian case. In *Man, Settlement, and Urbanization,* ed. P. J. Ucko, R. Tringham, G. W. Dimbleby, pp. 277–303. London: Duckworth
41. Denham, W. W. 1974. Population structure, infant transport, and infanticide among Pleistocene and modern hunter-gatherers. *J. Anthropol. Res.* 30:191–98
42. Dickson, D. B. 1978. *Tikal, Milpa agriculture and population in a simulation.* Presented at Soc. Am. Archaeol. Meet., 1978, Tucson
43. Divale, W. T. 1972. Systemic population control in the Middle and Upper Palaeolithic: inferences based on contemporary hunter-gatherers. *World Archaeol.* 4:222–37
44. Dumond, D. E. 1965. Population growth and cultural change. *Southwest. J. Anthropol.* 21:302–24
45. Dumond, D. E. 1972. Demographic aspects of the classic period in Puebla-Tlaxcala. *Southwest. J. Anthropol.* 28: 101–30
46. Dumond, D. E. 1975. The limitation of human population: a natural history. *Science* 187:713–21
47. Dyson-Hudson, R., Smith, E. A. 1978. Human territoriality: an ecological reassessment. *Am. Anthropol.* 80:21–41
48. Fairservis, W. A. 1967. The origin, character, and decline of an early civilization. *American Museum Novitiates* No. 2302, pp. 1–48
49. Fix, A. G. 1975. Fission-fusion and lineal affect: aspects of the population structure of the Semai Senoi of Malaysia. *Am. J. Phys. Anthropol.* 43:295–302
50. Flannery, K. V. 1969. Origins and ecological effects of early domestication in Iran and the Near East. In *The Domestication and Exploitation of Plants and Animals,* ed. P. J. Ucko, G. W. Dimbleby, pp. 73–100. Chicago: Aldine
51. Freeman, L. 1968. Discussions, Pt. V. See Ref. 16, p. 248
52. Freeman, M. M. R. 1973. A social and ecological analysis of systematic female infanticide. *Am. Anthropol.* 73:1011–18
53. Fried, M. H. 1967. *The Evolution of Po-*

litical Society. New York: Random House

54. Gibson, M. 1973. Population shift and the rise of Mesopotamian civilization. In The Explanation of Culture Change, ed. C. Renfrew, pp. 447–63. London: Duckworth

55. Glassow, M. A. 1978. The concept of carrying capacity in the study of culture process. In Advances in Archaeological Method and Theory, ed. M. B. Schiffer, 1:32–48. New York: Academic

56. Godelier, M. 1975. Modes of production, kinship and demographic structure. In Marxist Analyses and Social Anthropology, ed. M. Bloch, pp. 3–27. New York: Wiley

57. Gould, R. A. 1973. Australian archaeology in ecological and ethnographic perspective. Warner Modular Publ. 7:1–33

58. Hack, J. T. 1942. The Changing Physical Environment of the Hopi Indians of Arizona. Pap. Mus. Am. Archaeol. Ethnol. Harvard Univ., 35–85

59. Hallowell, A. I. 1949. The size of Algonkian hunting territories: a function of ecological adjustment. Am. Anthropol. 51:35–45

60. Hammel, E. A. 1964. Territorial patterning of marriage relationships in a coastal Peruvian village. Am. Anthropol. 66:67–74

61. Hammel, E. A. 1977. The influence of social and geographical mobility on the stability of kinship systems: the Serbian case. In Internal Migration: a Comparative Perspective, ed. A. A. Brown, E. Neuberger. New York: Academic

62. Harner, M. J. 1970. Population pressure and the social evolution of agriculturalists. Southwest. J. Anthropol. 26:67–86

63. Harris, M. 1977. Cannibals and Kings: The Origins of Cultures. New York: Random House. 351 pp.

64. Hassan, F. A. 1973. On mechanisms of population growth during the Neolithic. Curr. Anthropol. 14:535–40

65. Hassan, F. A. 1974. The Archaeology of the Dishna Plain, Egypt. Cairo: Geol. Surv. Egypt, Pap. 59

66. Hassan, F. A. 1974. Population growth and cultural evolution. Rev. Anthropol. 1:205–12

67. Hassan, F. A. 1975. Determinants of the size, density, and growth rate of hunting-gathering populations. See Ref. 20, pp. 27–52

68. Hassan, F. A. 1976. Prehistoric studies of the Siwa Oasis region, preliminary report, 1975 season. Nyame Akuma

9:18–34. Calgary: Dept. Archaeol. Univ. Calgary

69. Hassan, F. A. 1978. Demographic archaeology. See Ref. 55, 1:49–103

70. Hassan, F. A. 1978. Prehistoric Studies of Northern Egypt. Rep. Natl. Sci. Found. Pullman: Washington State Univ.

71. Hassan, F. A. 1978. Archaeological explorations of the Siwa Oasis region, Egypt. Curr. Anthropol. 19:146–48

72. Hassan, F. A. 1979. Prehistoric settlements along the main Nile. In The Sahara and the Nile, ed. M. Martin, H. Faure. In press

73. Haviland, W. A. 1969. A new population estimate for Tikal, Guatemala. Am. Antiq. 34:429–32

74. Hayden, B. 1972. Population control among hunter/gatherers. World Archaeol. 4:205–21

75. Hayden, B. 1975. The carrying capacity dilemma. See Ref. 121, pp. 11–21

76. Henneberg, M. 1976. Reproductive possibilities and estimation of the biological dynamics of earlier population. In The Demographic Evolution of Human Populations, ed. R. H. Ward, K. M. Weiss, pp. 41–48. New York: Academic

77. Hole, F., Flannery, K. V., Neely, J. A. 1969. Prehistory and human ecology of the Deh Luran plain: An early village sequence from Khuzistan, Iran. Memoirs No. 1. Ann Arbor: Univ. Michigan Mus. Anthropol.

78. Isaac, G. L 1. 1969. Studies of early culture in East Africa. World Archaeol. 1:1–28

79. Isaac, G. L 1. 1972. Early phases of human behaviour: models in Lower Palaeolithic archaeology. In Models in Archaeology, ed. D. L. Clarke, pp. 167–99. London: Methuen

80. Jochim, M. A. 1976. Hunter-Gatherer Subsistence and Settlement: A Predictive Model. New York: Academic. 206 pp.

81. Johnson, G. A. 1972. A test of the utility of central place theory in archaeology. See Ref. 40, pp. 769–85

82. Klein, R. 1969. Man and Culture in the Late Pleistocene: A Case Study. San Francisco: Chandler. 259 pp.

83. Kunstadter, P. 1972. Demography, ecology, social structure, and settlement patterns. In The Structure of Human Populations, ed. G. A. Harrison, A. J. Boyce, pp. 313–51. Oxford: Clarendon

84. Lee, R. B. 1972. !Kung spatial organization: an ecological and histological perspective. Hum. Ecol. 1:125–47

85. Lewis, H. T. 1972. The role of fire in the domestication of plants and animals in S.W. Asia: a hypothesis. *Man* 7:195–222

86. Little, M. A., Moran, G. E. B. Jr. 1976. *Ecology, Energetics, and Human Variability.* Dubuque: Brown

87. Mellars, P. A. 1972. The character of the middle-upper palaeolithic transition in southwest France. See Ref. 40, pp. 255–76

88. Mongait, A. L. 1961. *Archaeology in U.S.S.R.* Baltimore: Penguin. 320 pp.

89. Moseley, M. E. 1972. Subsistence and demography: an example of interaction from prehistoric Peru. *Southwest. J. Anthropol.* 28:25–50

90. Naroll, R. 1956. A preliminary index of social development. *Am. Anthropol.* 68:687–715

91. Nash, J., Nash, M. 1963. Marriage, family and population growth in Upper Burma. *Southwest. J. Anthropol.* 19:251–66

92. Naveh, Z. 1975. The evolutionary significance of fire in the Mediterranean region. *Vegetation* 29:199–208

93. North, D. C., Thomas, R. B. 1977. The first economic revolution. *Econ. Hist. Rev.* 30:229–44

94. Owen, R. C. 1965. The patrilocal band: a linguistically and culturally hybrid social unit. *Am. Anthropol.* 67:675–90

95. Polgar, S. 1972. Population history and population policies from an anthropological perspective. *Curr. Anthropol.* 13:203–11, 260–62

96. Randsborg, K. 1974. Prehistoric populations and social regulation. *Homo* 25:59–67

97. Randsborg, K. 1975. Social dimension of early Neolithic Danemark. *Proc. Prehist. Soc.* 41:105–18

98. Rapport, D. J., Turner, J. E. 1977. Economic models in ecology. *Science* 195:367–73

99. Redman, C. L. 1978. *The Rise of Civilization.* San Francisco: Freeman. 367 pp.

100. Renfrew, C. 1972. *The Emergence of Civilization.* London: Methuen

101. Sahlins, M. D. 1968. Notes on the original affluent society. See Ref. 16, pp. 85–89

102. Sahlins, M. D. 1972. *Stone Age Economics.* Chicago: Aldine-Atherton. 348 pp.

103. Sanders, W. T. 1972. Population, agricultural history, and societal evolution in Mesoamerica. See Ref. 115, pp. 101–53

104. Sanders, W. T. 1974. Chiefdom to state: political evolution at Kaminaljuyu, Guatemala. In *Reconstructing Complex Societies: An Archaeological Colloquium,* ed. C. B. Moore, pp. 97–113. Suppl. Bull. Am. Sch. Orient. Res. No. 20

105. Sauvy, A. 1969. *General Theory of Population* (Transl.) New York: Basic Books

106. Schaller, G. B., Lowther, G. R. 1969. The relevance of carnivore behavior to the study of early hominids. *Southwest. J. Anthropol.* 25:307–41

107. Schrire, C., Steiger, W. L. 1974. A matter of life and death: an investigation into the practice of female infanticide in the Arctic. *Man* 9:161–84

108. Service, E. R. 1966. *The Hunters.* Englewood Cliffs: Prentice-Hall. 118 pp.

109. Service, E. R. 1971. *Origins of the State and Civilization: the Process of Cultural Evolution.* New York: Norton. 361 pp.

110. Shawcross, W. 1967. An investigation of prehistoric diet and economy on a coastal site at Galatea Bay, New Zealand. *Proc. Prehist. Soc.* 33:107–31

111. Sherratt, A. G. 1972. Socio-economic and demographic models for the Neolithic and Bronze Ages of Europe. See Ref. 79, pp. 479–542

112. Smith, P. E. L. 1972. Changes in population pressure in archaeological explanation. *World Archaeol.* 4:5–18

113. Smith, P. E. L. 1976. *Food Production and its Consequences.* Menlo Park, Calif: Cummings. 120 pp.

114. Smith, P. E. L., Young, T. C. Jr. The evolution of early agriculture and culture in greater Mesopotamia: a trial model. See Ref. 115, pp. 1–59

115. Spooner, B., ed. 1972. *Population Growth: Anthropological Implications* Cambridge: M.I.T. Press

116. Steward, J. H. 1937. Ecological aspects of southwestern society. *Anthropos* 32:87–104

117. Steward, J. H. 1949. Cultural causality and law: a trial formulation of the development of early civilizations. *Am. Anthropol.* 51:1–27 (Reprint)

118. Steward, J. H. 1955. *Theory of Culture Change.* Urbana: Univ. Illinois

119. Street, J. 1969. An evaluation of the concept of carrying capacity. *Prof. Geogr.* 21:104–7

120. Suttles, W. 1962. Variations in habitat and culture on the Northwest Coast. *Proc. Int. Congr. Americanists, 34th, Horn-Vienna.* Austria: Verlag Berger

121. Swedlund, A. C., ed. 1975. Population studies in archaeology and biological

anthropology: a symposium. *Am. Antiq.* 40 (2), Mem. 30

122. Swedlund, A. C., Armelagos, G. J. 1976. *Demographic Anthropology.* Dubuque, Ia: Brown

123. Thomas, D. H. 1973. An empirical test for Steward's model of Great Basin settlement patterns. *Am. Antiq.* 38:155–77

124. Turner, B. L. II. 1967. Population density in the classic Maya lowlands: new evidence for old approaches. *Geogr. Rev.* 66:73–82

125. Turner, B. L. II. 1974. Prehistoric intensive agriculture in the Mayan lowlands. *Science* 185:118–24

126. Weiss, K. M. 1976. Demographic theory and anthropological inference. *Ann. Rev. Anthropol.* 5:351–81

127. Wendorf, F., ed. 1968. *The Prehistory of Nubia.* Dallas: Southern Methodist Univ. Press. 2 vols.

128. Wendorf, F., Schild, R. 1976. *Prehistory of the Nile Valley.* New York: Academic. 440 pp.

129. White, B. 1973. Demand for labor and population growth in colonial Java. *Hum. Ecol.* 1:217–36

130. White, L. 1949. *The Science of Culture.* New York: Grove

131. Whittle, A. W. R. 1978. Resources and population in the British Neolithic. *Antiquity* 52:34–42

132. Wiens, J. A. 1977. On competition and variable environments. *Am. Sci.* 65:590–97

133. Wilkinson, P. F. 1972. Ecosystem models and demographic hypotheses: predation and prehistory in North America. See Ref. 79, pp. 543–76

134. Williams, B. J. 1974. A model of band society. *Am. Antiq.* 39 (2), Mem. 29

135. Wilmsen, E. 1973. Interaction, spacing, behavior, and the organization of hunting bands. *J. Anthropol. Res.* 29:22–25

136. Wobst, H. M. 1971. *Boundary conditions for Paleolithic cultural systems: A simulation approach.* PhD thesis. Univ. Michigan, Ann Arbor, Mich.

137. Wobst, H. 1974. Boundary conditions for Paleolithic social systems: a simulation approach. *Am. Antiq.* 39:147–78

138. Wobst, H. 1975. The demography of finite populations and the origins of the incest taboo. See Ref. 121, pp. 74–81

139. Wobst, H. M. 1976. Locational relationships in Paleolithic society. See Ref. 76, pp. 49–58

140. Wright, H. T., Johnson, G. A. 1975. Population, exchange, and early state formation in Southwestern Iran. *Am. Anthropol.* 77:267–89

141. Yellen, J. 1977. *Archaeological Approaches to the Present.* New York: Academic

142. Yellen, J., Harpending, H. 1972. Hunter-gatherer populations and archaeological inference. *World Archaeol.* 4:244–53

143. Yessner, D. R. 1977. Resource diversity and population stability among hunter-gatherers. *West. Can. J. Anthropol.* 3:18–59

144. Young, C. T. 1972. Population densities and early Mesopotamia urbanism. See Ref. 40, pp. 827–42

145. Zimen, E. 1976. On the regulation of pack-size wolves. *Z. Tierpsychol.* 40:300–41

146. Zubrow, E. B. W. 1971. Carrying capacity and dynamic equilibrium in the prehistoric southwest. *Am. Antiq.* 36:127–38

147. Zubrow, E. B. W. 1975. *Prehistoric Carrying Capacity: A Model.* Menlo Park: Cummings

Ann. Rev. Anthropol. 1979. 8:161–205

FAMILY AND HOUSEHOLD: ♦9631
THE ANALYSIS OF
DOMESTIC GROUPS

Sylvia Junko Yanagisako

Department of Anthropology, Stanford University, Stanford, California 94305

INTRODUCTION

In 1913, Malinowski (91) introduced his disquisition on the family among the Australian Aborigines with the contention that a careful investigation of the facts of family life in Australia was urgently needed. He claimed that the confusion and contradiction in extant depictions of the Australian family were due to certain theoretical postulates and axioms adopted by some ethnographers. Principal among these was the attribution of European characteristics to the aboriginal family without adequate investigation of the details of actual family relationships. As an antidote to such inclinations, Malinowski proposed that we begin the study of the family in societies different from our own by attaching only a vague meaning to the term "individual family."

> For the essential features of the individual family, as of all other social institutions, depend upon the general structure of a given society and upon the conditions of life therein. A careful and detailed analysis of family life and of different aspects of the family unit in connection with other social phenomena is therefore necessary. Such an analysis enables us to describe the said unit in a complete and exact way (91, p. 6).

In the more than half-century that has passed since Malinowski expounded on the procedure for arriving at a "scientific, correct, and useful definition of the family in Australia" (91), it has become commonplace to charge him with having fallen far short of these goals. Less often evaluated is the success that anthropologists in general have attained in illuminating

161

0084-6570/79/1015-0161$01.00

the dynamic structures of those units we call families. This review is an attempt at such an evaluation, not by way of an analysis of the historical developments in anthropological research on the family, but through an examination of a cross-section of literature published mainly within the last decade.

A proper review of current anthropological discussions on the family must necessarily include the literature on households as well. For, over the years, the social units which in Malinowski's day were customarily referred to as families have come to be differentiated into "families" and "households." To introduce the reader to the conventional distinctions drawn between these two terms and to the notions underlying the meanings attributed to them, I begin with an examination of attempts to define the family and household. This is followed by a critical survey of the ways in which anthropologists interpret and explain observed variations in the social forms included under these rubrics. I then proceed to extract from this literature the basic conceptions and encompassing framework shared by its authors. My argument is that despite our repudiation of Malinowski's reduction of all kinship relationships to mere extensions of the emotional and psychological correlates of intimate family associations, most of our analyses of domestic groups remain fundamentally rooted in his conceptions of the family. Following this discussion, I introduce alternative analytic frameworks which have been applied productively to family and household relationships and evaluate their contributions and current limitations. I postpone until last a discussion of the universality of the family, because this issue can be addressed adequately only after I have elucidated the nature of anthropological discourse on the family and household.

DEFINITIONS OF FAMILY AND HOUSEHOLD

Although anthropologists commonly employ the terms family and household loosely without attaching to them rigorous, formal definitions, at the same time most recognize some sort of distinction between the two. The distinction that appears to be most widely accepted by anthropologists (8, 9, 17, 21, 29, 45, 74, 80, 81, 108, 128) contrasts kinship and propinquity as the essential features that define membership in the family and household respectively. Bender (8) contends that the grounds for analytically separating families and households lie in the recognition that they are both "logically distinct" and "empirically different" (8, p. 493). The logical distinction is apparent because the referent of the family is kinship, while the referent of the household is geographical propinquity or common residence. Following Bohannon (17, p. 86), who claims that kinship and propinquity "do not even belong to the same universe of discourse," and F.M. Keesing (80, p. 271), who views kinship and locality as two distinct principles of organization, Bender maintains that " . . . families, as kinship units, must be defined strictly in terms of kinship relationships and not in terms of co-residence" (8, p. 493). For Bender, the empirical difference derives from the observation that in numerous societies families do not form households, and in even more instances, households are not composed of families.

The contrast between kinship and locality as different principles of organization also lies behind the more specific distinction between family and household which prevails in studies of peasant communities. Here the family as a jurally defined, corporate kin group is distinguished from the household as a collection of kin and sometimes nonkin who share a common residence. The corporate nature of the family derives from the jural rights to property, usually land, which its members hold in common (29, 51, 106, 151). Accordingly, for Freedman (51, p. 9) a joint family exists in China whenever two or more men are coparceners of a *chia* (family) estate, regardless of whether these men are married or whether they and their respective wives and children live in different residences. An obvious consequence of this jural definition of the family is that in societies such as China and India, men, as inheritors of property, are placed at the core of the family, while women are classified as "subordinate or fringe members" who have lesser rights of ownership in the estate (151).

The focus on property rights attaches to the family the specific function of control over property, including its transmission. But the more general distinction between the family as a kinship unit and the household as a residential unit, which Bender carries further than anyone else, is an attempt to avoid a functionalist definition of the family. Bender asserts that functional definitions of the family are inadequate because many of the functions that have been construed as "family functions" are sometimes fulfilled by coresidential groups that are not based on kinship relationships and are in other instances carried out by neither families nor households. As an alternative, he proposes that we define the family in purely "structural" terms, because in all societies people recognize kinship relationships and use these to form social groups, and because these relationships can be organized in only a limited number of logical ways. Like the others who pose this distinction, Bender never makes explicit precisely what he means by "kinship" relationships or "kinship" units as distinct from coresidential relationships or relationships arising from propinquity. Yet it is evident from Bender's amplifications on the subject that by "kinship" relationships he means genealogically defined relationships; that is to say, relationships that can be traced through one or more parent-child or marriage linkages.

In his attempt to formulate a universal, parsimonious definition of the family for comparative purposes, Goodenough (58) likewise tries to divorce the family from specific functions. He defines the nuclear family group present in all human societies as a woman and her dependent children. When the woman's sexual partner is added to this group "in a functionally significant way" the result is an elementary conjugal family (Murdock's nuclear family). When the woman's brothers (and other close consanguines) are added to the group "in a functionally significant way," the result, according to Goodenough, is a consanguine family. The vagueness of the phrase "in a functionally significant way" is a conscious effort by Goodenough to avoid linking the family to a specified function or set of functions. In contrast to Bender, who does not specify the genealogical link or links that form the core of the family, Goodenough identifies the mother-child link as the nucleus of all family groups.

That both Bender and Goodenough would try to detach the definition of the family from particular functions is not surprising in light of the failure of past attempts (96, 143) to define the family on a functional basis. There appears to be no single function—and certainly no set of functions—that is invariably fulfilled by a set of genealogically linked individuals. In the final section of this paper, I will return to this issue to argue that in spite of their eschewal of a functional definition of the family, both Bender's and Goodenough's definitions are rooted in a functional view of the family.

While all the distinctions between family and household settle on residential propinquity as the criterion for the household, there remains still the question of what we mean by residential propinquity or coresidence. Innumerable problematic cases in the ethnographic literature can be adduced to illustrate the difficulties in defining the boundaries of households. These cases raise questions about how to treat residential groupings that move through a seasonal cycle of dispersal and concentration, how to handle the movement of personnel between dwelling units, particularly in societies where there is great mobility between these units (78, 145), whether to define as a single household the huts or houses that share a common yard, which may or may not be enclosed from other yards (39), and whether to include servants, apprentices, boarders, and lodgers as members of the household (74, 86, 156). Certainly there are discrepancies in our usage of the term household if its sole referent is residential propinquity. Why then do we regard solitaries (individuals living alone) as constituting households, while we exclude institutions like orphanages, boarding schools, men's houses, and army barracks?

The answer is that although the primary referent of the term household is spatial propinquity, in actual usage more is usually meant (8). Generally the term refers to a set of individuals who share not only a living space but also some set of activities. These activities, moreover, are usually related to food production and consumption or to sexual reproduction and childrearing, all of which are glossed under the somewhat impenetrable label of "domestic" activities. Yet since all the activities implicitly or explicitly associated with the term household are sometimes engaged in by sets of people who do not live together, several anthropologists (8, 22, 128) contend that we would do better to employ alternative terms in our ethnographic descriptions. Bulmer (22), for one, questions the adequacy of the term "household" for describing a situation where overlapping sets of people participate in meal sharing, gardening, and coresidence. He proposes that in these circumstances the "domestic group," in which people acknowledge common authority in domestic matters, is a more salient social unit. Seddon (128) offers the term "budget unit" to refer to a group of individuals having a common "fund" and exchanging goods among each other without reckoning, as distinct from individuals who live together within one homestead. In the same vein, Bender (8) points out that because the term household is always tainted by an implicit association with certain domestic functions it is often misused and consequently is not useful for comparative purposes. He suggests that we substitute the term "coresidential group" for household and that we draw a clear distinction between such groups and any functions they might fill. In the case of a society like the Mundurucu then, Bender identifies two kinds of coresidential units: one composed of adult males living in men's houses and the other composed of groups of women and children. By labeling these units coresidential groups rather than households, we avoid making the false assumption that either of these coresidential units are the most important groups for the performance of domestic functions in Mundurucu society. We would recognize, furthermore, that because domestic functions are for the most part carried out through reciprocal interactions between adult males as a group and adult females as a group, "the whole village forms the domestic unit, the sexual division of labor in domestic activities being at the village level" (8, p. 495).

Bender's separation of families, coresidential groups, and domestic functions is useful to the extent that it prods the ethnographer to explicate the exact nature of the social unit he is labeling a family or coresidential unit and to describe precisely the functions it performs rather than assuming them or leaving the reader to fill in with his own cultural assumptions. In addition, by substituting the term coresidential group for household, Bender allows for the coexistence of several types of coresidential groups at different levels within the same society. An individual may simultaneously belong to two or more nested coresidential groups: for example, a nuclear family hut, in a patrilaterally extended family compound, within a patrilineal descent-based settlement.

On the other hand, Bender's terminological scheme leads us directly back to the most troublesome issue confronting definitions of family and household; namely, what are domestic functions? When examined closely, all the above definitions can be shown to radiate from one central point: the notion that *domestic* functions, *domestic* activities, and *domestic* organization are what families and households are fundamentally all about. Yet "domestic" remains a rather poorly explicated term. We have Bender's (8, p. 499) uncharacteristically imprecise definition of "domestic" activities as those that "are concerned with the day-to-day necessities of living, including the provision and preparation of food and the care of children." Even more vague is Fortes's (45, p. 8) definition of the domestic group as "a householding and housekeeping unit organized to provide the material and cultural resources needed to maintain and bring up its members," and his definition of the domestic domain as "the system of social relations through which the reproductive nucleus [the family] is integrated with the environment and with the structure of the total society." Despite the imprecision of these definitions, at the core of most conceptions of "domestic" (8, 45, 47, 60, 74, 138) are two sets of functional activities: those pertaining to food production and consumption and those pertaining to social reproduction, including child-bearing and child-rearing.

Having arrived at what I consider to be the key to our conventional understanding as well as to the ambiguities of the terms family and household, I will postpone further consideration of what this tells us about the prevailing conceptual framework ordering anthropological discussions of domestic organization, leaving it to be taken up again in later sections of this article.[1] I want first to examine the manner in which anthropologists describe and explain the diverse social forms that they include under the rubrics of family and household. For the present, I will use the terms family and household as the authors being reviewed use them. The terms "domestic group" and "domestic unit" will be employed to refer more generally to both family and household, particularly where it is unclear whether the referent corresponds more closely to the conventional meaning of either term.

VARIATIONS IN DOMESTIC ORGANIZATION

The literature in which variations in domestic groups are described and explained can be divided conveniently into two sections: discussions of cross-societal and intrasocietal variations and discussions of variations over time.

[1]See Variations in Domestic Organization: An Underview, and Conclusion: A Return to Definitions and the Search for Universals.

Cross-societal and Intrasocietal Variations

Two related questions have been asked of the variations observed among domestic groups in the same society and in different societies. First, why do we find in some societies domestic groups, whether these are coresidential groups or dispersed families, which have a different composition and structure from those in other societies? And second, where the members of a society agree that a particular household or family form is the ideal, why do we so often discover that a significant percentage of the households or families in that society diverge from the ideal? Three sets of variables have been adduced to explain these interlinked questions: demographic variables, including the developmental cycle of domestic groups, economic variables, and stratification variables.

DEMOGRAPHIC DETERMINANTS AND THE DEVELOPMENTAL CYCLE OF DOMESTIC GROUPS   By now it has been well established that demographic processes affect the size and composition of domestic groups, thus acting as constraints on the attainment of the culturally ideal household or family type (23, 89, 162). Age at marriage, life expectancy, and fertility levels all have an impact on the composition of households and families in a community. For example, in the case of the Yugoslavian zadruga (a joint household of either the paternal-filial or fraternal type), Hammel (72) contends that if age at marriage is early, the period of overlap in the married lives of fathers and sons will be relatively great and the possibility of paternal-filial zadrugas increases.

Demographic processes may also have a significant impact on the economy of the household. Following the Russian economist Chayanov (25), Sahlins (120) claims that among peasants, where the household is the unit of production, changes in the demographic structure of the household as it moves through the developmental cycle will entail changes in the ratio of consumers to workers. As the number of dependent children increases while the number of adult workers remains constant, each family worker must farm a greater amount of land and work longer hours. Thus, the amount of time a family member works will be proportional to the dependency ratio (the number of consumers divided by the number of workers) of the household. Moreover, in a society where the household is the unit of production, some percentage of the households will not be able to support themselves because of an unfavorable dependency ratio (120, p. 74).

In attending to demographic factors, however, we must avoid treating observed demographic processes as exogenous, biologically given constraints which determine the composition and economy of households. To do so would be to confuse social replacement with biological replacement (122, 123) and to overlook the strategies that people employ to exercise control over household size and composition, many of which are embedded in "kinship" customs such as marriage and adoption practices and the timing of family division. For instance, in a remarkable piece of detective work in historical demography, T. C. Smith (140) discloses how in at least one village in eighteenth century Japan, peasants were able to prolong the family's phase of "maximum farming efficiency" by postponing the inheriting son's marriage as long as possible and in the meantime detaining the departure of his siblings from the household. Furthermore, we cannot assume, as do Chayanov and Sahlins, that because wage-labor is absent, households have access only to their own labor. As Donham (37, 38) convincingly argues, there may be other institutional contexts in which labor is transferred from one household to another. Accordingly, the members of households among the Malle of southwestern Ethiopia work about the same lengths of time regardless of the household's dependency ratio and stage in the developmental cycle. Rather than working longer hours, middle-aged men sponsor more work parties through which they are able to gain in the net transfer of labor between households (37).

Fortes's (45) model of the developmental cycle of domestic groups also relies on demographic processes to explain the varieties of domestic groups found in a community. According to Fortes, " . . . when it is recognized that these so-called types are in fact phases in the developmental cycle of a single general form for each society, the confusion vanishes" (45, p. 3). The various domestic groups observed at one point in time can be ordered into a single developmental sequence, as in the case of matrifocal families in (formerly) British Guiana (136). Hence, the developmental cycle may explain why a census shows only a small percentage of the households in a community conforming to the ideal type (10, 72). As all domestic groups pass through different stages of the developmental cycle at different times, a census will catch only a few in the ideal, complete phase. For this reason, an ideal household type such as the Eastern European zadruga is better regarded " . . . *not as a form,* but as a transitory state in the development of the household" (72, p. 142).

While the developmental cycle must be reckoned with in any analysis of household or family form, in most cases it cannot explain all the observed variation because factors other than those stemming from the process of social reproduction may operate to produce a diversity of domestic groups (29, 59, 141). E. N. Goody's study (59), for example, reveals that the developmental cycles of compounds are characteristically different among the three estates (commoner, Muslim, and ruling) in the divisional capitals of central Gonja. Hence, as Fortes (47, p. 18) now concedes, a model of a uniform developmental cycle cannot explain why the actual histories of different families entail different developmental sequences.

The limitations of Fortes's initial (45) concept of the developmental cycle derive from his attachment of the successive phases of the cycle to the individual's passage through the life cycle (29, 139). But changes in family structure can be kept distinct from changes in family personnel (29). Families can replenish their membership without undergoing changes in structure, and they can spawn other families that pass through divergent sequences.

Fortes's former assumption that in each society there is a single, uniform developmental sequence through which all domestic groups pass may also blind us to historical changes in domestic organization. If we order all the different household forms we observe at one point in time along a single developmental sequence, we may well fail to realize that more recently formed households are embarking on a different sequence than older households. To recognize historical change we must collect longitudinal data on domestic groups by utilizing historical sources, such as household registers, or by reconstructing the histories of individuals and families through retrospective accounts. By using the technique of cohort analysis developed by demographers, we can discern whether members of successive cohorts (whether these are birth cohorts, marriage cohorts, or whatever other cohorts emerge as historically significant in a particular population) have the same or different domestic histories.

Despite these limitations, the concept of the developmental cycle of domestic groups has been extremely useful in displaying the impact of events such as marriage, birth, death, and division of property on the composition of families and households. Although the timing and sequencing of these events have been shown to be complexly shaped by a wide range of cultural, political, and economic processes, these events clearly mediate between the complex causal factors and the shape of domestic groups.

ECONOMIC DETERMINANTS Economic variables are predominant among those adduced to explain family and household structure. At times a diverse mix of "economic" or "ecological" factors, including labor needs in production, defensive needs, care of children, taxation, and conscription practices of the state, are cited as the "underlying functional reasons" for the presence of a particular type of domestic group (72, p. 142). As often, however, one economic factor is singled out as the primary or causally prior determinant of domestic group structure.

Property is a common focus in discussions of family form, although it may be approached in different ways. One approach, which I have already touched upon in my discussion of definitions, views property relationships from a jural perspective and therefore does not cast it as an economic determinant. A second approach treats property as a resource and goal which shapes the actions of maximizing individuals. The two views are well illustrated in the literature on Chinese families, where most researchers (1, 28, 29, 51, 158) appear to agree on the pivotal role of property, but disagree over the manner by which property rights are transmitted from one generation to the next and, consequently, over what determines the timing of property division. According to Freedman (50, 51) and Ahern (1), the Chinese father has jural authority over the family property until his death. Cohen (28, 29), in contrast, maintains that as soon as a son marries he becomes his father's jural equal and can demand division of the family estate. For Freedman, the greater the authority of the father, that is, the more his authority is buttressed by his political and economic position in extradomestic spheres, the longer he can delay division of the estate by his sons. For Cohen, what determines the timing of division is not the extent of the father's authority over sons who wish to be free of it, but the economic self-interest of the sons. The pursuit of this disagreement, which may derive in part from actual regional differences, would hardly seem to be productive as it would lead only to further reifying the faulty dichotomy of jural and economic spheres which muddles discussions of property relationships. To view property either as the mere vehicle of jural relationships (46) or as an economic relationship between people and things (29) is to misconstrue what is more correctly an "entire system of rules, rights, and expectations of role" (73, p. 207) or a "system of social relationships" (16, p. 204) which must be explained rather than adduced as explanation.

In the same light, we must eschew narrow conceptions of property relationships as man-land relationships determined by "ecological factors." The limitations of a narrow ecological framework are well documented in G. A. Collier's (30) study of family organization and land tenure in six Maya communities. Although he began with a cultural ecological framework emphasizing the local adaptation of people to resources, Collier became increasingly aware that an adequate explanation of the relation between family organization and land tenure required an understanding of the region-wide system of interethnic and interclass relationships linking families to hamlet, township, state, and national processes. Goldschmidt & Kunkel (55) reach a similar conclusion in their cross-cultural survey of the relationship between degree of land scarcity, pattern of land inheritance, and "family structure" (by which they mean household composition) in 46 peasant communities. They find that the "ecological context" suggested by E. R. Wolf (159) cannot explain the different patterns of land inheritance in these communities because there is no conclusive pattern of association between land scarcity and either residence or inheritance patterns. Consequently, they direct our attention to Wolf's (159) "hierarchical social context" by suggesting several ways in which the relationship between peasants and the elites who control state organization (and thereby land tenure patterns) shapes the form of inheritance and, consequently, peasant family structure.

Goody's (61, 62) grand theory of the evolution of domestic organization also focusses on the transmission of property as a key feature of the domestic domain. Goody proposes to explain not just the structure of domestic groups, but a whole cluster of interlinked elements, including marriage transactions, inheritance patterns, descent groups, form of marriage, domestic roles, and kinship terminology. Central to his theory is the contrast he draws between African bridewealth societies and European and Asian dowry societies, in which two very different forms of marriage transactions generate far-reaching consequences for domestic organization. Bridewealth, as a transaction between the kin of the groom and the kin of the bride, forms part of a circulating societal fund which has a leveling effect on wealth differences. In contrast, dowry, as a type of premortem inheritance of the bride, sets up a conjugal fund for a married couple, thereby reproducing wealth differences. As different mechanisms for redistributing property, these marriage transactions are linked by Goody (61) to other aspects of social organization. Dowry systems are seen as inherently bilateral, because they distribute rights in a manner that does not link property to sex. Furthermore, as a form of "diverging devolution," dowry entails the transmission of property outside the unilineal descent group, thus weakening the corporate nature of these descent groups. In comparison, inheritance within the unilineal descent group in African bridewealth societies strengthens their corporate nature. Finally, bridewealth and dowry have different consequences for the "domestic role compendia" (62, p. 41). The status of women as heirs to significant property in a dowry system leads to monogamy (sometimes accompanied by concubinage), the concept of conjugal love, and the individualization of the mother (61, p. 37; 62, pp. 42, 51). In contrast, bridewealth is associated with polygyny, diffuse domestic relationships, and the classificatory role of mother.

There can be little doubt that Goody's typological scheme deserves to be a major focus of discussion and research on marriage transactions and domestic organization for some time to come. Most provocative are the questions raised about how the transmission of property—whether in the form of marriage payments, premortem inheritance, or postmortem inheritance—shapes both the internal structure of domestic units and economic and political processes usually construed as external to the domestic domain. What remains to be deliberated and further researched is the empirical generality and analytic utility of his typology. For example, there is ample evidence in the ethnographic literature on bridewealth transactions in cognatic societies (e.g. 6) and in the more "loosely structured" unilineal descent societies of highlands New Guinea (e.g. 149), which does not appear to fit well with his African bridewealth model. Indeed, one wonders whether we are due for another round of debate over the utility of "African models" as was our fate in the case of unilineal descent systems.

Even more disputable is Goody's characterization of dowry in European and Asian societies. Accounts of dowry transactions in Japan (140), southern Italy (33), and China (93) do not sustain Goody's claim that dowry is best seen as a form of female inheritance of "male property." Even Goody's coeditor Tambiah (151) cites critical differences among the South Asian societies of northern India, southern India, Ceylon, and Burma in jural conceptions of female rights to property, in the manner in which property is actually transmitted to women, and in the consequences of these transmissions for domestic organization. These recalcitrant cases, of which I suspect we will hear more in the future, are ample reminders that the task awaiting us is to "decompose the property of the family or the conjugal estate into its explicitly recognized components and see what rights husband and wife enjoy in relation to them at marriage and divorce" (151, p. 153).

Although it requires refinement, Goody's contrast between bridewealth and dowry, at least as two ideal types, provides a promising insight into the impact of marriage and its accompanying transactions in the shaping of domestic relationships. His causal model in which technological factors of production are the primary movers in the evolution of domestic organization probably will not stand so well against the test of time. His attempt to derive historical inferences from cross-sectional data by subjecting correlations between mode of property transmission and societal institutions to path analysis does little justice to the complexity of historical developments that have led to the kind of dowry system he describes [see Stone (146, 147) for a discussion of the significant changes that occurred in early modern England with regard to the control of property by family heads and women's legal rights to property]. The problem, of course, is inherent in any evolutionary scheme that rests on a crude succession of types. For however sophisticated the quantitative hardware, one cannot derive historical process from ahistorical, cross-sectional data.

There is a final issue that I fear will be overlooked in the debate over Goody's typology and evolutionary scheme, because it is so embedded within Goody's discussion that it is likely to go unnoticed. In Goody's evolutionary account of the shift from a bridewealth to a dowry system, radical transformations occur in mode of production, division of labor, stratification, property relations, centralization of political authority, marriage forms, kin terminology, and domestic role relationships. Yet one thing remains constant: the nuclear family is the basic productive unit of society (62, p. 20). Because he sees the nuclear family as everywhere and for all time the basic and natural unit of society, Goody never feels compelled to explain why, when intensive agriculture created greater production surpluses and differences in styles of life, people became concerned to reproduce these life-styles in their own progeny as *against* the members of the lineage or other kinship or locality grouping. For Goody, there is no need to explain the emergence of the nuclear family as a socially and culturally significant unit because it was already, and always, present. In the final section of this paper, I will return to a critical commentary of this assumption, which is held by many more anthropologists than just Goody.

A second productive resource cited as a determinant of household structure is labor. Labor requirements are singled out by Pasternak, Ember & Ember (108) as the most powerful determinant of the formation of extended family households. Using a randomly selected sample of 60 societies, they test their hypothesis that

> ... extended family households are likely to emerge and prevail in a society when (in the absence of slave or hired labor) work outside the home makes it difficult for a mother to tend children and/or perform her other regular time-consuming domestic tasks, or when the outside activities of a father make it difficult for him to perform his subsistence work (108, p. 121).

They assume that in the absence of such activity requirements, extended family households would not emerge in any society because they would be plagued by the "ordinary difficulties of extended family dynamics," including jealousies and problems of authority (108, p. 121). Having shown that the statistical association between presence of "incompatible activity requirements" and presence of "extended family households" is stronger than that predicted by Nimkoff & Middleton's (103) hypothesis (which attributes extended family households to agricultural subsistence), they conclude that labor requirements per se are better predictors of extended family households than type of subsistence activity. The problem with this conclusion, as the authors themselves point out (108, p. 121), is that they have no justification for positing a causal relationship between the purported independent variable (incompatible activity requirements) and the purported dependent variable (presence of extended family households) on the basis of correlational evidence. Hence, they must resort to insisting that it is more plausible that incompatible activity requirements cause extended family households rather than vice versa. But it is just as reasonable to argue that extended family households encourage women to work outside the home, particularly if we accept Pasternak, Ember & Ember's characterization of such households as riddled with tensions and conflicts. Even more dubious is their construction of arbitrary, crude measures such as the presence of "incompatible activity requirements," which they define for women as "work away from the home for more than half the day for at least (cumulatively) 30 days of the year" (108, p. 118).

The most vexatious issue that Pasternak, Ember & Ember and the others (55, 62) who attempt statistical cross-societal comparisons encounter is whether the units they have selected are appropriate for comparative purposes. The evidence that societies contain different frequencies of a range of household types surely challenges the classification of whole societies into two categories of those with "extended family households" versus those with "independent family households." Our goal of understanding and explaining domestic organization may be better achieved by investigations of the diversity of domestic units in societies and the articulation of these domestic units with one another, rather than by comparisons that reduce whole societies to a single household type, family structure, or marriage transaction.

Just as labor requirements are used to explain cross-societal variations in domestic groups, so a large number of researchers have used it to explain the frequency with which a particular household type appears in a society or segment of a society. In reviewing ecological studies, Netting (102) cites several studies which purportedly show that household composition among horticulturists and agriculturalists varies with the type and amount of labor required for effective crop production. In his own study, for example, he attributes the differences between the large, extended families of shifting cultivators and the nuclear family households of intensive agriculturalists in the same Nigerian plateau environment to differing labor requirements (100, 101). Along the same lines, Sahlins (119) argues that under conditions of widely dispersed resources the extended family provides a more efficient productive unit. Nakane (97) attributes the larger-than-average mean household size in two Japanese communities to the labor requirements of their productive activities (fishing in one, silk cultivation in the other), and Dorjahn (39) cites labor demands of upland rice farming as the prime factor in household size and type among the Mayoso Temne. In the case of the Chinese family, both Pasternak (107) and Cohen (29) stress the need for the efficient allocation of labor as a primary determinant of family form.

In all these studies, the authors assume that once having identified the productive activity of the household, they can ascertain the technologically determined labor requirements of that activity and proceed to show that the household efficiently meets these labor requirements. They fail to explain adequately, however, that it is not merely the technological requirements of production which necessitate a particular household type, but the entire manner in which production is socially organized. In other words, a productive activity can be accomplished by a variety of household types depending on how that production is socially organized, including the division of labor by sex and age, the use of hired labor, cooperation in productive tasks among households, and the exchange of labor between households. Like Chayanov and Sahlins, these authors are inclined to assume that the household is a self-contained labor unit, and so they fail to investigate sufficiently the existence of other forms of productive organization. Yet the salient units engaged in production may not be the same at different phases of the productive cycle; for example, different social groups may engage in the transplanting, weeding, and harvesting of rice (32). Once we realize that a particular productive enterprise can be accomplished by a variety of productive units, depending on how production is organized, it becomes apparent that to attribute household composition to labor requirements is to beg the question, because to do so we have to assume the prior existence of an entire institutional framework for production (38). To overcome this overly restricted focus on technologically derived factors of production we need to investigate a wider range of social, political, and economic forces shaping productive relationships both within and between domestic groups.

SOCIAL STRATIFICATION AND THE DIVERSITY OF DOMESTIC GROUPS Our past tendency to neglect stratification in the analysis of domestic organization seems to have derived from our notion of the basic homogeneity of the communities we have studied. In the case of peasant communities, for example, the contrast between the peasants we have studied and the landlords whom we generally have not has made the peasants look rather uniform. Hence, even though Freedman (50, 51) suggests that it was among the landed gentry in China that one found a significant proportion of joint families, while among the peasantry one found only nuclear and stem families, Cohen (29) finds it easy to dismiss stratification as a significant factor in his village because it contains only "dirt farmers," none of whom could be construed as members of an elite gentry. Cohen is right that wealth differences among the villages of Yen-liao are small in comparison to wealth differences between peasants and landed gentry. But his own data (29, pp. 239–42) indicate that per capita landholdings are consistently larger among the tobacco-growing households, many of whom also have diversified into capitalized, nonagricultural enterprises, than among the rice-growing households whose members appear to provide the hired labor for the larger, tobacco-growing households.

The failure to take adequate account of the internal differentiation among the peasantry has been redressed in a number of recent studies (95, 129, 130, 140, 156). As Mintz states, " . . . peasantries nowhere form a homogeneous mass or agglomerate, but are always and everywhere typified themselves by internal differentiation along many lines" (95, p. 3).

Part of the difficulty in recognizing significant wealth differences which generate structural differences in the households of a peasant community stems from their social mobility. Since peasant households function as small production units with extremely limited resources and are greatly subject to the forces of nature, the market, and the state, they experience some degree of random oscillation in social mobility (129, p. 112). Among the Russian peasantry in the early twentieth century, for example, there was considerable multidirectional and cyclical mobility of households (129). T. C. Smith (140) also characterizes the situation in Tokugawa Japan as one in which farm families were not likely to enjoy an economic advantage over their neighbors for many years. On the other hand, it would be wrong to conclude that because of this mobility observed differences in wealth are mere transitory advantages that have no consequence for domestic organization. Despite the mobility in Smith's village, the highest probability was for a family to remain in the same landholding category from one tax register to another—an average interval of 12 years (140, p. 119).

Significant differences in wealth among peasants also may be overlooked because they are so often obscured by kinship relationships which bind the landed to the landless and the land-rich to the land-poor (95, 129, 130). Consequential wealth differences may exist between the smaller coresidential units of a single kin-based compound (54) or between brothers who head the main and branch households of a family (140).

The complexity of the internal differentiation of the peasantry, or of any kind of community, should not deter us from investigating its relation to the variations we observe in the composition and internal structure of domestic groups, as well as in their external relationships. Indeed, it is this very complexity—the fluctuations in size and wealth, the social mobility, and the kin ties that bind together households in different strata—that underlines our need to investigate the economic and social interdependence of different sectors of society.

Variations over Time

In considering recent publications which address the topic of change in family and household structure, I have gone beyond the boundaries of our own discipline to include the burgeoning literature being produced by family historians. Given the limitations of space and my acquaintance with this literature, I have not attempted a broadly inclusive review of the history of the family. My purpose instead is to evaluate some of the historical studies that speak directly to our theoretical interest in changing domestic organization. Of course, as anthropologists become increasingly immersed in the study of literate societies with recorded pasts, an acquaintance and facility with the historian's methods of analyzing documentary materials becomes a necessity. My review of the work of historians, however, is intended partly as a didactic exercise directed toward exhibiting the predominant conceptions and theoretical orientations guiding our own analyses of family and kinship change as much as theirs, since many of their notions have been borrowed from anthropology and sociology. Indeed, the common guiding frameworks may be more easily discerned in the context of a newly developing field of inquiry such as the history of the family. After I discuss the methods and analytical strategies employed by family historians, I move on to a review of anthropological studies of family and kinship change.

THE HISTORY OF THE FAMILY   The emergence of historians' interest in the family is properly placed within the context of a more general trend in historical research, the shift away from a history focused primarily on the description and interpretation of particular historical events—a history that has been dominated by the ideas and actions of a few—to a history concerned with the everyday lives of the many (118). The "new social history" necessarily has been accompanied by a change in the kinds of data sources and methods of analysis historians employ. The social historian sifts through records of births, marriages, deaths, and household lists contained in censuses, parish registers, and government reports, rather than through political treatises, autobiographies, and philosophical tracts. Given the kinds of events in the lives of the commonfolk which get recorded, much of the new social history has been directed toward reconstructing the family experience of historical populations.[2]

To utilize quantifiable enumerative materials, historians of the family have added two methods of analysis to their more traditional tool kit. These are: (a) the method of family reconstitution developed by the French historical demographer Louis Henry, which entails reconstruction of the demographic history of individual families from entries in parish registers (64, 161, 162); (b) aggregate data analysis, which uses nominal census lists or surveys taken at different points in time to construct a picture of statistical trends over time (10, 69, 86, 132, 133). Historical demographers employ these methods to discern demographic changes in death, birth, and illegitimacy rates, age at marriage and other events that have consequences for family size and composition. By supplementing the quantitative results achieved by these methods of analysis with qualitative source materials, family historians attempt to describe and analyze family and household patterns in different time periods and different locales, although primarily in Western Europe and the United States.

An emphasis on quantitative analysis is reflected in the work of the Cambridge Group for the History of Population and Social Structure co-

---

[2] A review of the *Journal of Family History,* the *History of Childhood Quarterly,* the *Journal of Interdisciplinary History,* the *Annales* (France), and *Past and Present* (England) confirms this concern with the family.

directed by Laslett. The main thrust of Laslett's work (85–87) is the refutation of the theory that a shift from an extended family system to a nuclear family system accompanied European industrialization. His discovery that early census materials show the small, nuclear family household to have predominated in England before the industrial revolution is ample evidence of the contribution that historical demography can make to the construction and revision of hypotheses about the history of the family. Having found similar evidence of the predominance of small households elsewhere in preindustrial Western Europe and even in Tokugawa Japan (76), however, Laslett boldly extends his thesis to assert that "little variation in family organization can be found in human history" (86, p. 1x). While he is aware of the distinction between household size and family organization, at times Laslett lapses into the unfortunate practice of confusing family organization with residence patterns. Because he relies primarily on aggregate data on household size and composition, Laslett's work suffers from a narrowness as well as a plethora of methodological and conceptual problems [see (12) for an excellent critique of Laslett's work]. A few of these problems are worth listing here because they plague the work of other quantitative historians of the family: equating residence patterns with family structure and even kinship organization, paying little heed to relationships between residential units, failing to consider regional diversity, failing to take into consideration the developmental cycle of domestic groups, and making unwarranted assumptions about the common criteria for defining households used by census takers in different societies.

These conceptual and methodological muddles are well illustrated by the literature on the history of the black family in the United States. In reassessing the slave experience through reconstructing the history of black families, scholars like Gutman (69, 70) assert that, contrary to received wisdom, blacks in the United States lived predominantly in two-parent households both before and after emancipation. Gutman's figures certainly attest to the need for a reassessment of popular notions of the black family. But he and other family historians (53) muddle the issue by assuming that if husbands are present in the household, they play a central role in the family and, therefore, that these cannot be "matrifocal," "matriarchal," or female-headed households. Yet the point that presence or absence in a household is quite a different thing from an individual's structural role in the family was made convincingly clear 20 years ago by R. T. Smith (136).

Fortunately, not all family historians who rely on quantitative methods suffer from these failings. Some historians of the black family (77, 131) are quite cognizant of the distinction between household composition and family structure; and those anthropologists whose works appear in historical anthologies have tried to drive home this distinction (60, 71). The most analytically refined works seem to come from historians who use a broader range of source materials in conducting intensive research on a specific locality at a single point in time, thus avoiding an unhealthy reliance on aggregate figures which obscure substantial differences among strata, regions, and ethnic groups. In some historical studies of the family, the authors take into account the developmental cycle of domestic groups, even in using aggregate data (10, 13), place the household within its proper kinship context (82, 156), attend to local variations (65, 142), and pay heed to the influence of other cultural domains, such as religion, on family ideology (7, 88). Greven (67, 68), for example, utilizes both the genealogical histories of specific families and aggregate data on the entire population in his case study of population, land, and family in a seventeenth-century New England town. His reconstruction of the household and kinship networks in the community enables him to interpret the organizational structure of individual households within the context of their relationships with other households. Similarly, Kent's study (82) of fifteenth-century aristocratic families in Florence shows the relations among the individual, household, and lineage to be more subtle than is suggested by overly dichotomized conceptual frameworks which portray the household and lineage as inherently antagonistic structures. Finally, historical research on inheritance systems in different regions of Western Europe (14, 153) promises to provide us with useful analyses of the interplay between the inheritance laws of the state, local customs, and the actual inheritance practices of different sectors of society.

Like anthropologists, social historians are searching for analytically productive ways to identify and describe family change. Stone's (146, 147) efforts to display the changes in English family structure in the early modern period lead him to the construction of a typology of three successive family types. While there is much that can be objected to in his interpretation of evidence (154), his attention to public ideologies of the family as well as to family functions contributes much richer material for an analysis of historical change than the absorption with surface level similarities of demographic statistics can offer.

The most formidable problem which confronts historians of the family is the matching of data sources with the right kinds of questions. Where they are least successful in their endeavors is when, like Laslett (86) and Gutman (69, 70), they attempt to answer questions about family structure for which their quantitative sources are ill suited, or when, like Shorter (132, 133), they try to "extract emotional motivations from unwilling statistics" (C. Daniels, unpublished paper). They are most successful when, like T. C. Smith (140), they make creative but judicious use of quantitative materials to calculate measures of age-specific mortality and fertility, life expectancy, nuptiality, and birth spacing, and supplementing these with literary and legal records, arrive at conclusions about population growth, infanticide, and the dynamics of the household in a specific locality.

Although the research of historians has certainly yielded much of substantive interest and significance for discussions of the history of the Western family, the implications of these results for our understanding of family change are obscured by the absence of a coherent theoretical framework. A rather odd grab-bag of conceptual tools and analytic strategies has been lifted from the social sciences by historians. Perhaps most ill-advised is the proclivity of some social historians (86, 87, 132, 133) to infer changes in sentiments and cultural conceptions from alterations in demographic patterns. Because the illiterate masses leave behind mainly vital statistics which do not speak of attitudes and beliefs, they are particularly vulnerable to this kind of interpretation. Given the available source materials, the adoption of psychoanalytic models to speculate about the historical consequences of childhood experiences in different periods also seems particularly inappropriate. Few historians go as far as deMause (35) to propose a "psychogenic theory of history" which applies Freudian and neo-Freudian theories to the history of childhood, but an emphasis on socialization and an implicit, if undeveloped, theory of the importance of early childhood experience in shaping personality and culture is present in the works of other family historians (86, 87). It is because of this socialization bias that Laslett chooses as the predominant familial type in a society the form in which the largest percentage of children have grown up "in their most impressionable years" (86, p. 67). This reinvention of personality and culture theory leads historians like Laslett to place an inordinate emphasis on a single family function to the detriment of other, no less important, functions (12, 156).

The most popular import from the social sciences, however, has been a somewhat loosely conceptualized, Parsonian equilibrium model of society. In general, family structure and function are seen as adjusting to the shifting external conditions of the economy and political organization (11, 118, 146, 147). Economic factors may be singled out as having a major causal influence on the family, as in Greven's study (67) where the control of land by the town's founding fathers leads to the establishment of "extended patriarchal families." In any event, alterations in family form and functions are portrayed as attempts to make domestic relationships more congruent with the outside social environment. I include within the general category of a Parsonian equilibrium framework the "actor-oriented" approaches (4, 5, 118) which purport to explain particular family structures by reconstructing the social options open to maximizing individuals. For despite the interest of historians such as Anderson (4, 5) in decision-making processes and the inclusion of formalist premises such as "all actors have a number of goals, the attainment of which would maximize their satisfactions or psychic rewards" (4, p. 8), in the end the explanation of family relationships is a functionalist one. Hence to explain the high incidence of coresidence of married children and parents in the early industrial English town of Preston, Anderson (4) cites the economic benefits for both the married couple and parents. Much rarer are the historians like N. Z. Davis who recognize the conflicts and tensions as well as the consistencies between family life and political, economic, and religious institutions. Davis's discussion (34) of the disjuncture between "privatistic family values" and the "more corporate values" held by the same families in early modern France conveys a more refined notion of cultural systems than do the analyses of family historians who are inclined toward tightly integrated functionalist schemes.

Several family historians (e.g. 63, 133) have been attracted to the simple dichotomies of traditional vs modern, rural vs urban, mechanical solidarity vs organic solidarity and instrumental vs affective families. While this is hardly the place to review the shortcomings of a modernization framework, suffice it to say that it is somewhat ironic that historians would find a static functionalist perspective so appealing just at a time when anthropologists and sociologists are searching for more dynamic models of society.

As I implied in the beginning of this section, the answer to the question of why historians have not been more successful in integrating their findings into a unified theory of family change lies, at least in part, in the shortcomings of our own discipline. It is to this body of literature that I now turn.

ANTHROPOLOGICAL STUDIES OF CHANGE IN FAMILY AND HOUSEHOLD   A good deal of anthropological publications of family and household change can be categorized as refutations or at least refinements of a Parsons-Redfield-Durkheim model of the evolution of the family in industrial-urban society. Hammel & Yarbrough (75) summarize well the received hypothesis of family breakdown and the contrasting view of the family as a durable institution:

> ... a conservative and often romantic view has prevailed, beginning perhaps with LePlay and Durkheim, that upheaval, social change, and increasing division of labor destroy fundamental values, divide the primary group, and disrupt the relationships between its members. The family, in particular, has been seen as a victim, reduced from a solidary fortress protecting the social and psychic welfare of its members to a temporary abode for transient seekers of self-interest, losing its function as the incubator of social virtue to the market place and the peer group. More recent, and it is probably fair to say, more empirical research has suggested that the family is an extraordinarily durable institution, even under conditions of extreme social change and social mobility (75, p. 145).

Hammel (71) concludes that industrialization, urbanization, and integration into a money economy have not weakened the Balkan extended family, but rather have strengthened it. Similarly, Carlos & Sellers (24), in reviewing publications on the family in Latin America, contend that "the modernization process is being molded to existing family and kinship institutions and areas of traditional family function" (24, p. 113). They suggest that Goode's (57) propositions about industrialization and family change be modified because studies in Latin America disclose that geographic mobility and class differential mobility do not weaken intimacy and contact in the kin network and that industrialization does not create a new value structure emphasizing achievement over ascription. Other researchers (150) report that kinship ties endure under conditions of social change and that new functions are assumed by kinship units. Still others (106, 135) find that in developing nations such as India it is particularly entrepreneurs and the leaders of modern industry who are members of joint families. Hence, the most "well-adjusted" and financially successful sectors of society have a family structure that modernization theory would characterize as "traditional." At the same time, research in rural areas confirms that migration and increasing integration into a market economy do not inevitably spell decline in family unity. Urban migration may increase family solidarity and widen kin ties in the rural community (19), and wage-labor migration may contribute to the maintenance of extended family households (104, 105).

The above studies provide a necessary corrective to the excessively broad hypothesis that with "modernization" kinship structures decline. At the same time, however, they often replicate the shortcomings of those whom they criticize by using the same problematic terms, like "modernization" (24, p. 114). At other times, the argument over whether extended families deteriorate in the face of industrial change seems little more than an outcome of the inconsistent usage of the term "extended family." Firth, Hubert & Forge (44) point out that there is no inherent contradiction between the view that modern industrial society favors the development of the nuclear family at the expense of the extended family and the view that the extended family remains important. They suggest that it all depends on what we mean by the extended family. To resolve what they see as a needless debate, Firth, Hubert & Forge suggest that we distinguish between two uses of the term by asking where authority lies. In *extended families,* authority normally resides with the senior male; in a set of *extrafamilial kin,* authority is dispersed. Having made this distinction, they concur with Parsons on the relative isolation of the nuclear family in urban-industrial society, because

... except for family firms and some control of joint property, decisions in the set of extra-familial kin in a modern Western urban society are made in nuclear family units, however influenced they may be by kin ties outside (44, p. 456).

Firth, Hubert & Forge are right that some of the debate is created by researchers who tend to overstate the significance of kin ties. But in addition to its androcentric bias, their distinction gives undue weight to centralized authority as the defining feature of the extended family. Kin groups can make decisions and take cooperative action without a central authority. And even when a dispersed family is not specifically a political or economic *group,* this does not mean that it cannot be used for political or economic purposes (15). It is wrong, therefore, to accept the absence of kin groups resembling those found in lineage societies as evidence of a decline in the importance of the extended family.

If we are to refine our analysis of family and household change, we must begin to ask new questions of our data. Questions as to whether or not the extended family or kinship in general has declined in industrial-urban society or whether the family has endured even under conditions of rapid social change have impeded our progress toward a more refined analysis of change. After all, structural change and structural continuity in family and kinship institutions are not mutually exclusive phenomena (135, 163). One way to move toward a more refined analysis of change in family and kinship is to examine the relationship between change in the ideology of family and kinship and change in actual institutional arrangements. In the case of the Balkan zadruga, Hammel (71) concludes that recent changes can be attributed largely to alterations in demographic rates and external constraints while the underlying kinship principles (e.g. virifocality, agnatic bias, patrifocality, and lineage organization) have remained relatively unmodified. Brown (20) suggests similarly that we cannot assume that industrial-urbanization in Japan has necessarily resulted in the demise of the dozoku (a group of households related in a network of main and branch ties) even though the classic type of dozoku with its economic correlates is no longer viable. The ideology which has yielded dozoku organization can persist despite alterations in the observable organizational forms.

The critical question which arises when we employ this analytical strategy is how do we identify the underlying, ideological principles of forms like the Balkan zadruga and the Japanese dozoku to discern whether ideological change has occurred? For the zadruga, the underlying kinship principles extracted by Hammel (71) consist of an assortment of things, some of which appear to be normative rules or preferences (patrifocality), other of which are observable behavioral tendencies (agnatic bias), and still others of which (virifocality) are ambiguously either observable patterns or normative rules.

As some of the basic principles are outcomes of other principles when they are combined with certain demographic and social constraints, the meaning of "ideological principles" is equivocal.

The assessment of ideological change, of course, is difficult where the anthropologist, like the historian, does not have direct evidence of former cultural ideals, values, and meanings. Most commonly, the anthropologist is forced to reconstruct past ideologies from contemporary accounts. If he then compares this abstracted ideology of the past with the more richly contextualized contemporary ideology, his evaluation of change may be limited by the vagueness of his constructed model of the past. If we are to bring to our analysis the knowledge that change in observable behavior does not necessarily mean that cultural ideologies have altered, we need a conceptual framework that can help us to systematically differentiate and display the interaction between these aspects of family and kinship. The great promise of such an analytic strategy lies in its capacity to identify the dynamic tension between ideology and action as a possible source of change (163), thereby transcending the limitations of an analytic framework that invariably attributes change to the constraints imposed by factors external to family, household, and kinship.

Variations in Domestic Organization: An Underview

Having surveyed the recent literature on variations in domestic groups across societies, within societies, and over time, I want to pause here to address the question of what holds all these works together. Do these diverse inquiries into the structure and function of domestic groups share any mutual conceptions or analytic categories? The answer, I contend, is yes; however, to unearth this common ground we must first turn the question around and ask not what we see in common in the explanations, but what we see in common in the depictions of the phenomena being explained. In other words, when anthropologists treat the family and household as the thing to be explained, the dependent variable, how do they describe its features?[3]

My preceding commentary by now must have made it apparent that when they attempt to explain variations in domestic groups most authors settle on the genealogical composition of the domestic group as its most salient feature. Terms such as "nuclear family" and "nuclear family household," or "stem family" and "stem family household" classify a do-

[3]I should point out here that there are anthropological studies which treat the family or household as an independent variable, that is, as the explanation for such things as child-rearing practices and personality structure. I have not included these studies in this review.

mestic unit on the basis of the genealogically defined kin types contained within it, regardless of whether the unit is a coresidential group or a spatially dispersed family. In addition, the group is usually labeled according to the tie between its most genealogically "close" members, because it is presumed that this relationship forms its structural core. If it contains two adult brothers, their wives and children, it is labeled a fraternal-joint family or household. In other words, for a fraternal-joint household, the assumption is that the brother-brother relationship is the structurally dominant relationship which binds together the rest of the members of the household. Furthermore, in studies that consider the developmental cycle of the domestic group, what is usually described as changing over the course of time is the genealogical composition of the group (10, 48, 72, 129).

The classification of households and families on the basis of their genealogical makeup conveys the implicit notion that there is a fundamental similarity in the structures of the units which share the same label. In cross-societal comparisons or historical investigations, the presumption is that a stem family at one time and place has the same organizational structure as a stem family at another time and place. Yet obviously there is more to "family structure" than genealogical composition. The structure of a family, household, or any other social unit is not merely the sum of its genealogical ties, but the total configuration of social relationships among its members. There is a plethora of early and recent ethnographies (29, 59, 136, 144, 145, 149) which provide rich accounts of the continually shifting relationships of authority, influence, emotional solidarity, and conflict which characterize families and households. And yet when *explanations* of these variations in domestic relationships are attempted, the tendency is to divest them of their interactional and meaningful dimensions, leaving only the genealogical dimension as the salient feature to be compared and explained. Aside from comparing the configuration of actual domestic relationships, comparative studies might alternatively treat the family as a ". . . normative system composed of those interrelated norms which define the proper modes of interactions between persons performing familial roles" (137, pp. 59). Unfortunately, when a term is proposed as a label for a dynamic system of normative role relationships, as in the case of the term "matrifocal family structure" (136), it is often mistaken for a description of household composition (83).

The failure to bring into our comparative analyses the dynamic configuration of role relationships of families and households extends to relationships between domestic groups. As I explained in my critique of explanations that center on the labor requirements of households, to focus on households as self-contained units which fulfill some set of specified domestic functions may be altogether the wrong strategy. This is true of sets of households that share a corporate identity as well as those that do not, but which may have other significant relationships. It is too often thought that by labelling a domestic unit a "stem-family" we have adequately described both its internal organizational structure and the relationships that articulate it with groups and individuals outside it. But if we compare, for example, stem family households in eighteenth century Austria (10) with stem family households in eighteenth century Japan (140), the economic relationships between households in these two societies are clearly different.

One kind of analytic advance we can make is illustrated by Cohen's (29) dissection of Chinese family organization. He observes that while the Chinese family (chia) is a discrete kin group,

> it can display a great deal of variation in residential arrangements and in the economic ties of its members. For purposes of analysis the chia estate, economy, and group can be considered as three basic components in chia organization (29, p. 58).

The chia estate is "that body of holdings to which the process of family division is applicable," the chia group is "made up of persons who have rights of one sort or another to the chia estate at the time of family division," and the chia economy "refers to the exploitation of the chia estate as well as to other income-producing activities linked to its exploitation through remittances and a common budgetary arrangement" (29, p. 59). By examining variations in the connections between chia components, Cohen succeeds in clarifying some of the problems encountered when the Chinese family is described in terms that wrongly assume an ideal chia in which the estate, group, and economy are unified.

An analytic framework such as Cohen's, of course, is useful only when applied where the common ownership of property is the key element binding together domestic units. Where this is not the case, as among landless peasants, hunter-gatherers, or wage-laborers, we may usefully identify other significant components of family organization, including the commensal group, the production group, and the budget group in which reciprocal exchange occurs without accounting (cf 90, 128). However, as I have already remarked, the aggregate of people engaged in any of these activities may change throughout the production cycle, the exchange cycle, or the individual's life cycle. Consequently, it seems more analytically strategic to begin with an investigation of the *activities* that are central to the domestic relationships in each particular society, rather than with its domestic groups. If we start by identifying the important productive, ritual, political, and exchange transactions in a society and only then proceed to ask what kinds of kinship or locality-based units engage in these activities, and in what manner, we decrease the likelihood of overlooking some of these salient units, particularly those that do not fit our conventional notion of a household.

A consideration of the second area of common ground in the literature reviewed takes us back to the conception of the "domestic" which I said lies at the heart of definitions of the family and household. I observed that in spite of their imprecision, definitions of "domestic" activities, "domestic" groups, and the "domestic" domain coverge on two sets of functional activities: food production and consumption and social reproduction. Now that we have seen how anthropologists describe and explain the structures of social units which engage in these activities, we can elicit a further component in the conception of the domestic. This facet derives from the conceptual opposition drawn between the "domestic" domain and the "politico-jural" domain. The most ardent advocate of the heuristic advantages of this distinction is Fortes, who views human social organization everywhere as "a balance, stable or not, between the political order—Aristotle's polis—and the familial or domestic order—the oikos—a balance between polity and kinship" (47, p. 14). For Fortes, the two domains can be "analytically and indeed empirically distinguished even where the two orders appear to be fused together in a single kinship polity, as among the Australian aborigines" (47, p. 15).

In unilineal descent societies like Ashanti, the family and interpersonal relations among kin and affines belong to the domestic domain, while the lineage belongs to the politico-jural domain. The critical feature differentiating the two domains is the type of normative premise which regulates each domain. Underlying the politico-jural domain are jural norms guaranteed by "external" or "public" sanctions which may ultimately entail force. In contrast, the domestic or familial domain is constrained by "private," affective and moral norms, at the root of which is the fundamental axiom of prescriptive altruism (46, pp. 89, 250–51).

Fortes warns against the reification of this methodological and analytic distinction by stating that "the actualities of kinship relations and kinship behaviors are compounded of elements derived from both domains" (46, p. 251). But when the distinction is used by other anthropologists, his caveats often fall by the wayside. There is, in fact, a tendency for the terms to be employed to refer to whole social relations (rather than to their contexts and implications) and to entire social institutions (rather than to facets of social institutions). Moreover, as Bender perspicaciously notes, most social scientists employ the term "domestic" as an unmodified folk concept to refer to "those activities associated with the household or home" and to "female activities more than male activities" (8, p. 498).

The pervasive and unreflective usage of this distinction in anthropological studies has had an important and as yet little recognized consequence for research on families and households. Two studies by anthropologists who otherwise represent divergent conceptual approaches will illustrate this consequence.

Pasternak's (107) study of family and lineage organization in two Taiwanese villages exhibits a common unevenness found in many ethnographies of family and lineage organization. In separate sections of his book, he proposes to explain differences in the strength of agnatic ties in the lineages of the two villages and differences in the frequency of joint families in the same two villages. If we compare his two discussions, we notice a marked contrast between his analysis of agnatic organization and his analysis of family form. In the case of lineage organization, Pasternak considers several possible sources of variability in the strength of agnatic ties, including urbanization, industrialization, ethnicity, Japanese colonial policy, and the conditions of initial settlement. In the case of differences in family form, he considers only ethnicity and productive labor needs, rejecting the former (for good reason) and settling on the latter as *the* explanatory variable. For a researcher who handles causal complexity with great sophistication, as he does in his discussion of lineage organization, Pasternak is surprisingly content to have found a single determinant of family form. Moreover, the two features of kinship organization—agnatic organization and family form —are treated as if they were rather isolated features of social structure instead of facets of an integrated kinship system requiring a unified explanation.

Geertz & Geertz's (54) analysis of Balinese kinship suffers from the usage of a similar dichotomy. In this case, the authors are quite explicit about their reasons for dividing their discussion of kinship institutions and practices into two domains: the private or domestic domain versus the public or civil domain. The reason is that the Balinese themselves make this distinction with great clarity. The domestic affairs conducted within the houseyard walls of Bali are considered fundamentally different from the affairs of the society at large (54, p. 46). While there is thus ample justification for elucidating this cultural distinction of Balinese kinship, the distinction has its drawbacks as an analytic frame. A comparison of Geertz and Geertz's chapter on kinship in the private domain with their chapters on kinship in the public domain shows the former to be uncharacteristically thin and unrevealing. Furthermore, whereas they discuss kinship in the public domain for the gentry and kinship in the public domain for the commoners in separate chapters, the two strata are considered together in a single chapter on kinship in the private domain because the authors view it as essentially the same for commoners and gentry (54, p. 47). One wonders if this is really the case or whether their unified treatment stems more from their approach to the domestic domain. Their discussion of the politics of marriage among the gentry (54, p. 131) makes it clear that there is much more complexity in marriage relationships among the gentry than among commoners and consequently greater status distinction among gentry siblings. If this is the case, we would expect to find some salient differences between commoner and gentry sibling relationships and in the relationships between households within a common houseyard which are linked by a sibling tie. These matters are never discussed, however, and we are led to believe that despite significant differences between the two status groups in the operation of public kinship institutions, kinship in the private domain is essentially the same for both.

This kind of oversight occurs, it seems, because Geertz and Geertz begin their analysis of kinship with a discussion of the domestic domain and then never return to it after they have extensively analyzed the public domain. As a result, their analysis of interpersonal relationships in the domestic domain does not benefit from their exposition of the complex forces shaping the public domain of kinship. Indeed one wonders whether the thinness of our descriptions of domestic relationships is partly an artifact of our habit of beginning with the domestic and then moving to the politico-jural—a habit that we may have unthinkingly inherited from Malinowski.

The distinction between the domestic and politico-jural domains (or the private and public domains) calls for strict scrutiny not just because of its analytical consequences, but because it is the encompassing framework for a cluster of notions which pervade anthropological studies on the family and household. Included within this dense conceptual network is the conviction that the core of domestic relations is the mother-child bond. While there may be differences in the manner in which the mother-child unit is linked to larger organizational structures, the bond itself is perceived as essentially the same everywhere and derived from the biological facts of procreation and nurturance (45, p. 8; 46, pp. 251, 255–56; 47, p. 21; 49, p. 37; 58, p. 18). Closely tied to this notion is the idea that the mother-child relationship is constrained by affective and moral convictions generated by the experience of "mothering" necessary for the biological survival of human offspring. These affective and moral constraints permeate the entire domain of domestic relationships, thereby distinguishing them from those relationships which are ordered by political and jural principles. Finally, as was seen in the attempts to define family and household, there is the belief that reproduction—that is, the provision of properly enculturated personnel to fill social positions necessary for the perpetuation of the social order—is the primary activity of the domestic domain.

NEW PERSPECTIVES ON DOMESTIC ORGANIZATION

Within the past decade, alternative perspectives on domestic groups have been generated primarily by anthropologists concerned with a set of issues which have consequential implications for our conceptualization of domestic relationships. Although they overlap to some degree, these explorations can be loosely categorized into three groups: the study of gender and sex-role systems, particularly women's roles in domestic groups, the study of kinship as a symbolic system, and the study of social inequality.

Women in Domestic Groups

Anthropologists interested in gender and sex roles have had to confront the issue of women's status and roles in domestic groups. In their efforts to transcend the limitations of previous analyses of gender and sex roles, many researchers have come to question the utility of extant analytic categories, including the domestic versus public (political) dichotomy. There now appears to be a growing consensus among these anthropologists that past research tended to overlook the political consequences and motivations of women's actions in domestic groups (31, 36, 84, 112, 160). M. Wolf's (160) portrayal of Taiwanese families reveals that family division is as much a result of women's attempts to advance their own interests and those of their "uterine family" as it is an outcome of conflicts of interest between brothers. J. F. Collier (31) and Lamphere (84) suggest that this is a general phenomenon in societies where men gain political power by having large, cohesive bodies of coresident kin, but where women (particularly young women) gain power by breaking up these units. These authors note that the political nature of these conflicts is usually obfuscated by cultural perceptions of women as quarrelsome, selfish, and irresponsible by nature. Folk explanations of the division of patrilaterally extended joint families, for example, commonly stress women's petty jealousies, thereby masking the extent to which women's actions are politically motivated rather than generated by emotional predispositions. Rogers (112) attributes some of our past failure to recognize the political nature of women's actions in domestic groups to our attentiveness to authority visible in formal power structures (legitimized power) rather than to informal power. However, by viewing women as political actors and by viewing the developmental cycle of domestic groups from a female-ego's perspective, we enlarge our understanding of the dynamic tensions operant within domestic groups. Such an approach enables us to recognize that virilocal extended households are as much faced with the problem of incorporating outsiders as are uxorilocal extended households (36).

Inquiries into women's relationships with people outside their own domestic group refute the notion that it is invariably men who link mother-child units to larger institutional structures in society. Women's involvements in exchange transactions (149, 155), in informal women's communities (99, 111, 160), and in urban kin networks (164) are now interpreted as having significance for extradomestic arrangements rather than as mere extensions of women's domestic orientation [see for example (56)]. Moreover, domestic relationships are often so inextricably inter-meshed with relationships of political alliance that to separate the domestic aspects from the political aspects is to misconstrue these relationships. M. Strathern's (149) discussion of divorce and the attribution of blame for divorce on women's "will" by Mt. Hageners is a particularly telling demonstration that "domestic" aspects of the conjugal relationship sometimes cannot be usefully separated from the alliance aspects of the relationship.

Taken together, these studies push beyond the recognition that domestic relationships are influenced by extradomestic, politico-jural considerations to the realization that domestic relationships are part and parcel of the political structure of a society. Although some initial explorations on sex roles may have been guided by a domestic versus public distinction (52, 113, 121), more recently there appears to be an emerging consensus that this dichotomy is analytically unproductive and empirically unfounded (109, 110, 114). Too many studies of women's "domestic" activities have disclosed that these have political as well as reproductive consequences for us to continue to accept the domestic/public dichotomy as a description of social reality. It now seems more productive to interpret the dichotomy as "a cultural statement masking relations which are highly problematic" (110).

As research on women has taken a closer look at gender ideologies, it has also begun to dispute the notion that the biological facts of reproduction produce an immutable mother-child relationship. "Motherhood," it turns out, is not everywhere construed in the same manner, nor do all gender ideologies place equal emphasis on "motherhood" as an aspect of woman-hood (115, 116). Revelations about nannies, wet nurses, and other "surrogate" mothers disclose that even in our own Euro-American history one cannot assume that "motherhood" has always entailed the same functional components or the same components of meaning (18, 40).

Symbolic Approaches to the Family and Kinship

The analysis of kinship as a system of symbols and meanings has likewise shown that relationships diagrammed similarly on genealogical charts do not necessarily have the same meanings across cultures. Schneider (122, 124, 126) contends that the study of kinship as a symbolic system must be undertaken if we are to produce *cross-cultural* comparisons of kinship rather than *cross-societal* comparisons which divorce components of behavior from their symbolic meanings. In a *cultural* (symbolic) analysis of kinship, one does not define the domain of kinship

> ... *a priori* by the bio-genetic premises of the genealogically-defined grid ... [in contrast to Morgan and his followers who] take it as a matter of definition that the invariant points of reference provided by the facts of sexual intercourse, conception, pregnancy and parturition constitute the domain of "kinship" (126, p. 37).

Instead one asks what the definition of the domain of kinship is for each culture studied. By abstracting normative rules from concrete, observable actions (which includes verbal statements), the anthropologist derives the system of symbols and meanings pertaining to kinship relationships (126, p. 38).

Because it directs us to conduct thorough investigations of native conceptual categories, symbolic analysis produces richer and more precise ethnographic accounts than do analyses that fail to interpret social units and actions within their relevant contexts of meaning. The advantages of symbolic analysis as an analytic tool for the comparative study of family and kinship are attested to by studies (79, 127, 134, 157, 165) that employ Schneider's approach. For example, Inden & Nicholas (79) demonstrate that a Bengali kinship unit, which from a purely genealogical perspective appears to be identical to the Euro-American "nuclear" family, is constructed out of very different cultural meanings and normative expectations than are Euro-American families. In addition, symbolic analysis enables us to see that native kin categories, including family and household, are often polysemic, that is, they encompass a range of different meanings (26, 40, 98, 117, 134, 165). R. I. Rosaldo's analysis (117) reveals that the Ilongot category name "be:rtan" is used in a number of different senses that cannot be conveyed adequately by any single, reduced anthropological concept, such as the deme or nonunilineal descent group. By introducing a diachronic perspective, he is able to show that these category names are best interpreted as "a means of identifying bounded groups at different phases in a single historical process" (117, p. 18). In my analysis of Japanese-American kinship (165), I conclude similarly that the category "relative" has different meanings and is composed of different types of units depending upon the cultural context. Hence, if we are to understand the nature of kinship categories in a society, we must investigate the diverse meanings attached to them in actual usage. And contrary to the claim that this kind of ethnographic specificity makes comparative studies unfeasible, Needham (98) and others (117, 124) argue persuasively that it puts us in a better position to make comparisons because it allows us to "see the social facts in a less distorted way." (98, p. 70).

Symbolic approaches to kinship also have contributed to our under-standing of the interpenetration of kinship and other cultural domains. Although "kinship" relationships may have symbolic meanings that are not reducible to other relationships (e.g. economic relationships), at the same time several studies (2, 3, 26, 125, 127, 165) demonstrate that "kinship" is not a discrete, isolable domain of meaning. Rather, the meanings attributed to the relationships and actions of kinsmen are drawn from a range of cultural domains, including religion, nationality, ethnicity, gender, and folk concepts of the "person." One cannot, for example, explain why Japanese-Americans evaluate the actions of parents and children differently in spe-cific contexts unless one understands their historically derived system of ethnic constructs (165).

A further advantage of analyzing kinship as a symbolic system lies in its ability to help us make sense of the diversity in family and kinship organiza-tion within a single society. Geertz & Geertz (54) employ the analytic strategy of differentiating the cultural dimension of kinship from its social structural dimension to bring together "as aspects of a single structure of meaning" what seem to be "puzzlingly irregular and contradictory" Bali-nese kinship customs and practices (54, p. 3). They conclude that the diversity of kin groups observed in Bali are all "variations on a set of common ideational themes. . . . which permeate and inform the whole of Balinese life" (54, p. 3).

Caution must be exercised, however, lest we assume that all variability in domestic arrangements is produced by diverse external (i.e. economic, political, ecological) constraints rather than by differences in cultural values and meanings. Efforts to encompass all the sectors of a complex society, including the United States, within a unitary model of the cultural system of kinship may undermine the very strengths of a symbolic approach (165). The question of whether our discovery of cultural uniformity in the midst of social diversity is an artifact of our relative lack of facility in recognizing diversity in symbolic systems can only be answered by further research and by the refinement of our conceptual armature for eliciting and displaying the symbolic components of family and kinship.

Social Inequality and Domestic Organization

One of the lacunae in past studies of the family and household has been the investigation of social inequality both within and between the domestic units of a society. Although factors such as wealth and property have been considered as variable constraints impinging on different segments of soci-ety, researchers generally have failed to focus on *relations* of inequality themselves as determinants of the total configuration of domestic groups. Three recent works illustrate provocative new ways of bringing relations of inequality into the heart of our analysis of domestic organization.

At the core of J. F. Collier's analysis[4] of the political-economy of three nineteenth century Plains Indian tribes is her investigation of the relations of inequality *within* households. Collier examines the inequalities between men and women and between seniors and juniors which underlie household production units and discloses how the socially created norms of kinship structure the social relations of production. Following Meillasoux's (94) and Terray's (152) concern for matrimonial policy, she looks carefully at the connection between bridewealth and social inequality, because ". . . it is through bridewealth exchanges that the material products of economic activity are converted into kinship relations which determine the nature and organization of those groups which cooperate in production" (J. F. Collier, unpublished manuscript, p. 86). For example, in discussing Cheyenne society with its uxorilocal extended households, she maintains that property exchanges occurring at marriage "contributed to the subordination of the young *within* production units by ensuring the dependence of all youths" and at the same time "contributed to the creation of unequal relations *between* production units by giving the rich an opportunity to accumulate kin at the expense of the poor" (J. F. Collier, unpublished manuscript, p. 27). A major advantage of Collier's analysis is its tying together of the two ends of the stratification spectrum in Cheyenne society by showing how large, wealthy households required the simultaneous existence of small, poor households. Her use of a political-economy perspective, moreover, enables her to break through the domestic/politico-jural dichotomy and place domestic relationships at the core of the political and economic processes of society.

Martinez-Alier (92) also focuses on marriage as a key element in her inquiry into the color/class stratified society of nineteenth century Cuba. By way of her analysis of the marriage practices of the upper class and lower class, she arrives at a compelling historical interpretation of matrifocality in Cuba. She contends that

> . . . the existence of slavery produced a social order which assigned to the coloured people, whether slave or free, the lowest rank in the social hierarchy . . . to perpetuate this hierarchy it was essential to proscribe marriage between the dominant and the dominated groups. Yet, partly for demographic reasons, white men had to resort to the coloured community for women. By virtue of the hierarchical nature of the society these unions as a rule took on the form of sporadic or stable concubinage. Both the free men and the slave women acquiesced in this inferior form of mating because, due to the racial overtones of the system, it was a most effective means of social advance to them and particularly to their offspring. The principle of hypergeneration applies as well to intraracial unions (92, p. 124).

[4]J. F. Collier. "Women's Work, Marriage, and Stratification in Three Nineteenth Century Plains Tribes." Unpublished manuscript, Stanford University.

Hence, it was the hierarchical nature of the social order that produced the "sexual marginalization" of colored women, and this in turn produced concubinage and matrifocality.

As R. T. Smith (139) perceptively notes, Martinez-Alier's analysis eclipses other explanations of matrifocality in the Caribbean because it does not focus on isolated "economic factors" like income or occupation, which cannot adequately account for the diverse types of domestic union observed. By focusing on relations of inequality, including conjugal unions, *between* members of different strata, she casts light onto the marriage relations and forms of domestic union *within* each stratum.

A third study that brings social inequality into a discussion of domestic organization is Gough's (66) reanalysis of Nuer society as a society in transition rather than in timeless equilibrium. Gough's reexamination of Evans-Pritchard's (41, 42) data on Nuer domestic relations uncovers the fact that a large proportion of the population did not conform to the "agnatic principle." By presenting evidence of the differences between Nuer aristocratic lineages and Dinka or Nuer commoner lineages in forms of domestic union, postmarital residence, and the tracing of descent, Gough is able to argue persuasively that Evans-Pritchard overlooked a marked "skewing" in the operation of the agnatic principle among different segments of the population. Having recognized this unevenness in the operation of the agnatic principle, she offers a compelling historical explanation of this variability.

What is particularly notable in Gough's analysis is that she draws on two different sets of materials, each of which Evans-Pritchard presented in a separate monograph (41, 42). Evans-Pritchard, of course, was committed to the idea that ". . . the relations between the sexes and between children and adults belong rather to an account of *domestic relations* than to a study of political institutions" (41, p. 178) Consequently, he excluded such relations from his analysis of Nuer social structure and relegated them instead to a second volume in which he discussed incest prohibitions, marriage, types of domestic unions, and interpersonal kinship relationships. Gough's creative contribution derives from her unwillingness to accept this separation of the domestic and political spheres. By bringing together in a single analysis what Evans-Pritchard separated into two, she elucidates the workings of a social system that is as much produced by relations between the sexes and between children and adults as it is produced by relations between men. Her reanalysis should lay to its final rest the false notion (cf 49, p. 22) that one can describe the political system of a society without taking into account the web of interpersonal relationships of kinship.

All three of these works show marriage to be central to the creation of different types of domestic groups. All three are able to display the interrelationship between the domestic structures of different segments of society. Together they demonstrate the necessity of bringing relations of inequality within and among domestic groups into our analysis of the political and economic processes of society.

CONCLUSION: A RETURN TO DEFINITIONS AND THE SEARCH FOR UNIVERSALS

At the outset of this review, I stated that it was my intention to save for the very last the question that most systematic reviews of the family begin by addressing, namely, is the family universal? To answer the question of whether the family (or the household) is universal, one must obviously be able to define it. Not every definition of the family, of course, need be an attempt to delineate an invariant social unit. We might instead propose a definition which could be used to assess the presence or absence of the family in each society. The fact that anthropologists have not been inclined to proceed in this manner with regard to the family, whereas they have been willing to do so in the case of the lineage, the clan, the state, and a host of other institutions, including the household, attests to the firmness of our belief in the functional necessity of the family for human survival. Given this conviction and the consequent intertwining of the issues of definition and universality, the question we inevitably encounter is whether there is a definition of the family that can stand the test of all ethnographic cases. There are, in essence, three candidates for the universal definition of the family.

The first of these candidates can be rather readily dismissed. By now most anthropologists (21, 27, 43, 46, 49, 58) acknowledge that the nuclear family or the elementary family as Murdock (96) defined it is not universal. According to Goodenough (58), exceptions like the Nayar castes of southwestern India, the kibbutz communities in Israel, and the matrifocal families in the Caribbean testify to our ethnocentrism in ". . . taking a functionally significant unit in our society . . . and treating the nearest functional equivalent elsewhere as if it were, in some fundamental way, the same thing" (58, p. 5).

Goodenough himself, along with Bohannan (17, p. 73), Fox (49, pp. 37–40), and Fortes (46, pp. 251–56; 47, p. 21), designates a woman and her dependent children as the nuclear familial group in human societies. As I related earlier, Goodenough consciously avoids specifying the functions which the family fulfills. Yet behind the studied ambiguity of his definition of the family as a "woman and her dependent children plus whomever else they are joined to through marriage or consanguinity in a minimal functioning group, whatever the group's functions may be" (58, p.

19) is the belief that the vital function of the family is the bearing and rearing of children. Otherwise there would be no reason for choosing mothers and children as the atom of the family. Goodenough's definition, therefore, ironically suffers from the same ethnocentrism that he attributes to Murdock's definition. By assuming that wherever we find mothers and children (a biological given) they form the core of the family, he has himself taken a functionally significant unit in our society and treated units that resemble it elsewhere as if they were fundamentally the same things. While he is undoubtedly right that in every human society mothers and children can be found, to view their *relationship* as the universal nucleus of the family is to attribute to it a social and cultural significance that is lacking in some cases. Merely because one can identify a relationship that bears a genealogical resemblance to our own mother-child relationship does not prove that people everywhere attach to this relationship the same cultural meanings and social functions, nor that it forms the structural core of larger kinship groups. We do not, after all, insist that unilineal descent groups are present everywhere just because in every society we can ferret out of genealogies a set of unilineal descent relationships. Just as a unilineal descent group requires the attachment of concrete functions and a culturally recognized identity, so any unit designated as the nuclear family must be shown to engage in some socially significant activity and to be imbued with some consequential meaning. Goodenough does not feel compelled to present us with proof that the mother-child dyad everywhere has a central functional and meaningful role, because he assumes that nurturance by the mother is required for the biological survival of human offspring and that, consequently, all people must attribute cultural import to this fact. But, as I indicated in the preceding section, closer scrutiny of the functional and meaningful entailments of "motherhood" does not sustain these assumptions (18, 40, 115, 116). We should no more infer that mothers and their dependent children are the irreducible core of the family, because everywhere they have some kind of socially recognized tie, than we should conclude that the sibling tie is the core of the family because it is likewise invariably recognized.

As the final candidate for a universal definition of the family, Bender's (8) characterization of the family as a strictly kinship phenomenon poses a slightly different set of problems. As people everywhere recognize "kinship" relationships, Bender might seem to have hit upon the sole invariant aspect of the family. Yet if we define the family in what has been disclosed to be strictly genealogical terms, how then do we recognize its boundaries? If we completely divorce the family from any functional considerations, there is but one way to decide who are the members of a family in a particular case: that is by asking the natives to identify the culturally meaningful "kinship" units in their society. The inescapable outcome of this procedure must be the discovery of *many* kinds of families, but no universal family. Although in part Bender adopts this procedure, he stops just short of its inevitable conclusion. While he discloses that in some societies, as among the Yoruba kingdom of Ondo, the idea of a distinctive family unit is not a cultural emphasis and that there are no terms used to designate particular forms of families or families in general, he concludes that here there are defacto families (9). Thus, even though there are no Ondo social groupings based exclusively or primarily on kinship relationships, he still holds that ". . . the *relationships* of which families are composed . . . are nearly universal" (9, p. 238). There is no uncertainty that what Bender means here by family relationships are really genealogical relationships and not role relationships, either normative or actual. Hence, because he equates genealogical relationships with "familial relationships" which have normative role entailments, Bender fails to recognize that a de facto family is no family at all.

Bender's methodical examination of the family, furthermore, suffers from the false premise that the family and household are always logically distinct, if not always empirically different, phenomena. In the face of contrary ethnographic examples (e.g. the Burmese ain-daung) where the "principles of propinquity and kinship are combined to form what are frequently designated as household groups" (8, p. 498), and where coresidence is not merely epiphenomenal to kinship principles, but is as much the basis for the existence of the group, he fails to see the fallacy in the statement that kinship and propinquity always belong to two different universes of discourse. Yet the Burmese ain-daung, along with numerous other ethnographic examples [for two particularly illuminating cases, see (117, 148)] affirms that in some cultural systems kinship and propinquity not only belong to the same universe of discourse, but are so intermeshed that to separate them would be to undermine the integrity of cultural principles.

The concentration of genealogical relationships, the equation of these with role relationships, and the unstated focus on the nuclear family in his discussion of de facto families, display Bender's commitment to reproduction as the essential function of the family. This commitment is most clearly reflected in his statement that

> . . . the legitimization of children, rights in children and exchange of sexual and other rights are nearly everywhere associated with unions between men and women. It follows from the universality of kinship and the near universality of marriage that, by definition, family relationships are nearly universal (9, p. 238).

A similar commitment to the reproductive functions of the family underlies Goody's conclusion that the "domestic family was never extended to any degree" and that there are "basic similarities in the way that domestic groups are organized throughout the whole range of human societies" (60, pp. 118, 124). This minimization of domestic variability springs forth from Goody's assumptions about the way in which the physiological and psychological concomitants of childbearing, childrearing, and food preparation structure the activities of domestic units (139). The reluctance to recognize that in different societies widely varying and shifting assemblages of people participate in these activities bespeaks of an unstated absorption with the biological requirements of sexual reproduction.

To commence a search for "the family," whether general or particular, by seeking out genealogical relationships is to begin with the assumption that reproduction is the primary function of the family. For if our investigation begins with the identification of affinal and filial links and then proceeds to discover the groupings formed out of these bonds, parenthood and marriage and, inevitably, reproduction must by definition emerge as the irreducible core of the family. As Schneider (126) rightly argues, the use of the genealogical grid in kinship studies commits us to the position that the biological facts of reproduction are what kinship is all about.

The conviction that the reproduction of society's members is the essential function of the family reveals that we have not progressed as far past a Malinowskian conception of the family as we would like to claim. We may have recognized the error in Malinowski's reduction of all kinship institutions to extensions of relationships within the elementary family, but we continue to accept many of his notions about the nature of the family itself. Our placement of the family within the domestic domain with its moral and affective constraints, our fixation on genealogical definitions of the family, and, underlying all, our emphasis on reproduction as the core of the family's activities all betray our Malinowskian heritage.

The belief that the facts of procreation and the intense emotional bonds that grow out of it generate an invariant core to the family is what sustains our search for universals. But the units we label as families are undeniably about more than procreation and socialization. They are as much about production, exchange, power, inequality, and status. When we fully acknowledge that the family is as much an integral part of the political and economic structures of society as it is a reproductive unit we will finally free ourselves from an unwarranted preoccupation with its procreative functions and all the consequent notions embodied within such a stance. There is nothing wrong, of course, with a functional analysis of the family; for if the family is a salient unit in any society it must have attached to it some functions—whether these are symbolic functions, activity functions, or both. What is wrong is to decide a priori that the diverse array of social units we call families fulfill the same set of functions or that their primary function is always the same. If we are to cast aside this premise and instead seek out the functions of the family in each society, we must at the same time abandon our search for the irreducible core of the family and its universal definition. Our usage of the terms "family" and "household" will then reflect an awareness that they are, like "marriage" and "kinship," merely "odd-job" words, which are useful in descriptive statements but unproductive as tools for analysis and comparison (98, p. 44). The dilemmas we encounter in cross-cultural comparisons of the family and household stem not from our want of unambiguous, formal definitions of these units, but from the conviction that we can construct a precise, reduced definition for what are inherently complex, multifunctional institutions imbued with a diverse array of cultural principles and meanings. Indeed, the only thing that has thus far proved to be unvarying in our search for the universal family is our willingness to reduce this diversity to the flatness of a genealogical grid.

ACKNOWLEDGMENTS

I am grateful to Ruth Borkner, George Collier, Jane Collier, Danny Maltz, Brigette O'Laughlin, Rayna Rapp, Michelle Rosaldo, Renato Rosaldo, G. William Skinner, Raymond T. Smith, Arthur Wolf, and Margery Wolf for their suggestions and comments at various stages in the development of this paper. I am particularly indebted to Jane Collier and Michelle Rosaldo for suggesting the relevance of Malinowski's conception of the family within the context of their research seminar on sex roles among Australian Aborigines.

Literature Cited

1. Ahern, E. M. 1973. *The Cult of the Dead in a Chinese Village.* Stanford: Stanford Univ. Press. 280 pp.
2. Alexander, J. 1977. The role of the male in the middle-class Jamaican family. *J. Comp. Fam. Stud.* 8:369–89
3. Alexander, J. 1978. The cultural domain of marriage. *Am. Ethnol.* 5:5–14
4. Anderson, M. 1971. *Family Structure in Nineteenth Century Lancashire.* Cambridge, England: Cambridge Univ. Press. 230 pp.
5. Anderson, M. 1972. Household structure and the industrial revolution: mid-nineteenth-century Preston in comparative perspective. In *Household and Family in Past Time,* ed. P. Laslett, R. Wall, pp. 215–36. London: Cambridge Univ. Press, 623 pp.
6. Appell, G. N. 1976. The Rungus: social structure in a cognatic society and its ritual symbolization. In *The Societies of Borneo: Explorations in the Theory of Cognatic Social Structure,* ed. G. N. Appell, pp. 66–86. Washington DC: Am. Anthropol. Assoc. 160 pp.
7. Auwers, L. 1978. Fathers, sons, and wealth in colonial Windsor, Connecticut. *J. Fam. Hist.* 3:136–49
8. Bender, D. R. 1967. A refinement of the concept of household: families, co-residence, and domestic functions. *Am. Anthropol.* 69:493–504
9. Bender, D. R. 1971. De facto families and de jure households in Ondo. *Am. Anthropol.* 73:223–41
10. Berkner, L. K. 1973. The stem family and the developmental cycle of the peasant household: an 18 century Austrian example. In *The American Family in Social-Historical Perspective,* ed. M. Gordon, pp. 34–58. New York: St. Martin's. 428 pp.
11. Berkner, L. K. 1973. Recent research on the history of the family in Western Europe. *J. Marriage Fam.* 35:395–405

12. Berkner, L. K. 1975. The use and misuse of census data for the historical analysis of family structure. *J. Interdiscip. His.* 5:721–38

13. Berkner, L. K. 1976. Inheritance, land tenure, and peasant family structure: a German regional comparison. In *Family and Inheritance: Rural Society in Western Europe, 1200–1800,* ed. J. R. Goody, J. Thirsk, E. P. Thompson, pp. 71–95. Cambridge, England: Cambridge Univ. Press. 421 pp.

14. Berkner, L. K., Shaffer, J. W. 1978. The joint family in the Nivernais. *J. Fam. Hist.* 3:150–62

15. Bloch, M. 1971. *Placing the Dead: Tombs, Ancestral Villages and Kinship Organization in Madagascar.* London: Seminar. 241 pp.

16. Bloch, M. 1975. Property and the end of affinity. In *Marxist Analyses and Social Anthropology,* ed. M. Bloch, pp. 203–28. New York: Wiley. 240 pp.

17. Bohannan, P. 1963. *Social Anthropology.* New York: Holt, Rinehart & Winston. 421 pp.

18. Boon, J. A. 1974. Anthropology and nannies. *Man* 9:137–40

19. Brandes, S. 1975. *Migration, Kinship and Community: Tradition and Transition in a Spanish Village.* New York: Academic. 220 pp.

20. Brown, K. 1968. The content of dozoku relationships in Japan. *Ethnology* 7:113–38

21. Buchler, I. R., Selby, H. A. 1968. *Kinship and Social Organization.* New York: Macmillan. 366 pp.

22. Bulmer, R. N. H. 1960. *Leadership and social structure among the Kyaka people of the western highlands district of New Guinea.* PhD thesis. Australian National Univ., Canberra, Aust.

23. Burch, T. K. 1972. Some demographic determinants of average household size: an analytic approach. See Ref. 5, pp. 91–102

24. Carlos, M. L., Sellers, L. 1972. Family, kinship structure, and modernization in Latin America. *Lat. Am. Res. Rev.* 7:95–124

25. Chayanov, A. V. 1966. *The Theory of Peasant Economy,* ed. D. Thorner, B. Kerblay, R. E. F. Smith. Homewood, Ill: Irwin. 317 pp.

26. Chock, P. P. 1974. Time, nature and spirit: a symbolic analysis of Greek-American spiritual kinship. *Am. Ethnol.* 1:33–46

27. Clignet, R. 1970. *Many Wives, Many Powers: Authority and Power in Polygynous Families.* Evanston: Northwestern Univ. Press. 380 pp.

28. Cohen, M. L. 1970. Developmental process in the Chinese domestic group. In *Family and Kinship in Chinese Society,* ed. M. Freedman, pp. 21–36. Stanford: Stanford Univ. Press. 269 pp.

29. Cohen, M. L. 1976. *House United, House Divided: the Chinese Family in Taiwan.* New York: Columbia Univ. Press. 267 pp.

30. Collier, G. A. 1975. *Fields of the Tzotzil: The Ecological Bases of Tradition in Highland Chiapas.* Austin: Univ. Texas Press. 255 pp.

31. Collier, J. F. 1974. Women in politics. In *Woman, Culture and Society,* ed. M. Z. Rosaldo, L. Lamphere, pp. 89–96. Stanford: Stanford Univ. Press. 352 pp.

32. Crain, J. B. 1976. Ngerufan: ritual process in a Bornean rice harvest. In *Studies in Borneo Societies,* ed. G. N. Appell, pp. 51–63. Northern Illinois Univ. Center for Southeast Asian Studies Spec. Rep. 12. De Kalb: Center for Southeast Asian Studies, Northern Illinois Univ. 157 pp.

33. Davis, J. H. 1973. *Land and Family in Pisticci.* London: Athlone. 200 pp.

34. Davis, N. Z. 1977. Ghosts, kin and progeny: some features of family life in early modern France. *Daedalus* 106: 87–114

35. deMause, L. 1974. The evolution of childhood. In *The History of Childhood,* ed. L. deMause, pp. 1–73. New York: Psychohistory Press. 450 pp.

36. Denich, B. S. 1974. Sex and power in the Balkans. See Ref. 31, pp. 243–62

37. Donham, D. L. 1977. *A field theory of household production.* Presented at Ann. Meet. Am. Anthropol. Assoc., 76th, Houston

38. Donham, D. L. 1978. *Production in a Malle community, Southwestern Ethiopia, 1974–75.* PhD thesis. Stanford Univ., Stanford, Calif. 309 pp.

39. Dorjahn, V. R. 1977. Temne household size and composition: rural changes over time and rural-urban differences. *Ethnology* 16:105–28

40. Drummond, L. 1978. The transatlantic nanny: notes on a comparative semiotics of the family in English-speaking societies. *Am. Ethnol.* 5:30–43

41. Evans-Pritchard, E. E. 1940. *The Nuer.* Oxford: Clarendon. 271 pp.

42. Evans-Pritchard, E. E. 1951. *Kinship and Marriage among the Nuer.* Oxford: Clarendon. 183 pp.

43. Fallers, L. A., Levy, M. J. Jr. 1959. The

family: some comparative considerations. *Am. Anthropol.* 61:647–51

44. Firth, R. W., Hubert, J., Forge, A. 1969. *Families and their Relatives: Kinship in a Middle-Class Sector of London: an Anthropological Study.* London: Routledge & Kegan Paul. 476 pp.

45. Fortes, M. 1958. Introduction. In *The Developmental Cycle in Domestic Groups,* ed. J. R. Goody, pp. 1–14. Cambridge, England: Cambridge Univ. Press. 145 pp.

46. Fortes, M. 1969. *Kinship and the Social Order.* Chicago: Aldine. 347 pp.

47. Fortes, M. 1978. An anthropologist's apprenticeship. *Ann. Rev. Anthropol.* 7:1–30

48. Foster, B. L. 1975. Continuity and change in rural Thai family structure. *J. Anthropol. Res.* 31:34–50

49. Fox, R. 1967. *Kinship and Marriage.* Middlesex, England: Penguin. 271 pp.

50. Freedman, M. 1958. *Lineage Organization in Southeastern China.* London: Athlone. 151 pp.

51. Freedman, M. 1970. Introduction. See Ref. 28, pp. 1–20

52. Friedl, E. 1975. *Women and Men: an Anthropologist's View.* New York: Holt, Rinehart & Winston. 148 pp.

53. Furstenberg, F. F. Jr., Hershberg, T., Modell, J. 1975. The origins of the female-headed black family: the impact of the urban experience. *J. Interdiscip. Hist.* 6:211–34

54. Geertz, H., Geertz, C. 1975. *Kinship in Bali.* Chicago: Univ. Chicago Press. 213 pp.

55. Goldschmidt, W., Kunkel, E. J. 1971. The structure of the peasant family. *Am. Anthropol.* 73:1058–76

56. González, N. L. 1970. Toward a definition of matrifocality. In *Afro-American Anthropology: Contemporary Perspectives,* ed. N. E. Whitten Jr., J. F. Szwed, pp. 231–44. New York: Free Press. 468 pp.

57. Goode, W. J. 1963. *World Revolution and Family Patterns.* New York: Free Press. 432 pp.

58. Goodenough, W. H. 1970. *Description and Comparison in Cultural Anthropology.* Chicago: Aldine. 173 pp.

59. Goody, E. N. 1973. *Contexts of Kinship: an Essay in the Family Sociology of the Gonja of Northern Ghana.* Cambridge, England: Cambridge Univ. Press. 335 pp.

60. Goody, J. R. 1972. The evolution of the family. See Ref. 5, pp. 103–24

61. Goody, J. R. 1973. Bridewealth and dowry in Africa and Eurasia. In *Bridewealth and Dowry,* ed. J. R. Goody, S. J. Tambiah, pp. 1–58. Cambridge Univ. Press. 169 pp.

62. Goody, J. R. 1976. *Production and Reproduction: A Comparative Study of the Domestic Domain.* Cambridge, England: Cambridge Univ. Press. 157 pp.

63. Gordon, M. 1973. Introduction. See Ref. 10, pp. 1–16

64. Goubert, P. 1970. Historical demography and the reinterpretation of early modern French history: a research review. *J. Interdiscip. Hist.* 1:37–48

65. Goubert, P. 1977. Family and province: a contribution to the knowledge of family structures in early modern France. *J. Fam. Hist.* 2:179–95

66. Gough, K. 1971. Nuer kinship: a reexamination. In *The Translation of Culture: Essays to E. E. Evans-Pritchard,* ed. T. O. Beidelman, pp. 79–121. London: Tavistock. 440 pp.

67. Greven, P. J. Jr. 1970. *Four Generations: Population, Land and Family in Colonial Andover, Massachusetts.* Ithaca: Cornell Univ. Press. 329 pp.

68. Greven, P. J. Jr. 1973. Family structure in seventeenth-century Andover, Massachusetts. See Ref. 10, pp. 77–99

69. Gutman, H. G. 1975. Persistent myths about the Afro-American family. *J. Interdiscip. Hist.* 6:181–210

70. Gutman, H. G. 1976. *The Black Family in Slavery and Freedom, 1750–1925.* New York: Pantheon. 664 pp.

71. Hammel, E. A. 1972. The zadruga as process. See Ref. 5, pp. 335–74

72. Hammel, E. A. 1975. Reflections on the zadruga. *Ethnol. Slav.* 7:141–51

73. Hammel, E. A. 1978. Review of family and inheritance, ed. J. Goody, J. Thirsk, E. P. Thompson. *J. Fam. Hist.* 3:203–10

74. Hammel, E. A., Laslett, P. 1974. Comparing household structure over time and between cultures. *Comp. Stud. Soc. Hist.* 16:73–109

75. Hammel, E. A., Yarbrough, C. 1973. Social mobility and the durability of family ties. *J. Anthropol. Res.* 29:145–63

76. Hayami, A., Uchida, N. 1972. Size of household in a Japanese county throughout the Tokugawa period. See Ref. 5, pp. 473–516

77. Higman, B. W. 1975. The slave family and household in British West Indies, 1800–1834. *J. Interdiscip. Hist.* 6:261–88

78. Howard, A. 1971. Households, families and friends in a Hawaiian-American community. *Work. Pap. East-West Popul. Inst.* No. 19. Honolulu: East-West Center. 117 pp.

79. Inden, R. B., Nicholas, R. W. 1977. *Kinship in Bengali Culture.* Chicago: Univ. Chicago Press. 139 pp.

80. Keesing, F. M. 1958. *Cultural Anthropology.* New York: Rinehart. 477 pp.

81. Keesing, R. M. 1973. *Kinship studies in current and future anthropology.* Presented at 9th Int. Congr. Anthropol. Ethnol. Sci., Chicago

82. Kent, F. W. 1977. *Household and Lineage in Renaissance Florence: the Family Life of the Capponi, Ginori, and Rucellai.* Princeton: Princeton Univ. Press. 325 pp.

83. Kundstadter, P. 1963. A survey of the consanguine or matrifocal family. *Am. Anthropol.* 65:56–66

84. Lamphere, L. 1974. Strategies, cooperation, and conflict among women in domestic groups. See Ref. 31, pp. 97–112

85. Laslett, P. 1971. *The World We Have Lost.* London: Methuen. 2nd ed.

86. Laslett, P. 1972. Introduction: the history of the family. See Ref. 5, pp. 1–90

87. Laslett, P. 1977. *Family Life and Illicit Love in Earlier Generations.* Cambridge, England: Cambridge Univ. Press. 270 pp.

88. Levy, B. 1978. "Tender plants:" Quaker farmers and children in the Delaware Valley, 1681–1735. *J. Fam. Hist.* 3:116–35

89. Levy, M. J. Jr. 1965. Aspects of the analysis of family structure. In *Aspects of the Analysis of Family Structure,* ed. A. J. Coale, L. A. Fallers, J. J. Levy Jr., D. M. Schneider, S. S. Tomkins, pp. 1–64. Princeton: Princeton Univ. Press. 248 pp.

90. Lomnitz, L. A. 1977. *Networks and Marginality: Life in a Mexican Shantytown.* Transl. C. Lomnitz. New York: Academic. 230 pp.

91. Malinowski, B. 1963. *The Family among the Australian Aborigines: A Sociological Study.* New York: Schocken. 322 pp. Original publ. 1913

92. Martinez-Alier, V. 1974. *Marriage, Class and Colour in Nineteenth-Century Cuba: A Study of Racial Attitudes and Sexual Values in a Slave Society.* London: Cambridge Univ. Press. 202 pp.

93. McCreery, J. L. 1976. Women's property rights and dowry in China and South Asia. *Ethnology* 15:163–74

94. Meillasoux, C. 1972. From reproduction to production. *Econ. Soc.* 1:93–105

95. Mintz, S. 1973. A note on the definition of peasantries. *J. Peasant Stud.* 1:91–106

96. Murdock, G. P. 1949. *Social Structure.* New York: Macmillan. 387 pp.

97. Nakane, C. 1972. An interpretation of the size and structure of the household in Japan over three centuries. See Ref. 5, pp. 517–44

98. Needham, R. 1974. *Remarks and Inventions: Skeptical Essays about Kinship.* London: Tavistock. 181 pp.

99. Nelson, C. 1974. Public and private politics: women in the Middle Eastern world. *Am. Ethnol.* 1:551–64

100. Netting, R. McC. 1965. Household organization and intensive agriculture: the Kofyar case. *Africa* 35:422–29

101. Netting, R. McC. 1968. *Hill Farmers of Nigeria: Cultural Ecology of the Kofyar of the Jos Plateau.* Seattle: Univ. Washington Press. 259 pp.

102. Netting, R. McC. 1974. Agrarian ecology. *Ann. Rev. Anthropol.* 3:21–56

103. Nimkoff, M. F., Middleton, R. 1960. Types of family and types of economy. *Am. J. Sociol.* 68:215–25

104. Nutini, H. G. 1968. *San Bernadino Contla: Marriage and Family Structure in a Tlaxcalan Municipio.* Pittsburgh: Univ. Pittsburgh Press

105. Nutini, H. G., Murphy, T. D. 1970. Labor-migration and family structure in the Tlaxcala-Pueblan area, Mexico. In *The Social Anthropology of Latin America: Essays in Honor of Ralph Leon Beals,* ed. W. Goldschmidt, H. Hoijer, pp. 80–103. Los Angeles: Lat. Am. Cent., Univ. Calif., Los Angeles. 369 pp.

106. Owens, R. 1971. Industrialization and the Indian joint family. *Ethnology* 10:223–50

107. Pasternak, B. 1972. *Kinship and Community in Two Chinese Villages.* Stanford: Stanford Univ. Press. 174 pp.

108. Pasternak, B., Ember, C. R., Ember, M. 1976. On the conditions favoring extended family households. *J. Anthropol. Res.* 32:109–23

109. Rapp, R. 1978. Family and class in contemporary America: notes toward an understanding of ideology. *Sci. Soc.* 42:278–300

110. Rapp, R. 1979. Review essay: anthropology. *Signs: Journal of Women in Culture and Society.* In press

111. Reiter, R. R. 1975. Men and women in the south of France: public and private domains. In *Towards an Anthropology*

of Women, ed. R. R. Reiter, pp. 252–82. New York: Monthly Review Press. 416 pp.

112. Rogers, S. C. 1975. Female forms of power and the myth of male dominance: a model of female/male interaction in peasant society. Am. Ethnol. 2:727–56

113. Rosaldo, M. Z. 1974. Woman, culture, and society: a theoretical overview. See Ref. 31, pp. 17–42

114. Rosaldo, M. Z. 1978. Thoughts on domestic/public. Presented at Rockefeller Found. Conf. Women, Family, Work, New York

115. Rosaldo, M. Z., Atkinson, J. M. 1975. Man the hunter and woman. In The Interpretation of Symbolism, ed. R. Willis, pp. 43–76. London: Malaby, 181 pp.

116. Rosaldo, M. Z., Collier, J. F. 1979. Politics and gender in "simple" societies. In Sexual Meanings, ed. S. Ortner, H. Whitehead. Submitted for publication.

117. Rosaldo, R. I. 1975. Where precision lies. See Ref. 115, pp. 1–22

118. Rosenberg, C. E. 1975. Introduction. In The Family in History, ed. C. E. Rosenberg, pp. 1–12. Philadelphia: Univ. Pennsylvania Press. 210 pp.

119. Sahlins, M. D. 1957. Land use and the extended family in Moala, Fiji. Am. Anthropol. 59:449–62

120. Sahlins, M. D. 1972. Stone-Age Economics. Chicago: Aldine-Atherton. 348 pp.

121. Sanday, P. R. 1974. Female status in the public domain. See Ref. 31, 189–206

122. Schneider, D. M. 1964. The nature of kinship. Man 64:180–81

123. Schneider, D. M. 1965. Kinship and biology. See Ref. 89, pp. 83–101

124. Schneider, D. M. 1968. American Kinship: A Cultural Account. Englewood Cliffs: Prentice-Hall. 117 pp.

125. Schneider, D. M. 1969. Kinship, religion, and nationality. In Forms of Symbolic Action, ed. V. Turner, pp. 116–25. Seattle: Univ. Washington Press

126. Schneider, D. M. 1972. What is kinship all about? In Kinship Studies in the Morgan Centennial Year, ed. P. Reining, pp. 32–63. Washington DC: Anthropol. Soc. Washington. 190 pp.

127. Schneider, D. M., Smith, R. T. 1973. Class Differences and Sex Roles in American Kinship and Family Structure. Englewood Cliffs: Prentice-Hall. 132 pp.

128. Seddon, D. 1976. Aspects of kinship and family structure among the Ulad Stut of Zaio rural commune, Nador province, Morocco. In Mediterranean Family Structures, ed. J. G. Peristiany,

pp. 173–94. Cambridge, England: Cambridge Univ. Press. 414 pp.

129. Shanin, T. 1972. The Akward Class: Political Sociology of Peasantry in a Developing Society: Russia 1910–1925. London: Oxford Univ. Press. 253 pp.

130. Shanin, T. 1973. The nature and logic of the peasant economy, 1: a generalization. J. Peasant Stud. 1:63–80

131. Shifflett, C. A. 1975. The household composition of rural black families: Louisa County, Virginia, 1880. J. Interdiscip. Hist. 6:235–60

132. Shorter, E. 1973. Female emancipation, birth control and fertility in European history. Am. Hist. Rev. 78:605–40

133. Shorter, E. 1975. The Making of the Modern Family. New York: Basic Books. 369 pp.

134. Silverman, M. G. 1971. Disconcerting Issue: Meaning and Struggle in a Resettled Pacific Community. Chicago: Univ. Chicago Press. 362 pp.

135. Singer, M. 1968. The Indian joint family in modern industry. In Structure and Change in Indian Society, Ed. M. Singer, B. S. Cohen, pp. 423–54. Chicago: Aldine. 507 pp.

136. Smith, R. T. 1956. The Negro Family in British Guiana. London: Routledge & Kegan Paul. 282 pp.

137. Smith, R. T. 1970. The nuclear family in Afro-American kinship. J. Comp. Fam. Stud. 1:55–70

138. Smith, R. T. 1973. The matrifocal family. In The Character of Kinship, ed. J. R. Goody, pp. 121–44. London: Cambridge Univ. Press. 251 pp.

139. Smith, R. T. 1978. The family and the modern world system: some observations from the Caribbean. J. Fam. Hist. 3:337–60

140. Smith, T. C. 1977. Nakahara: Family Farming and Population in a Japanese Village, 1717–1830. Stanford: Stanford Univ. Press. 183 pp.

141. Solien de González, N. 1965. The consanguineal household and matrifocality. Am. Anthropol. 67:1541–49

142. Spagnoli, P. G. 1977. Population history from parish monographs: the problem of local demographic variations. J. Interdiscip. Hist. 7:427–52

143. Spiro, M. E. 1954. Is the family universal? Am. Anthropol. 56:839–46

144. Spiro, M. E. 1977. Kinship and Marriage in Burma: A Cultural and Psychodynamic Analysis. Berkeley: Univ. Calif. Press

145. Stack, C. B. 1974. All Our Kin: Strategies for Survival in a Black Community. New York: Harper & Row. 175 pp.

146. Stone, L. 1975. The rise of the nuclear family in early modern England. See Ref. 118, pp. 13–58
147. Stone, L. 1977. *The Family, Sex, and Marriage in England 1500–1800.* London: Weidenfeld & Nicolson. 800 pp.
148. Strathern, A. 1973. Kinship, descent and locality: some New Guinea examples. See Ref. 138, pp. 21–34
149. Strathern, M. 1972. *Women in Between: Female Roles in a Male World: Mount Hagen, New Guinea.* London: Seminar. 372 pp.
150. Talmon-Garber, Y. 1970. Social change and kinship ties. In *Families in East and West: Socialization Process and Kinship Ties,* ed. R. Hill, R. Konig, pp. 504–24. The Hague: Mouton. 630 pp.
151. Tambiah, S. J. 1973. Dowry and bride-wealth and the property rights of women in South Asia. See Ref. 61, pp. 59–169
152. Terray, E. 1972. *Marxism and "Primitive" Societies.* Transl. M. Klopper. New York: Monthly Rev. Press. 186 pp.
153. Thirsk, J. 1976. The European debate on customs of inheritance, 1500–1700. See Ref. 13, pp. 177–91
154. Thomas, K. 1977. The changing family. *Times Lit. Suppl.* 3943:1226–27
155. Weiner, A. B. 1976. *Women of Value, Men of Renown: New Perspectives in Trobriand Exchange.* Austin: Univ. Texas Press. 299 pp.

156. Wheaton, R. 1975. Family and kinship in Western Europe: the problem of the joint family household. *J. Interdiscip. Hist.* 5:601–28
157. Witherspoon, G. 1975. *Navaho Kinship and Marriage.* Chicago: Univ. Chicago Press. 137 pp.
158. Wolf, A. P. 1976. *Chinese domestic organization: the view from Taiwan.* Presented at Conf. Anthrop. in Taiwan, Portsmouth, New Hampshire
159. Wolf, E. R. 1966. *Peasants.* Englewood Cliffs: Prentice-Hall. 116 pp.
160. Wolf, M. 1972. *Women and the Family in Rural Taiwan.* Stanford: Stanford Univ. Press. 229 pp.
161. Wrigley, E. A. 1966. Family reconstitution. In *An Introduction to English Historical Demography,* ed. E. A. Wrigley, pp. 96–159. London: Weidenfeld & Nicolson. 283 pp.
162. Wrigley, E. A. 1969. *Population and History.* New York: McGraw-Hill. 256 pp.
163. Yanagisako, S. J. 1975. Two processes of change in Japanese-American kinship. *J. Anthropol. Res.* 31:196–224
164. Yanagisako, S. J. 1977. Women-centered kin networks in urban bilateral kinship. *Am. Ethnol.* 4:207–26
165. Yanagisako, S. J. 1978. Variance in American kinship: implications for cultural analysis. *Am. Ethnol.* 5:15–29

Ann. Rev. Anthropol. 1979. 8:207–30
Copyright © 1979 by Annual Reviews Inc. All rights reserved

ANTHROPOLOGICAL GENETICS OF SMALL POPULATIONS

♦9632

Alan G. Fix

Department of Anthropology, University of California,
Riverside, California 92521

INTRODUCTION

Anthropological genetics encompasses a wide spectrum of interests centered on the explanation of genetic variation in human populations. The methods and theories of anthropological genetics are derived from population genetics, one of the most mathematically developed areas of biology. In theory, the behavior of gene frequencies under a variety of conditions can be accounted for. However, basic disagreements persist concerning the interpretation of variation in real populations (55). Controversy stems in part from the very general assumptions required by the mathematical theory. These assumptions often seem to be forgotten and models are applied to empirical situations for which they were never intended (9). Another problem has been the difficulty in measuring in real populations the quantities required by the theories (55).

These major problems are unlikely to be solved by an exclusive concern with human populations. Nevertheless, the detailed analysis of human populations can provide perspective on assumptions and allow measurements of variables which would be difficult if not impossible to examine in natural populations of other organisms. Ward (107) has clearly expressed this point of view: "the very general insights into the intimate working of a biological population, gained by the cautious and pragmatic analysis of human data, may do more to advance the theory of population genetics than the uncritical application of the latest mathematical model to populations where the basic assumptions can never be tested."

This holistic and empirical approach is often characterized as the study of "population structure." Although the term is somewhat variably defined,

207

the view of Mielke et al (64), following Harrison & Boyce (37), is representative. They state that "the total description of population structure ... requires the integration of biological, social, and demographic data set in an ecological framework." Additionally, as they comment, an important research goal is to see how this complex structure changes and evolves through time.

For both historical and methodological reasons, population structure studies have usually concentrated on small populations. Anthropologists have traditionally studied technologically "primitive" societies within which local populations are typically small. Probably more importantly, the intensive methods of anthropology have led to studies of small isolates or groups of semi-isolated communities. Thus, even when the total population aggregate is large, the analysis generally deals with subdivisions of the whole.

One aim of this review is to show how recent empirical studies of human population structure have led to reassessments of some critical assumptions in genetic evolutionary theory. Many of these studies combine a large body of genetic data with detailed anthropological work on social structure, demographic structure, and history (written or inferred). This consideration leads to the second goal of the essay; to point out a number of areas where cultural and biological anthropologists might cooperate on problems of mutual interest such as mating structure and endogamy, the role of geographic distance in human interaction, the stability of local population groups, and migration patterns.

Neither of these goals is exhaustively pursued; however, selected examples and problem areas are used to illustrate and examine some major issues. Some topics are not covered in detail. Demographic anthropology, a rapidly growing area of great relevance to anthropological genetics, has been reviewed recently (105, 110). The extensive theoretical and methodological literature on subjects related to population structure has received numerous recent reviews (9, 11, 14, 26, 34, 85, 96, 97, 101) and will not be reconsidered here. Other theoretical work in general population genetics has sought to add realism to the classic models along an ecological dimension; Hedrick et al (38) should be consulted for a review.

In few areas is the potential combination of anthropological insight and importance to theory more apparent than in the analysis of the basic population unit. The definition of the population begins this review and serves as a tertiary theme throughout the work.

THE DEFINITION OF THE POPULATION

The most inclusive Mendelian population, the species, is well defined. Yet the total species population is rarely the unit of genetic analysis. Local or regional populations, often defined on political or geographic bases, are the usual study units. In fact, population definition is generally considered to be arbitrary, depending on the sampling procedure in the genetic survey (15). Villages, parishes, counties, districts, or countries are all equally valid units.

Population definition is nonetheless important. As Cavalli-Sforza & Bodmer (15) state: "a central problem in the analysis of population structure is the determination of N, the effective population size." The expected amount of genetic drift is one obvious process dependent on N. Since this expectation is often used (rightly or wrongly) to decide the critical question of the relative roles of drift and natural selection, N is very important. Yet it is N which is used by Lewontin (55) as an example of an unmeasurable parameter in current models. In his view, this inability to measure N obviates much of stochastic population genetics theory since most of its predictions depend on products of N with other equally difficult to measure quantities such as the migration rate (which also depends on the definition of the population unit) and the selection coefficient.

The relevance of accurate population size measurement can be seen in two recent studies of the high frequency of Tay-Sachs disease among Ashkenazic Jews. Both studies used the same basic data but they arrived at opposite conclusions. One (106) favored a drift explanation; the other (17) implicated natural selection. Ewens (24) showed that some of the discrepancy in views followed from different values of N_e assumed by the authors. Precise measurement of the varying population size through time, properly correcting for bottlenecks, might be impossible for this population. However, in the absence of good data on the population, the conclusions become a function of the assumptions.

The importance of assumptions about population size also may be seen in several current models of population structure, most notably migration matrices (4). These models require that local gene frequencies be stabilized by some linear systematic force. This is usually taken to be migration from "outside." But in order to maintain a constant gene frequency through time, the outside population must be essentially infinite in size and therefore not subject to genetic drift itself. This is the classic island model where migrants come from a large homogeneous continental population. It is possible that some real islands may fit the model, but it seems most unlikely for other empirical cases [see Hiorns et al (40) for a discussion]. In those studies where migration matrices have been used, the procedure has been to define the populations of interest as small and subject to drift and local migration. Populations outside the area of study are lumped in the "outside world" and are defined as an infinite pool. Here, by an arbitrary process of definition, an evolutionary result is obtained: local populations reach an equilibrium gene frequency [see Fix (29) for further details].

Population definition is equally critical for comparative studies of human populations. As long as internal comparisons are being made, the population unit may be arbitrarily defined. As problems and foci of interest shift between the study of drift likelihoods, migration patterns, or natural selection, different units will be appropriate. Once comparisons are to be made between different studies, however, the question of comparability of units becomes crucial. As Harpending (34) noted, "one investigator's subdivision might be another's total sample."

Speilman et al (101) make clear the importance of comparable population units in their discussion of the "paradox of Brazil and Japan" (see also 31, 77). Previous studies had found that "local inbreeding" (in this case, Morton's ϕ_{ii}) in the Brazilian population, which comprises peoples of heterogeneous ethnic background, exceeded that of the ethnically more homogeneous population of Japan. This strange conclusion can be partially accounted for by a difference in local population definition between the two populations. The Brazilian *distrito* of mean radius 10 km was compared with the Japanese prefecture of radius 45 km. This size difference suggests that "local" inbreeding might appear to be higher in Brazil simply because numerous actual local breeding communities were lumped together in the prefectures of Japan.

Another clear demonstration of this point can be seen in the Finnish data of Workman et al (118). They show how "inbreeding" (here R_{ST}, the Wahlund variance reflecting local differentiation) depends on the hierarchical population level chosen for analysis. When counties are the population unit, $R_{ST} = 0.002$; for districts, $R_{ST} = 0.005$; at the community level, it would be considerably greater. Thus lists of comparative population structure statistics (30) or Wahlund coefficients (36), if not meaningless, are at least to be treated as highly suspect in the absence of good information on the population units being represented.

Different problems will require different population levels of analysis in the hierarchy from local deme to the species population, and in this sense the definition of the population unit is arbitrary. This does not mean that the definition should not be an operational one. However, even the local breeding unit may be difficult to define as can be seen, for instance, in the discussion of Wiesenfeld & Gajdusek (112). Recent administrative changes in New Guinea have produced artificial villages which include several previous social groups with very different mating patterns. Similarly, "tribes" may be administrative units rather than interbreeding units. Villages, tribes, districts or any other unit of analysis should not be assumed to be local breeding populations. Measuring the degree of endogamy is the relevant operation. Ideally, comparisons of genetic interest could then be made between comparable units.

Endogamy is also a topic of interest to cultural anthropologists. A recent study by Adams & Kasakoff (1) looked at the relationship between percentage of endogamy and population size for 21 ethnographically known societies of varying socioeconomic pattern. In each society they examined, a threshold in group size existed at approximately an 80 percent endogamy rate (ranging from 70 to 90 percent). There was considerable variation in the size of these 80 percent groups but they were clearly recognizable. Above the 80 percent endogamy rate, the size of the higher level group increased dramatically for each small increase in endogamy rate such that higher level groups comprised entire ethnic groups or nations.

Population density appeared to be a strong factor in accounting for the range in size of the 80 percent groups. Numerous isolating factors have been documented in human populations [see Roberts (92)], although propinquity is often given primary consideration. Adams and Kasakoff found that geographic distance was a significant factor in their data; however, for very low and very high density populations, other factors also become important. For sparse populations, minimum population size (58) is relevant. The rationale behind this work is that below a critical level of population numbers, insufficient potential mates will be available to spouse-seekers and marriage will of necessity be exogamous. Individuals will go farther to find mates, and the geographic extent of the breeding population will be larger than in more densely populated situations. In very dense populations, other factors such as social class or caste may be more important in structuring the marriage universe (1). These considerations should be taken into account in comparative studies of populations at different socioeconomic levels (e.g. hunter-gatherers vs horticulturalists—see also the discussion under GEOGRAPHIC DISTANCE).

If the 80 percent group is of as wide an occurrence as Adams and Kasakoff suggest, it would constitute a very useful, even "natural," unit for studies of inbreeding levels and microdifferentiation. Nonetheless, comparative analysis of genetic differentiation does not depend on the use of such units and, if they turn out to be rarer than presumed here or difficult to identify, more "arbitrary" units will suffice. For example, a procedure suggested by Cavalli-Sforza & Bodmer (15, p. 481) is one possibility. The breeding group is seen by them as the sum of all the groups from which an individual might find a mate, taking into account the probability of the mate actually being chosen in that population. As they note, this definition might be most useful for studying social (or other) restrictions on marriage, but it also provides the detailed data which would allow direct comparison between different studies, or aggregation of the breeding groups into arbitrary units which are well defined in terms of breeding behavior. The study of migration matrices (4) follows naturally from this definition of the breeding population. In fact, whether an individual is considered a member of the population or a "migrant" depends on the definition of the population.

To this point, the breeding population has been defined on the basis of *current* mating practices. The 80 percent group refers to endogamous marriages of individuals of a single generation. However, as Smith (96) makes clear, populations extend in time as well as in space. At 20 percent per generation in-migration, over the long term the population must change considerably in composition. The breeding unit considered on a time scale of many generations will encompass a much larger geographic extent than the single generation population. Again, this distinction might be considered arbitrary since for some problems the results of considering a set of 80 percent groups undergoing migration over 10 generations will not be very different from taking the whole group as one big population. For other problems, the analysis might as easily differ.

This extensive discussion of population definition contrasts with the attention usually given the subject in genetic surveys. In comparison with laboratory techniques and genetic methods, characterization of the populations sampled are generally quite casual. Because the population unit is "arbitrary," it seemingly is assumed to be less important than these other concerns; yet for exactly this reason, it is crucial that it be carefully defined for each study. Particularly if comparisons are to be made between mathematical models and empirical studies, the correspondence between the assumptions about the population and the actual case needs to be carefully specified. The confusion resulting from the failure to make these specifications will be seen at several points in the sections which follow.

GEOGRAPHIC DISTANCE

Distance clearly has a strong effect on probabilities of mating, the degree of isolation of local populations, and, therefore, the pattern of genetic diversity among populations. This importance is recognized in a number of models which incorporate geographic distance as a critical parameter. One of the most widely applied of these is Malécot's isolation by distance theory as championed by Morton and his colleagues. The merits of the Malécot/ Morton approach have been debated for several years without obvious resolution (see 14, 25, 34, 50, 69–71).

Of more interest in the present context is Morton's (71) claim that the Malécot model has provide an "acceptable" fit to many human populations. As Morton admits (71) the model "provides a less complete and reliable prediction" than more detailed analyses such as migration matrices. Still it is a very general and, Morton says, widely applicable model. The generality of the model, however, is attained by sacrificing concern for a more precise relationship between distance and genetic similarity. So, for example, it may be sufficient to know that genetic similarity declines sharply with distance among continental isolates and less so among hunter-gatherers and oceanic islanders (67). On the other hand, careful attention to the levels of subdivision and the actual relationship of genetic similarity to distance shows that distance is not all-important in determining genetic similarity nor is its effect uniform at all levels of population partition (64, 117, 118).

A less generalized method than the Malécot model compares geographic maps with two-dimensional scales of genetic similarities (49, 116). These studies tend to show "clear relationships" between genetic similarity and geographic location (51), although the fit is far from perfect. Workman et al (117), for instance, find only about 25 percent of genetic distance can be accounted for by map location of Sardinian villages.

Where hierarchic population levels have been considered, as in the Finnish study of Workman et al (118), isolation by distance is most apparent at the local breeding population level and less clear at higher levels. Analysis of Finnish archival data from the period 1790 to 1815 showed that only 1.1 percent of marital birthplaces were more than 25 km apart. However, at the next level of analysis, variation between districts of the country, there was no case (of 27 districts) where genetic kinship declined with increasing distance. Indeed, the plots of kinship to distance have sawtooth appearances. Even more interesting is the observation that when districts are aggregated into simple distance classes, the relationship between distance and kinship reappears. Workman and associates (118) interpret these results as showing that distance per se has no systematic effect, but rather the "relationship" implied by the aggregated data is due to the "geographic and genetic regional substructure" which they go on to analyze in detail. Similarly, Mielke et al (64) show how the relationship between kinship and geographic distance varies between different regions of the Åland Islands, partially due to differences in transportation opportunities.

As in the analysis of breeding populations, several disciplines might cooperate to explore the role of distance in human movement. Current interest among anthropologists and geographers in regional analysis could provide many examples of work relevant to population structure studies. For instance, Jackson's (44) material on marriage among Indians in the Vaupés region of the Amazon showed how geographic distance and socially defined kinship distance both structure the mating network; indeed, how geographic distance, travel distance, and the degree of social interaction between villages interact to influence mating. Fix (27) described a similar situation among the Semai Senoi of Malaysia. These studies emphasize the wide-ranging regional nature of marriage in a way reminiscent of hunter-gatherer groups (119) and suggest that simplistic classification of hunter-gatherers, tropical swiddeners, and "continental isolates" may not be a particularly significant dimension of comparison. Perhaps Jackson's (44) distinction of low density, dispersed populations as networks vs higher density central-place systems may be a more fruitful scale than hunter-gatherers vs horticulturalists in viewing changes in population structure across populations and time.

SOCIAL STRUCTURE

From the beginnings of the discipline, anthropological genetics has been concerned with the effects of social structure and cultural practices on genetic structure. A paper by Kluckhohn & Griffith (48), presented at the 1950 Cold Spring Harbor Symposium on Quantitative Biology, a seminal contribution to the founding of the field (104), clearly stated the relationships between population genetics and social anthropology. The major concern was kinship systems and inbreeding, a topic which remains a focal one in recent work (53, 88), but other areas were discussed and have been studied in the intervening years. For instance, in the same volume, Birdsell (3) showed how Australian tribal organization acted to limit gene flow.

There has been a continuing interest in the segmentation of populations on the basis of social categories, a topic directly relevant to the analysis of breeding populations. Clans are one sort of social division which has been studied by geneticists. Morton and his associates (72) and Cannings & Skolnick (10) concluded that clans had essentially no effect on the mean coefficient of genetic kinship between random individuals and could therefore be ignored. However, in both studies, clans were exogamous and, in the Morton et al formulation, mating between clans was random. The conclusion that such entities are not strong genetic barriers is therefore not surprising. Where the "clan" has been used as the basic unit of genetic analysis, as in the empirical study of Malcolm et al (59), it was shown to be a more or less geographically localized group with varying rates of endogamy depending on clan size. Consistent with the generally low rate of endogamy in the groups, genetic heterogeneity between clans was low. Hetereogeneity predictably increased when the entire group was compared with neighboring tribes. The fairly obvious conclusion is that "clans," insofar as they are exogamous, are inappropriate units for studying genetic differentiation.

In kinship-based societies, the stability of local groups and the composition of migrant groups may be strongly influenced by social factors. Thus among several South American Indian tribes, villages are composed of groups of kin. These local groups are politically unstable and periodically split up to either form new local groups or fuse with other established groups. In addition, these fission groups are generally composed of biologically related individuals, a phenomenon Neel (74) has termed the "lineal effect." The genetic effect is to reduce the number of independent genomes in splinter groups, thereby augmenting the nonrepresentativeness of the genetic sample.

This fission-fusion structure contrasts sharply with the long-term localization and stability of most genetic models. No new formal approaches comparable to the various extant population structure models have been proposed on the basis of this work. However, the implications of the fission-fusion structure and the lineal effect process for the genetic structure of populations have been explored in a long series of papers by Neel and his colleagues beginning in 1964 (2, 74–76, 79–81, 107).

Perhaps the most striking inference obtained from these studies is that a high percentage (circa 68%) of the genetic differences between South American Indian tribes arises from the initial splitting of the populations (107). This contrasts with traditional formal models of gradual population differentiation due to isolation and intergenerational genetic drift over relatively long time periods [although others had observed that a small founder group could well differ genetically from its parental population (61)].

The importance of this structure depends to some extent on its generality. As Roberts (91) notes, this type of social organization is well known to anthropologists. Kunstadter's (48a) comparison of Lua' and Karen of Thailand illustrates some of the social structural conditions promoting or retarding fission-fusion of local populations. Chagnon's (15a) description of the Yąnomamö emphasizes patrilineal descent and alliance patterns in warfare and suggests that many of the features of Yąnomamö social structure are widespread in tribal societies. Yet the fission-fusion pattern does not seem necessarily linked to specific descent systems nor particular culture practices. Local groups of Semai Senoi, Malaysian swiddeners, whose social structure differs from the Yąnomamö in numerous basic respects (bilateral descent, no warfare, etc) also periodically split along kinship lines (28). Wiesenfeld & Gajdusek (112) also suggest that fission and fusion are characteristic of the populations of the eastern highlands of New Guinea. Others have noted nonrandom fission along family lines or the likelihood of founder groups being biologically related in non-"primitive" societies (60, 64). In fact, there are some indications that "lineal" fissioning occurs among nonhuman primates (18, 20), although it does not appear to have a great effect on genetic variation among populations in these studies. On the other hand, Friedlaender (32) presents the villages of Bougainville as extremely sedentary and stable and suggests that this is typical of "tropical swiddeners."

That differences between societies in local group stability exist is to be expected. Here again would seem to be a topic for cooperative research between the subdisciplines within anthropology. The basic data required are

genealogies and village histories, materials which many cultural anthropologists collect for their own research goals. To apply these data to
considerations of population structure, migration, and fission-fusion should
be relatively straightforward.

Ideally such a comparative study would produce not only a catalog of
fission-fusion societies but would also identify the critical variables determining the magnitude and frequency of such splitting. Beyond this, it would
be extremely interesting to know how prevalent such social structures were
in earlier periods of human evolution. This consideration raises the difficult
problem of the validity of ethnographic analogy. Is it possible to infer the
social conditions under which human evolution occurred from extant populations, or would any view based on these data "remain essentially philosophical" (107, p. 369)? It would seem that anthropologists interested in
this question are in the same boat with the prehistoric archaeologists. Only
the most sanguine can hope for full understanding; the alternative to this
sort of reconstruction, however, does not seem obvious if we are to know
anything about human evolution in earlier times.

Whether ubiquitous in prehistory or not, the genetic consequences of the
fission-fusion pattern are numerous. Most of these effects increase the random component of genetic variation and many of the conclusions to be
drawn are cautionary. The detection of natural selection is particularly
complicated in these populations. Even the presence of statistically significant clines, generally thought to result only from the systematic forces,
migration or selection, seem due to chance effects in the Yanomama (109).
Another predicted outcome of natural selection, gametic disequilibrium, is
also attributed to random events (98).

Although the fission/fusion pattern promotes genetic drift in the wide
sense, its recognition may actually decrease confidence in drift explanations.
Consider the example given by Neel (77): The classic Parma study by
Cavalli-Sforza (12) and his colleagues compared expectations of genetic
variability on a drift model to actual gene frequencies and concluded that
drift provided an adequate explanation. However, if the initial gene frequencies of the Parma populations were highly differentiated, as would be expected on a lineal effect model, the predicted present genetic variability
would be affected and, as Neel argues, natural selection could no longer be
excluded as a relevant factor.

Simiarly, Fix (29) has shown that migration in a fission-fusion type
population may be less effective than is generally supposed in reducing
variation among subpopulations arising from intergenerational genetic
drift. This result is based on the kinship structuring of migrant groups of
individuals in these populations. Migrants are not necessarily independent
random samples of the donor gene pool (see also 46). As groups of kinsmen

migrate from one local population to another, gene frequencies fluctuate. Predictions depending on internal migration as a homogenizing force as, for example, the migration matrix model, may be inaccurate as a result. Moreover, when it is remembered that the overall stabilization of gene frequencies depends on α, outside migration, which is in itself something of a convenient fiction, it may once again be impossible to exclude balancing selection. It should be noted that Bodmer & Cavalli-Sforza do not ignore this possibility [see (5) for a thoughtful discussion of this and several other points relevant to the use of migration matrices].

A more basic assumption of the migration matrix model, and for that matter almost all models in population genetics, involves the attainment of equilibrium. In the migration matrix formulation, current estimates of migration between local populations are assumed constant over long time periods. The technique requires powering the matrix for as many generations as are required to achieve equilibrium in genetic variance (4, 43). As Friedlaender (33), points out, even for the highly localized Bougainville islanders, 50 generations of the same mating pattern "pushes reality." For fission-fusion populations such as the Yanomama Indians, after only a few generations the migration pattern could be expected to be radically different (79, 108). Bodmer & Cavalli-Sforza (5) recognize this difficulty but suggest that the approach is useful even under these circumstances as a device to compare with empirical observations. Wood (114) has also commented on the problem and provided a test of the equilibrium assumption. The test is based on the demographic fact that migration matrices which would result in exponentially growing or declining subpopulations could not persist indefinitely. But, as he notes, the method only excludes impossible situations; where fission-fusion is occurring, even migration rates that could persist probably will not.

Although the migration matrix model was singled out in the discussion of equilibrium assumptions, the arguments apply more strongly to most stochastic theory. This theory assumes the gene frequencies have reached their stationary states. As Ewens (23) points out, an extremely long time would have had to elapse for several processes involving mutation to reach stationarity. Fixation, for example, may require so long a time as to be unlikely for any population, fission-fusion or not. However, in contrast to the relative definiteness of the assumptions of the migration matrix argument, much of this theory is sufficiently abstract and generalized that long persistent populations may be among the least of its departures from reality (see 55).

If stochastic theory is based on long-term equilibrium assumptions, measurements in populations often reflect short-term events. Spielman et al (101) reiterate this fact with regard to inbreeding. Since inbreeding accumulates in each generation, the actual level of identity by descent in small-scale populations may be several times that ascertained from gene frequencies (let alone pedigrees). For Yanomama villages, they suggest that identity by descent may be as high as 0.5, based on the New World founder population as reference generation (circa 20,000 years ago). This high value is a consequence of the long time span but also the social structure of the Yanomama, primarily preferential cousin marriage.

Nei's (83) "variable allele" model makes identity by descent even more frequent. On this view essentially all homozygotes are identical by descent by definition. This follows from the belief that mutations are unique or nearly so and that equilibrium, whether due to opposed backward-forward mutation or otherwise, is rare. As has been pointed out by Jacquard (45), inbreeding has multiple meanings corresponding to several uses of the concept. For comparing species populations over long periods of evolutionary time, Nei's (84) view makes considerable sense, particularly if most alleles are selectively neutral. On the other hand, problems focusing on a shorter time scale may continue to study regional differentiation and other factors commonly considered under inbreeding.

The significance of the implications of the fission-fusion pattern is somewhat controversial. Some doubt whether it was ever a widespread feature of the species and assert that local differentiation, even if it had existed, was probably of little long-term importance (34). Others compare the fission-fusion structure with that suggested by Sewall Wright as optimum for rapid evolution of a species (e.g. 79, 82). These differences of opinion are partly empirically resolvable (Was fission-fusion widespread? Does it have an effect?) and partly a consequence of differing research goals (What is "important"?). None of these questions are easily answered.

HISTORY

"The great virtue of the study of human populations is that it introduces *history* into evolution" (56, p. viii). Lewontin goes on to point out that most theoretical studies in evolutionary genetics involve assumptions of equilibrium. In order to check those assumptions, the history of the population should be known, a difficult if not impossible task for most natural populations of other animals.

In addition to evaluating assumptions, detailed history may also help to decide between alternative evolutionary hypotheses (64). The current genetic structure of a population observed in a genetic survey will be the result of some mix of evolutionary processes. For almost any genetic structure there are several possible alternative explanations. When history is known, particularly demographic history allowing estimates of population sizes and migration rates, inferring process is possible. The more detailed the history, the more likely this becomes.

The degree to which actual history will be known and can be utilized depends on the population. The Yąnomamö Indians, for example, do not have a written history; still Chagnon's (16) analysis of oral histories, individual life histories, genealogies, and other anthropological data provides historical material beyond anything usually available for nonhuman populations. Fission and fusion are regularities or patterns derived from this "historical" analysis; the observed genetic variability among the Yąnomamö may be evaluated in the light of reconstructed fissions and fusions (107).

Comparative linguistics can also be used to provide some historical perspective in nonliterate human population studies. The assumption here is that linguistic similarity is a measure of historical relatedness. This may occasionally be a dangerous supposition since languages may reflect history other than descent from a common ancestor. For example, the various Pygmy groups who speak unrelated languages (which are, in fact, the languages of surrounding horticulturalists) are almost certainly biologically related (14). Still, many studies have shown "reasonable congruence" between language and genetics (33, 100) and, as Spuhler (103) comments, linguistics may be the only way to get a really long time perspective on human groups and therefore it will remain a useful, if cautiously used, tool.

For some populations, abundant archival material is available representing considerable time depth and extensive demographic information on the populations (21, 64, 89, 117, 118). Family sizes, migration rates, and population sizes through time can often be estimated in these populations (52). As anthropologists turn increasingly to studies of literate populations, many more detailed demographic histories should become available (105).

Results from these studies have often seemed very particularistic. Morton (68, 73), for instance, states that one of the principal objectives of historical genetics is to analyze the contemporary gene pool of small isolates in terms of the constitution of founding members of the population. This leads to explanations of locally high concentrations of some genes in terms of unique sets of founders (22, 42, 62). On the other hand, studies of this sort have been among the classics of anthropological genetics. Certainly one of the most convincing descriptions of the changing composition of a population came from the detailed history of the island population of Tristan da Cunha (89–91). Likewise, the Parma Valley genetic drift argument was made much more compelling by the availability of a long historical record (13).

Good historical evidence on small relatively isolated populations has now documented a pattern of intermittent population size reduction due to various natural or human catastrophes (typhoons, accidents) and the potential genetic effects of these population bottlenecks (73, 89). It has also been shown that these populations are very resilient. Once decimated, small human populations have the ability to grow rapidly (64, 66, 90). If it may be assumed that most populations began as relatively small groups which grew rapidly in the initial phases of settlement, founder effect and/or lineal effect may be of considerable importance in explaining the overall gene distribution. Indeed, some have suggested even more global effects from such historical events, including an important role for founder effect in some types of speciation (8, 113).

To this point the argument has been that history provides an extra dimension to studies of human populations, thereby making genetic structure more intelligible. Thus, when we know that a small population has grown rapidly from a few founders, we should expect that some genetic diseases (say) will be found in higher than "normal" frequencies; to know that large components of the Finnish population derives from in-migration from Scandanavia makes understandable the cline in gene frequencies from coastal areas toward the northeast (118) and so on.

If the relationship between history and genetic structure is viewed as simply a correlation, then there should be no reason why the inference could not go the other way: similarity in gene frequencies implies common historical derivation of the populations. "The cumulative genetic difference between two populations can be expected to be a summary of their evolutionary history, being proportional to the time of separation and inversely related to the intermigration between them" (63, p. 786). Indeed, this is a very old idea in physical anthropology. Genetical anthropology began in this tradition as is obvious from Boyd's "Four Achievements of the Genetical Method in Physical Anthropology" (7). Some continue to see this as the principal achievement of small population genetics (34). Genetic similarity, then, becomes a tool used by archaeologists and ethnohistorians to reconstruct regional history.

As appealing as this idea may be, probably only the barest outline of history can be recovered from the distributions of genetic traits. This uncertainty follows from the fact noted at the beginning of this section that present genetic structure can be the result of several distinct processes. Different processes can lead to similar genetic outcomes. Unraveling this mix without external information is logically impossible. In those cases where detailed history has been known, historical relations generally account for some but not by any means all of the genetic relationships. So, for instance, with regard to the well-documented Åland Island study, Meilke et al (64, p. 290) state that ". . . for historical inference from genetic structure, present day distributions of gene frequencies would not be of much use without the information supplied by the historical material".

A better procedure is to see historical relatedness as an hypothesis to be tested by as many different methods as is possible. In the absence of external evidence for historical relations (linguistic, archaeological, ethnohistorical), history should have no special place as an explanation, as most would agree in extreme cases; e.g. biological similarities between African and Oceanic Negritos are not very likely to be due to common ancestry.

Menozzi et al (63) provide a nice example of this point. They examined an historical question, the spread of farming through Europe as a wave of population advance, on the basis of present-day gene frequencies. However, the historical spread of agriculture is well known. The hypothesis is based on independent archaeological data, and there is a definite expectation for both null and alternative hypotheses. As expected on the basis of demic diffusion, they demonstrate the presence of clines in composite variables reflecting gene frequencies at numerous loci. However, as they note, these clines do not constitute proof of their hypothesis (although the data are compatible with the physical spread of Neolithic farmers) since other alternative explanations are possible.

THE APPORTIONMENT OF HUMAN DIVERSITY

The early exponents of anthropological genetics shared the same concerns for racial taxonomy as traditional physical anthropologists (e.g. 6). This interest has waned considerably in recent years. It may be noted, for example, that race was not mentioned during a recent symposium on natural selection in the human population (94). While no longer the central concern of physical anthropology, taxonomic questions continue to occupy many investigators.

A number of recent studies have discussed the degree of genetic variation within and between the "major" races of *Homo sapiens* (13, 54, 65, 86, 87, 93, 111). The relevant question in these studies is whether or not the "racial" subdivision of the human species population is a significant one. That is, human races might constitute fundamental divisions of the species reflecting long periods of isolation during which time genetic differences arose through random processes and/or adaptations to differing geographic selective factors (13, 19). On the other hand, it may be that the traditionally identified major races are so biologically heterogeneous that little is learned by distinguishing them (102).

Lewontin (54) and Nei & Roychoudhury (86, 87), using different metrics, arrived at similar conclusions on this question. Both studies suggest that variation within the races is great compared to variation between the major racial groups. Indeed, Lewontin allocates over 85 percent of human diversity to individual variation within local populations; of the remaining 14 percent of total species diversity, 8 percent is due to variation between populations within the major racial groups and only 6 percent remains to be accounted for by racial subdivision.

Mitton (65) has criticized these conclusions on the basis of the insensitivity of the statistic used by Lewontin and on the use of monomorphic loci by Nei and Roychoudhury in their comparison set. He goes on to show that when multiple-locus comparisons are made, races are distinguishable. But as Weiss & Maruyama (111) point out, the question of whether races can be discriminated is not at issue. By looking at the joint frequencies of *enough* loci, every individual would be unique and thus distinguishable. Monomorphic loci would not be good discriminant variables, but if races are thought to result from a long period of relative isolation, this is not a valid point. Monomorphisms should be included since a representative sample of the whole genome is required to gauge the total degree of differentiation. On this view, the criticism cuts the other way; i.e. because monomorphisms are probably less likely to be discovered (particularly for blood antigens), they may be *insufficiently* represented in the gene set. Thus Lewontin and Nei and Roychoudhury try to support the representativeness of the gene sample by showing that average heterozygosity of the species appears to be reaching an asymptotic value, new discoveries not changing it in recent years. However, Lewontin estimated this value to be 16 percent and Nei and Roychoudhury 2 years later claim 13 percent or less (see also 39). Moreover, the loci considered are mainly blood substances (enzymes and antigens) for the obvious reason that blood is the easiest tissue to sample. This should also pose problems of representativeness.

Interestingly, Nei and Roychoudhury do not consider the question of representativeness of the populations making up their races. Their genetic data came primarily from American "Caucasoids" and American "Negroids," with the Japanese population being the almost exclusive representative of the "Mongoloids." Other large geographic divisions of the species such as American Indians (93) are not "major" races. Other judgments such as whether South Asians are "Caucasoids" or not (65) seem to be made arbitrarily. Lewontin, on the other hand, discusses at some length the composition of the major races. As he notes, this is not a trivial problem. In fact, as he suggests, racial categories can be *constructed* in such a way as to maximize internal homogeneity. Weiss & Maruyama (111) make this point even more strongly. Following an argument by Hulse (41), they relate the present importance in numerical proportions of modern populations to cultural factors. On the basis of these and other demographic arguments, they conclude that racial classification is a "tenuous pursuit."

This review is not the place to explore the long history of the race concept; however, these recent studies raise again the issue of the purpose of human racial taxonomy. As a multitude of anthropologists should by now have made clear, the concept of race includes a wide variety of very different concerns (e.g. 47). It is worth recalling this in the light of recent calls for a more "global" approach to human diversity (34).

One issue is whether or not traditionally defined "major" races are distinguishable. This is obviously true (and, as noted already, could probably be made true for almost any split of the species). A second issue is how much of the total species variation exists at various levels of partition of the species. According to Lewontin and Nei and Roychoudhury, the racial level is insignficant.

A third procedure has been to construct dendrograms which purport to show the pattern of genetic differences between racial populations as a tree structure. This has been a common recent exercise in classification at the local population level, but racial groupings have also been used as the units to be clustered (13). The tree structure suggests a phylogenetic interpretation; however, since races are not reproductively isolated, this interpretation is inappropriate (57). Moreover, the initial decision to cluster "races" presumes that the categories are already defined. These initial racial groupings mix together geography, presumed history, selected biological characteristics, and folk prejudices as attributes of definition. They are poor candidates for even phenetic classification.

There are certainly good reasons for aggregating local breeding populations into larger units of analysis. Small populations are notoriously too "noisy" as a result of random variation to detect natural selection statistically. To demonstrate small fitness differentials among genotypes with any confidence would require sample sizes beyond that obtainable in most small population work. Livingstone (57) makes a good case for analyzing genetic variation in terms of larger regional population units. Such analysis often shows more systematic and regular trends which may reveal the operation of natural selection. This argument is particularly convincing when illustrated by hemoglobin and G6PD data. Gene frequencies in local breeding populations vary due to random fluctuations; larger scale regional trends seem explicable on the basis of deterministic factors.

In order to study natural selection, not only are large populations required for statistical reasons, but, more important biologically, they need to be homogeneous with respect to the purported selective factor. Large heterogeneous populations will not solve the problem. Thus Livingstone's prescription must be taken judiciously, and breeding populations must be combined into large units of analysis with some attention to the purpose of the analysis.

Many large populations in the modern world are aggregates of numerous subpopulations of differing historical, environmental, cultural, and ethnic backgrounds. This mixture has made the task of sorting out the causes of modern biological variation extremely complex (33). In considering the current diversity of alleles and high heterozygosity of the "European" population, for example, it might be well to attend to Neel's (77, 101) suggestion that this situation is due to the fusion of many original tribes, each of which would have been relatively homogeneous. This, along with the well-documented historical breakdown of rural isolation in Europe, must be taken into account if the "European population" is to be a unit of long-term evolutionary analysis.

Pooling of local breeding populations into larger units may also be useful for studies which do not involve selection. Workman et al (118) provide a good discussion of the trade-offs between different levels of population partition. As they note, deciding on the "appropriate number and composition of the aggregates is probably the most difficult problem in the analysis of large continental populations" (p. 365).

Smouse & Ward (99) show how comparison of grouped historically related village populations at the "cluster" level illuminates the genetic effects of demographic and sociocultural factors. Among-village variation is similar between the Ye'cuana and Yanomama Indian tribes; however, clusters of related villages are significantly more variable among the Yanomama, a result explicable in terms of differences between the tribes in population growth, fissioning, and migration rates. (This paper is also of methodological interest as it describes a likelihood procedure for testing population differences.)

Depending on the problem of interest, then, useful studies might range from individual phenotype data (to analyze clines, for instance) through local breeding populations (for inbreeding or isolation by distance) to regional populations (to study overall patterns). A comprehensive study involving variation over time as well as space would require a combination of these levels of analysis emphasizing different aspects of the structure. In short, good large-scale analysis depends on the careful specification of levels in the population hierarchy and attention to the appropriate level for a given analysis.

The apportionment of human diversity is not simply a question of how many human races exist, or even whether or not races exist, but rather, as Lewontin (54) emphasizes, the relative importance of intragroup or intergroup variation. There is no single correct partition; only different problems requiring different levels of analysis. The traditionally defined races, because they are often represented as all-purpose "natural" categories, are best discarded. It might be possible that they correspond to some useful division of the species, but after generations of controversy, this remains to be shown.

SUMMARY AND CONCLUSIONS

Anthropological genetics is in one sense a branch of evolutionary genetics. Theoretical and methodological advances in the genetics of human populations generally mirror those of the parent discipline. Equally, controversies such as the continuing neutralist/selectionist debate (55) are reflected in anthropological work (115). Human data, because it is rich in demographic and historical detail, has been important in some of these discussions, and some models seem most adapted to the human situation (4, 95), but the theories have not been specific to human populations.

Anthropological genetics is also a branch of anthropology. Here also theories and methods overlap with other anthropological disciplines. Most notable is the shared concern with patterns of mating (88); for genetics, this leads to studies of inbreeding and rates of endogamy, the defining characteristic of the deme. I have emphasized the analysis of the hierarchy of Mendelian populations more than might be justified on the basis of current research, partially because it seems to me that this is an important problem where anthropologists can contribute to evolutionary understanding. Population genetic theory is based on the breeding population as the unit of evolution, but little attention has been given to the complex set of hierarchic levels between the deme and the total species population (104). For a variety of problems, careful specification of appropriate population levels is required, and anthropological methods seem best suited for this analysis.

The anthropological approach has also led to the study of population structure which combines geographical, demographic, sociocultural, and historical factors in a holistic framework. This work has not resulted in any startling new theories of the evolutionary process; however, a number of assumptions have been clarified and evaluated by these studies. Thus it has been shown that geographic distance is a determinant of genetic similarities in only a very general sense (57, 118). Certainly geography is important in structuring populations, but to ignore other factors produces a very simplistic view of human mating and migration patterns. Social structure is one additional factor of long-standing anthropological interest. Some features of social structure are probably irrelevant to genetic structure, but the importance of fission-fusion and lineal effect have now been extensively documented by Neel and others. History provides another set of factors which are particularly salient in studies of human populations due to the availability of historical materials (written or inferred from genealogies, etc). Thus the history of the human species and of particular populations suggests that long-term equilibria, an assumption of many genetic models, is only a convenient mathematical fiction (77).

Populations are structured geographically or socially at any one point in time; however, migration patterns, cultural practices, and demographic processes change through time. Current gene frequencies provide a cross-section of genetic structure. To infer how these frequencies arose, time perspective is required. Thus independent historical sources become extremely useful to correct interpretation. On the other hand, the fact that different evolutionary processes can lead to equivalent genetic outcomes limits the use of gene frequencies in historical reconstruction.

Although anthropological geneticists have concentrated on small relatively homogeneous populations, it has often been assumed that the results of these studies will be applicable to species-wide problems. From all indications, prehistoric human populations were small and subdivided. Despite the difficulties and uncertainties, modern small-scale or "primitive" populations provide the best models for these populations and, therefore, for the range of conditions under which most of human evolution occurred (78).

Others have argued that current conceptions emphasizing marked microdifferentiation in these populations are incorrect and give too much weight to random noise or "ripples on the gene pool" (34, 35). According to this view, a broader perspective is required for understanding human evolution. This does not mean that large heterogeneous populations will provide better estimates of natural selection (77). Races, for example, are ill-defined and heterogeneous assembleges of populations of uncertain relevance to evolutionary problems (111).

The view of anthropological genetics presented here has emphasized the intensive holistic study of small-scale populations. A variety of problems have been investigated in a broad range of populations (certainly not limited to "primitive" populations). As foci of interest of different studies shift from genetic drift to natural selection to overall species heterozygosity, the detailed social, historical, and demographic data obtainable for human populations should allow the meaningful aggregation of individuals into local breeding populations which, in turn, may be further combined for regional analysis, and so on. Thus the understanding of human diversity on a species-wide scale may be enriched by the intensive anthropological study of small populations.

Literature Cited

1. Adams, J. W., Kasakoff, A. B. 1976. Factors underlying endogamous group size. In *Regional Analysis*, Vol. 2, Social systems, ed. C. A. Smith, pp. 149–73. New York: Academic. 381 pp.
2. Arends, T., Brewer, G., Chagnon, N., Gallango, M. L., Gershowitz, H., Layrisse, M., Neel, J., Shreffler, D., Tashian, R., Weitkamp, L. 1967. Intratribal genetic differentiation among the Yanomama Indians of Southern Venezuela. *Proc. Natl. Acad. Sci. USA* 57:1252–59
3. Birdsell, J. B. 1950. Some implications of the genetical concept of race in terms of spatial analysis. *Cold Spring Harbor Symp. Quant. Biol.* 15:259–311
4. Bodmer, W. F., Cavalli-Sforza, L. L. 1968. A migration matrix model for the study of random genetic drift. *Genetics* 59:565–92
5. Bodmer, W. F., Cavalli-Sforza, L. L. 1974. The analysis of genetic variation using migration matrices. In *Genetic Distance*, ed. J. F. Crow, C. Denniston, pp. 45–61. New York: Plenum. 195 pp.
6. Boyd, W. C. 1950. *Genetics and the Races of Man*. Boston: Little, Brown. 453 pp.
7. Boyd, W. C. 1963. Four achievements of the genetical method in physical anthropology. *Am. Anthropol.* 65:243–52
8. Bush, G. L. 1975. Modes of animal speciation. *Ann. Rev. Ecol. Syst.* 6: 339–64
9. Cannings, C., Cavalli-Sforza, L. L. 1973. Human population structure. *Adv. Hum. Genet.* 4:105–71
10. Cannings, C., Skolnick, M. H. 1975. Genetic drift in exogamous marriage systems. *Theor. Popul. Biol.* 7:39–54
11. Carmelli, D., Cavalli-Sforza, L. L. 1976. Some models of population structure and evolution. *Theor. Popul. Biol.* 9:329–59
12. Cavalli-Sforza, L. L. 1969. Genetic drift in an Italian population. *Sci. Am.* 21:30–37
13. Cavalli-Sforza, L. L. 1969. Human diversity. *Proc. 12th Int. Congr. Genet.* 3:405–16
14. Cavalli-Sforza, L. L. 1973. Some current problems of human population genetics. *Am. J. Hum. Genet.* 25:82–104
15. Cavalli-Sforza, L. L., Bodmer, W. F. 1971. *The Genetics of Human Populations*. San Francisco: Freeman. 965 pp.
15a. Chagnon, N. A. 1972. Tribal social organization and genetic microdifferentiation. See Ref. 37, pp. 252–82
16. Chagnon, N. A. 1974. *Studying the*

Yanomamö. New York: Holt, Rinehart & Winston. 270 pp.
17. Chakravarti, A., Chakraborty, R. 1978. Elevated frequency of Tay-Sachs disease among Ashkenazic Jews unlikely by genetic drift alone. *Am. J. Hum. Genet.* 30:256–61
18. Cheverud, J. M., Buettner-Janusch, J., Sade, D. 1978. Social group fission and the origin of intergroup genetic differentiation among the Rhesus monkeys of Cayo Santiago. *Am. J. Phys. Anthropol.* 49:449–56
19. Coon, C. S. 1962. *The Origin of Races*. New York: Knopf. 724 pp.
20. Duggleby, C. R. 1977. Blood group antigens and the population genetics of *Macaca mulatta* on Cayo Santiago. II. Effects of social group division. *Yearb. Phys. Anthropol.* 20:263–71
21. Ellis, W. S., Starmer, W. T. 1978. Inbreeding as measured by isonymy, pedigrees, and population size in Törbel, Switzerland. *Am. J. Hum. Genet.* 30:366–76
22. Eriksson, A. W., Eskola, M., Fellman, J., Forsius, H. 1973. The value of genealogical data in population studies in Sweden and Finland. See Ref. 68, pp. 102–18
23. Ewens, W. J. 1977. Population genetics theory in relation to the neutralist-selectionist controversy. *Adv. Hum. Genet.* 8:67–134
24. Ewens, W. J. 1978. Tay-Sachs disease and theoretical population genetics. *Am. J. Hum. Genet.* 30:328–29
25. Felsenstein, J. 1975. A pain in the torus: some difficulties with models of isolation by distance. *Am. Nat.* 109:359–68
26. Felsenstein, J. 1976. The theoretical population genetics of variable selection and migration. *Ann. Rev. Genet.* 10:253–80
27. Fix, A. G. 1974. Neighbourhood knowledge and marriage distance: the Semai case. *Ann. Hum. Genet.* 37:327–32
28. Fix, A. G. 1975. Fission-fusion and lineal effect: aspects of the population structure of the Semai Senoi of Malaysia. *Am. J. Phys. Anthropol.* 43: 295–302
29. Fix, A. G. 1978. The role of kin-structured migration in genetic microdifferentiation. *Ann. Hum. Genet.* 41:329–39
30. Friedlaender, J. S. 1971. The population structure of South-Central Bougainville. *Am. J. Phys. Anthropol.* 35:13–26
31. Friedlaender, J. S. 1974. A comparison of population distance and population

structure techniques. See Ref. 5, pp. 167–87
32. Friedlaender, J. S. 1975. Models of population structure and reality. In *The Role of Natural Selection in Human Evolution,* ed. F. M. Salzano, pp. 121–32. New York: Am. Elsevier
33. Friedlaender, J. S. 1975. *Patterns of Human Variation.* Cambridge: Harvard Univ. Press. 252 pp.
34. Harpending, H. 1974. Genetic structure of small populations. *Ann. Rev. Anthropol.* 3:229–43
35. Harpending, H., Chasko, W. 1976. Heterozygosity and population structure in Southern Africa. In *The Measures of Man,* ed. E. Giles, J. Friedlaender, pp. 214–29. Cambridge, Mass: Peabody Mus. Press
36. Harpending, H., Jenkins, T. 1974. !Kung population structure. See Ref. 5, pp. 137–65
37. Harrison, G. A., Boyce, A. J. 1972. Migration, exchange, and the genetic structure of populations. In *The Structure of Human Populations,* ed. G. A. Harrison, A. J. Boyce, pp. 128–45. Oxford: Clarendon. 447 pp.
38. Hedrick, P. W., Ginevan, M. E., Ewing, E. P. 1976. Genetic polymorphism in heterogeneous environments. *Ann. Rev. Ecol. Syst.* 7:1–32
39. Hedrick, P. W., Murray, E. 1978. Average heterozygosity revisited. *Am. J. Hum. Genet.* 30:377–82
40. Hiorns, R. W., Harrison, G. A., Gibson, J. B. 1977. Genetic variation in some Oxfordshire villages. *Ann. Hum. Biol.* 4:197–210
41. Hulse, F. S. 1957. Some factors influencing the relative proportions of human racial stocks. *Cold Spring Harbor Symp. Quant. Biol.* 22:33–45
42. Hussels, I. E., Morton, N. E. 1972. Pingelap and Mokil atolls: Achromatopsia. *Am. J. Hum. Genet.* 24:304–9
43. Imaizumi, Y., Morton, N. E., Harris, D. E. 1970. Isolation by distance in artificial populations. *Genetics* 66:569–82
44. Jackson, J. E. 1976. Vaupés marriage: a network system in the Northwest Amazon. See Ref. 1, pp. 65–93
45. Jacquard, A. 1975. Inbreeding: one word, several meanings. *Theor. Popul. Biol.* 7:338–63
46. Johnston, F. E., Albers, M. E. 1973. Computer simulation of demographic processes. In *Methods and Theories of Anthropological Genetics,* ed. M. H. Crawford, P. L. Workman, pp. 201–17. Albuquerque: Univ. New Mexico Press. 509 pp.

47. Kelso, A. J. 1974. *Physical Anthropology: an Introduction.* Philadelphia: Lippincott. 357 pp. 2nd ed.
48. Kluckhohn, C., Griffith, C. 1950. Population genetics and social anthropology. *Cold Spring Harbor Symp. Quant. Biol.* 15:401–8
48a. Kunstadter, P. 1972. Demography, ecology, social structure, and settlement patterns. See Ref. 37, pp. 313–51
49. Lalouel, J. M. 1973. Topology of population structure. See Ref. 68, pp. 139–49
50. Lalouel, J. M. 1976. The conceptual framework of Malecot's model of isolation by distance. *Ann. Hum. Genet.* 40:355–60
51. Lalouel, J. M., Morton, N. E. 1973. Bioassay of kinship in a South American Indian population. *Am. J. Hum. Genet.* 25:62–73
52. Lee, R. E., ed. 1977. *Population Patterns in the Past.* New York: Academic. 376 pp.
53. Leslie, P. W., MacCluer, J. W., Dyke, B. 1978. Consanguinity avoidance and genotypic frequencies in human populations. *Hum. Biol.* 50:281–99
54. Lewontin, R. C. 1972. The apportionment of human diversity. *Evol. Biol.* 6:381–98
55. Lewontin, R. C. 1974. *The Genetic Basis of Evolutionary Change.* New York: Columbia Univ. Press. 346 pp.
56. Lewontin, R. C. 1975. Foreword. See Ref. 33, pp. vi–ix
57. Livingstone, F. B. 1973. Gene frequency differences in human populations: some problems of analysis and interpretation. See Ref. 46, pp. 39–66
58. MacCluer, J. W., Dyke, B. 1976. On the minimum size of endogamous populations. *Soc. Biol.* 23:1–12
59. Malcolm, L. A., Booth, P. B., Cavalli-Sforza, L. L. 1971. Intermarriage patterns and blood group gene frequencies of the Bundi people of the New Guinea highlands. *Hum. Biol.* 43:187–99
60. Martin, A. O. 1973. An empirical comparison of some descriptions of population structure in a human isolate. See Ref. 68, pp. 195–202
61. Mayr, E. 1963. *Animal Species and Evolution.* Cambridge, Mass: Belknap Press and Harvard Univ. Press. 797 pp.
62. McKusick, V. A., Hostetler, J. A., Egeland, J. A., Eldridge, R. 1964. The distribution of certain genes in the Old Order Amish. *Cold Spring Harbor Symp. Quant. Biol.* 29:99–114
63. Menozzi, P., Piazza, A., Cavalli-Sforza, L. L. 1978. Synthetic maps of human

gene frequencies in Europeans. *Science* 201:786–92

64. Mielke, J. H., Workman, P. C., Fellman, J., Eriksson, A. W. 1976. Population structure of the Åland Islands, Finland. *Adv. Hum. Genet.* 6:241–321

65. Mitton, J. B. 1977. Genetic differentiation of races of man as judged by single-locus and multilocus analyses. *Am. Nat.* 111:203–12

66. Morgan, K. 1973. Historical demography of a Navaho community. See Ref. 46, pp. 263–314

67. Morton, N. E. 1972. The future of human population genetics. *Prog. Med. Genet.* 8:103–24

68. Morton, N. E., ed. 1973. *Genetic Structure of Populations.* Honolulu: Univ. Hawaii Press. 313 pp.

69. Morton, N. E. 1973. Isolation by distance. See Ref. 68, pp. 76–77

70. Morton, N. E. 1974. Controversial issues in human population genetics. *Am. J. Hum. Genet.* 26:259–62

71. Morton, N. E. 1977. Isolation by distance in human populations. *Ann. Hum. Genet.* 40:361–65

72. Morton, N. E., Imaizumi, Y., Harris, D. E. 1971. Clans as genetic barriers. *Am. Anthropol.* 73:1005–10

73. Morton, N. E., Lew, R., Hussels, I. E., Little, G. F. 1972. Pingelap and Mokil atolls: historical genetics. *Am. J. Hum. Genet.* 24:277–89

74. Neel, J. V. 1967. The genetic structure of primitive human populations. *Jpn. J. Hum. Genet.* 12:1–16

75. Neel, J. V. 1970. Lessons from a primitive people. *Science* 170:815–21

76. Neel, J. V. 1972. The genetic structure of a tribal population, the Yanomama Indians. I. Introduction. *Ann. Hum. Genet.* 35:255–59

77. Neel, J. V. 1973. Inferences concerning evolutionary forces from genetic data. *Isr. J. Med. Sci.* 9:1519–32

78. Neel, J. V. 1976. The circumstances of human evolution. *Johns Hopkins Med. J.* 138:233–44

79. Neel, J. V., Layrisse, M., Salzano, F. M. 1977. Man in the tropics: the Yanomama Indians. In *Population Structure and Human Variation,* ed. G. A. Harrison, pp. 109–42. Cambridge: Cambridge Univ. Press. 342 pp.

80. Neel, J. V., Salzano, F. M. 1967. Further studies on the Xavante Indians X. Some hypotheses-generalizations resulting from these studies. *Am. J. Hum. Genet.* 19:555–73

81. Neel, J. V., Salzano, F. M., Junqueira, P. C., Keiter, F., Maybury-Lewis, D.

1964. Studies on the Xavante Indians of the Brazilian Mato Grosso. *Am. J. Hum. Genet.* 16:52–140

82. Neel, J. V., Ward, R. H. 1970. Village and tribal genetic distances among American Indians, and the possible implications for human evolution. *Proc. Natl. Acad. Sci. USA* 65:323–30

83. Nei, M. 1973. The theory and estimation of genetic distance. See Ref. 68, pp. 45–51.

84. Nei, M. 1975. *Molecular Population Genetics and Evolution.* Amsterdam: Am. Elsevier/North Holland. 288 pp.

85. Nei, M. 1977. F-statistics and analysis of gene diversity in subdivided populations. *Ann. Hum. Genet.* 41:225–33

86. Nei, M., Roychoudhury, A. K. 1972. Gene differences between Caucasian, Negro, and Japanese populations. *Science* 177:434–36

87. Nei, M., Roychoudhury, A. K. 1974. Genic variation within and between the three major races of man, Caucasoids, Negroids, and Mongoloids. *Am. J. Hum. Genet.* 26:421–43

88. Reid, R. M. 1973. Inbreeding in human populations. See Ref. 46, pp. 83–116

89. Roberts, D. F. 1968. Genetic effects of population size reduction. *Nature* 220:1084–88

90. Roberts, D. F. 1968. Genetic fitness in a colonizing human population. *Hum. Biol.* 40:494–507

91. Roberts, D. F. 1973. Anthropological genetics: problems and pitfalls. See Ref. 46, pp. 1–17

92. Roberts, D. F. 1975. Genetic studies of isolates. In *Modern Trends in Human Genetics,* ed. A. E. H. Emery, pp. 221–69. London: Butterworths

93. Roychoudhury, A. K. 1978. Genetic distance between the American Indians and the three major races of man. *Hum. Hered.* 28:380–85

94. Salzano, F. M. 1975. Some key problems in the study of natural selection in man. See Ref. 32, pp. 407–24

95. Smith, C. A. B. 1969. Local fluctuations in gene frequencies. *Ann. Hum. Genet.* 32:251–60

96. Smith, C. A. B. 1974. Measures of homozygosity and inbreeding in populations. *Ann. Hum. Genet.* 37:377–91

97. Smith, C. A. B. 1977. A note on genetic distance. *Ann. Hum. Genet.* 40:463–79

98. Smouse, P. E., Neel, J. V. 1977. Multivariate analysis of genetic disequilibrium in the Yanomama. *Genetics* 85:733–52

99. Smouse, P. E., Ward, R. H. 1978. A comparison of the genetic infrastructure

of the Yecuana and the Yanomama: a likelihood analysis of genotypic variation among populations. *Genetics* 88: 611–31

100. Spielman, R. S., Migliazza, E. C., Neel, J. V. 1974. Regional linguistic and genetic differences among Yanomama Indians. *Science* 184:637–44

101. Spielman, R. S., Neel, J. V., Li, F. H. F. 1977. Inbreeding estimation from population data: models, procedures and implications. *Genetics* 85:355–71

102. Spiess, E. B. 1977. *Genes in Populations.* New York: Wiley. 780 pp.

103. Spuhler, J. N. 1972. Genetic, linguistic, and geographic distances in native North America. In *The Assessment of Population Affinities in Man,* ed. J. S. Weiner, J. Huizinga, pp. 72–95. Oxford: Clarendon. 224 pp.

104. Spuhler, J. N. 1973. Anthropological genetics: an overview. See Ref. 46, pp. 423–51

105. Swedlund, A. C. 1978. Historical demography as population biology. *Ann. Rev. Anthropol.* 7:137–73

106. Wagener, D., Cavalli-Sforza, L. L., Barakat, R. 1978. Ethnic variation of genetic disease: roles of drift for recessive lethal alleles. *Am. J. Hum. Genet.* 30:262–70

107. Ward, R. H. 1973. Some aspects of genetic structure in the Yanomama and Makiritare: two tribes of southern Venezuela. See Ref. 46, pp. 367–88

108. Ward, R. H., Neel, J. V. 1970. Gene frequencies and microdifferentiation among Makiritare Indians. IV. A comparison of a genetic network with ethnohistory and migration matrices; a new index of genetic isolation. *Am. J. Hum. Genet.* 22:538–61

109. Ward, R. H., Neel, J. V. 1976. The genetic structure of a tribal population.

XVII. Clines and their interpretation. *Genetics* 82:103–21

110. Weiss, K. M. 1976. Demographic theory and anthropological inference. *Ann. Rev. Anthropol.* 5:351–81

111. Weiss, K. M., Maruyama, T. 1976. Archeology, population genetics and studies of human racial ancestry. *Am. J. Phys. Anthropol.* 44:31–49

112. Wiesenfeld, S. L., Gajdusek, D. C. 1976. Genetic structure and heterozygosity in the kuru region, Eastern Highlands of New Guinea. *Am. J. Phys. Anthropol.* 45:117–89

113. Wilson, A. C., Bush, G. L., Case, S. M., King, M.-C. 1975. Social structuring of mammalian populations and rate of chromosomal evolution. *Proc. Natl. Acad. Sci. USA* 72:5061–65

114. Wood, J. W. 1977. A stability test for migration matrix models of genetic differentiation. *Hum. Biol.* 49:309–20

115. Wood, J. W. 1978. Population structure and genetic heterogeneity in the Upper Markham Valley of New Guinea. *Am. J. Phys. Anthropol.* 48:463–70

116. Workman, P. L., Harpending, H., Lalouel, J. M., Lynch, C., Niswander, J. D., Singleton, R. 1973. Population studies on southwestern Indian tribes. VI. See Ref. 68, pp. 166–94

117. Workman, P. L., Lucarelli, P., Agostino, R., Scarabino, R., Scacchi, R., Carapella, E., Palmarino, R., Bottini, E. 1975. Genetic differentiation among Sardinian villages. *Am. J. Phys. Anthropol.* 43:165–76

118. Workman, P. L., Mielke, J. H., Nevanlinna, H. R. 1976. The genetic structure of Finland. *Am. J. Phys. Anthropol.* 44:341–67

119. Yellen, J., Harpending, H. 1972. Hunter-gatherer populations and archaeological inference. *World Archaeol.* 4: 244–53

Ann. Rev. Anthropol. 1979. 8:231–66

THE ANTHROPOLOGY
OF INDUSTRIAL WORK

◆9633

Michael Burawoy[1]

Department of Sociology, University of California, Berkeley, California 94720

The anthropology of industrial work has had a relatively short although turbulent history. During the last 50 years the study of the shop floor has spawned a number of theories, each asserting its claim to universal validity. In this essay I propose to resolve the differences among these general theories by restoring them to the specific context in which they were germinated—a particular period in capitalist development, a particular sector of the capitalist economy, or a particular capitalist society. By interpreting the multiplicity of general theories as reflecting the diversity of the capitalist labor process we can begin to grasp its underlying unity as well as understand the forms and causes of its variation.

OVERVIEW

The first chapter of industrial anthropology was inspired by its arch-priest —Elton Mayo. He helped to direct the first systematic, detailed and intensive studies of the organization of work undertaken at the Hawthorne plant of the Western Electric Company between 1927 and 1933 (3, 24, 66, 94, 123). Drawing on these studies, Mayo pioneered what has come to be known as the human relations school, with its uninhibited focus on the "human" dimension of work (76, 77). This school of thought was a retreat from the examination of the objective conditions of work, from studies of fatigue and monotony, and from an image of men and women as machines, espoused by such representatives of scientific management as Frederick Winslow Taylor (115). It was a turn toward constituting men and women

[1] I should like to thank Gretchen Franklin, Kathy Keilch, and Erik Wright for their comments and assistance.

231

0084-6570/79/1015-0231$01.00

as social and sentient beings with the capacity to construct subjective experiences at work, independent of and in adjustment to its objective constraints. Mayo's perspective eschewed conflict as pathological and isolated the work place from its environment. Many of his ideas are elaborated in the sociological writings of William Foot Whyte (124, 125), Burleigh Gardner and David Moore (48), as well as the more psychological work of Chris Argyris (4) and Rensis Likert (68).

The Mayo school and its descendants were rooted in the concrete realities and aspirations of welfare capitalism—a system of paternalistic industrial relations and company unions which large corporations such as Western Electric embraced during the 1920s. Yet at the very time that Mayo was drawing on the Hawthorne studies to sustain visions of industrial collaboration, the basis of those visions was collapsing. The destruction of welfare capitalism in the 1930s and the militant struggles between capital and labor required a very different framework of analysis than the one offered by the human relations school. Thus, in their study of a strike in 1933 at Yankee City, Warner & Low (121) trace the source of industrial conflict to the progressive loss of control over the labor process experienced by operatives during the twentieth century. In pointing to the conditions for the destruction of skill and concentration of capital, Warner and Low provide explanations for the unevenness of changes in the labor process, in particular the separation of mental and manual labor.

Once crafts are destroyed what new forms of work organization arise to take their place? Answers can be found in the general theories developed as a response to Mayo but which nevertheless reflected particular features of twentieth century capitalism and accentuated particular aspects of its labor processes. The substitution of collective bargaining for paternalism after the depression led both radicals and economists to attack Mayo for failing to come to terms with industrial conflict (9, 64, 81). Economist Clark Kerr, for example, saw the trade union as an instrument for regulating and institutionalizing conflict rather than the implacable enemy of management (62, 63). But his view was and continues to be a partial one, expressing what is more distinctive of the organized "monopoly" sector of industry rather than the unorganized "competitive" sector. A second group of studies responded to the human relations school by emphasizing the constraints new types of technology imposed on management's ability to reconstruct work experience through "person-oriented supervision" and treating employees as "integrated individuals" (14, 119). In Britain the Tavistock Institute inaugurated a new human relations school which paid explicit attention to the constraints of technology (91, 117), while Joan Woodward (127) developed theories in which technological complexity and thus the organization of work were shaped by the size and standardization of the product market.

A third group of studies began to investigate the structure of management. Where Mayo had treated management as a cohesive and isolated bloc distinct from workers, the new studies drew attention to divisions within management and problems of dealing with "environments," categorized as stable or unstable, homogeneous or heterogeneous, differentiated or undifferentiated (37, 116). Out of the study of the environment and its impact on the structure and operation of the firm there grew over-arching theories of organizations which embraced hospitals, prisons, trade unions, political parties, and so on, as well as industrial enterprises (67, 72, 92, 107, 116). But in striving for ahistorical generalizations appropriate to all organizations, the concrete world was left behind and industrial anthropology disappeared in a welter of abstract categories. This assimilation of industrial to all organizations is the reflection in theory of a movement in reality, namely the penetration of bureaucratic patterns into ever wider arenas of social life. The study of bureaucracy became the focus of another school which emerged after World War II under the guidance of Robert Merton. Pushing aside Mayo's concern with harmony, Merton and his students took Max Weber as their point of departure and in a series of case studies showed how the adoption of rules undermined organizational goals (13, 52, 104). Their conclusions seemed as applicable to government agencies, military organizations, and other bureaucratic systems as they were to industrial concerns.

However, in the arena of industrial relations the emergence of rules to regulate relations between capital and labor, management and unions was not only historically specific but also geographically specific. As I suggest in the final part of this essay, much of what is taken for granted by industrial anthropology no longer holds in other countries outside the United States. American industrial anthropology turns out to be the anthropology of industrial work in the United States. It then becomes necessary to incorporate national characteristics such as the history of class struggles, the form of the state, and the manner and timing of insertion into the world capitalist order so as to reach a more complete understanding of the forms and causes of variations in the labor process.

WELFARE CAPITALISM AND THE ROOTS OF INDUSTRIAL ANTHROPOLOGY

Welfare capitalism emerged during World War I as a managerial strategy to preempt unionization (16). One of the earliest schemes followed the Ludlow Massacre of 1914, in which battles raged between the National Guard and battalions of armed miners from the Colorado Fuel and Iron Company. As chief executive of the company, John D. Rockefeller brought in Ivy Lee and Mackenzie King to set up a system of "industrial democracy" which would offer wage guarantees and fringe benefits and would erect a grievance machinery and a plan for employee representation. According to the new welfare philosophy, industrial strife was the product of misunderstanding and the failure of different sides of industry to treat one another as human beings:

> It follows, therefore, that the relations of men engaged in industry are human relations. Men do not live merely to toil; they also live to play, to mingle with their fellows, to love, to worship. The test of success of our social organization is the extent to which every man is free to realize his highest and best self. . . . If in the conduct of industry, therefore, the manager ever keeps in mind that in dealing with employees he is dealing with human beings, with flesh and blood, with hearts and souls; and if likewise the workmen realize that managers and investors are themselves also human beings, how much bitterness will be avoided (93, p. 12).

During the 1920s, welfare capitalism became the dominant ideology of enlightened business, and many large corporations adopted one of its plans. After becoming president of General Electric, Gerald Swope spread the gospel to plant officials:

> production, costs, and relations with men. Usually . . . we think of the first two only. . . . The last thing our foremen will remember is the relations with men who work for him and that, as a matter of fact, is the most important consideration that bears on the results that any executive is to achieve.

As Charles Swab, head of Bethlehem Steel, put it, "Industry's most important task in this day of large-scale production is management of men on a human basis" (cited in 20, pp. 152–53).

The school of human relations founded by Elton Mayo was but a continuation in academic garb of what was being preached in industry by corporate executives. It is no accident that the first major investigations into human relations in industry should be supported by the Rockefeller Foundation and located in a plant of a leading practitioner of welfare capitalism. It fell to Harvard Business School and Elton Mayo in particular to use these early investigations to bestow legitimacy and universality on the words of John D. Rockefeller. Mayo sought to recreate the emotional bonds of the human group, which were breaking down outside the factory gates, on the shop floor. There individuals would give free reign to their repressed propensity toward spontaneous collaboration. Drawing on Durkheim, Pareto, Malinowski, and Warner, Mayo aimed to install the mechanical solidarity of preindustrial societies inside the industrial plant. The large corporation would become the home of solidarity, binding people together in the pursuit of common goals.

Following studies of industrial fatigue and monotony in Britain and of the causes of labor turnover in a textile mill near Philadelphia, the Hawthorne experiments were designed to explore the effects of changes in working conditions such as rest pauses, length of working day, length of week, wage incentives, and illumination on worker output. The series of experiments all showed that variations in hourly or weekly output could not be linked to any one of these factors. Rather, it was argued (76, 94), variation in output had to be understood as the interrelated effect of objective conditions on the sentiments of the work group. In line with this interpretation, the final phase of the Hawthorne studies was directed toward examining the work group as a whole and not merely measuring the impact of different isolated variables. This was the famous bank wiring room experiment. The "relay assembly" and "mica splitting" experiments seemed to suggest that if management were to seek the cooperation of the informal work group which naturally springs up at the work place, through paying attention to employees' social and psychological needs, worker output would increase. The bank wiring room, however, seemed to illustrate the opposite tendency, namely the capacity of the informal group to enforce definite limits on worker output. Mayo (76) argued that the spontaneous solidarity that emerged on the shop floor could undermine managerial logic if workers did not understand that logic or acted out of irrational fear. Restriction of output was presented as an irrational response to the economic rationality of management.

Given rising levels of unemployment and the widespread adoption of Taylorism, the fear that speed-up or rate increases would result from breaking output norms was far from irrational. As Kerr & Fisher (64) were to point out after World War II, when collective bargaining had been established, Mayo's insistence on regarding the work place as the locus of harmony and spontaneous consent was at odds with the reality of industrial life. Workers were not "aborigines." Instead, Kerr and Fisher preferred to view industrial behavior as an expression of conflict or competition among economically rational individuals. Support for such an interpretation is to be found in Roy's study of output restriction among machine operators at the end of World War II (95–98). Roy highlights two particular forms of restriction. In the first—goldbricking—workers respond to impossible piece rates by not attempting to make the quota, content to earn the minimum guaranteed wage. In the second—quota restriction—workers respond to easy rates by keeping their output within a well defined upper limit for fear that exceeding this bound would cause management to cut the prices. This fear was grounded in the presence of time-study men stalking the aisles with stop watches in hand. Even more significantly, Roy shows that in order to make any of the rates, workers had to erect informal groups to counter managerial inefficiency and managerial regulations which obstructed the smooth operation of the machine shop. Thus, it was the economic *rational-*

ity of workers which led them to establish informal groups designed to defeat *managerial irrationality*.

This turning of Mayo's world on its head is not quite the demolition it appears. A closer reading of Roy's work reveals a number of significant departures from the rational pursuit of economic advantage. First, there are limits beyond which the search for increasing rewards becomes too costly. Exactly where that limit lies is not arrived at through rational calculation but through socially defined norms. The rationality of shop floor behavior, although couched in the idiom of dollars and cents, is nonetheless the product of a piece rate game—making out—which defines the rules and goals of the working activities of each operator. Second, as Mathewson (75) suggested and as Roy's study demonstrates, far from springing from autonomous resistance to management, making out is facilitated, encouraged, and in part organized by shop floor management in opposition to directives from higher management.

In other words, closer examination of the machine shop does vindicate an essential postulate of the Mayo school: that worker behavior cannot be understood outside of the particular culture (ideology) created in the work place. However, where Mayo might look upon the informal group as constituting an opposition to management, more careful analysis of both the bank wiring room and the machine shop indicates that management depends on the informal group to elicit the cooperation of workers. At the same time, this cooperation is not a manifestation of some universal human propensity to spontaneous collaboration, but is something produced and reproduced on the shop floor. Thus, to criticize Mayo for not recognizing the inevitable, structured conflict of interests between workers and management (17, 81) is to commit the same fallacy which Mayo himself commits in insisting on an underlying harmony. Interests are not given primordially but are organized and shaped by the labor process itself. The point is not to *assume* consensus or conflict but to *explain* them.

With labor wars being waged in other corporations around unionization, how was it possible for Hawthorne management to continue to achieve such a level of cooperation? What had happened to the labor struggles prior to the rise of welfare capitalism—struggles which had in fact brought about welfare capitalism? In part the answer is hidden in the Hawthorne data themselves, but has remained obscure until recently. The conventional interpretations (76, 94) share a vision restricted by their roots in welfare capitalism. The independent variables used to explain variation in output are precisely the ones subject to managerial manipulation. When these do not account for the observed changes, Roethlisberger, Dickson, and Mayo invoke the metaphysic of "human relations" as the missing link. In a remarkable reanalysis of the data from the first relay assembly experiment which lasted the entire 5 years, Franke & Kaul (43) demonstrate that shifts in output can be explained by variables that were not examined by Roethlisberger and Dickson either because they were beyond managerial control (economic depression) or because they were not deemed important (intensification of supervision). The reanalysis shows that an amazing 78.7 percent of the variation in output can be attributed to the enforcement of tighter discipline occasioned by the replacement of two members of the work group after nine months; 14.5 percent can be attributed to the onset of the depression after another 19 months; and a further 3.9 percent to changes in scheduled rest times, leaving 3 percent unexplained. So much for human sentiments. Moreover, although the quality of output also diminished during this period, 65 percent of the decline was due to defective materials, 14 percent to changes in rest stops, while only 5 percent was due to the economic depression.

Franke and Kaul go no further than to present their results, but the story cannot rest here. How do these results match those obtained from the other Hawthorne experiments? In the case of the bank wiring room the level of output remained fairly steady despite the development of the depression's effects, in particular a shorter working week. Since there is no record of supervision changing in the bank wiring room, one may conjecture that the depression had no effect on output due to the absence of managerial intervention. Equally, without the coercive sanctions implicit in increasing levels of unemployment and shortage of work, the intensification of supervision might not have been attempted, or could have been resisted.

In summary, our brief return to the Western Electric Studies and their reinterpretation leaves us with three sets of questions. First, how is consent organized on the shop floor and under what conditions might it break down? Second, does the intensification of coercion always have the effect of increasing output? If not, on what does it depend? Third, what is the impact of the environment on the organization of work and the activities of workers? How is the labor process shaped by factors that are beyond managerial control? We shall carry these questions into the remainder of the essay, but they can only be answered by going beyond the Western Electric studies both in time and place.

THE UNEVEN DESTRUCTION OF SKILL

Welfare capitalism might have continued were it not for the depression. Companies could no longer afford to maintain wage levels and extend welfare concessions. They defaulted on the promises of paternalism (20). The ensuing struggles for union recognition were bitter and violent. Only after the state intervention of the New Deal, in particular the Wagner Act of 1935, did the ideology of benevolence give way to collective bargaining. Just as welfare capitalism was antithetical to independent unionism, so its representation in theory—Mayo's school of human relations—had difficulty in recognizing the company as made up of disparate interests. Attempts to develop the framework so as to be in tune with changes in the pattern of industrial relations often sought to present the union as an instrument of collaboration, a means of facilitating communication between managers and managed rather than a bargaining opponent (125). Strikes were interpreted as breakdowns of communication between workers and management (103) rather than a fundamental conflict that divided the corporation into two antagonistic camps.

To understand the development of class struggle and the collapse of paternalism, a new perspective would have to emerge: it would have to incorporate the work place as part of, and influenced by, a wider set of factors which the earlier studies had either ignored or taken for granted. Paradoxically, it was Lloyd Warner, strongly identified with the human relations approach, who continued where Mayo left off. In a study that deserves much more attention than it has received, Warner & Low (121) examine the economic, political, and social forces which were transforming relations between capital and labor in the 1930s.

In normal times the various parts of the capitalist world appear fragmented and disconnected. The work place appears separate and relatively insulated from family life, distant markets, and so on. Appearances hide the links which bind the disparate parts of society together. In times of crisis, however, these bonds become transparent. Thus, in their interpretation of the causes of a 1933 community-wide strike by the workers of Yankee City's major industry—shoe-making—Warner and Low are forced to move far beyond those shop floor conditions which can be marginally manipulated by management to the factors contributing to the changing patterns of labor control and worker solidarity that had been emerging in the twentieth century.

The factors precipitating the strike were closely linked to the economic depression: wage cuts threatened minimal livelihood even for those with jobs; workers spent a great deal of their time waiting for jobs and were paid nothing for the waiting periods; as a result of attempts to boost sales, retail outlets were continually introducing new styles of shoes, which for the factory operatives meant more work for the same pay. Underlying these immediate grievances, however, were broader changes to which workers and managers sometimes alluded when explaining why there had never been a major strike in Yankee City before and why for the first time workers were united behind a union leadership. First, operatives were losing control over the labor process as a result of mechanization and fragmentation of jobs.

Second, control of the shoe companies themselves was passing out of the hands of the community and into the hands of financial bodies in distant centers such as New York. Major retail outlets were now dictating terms to the manufacturers in Yankee City, and residents had to confront the prospect of companies moving out of town and relocating in other cities where labor was cheaper or which were closer to the major consumer markets. The concentration of capital outside the community forced labor to similarly organize on a regional basis. The industrial union was the new vehicle which labor adopted to combat the vertical and horizontal integration of the shoe industry. To highlight the changes that had overtaken shoe-making, Warner and Low describe how mechanized, assembly line mass production for national markets, monopolized by one or two retail outlets and ultimately controlled by a distant complicated financial structure, emerged from the family-controlled craft production for local demand which had prevailed at the beginning of the seventeenth century.

Inasmuch as they examine workshop behavior, Warner and Low present a stark contrast with the exponents and philosophers of the Western Electric Studies. Where the latter stress the subjective dimension of adaptation to the inexorable features of industrial work, the former focus on the objective changes in the labor process, with little attention given to social and psychological mechanisms of adjustment. With the destruction of skills, wages are increasingly determined by the solidarity that workers can achieve in opposing management. This is as true at the collective level of the industry as it is for particular groups of workers within a single company. Thus, they argue that because women have not been able to build resistance to management, "women's work" is paid less than men's work irrespective of any skill. Similarly the newer ethnic groups—"the foreigners"—being socially insecure are more compliant and less assertive than the Yankees, the Irish, or the French. This is reflected in their earnings. By allocating jobs on the basis of gender and ethnicity, management creates antagonistic divisions within the labor force and thereby undermines its collective strength.

In their analysis of the fate of Yankee City shoemakers, Warner and Low anticipated Braverman's work (17), which has recently sparked a resurgence of interest in the labor process. Drawing on Frederick Winslow Taylor as the apostle of managerial control, Braverman elevates what Warner and Low call the "break in the skill hierarchy" to a defining developmental law of the labor process under monopoly capitalism. Unaware of the work of Warner and Low, Braverman refers to the process of deskilling as the separation of manual and mental labor or, more usually, of conception and execution. However, his argument is overly deterministic and functional in that what he describes as the separation of conception and execution is explained in terms of its necessity for the survival of capitalism. He does not examine why the process of deskilling proceeds unevenly, transforming sectors of the economy in different countries at different times and leaving some industries altogether untouched. Warner and Low at least suggest definite conditions for the development of the "break in the skill hierarchy," and therefore provide the basis for examining the generality of Braverman's tendential law.

What significance can we attach to the absence of a permanently organized union in Yankee City? What role does unionization play in labor's ability to resist the expropriation of skill and loss of control over the labor process? Certainly nineteenth-century craft unions provided a powerful bulwark against managerial encroachments on the craft workers' autonomy. In a survey of the United States during the second half of the last century, Montgomery (84) delineates three stages in the struggle for the retention, and in some instances expansion, of worker control over production: the functional autonomy of the craft worker, the use of union work rules, and the mutual support of diverse trades in rule enforcement and sympathetic strikes. However, at the beginning of the twentieth century many craft unions buckled in the face of the onslaught of scientific management and the open shop drive (11, 18, 19, 112). Hobsbawm (57, Chap. 9), in an analysis of British gas workers at the end of the nineteenth century, shows how unionization led to the expropriation of skill. Since the gas industry was a monopoly, changing patterns of competition were not the factor instigating the transformation of the labor process. Similar events in California agribusiness suggest that mechanization of picking has been a response to the growing strength of labor and the organization of the United Farm Workers. The technology for mechanized picking had been available to growers for some time, but they only introduced machines into the tomato and lettuce fields when they were faced with unionization and new labor legislation (44, 45).

In addition to class struggle, changing patterns of competition often provide the impetus for the destruction of crafts. In her study of glass workers at Carmaux in southwest France, Scott offers a detailed analysis of how just such a process of deskilling was spurred by domestic and British competition (102). Efficiency rather than struggle was the force behind technological change which undermined craft control over the labor process. Unionization was the consequence rather than the cause of these changes, and it failed to reverse the trend toward the separation of conception and execution. In other situations, rather than fighting such changes, unions become the vehicle for bargaining away labor's rights of directing the labor process in return for certain material benefits (83). More generally, the productivity deal has become the typical instrument through which labor is forced to give up what little control of production it still has (29). In short, the link between unionization and the uneven degradation of work is a complicated one which would bear careful study.

Rather than focus on the organization of labor, it might be as fruitful to examine the conditions which circumscribe the power of capital. In the study of Yankee City one of the major factors in favor of the manufacturers was the threat to move. What happens when capital is rooted to a given place, as in extractive industries like mining? A series of studies of the British coal-mining industry begin to respond to this question. In Britain the Tavistock Institute has taken the Mayo school of human relations one step forward in its pioneering of the sociotechnical systems perspective. These investigations go beyond the Hawthorne experiments in that they advocate broader changes in the organization of social relations in production. Technology, they argue, does not uniquely determine these relations and, moreover, technology itself should be treated as a variable. By shaping the social and technical organization of work in accordance with the social-psychological needs of workers, management can promote the effectiveness of the system as a whole. In their interpretation of a series of controlled experiments, Trist et al (117) claim that mechanization of mining, which involves the fragmentation of work and the break-up of the self-regulating, self-selecting work group, leads to higher levels of stress, higher rates of absenteeism, and lower levels of productivity than a system which involves the mutual adaptation of men and machines in the retention of the relatively autonomous work group of the single-place tradition. Thus, whereas management naturally chose to use mechanization to appropriate control from the colliers—conventional long-wall mining—Trist and company suggest that the transition to a "composite work organization" in which miners collectively decide how and when to use machines would be more effective.

As in the Western Electric studies, little attention is directed to changes in the environment during the period of observation. Their claim is a general one, that machines should not be designed or used to fragment work or appropriate control but rather should be used to consolidate the responsible autonomy of the primary work group. Although this has been the philosophy behind many so-called job enrichment schemes, one wonders why it has not been adopted more widely if it is so beneficial for all. The answer may be sought in the particular conditions under which such a strategy is most successful. When workers are organized in a tightly knit trade union with a strong community base and management is rooted in a particular geographical area and is unable to draw upon an alternate labor supply, a coercive regime of control may meet with too much resistance to be effective. In other words, the success of particular managerial strategies for organizing work is critically dependent on the level of class struggle.

There is yet another reason why breaking the skill hierarchy is likely to be ineffective in mining. Given the hazards and uncertainty of the physical environment underground, the routinization of coal mining could only be accomplished with a degree of coercion that would arouse so much opposition, at least in Britain, as to make it infeasible. However, as I shall suggest later, where such a regime of coercion can be enforced, mining may be organized along militaristic lines of discipline.

The more restricted the movement of capital and the labor supply upon which it may draw and the more uncertain the conditions of production, the more likely labor will be able to resist the expropriation of skill. This conclusion is well illustrated by the organization of construction work. Attempts to introduce a centralized managerial authority and eliminate subcontracting are known to be "inefficient" [Stinchcombe (110)]. In part this is because the administration of construction has to be limited to a given geographical region, which reduces the power of management while increasing the variability of volume and product mix. Indeed, it is fluctuations in output according to season and consumer demand that account for labor's capacity to make craft administration more "efficient" than bureaucratic administration. Stinchcombe, however, downplays the importance of the organization of labor, seeing this more as a consequence than a cause of the particular form of labor process. In practice it is both, but more important the very notion of "efficiency" has to be understood as relative to the level of struggle between capital and labor. Comparisons with the organization of building industries in other countries where labor is not organized into a craft union might suggest alternative patterns. The International Typographers Union is another instance of a craft union resisting deskilling for a long time because of the late development of a technology that might preempt the powerful resistance of labor, which is tightly organized into relatively autonomous and democratic locals (69).

In summary, we have seen how competition among employers and struggle between classes can be both cause and consequence of the destruction of skill and how this process is influenced by the organization of labor and mobility of capital, as well as by market and other uncertainties.

FROM COMPETITIVE TO MONOPOLY CAPITALISM

So far we have examined some of the factors which account for the uneven development of the degradation of work. We now have to account for its reconstitution—the form of controls that emerge to take the place of craft administration. In giving scant attention to the ways management elicits consent and organizes work once skill is appropriated, Braverman recognizes the fact but not the significance of the uneven progress of the separation of conception and execution. The historical timing of the separation of conception and execution determines the new relationship between the two, the manner in which conception dictates to execution.

A wide range of historically specific conditions shapes the particular form of labor process which replaces craft organization. Moreover, as both Blauner (14) and Stinchcombe (111) point out, an organizational structure tends to persist in its original form despite changes in its "environment." The vesting of interests, sunk costs, and monopoly markets are among the factors that might make its transformation unlikely. Thus Stinchcombe shows how the level of bureaucratization, as measured by the relative proportion of administrative staff in an industry, is correlated with the age of its organizational form. Blauner explores the development of four different industries—printing, textiles, automobiles, and chemical—established at different periods and shows how they continue to possess features associated with the technology current at the time of their formation. Although these analyses do not give sufficient attention to the dynamics of the labor process and the way this shapes the impact of change external to the firm, the essential point remains: the character of labor processes can be traced to their points of origin, and there is no necessary convergence to a common form.

Change in the labor process then cannot be understood outside of the technological, economic, and political context of the formation of the labor process as well as of its development. How should this context and its change be examined? One could simply take external factors as given and describe how their variation affects the labor process, as Stinchcombe and Blauner tend to do. However, in order to develop an understanding of the historical tendencies of the labor process, it would also be necessary to place the changes of the context within a theory of the development of capitalism. Here I propose a scheme that distinguishes between competitive and monopoly capitalism, based first and foremost on the changes in relations among capitalists. Between 1890 and 1920 the United States and, to a less clear extent, other advanced capitalist societies went through the transition from competitive to monopoly capitalism.

As a result of their subordination to the "anarchy" of the market, individual capitalists under competitive capitalism had no alternative but to innovate and change with their competitors if they were to survive. The search for profit also intensified the struggle between capital and labor. Except for those who could cling to some monopoly or craft, anarchy in the market meant despotism in the factory. As Schumpeter (101) and Polanyi (90) have both argued, either capitalism would destroy itself or it would have to be converted into a form which restricted competition among capitalists and organized struggles between capital and labor in ways which did not threaten the economic order. Precisely how this took place is not my concern here; suffice it to say that in each case the transition had two aspects. First, the vertical and horizontal integration of firms led to the emergence of the large corporation which dominated supply and labor markets. The large corporation was also able to mobilize its resources to regulate struggles between capital and labor initially, in many companies, through some form of welfare capitalism and, after this collapsed in the depression, through unionization. The second feature of the transition from competitive capitalism was the active involvement of the state in regulating relations among capitalists and between capital and labor. This section will be devoted to examining the impact of both sets of factors on the labor process.

Competitive and Monopoly Firms

The rise of the large corporation in the monopoly sector[2] by no means spelled the downfall of the small firm in the competitive sector. On the one hand, in many branches of industrial production the competitive structure persisted relatively unchanged into the period of monopoly capitalism. We have already seen this in the uneven destruction of skill in such craft-dominated industries as printing and construction. On the other hand, monopoly capital also *generates,* as a condition of its own existence, a corresponding competitive sector. What the large corporation can't produce in a capital-intensive fashion it frequently contracts out to one of a number of small competitive firms. In this way it gains flexibility in adapting to fluctuations in demand without laying off so many of its own workers, and also takes advantage of the lower wages in the nonunionized or weakly unionized competitive sector. In other words, the small firm which makes car locks, for example, absorbs uncertainties and in effect transfers surplus to the automobile assembly company upon which it depends for survival (46).

How does the competitive structure of an industry affect its characteristic labor process? Lupton (71) worked in two different firms in Manchester, England. At Wye Garment Company he made waterproof clothing and at Jay's Electrical Components he made transformers. Briefly, he discovered that at Wye workers did not exercise much control over productive activities or the system of piece rates whereas at Jay's workers were able to manipulate the productive process and the incentive scheme, thus exercising both individual and collective control over output and earnings. Lupton first tries to explain this discrepancy by reference to factors "internal" to

---

[2]Following conventional usage, the monopoly sector refers to industries in which a few large companies dominate the product market. These are, of course, not actually monopolies but oligopolies.

the workshops, namely the different methods of wage payment, the productive system as measured by the degree of fragmentation of tasks, the nature of sociable groupings and their relation to production groupings, the gender of the workers, and the structure of management/worker relations. However, rather than treating these factors as explanations in themselves, he proceeds to treat them as phenomena to be explained by a series of "external factors": the stability, size, and content of the product market; the competitive structure of the industry; the scale and location of the industry; union organization; and the proportion of total costs going to labor. At Jay's a strong union with low labor costs and high profit margins, plus a large and stable market for capital goods with collusive price agreements among a few large firms, shaped an organization of work in which workers were able to exercise control over output and earnings. At Wye, a weak union with relatively high labor costs and low profit margins, subject to a small seasonally variable market for consumer goods in a competitive industry of many small firms concentrated in a small region, led to a rigid organization of work in which workers had little room for maneuver without putting the company out of business. Lupton suggests that the two clusters of internal variables correspond to the two clusters of "external" variables, although he is not prepared to nominate any one factor to causal primacy.

What aspects of the labor processes at Wye and Jay's are characteristic of the competitive and monopoly sectors of an advanced capitalist economy? Where an industry is dominated by a few large firms, it is likely that formal or informal price fixing will occur. Increases in labor costs can be pushed onto the purchaser, while trade unionism organized on an industry-wide basis can be both strong and a stabilizing factor in management-worker relations. Furthermore, those uncertainties that cannot be absorbed or contained by the large firm can be externalized to smaller firms in the competitive sector. In such "monopoly" corporations unionization usually guarantees an "acceptable" minimum wage which allows workers a certain room for maneuver and bargaining power on the shop floor. As we shall see, when reward is no longer directly dependent on effort, new methods of ensuring the cooperation of workers must be invoked.

In the competitive sector, subordination to the market and the inability to manipulate product prices leads to low profit margins with labor costs assuming a high proportion of total costs. Here we find weak unions and a direct link between reward and effort, engineered either through a piece rate system without minimum wage guarantees or the threat of dismissal when output falls short of acceptable quotas. The economic compulsion of a wage system shapes a coercive regulation of work.

However, the distinction between competitive and monopoly sectors can explain only so much of the variation in the labor process. Differences within each sector are probably as great if not greater than differences between sectors. How can we characterize variation within sectors? Fox (41) uses "discretion" inherent in jobs or the amount of "trust" management is compelled to place in its workers, while Crozier (31) takes "uncertainty" and the derivative "power" it offers workers to be a key factor in shaping the labor process. For Friedman (46) this dimension of "uncertainty" and "trust" leads to two distinct managerial strategies: "direct control" and "responsible autonomy." Within the same firm we may encounter the deployment of both strategies, and the predominance of one or the other will vary from industry to industry. Apart from the competitive structure of the firm, what shapes these variations in the organization of work?

The Structure of the Product Market

Baran & Sweezy (8) have persuasively argued that the transition to monopoly capitalism has meant that firms compete less over their ability to increase profit through mechanization and intensification of labor and more over the slice of the market they can capture. The problem of overproduction becomes increasingly important, as witnessed by the growing energies devoted to sales and marketing as well as research and development of new products. Earlier we remarked that one of the precipitating factors in the 1933 strike at Yankee City was the inability of operatives to make their regular earnings as a result of changes in shoe styles. In order to boost sales, retailers were orchestrating changes in fashion, a strategy that has become part and parcel of contemporary capitalism. As far as the labor process is concerned, this makes standardization and therefore mechanization more difficult.

The garment industry faces a similar problem. In drawing the contrast between Wye and Jay's, I stressed the competitive structure of the garment and electrical components industries rather than the structure of the product market. As compared to other companies in the garment industry, Wye's relatively large size and ability to attract government contracts made it somewhat unusual. Although subject to seasonal fluctuations, business cycles, and the demand for a variety of garments, Wye's market was nevertheless relatively stable. This was reflected in the production process which involved an advanced separation of conception and execution with each operator working on only a small fraction of the garment. The organization of production had been carefully planned out by management according to the latest "scientific" techniques of time and motion study to allow workers to make a reasonable wage without interupting a smooth flow of production. In practice there was an endemic conflict due to the clash between a system of piece rates based on individual output and a system of production based on interdependence and cooperation (74).

Cunnison's study (32) of Dee, another Manchester factory producing waterproof clothing, portrays the more conventional make-through method of production. Here maker and machinist work together to produce the entire garment. Workers exercise both skill and discretion in the manufacture of garments to a much greater degree than at Wye. They depend less on the completion of work by other makers or machinists. At the same time, although the workers at Dee exercised more individual control over the labor process, their earnings were much more erratic than those at Wye. At Dee the manager used his personal discretion in deciding who should receive "good" and "bad" work (reflected in the looseness of piece rates), cheap and quality work, and who should be laid off or face a reduced work load when there was a shortage of orders. The particularism inscribed in the distribution of work created much hostility and jealousy among the operatives, but they were powerless to resist as this would jeopardize the very existence of the firm as well as their own livelihood.[3]

Just as Wye was not typical of the competitive sector, so Jay's was not typical of the monopoly sector. Variability in the product market affects the labor process no less in the monopoly sector than in the competitive sector. Jay's manufactured capital goods, but there are "monopoly" corporations which engage in mass production of consumer items such as the electronic and automobile industries. Where the product—television or car—can be marketed on a mass scale and more or less standardized, some more technically complex labor process such as the assembly line can be introduced. Many changes in style and design can be accommodated within an unchanged organization of work; those which cannot are contracted out to smaller firms.

In a more general scheme that cuts across the distinction between competitive and monopoly industries, Woodward (127) argues that the volume and variety of market demand shapes the potential for control and prediction in the production process, that is, what she calls the level of technical complexity. She discovers that industries in each of her three basic types

[3]A comparison of Dee and Jay's brings out more clearly the implications of being in a competitive rather than monopoly firm. At Dee prices for piece work were decided at the industry level outside the firm, although some managers might make additional concessions. At Jay's operators, supported by the shop steward, would battle with the time-study man on the shop floor over piece rates. At Dee the manager would try and guarantee his workers a certain minimal wage each week by paying them for work they had not yet completed. This system, known as the dead horse, is frequently found in the garment industry and is associated with the make-through process of production. Entering into a debtor's relationship with one's employer only enhances the employer's power to forestall any resistance. Interestingly, at Jay's the opposite system operated: workers banked unpaid work which they could release when and how they liked. This was used to strengthen their bargaining position with management, particularly when they were handed "bad" work.

—unit and small-batch production, large-batch production, and process production—share certain organizational characteristics such as levels of authority, ratio of salaried administrative and clerical workers to hourly paid employees, specialization of managerial functions, and the degree of separation of administration from production. She also suggests that the form of technology defines the character of "human relations" and, like Blauner (14), argues that relations between workers and managers "deteriorate" as one moves from unit and small-batch production to large-batch and mass production, but then "improve" in the shift to process production. This curvilinear relationship between the development of technology and the level of alienation experienced by wage labor has been vigorously contested by Nichols & Beynon (86). According to their study of a large chemical plant in southern England, continuous flow technology in no way reduces boredom, oppressive working conditions, or coercive routines.

In approaching a technological determinism, both Blauner and Woodward present an important corrective to the human relations approach but at the same time ignore what we emphasized earlier—the level of concentration of firms in the same industry. In addition, they present the development and adoption of technology as unproblematic. Yet this depends on the harnessing of science and industry and is therefore usually restricted to the monopoly sector.

Corporate Management and the Application of Science

The emergence of complex systems of corporate management is our third feature of the development of monopoly capitalism. So far we have merely pointed to the logic behind the links between the organization of the labor process and certain situational factors such as markets. We must now briefly pose the problem of how such external factors become translated into managerial strategies for the organization of work.

Chandler's history of the transformation of the organizational structure of major United States corporations (27) examines the influence of changing conditions under monopoly capitalism. He argues that successful enterprises adapted to changes in technology, markets, and supply factors by shifting from a structure of centralized, functionally departmentalized divisions to decentralized multifunctional divisions. Those who made the transition early gained considerable competitive advantage over those who made it later, and he describes the trials and errors experienced by some of the largest corporations in the process. Lawrence & Lorsch (67) study the adaptations of firms to "environmental" change in three industries—plastics, containers, and food. Focusing primarily on the fluctuating markets, production organization, and scientific development as the source of "contingencies," they try to demonstrate the necessity of departments having sufficient autonomy to adapt to their respective "environments." This leads to functional "differentiation" of departments and the problem of their "integration" and the "resolution of conflict" among them. They examine how this is accomplished through "integrators" whose function is to coordinate the operations of differentiated departments.

Burns & Stalker's study of the electronics industry in Scotland and England (23) relies less on formal questionnaires as the source of information and more on nonparticipant observation and in-depth interviews. They set out to investigate why some companies proved more able to take advantage of governmentally subsidized research in the burgeoning field of electronics after World War II. Their findings indicate that those organizations which developed what they call an "organic" management structure were more likely to succeed in conditions of continual change and innovation such as is found in many branches of the electronics industry, whereas the adoption of what they call a "mechanistic" structure was better suited to stable conditions. Within a mechanistic organization roles are well defined and arranged in a permanent hierarchy of authority, with those at the top monopolizing the power of decision-making. An organic system, by contrast, is distinguished by its flexibility. Roles and responsibilities are continually being redefined. Communication is not something that always flows in a vertical direction but rather tends to take the form of lateral consultation. Authority is decentralized and the head of the concern is no longer the omniscient presence which he is under more rigid structures.

But Burns and Stalker are not content to advertise their prescription for managerial effectiveness. They attempt to establish a framework for understanding why some firms follow the prescription and some do not. They start from the assumption that the firm must be conceived of as the intersection of a number of social systems with goals and values that may not be in accord with those of the organization. Here Burns and Stalker begin to make a major advance on the notion of informal organization conjured up by the human relations school as a residual category for all that was not explicitly acknowledged by management as an essential feature of the firm (10, 33, 94). In drawing attention to the realms of political struggles and status striving, they are able to explain why managerial systems differ in their responses to similar environments. However, it still is important to develop an understanding of how the political and status orders interrelate with the prerequisites of organizational survival.

Much work has yet to be undertaken in this area. By abandoning the concern for prescription, by substituting participant observation for surveys and interviews, and by developing new frameworks which incorporate as central features the political and ideological dimensions of industrial concerns, the mists of managerial rationalization and organization theory will be more easily distinguished from the realities of corporate life. Departments do have their particularistic interests to pursue, and they do couch and defend those interests in the name of the interest of the firm as a whole. How do different fractions of management form coalitions? Which fractions constitute the dominant power bloc and direct the firm in their particular interest? Under what conditions do coalitions among departments break down and crises emerge? What forces are brought to bear to contain conflict within limits defined by the survival of the enterprise? Above all, how do the coalitions, alliances, and blocs among different fractions and strata of management shape the struggles between management and workers? And how, in turn, do these struggles shape the organization of management? These are issues that lurk behind the "integrators" who "resolve conflicts" between "differentiated" departments.

In the examination of the "environment" and the development of a "contingency theory of organization" (67, 116) based on "uncertainty" outside the enterprise, we have come a long way from the Western Electric Studies. For Mayo and his colleagues management presented itself as a single monolith which had to be persuaded to treat its workers as human beings. The problems that concerned Mayo were those of conflict between management and worker. In the organization theory which has supplanted the human relations approach, either the worker no longer exists or everyone is a worker. In either case the problem of eliciting the cooperation of those who only receive instructions and have no recognizable say in the organization of work has disappeared. Apparently Mayo's wildest hopes—the restoration of humanity's capacity for spontaneous cooperation (94, p. xiv)—have been realized.

This shift in the focus of the literature toward problems of conflict within managerial hierarchies does perhaps express, albeit in a concealed form, some very real trends in the postwar United States: the incorporation of wage-laborers in large firms of the monopoly sector. And it is this fact that now presents itself in the guise of disunity within the ranks of management. Ironically, it may be the very solution of the problem that defined the human relations approach that now generates the new problem of managerial divisiveness. Rather than attribute such conflict within management to the growing turbulence of the "environment," for which there is not much evidence, one might explain it in terms of declining threats to corporate survival, in particular the successful containment of capital/labor struggles. If this is true, then it is not something to be ignored but something to be explained. How have workers been persuaded to subordinate themselves to the direction of management? What has happened to all the conflict that Mayo bewailed—the struggle for union recognition in the 1930s?

Part of the answer must lie precisely in the application of science to the labor process (87). "The skill once 'owned' by the worker and sold as a service is now possessed by the manager in the form of the machine" (121, p. 190). But what is it about the machine that fosters the subordination of workers and their cooperation in the pursuit of profit? What determines the design of the machine? What function is it supposed to perform? Warner and Low pose a provocative answer:

> Since the shoe-factory workers holding high-skilled jobs are a potential threat to management's control of shoe operatives, inventors apparently are encouraged to break down complex jobs into series of simple, easily standardized operations. An important result of their work, therefore, is to eliminate more and more of the skilled jobs from shoemaking, tending to accelerate the leveling of technological jobs in the shoe factory to a common low order of skill. To a lesser extent, research departments in other industries (chemistry is a case in point) also reduce the number of high-skilled jobs in the shoe factories by developing new substances which simplify shoemaking. Designing departments and the skilled jobs in connection with them have been almost eliminated from modern shoe factories (121, pp. 81–82).

If control is one factor, efficiency is clearly another, since breaking down a craft into unskilled or semiskilled jobs increases the labor supply and can bring about a decline in wages and, with mechanization, an increase in output. What motivates management in the development and adoption of machines: efficiency, control, or both? Or are they indistinguishable? One answer is to be found in Noble's study of automation in the metal-working industry (88). Manufacturers of machine tools faced a choice between two technologies: "record play-back" which could be adopted by smaller machine shops, and "numerical control" which was more complex, more expensive, and beyond the means of most buyers. Whereas "record play-back" retained a central role for the skilled machinist, numerical-control systems involved the elimination of any machinist skill and its replacement by trained computer programmers. Noble shows how, and suggests why, the users of the new technology, in particular the Air Force, opted for the more expensive and comprehensive numerically controlled machinery that removed any control over the labor process from the shop floor.

Although it is not clear whether Noble's study is exceptional, it does seem to uphold the observations of Warner and Low concerning the purpose of mechanization. But what neither analysis examines is the response of the now unskilled workers. How do they "adapt" or "resist" the introduction of machines? Their services are still required and their cooperation is still essential. One approach has been developed by Baldamus (6), who examines the deprivation inherent in work, what he calls effort. There are three sources of effort: physical conditions which lead to "impairment," repetitiveness which leads to "tedium," and coercive routines which lead to "weariness." To the extent that workers regard these forms of effort as unavoidable, they attempt to achieve corresponding relative satisfactions by becoming accustomed to physical conditions (inurement), generating a feeling of being pulled along by work (traction), and being in the mood for work (contentment). But these satisfactions are always relative to the more fundamental and inescapable deprivation.

Baldamus does not examine the equally important response to the strictures of work noted by many others (12, 13, 31, 34, 58, 94, 96–99, 114, 126), namely the constitution of "games," whose objectives usually involve regaining a certain marginal control over the labor process. Such reunification of conception and execution is frequently regarded as disruptive by higher management, but in practice can often turn out to be critical for effective cooperation. Indeed, where the reunification of conception and execution is impossible, as is the case for numerically controlled machine tools, the labor process frequently breaks down. It would seem that every labor process depends on a certain spontaneous collaboration of the worker.

There is a further assumption behind the postulates of Noble, Warner, and Low concerning machine design, which also threads through the technological determinism of writers such as Blauner (14) and Woodward (127), namely that technology to a lesser or greater extent shapes the form of the labor process. There are undoubtedly technical imperatives that are rooted in the particular machinery adopted, what I shall call the technical relations in production. But as the work of Rice (91), Trist et al (117), and others of the Tavistock Institute have demonstrated, there are also aspects of the labor process that are not determined by technology, which I shall call the social relations in production. We have discussed some of the issues in the determination of machinery and thus of the technical relations in production, but what determines the social relations in production? In the case of mining, I earlier suggested that these may be the outcome of struggles, and I shall offer some further answers to this question in the last section. First I want to pose the question in an alternative way: in the absence of machines what forces shape the labor process once deskilling has occurred?

The Penetration of Bureaucratic Patterns

If administrative apparatuses have grown within industry, their proliferation outside industry is even more pronounced. The expansion of the state and service sectors of the economy has entailed the spreading and at the same time deskilling of office work (17, 70, 82). How is skill first appropriated from white collar workers and then restored as an alien power over them? What comes to replace their lost skill? The answer lies in part in the "rule" which assumes the same role in the office that the machine plays in the factory. Like the machine, the rule is as much an instrument of exercising control as it is of increasing efficiency. However, it is the latter feature which has captured the imagination of Merton (79) and his students such as Blau (13), Selznick (104), and to a lesser extent, Gouldner (52). As their point of departure they take Weber's appraisal of bureaucracy as the most efficient form of organization [(122) particularly Vol. I] and demonstrate how and why it fails to live up to expectations. Thus Selznick shows how a government agency—TVA—cannot achieve its stated goal because of concessions it has to make to various external interest groups. Just as factory workers turn production into "games" with, against, and around machines, office workers do the same with rules by ritualizing responses (78, Chap. 8), manipulating them in their own interests (13), or using them to protect themselves from face-to-face interaction with supervisors (31). In each case adaptation to rules leads to "goal displacement" or "inefficiency," so that for Crozier the defining characteristic of the bureaucracy is its inability to correct its own errors.

In concentrating on the inefficiency of bureaucracy, these studies underplay the other theme in Weber's discussion, that of domination. Somewhat exceptional, therefore, are Gouldner's discussion of the way that rules obscure and reduce conflict while facilitating the exercise of control (52) and Etzioni's discussion of the different forms of compliance in organizations (40). A second problem in much of Merton's work and that of his followers is the presumption that inefficiency and goal displacement are some *unintended* consequence. In practice bureaucracies may deliberately foster "inefficiency" through the proliferation of rules. Thus Piven & Cloward (89) demonstrate that the dominant objective of the welfare agency is to instill the work ethic rather than distribute assistance. The addition of another rule to regulate relations either between the agency and its clients or within the agency itself may have the *intended* effect of reducing the number of welfare recipients. Were the welfare agency more eager to distribute assistance it would, following Burns & Stalker (23), assume a much less rigid structure so as to be responsive to the unpredictable and insecure lives of the unemployed and underemployed people seeking welfare (113).

The welfare agency is merely a single illustration of a general principle that Weber understood only too well, namely the manner in which formal rationality (the use of rules to regulate behavior) comes to dominate substantive rationality (the rational goals of human endeavor). Formal rationality becomes substantive irrationality (54, Chap. 6; 58; 73, Chap. 8). In the name of efficiency or science, rules serve to hide the true objectives of the bureaucratic organization. As with machines, efficiency becomes domination. Just as in the conventional literature on technology, it is the fact of mechanization rather than the specific form of machines that is usually discussed; in the literature on bureaucracy it is the proliferation of rules rather than their content that receives attention. But who decides what those rules shall be and with what ends in mind? Is the content of rules shaped in struggle or is it designed to preempt struggle? Do rules and machines have to be associated with debilitating restrictions? Or are there particular incarnations which liberate rather than fetter human creativity?

Rules, of course, are often used as an adjunct to machines. Where Blau (13) examines the administration and enforcement of rules through the rule-bound organizations of two government agencies, Gouldner (52) investigates the administration of production through rules in a gypsum plant. He identifies three patterns of industrial bureaucracy: the mock bureaucracy in which there are few rules and little conflict between management and workers; the representative bureaucracy in which rules are legitimated by both management and workers; and finally the punishment-centered bureaucracy in which rules are enforced by management against an unwilling and resistant labor force through the application of disciplinary sanctions. Gouldner describes a transition from the indulgency pattern of the mock bureaucracy to the more coercive pattern of the punishment-centered bureaucracy in terms of the social and political processes of managerial succession from the "local" Old Doug to the "cosmopolitan" Peele. Toward the end of the field research, 2 years after the succession, there was a wildcat strike (53).

The significance of Gouldner's study can be most easily appreciated through a comparison with Warner and Low's treatment of the shoe strike in Yankee City 17 years before. There the major underlying cause of the strike was not so much the destruction of the shoemakers' craft but their loss of control over management as it became increasingly responsive to the needs of New York bankers and national markets. The community had lost its influence over the owners of the company, who threatened to move the company to a more convenient place. This was not a possibility at Gouldner's gypsum plant which was rooted in a particular geographical location. Here a major underlying cause was the workers' loss of control over the labor process, occasioned by the enforcement of restrictive rules. In both instances the strike was seen as a reactive protest against a defeat which workers had already sustained. But where Warner and Low do not see any way of resolving such protest, except possibly by creating new channels of mobility through education (see also 28), Gouldner's analysis suggests that the rise of a punishment-centered bureaucracy may also be a solution to the conflict it instigates and to the reduction of the working class to homogeneous unskilled laborers hostile to capital. The punishment-centered bureaucracy becomes a way of organizing conflict in ways that do not threaten the survival of the firm.

However, Gouldner does not adequately appreciate the historical specificity of the emergence of his patterns of industrial administration. His punishment-centered bureaucracy arose during World War II and was consolidated after the war. With the assistance of industrial trade unions, management was now able to return to its earlier interest in welfare capitalism. Although it occasionally breaks out in wildcat strikes, conflict on the shop floor is normally either transferred to the bargaining table where contracts are renegotiated or channelled into a grievance procedure. Collective bargaining confines conflict within limits defined not only by the survival of the firm but also by its expansion, which guarantees *future* increases in wages and benefits. The grievance procedure turns struggles between classes into struggles between the individual and the company. The system of day-to-day factory administration represents workers as industrial citizens—individuals with rights and obligations (105). The possessive individualism created by the "external" labor market is reconstituted within the firm through the organization of job mobility. The bidding system allows workers to compete for vacancies in the plant or department largely on the basis of seniority. Seniority also governs the length of vacations, pay, supplementary unemployment benefits, and other fringe benefits. Thus the consequences of seniority clauses combine with those of collective bargaining to attach individual workers to the present and future interests of the company rather than to the interests they share with other workers, particularly workers in other firms.

This interpretation of Gouldner's study complements and adds a new dimension to the findings of Lupton (71) and Cunnison (32), for the reconstitution of welfare capitalism presumes a capacity to extend benefits and administer relations between workers and management through rules. It presumes definite restrictions on managerial discretion which may be incompatible with the conditions of uncertainty in the competitive sector. In a company such as Dee there can be little incentive for management to stabilize industrial relations through collective bargaining, grievance procedures, or bidding systems so long as the product market is unpredictable. On the other hand, the erection of such administrative structures in the monopoly sector, inasmuch as the firm can externalize increased labor costs through increased prices, is not only possible but desirable. The advantages of containing one source of uncertainty, such as the product market, can only be fully realized when all other sources of uncertainty, such as labor market and management/worker relations, are also contained.

The presence or absence of a rule-bound administration of work becomes critical in shaping the impact of external roles on industrial behavior. The attempt by Goldthorpe and company (51) to stress the importance of "external orientations" to work misses this point. Thus at Dee sex, religion, and age had important effects on workshop activities. The competitive sector firm often approximates an open system of overlapping and competing roles, whereas in the monopoly sector firm the administrative structures create a more closed system in which "extrinsic" attributes are of less significance in the organization of production and in molding productive activities. Thus Kornblum (65) suggests that race and ethnicity have diminishing impact on patterns of behavior in the steel mills as seniority systems become entrenched. However, if race, sex, and ethnicity have declining significance inside the factory, that is not to say they are no longer significant there nor that they do not have increasing significance outside the factory as, for example, in shaping access to different labor markets (15, 36, 56, 80). (Even here affirmative action may have had some influence on the recruitment policies of corporations which are dependent on government contracts.)

In summary, the proliferation of bureaucratic patterns is rooted in the growth of government and service sectors on the one hand and in the changes in the organization and administration of the labor process on the other (109). However, the shift from the decline in welfare capitalism, epitomized by Warner and Low's study, to its reconstruction, expressed in Gouldner's study, is also a geographically specific trajectory. As Lupton's description of Jay's suggests, British monopoly industry has not trodden the same path of bureaucratization. To understand this and the corresponding particularity of much of United States' industrial anthropology we must briefly consider international variations in the labor process and its administration.

UNEVEN DEVELOPMENT OF THE LABOR PROCESS ON A WORLD SCALE

Not too long ago, the secret of economic development was seen to reside in replicating the material and ideological conditions of the first capitalist nations. Capital importation, the adoption of democratic institutions, and the penetration of "modern" values were seen as essential ingredients of Third World development in the twentieth century. Baran (7), Emmanuel (38), Frank (42), Amin (2), Wallerstein (120), and many others have now demolished the myths of "modernization" theory. It is one thing to attempt capitalist accumulation when there are no other capitalist countries around; it is quite another to do so in the face of already powerful capitalist nations. The expansion of capitalism in "core" countries becomes the condition for its underdevelopment or failure to develop in other countries, although, of course, there are exceptions to this rule.

We have already observed how the uneven accumulation of capital within a single nation leads to the uneven development of the labor process. First the structure of the work is critically shaped by technological, economic, and political conditions existing at the time of its formation. Organizational forms tend to bear the marks of their origin. Second, the domination exercised by the monopoly sector over its various markets allows it to absorb increasing labor costs by draining surplus from the competitive sector. As Friedman (46) has noted, a center and periphery emerge within the advanced capitalist economy with "hegemonic" forms of labor process appearing in the former and more "despotic" forms appearing in the latter. Both principles operate in the uneven development of the labor process on a world scale. I shall deal with each in turn as late development and unequal development.

Late Development

Those countries which embark on capitalist accumulation relatively late, although hampered in their progress by advanced capitalist countries, frequently adopt the latter's latest technology, organizational skills, and norms of industrial practice. This is what Gerschenkron (49) has called the late development effect, and it has recently been used by Dore (35) to interpret differences in Japanese and British employment systems. Basing his comparison on a detailed study of two Hitachi and two English Electric factories, Dore claims that the essential characteristics of the Japanese system are "lifetime employment, a seniority-plus-merit wage system, an intra-enterprise career system, enterprise training, enterprise unions, a high level of enterprise welfare, and the careful nurturing of enterprise consciousness." This is in contrast to the British system, which has "considerable mobility of employment, a market-based wage and salary system, self-designed mobile rather than regulated careers, publicly provided training, industrial and craft unions, more state welfare and a greater strength of professional, craft, regional or class consciousness" (35, p. 264).

In explaining the different patterns of industrial relations, Dore compares the conditions under which Japan began its major industrialization in 1900–1920 with conditions during the middle of the nineteenth century when Britain's employment system was established. Thus the distinctive consequences of Japan's late development are the lesser significance of laissez-faire market principles, the rapidity of the transition to capitalism and the absence of intermediary structures such as putting-out systems, the emergence of school systems before the development of a substantial manufacturing sector, the technological and organizational leap made possible by adoption from already advanced industrial nations, and the sharper dualism between monopoly and competitive sectors (35, chap. 15). He refuses to single out any of these consequences of late development as being of primary importance; they must be treated together.

An alternative approach, following our earlier discussion of the transition from competitive to monopoly capitalism, would be to examine how late development affects competition among capitalists and struggle between capital and labor, and how in combination these then shape the labor process. In order to be competitive on a world market, Japanese firms had to operate on the same scale and with the same technology as advanced capitalism. With state intervention playing a key role, Japan was able to build a viable monopoly capitalism without the intense class struggles associated with the transition from competitive capitalism and the destruction of crafts. Instead, the monopoly firm secured the support of labor through establishing enterprise trade unions. As in other countries, the monopoly sector created a competitive sector as a condition for its own existence. But labor in the competitive sector was particularly weak in Japan because of the absence of a legacy of organization from an earlier period of capitalism. This led to the accentuation of dualism with sharp disparities between conditions and industrial relations in the two sectors (30).

By contrast, the transition to monopoly capitalism in Britain had to overcome resistance built up under competitive capitalism. Most significant was the strong trade union movement that emerged through the self-organization of the British working class during the nineteenth century. Organizational changes that undermined worker control over the labor process were actively resisted. The heritage of shop floor militancy has continued to pose obstacles to mechanization, bureaucratization, and speed-up. The relative strength of labor in the competitive sector has retarded tendencies toward the dualistic disparities that emerged rapidly in Japan.

The United States holds a position in between Japan and Britain. During the era of competitive capitalism American labor did not develop the same organizational strength as in Britain, in part because working class struggles over political issues were less significant. The bloody massacres of workers that recur throughout United States history are testimony to their courage but also their weakness. During the transition from competitive to monopoly capitalism labor made few if any gains, and the emergence of industrial unionism was further stalled by welfare capitalism. As in Japan, it was only after craft workers had come under major assault and mechanization had revolutionized production that industrial unions were born. Thus, the distinctive character of industrial relations in the monopoly sector firm—the system of collective bargaining, grievance machinery, and seniority systems controlled by management—are more akin to the Japanese model than to the British pattern in which workers continue to retain greater control over the administration of production. A comparison of anthropological studies of machine shops (22, 35, 71, 95) and of assembly line production in auto companies (5, 12, 30, 119) suggests that the character of shop floor politics in a United States monopoly firm falls between the confrontational pattern with militant shop stewards often found in England and the corporatist pattern based on union management cooperation frequently found in Japan. Dualism in the three countries seems most accentuated in Japan and least in Britain, although such international comparisons have hardly begun.

Unequal Development

More often than not late development means underdevelopment and unequal development. In its simplest form this involves the transfer of surplus from the "backward" country to the "advanced" country, from the periphery to the core, from the colony to the metropolis. The state plays a critical role in facilitating this transfer of surplus but it also plays another role—organizing the conditions for the production of profit. Thus, the imperatives of the colonial state are to allow the repatriation of surplus and its extraction through the most profitable means consistent with the existing political and economic situation. Insofar as a system of wage labor is established in the colony, a distinctive form of the capitalist labor process emerges. In order to highlight its typical features I will contrast it with corresponding labor processes in advanced capitalist nations.

I confine myself here to an examination of a colonial system of mining. In discussing alternative techniques of organizing underground mining, Trist et al write:

> Longwall systems, because of their greater degree of differentiation, require much more integration than single place systems; but the conventional pattern of organization has broken up the traditional, self-regulating cycle group into a number of segregated single task groups each bound within its own concerns. These groups depend entirely on external control in order to carry out the indivisible primary task of completing the cycle. The existing pattern of management through the wages system can only partially supply this control. Full control would require either a degree of coercion which would be both impracticable and unacceptable or a degree of self-regulation which implies a different organizational pattern (117, pp. 66–67).

Trist and company suggest that full control can be exercised by reconstructing a self-regulating group around the newly developed machinery. However, the mining of gold and diamonds in South Africa (60; 108, Chap. 2–4), of gold and coal in Southern Rhodesia (118), and of copper in Northern

Rhodesia (now Zambia) (39) were all organized using a degree of coercion "which would be both impracticable and unacceptable" in Britain. How has this been possible?

The colonial state creates two labor markets—one organized by taxing Africans and dispossessing them of their land, and one organized by inducing white workers to leave the metropolis for the colony, where they often become settlers. Whereas the colonized populations have to obtain jobs of an unskilled or semiskilled nature, the colonizing populations take up skilled and supervisory positions in the mine. A color bar rigidly separates the jobs allocated to the different populations so that no white worker ever takes orders from a black worker. The labor process is controlled by the white boss who commands untrammeled and arbitrary power over his black subordinates. The company's administrative apparatus sanctions the coercive regulation of work through the perpetration of physical brutality and the arbitrary firing of African laborers. Its totalitarian rule extends into the life of the mine compound (118). The powerlessness of Africans to resist ultimately rests on the ability of the colonial state to recognize few if any rights of the colonized. The state's role is to protect the external conditions of colonial despotism—the regulation of a system of migrant labor that feeds the mines, the construction of economic infrastructure, and so on.

It becomes apparent after political independence that colonial despotism at the point of production depends on the colonial state. Thus, the mining companies in Zambia could no longer uphold the arbitrary dictatorship of the white boss. However, the heritage of colonialism presented serious obstacles to the effective transition to an administrative apparatus similar to ones found in advanced capitalist countries. The new Zambian supervisor could no longer exercise the same arbitrary power of his predecessor, yet this was often the only effective system of control under the prevailing technology and mining excavation which had been established on the basis of cheap colonized labor power (21). In other words, the legacy of a colonial labor process in a postcolonial period created much tension and conflict. Technology and organization shaped in one political context cannot be easily transformed when the context changes.

The colonial state did not intervene directly in the labor process itself. In other countries, however, the state does become directly involved in the administration of industrial work through such organs as the trade union and the political party. The contrast between such systems of "bureaucratic despotism" and the bureaucratic patterns of the United States is highlighted by a comparison of Roy's study of Geer Company in South Chicago (95) and Haraszti's study of Red Star Factory in Hungary (55). The machine shops they examine share similar technology and payment systems but differ markedly in other aspects of the organization of work. At Red Star the union and party were harnessed to and buttressed the arbitrary rule of the foreman, whereas at Geer the union acted as a limited restraint on managerial discretion. At Red Star work was constituted as a piecework "game," but it differed from that described by Roy and also Lupton (71, Chap. 7–12) in several ways. First, the absence of effective minimum wages precluded goldbricking, while arbitrary price cutting undermined the rationale behind quota restriction. Second, economic survival, according to Haraszti, depended on making one's quota and this often involved the remarkable feat of running two machines at once. Third, exceeding the norm (100 percent level) was expected at both Geer and Red Star, but in the latter it was referred to as "looting" (cheating the norm) while in the former it was called "making out." Whereas looting justified arbitrary managerial assaults on piece rates, making out, as long as it was within definite limits, rarely prompted such attacks. Finally, banking work to cover "bad" jobs was possible at Geer but not at Red Star. Indeed, the organization of work at Red Star was more reminiscent of the "market despotism" of early capitalism, but with direct state intervention in the factory rather than of the "hegemonic" systems of late capitalism.

These two examples offer clues as to the role of technology and politics in the formation of the labor process. In the first, technology was itself shaped by the colonial political order, and furthermore, this technology imposed certain constraints on the form of the labor process. By extension, one may speculate on the existence or potential existence of socialist machines whose techincal imperatives do not involve the fragmentation of work but allow workers to regain collective, if not individual, control over the labor process. In the second example we demonstrated variations, according to political context, of the organization of work around the same technology and system of payment.

In both examples, as well as in our discussion of late development, the role of the state was critical. It shaped the form of the labor process either directly, through intervening within the factory, or more usually indirectly, by guaranteeing certain external conditions, whether these were relations among capitalists or between capital and labor, or the reproduction of supplies of cheap labor power. In the latter instance I am not only referring to the organization of migrant labor either in the Third World or in Europe (25, 26) and the United States (47, 100), but to a more general creation of reserves of politically weak labor power composed of women, blacks, and other "minorities." What effect, for example, has the availability of female labor had on the form of the labor process? Has it merely delayed mechanization as in the recruitment of migrant workers to the fields of California agribusiness? In what ways has the balkanization of the labor force into weak and strong, organized and unorganized, accentuated its dualistic character and to what extent does the dualism determine the weakness of women and minority workers? More generally, how does the labor process shape the labor force and, conversely, how does the labor force shape the labor process?

Finally, in highlighting the international variation of the labor process, this last section provides a corrective to the more conventional development literature which on the one hand misses the geographical specificity of the labor process and on the other hand emphasizes attitudes, orientations, commitments, primordial loyalties, and so on as the sources of variations in industrial behavior (11, 63, 85). The alternative approach, long since the cornerstone of the Manchester School's "situational analysis" (39, 50, 61, 106), draws attention to the context of industry itself and not the "belief systems" people carry around in their heads, although these can be crucial in situations of uncertainty or crisis. Nor do we have to resort to elements of cultural reductionism, found for example in Crozier (31) and Abegglen (1), to explain variations in the capitalist labor process. Instead I have pointed to the articulation of competition among capitalists with the struggle between capital and labor as shaped by organs of the state in the context of its historical involvement in a world capitalist order.

CONCLUSION

Out of the variety of theories competing to explain a single labor process I have begun to construct a single theory to explain a variety of labor processes. The essay began with the Hawthorne experiments which Elton Mayo used to project as a global theory what was in fact largely confined to a particular type of company at a particular point in time. Theoretical advances depended on making problematic what Mayo took for granted. First, although it might have been possible to ignore the political and economic context of the Hawthorne plant for some purposes, this possibility must be explained, not assumed. I have tried to examine some of the mechanisms through which the relative insulation of the labor process is preserved and the conditions under which this insulation can break down. Second, variations in the organization of work that emerge through comparative and historical studies can only be explained by stepping outside of the factory and examining its changing context, in particular the patterns of competition among capitalists and struggles between capital and labor as organized by the state. Third, by expanding the context to ever more remote arenas, different forces emerge as fundamental to shaping the labor process. For example, the effect of those factors constant within national boundaries, such as the history of class struggles, may only be readily appreciated when we compare factories adopting a similar technology but situated in different countries. In the area of national, let alone international, variation the study of the labor process is only just beginning. Fourth, the dynamics of the labor process is a problem I have addressed but inadequately. What are the forces that lead to the destruction of crafts and to the particular reconstitution of the labor process? How do we understand the interaction of external factors on dynamics inscribed in the structure of work so as to explain changes in the labor process over time? And how should we study such changes? Perhaps one way would be to revisit the classical sites of industrial anthropology—Hawthorne, Wye, Geer, Jay's and so on.

In exploring changes in the labor process either over time or between places, we are simply trying to approach the limits of variation of the capitalist labor process, that is, its capitalist essence. And to appreciate the limits of what is possible under capitalism is to begin to grasp the conditions for realizing what is impossible under capitalism.

Literature Cited

1. Abegglen, J. C. 1958. *The Japanese Factory.* New York: Free Press
2. Amin, S. 1976. *Unequal Development.* New York: Monthly Rev. Press
3. Arensberg, C., ed. 1957. *Research in Industrial Human Relations.* New York: Harper & Row
4. Argyris, C. 1964. *Integrating the Individual and the Organization.* New York: Wiley
5. Aronowitz, S. 1973. *False Promises: The Shaping of American Working Class Consciousness.* New York: McGraw Hill
6. Baldamus, W. 1961. *Efficiency and Effort.* London: Tavistock Inst. Hum. Relat.
7. Baran, P. 1957. *The Political Economy of Growth.* New York: Monthly Rev. Press
8. Baran, P., Sweezy, P. 1966. *Monopoly Capital.* New York: Monthly Rev. Press
9. Baritz, L. 1965. *The Servants of Power: A History of the Use of Social Science in American Industry.* New York: Wiley
10. Barnard, C. I. 1938. *The Functions of the Executive.* Cambridge, Mass: Harvard Univ. Press
11. Bendix, R. 1956. *Work and Authority in Industry: Ideologies of Management in the Course of Industrialization.* New York: Wiley
12. Beynon, H. 1973. *Working for Ford.* London: Lane
13. Blau, P. 1955. *The Dynamics of Bureaucracy.* Chicago: Univ. Chicago Press
14. Blauner, R. 1964. *Alienation and Freedom.* Chicago: Univ. Chicago Press
15. Blaxall, M., Reagan, G., eds. 1976. *Women and the Workplace.* Chicago: Univ. Chicago Press
16. Brandes, S. 1976. *American Welfare Capitalism 1880–1940.* Chicago: Univ. Chicago Press
17. Braverman, H. 1974. *Labor and Monopoly Capital.* New York: Monthly Rev. Press
18. Brody, D. 1960. *Steelworkers in America: The Nonunion Era.* Cambridge, Mass: Harvard Univ. Press
19. Brody, D. 1965. *Labor in Crisis.* Philadelphia/New York: Lippincott
20. Brody, D. 1968. The rise and decline of welfare capitalism. In *Change and Continuity in Twentieth Century America: The 1920s,* ed. J. Braeman, R. Brenner, D. Brody, pp. 147–78. Columbus: Ohio State Univ. Press
21. Burawoy, M. 1978. *The transition to post-colonial politics of production: The case of the Zambian mining industry.* Presented at SSRC Conf. Politics Common People in Africa, New York
22. Burawoy, M. 1979. *Manufacturing Consent: Changes in the Labor Process under Monopoly Capitalism.* Chicago: Univ. Chicago Press
23. Burns, T., Stalker, G. M. 1961. *The Management of Innovation.* London: Tavistock
24. Carey, A. 1967. The Hawthorne studies: A radical criticism. *Am. Sociol. Rev.* 32:403–16

25. Castells, M. 1975. Immigrant workers and class struggles in advanced capitalism: The Western European experience. *Polit. Soc.* 5:33–66
26. Castles, S., Kosack, G. 1973. *Immigrant Workers and Class Structure in Western Europe.* London: Oxford Univ. Press
27. Chandler, A. 1962. *Strategy and Structure: Chapters in the History of the American Industrial Enterprise.* Cambridge: MIT Press
28. Chinoy, E. 1955. *Automobile Workers and the American Dream.* New York: Doubleday
29. Cliff, T. 1970. *The Employer's Offensive.* London: Pluto
30. Cole, R. E. 1971. *Japanese Blue Collar.* Berkeley/Los Angeles: Univ. California Press
31. Crozier, M. 1964. *The Bureaucratic Phenomenon.* Chicago: Univ. Chicago Press
32. Cunnison, S. 1966. *Wages and Work Allocation.* London: Tavistock
33. Dalton, M. 1966. *Men Who Manage.* New York: Wiley
34. Ditton, J. 1977. Perks, pilferage, and the fiddle. *Theory Soc.* 4:39–71
35. Dore, R. 1973. *British Factory—Japanese Factory.* Berkeley/Los Angeles: Univ. California Press
36. Edwards, R. 1975. The social relations of production in the firm and labor market structures. *Polit. Soc.* 5:83–108
37. Emery, F. E., Trist, E. L. 1963. The casual texture of organization environments. *Hum. Relat.* 18:20–26
38. Emmanuel, A. 1972. *Unequal Exchange.* New York: Monthly Rev. Press
39. Epstein, A. L. 1958. *Politics in an Urban African Community.* Manchester: Manchester Univ. Press
40. Etzioni, A. 1961. *A Comparative Analysis of Complex Organizations.* New York: Free Press
41. Fox, A. 1974. *Beyond Contract: Work, Power and Trust Relations.* London: Faber & Faber
42. Frank, G. 1969. *Latin America: Underdevelopment or Revolution.* New York: Monthly Rev. Press
43. Franke, R. H., Kaul, J. D. 1978. The Hawthorne experiments: First statistical interpretation. *Am. Sociol. Rev.* 43:623–43
44. Friedland, W., Barton, A. 1975. *Destalking the Wily Tomato.* Dep. Appl. Behav. Sci., Coll. Agric. Environ. Sci., Univ. California, Davis
45. Friedland, W., Barton, A., Thomas, R. 1978. *Manufacturing Green Gold: The Conditions and Social Consequences of Lettuce Harvest Mechanization.* Unpublished manuscript, Univ. California, Santa Cruz
46. Friedman, A. L. 1977. *Industry and Labour.* London: MacMillan
47. Galarza, E. 1964. *Merchants of Labor.* Santa Barbara, Calif: McNally & Loftin
48. Gardner, B. B., Moore, D. G. 1950. *Human Relations in Industry.* Chicago: Irwin
49. Gerschenkron, A. 1962. *Economic Backwardness in Historical Perspective.* Cambridge, Mass: Harvard Univ. Press
50. Gluckman, M. 1961. Anthropological problems arising from the African industrial revolution. In *Social Change in Modern Africa,* ed. A. Southall, pp. 67–82. London: Oxford Univ. Press for Intern. Afr. Inst.
51. Goldthorpe, J., Lockwood, D., Bechhofer, F., Platt, J. 1968. *The Affluent Worker: Industrial Attitudes and Behavior.* New York: Cambridge Univ. Press
52. Gouldner, A. W. 1954. *Patterns of Industrial Bureaucracy.* New York: Free Press
53. Gouldner, A. W. 1954. *Wildcat Strike.* Antioch: Antioch Press
54. Habermas, J. 1970. *Toward a Rational Society.* Boston: Beacon
55. Haraszti, M. 1977. *A Worker in a Worker's State.* Harmondsworth, England: Penguin
56. Harrison, B. 1972. Public employment and the theory of the dual economy. In *The Political Economy of Public Service Employment,* ed. H. L. Sheppard, B. Harrison, W. J. Spring, pp. 41–76. Lexington, Mass: Heath-Lexington
57. Hobsbawn, E. 1964. *Labouring Men.* London: Weidenfeld & Nicolson
58. Homans, G. C. 1955. *The Human Group.* New York: Harcourt, Brace
59. Horkheimer, M. 1974. *The Eclipse of Reason.* New York: Seabury
60. Johnstone, F. 1976. *Class, Race and Gold.* London: Routledge & Kegan Paul
61. Kapferer, B. 1972. *Strategy and Transaction in an African Factory.* Manchester: Manchester Univ. Press
62. Kerr, C. 1964. *Labor and Management in Industrial Society.* New York: Doubleday
63. Kerr, C., Dunlop, J. T., Harrison, F. H., Myers, C. A. 1960. *Industrialism and Industrial Man.* Cambridge, Mass: Harvard Univ. Press
64. Kerr, C., Fisher, L. 1964. Plant sociology: The elite and the Aborigines. See Ref. 62, pp. 43–82

65. Kornblum, W. 1974. *Blue Collar Community.* Chicago: Univ. Chicago Press
66. Landsberger, H. 1958. *Hawthorne Revisited.* Ithaca: Cornell Univ. Press
67. Lawrence, P., Lorsch, J. 1967. *Organizations and Environment.* Boston: Grad. Sch. Bus. Adm., Harvard Univ. Press
68. Likert, R. 1961. *New Patterns of Management.* New York: McGraw Hill
69. Lipset, S. M., Trow, M., Coleman, J. 1956. *Union Democracy.* Glencoe: Free Press
70. Lockwood, D. 1958. *The Blackcoated Worker: A Study in Class Consciousness.* London: Allen & Unwin
71. Lupton, T. 1963. *On the Shop Floor.* Oxford: Pergamon
72. March, J., Simon, H. 1958. *Organizations.* New York: Wiley
73. Marcuse, H. 1968. *Negations.* Boston: Beacon
74. Martin, R. 1978. *Resistance and control on the shop floor: The dynamics of the labor process in a garment factory.* B. A. honors thesis. Univ. California, Berkeley
75. Mathewson, S. 1931. *Restriction of Output Among Unorganized Workers.* New York: Viking
76. Mayo, E. 1933. *The Human Problems of an Industrial Civilization.* New York: Macmillan
77. Mayo, E. 1945. *The Social Problems of an Industrial Civilization.* Cambridge, Mass: Harvard Univ. Press
78. Merton, R. K. 1968. *Social Theory and Social Structure.* New York: Free Press
79. Merton, R. K., Gray, A. P., Hockey, B., Selvin, H., eds. 1952. *Reader in Bureaucracy.* New York: Free Press
80. Milkman, R. 1976. Women's work and the economic crisis: Some lessons from the Great Depression. *Rev. Radical Polit. Econ.* 8(1):73–97
81. Mills, C. W. 1948. The contributions of sociology to studies of industrial relations. *Proc. First Ann. Meet. Ind. Relat. Res. Assoc.* 1:199–222
82. Mills, C. W. 1956. *White Collar.* New York: Oxford Univ. Press
83. Mills, H. 1977. The San Francisco waterfront: The social consequences of industrial modernization, Pt. 2: "The Modern Longshore Operations." *Urban Life* 6:3–32
84. Montgomery, D. 1976. Workers' control of machine production in the nineteenth century. *Labor Hist.* 17:485–509
85. Moore, W. E., Feldman, A. S. 1960. *Labor Commitment and Social Change in Developing Areas.* New York: Soc. Sci. Res. Council
86. Nichols, T., Beynon, H. 1977. *Living with Capitalism: Class Relations and the Modern Factory.* London: Routledge & Kegan Paul
87. Noble, D. 1977. *America By Design: Science, Technology, and the Rise of Corporate Capitalism.* New York: Knopf
88. Noble, D. 1978. *Before the fact: Social choice in machine design.* Presented at Natl. Conv. Organ. Am. Hist.
89. Piven, F. F., Cloward, R. A. 1971. *Regulating the Poor: The Functions of Public Welfare.* New York: Random House
90. Polanyi, K. 1944. *The Great Transformation.* New York: Reinhart
91. Rice, A. K. 1958. *Productivity and Social Organization: The Ahmedabad Experiment.* London: Tavistock
92. Rice, A. K. 1963. *The Enterprise and its Environment.* London: Tavistock
93. Rockefeller, J. D. 1916. Labor and Capital—Partners. *Atlantic Monthly* Jan.: 12–21
94. Roethlisberger, F. J., Dickson, W. 1939. *Management and the Worker.* Cambridge: Harvard Univ. Press
95. Roy, D. 1952. *Restriction of output in a piecework machine shop.* PhD Thesis. Univ. Chicago, Chicago, Ill.
96. Roy, D. 1952. Quota restriction and goldbricking in a machine shop. *Am. J. Sociol.* 57:427–42
97. Roy, D. 1953. Work satisfaction and social reward in quota achievement. *Am. Sociol. Rev.* 18:507–14
98. Roy, D. 1954. Efficiency and the fix: Informal intergroup relations in a piecework machine ship. *Am. J. Sociol.* 60:255–66
99. Roy, D. 1959. 'Banana Time': Job satisfaction and informal interaction. *Hum. Organ.* 18:158–168
100. Samora, J. 1971. *Los Mojados: The Wetback Story.* Notre Dame, Ind: Univ. Notre Dame Press
101. Schumpeter, J. A. 1950. *Capitalism, Socialism, and Democracy.* New York: Harper
102. Scott, J. 1974. *The Glassworkers of Carmaux.* Cambridge, Mass: Harvard Univ. Press
103. Scott, J. F., Homans, G. C. 1947. Reflections on the wildcat strikes. *Am. Sociol. Rev.* 12:278–87
104. Selznick, P. 1949. *TVA and the Grass Roots.* Berkeley: Univ. California Press
105. Selznick, P. 1969. *Law, Society and Industrial Justice.* New York: Sage

106. Sheth, N. R. 1968. *The Social Framework of an Indian Factory.* Manchester: Manchester Univ. Press

107. Simon, H. A. 1976. *Administrative Behavior.* New York: Free Press

108. Simons, H. J., Simons, R. E. 1969. *Class and Colour in South Africa 1850–1950.* Harmondsworth, England: Penguin

109. Singelmann, J., Wright, E. O. 1978. *Proletarianization in advanced capitalist societies: An empirical intervention into the debate between Marxist and post-industrial theorists over the transformations of the labor process.* Presented at Ann. Meet. Am. Sociol. Assoc., San Francisco

110. Stinchcombe, A. L. 1959. Bureaucratic and craft administration of production: A comparative study. *Adm. Sci. Q.* 4:168–87

111. Stinchcombe, A. L. 1965. Social structure and organizations. In *Handbook of Organizations,* ed. J. March, pp. 142–69. New York: Rand McNally

112. Stone, K. 1974. The origins of job structures in the steel industry. *Rev. Radical Polit. Econ.* 6:113–73

113. Susser, I. 1979. *Poverty and politics in a New York City neighborhood.* PhD thesis. Columbia Univ., New York, NY

114. Swados, H. 1957. *On the Line.* Boston: Little, Brown

115. Taylor, F. W. 1947. *Scientific Management.* New York: Harper

116. Thompson, J. 1967. *Organizations in Action.* New York: McGraw Hill

117. Trist, E. L., Higgin, G. W., Murray, H., Pollack, A. B. 1963. *Organizational Choice.* London: Tavistock

118. Van Onselen, C. 1976. *Chibaro.* London: Pluto

119. Walker, C. R., Guest, R. H. 1957. *The Man on the Assembly Line.* New Haven: Yale Univ. Press

120. Wallerstein, I. 1974. *The Modern World-System.* New York: Academic

121. Warner, W. L., Low, J. 1947. *The Social System of a Modern Factory.* New Haven: Yale Univ. Press

122. Weber, M. 1968. *Economy and Society.* New York: Bedminster. 3 vols.

123. Whitehead, T. N. 1938. *The Industrial Worker.* Cambridge, Mass: Harvard Univ. Press

124. Whyte, W. F. 1948. *Human Relations in the Restaurant Industry.* New York: McGraw Hill

125. Whyte, W. F. 1951. *Pattern for Industrial Peace.* New York: Harper

126. Whyte, W. F. 1955. *Money and Motivation.* New York: Harper

127. Woodward, J. 1958. *Management and Technology.* London: HMSO

Ann. Rev. Anthropol. 1979. 8:267–307

ETHNOART

♦9634

Harry R. Silver

Department of Anthropology, University of Denver, Denver, Colorado 80210

INTRODUCTION

Anthropology's fascination with the diversity and significance of art is as old as the discipline itself. Not surprisingly, studies on ethnoart have often reflected, in microcosm, the dominant theoretical approaches of their day. By examining the works of ethnologists and, where appropriate, of art historians and others, this essay will review a number of the major theoretical issues that have captured scholars' attention both in the past and today.

The already substantial literature of ethnoart continues to grow, presenting numerous options for organization. However, the central focus here will be upon art as a dynamic process. Mills (76) has isolated salient features of the artistic process, including the public object itself, the sociocultural context in which it functions, and the social and cognitive matrix in which creation and appreciation take place. The public object and its sociocultural context are dealt with in the sections on the analytic implications of style and symbolism, respectively. We will also examine the social framework of creativity and the position of "artist" as a differentiated role. Anthropological attempts to understand the nature of the aesthetic experience and the information communicated through it are also included as keys to the substantive workings of the art process.

Apart from the above topics, several specialized areas with a considerable literature of their own are also examined. These include speculations on the origins of art as well as treatments of the contemporary arts of acculturation the world over. Before turning to these theoretical issues, however, let us begin by briefly surveying the historical context within which interest in ethnic arts has arisen.

TERMINOLOGY AND PARAMETERS

A survey of literature on the anthropology of art reveals a tremendous variation in those terms used to describe the actual materials under investi-

267

0084-6570/79/1015-0267$01.00

gation. "Primitive," "tribal," "non-Western," and "traditional" have all been so employed. However, each of these terms leaves something to be desired (26). "Primitive art" defeats the spirit of most anthropological investigations, which typically strive to demonstrate the subtlety and sophistication of these works. "Non-Western art" fails to acknowledge the distinctions between "great" and "little" traditions. A term which, on a formal basis, lumps the arts of the Sepik with those of Ming-dynasty China cannot help but occasionally cloud analysis. "Tribal art" similarly fails because first, the concept of tribe is itself a much-debated one (45), and second, anthropologists are just as likely to study the art of societies with band, chiefdom, or state levels of organization.

Does any dimension unite these disparate groups targeted in the anthropological literature? Perhaps "preliterate" provides the key. For ancient societies lacking cipherable recorded history, art offers the social scientist a variety of means for reconstructing patterns of sociocultural life. Similarly, in contemporary nonliterate societies, analysis of art in its cultural context may illumine other less immediately accessible aspects of cognitive and symbolic organization. Still, the increasing attention paid by ethnologists to analyzing both Western art (2, 23) and the arts of acculturation among modernizing groups (50) makes "preliterate" less satisfactory as a generic term subsuming the focus of anthropological studies.

The terms "folk," "native," and "ethnic" art also have common currency in the field. These categories suggest minority traditions operating outside of, but not totally divorced from, dominant or "great" civilizations. Once again, these terms may account for some, but not all, of the extreme topical variance in the anthropological literature on art. For example, the great pre-Columbian traditions can hardly be considered "folk arts." Still, these terms do seem appropriate for the arts of many smaller-scale social groups.

Finally, we turn to the title term of this essay. "Ethnoart" suggests not merely a specific aesthetic tradition, but rather a broader orientation toward the problem of studying art as a whole. Semantically akin to "ethnoscience," the term denotes the study of art from an emic perspective, seeking its meaning and significance for a society's constituent members and institutions. This may range from efforts to actually reconstruct native categories to less systematic investigations which, through the ethnographer's own interpretive powers, seek a given art's function in its own sociocultural context.

When conscientiously applied, this approach minimizes temptations to apply Western evaluative standards to the analysis of non-Western art. In fairness, however, it must be said that many valuable and objective studies minimize or eliminate analysis from an emic or culturally embedded perspective, instead addressing supracultural themes or theories and employing specific ethnographic cases for cross-cultural data to verify hypotheses.

Thus, to apply the term "ethnoart" as a gloss for all anthropological studies in the field is somewhat misleading. Still, given that "ethnoart" connotes the anthropologically attractive notion of an "ethnic art" as well, the term is probably, on balance, as evocative as possible. Perhaps more than any other, it does succeed in conveying the idea of a uniquely anthropological view of art concentrating not only upon objects, but also upon the sociocultural processes molding their production, use, meaning, and appreciation.

DEVELOPMENT OF INTEREST IN ETHNOART

Western interest in "exotic art" has a long tradition. Fraser (40) dates serious appreciation of these arts at least to the late Renaissance, when Dürer expressed his wonder at the treasures brought from the New World. Later, in the seventeenth and eighteenth centuries, missionaries and explorers customarily made gifts of native curios to their patrons and royal benefactors, or otherwise distributed objects to the rare collectors of the day (43). Royalty might store these pieces in their curiosity cabinets—which came to form the nuclei of many national museum collections in the nineteenth century.

In addition to the formal organization of many royal collections, the nineteenth century also witnessed another development contributing to the wider appreciation of native arts. As imperialism grew in the latter half of the century, many European capitals organized major exhibitions incorporating works from distant regions of their empires. Thousands of people, including many prominent artists, gained their first introduction to so-called primitive art through these exhibits. By 1907, the influence of these arts in the work of European artists, such as Picasso, began to be visible. African art was particularly influential, though by the 1940s men such as Ernst had also come to appreciate Northwest Coast traditions. Various schools of "primitivism" arose in Europe, and nowhere are they chronicled better than in Goldwater's classic work (48). While foreign arts clearly affected these European schools, Goldwater stresses that the "primitivism" of modern Western art is conceptually distinct, noting that through either formal simplification or iconographic generalization, in Primitivism an object, as symbol, is imbued with universal reference. He suggests that in true "primitive art," symbolic referents are far more limited—they must always be accurate and recognizable to be effective. This seems an overbold statement since, as Goldwater himself allows, native symbolic referents may be multiple and even ambivalent, a fact which Turner (100) has admirably demonstrated.

Initial Western interest in "primitive" art, however, was certainly not limited to fine artists alone. Many pioneers in anthropology focused on it as a means of addressing larger theoretical issues. Early debates between the evolutionist and diffusionist schools often used the development and distribution of artistic styles or traits as evidence for their theoretical claims, even when documentation on pieces' provenience or age was inconclusive. A review of this debate provides excellent entry into a discussion of those elements of the art process among the first to be systematically studied within anthropology—the public object and the sociocultural significance of formal style.

STYLE

An analysis of "style" presents two problems for the social scientist: (*a*) to define adequately what is meant by style, and (*b*) to determine what relationship art styles bear to the civilizations which produce them. This section will concentrate upon the latter problem, adopting a broad "common sense" definition of style which attends to formal features characterizing individual works of art. Where clusters of features repeatedly co-occur in the corpora of numerous artists, we may speak meaningfully of stylistic trends. Common sociocultural characteristics of producers or common uses of objects may also allow us to situate these styles in an appropriate sociocultural matrix. For example, examination of a large sample of goods carved by Ashanti artists may reveal sufficient formal similarities to justify identification of an Ashanti "style." And, within a culture, we can often identify secular as versus sacred art styles. Recent anthropological work (36, 99) has also made progress in identifying the emergence and development of individual styles within these broader cultural frameworks. Bascom (8) provides an excellent systematic overview of style types, with special reference to the range of individual creative latitude allowed.

Of course, the search for common features should be conducted on as concrete a basis as possible. Imbuing formal traits with anthropopsychic qualities is a particularly dangerous pitfall for anthropologists, who must ever beware of ethnocentric bias. Hence, classifying works as sharing a common style because of their "grotesque" or "heroic" qualities is always questionable unless such judgments can be supported with rigorous ethnographic documentation validating these interpretations from an "etic" as well as an "emic" standpoint.

Diffusion and Evolution

Turning now to the significance of style for the study of civilization, early anthropological interest in non-Western art styles was typically couched in terms of two basic theoretical orientations—evolution and diffusion. The reaction of Victorian observers to the art of "primitive" peoples was generally not one of enthusiasm. Most scholars limited their analyses to appraisals of the ornamental motifs found on isolated objects resting in European museums. Often even the actual chronology of these pieces relative to one another was unknown. For many years, debates raged over whether the origins of primitive design lay in naturalistic or geometric forms. Nineteenth century theorists such as Haddon, Balfour, and Stolpe contended that the earliest primitive art forms sprang from attempts at naturalistic representation. They hypothesized that, over time, the original naturalistic forms succumbed to geometric stylization as a result of a ". . . lack of skill on the part of a series of savage artists, who copied, or rather tried to copy, each other because they were not equal to copying from nature" (48, p. 20). To an evolutionist, of course, these findings provided yet another example of fixed developmental sequences in culture.

The study of art, and material culture in general, also bulked large in diffusionism. In the nineteenth century, the term "diffusion" typically referred to either the borrowing of culture traits between settled groups or the physical migration of an established group and its traits to a new geographical area. Both lines of diffusionist reasoning claimed that the invention of new traits was a rare occurrence. Several important anthropological schools were rooted in a basically diffusionist philosophy—the two most influential being, of course, the Kulturkreis and culture-area schools. The latter in particular involved an analysis of material culture traits, including styles of native arts and industries. In fact, this approach arose originally as a technique for organizing museum collections, in which the distribution of selected traits was first mapped and then underlying geotechnological and sociocultural patterns were sought. Culture areas were seen as organized around innovative centers from which traits diffused by borrowing to adjacent peoples, and bounded usually by environmental barriers. Perhaps the leading exponent of culture area studies was Wissler, although other American anthropologists such as Kroeber and Spier utilized very similar concepts.

The Kulturkreis school developed in Germany and Austria and was led by Graebner and Schmidt. Kulturkreise were large complexes of culture traits; scholars suggested that all world cultures stemmed from the diffusion of a limited number of original Kreise. Diffusion was said generally to occur through human migrations rather than simply through borrowing. Kulturkreis scholars were somewhat less dependent upon the analysis of material traits—including visual art styles—than were culture-area theorists.

Predictably, Kulturkreis, culture-area, and other diffusionist schools were basically incompatible with most evolutionary theory. By claiming invention to be a rarity, diffusionists rejected the likelihood that fixed laws of development independently guided unrelated societies down identical cultural paths. Implicit also in these arguments was a comment on the limitations to human creativity, a subject of great concern to those interested in the arts.

It is within the context of these debates on evolution and diffusion that Franz Boas's contribution to the study of art styles must be assessed. Boas was instrumental in dispelling many evolutionist dogmas—and without slipping into the weaknesses of extreme diffusionist views. For example, his article on Alaskan needle cases (15) demonstrates that natural forms in art may develop out of geometric design elements. He thereby effectively destroyed evolutionist claims that geometric style was inevitably a later artistic development representing a gradual degeneration from early naturalism. Boas's approach still stands as a model of balanced reasoning and careful research.

Surely there is no finer critique of the evolutionist-diffusionist debate on the arts than Munro's definitive text, *Evolution in the Arts* (83). Munro recognizes the danger of oversimplified and programmatic statements in either theoretical direction and demonstrates that certain sociocultural factors tend to encourage the development of large-scale uniformities while others promote local-level divergences. Munro views historical developments in the arts as a process of "multiple dialectic"; single dichotomies are not always sufficient to explain the subtleties of history—particularly in complex sociocultural milieux. One artistic movement may provoke numerous rival reactions, not simply a single neat antithesis. Resolution, if it occurs at all, may take centuries.

Style, Psyche, and Civilization

In addition to evolutionary concerns, Boas explained both the techniques of artistic execution and the interpretation of symbolic motifs (16). He believed that the excellence and formal diversity of a given art style hinged upon the perfection of technique. He wrote that ". . . the more fundamental the motor habits that determine the form of an implement, the less likely will be a deviation from the customary" (16, p. 146). Yet a knowledge of technique must be accompanied by an understanding of the attitudes of artists themselves. Boas recognized that the play of the individual imagination deeply influences the development of art styles. In the realm of meaning, associative processes act to instill conventionalized forms with symbolic significance. Differences in individual expertise may also produce variations within a style. He therefore stressed the imperativeness of a balanced appreciation of material, technical, and psychological factors to a proper understanding of how art styles develop and how their meanings can best be interpreted.

Boas's interest in stylistics was shared by many of his students, including Bunzel and Kroeber, although they did not necessarily share his attitudes toward art. Kroeber, in particular, felt that Boas approached art too much like a "physicist," taking style as a mere departure-point for analyzing a specific theoretical problem, such as the processes of conventionalization. He attacked Boas's lack of real sensitivity to "the essential qualities" of the styles themselves, purely from their standpoint as fascinating phenomena (see 54, p. 276).

Bunzel, on the other hand, saw art styles as intimately related to their artists' mental processes and arising from artists' dependence upon visual images, either consciously evoked or dreamed. The modes of acceptable expression for these images are always clearly definable through formal analysis. However, Bunzel stressed that the limits of acceptability in style are constantly shifting. The degree of variability may be related to the number of artists working in the style and even to the nature of the style itself—some allowing more room for innovation than others. Bunzel did not believe that technique exerts a powerful influence on stylistic change; she states that a wide variety of styles may develop out of basically similar techniques. Of further interest are Bunzel's views on the relationship between art and society. On the basis of her work in the American Southwest, she saw in ceremonials and other aspects of social life a congruence with stylistic principles similar to those of local art. She generalized this further to state that ". . . we are working towards a definition of art. It is the elaboration of the formal elements of objects and activities for their own sake. By this means civilizations achieve style" (22, p. 89).

Kroeber also attempts to develop a theory of the interrelation of style and civilization (59). His notion of an art style refers generally to form rather than content. He recognized that individual artists may have distinctive styles, but his major concern was with the historical development of art styles among whole cultures. When he stressed this latter interest, analysis of individual "idiosyncracies" was subordinated to the course of the style as a whole: "It is the interrelations of the persons that count now, rather than the persons in themselves" (59, p. 59).

Kroeber believed that "historical styles" pass through a series of stages embodying a general cycle of growth and decay. In his view, styles are inherently dynamic and it is rare for them to become static without deteriorating. Stylistic revolutions come about when individuals sense that an existing style has exhausted its potential. Kroeber found that a developmental flow through stages of growth and decay was one of the most characteristic qualities of style.

Of course, Kroeber was also interested in the study of total cultural patterns. An art style can be a sensitive indicator of a civilization's general profile; but social, ethical, and economic phenomena may have styles of their own which also contribute to the culture's "master pattern" (60, p.

126). Implicit in this notion is the element of choice; one line of procedure out of several must be selected and adhered to. However, Kroeber was by no means dogmatic in his pronouncements on culture patterns, for he appreciated the difficulties involved in accurately defining them. For example, in art, it is not necessarily true that all artists in a given culture and time come, through their interrelations, to pursue a single stylistic line. Data from my own field study among the Ashanti illustrate this point (95). There I found two distinct art styles coexisting contemporaneously in the same site—one geometric and static, the other more naturalistic and dynamic—with neither showing any signs of immediate disappearance or decay. In this case it would be difficult, to say the least, to employ art style as an indicator of a coherent master pattern representative of the whole of modern Ashanti society.

It is interesting that when anthropologists required a definitive statement on style for *Anthropology Today* (90) they turned to an art historian for an overview of the subject. Schapiro's discussion of the concept of style still stands as one of the most intensive treatments of the topic. For him, style is founded in form; but he emphasizes that art forms are usually instilled with an emotional expressiveness conveying impressions of the artist's personality and his culture's general "outlook." A proper study of style therefore demands an appreciation of both compositional pattern and expressive quality.

As for the relation between form and subject matter, Schapiro is sympathetic to the view that style may at times be a vehicle of content,

... a means of communication, a language not only as a system of devices for conveying a precise message by representing or symbolizing objects and actions but also as a qualitative whole which is capable of suggesting the diffuse connotations as well, and intensifying the associated or intrinsic affects (90, p. 304).

Using experience as a guide, an artist imaginatively searches for the formal relationships which will best express contextual values in an aesthetically satisfying manner. Out of many attempts in this respect, the most successful are duplicated by others and, over time, come to constitute the stylistic norm.

Schapiro vacillates somewhat on the precise relationship of art styles to other aspects of society. On the one hand, he states that style and content are parallel products of the emotional and intellectual disposition common to a whole culture. However, he also recognizes that the extent to which an art style reflects a common "world view" is highly variable. An artist's work frequently displays clearly individual as well as conventional elements. And, as noted above, artists in a given society may be working in several styles simultaneously. Such problems make it difficult to reach reliable generalizations about a given culture on the basis of art styles.

The Cross-Cultural Approach

Though the difficulties in extrapolating from art styles to other aspects of culture are great, they have seldom deterred speculation upon the nature of these relationships. A considerable literature has emerged from cross-cultural statistical attempts to establish broad correlations between a group's art forms and its other sociopsychological orientations. Fischer (38), Barry (7), and Wolfe (105) are major exponents of this method.

For Fischer and Barry, art styles are objectifications of pervasive socio-cultural preferences; they reveal information about communal values, economics, politics, and social stratification. These authors elaborate hypotheses about the exact nature of these relationships, then test them by first classifying a large number of societies and their associated art forms according to the criteria in question, and next determining statistically whether the criteria are significantly correlated.

For example, Barry (7) attempts to relate art styles and patterns of socialization—specifically, design complexity and severity of child rearing —by having panels of expert judges rate selected cultures and art styles along these dimensions. Barry does find a significant link between the two, and attributes this to the fact that socialization patterns help create the personalities of a society and its artists. These latter, then, presumably produce their objects in a style which in some way reflects their personalities. In this particular instance, Barry argues that in most cultures with complex art styles, individuals are pressured to learn self-reliant behavior, with punishment accorded to overt dependence. To his credit, Barry recognizes the limitations of such findings, since it is never clear just why design complexity should be associated with severity of socialization. In short, though the statistical correlations may be significant, the causal mechanism is missing.

Fischer (38), employing a similar approach, establishes his causal arguments much more clearly. First, he endeavors to show that design elements reflect a society's level of hierarchical development. To take one example, Fischer states that a design which repeats "... simple elements should characterize egalitarian societies, designs integrating a number of unlike elements should be characteristic of hierarchical societies" (38, p. 81). The rationale is as follows: in egalitarian societies security comes from having many comrades of similar status; in a hierarchical society it stems from establishing functional relations with a wide variety of different persons within the hierarchy. Therefore, in the "egalitarian designs" the artist symbolically multiplies equal allies, while in the "hierarchical designs" personal differentiation is stressed within a broader scheme of integration. Fischer presents further hypotheses on design and hierarchy, as well as still others linking design and the prestige/security of the sexes. In all cases his hypotheses are borne out through statistical testing. He even attempts to explain Barry's results by arguing that in egalitarian societies individual differentiation is not encouraged, while in hierarchical ones it can be tolerated—thereby rationalizing the link between design complexity and independence.

Wolfe (105) offers a sophisticated statistical analysis of a proposition linking advanced art production with societies characterized by fixed, nucleated settlements and significant social cleavages among male members. He rather vaguely attributes this to a connection between the emotions associated with art production and with social barriers between males. Wolfe presents no clear causal rationale for why these dimensions should be related; but his statistical survey of 53 African societies bears out his hypothesis. Societies were ranked by independent raters on the basis of art development (both quantitative and qualitative) and were further identified according to 105 sociocultural variables, with settlement pattern and non-kin sodalities leading the list of variables associated with art through factor analysis and other statistical techniques. Wolfe also directly addresses Galton's problem, convincingly demonstrating that diffusion alone cannot account for his findings. He believes he has clearly identified correspondences between cognitive processes inducing the development of art and other emotions or feelings generated by certain sociocultural institutions.

Before turning to a brief critique of the cross-cultural or statistical approach, the work of one other author should be mentioned. Kavolis (57) aims to draw very broad correlations between stylistic features and stratificational, economic, political, ideational, and value systems. The breadth of Kavolis's scholarship is impressive and his hypotheses provocative. With regard to stratification, for example, he tenders a causal mechanism by suggesting that certain social classes have characteristic fantasy dispositions —dispositions which in turn receive expression in art. Later, drawing upon F. Kluckhohn and others in classifying differing schemes of value orientations, Kavolis seeks to demonstrate how these orientations can be translated into visual expression. This is consistent with his basic view of style as a ". . . projection of subjective perceptions of, and responses to, situations of action" (57, p. 6). To his credit, Kavolis pursues his research in a spirit of open inquiry. Statistical confirmations are lacking and certain arguments seem impressionistic; but, on the whole, his book suggests many potentials for further empirical research. His hypotheses are both numerous and, if one accepts their basic premises, well founded and logical. However, these premises bear closer scrutiny.

Cross-cultural studies of the type described above are intriguing but also highly problematic. It is debatable whether societal values are so homogeneous that one orientation alone can adequately represent a large, complex social group. Further, as noted earlier, a variety of art styles may coexist in the same community. These facts greatly undermine the validity of drawing one-to-one correspondences between values and style, even in a single community.

Another weakness in this technique is that the rationale for hypotheses is often drawn from general psychological studies of individuals who were not themselves artists. I believe that the test response of untrained individuals are not directly comparable to the expressive values of professional artists working within a preexisting tradition. An artist's work may include traditional elements whose original meanings do not entirely reflect the creator's, or even the society's, current values; but these elements may still be widely known by the public and capable of communicating other messages. For example, a newcomer to modern American art might consider Warhol's giant soup cans a sincere and heroic celebration of a popular food, whereas in reality they constitute a satiric comment on American consumerism. In fact, it appears that the Fischer/Kavolis hypotheses would consistently hold true only if artists were considered ideal representatives of their culture—a proposition that is hardly universally valid.

Fischer (38) is not oblivious to the conceptual limitations underlying his arguments. He specifically addresses the problem of the artist's awareness and representativeness of his sociocultural milieu and the related problem of art that appears to reflect purely personal wish-fulfillment. Fischer argues that all sane individuals share in their culture's modal personality and that wish-fulfillment therefore usually involves some accommodation with sociocultural reality. A possible compromise position might involve a careful screening of cultures along a dimension of "artist's social representativeness," including in the final sample only those with a positive rating.

So far we have dealt with the public object from the perspective of formal style, noting that, both overtly and covertly, an art style may convey considerable information about its producers and their culture. Of course, style is by no means the only artistic dimension which can transmit information. The following section will deal with a multiplicity of approaches to the study of meaning in art, whether this meaning be conveyed through style, context, or thematic content, either singly or jointly.

SYMBOLISM

Approaches to the analysis of symbolism in art vary tremendously. Here we can only touch on a few of the most challenging theories. First, however, mention should be made of two authors who endeavor to establish sound frameworks within which to study symbolism.

Iconography and Iconology

Panofsky (86) develops a tripartite system for the study of symbols which covers virtually all levels of meaning. He distinguishes between preiconographical, iconographical, and iconological acts of interpretation. The preiconographical level is rooted in the analysis of form. All art styles employ certain formal conventions for representing objects, events, and emotions. An informed viewer must have at least some acquaintance with an object's stylistic context in order to "read" its formal components properly. Real considerations of symbolism, however, do not enter in until the iconographical level. Iconography demands that the viewer relate visual motifs to their appropriate cultural referents. As Panofsky (86, p. 35) points out, to Australian bushmen, the *Last Supper* is simply an excited dinner party. A knowledge of appropriate cultural themes or concepts is necessary to understanding at this level, although, depending on the piece under consideration, varying levels of expertise may be needed for accurate interpretation.

Finally, beyond inconographical analysis lies the more intuitive level of iconology. Here the observer appreciates the symbol in the broadest context possible. The symbol is now seen as a key to unlocking the secret of how, ". . . under various historical conditions, the general and essential tendencies of the human mind were expressed by specific themes and concepts" (86, p. 39). To accomplish this feat of synthetic intuition as reliably as possible, observers must thoroughly familiarize themselves with available supplementary materials (be they philosophical, poetical, political, or religious) which further elucidate the "Weltanschauung" of the era in question.

Like Panofsky, Turner (100) develops a tripartite scheme for the analysis of symbols, distinguishing three types of meaning. Exegetical meaning is obtained by eliciting the opinions of indigenous informants about a symbol's significance. Operational meaning tends to equate meaning with use and is discerned by observing how people actively react to symbols. Finally, the positional meaning of the symbol derives from its relation to other symbols in the total structure of an object or event. Context often clarifies a symbol's significance where several meanings are possible. Turner is particularly interested in the role of symbols in ritual. However, his scheme may be applied usefully to the study of visual art as well. Exegetical meaning may be approached emically by interviewing artists and audience to discover the structure of ethnoaesthetic systems. This approach can be combined with etic observation of the object in its social context.

Works of art may contain a multitude of symbols. Some may be understood in their own terms but others may only be comprehensible when the
messages of several symbols are combined. Using Turner's terminology, the
positional meaning of a visual symbol may be compounded on two different
levels: the symbol's meaning may depend upon its position relative to other
visual motifs in the object itself or it may be heavily influenced by the
context of action in which it appears. This is particularly true for objects
which have dynamic social functions, as is often the case for tribal arts.

Turner recognizes that the psychological foundations of symbolism are
important to the understanding of meaning. Meaning is bounded by both
ideological and sensory poles. Ideological significata order the norms and
values guiding individual behavior in social groups, while sensory significata
are emotive. A given symbol may appeal to both. Once again, this is particularly true in ethnic arts, where ideational function and dramatic embellish-
ment are typically intertwined.

Structuralism

As the foregoing suggests, symbolically oriented researches usually seek the
underlying motivations and meanings conveyed through the form and content of art. The most sophisticated studies link the logic motivating art
production with the rationale behind numerous other cultural patterns in
the society. For this purpose, many anthropologists find structuralism an
especially compelling strategy. Naturally, Lévi-Strauss is a key figure in the
structural study of art. An exhaustive discussion of Lévi-Straussian theories
of non-Western art is not possible here, but we will recapitulate three of his
major concept areas.

First, in his article on split representation, Lévi-Strauss (66) systematically appraises the formal stylistic features which he feels are shared by the
arts of four distinct cultures, addressing both the manner in which certain
stylistic motifs are representative of broader social and psychological dispositions and general questions of historical reconstruction through analysis
of art. With regard to the former, Lévi-Strauss rejects the claim that split
representation arises merely as a natural result of the extension to flat or
angular surfaces ". . . of a technique which is naturally appropriate in the
case of three-dimensional objects" (66, p. 253). The definitive significance
of an object is achieved only through the successful integration of structure,
decoration, and function. The dualism between the plastic and graphic
components in objects displaying split representation reflects other kinds of
dualism in society as well—including ". . . person and impersonation, individual existence and social function, community and hierarchy" (66, p.
255). Lévi-Strauss suggests that in societies where split representation is

found, masking is also an important cultural trait, emphasizing a further dualism between actor and roles. In these societies, masks are the vehicles by which "chains" of privilege and prestige ". . . validate social hierarchies through the primacy of genealogies" (66, p. 258). In such cultures, ancestors confer titles and positions on living persons in the social world. Lévi-Strauss summarizes this analysis of the relation between an art style and other social patterns thus:

> The mutual independence of the plastic and graphic components corresponds to the more flexible interplay between the social and supernatural orders, in the same way that split representation expresses the strict conformity of the actor to his role and of social rank to myths, ritual, and pedigrees (66, p. 259).

Lévi-Strauss also addresses the implication of his approach for historical studies. Again, in comparing the art styles of four geographically diverse populations (Maori, Chinese, Caduveo, and Northwest Coast) he claims that while direct historical influences between the groups are unlikely, similarities can be explained by other means, such as psychology or the structural analysis of forms. In fact, even when historical contacts can be documented, a mere demonstration of a diffusion's authenticity is not sufficient to explain why it becomes accepted. "External connection can explain transmission, but only internal connection can account for persistence" (66, p. 258).

A second central topic in other of Lévi-Strauss's writings on art is its psychological foundations (65). For him, art lies midway between scientific knowledge and mythical thought. Like a bricoleur, the artist creates structures from a set of contingent materials and events. Art synthesizes the intrinsic properties of an object with other properties which depend upon its specific spatial, temporal, and social environment. The artist unites internal and external knowledge, i.e.

> . . . the aesthetic emotion is the result of a union between the structural order and the order of events, which is brought about within a thing created by man and so also in effect by the observer who discovers the possibility of such a union through the work of art (65, p. 25).

Observers of art objects may also mentally note numerous other possible permutations of components beyond that which the artist chose; this process helps the observer both to understand the artist's intentions and to engage in a creative act of his own.

Though art has semantic functions in all societies, a third major notion of Lévi-Strauss's is that certain basic differences in the orientation of these functions separate primitive from Western art in a meaningful way. For example, he finds primitive art especially effective at linking individual and collective impulses. Since the opposition between individual and collective consciousness is regarded as an important psychological phenomenon, Lévi-Strauss applauds primitive art's very lucid handling of these subtle functions of the mind.

He also finds the concept of academicism, common in Western art, inapplicable to primitive traditions. Academicism implies that aesthetic activity stands in direct relation to artistic traditions, not to objects themselves. Lévi-Strauss feels that such a concept could not apply to primitive art because "... the continuity of tradition is assured" (23, p. 68). In primitive art, changes in style are often rejected because they may cloud the semantic function of the art, thereby threatening its social utility. Western art, particularly that of recent origin, is more amenable to stylistic change because its semantic statement may be simply a highly specialized comment on the nature of style itself.

Of these three spheres of interest in art, it is probably through the first that Lévi-Strauss has primarily influenced anthropological thought on the topic. In recent years, an increasing number of students have endeavored to relate the structural principles motivating artistic production to other structural patterns essential to societal functioning. Munn (82) engages in a complex dissection of Walbiri graphic art to demonstrate how visual elements are assigned meanings and how, in the case of composite visual categories, items can be broken down into core and adjunct features. Complex, contrastive designs representing totems are constructed from a limited range of elementary forms. Munn believes that these design patternings parallel the ordering principles inherent in totemism itself:

> On the one hand, each species is distinctive and functions as the symbol of a particular clan; on the other hand, each can be analyzed into a set of parts shared with the other totemic animals and intersecting these species' differences (82, p. 945).

Still other Walbiri cosmological theories are reflected in the structure of graphic designs, which Munn takes as visual models of these abstract principles. Munn's analytical scheme offers an intriguing guide for future discussions of other graphic systems such as, for example, Ashanti adinkra symbols.

In another excellent study examining the manner in which art styles reflect aspects of social life, Fernandez (37) shows that for the Fang, balanced opposition among forms imparts a perceived vitality to art that is aesthetically valued. Achievement of this same balance is also sought in the social realm—both on the individual level of personal maturity and within the broader scope of interclan relations.

Studies in the structuralist mode are clearly both insightful and stimulating. At their best they reveal underlying continuities of process and pattern which further our understanding of the integrative dynamics of culture.

However, there is always the danger of the ethnologist's succumbing to flights of analytical fancy. Still, this risk can be minimized by insisting, as any good researcher should, that analysis of deep structures be firmly rooted in sound empirical data.

Psychological and Psychoanalytic Theories

Structuralism is by no means the only possible approach to the study of symbols. A number of other views seek to relate art to key elements of social and cultural life. One such is the explication of artistic symbols through psychological, and often psychoanalytic, interpretation.

The interest of psychoanalytic theorists in art can be traced to Freud himself. As an exercise in method, anthropologists can profit from Freud's study of Da Vinci. Freud (44, 91) analyzes Leonardo's genius from his early memories of infancy to the development of such masterpieces as *The Virgin and St. Ann.* To Freud, the experiences of Leonardo's early childhood are never far beneath the surface of his masterpieces. To his credit, Freud recognized that psychoanalytic investigations simply touch the superficies of creativity and genius. He saw his approach not as a cold scalpel dissecting beauty but rather as one among many possible tools for clarifying problems in interpretation.

Given Freud's interest in the Western tradition, how then is his method relevant to the study of native arts? Freud felt that for centuries Western art had repressed all concerns with sex. In earlier ages in the West and among contemporary primitives today, relationships between art and sex are much more openly expressed. In such societies, reasoned Freud, sexual concerns are an integral part of religious beliefs and consequently are reflected in art, which is itself tied into the dominant religious-symbolic system of society. In this view, the method and terminology of psychoanalysis provide an excellent framework within which to examine these interrelationships.

Let us now consider the work of several psychoanalytically oriented critics who address primitive art directly. Muensterberger (81) sees fertility, potency, and death as major elements in the arts of non-Western peoples. His arguments are frequently ingenious and merit close inspection even from skeptics of Freudian analysis. Like most psychoanalytic interpreters, he is inclined to see a plethora of phallic symbolism inhabiting the aesthetic landscape. From animal tusks to elongated noses, the potential for identifying phallic symbolism in art seems unlimited. Muensterberger believes that such symbols are often universal—thus implying that at some primal level even Westerners are ready to accept and understand the messages of primitive art.

The relationship of death and the ancestors to sex and potency is another common theme in psychoanalytic interpretations. Art may play a central role in mediating between these elements. In some instances, an art object may actually become a repository for an ancestor or spirit, while in performance art, the performer, upon donning the object, may himself become the spirit-hero. For example, in their ritual context, masks may portray dead ancestors or supernatural enemies. Donning an ancestor mask is seen as a means of adding the latent sexual strength of the ancestor to one's own powers. Similarly, through the proper performance of a religio-aesthetic ceremony, one can confront a potent enemy spirit, defeat this hostile strength, capture it, and add it to one's own prowess. The association between object and spirit need not be completely abstract; an art object may actually incorporate parts of a deceased ancestor or enemy.

Taking a Freudian outlook, investigators may attempt to integrate such observations into a wider interpretive framework. For example, in the above case, Muensterberger argues for a measure of identification between ancestors, enemies, and an overarching father-figure concept. Father/ancestor/enemy are one in the oedipal situation. From this standpoint, the use of art in augmenting potency is also a mechanism for combating one's fears of castration at the hands of the father.

While the example cited deals primarily with males, Freudians are equally vigorous in searching out themes related to a so-called female sphere. Most notable of these is the theme of fertility, with its associated breast and womb symbolism. Sexual dimorphism may exist on the symbolic plain, but proper propitiation of both dimensions is seen as essential to the healthy functioning of society. Symbols from each dimension frequently intertwine and even overlap, whether within the context of whole rituals or within a single object itself.

Sexual dimorphism extends beyond the realm of ritual and symbolism into the concrete dynamics of production. Cross-cultural tabulations reflect a remarkable tendency to divide the manufacture of material objects, including art, along sex lines (29). Domains of production are often jealously guarded by the sexes. In many societies, particularly Africa and Oceania, it is not at all uncommon for male artists to be forbidden contact with females while they work. At one level, an explanation may be advanced that this dimorphism in the realm of art production reflects a general cultural fear of clouding the boundaries between male/female categories. Neo-Freudians, however, locate these phenomena deep in the psyche's innermost recesses. In this view, a male artist's fear of women represents a kind of regression, the desire for affect being shifted from external sources to a narcissistic isolation. As usual, culture is largely reduced to an Oedipal battlefield in which conflicting sociosexual desires struggle for supremacy. The male artist retreats from the tempting threat of the Oedipal mother, yet seeks out a creative force which psychoanalysts equate with the nurturing mother of the pre-Oedipal phase (81, p. 128). Presumably, the mysteries of female artistic creativity must be read in a different light, although they are not directly treated.

Psychoanalytic approaches are employed by other scholars as well. Devereux (34) attempts to outline a programmatic relationship between art and other dimensions of societal and individual consciousness by summarizing art as "stylized communication," with the conventions of style playing, in a very real sense, the role of an alibi or bribe to the superego. The forbidden content is deemed by society as subordinate to form, with an added element of psychic "distance" between object and creator which allows the creator or audience the option of repudiating the object's darker connotations. Taboos treated in art may include the universally human, the culturally specific, and the idiosyncratic—the latter, however, seldom being completely divorced from the cultural. Truly great works, in Devereux's view, tackle taboo at multiple levels. Art takes potentially disruptive impulses and rechannels them in socially acceptable directions. The anthropologist's "mission" therefore includes identifying the types of tabooed materials that a given society approves for expression in art; chronicling the rules governing expression; and finally, describing the skills necessary for properly executing a work which subliminally titillates beneath the culture-specific cloak of propriety.

Strict Freudian, or even neo-Freudian, analysis is no longer so major a force in anthropology. Its decline is well documented (54) and need not be pursued here. Topics such as sex and taboo—previously the preserve of Freudians—are now open to broader types of cognitive and symbolic interpretation. The work of Forge (39) provides an excellent example of how sexual symbolism in art can be treated from a nonpsychoanalytic standpoint. Phallic and womb symbols abound in the ceremonial arts and architecture of the Sepik. Forge successfully accounts for the "deep-structure" significance of these symbols to local populations without conjuring up the id/ego/superego ghost for support. Using controlled comparisons, he demonstrates these symbols' integration into wider cosmological and technoenvironmental contexts. Like Devereux, Forge recognizes that art may communicate messages which fail to find a voice in other areas of culture. Comprehension of these messages, however, does not require a Freudian model limited to the use of a psychoanalytic "decoder." Leach's (63) classic analysis of the "Trobriand Medusa" provides another nice study in this vein.

Symbols and Social Action

As the above sections suggest, while symbolism may be interpreted from a variety of theoretical perspectives, the social scientist must always recognize that symbols are ultimately rooted in human action. The visual and per-

forming arts may vividly manifest a society's broad symbolic system, which
in turn often reinforces the existing power structure both at state and local
levels. Fraser & Cole's (42) anthology documents numerous instances of the
articulation between the ritual-aesthetic and power spheres in Africa. For
example, the Ashanti forced constituent members to their confederacy to
employ Ashanti ceremonial regalia, hoping thereby to impose on a psy-
chosymbolic level a hegemony already established through armed force.
Further, possession of the appropriate regalia was itself a crucial factor in
legitimizing claims to authority; and the use of selected symbolic motifs
could make significant comments on the nature of the social event taking
place (18, 41, 95). Interestingly, Kubler (61) similarly notes that in colonial
Hispanic America, all symbolic expressions, including undestroyed indigenous ones, eventually became reinforcements of the colonial state's power.
Ironically, the Inca laid the pattern for this development in Andean America through their own systematic institution of the state religion—of which
the head of state was also the divine leader—and its associated symbols and
rituals throughout the empire. These and other examples attest to the
dynamic power of symbols, visual and otherwise, in social interaction.

ANTHROPOLOGICAL APPROACHES
TO AESTHETIC SYSTEMS

In addition to style and meaning, anthropologists also study the conceptual
and physical parameters which define a work of art in a given culture. Once
these have been identified, they proceed to the dimensions along which
evaluative judgments are made. Studies of this latter topic span a spectrum
of both emic and etic strategies.

Common Western usage of the term "aesthetic" often distinguishes between the "abstract" notion of aesthetic and aesthetics proper—which pertain, respectively, to our concepts of beauty and emotive sensuality, and to
the discipline of abstracting basic principles from those qualities of form and
feeling perceived in works of art. Our terms "beauty" and "art," of course,
are cognitively tied to congeries of Western values and concepts. Other
cultures may lack similar categories, causing no end of confusion in culture
contact situations. The literature on "primitive" art abounds with statements that given cultures lack a concept of art or aesthetics.

Process, Culture, and Qualitative Experience

In this brief essay we can only allude to a few of anthropology's contributions to aesthetic theory. An excellent entry into the field is furnished by
d'Azevedo's (31) and Mills's (77) outlines of the basis for an anthropological understanding of art.

Both authors seek to embed aesthetic process in the matrix of human action. Both stress an experiential approach to aesthetics; aesthetic phenomena are experiences in the qualitative mode. Producer, audience, and object dynamically interact, each contributing toward an experience that is both *aesthetic* and *artistic*. It is important to distinguish these two concepts. Objects and events may stimulate aesthetic responses in perceivers but, as d'Azevedo cautions, aesthetic values are not intrinsic in these stimuli. We must therefore ask to what extent are such values culturally conditioned, and to what extent are they a product of more "innate" panhuman proclivities. Naturally, anthropologists are more interested in the former question.

Segall, Campbell & Herskovits (94) have presented both an original study and a thorough-going literature review which convincingly contend that human perception is heavily influenced by cultural conditioning. Relatedly, Cole & Scribner (27) wrestle with the problem of whether basic human cognitive processes differ between cultures. While noting that the question is open to a great deal more research, they are nevertheless skeptical that the basic processual components of cognition (such as abstraction, inferential reasoning, and categorization) vary much cross-culturally, although sociocultural factors may influence which processes are actualized in given performance situations. They urge investigation of cognitive processes as functional systems, realizing full well that methical researches in this vein must be carefully constructed due to the danger of experimental artifact.

The determination of exactly what constitutes the nature of an aesthetic experience is similarly problematic, for both emotion and cognition are involved in what seems to be the enjoyment of experience for its own sake. d'Azevedo clarifies this hazy notion of aesthetic effect somewhat:

> The esthetic effect is more precisely identified as the especially meaningful, the new insight, the conscious unit of feeling, or the shock of recognition emerging from the correspondences perceived between the qualities of an esthetic object and their affinities in the subjective experience of the individual (31, p. 708).

Idiosyncratic, situational, and cultural factors all contribute to the creation of these qualitative events.

The preceding paragraphs have considered the place of the "aesthetic" experience in its sociopsychological matrix but, as both Mills and d'Azevedo point out, there is more to art than simply aesthetic appreciation. As early as the time of Boas, anthropologists, like philosophers, recognized that no clear analytical line may be drawn between the aesthetic enjoyment engendered by a sunset or a Cezanne. The artistic object or event demands the added element of human workmanship and organization. The artist takes a knowledge of both the available techniques and the existing aesthetic canons and applies it to an appropriate medium. The resultant objects constitute foci for new "aesthetic" experiences—this time specifically "artistic," since part of the act of appreciation now involves an evaluation of excellence or pleasingness in skill and style. The artist organizes, both consciously and at times unconsciously, formal elements of his media to approximate his subjective intentions—usually with varying degrees of success. Just as the appreciator's reaction may be molded by influences ranging from the idiosyncratic to the cultural, so too the artist's final work is the product of numerous contingencies which, once again, must be related to a broader social matrix. As d'Azevedo succinctly states:

> The conditions of art in a given society may be stated as the repertoire of technologies of that society, its available and prescribed media, and the particular systems of value which orient selection and organization of the qualitative aspects of experience. Reference must also be made to a tradition of conventional specifications, uses, incentives, and evaluations relating to the products of artistic activity (31, p. 711).

Anthropologists can make a major contribution toward understanding these processes through investigation of the sociocultural influences upon artistic production and appreciation—specifically, how these influences are formed, transmitted, and activated in the social world.

Summarizing to this point, we have outlined an approach to aesthetic phenomena which might be called "the social construction of art." Mills stresses the point that art is a dynamic process involving the creation of public objects or events that stimulate qualitative experiences. However, some art forms, through either accident or design, show markedly greater success than others in engendering these qualitative responses. Mills's formulation also implies that anthropologists should pay closer attention to the qualitative side of *all* experiences than they have heretofore—a proposition with which (especially at the time of Mills's writing) the sympathetic reader could hardly take umbrage.

Art and Communication

Inherent in the above arguments are two basic and apparently cross-culturally valid premises: (*a*) that an artistic process exists, incorporating as basic elements artists, objects/events, and appreciators; and (*b*) that at varying processual levels, considerable communication is taking place. The latter has led some researchers to apply a formal communications model as a heuristic for studying the art process—although, as Green & Courtis (52) have demonstrated, too literal an application of information theory to figure perception is unsatisfactory. They attack the notion that artistically generated figures, founded in innate objective formal properties, communicate information to the universe of perceivers in maximally predictable ways. As already noted, a social science approach cannot be overly object-centered.

Green and Courtis reiterate this point: "In real life the amount and location of information [in a figure] is a function of the percipient. What has to be measured is not something in the source, but something about the process of perceiving" (52, 26). Once again, personal, situational, and even cultural contingencies in the perception process may affect the substance of what is communicated.

Despite this skepticism, Green and Courtis, like many others, agree that the communications model is a stimulating metaphor which, on a limited scale, can be both useful and illuminating. Alland (2), drawing upon the work of Moles (78), states the case in pro in a straightforward fashion. The sender-channel-receiver model of communication theory can be applied loosely to the artist-object-appreciator triad. The flow of information is not unidirectional; feedback is a major factor in the system. Messages travel along visual or auditory channels. To comprehend the dynamics of the system, one must appreciate both the nature of information and the contribution of redundancy. In formal theory, information consists of messages containing new or unpredictable elements. A message which contains no predictable elements to orient the receiver, however, may be high on information but very low on intelligibility. At least some measure of redundancy is necessary—i.e. in the case of art, a degree of conformity with culturally recognized stylistic or thematic conventions. Complete deviation from them results in chaos, but too great a reliance upon the redundant reduces a work to the mundane. The "culturally well-adjusted" artist must strike a balance between information and redundancy which best fits cultural expectations; this balance will naturally vary across societies.

In this scheme, aesthetic information is conceived as less concretely expressible than semantic information—again, because it operates more in the qualitative realm of mood and state (although a given work of art may also certainly have a semantic component). Hence, the communication of aesthetic information allows more openness and even ambiguity, encouraging multiple and changing interpretations of messages (2).

Before turning to specific ethnographic studies in aesthetics, let us note one other major investigator's work dealing with the human capacity for processing messages conveyed visually. Among nonpsychoanalytic writers, Arnheim (3–5) was the first to apply Gestalt theories such as Koffka's and Gottschaldt's directly to the visual arts. He points up analogies between states of the dynamic equilibrium in nature and the balance in art, warning against theories of artistic expression which draw too heavily upon anthropopsychic projection. Arnheim instead urges that research focus upon those formal aesthetic elements serving as vehicles of expression (i.e. symmetry, line, balance, etc). Once these are firmly established, the cognitive processes involved in producing and reacting to them should be investigated, as well as the manner in which people come to learn the significance of these expressive elements.

The spirit of Arnheim's quest for a scientific approach to expression is heartening for anthropologists, although we must heed Green and Courtis's warning about situating too exactly the "objective" loci of information within the object itself. Still, as Arnheim agrees, researchers (particularly anthropologists) must be highly sensitive to any components of anthropopsychic projection. For the ethnographer to evaluate expressive messages as sad, happy, powerful, etc based upon his own opinions is obviously extremely dangerous and renders suspect all subsequent analyses grounded in these evaluations. As we shall see, what strikes fear into the heart of one observer may merely engender confusion in another, especially if they are of different cultural backgrounds. Probably the only time that anthropopsychic qualities can be introduced validly into the ethnographic discussion of objects occurs when the ethnographer employs terms consistently applied by members of the producing culture. Although these terms have no universal objective validity, they will aid construction of a model of a local ethnoaesthetic system—a goal which may further understanding of the relation between art and other aspects of culture, social organization, religion, and economy which themselves conform to this system at different levels.

Ethnoaesthetic Research: Principles, Universals, and Informant Selection

Having acknowledged the potential theoretical problems facing systematic aesthetic analysis, let us now turn to several ethnographic studies which nonetheless have at least partially succeeded in reconstructing native aesthetic principles. From Africa, data are exceptionally good, although a growing body of world literature is emerging.

Schneider (93) describes the Pakot distinction between plain objects which simply are well made and useful (*karam*) and those which possess extraneous embellishments not contributing to basic utility (*pachigh*). Interestingly, an object may be *karam* along one dimension and *pachigh* along another. For example, a cloth may be strong and well made while also possessing a luminous shine. Schneider further notes that Pakot aesthetic evaluations may differ by sex—a finding that merits study in other cultures, including our own.

Thompson (98) and Crowley (28) also identify ethnoaesthetic categories in African societies. Thompson staunchly maintains that tribal peoples possess very sophisticated critical sensibilities. He identifies several canons of Yoruba taste, including "moderate" mimesis, visibility, luminosity, and symmetry. These may be purposely violated, however, for aims of satire or

intimidation. Masks that to Westerners appear clearly sinister and horrify-
ing when compared to "normal" Yoruba sculpture may, depending on
context, be deemed hilarious by the Yoruba themselves. Yet in other cases,
distorted eyes and facial proportions may indeed produce a sense of dread
among local viewers. The lesson is that in order to really understand the
impact of art upon a culture, one must carefully examine the native cognitive categories underlying perception.

A major work in this regard is Warren & Andrews' (102) study of Akan
aesthetics. Employing an ethnoscience approach, they convincingly outline,
for several media, dimensions along which the Akan themselves evaluate
art, and present a detailed taxonomy summarizing how the Akan generically classify those objects "made by hand." Theirs is a work of obvious
interest to Akan scholars and also a model for systematic research anywhere.

Limitations of space prevent discussion of numerous other ethnoaesthetic
studies, but a solid body of literature does exist. In North America, the
Navaho are the subject of several fine studies outlining their general aesthetic system with an eye to its significance in all areas of life (77, 104). For
Oceania, Maori aesthetic principles have been investigated (25, 67).
Mesoamerica is represented in Golde's (47) account of aesthetic values for
a Nahuatl pottery-producing community with special attention to intragroup variation along such dimensions as sex, "cosmopolitaness," and technical specialization. In addition, many ethnographies contain accounts
which with study can yield surprising insight into local aesthetic values.
Evans-Pritchard's (35) report of the Nuer's relation to their cattle is one
such.

Let us conclude this section with a comment on ethnoaesthetic studies
from the two poles of cultural universality and diversity. Can any generalizations be made concerning aesthetic universals? Conclusions are certainly
subject to debate, but some basic principles do emerge. First, every society
appears to have some sense of qualitative experience that we may denomi-
nate "aesthetic." There are also few, if any, societies which lack the deliberate production of objects/events stimulating these experiences (art).
Second, the Western dichotomy between form and function in art is by no
means clearly drawn cross-culturally. The care lavished on Eskimo tools,
for example, strongly suggests that they are a source of aesthetic satisfaction
as well as life-sustaining aids.

I would like to raise a possible third universal, too. In the visual arts, I
believe certain formal categories are universally attended to. These include,
at the very least, symmetry, proportion and balance, surface finish, and
where pertinent, structural soundness. Cultures may differ widely in terms
of what exactly is valued in these categories, but the categories themselves
are attended to by artist and audience alike. Each culture recognizes canons

in these areas, and their violation stems from either lack of skill or deliberate intent to jar the average viewer.

This last stance obviously differs from those who claim that universals exist in values as well as categories. Jung (53, 56) sought to locate symbols, in part, in the archetypes of the collective unconscious, with possible "racial" and individual variants built upon these universal archetypes. Symbols represent these archetypes, and some succeed on a more universal plane than others. While Jung's ideas remain popular in some circles today, they are of little importance in anthropology. A more satisfying argument for a "universal aesthetic" is provided by Child & Siroto (24). A sample of 39 Bakwele masks was shown to two target groups—one comprised of carefully selected Bakwele artists and connossieurs and the other of experts in New Haven, Connecticut. Subjects rated the masks according to personal aesthetic preference. Striking correlations emerged between the evaluations of both groups. Consistency within each group was also generally quite high. To their credit, Child and Siroto carefully weigh the implications of their findings, allowing that researcher artifact, the condition of the photographs employed, and the possible influence of Western values on young Bakwele may all have affected the outcome. Despite these reservations, however, they do believe the ratings reflect to at least some degree objective qualities of beauty universally recognized by all "art-involved" viewers.

This raises a final issue in the anthropological study of aesthetic systems —who shall serve as informants? Child and Siroto insist that they must be individuals who take an active interest in the arts. These authors feel that people lacking such interest consider aesthetics essentially irrelevant to their lives and hence their judgments may be random or facile. However, criteria must then be established to determine what individuals or groups constitute the "actively interested." Child and Siroto concentrate their attention solely on individuals occupying formal statuses involving the frequent production or use of art—including carvers, art students, and religious practitioners. The assumption that other individuals are *not* so interested in art, however, may be a dangerous one—particularly if the society is one in which art plays a dynamic role in politics and religion. In fact, Bohannan (17) has suggested that for the Tiv, artists are among the worst sources of information on aesthetics. They hesitate to criticize peers' work for fear of offending them and are also reluctant to single out those of their own creations they like best—rather like a parent's reluctance to name a favorite child. In contrast to this reticence on the part of the experts, other Tiv readily engaged in long and thoughtful discourses on local products.

Can this problem be solved? At best it seems that the careful ethnographer should sample as broadly as possible. Both experts and numerous other community members should be interviewed. The relative richness of their respective data will reveal which groups have the most to say about art and will prevent the ethnographer from overlooking valuable information due to his preconceived stereotypes (as Bohannan felt he did). In my own fieldwork among the Ashanti, I found that both experts and nonexperts alike were eager to talk about art and overall showed a remarkable similarity in views—a fact which I attribute to the importance and visibility of art in so many aspects of Ashanti life.

A final caveat should be issued, though. While in many societies aesthetic preferences may be sharply defined, overt expression of dislike may be bad manners. A piece deemed ugly is simply praised less or not at all, but is never insulted outright. A careless ethnographer may mistakenly take this as evidence of an underdeveloped aesthetic sense. An easy and effective way to surmount this obstacle is to follow Child & Siroto (24) and others in asking subjects to rate a representative sample of art which spans all ranges of content, style, and execution, thereby forcing informant decisions and allowing the ethnographer to elicit comments on the ratings. Once involved in the procedure, many people (including the so-called nonexperts) release a wealth of information which is otherwise almost impossible to obtain. By identifying common or competing themes in the resulting data, the ethnographer can approach a detailed portrait of the nature, range, and significance of aesthetic values in the social system under study.

THE ROLE OF THE ARTIST

We have seen how the construction of an analytic model of the art process distinguishes object/event, artist, and audience as the major components. Our discussions of style and symbolism have highlighted aspects of the public object which are of particular anthropological interest; similarly, audience response was considered from the standpoints of perceptive experience and public criticism. It now remains to investigate those anthropological studies which have focused upon artists themselves, assessing both the importance of individual input into native aesthetic traditions and the place of the artist in his larger sociocultural environment.

Role and Archetype

d'Azevedo's (32) discussion of occupational archetypes among the Gola proffers a formal definition of the parameters of an artist's role in tribal society. Role archetypes refer to a set of stereotypic personality traits or behaviors attached to, and assumed to co-occur in, a given role. If an individual displays certain of these traits, most people will expect him to possess all others in the set as well. Role incumbents recognize this and, in fact, may ultimately modify their behavior to conform to societal preconceptions and expectations.

Not all societies institutionalize artistry to the point of clearly differentiating the artist's role; and even fewer can support artists as fulltime specialists. Where a clearly delineated role of artist does exist, however, d'Azevedo distinguishes two polar "artist's ideals." In the first, ". . . artistry is a way of life, replete with an ideology and system of beliefs concerning the techniques and purposes of art as well as the personal conduct of the artist himself" (32, p. 3). In short, an archetype clearly exists in this ideal. In many such cases, the artist's role may be invested with both charisma and tension. The artist is respected for his esoteric knowledge and skill, but may be perceived as at odds with the general run of society. In this view, genius may make such heavy demands upon individuals that their ability to cope with mundanities is impaired. The romantic Western notion of the artist as a struggling nonconformist approximates this ideal. The Gola share a similar portrait of the artist as gifted but irresponsible—evidence that this ideal can exist in a wide range of differing sociopolitical orders.

In contrast, in the second model type, artists are ". . . primarily oriented to the application of their creative ideas and skills in the elaboration of standard forms that meet ready public approval and provide an income" (32, p. 3). Here the artist is not divorced from communal aspirations and ideals; charisma is minimal and no personality stereotypes adhere to the role. In short, though the role is differentiated, no archetype obtains. The Ashanti (95) exemplify this second type, as do the Anang of Nigeria (75).

d'Azevedo notes that in complex societies strains of both types may occur, though one will usually predominate. In the West, for example, we have long drawn distinctions between types of occupations involving the manipulation of varied media toward an end "product" or service. Common distinctions include "fine artist," "commercial artist," and "craftsman." In large part, judgments of beauty and utility in the objects produced by these individuals determine the practitioner's status (11). Accompanying behavioral stereotypes may or may not exist, however. Craftsmen and commercial artists produce functional items in which "beauty" is a desirable but not essential element. Community and personal goals overlap here, with no behavioral expectations adhering to the role. The fine artist, on the other hand, shuns function in order to fully serve—or at least comment upon—beauty. The public expects a certain nonconformity transcending the ordinary in the fine artist's lifestyle. Gaughin is a classic example. Even though reality may provide many counterexamples to the ideal, the stereotype nevertheless persists.

Identifying the presence or absence of an archetype may thus prove a useful starting point in analyzing the artist's situation in any given culture. However, care must be taken not to employ role classifications from one culture to analyze roles in another. For example, many authors have wrestled with the pseudoproblem of whether native practitioners are "artists" or "craftsmen." However, since function and beauty are usually combined in native art, the question is largely spurious; our own "art-craft" categories really do not apply (96). The best anthropological works strive to understand a culture's art production in that culture's own terms.

We have seen that art is a process involving both human behavior and the resultant material products. The artist's concept of himself as artist, as well as his concept of what constitutes an appropriate product, both influence his behavior, which ultimately affects his product's final form. Merriam (73) has suggested that the artist's behavior is an often neglected aspect of the art process that should be of especial interest to social scientists. Anthropological efforts to understand the behavioral processes underlying art production are best represented in the literature on creativity.

Innovation and Creativity

Perhaps the major polemic in this literature involves the link between creativity and innovation. Westerners have long assumed an intimate connection between the two. Lasswell (62), for example, sees creativity as simply the disposition to make or recognize valuable innovations—innovations themselves constituting previously unperceived assemblages of cultural or material structures. Ideally, since anthropologists are more sensitive to cross-cultural variation, they are less likely to equate the two so directly, particularly in non-Western societies. Mead (71), for one, stresses the sociopsychological function of the creative process as an end in itself. She cites cases where the magnitude of aesthetic innovation is almost imperceptible, yet claims that, even so, artists may fully experience the satisfying and possible therapeutic effects of the creative process. Among the Samoans, innovations were both expected and rewarded; yet on the whole, they were so slight that they generally preserved, rather than changed, style. From this perspective, the continued transmission of the traditional cultural order is essential to successful creativity, since expression must be at least partially channeled through recognizable forms to remain comprehensible. A traditional baseline is also necessary as a rule against which to measure the value of an innovation. Recall the communications model which stressed redundancy for message comprehension; similarly, the channel must take a form recognizable to the viewer. This is particularly so where art performs needed cultural functions and must therefore meet minimum standards of recognition and comprehension. This may explain why recent Western fine arts—which minimize function—have been able to accommodate and encourage radical innovation, while tribal arts generally seem to remain, in noncontact situations, more overtly conservative.

However, even among anthropologists, debate on this issue continues. Goodale & Koss (49) present a sophisticated analysis of creativity among the Tiwi, and tackle the question of innovation's role in the creative process. While these authors appreciate the need for innovations' continuity with established traditions, they follow Bruner (21) in basically defining creativity as a function of novelty—with the implicit assumption that both directly co-vary. They go on to explore the proposition that the structure of creative activity is basically universal, once again relying on Bruner's model of the "conditions of creativity." Fundamental features of this model include recognition of an artist's need to balance passionate immediate involvement with a more detached critical perspective. Though such propositions are difficult to test, few would take serious exception to them, and the authors convincingly demonstrate their presence in Tiwi burial pole carving.

Less compelling on a universal scale are Bruner's "internalized ideals" and "contemplative inspiration," as well as his proposition that at some point in its production a work develops an integrity of its own which demands completion in a certain manner, almost independent of the artist's own critical judgment. Goodale and Koss feel these are integral to the Tiwi creative process. While some measure of these dimensions may be present across cultures, their magnitude is certainly variable. Many Amerind artists show a remarkable facility for conceptualizing a work almost completely before beginning its execution. Thus, while Bruner's model may serve as a heuristic for the cross-cultural study of creativity, the ethnographer should, as always, keep an open mind when evaluating the importance of Bruner's conditions in a given culture. As Goodale and Koss themselves note, every culture has appropriate contexts for producing art and these in turn influence the nature of production.

Before abandoning the subject of creativity entirely, a corollary issue must be addressed. What is the impact of the individual artist upon his product's final form? Rephrased in a more anthropological vein, the question becomes, can individual styles be discerned in non-Western art? In contrast to Western production, native arts were for years viewed as emerging from a murky pool of anonymity. While ethnic styles could be identified, the weight of tradition within a group was seen as so great that no personal statements, even at the formal level, were possible. This belief was reinforced by the lack of first-hand documentation identifying the creators of these arts which are, of course, unsigned. The works of a single master may be scattered through collections the world over, with no overt marks or recorded history to identify them. It is therefore not surprising that recognition of individual styles has been slow.

Fagg (36) is one of the most vocal in calling for such recognition in native art. He has identified corpora of several ancient African masters, and has fared even better in attributing more recent (i.e. late nineteenth century to the present) pieces to individual creators. Artists adhere to basic tribal aesthetic norms in these pieces but also make personal interpretations. One of the most stunning analyses to date in this vein is Thompson's (99) on the Yoruba potter Àbátàn, in which he demonstrates that a tribal artist's work may be culturally well embedded and yet remain autonomous (99, p. 121). Thompson traces the evolution of Àbátàn's art over approximately 50 years. Much of her work is linked to the Yoruba Eyinle cult and responds to the changing needs of cult members during this century—as well as to Àbátàn's own personal development. Iconography, proportion, and the treatment of space are among the major formal dimensions which vary through time in her work. There is constant interplay between the revival of older traditional elements and the creation of new effects. Thompson is admirably thorough in documenting the cultural context and tradition in which Àbátàn's work is embedded and from which it creatively departs.

As stimulating as this study is, we must make one qualification: how feasible are such researches in most ethnographic situations? Even Thompson acknowledges that they are best pursued where there is ". . . a high incidence of creativity and also the means of isolating within the milieu a single master whose corpus of works is sufficiently ranged in time to yield developmental data" (99, p. 122). The question of accurate attribution is an obvious problem in prehistoric cases. Bernal (13) discourages any such attempts to identify corpora of individual masters in pre-Columbian art. He feels that the whole notion of individual genius and personal authorship is a Western obsession and violates what was probably the spirit of pre-Columbian production.

This raises an interesting point: can such microdevelopmental analyses only be achieved where the artist is alive to identify his work or, at the very least, where either other living people or existing documentation can make such identifications? If so, then there is an additional factor in considering the weight of personal expression in native art—that of Western contact. In many parts of the world, works (i.e. of the past 100 years) for which direct identification can be made have been produced in the shadow of Western influences, either direct or indirect. While this need not affect the importance of individuality in native art, there is no question that at times it may. In the American Southwest for example, traders often encouraged artists to develop interesting personal styles, even to the point of signing their work—cf the case of Maria Martinez and her descendents (70). Whether these overt expressions of personal style represent a complete break with the past or merely an exacerbation of preexisting proclivities toward individualism is difficult to say, but in any event, Western impact cannot be denied. Certainly some tribal societies do appear to have recognized and encouraged individual artistic achievement independent of Western influence. The Northwest Coast (55) and the Solomon Islands (30) are among many areas where regional or tribal styles are traditionally supplemented by readily recognizable individual style variations. Specific artists were acknowledged as masters by the public and were often sought out for commissions. An ethnographer interested in tracing the work of a particular artist should address the importance of individuality in both traditional and contemporary art in the given ethnographic milieu, for it is essential to understanding the broader dynamics of the interplay of culture and creativity in that situation.

The Social Matrix of Production

Let us conclude this section with a word on the training of artists. Is it true that where the artist's role is clearly differentiated, training procedures are more formal and rigorous? An initial sampling of the literature suggests this might be the case. In d'Azevedo's excellent collection on African artists (9), nearly every society cited possessed both clear role differentiation and specialized training procedures for artists. These latter procedures varied from formal apprenticeships, sometimes involving cash payments, for set periods of specialized instruction with a recognized master, to intensive training in a less personalized vein, such as Poro instruction for the Gola. While technical excellence is of course largely achieved, entry into these specialities may be partly ascribed. In many societies, including the Ashanti, artists' relatives have priority in formal training, although they have already learned a great deal informally before beginning direct instruction. Often official entry to this status is marked by an initiation ceremony. For a price, an outsider's child demonstrating special talent or interest may be allowed to study with a master, but where production is largely a family affair, outsiders may be kept to a minimum.

Almost universally, any facility a child shows for a given genre is seen as a divine gift, and perhaps also a partly inherited ability. Without this gift —whatever its source—even the most carefully trained individual will never amount to much as an artist. However, the mystique surrounding ability varies considerably across cultures. The Gola, for example, see genius as the result of contact with somewhat menacing supernatural beings; in contrast, the Ashanti largely view exceptional ability as the fruit of good training plus a certain innate vision, very much like Edison's "1% inspiration and 99% perspiration."

Where the artist's role is less clearly differentiated, training may be much less formal. Bohannan's (17) discussion of the Tiv and their communal approach to production lends credence to this observation. Most Tiv men do art work and, while some are better and busier than others, a true specialist is rare and training is not particularly exclusive. Aboriginal groups of Australia also seem to follow this pattern (80).

The recognition of role differentiation, however, does not automatically imply full-time specialization. Other sociocultural factors are necessary for this development, and there may even be considerable variation within a single society. Where there is no access to open art markets, most tribal specialists work on a commission basis. It takes either a large, well-established patron group or, in rare cases, an exceedingly talented artist to derive a comfortable living from art alone. In the first instance, a wealthy chiefdom or state may provide the resources to support a coterie of full-time specialists. In such circumstances, artists may control the flow of patronage through tightly organized professional groups resembling guilds, with a possible caste-structure overlay. Nadel's (84) excellent account of the Nupe probably provides the best ethnographic sketch of such a group. More commonly, specialists are forced to pursue basic subsistence activities to supplement their incomes. Bascom (9), Merriam (74), and Messenger (75) document this for the Yoruba carver, Bala musician, and the average Anang carver, respectively. In the precontact Ashanti state, although specialists were sent to live in craft villages and were always on call for commissions, they nevertheless derived day-to-day subsistence from farming (88). Gola artists also must generally rely on farming to supplement commissions, though most are viewed as singularly inept in such practical pursuits (32, 33).

In general, the social organization of artists, as well as the distribution channels for their products, are too little studied. The introduction of Western markets may significantly modify traditional systems of production and distribution. A common alteration occurs in the patronage system. As we have seen, most traditional ethnic arts were commissioned by specific patrons, usually political and religious leaders. Artists therefore knew, with varying degrees of accuracy, what kinds and numbers of objects to produce. The modern tourist market alters this system radically. Unless specifically commissioned by a resident Westerner or a commercial firm, the artist must now carefully gauge the quantity and type of his production to the vagaries of the market, taking into account both aesthetic fashions and tastes of the moment and the cost-efficiency of different items. Ben-Amos (12) gives an excellent account of these new factors in her discussion of the ebony-carvers of Benin. The impact of such new distribution procedures on both art and artists has also been extensively described for Brahmin artists of India (68), painters of Xalitla (97), and Amerind artists of the American Southwest (1, 46, 58).

In fairness it should be noted that the development of a commercial art need not automatically lead to the artist's direct articulation with an open market. Middlemen may aid the artist in his decision-making problems with their knowledge of prevailing market conditions and may even partially fill the position held by indigenous patrons in the past (95). In some cases, a national government or other dominant-culture institution may itself assume the middleman role (51, 103).

This last topic has touched upon another aspect of the art process so far only hinted at in this essay: the potentially enormous impact of Western contact on objects, artists, and their associated economic and cultural milieux. The following section will examine further regularities in these processes of artistic change.

ACCULTURATION AND CHANGE

The literature on culture change is vast and itself constitutes a common topic for review articles. Suffice it to say that ethnic arts have been exposed to tremendous pressure for change in the face of Western contact over the past several centuries. Truly sensitive studies of this process, however, are relatively rare. The general attitude has been to dismiss tourist arts as anything from "soulless" to outright grotesque. Fortunately, in recent years, a more discriminating eye has been turned to these arts, observing that they may make both revealing aesthetic statements and profound impact on the communities which produce them.

Graburn (50) offers a detailed classification of existing varieties of modern ethnic arts. His scheme incorporates variables across two dimensions: (a) the intended audience, whether the producing minority culture itself or an external civilization; and (b) the aesthetic-formal sources of the arts—from within the minority group or dominant society, or from novel syntheses of the two. Many such arts essentially conform to traditional models, even when they are produced for sale to a diverse public. Some arts utilize a traditional technology but develop new forms or themes which improve their marketability. The development of the Navaho rug from blanket production provides one such example of a "reintegrated art" (58). Conversely, traditional themes may be reinterpreted in new media borrowed from outside sources, as in Plains and Southwestern Indian painting (19, 20). Such pieces are generally produced for external consumption, but at times artists may employ new media or expressive forms to reinterpret traditional values in works for local consumption. Graburn terms these "popular arts"; they include such items as Navaho jewelry and African wall painting. Graburn also recognizes new "souvenir arts," which aim to satisfy outsiders' demands for items which often conform in curious ways to the ". . . consumer's popular notions of the salient characteristics of the minority group" (50, p. 6). Any one culture may produce items in several of these categories, e. g. Maori (72), while some art forms span several categories, e.g. Australian bark painting (103).

Graburn's anthology furnishes numerous excellent discussions of such works from throughout the world. He locates these arts and their producers in the "fourth world"—meaning "native and aboriginal" peoples existing within national boundaries the world over. This taxonomic distinction is admittedly better than the "primitive" it seeks to replace, but it may cause some confusion with recent reclassifications of the old tripartite system into "five worlds" along largely economic and social lines.

These new arts and the socioeconomic pressures which give them rise may profoundly affect traditional systems of production, distribution, and aesthetic values. The nature of this impact, however, may range from reasonably adaptive to clearly destructive. Eastern Eskimo carving and print-making, for example, have played a major role in helping Eskimos regain a measure of economic self-sufficiency in the face of increasing en-croachment by a Western government and a cash economy (51). The Hud-son's Bay Company upset aboriginal economic patterns both by encouraging intensive trapping and by fostering a "false" dependency on European goods. When trapping no longer proved profitable, new ways to obtain cash were sought, and carving presented the most attractive alterna-tive. A once casual art form produced for personal use was deliberately transformed into an intensive full-time occupation. Subsequent develop-ments contributed to both continuity and change. Male values once asso-ciated with hunting were reinterpreted into a "macho" philosophy of carving which stressed a man's ability to manipulate hard stone. Women and the aged have also played an important role in the growth of this lucrative enterprise; but contemporary iconography continues to show, through angularity and positioning, a sharp dichotomy between males and females consistent with traditional sex stereotypes. Therefore, from the socioeconomic standpoint, while Western contact initially played havoc with the aboriginal subsistence system, new artistic pursuits geared to a Western market allowed Eskimos to articulate successfully with the na-tional economy while still retaining, in modified form, some of the integrity of the traditional cultural system.

At the opposite extreme, Biebuyck's (14) account of Lega sculptural art chronicles the demise of a once distinguished carving tradition in the face of Western contact. This art was primarily linked with the *bwami* associa-tion, a graded organization with elaborate initiation rites requiring consid-erable regalia. Under colonial rule, however, *bwami* was surpressed as a threat to public stability. Regalia items were destroyed both by local author-ities and by devotees fearful of discovery. Association activities secretly continued, but the production of carved regalia declined drastically. New objects, including European-made "oddities," replaced traditional sculp-ture in the ceremonies. Over time, old skills were lost to a new generation of Lega carvers, who today pitifully copy traditional motifs in hopes of selling their carvings to foreigners.

From the socioeconomic standpoint, therefore, the effect of "arts of acculturation" on aboriginal art, and on the host society in general, is highly variable. Ideally, anthropologists should chronicle and interpret these transformations with minimal judgments as to whether they are for the best or not. Barnett (6) has noted that when a trait or idea is borrowed from another culture, the process of acceptance is neither passive nor noncreative. The borrowing may itself be modified or, at the very least, the way in which it is perceived, appreciated, or used in its new context will probably differ from that of its original source. The "Mickey Mouse" katchina of the Hopi is a splendid example of a reinterpretation incorporating a Western art motif into a traditional belief system. The converse may occur where traditional arts are modified in form or used to meet the demands of new institutions or ideas. Graburn's classificatory scheme neatly accommodates these developments, as well as virtually every other possible synthesis of tradition and borrowing in media, style, and iconography.

Ultimately, perhaps the most fruitful perspective from which to assess the significance of these new arts is that of ethnic identity (50). The revival of traditional aesthetic themes may facilitate powerful ethnic statements in the face of real or potential disruptive change. New aesthetic forms and statements may also serve an adaptive function. Peacock (87) sees contemporary popular theater in Indonesia as a kind of "mental gymnasium" in which modern values are subliminally learned and exercised. The Navaho squash blossom, itself a new "popular art," serves as both a badge of tribal identity to the outside world and a source of pride to the Navaho themselves. In Mesoamerica, the Cuna molas serve a roughly similar function for their makers (89).

At times, formerly autonomous and even antagonistic ethnic groups will effectively recategorize themselves along multi- or panethnic lines, employing art to express this new organization. In Ghana, for example, a Western-educated Ewe may proudly display an Ashanti stool or *akuaba* doll in his home, thereby asserting his "Africanness" to visitors without appearing overly provincial. Similarly, native Americans who have fairly successfully assimilated to American middle-class life may display a melange of Amerind artifacts in their homes. At times even whole new art styles may arise to signal new cross-ethnic lines of contact or integration. Ben-Amos [as quoted in (50)] has noted the advent of a pan-African art style which satisfied Africans as well as tourists. Such developments often reflect the desire of subcultural groups to retain some sense of traditional identity while still accommodating superposed economic or political systems. Interestingly, whole nations may draw upon the traditions of constituent subgroups to project a national cultural symbolism which both encourages "patriotism" at home and serves as a national badge of identity to the world community. However, such symbols ideally should not foster divisiveness. Mexico's borrowing of the artistic achievements of the long-dead Aztec is a case in point—a great irony when one considers that the one culture brought about the total destruction of the other whose heritage it now claims. Care must be taken in such situations to avoid projecting a national image which threatens to destroy multitribal or multiethnic integration by overly favoring any one group—as in many African nations. Monumental works in a pan-African style may avoid this pitfall, as may a judicious synthesis of varied local traditions, as illustrated in the parlimentary regalia of Ghana.

The preceding has highlighted a few of the many ways in which art, identity, and socioeconomic changes are intertwined. Let us now ask whether the arts of acculturation themselves show any formal similarities across cultures. Few overall generalizations can be drawn about the formal qualities of most arts included in Graburn's categories; the diversity is simply too great. However, Bascom (10) has demonstrated that, for Africa at least, commercial "touristic" arts follow one of two major stylistic tendencies. The first is toward naturalism, with an emphasis upon reproducing typical scenes of daily life. Ben-Amos (50) has suggested that the popularity of this trend is due to its success as a "minimal" visual system which maximizes the accessibility of art across cultural lines—rather like a pidgin language. Turning again to communication theory, we may say that such art is reasonably high in formal redundancy for viewers cross-culturally, with just enough thematic "information" to make it interesting while at the same time minimizing interfering "noise."

The other trend in African tourist arts is toward grotesqueness—a distortion of, but not a complete deviation from, the natural. By tampering with the familiar, grotesqueness creates a sense of the exotic and vaguely sinister —qualities which most Westerners attribute to African cultures and their art. Redundancy, therefore, is minimized on the formal level. However, complete deviation from the natural is relatively rare in ethnic arts.

What can be said of the artists' own attitudes toward these new works they produce for external markets? Are they merely cynical exploitations of a convenient market, with no significance for their producers and local audience? Once again, the data are inconclusive. In my own fieldwork among Ashanti carvers, both types of "touristic" statuary were produced —one a naturalism building on traditional themes, the other a grotesque style which aped the works of neighboring tribes. The Ashanti, whose traditional formal style is largely geometric, nevertheless love the new naturalistic works, often preferring them over traditional pieces. Yet they despise almost all of the distorted ones. In India, touristic paintings done by Brahmin artists are generally scorned by their creators (68). Nor do Benin ebony-carvers accord their work the prestige of traditional pieces (12). On the other hand, southwestern Amerinds often genuinely like many of their new handiworks. Perhaps indigenous appreciation of emerging art forms rests on two factors: (*a*) the strength and significance of preexisting traditions; and (*b*) where these are strong, the degree of indigenously perceived "fit" between the new and the traditional arts. Obviously, where a long-standing tradition in a given medium is lacking, innovation may be more easily tolerated. Such is the case with Navaho weaving (58) and silver jewelry. Similarly, a new art which develops in harmony with a strong tradition may have maximum chances of gaining local acceptance.

THE ORIGINS OF ART

This essay has focused primarily upon ethnographic accounts of living peoples and their arts. Before concluding, however, we should briefly review the substantial literature elaborated by anthropologists, archaeologists, and ethnologists on the possible origins and biological underpinnings of art.

Alland (2) discusses Moore's thesis linking art with play and autotelic learning. The action, in short, provided its own reward. In this view, art may have originated as an early effort to explore and manipulate the external environment, perhaps presaging later technological developments.

Schiller (92) and others (cf 79) have experimented with chimpanzees to discover to what degree principles of aesthetic ordering may be rooted in psychobiological imperatives. When given drawing implements, chimps will show some attentiveness to composition, balance, and preexisting outlines, as well as a very rudimentary development of "style" over time. However, as Schiller points out, there is no attempt at representation in any form. These data suggest that while certain very basic formal properties of composition may be linked to elementary primate processes of motor expression, the intricate representational and geometric arts of humans derive from a far more sophisticated conceptual organization. Numerous experiments performed by psychologists have shown that for humans (at least, in Western populations), visual features such as color, form, and composition are cognitively loaded along the dimensions of such semantic concepts as evaluation, potency, and activity—with artists and nonartists differing somewhat in their perceptions of "connotative meaning" (85).

The question of meaning and value arises again when scholars attempt to understand Paleolithic art. On the basis of intensive quantitative study, Leroi-Gourhan (64) has demonstrated an evolution of Paleolithic style across 20,000 years in the general direction of more realistic shape and movement. Standard interpretations of the meaning and function of these parietal expressions are based on the concept of sympathetic magic; they stress either hunting or fertility. Other theories suggest that the paintings are totemic or that they were done purely for pleasure and decoration. Ucko & Rosenfield (101) are highly skeptical of these various theories. Citing data from contemporary hunting and gathering groups, they argue that there is no particular reason to believe that Paleolithic man was excessively concerned with fertility, population increase, or an ever-increasing food supply. As for the decorative thesis, no clear correlation can be drawn between painting locations and areas of regular, intensive habitation.

How then are these paintings to be understood? Ucko and Rosenfield put forward the hypothesis that some of these works may have had important ceremonial functions. They also make the cogent point that different paintings may have been used for different purposes, including some of the possibilities mentioned above. Though function is ambiguous, the mere existence of these works may, on a different level, elucidate the origins of culture and language. Marshack (69) argues that because Mousterian art shows a level of complexity demanding advanced two-handed competence ". . . with a highly evolved right-handed, vision-oriented specialization for symbol forming aided by a left hand supplying a different input" (69), this level of "two-handedness" and concomitant symbolizing capacities suggest a cross-modal neurological development arising in conjunction with an increasing capacity for language. His discussion opens a fruitful area for further research into the origins of art and language, as well as their associated neurologic mechanisms.

CONCLUDING REMARKS

Having reviewed a number of significant contributions to the study of ethnoart, we must conclude by tendering some apologies. First, many of the articles discussed cover a wide range of substantive topics, and their inclusion under specific thematic headings sometimes does them the injustice of over-compartmentalization. Certainly other organizational strategies suggested themselves, but the highlighting of important elements in the art process, along with the more specialized problems of origins and modernization, probably allow for as comprehensive a survey of the subject as was feasible in the space allotted. Second, many issues of great interest in psychological or symbolic studies have been glossed over or omitted entirely because of the need to restrict our review primarily to anthropological researches in ethnoart. Similarly, many fine, and indeed classic, studies of native arts have of necessity also been omitted. Third, discussions have been largely restricted to the plastic arts—leaving the excellent and burgeoning literature of the performing arts for others to review. Fourth, in many places the author's African ethnographic bias is doubtless evident—sometimes perhaps at the expense of equally telling data from other world areas. However, despite these limitations, we can only hope that the reader may be stimulated to further investigate a field that is one of the most diverse and challenging in cultural anthropology today.

ACKNOWLEDGMENT

My special thanks to C. M. McCorkle for helpful comments throughout on both content and style.

Literature Cited

1. Adair, J. 1944. *The Navajo and Pueblo Silversmiths.* Norman: Univ. Oklahoma. 220 pp.
2. Alland, A. 1977. *The Artistic Animal.* Garden City: Doubleday/Anchor. 153 pp.
3. Arnheim, R. 1943. Gestalt and art. *J. Aesthet. Art Crit.* 2:71–75
4. Arnheim, R. 1949. The gestalt theory of expression. *Psychol. Rev.* 56:156–71
5. Arnheim, R. 1954. *Art and Visual Perception.* Berkeley: Univ. California. 485 pp.
6. Barnett, H. B. 1953. *Innovation: The Basis of Cultural Change.* New York: McGraw-Hill. 462 pp.
7. Barry, H. 1957. Relationships between childtraining and the pictorial arts. *J. Abnorm. Soc. Psychol.* 54:380–83
8. Bascom, W. 1969. Creativity and style in African art. In *Tradition and Creativity in Tribal Art,* ed. D. P. Biebuyck, pp. 98–119. Los Angeles: Univ. California. 236 pp.
9. Bascom, W. 1973. A Yoruba master carver: Dugn of Meko. In *The Traditional Artist in African Societies,* ed. W. L. d'Azevedo, pp. 62–78. Bloomington: Indiana Univ. 454 pp.
10. Bascom, W. 1976. Changing African art. In *Ethnic and Tourist Arts,* ed. N. H. H. Graburn, pp. 303–19. Berkeley: Univ. Calif. 412 pp.
11. Becker, H. 1978. Arts and crafts. *Am. J. Sociol.* 83:862–89
12. Ben-Amos, P. 1976. "A la recherche du temps perdu": On being an ebony-carver in Benin. See Ref. 10, pp. 320–33
13. Bernal, I. 1969. Individual artistic creativity in Pre-Columbian Mexico. See Ref. 8, pp. 71–83
14. Biebuyck, D. P. 1976. The decline of Lega sculptural art. See Ref. 10, pp. 334–49
15. Boas, F. 1908. Decorative designs of Alaskan needlecases: A study in the history of conventional designs, based on materials in the U.S. National Museum. *Proc. US Natl. Mus.* 34:321–44
16. Boas, F. 1955 (1927). *Primitive Art.* New York: Dover. 372 pp.
17. Bohannan, P. 1961. Artist and critic in an African society. In *The Artist in Tribal Society,* ed. M. W. Smith, pp. 85–94. London: Routledge & Kegan Paul. 150 pp.
18. Bravmann, R. A. 1972. The diffusion of Ashanti political art. In *African Art and Leadership,* ed. D. Fraser, H. M. Cole, pp. 153–72. Madison: Univ. Wisconsin. 332 pp.
19. Brody, J. J. 1971. *Indian Painters and White Patrons.* Albuquerque: Univ. New Mexico
20. Brody, J. J. 1976. The creative consumer: survival, revival, and invention in Southwest Indian arts. See Ref. 10, pp. 70–84
21. Bruner, J. 1963. The conditions of creativity. In *Contemporary Approaches to Creative Thinking,* ed. H. E. Gruber, G. Terrell, M. Wertheimer, pp. 1–30. New York: Atherton. 223 pp.
22. Bunzel, R. 1972 (1927). *The Pueblo Potter: A Study of the Creative Imagination in Primitive Art.* New York: Dover. 130 pp.
23. Charbonnier, G., ed. 1969. *Conversations with Claude Lévi-Strauss.* London: Cape. 159 pp.
24. Child, I. L., Siroto, L. 1965. Bakwele and American aesthetic evaluations compared. *Ethnology* 4:349–60
25. Chipp, H. B. 1960. Formal and symbolic factors in the art styles of primitive cultures. *J. Aesthet. Art Crit.* 19:150–66
26. Claerhout, A. G. H. 1965. The concept of primitive applied to art. *Curr. Anthropol.* 6:432–38
27. Cole, M., Scribner, S. 1974. *Culture and Thought.* New York: Wiley. 227 pp.
28. Crowley, D. J. 1966. An African aesthetic. *J. Aesthet. Art Crit.* 26:519–24

29. D'Andrade, R. 1974 (1966). Sex differences and cultural institutions. In *Culture and Personality*, ed. R. A. LeVine, pp. 16–39. Chicago: Aldine. 458 pp.

30. Davenport, W. H. 1968. Sculpture of the Eastern Solomons. *Expedition* 10: 4–25

31. d'Azevedo, W. L. 1958. A structural approach to esthetics: Toward a definition of art in anthropology. *Am. Anthropol.* 60:702–14

32. d'Azevedo, W. L. 1966. *The Artist Archetype in Gola Culture*. Reno: Univ. Nevada/Desert Res. Inst.

33. d'Azevedo, W. L. 1973. Sources of Gola artistry. See Ref. 9, pp. 282–340

34. Devereux, G. 1961. Art and mythology: a general theory. In *Studying Personality Cross-Culturally*, ed. B. Kaplan, pp. 361–86. Evanston: Row, Peterson. 687 pp.

35. Evans-Pritchard, E. E. 1940. *The Nuer*. Oxford: Oxford Univ. 271 pp.

36. Fagg, W. 1969. The African artist. See Ref. 8, pp. 42–57

37. Fernandez, J. 1966. Principles of opposition and vitality in Fang aesthetics. *J. Aesthet. Art Crit.* 25:53–64

38. Fischer, J. L. 1961. Art styles as cultural cognitive maps. *Am. Anthropol.* 63:79–93

39. Forge, A. 1965. Art and environment in the Sepik. *Proc. R. Anthropol. Inst. GB Irel.*, pp. 23–31

40. Fraser, D. 1971 (1957). The discovery of primitive art. In *Anthropology and Art*, ed. C. M. Otten, pp. 20–36. Garden City: Nat. Hist. Press. 440 pp.

41. Fraser, D. 1972. The symbols of Ashanti kinship. See Ref. 18, pp. 137–52

42. Fraser, D., Cole, H. 1972. Art and leadership: An overview. See Ref. 18, pp. 295–328

43. Frese, H. H. 1969. *Anthropology and the Public: The Role of Museums*. Leiden: Brill. 253 pp.

44. Freud, S. 1916. *Leonardo Da Vinci: A Psychosexual Study of an Infantile Reminiscence*. New York: Moffat, Yard. 130 pp.

45. Fried, M. H. 1977 (1975). The myth of tribe. In *Readings in Anthropology: 77/78*, ed. D. Rosen, pp. 40–44. Guilford: Duskin

46. Gill, R. R. 1976. Ceramic arts and acculturation at Laguna. See Ref. 10, pp. 102–13

47. Golde, P. 1973. Analysis of an aesthetic values test: Detection of the inter-subgroup differences within a pottery producing community in Mexico. *Am. Anthropol.* 75:1260–75

48. Goldwater, R. 1967. *Primitivism in Modern Art*. New York: Vintage. 289 pp. Rev. ed.

49. Goodale, J. C., Koss, J. D. 1966. The cultural context of creativity among Tiwi. In *Essays on the Verbal and Visual Arts*, ed. J. Helm, pp. 175–91. Seattle: Univ. Washington. 215 pp.

50. Graburn, N. H. H. 1976. The arts of the fourth world. See Ref. 10, pp. 1–32

51. Graburn, N. H. H. 1976. Eskimo art: The eastern Canadian Arctic. See Ref. 10, pp. 39–55

52. Green, R. T., Courtis, M. C. 1966. Information theory and figure perception: the metaphor that failed. *Acta Psychol.* 25:12–36

53. Hall, C. S., Nordby, V. J. 1973. *A Primer of Jungian Psychology*. New York: Mentor/New Am. Library. 142 pp.

54. Harris, M. 1968. *The Rise of Anthropological Theory*. New York: Crowell. 806 pp.

55. Hawthorn, H. B. 1961. The artist in tribal society: the Northwest Coast. See Ref. 17, pp. 59–70

56. Jung, C. G., et al 1964. *Man and His Symbols*. New York: Doubleday. 320 pp.

57. Kavolis, V. 1968. *Artistic Expression: A Sociological Analysis*. Ithaca: Cornell Univ. 272 pp.

58. Kent, K. P. 1973. Pueblo and Navaho weaving traditions and the Western world. See Ref. 10, pp. 85–101

59. Kroeber, A. L. 1957. *Style and Civilization*. Ithaca: Cornell Univ.

60. Kroeber, A. L. 1963 (1948). *Anthropology: Culture Patterns and Processes*. New York: Harcourt, Brace & World. 252 pp.

61. Kubler, G. 1961. On the colonial extinction of the motifs of Pre-Columbian art. In *Essays in Pre-Columbian Art and Archaeology*, ed. S. Lothrop, pp. 14–34. Cambridge: Harvard Univ. 507 pp.

62. Lasswell, H. 1959. The social setting of creativity. In *Creativity and Its Cultivation*, ed. H. Anderson, pp. 203–21. New York: Harper. 293 pp.

63. Leach, E. R. 1954. A Trobriand Medusa? *Man* 54:103–5

64. Leroi-Guurhan, A. 1968. The evolution of paleolithic art. *Sci. Am.* 218:58–70

65. Lévi-Strauss, C. 1966 (1962). *The Savage Mind*. Chicago: Univ. Chicago. 290 pp.

66. Lévi-Strauss, C. 1967. *Structural An-*

thropology. Garden City: Doubleday/
Anchor. 413 pp.

67. Linton, R. 1941. Primitive art. *Kenyon Rev.* 3:34–51

68. Maduro, R. 1973. The Brahmin painters of Nathdwara, Rajasthan. See Ref. 10, pp. 227–44

69. Marshack, A. 1976. Implications of the Paleolithic symbolic evidence for the origin of language. *Am. Sci.* 64:136–45

70. Maxwell Museum. 1974. *Seven Families in Pueblo Pottery.* Albuquerque: Univ. New Mexico. 112 pp.

71. Mead, M. 1959. Creativity in cross-cultural perspective. See Ref. 62, pp. 222–35

72. Mead, S. M. 1976. The production of native art and craft objects in contemporary New Zealand. See Ref. 10, pp. 285–98

73. Merriam, A. P. 1964. The arts and anthropology. In *Horizons in Anthropology,* ed. S. Tax, pp. 224–36. Chicago: Aldine. 288 pp.

74. Merriam, A. P. 1973. The Bala musician. See Ref. 9, pp. 230–81

75. Messenger, J. C. 1973. The role of the carver in Anang society. See Ref. 9, pp. 101–27

76. Mills, G. 1957. Art: An introduction to qualitative anthropology. *J. Aesthet. Art Crit.* 16:1–17

77. Mills, G. 1959. *Navaho Art and Culture.* Colorado Springs: Taylor Mus. 221 pp.

78. Moles, A. 1972. *Théorie de l'information et Perception Esthétique.* Paris: Denoël Ganthier

79. Morris, D. 1962. *The Biology of Art.* New York: Knopf

80. Mountford, C. P. 1961. The artist and his art in an Australian aboriginal society. See Ref. 17, pp. 1–13

81. Muensterberger, W. 1971 (1951). The roots of primitive art. See Ref. 40, pp. 106–28

82. Munn, N. D. 1966. Visual categories: an approach to the study of representational systems. *Am. Anthropol.* 68: 936–50

83. Munro, T. 1963. *Evolution in the Arts.* Cleveland: Cleveland Mus. 561 pp.

84. Nadel, S. F. 1942. *A Black Byzantium.* London: Oxford Univ. 420 pp.

85. Osgood, C. E., Suci, E. J., Tannebaum, P. H. 1957. *The Measurement of Meaning.* Urbana: Univ. Illinois. 346 pp.

86. Panofsky, E. 1955. *Meaning in the Visual Arts.* Garden City: Doubleday/Anchor. 374 pp.

87. Peacock, J. 1968. *Rites of Modernization.* Chicago: Univ. Chicago

88. Rattray, R. 1927. *Religion and Art in Ashanti.* Oxford: Oxford Univ. 414 pp.

89. Salvador, M. L. 1976. The clothing arts of the Cuna of San Blas, Panama. See Ref. 10, pp. 165–82

90. Schapiro, M. 1953. Style. In *Anthropology Today,* ed. A. L. Kroeber, pp. 287–312. Chicago: Univ. Chicago. 966 pp.

91. Schapiro, M. 1956. Leonardo and Freud: an art-historical study. *J. Hist. Ideas* 18:149–79

92. Schiller, P. H. 1951. Figural preferences in the drawings of a chimpanzee. *J. Comp. Physiol. Psychol.* 44:101–11

93. Schneider, H. K. 1956. The interpretation of Pakot visual art. *Man* 56:103–6

94. Segall, M. H., Campbell, D. T., Herskovits, M. J. 1966. *The Influence of Culture on Visual Perception.* Indianapolis: Bobbs-Merrill. 268 pp.

95. Silver, H. R. 1976. *The mind's eye: Art and aesthetics in an African craft community.* PhD thesis. Stanford Univ., Stanford, Calif. 364 pp.

96. Silver, H. R. 1979. Rethinking arts and crafts: A comment on Becker. *Am. J. Sociol.* In press

97. Stromber, G. 1976. The Amate bark-paper paintings of Xalitla. See Ref. 10, pp. 149–62

98. Thompson, R. F. 1968. Aesthetics in traditional Africa. *Art News* 66:44–45, 63–66

99. Thompson, R. F. 1969. Àbátàn: A master potter of the Ègbádò Yorùbá. See Ref. 8, pp. 120–82

100. Turner, V. 1967. *The Forest of Symbols: Aspects of Ndembu Ritual.* Ithaca: Cornell Univ. 405 pp.

101. Ucko, P. J., Rosenfeld, A. 1967. *Paleolithic Cave Art.* New York: McGraw-Hill. 256 pp.

102. Warren, D. M., Andrews, J. K. 1977. An ethnoscientific approach to Akan arts and aesthetics. *Working Papers in the Traditional Arts #3.* Philadelphia: Ishi. 42 pp.

103. Williams, N. 1976. Australian aboriginal art at Yirrkala: the introduction and development of marketing. See Ref. 10, pp. 266–84

104. Witherspoon, G. 1977. *Language and Art in the Navajo Universe.* Ann Arbor: Univ. Michigan. 214 pp.

105. Wolfe, A. 1969. Social structural basis of art. *Curr. Anthropol.* 10:3–44

Ann. Rev. Anthropol. 1979. 8:309–31

CROSS-CULTURAL COMPARISONS

◆9635

Joseph G. Jorgensen

Program in Comparative Culture, University of California,
Irvine, California 92717

The preeminent British cultural evolutionist of the nineteenth century, E. B. Tylor, is credited with inventing the method of "worldwide cross-cultural comparisons" (46). In the formative period of his career, Tylor (45) was concerned with explaining why such stunning differences in cultural achievements, political organizations, kinship organizations, and ideology (mind or spirit) obtained among the world's societies in the industrial era. Many of his predecessors in Europe and the United States had addressed this same question, as had many of his contemporaries (for review see 1, 20).

In the United States, Franz Boas, the highly influential German-American psychophysicist cum anthropologist, was impressed with Tylor's attempts to provide pancultural explanations of the evolution of culture. Yet Boas was immersed in the ethnographies, languages, environments, and human physical types that occurred within geographic regions during the period of early contact with Europeans. His field research among scores of societies in the Arctic and along the Northwest Coast of North America had sensitized him to similarities as well as differences in these factors from one local area to another, and he sought to explain the resemblances and differences within regions by appealing to all of these factors. In 1894 Boas (2) published the first formal statistical analysis in the genre that is now known as "continuous area cross-cultural comparisons."

It will not be our purpose here to trot out a history of worldwide and continuous area cross-cultural analyses, their accomplishments, and their problems. Several recent papers, one in this series, have covered these topics well. Excellent reviews of worldwide studies are by Naroll (35), Naroll, Michik & Naroll (38), Driver (10), and Udy (47). Encompassing reviews

309

of continuous area studies have been done by Driver (9, 11, 12) and White (48). Jorgensen (24) has critiqued both traditions.

We will devote some attention to the basic suppositions of each of these modes of inquiry, emphasizing the enduring questions that are asked by practitioners of each method, the persistent problems in data analysis and interpretation that have plagued both since their inception, and recent developments that have aided investigations in these complementary endeavors.

WORLDWIDE CROSS-CULTURAL ANALYSIS

Europe was not only industrializing and harnessing energy in new ways during the late nineteenth century—over 35,000 internal combustion engines were at work around the world by 1880—but also European nations had been busy colonizing the non-Western world for three centuries. The contrast was marked between industrial societies and their horticultural, pastoral, and hunting-gathering counterparts (those societies that European and American states and businesses often came to dominate through colonization and expropriation). These differences prompted scholars to provide what were conceived as scientific explanations of these phenomena.

A plethora of explanations, born of comparisons but more or less based on similar, informal, methodologies and applied to information culled from classical Greek and Roman sources, European peasant histories, chronicles of the Crusades, missionary, traveler, trader, trapper, government, and ethnographic reports, were advanced by cultural evolutionists to account for the differences and for the similarities among the world's societies. In all instances the library information was analyzed in ad hoc ways to illustrate that systems of thought, forms of organization, and various customs evolved from simple to complex in a predictable fashion and that cultural evolution could be postdicted from comparisons among the range of living societies. Thus the "evolution of culture," which presumably occurred over hundreds of thousands, perhaps millions, of years, was inferred from comparisons of roughly contemporary societies. The present was stood on its head in order to infer the past.

In order to account for the differences among the world's societies, Tylor assumed that humans were part of the natural biological order whose development was explainable by scientific laws. He further argued that culture, too, was a natural phenomenon whose development was explainable by laws. In a paper that is now recognized as an anthropological classic, Tylor (46) broke from the informal methodology used by his peers and by himself earlier in his life and created an explicit methodology to account for the evolution of culture from simple to complex. He applied his method-

ology specifically to the development of several institutions including marriage customs (whether cross-cousins marry, for instance), postnuptial
residence practices (the places where couples reside after marriage), descent
rules (the manner in which people reckoned their relatives by kinship), bride
capture, teknonymy (naming a parent after his child) and kin avoidance
customs (explicit avoidance behaviors between parents-in-law and children-
in-law). From the application of the method to data drawn from a large
sample of societies, Tylor concluded that the "paternal" stage of cultural
institutions evolved from the "maternal" stage through a "maternal-paternal" transitional stage.

In brief, Tylor collected information on a sample of 350 societies from
around the world. But rather than compare pairs of societies for their
similarities and differences, Tylor used tests of empirical probabilities to
determine whether relations among social institutions (variables in modern
statistical terminology), such as the joint occurrence of cross-cousin marriage, matrilocal residence, matrilineal descent, and mother-in-law/son-in-
law avoidance practices, were attributable to chance or to lawful processes.
Tylor called the relations between variables that proved to be significant
"adhesions." Thus, he centered his attention on the variables that comprise
culture rather than societies themselves. Inasmuch as Tylor believed that
culture's development was orderly and lawful, progressed from simple to
complex, and could be measured through the arrangements of parts of
culture in various configurations, he also believed that the results of his
empirical probability tests would allow him to determine the various configurations of institutions that "adhered" to one another in stages, and from
these configuration he could prove the laws of cultural evolution.

Tylor's method of comparison, in the terminology of contemporary matrix analysis, was R-mode, and R-mode type inquiry has dominated most
formal cross-cultural analyses of samples of societies from around the world
ever since. In R-mode analyses, societies are not the sampling units. Rather,
the variables or traits that comprise culture are the sampling units. For
instance, Table 1 organizes data from the 350 societies in Tylor's sample
to measure the relations between forms of residence and forms of in-law
avoidances. The figures in the table represent the number of societies in each
category, e.g. there were 14 societies in which upon marriage the husband
moved into or near his spouse's mother's home (matrilocal) and also
avoided speaking directly to, looking eye-to-eye with, or eating with his
mother-in-law. The figures in parentheses are the values expected by
chance. The discrepancy between actual and expected values have provided
most cross-cultural analysts with the information they have required to
decide whether their hunches ("laws" in Tylor's usage, "theories" or "hypotheses" in modern usage) have been empirically warranted. In general,

Table 1 Tylor's (1889) data on avoidance and residence[a]

Kin avoidance	Matrilocal	Residence matri-patrilocal	Patrilocal	Total
Husband avoids wife's kin	14 (8)	22 (19)	9 (18)	45
Both husband and wife avoid the other's kin	0 (2)	5 (3)	3 (3)	8
Wife avoids the husband's kin	0 (2)	5 (5)	8 (5)	13
Neither avoids affinal kin	51 (53)	113 (118)	120 (114)	284
Total	64	145	140	350
	$x^2 = 17.2$		$p = .01$	

[a] Driver's (8) reworking of Tylor's original data. Numbers in parentheses are frequencies, expected by chance.

the greater the difference between expected and chance values, the greater the probability that the relation is not fortuitous.

In Tylor's study, and in most subsequent studies conducted in this tradition, cultural evolution in general, rather than the evolution of specific societies, is the object of inquiry. Modern research need not be evolutionary. It can and does focus on any of a number of propositions that seek to account for the regularities in culture. Researchers have sought to validate generalizations for all of the world's societies in time and space from samples thought to be representative of the whole. By and large, because the history and peculiarities of each society are considered to be controlled through a broad-based sample, cross-cultural researchers have correlated variables with variables (as in the example from Tylor above) rather than societies with societies. Correlations, and tests of significance (probabilities) of those correlations, have usually been treated one at a time (first-order correlations) rather than through multivariate analyses that evaluate the relations among many variables in the same matrix. Yet in the narratives that accompany the statistical tests, the correlations are concatenated into causal sequences.

It is the assumption of causal sequences of independent inventions that makes worldwide studies interesting, but this same assumption, given the nature of the data used by cross-cultural researchers and the methodologies that they have employed, also makes worldwide studies most suspect. Hypotheses, or sets of statements about relations among variables, are postulated by cross-cultural researchers before inquiry is begun. Because many of these hypotheses have long histories, especially evolutionary and functional assertions about economic development, property control, social organization, social structure, and Freudian assertions about personality, the researchers have often claimed that they have only had to operationalize variables through clear definitions into mutually inclusive sets, draw samples, rate the coded variables for the sample societies, and test for the relations among the variables through descriptive and inferential statistics in order to evaluate their claims. Beginning with Tylor's (46) investigation, large problems have surfaced at each step in the inquiries of cross-cultural researchers—from defining variables to interpreting statistical results—and practitioners of the art have sought to solve these problems in ways that are often imaginative and sometimes impressive.

Sampling Independence

Among the problems that surfaced in Tylor's original study that have never been adequately resolved are (*a*) sampling adequacy and (*b*) making valid statements about causal relations from synchronic data. The two, of course, are related problems. The eminent statistician, Sir Francis Galton, heard Tylor read his paper. He raised an important but unresolvable problem about sampling and statistical inference when he asked Tylor about the independence of each unit (for example, each instance of patrilineal descent) in his worldwide sample of 350 societies. Tylor had not produced maps locating each society in his sample or locating the distribution of each variable with respect to the tribes that practiced them. The mapping of variables would have allowed Tylor to determine the propinquity at least of similar practices and hence provide a means to assess the likelihood, say, that the descent customs of some societies influenced the descent customs of other societies. Furthermore, Tylor had not determined whether some of the societies spoke closely related languages, another means to assess the likelihood that some societies were similar in their institutions or customs, such as in-law avoidance practices, because of common heritages from "mother" cultures. So, whereas Tylor had used simple tests of probabilities to determine whether relations among social institutions were attributable to chance or to lawful processes, he failed to distinguish which of the institutional similarities possessed by groups of tribes in his sample had been inherited from a protoculture (two or more societies speaking sister languages and sharing cultural features that they inherited from a mother society from which they splintered), or had been acquired through borrowing, and which of the institutional similarities among tribes had been independently invented. As Galton's comment implied, the statistic that Tylor employed to determine the probability of the joint occurrence of traits assumed independence of sample units. For example, each instance of matrilocal residence and each instance of mother-in-law avoidance in Tylor's sample was assumed to be independent (not influenced) of every other instance of those two phenomena. Moreover, Tylor went one step further and assumed that postnuptial residence forms preceded and determined the nature of the avoidance custom. Tylor could not answer Galton's question. Over the years, Galton's question has come to be known as "Galton's Problem" (36).

In the past three decades cross-cultural researchers have wrestled with the problem of sample independence. Murdock (29), the nonpareil cross-cultural scholar, collected a sample of 250 societies from around the world. Because he had no inventory of all the world's societies past and present, and because he assumed that the entire range of cultural complexity was available in the ethnographic literature, in selecting his sample he used his own judgment about which societies were most representative of the world's societies and which were the most independent. Thus, Murdock's sample was judgmental and based on his own knowledge of the range of variation among the world's societies. As a consequence, the sample was biased toward all of those things in the world's ethnographic literature that Murdock knew about, and biased as well toward all of those things that Murdock did not think about.

Over the years Murdock (30) expanded his judgmental sample, the *Ethnographic Atlas* (EA), to include over 1300 societies, and from it he and Douglas White developed a *Standard Cross-Cultural Sample* (SCCS) of 186 societies (32). Using Murdock's impressions as their guide, Murdock and White divided the world into six ad hoc geographical regions of "approximately equal numbers of distinct peoples and cultures, so that selection of roughly the same number of societies from each would produce a first approximation to a representative world sample for the statistical testing of cross-cultural hypotheses" (33). Murdock & White (32) carried this stratification further by subdividing the 1300 societies from these six regions into 186 cultural provinces. They felt that researchers could then select a single representative from the best reported societies (most complete ethnographic record) within each of these provinces and that the result would be a satisfactory stratified sample of the world's known societies. The sample would control for interdependence among societies (the effects of borrowing and inheritance) by excluding the most obvious instances of interdependent societies.

At about the same time that the SCCS was being developed, Naroll (34, 37) was developing a sample of 60 well-described societies, known both as the HRAF PFS (Human Relations Area Files Probability Files Sample) and HRAF Quality Control Sample, drawn at random from the more than 300 societies in the Human Relations Area Files (28).

The SCCS was created to exercise controls for historical relatedness and to give representation to the society with the most comprehensive data base in each of 186 cultural-geographic provinces around the world. The HRAF PFS was created with the intention of giving each well-described society in the HRAF an equiprobable chance for selection. Yet both the HRAF and the EA are judgmental lists of the world's societies, and as I have pointed out elsewhere, drawing a sample from a judgmental sample that "controls" for time and space by disregarding both is still a judgmental sample of societies with unknown interdependencies (22, 24). This criticism still holds, although Murdock argues, and this reviewer concurs, that the SCCS is preferable to the HRAF probability sample. Nevertheless, the preferability does not extend to the application of probability measures that assume independence of sample units. Neither the SCCS or HRAF PFS satisfies this requirement, and each excludes the very information that is necessary in order to assess degrees of interdependence among societies. The *most* that can be claimed for statistical analyses of data from either the SCCS or the HRAF is that the results are generalizations *for* those societies, i.e. they are summaries for the HRAF PFS or the SCCS. The results, usually correlation coefficients and statements of probability, do not provide inferences *to* a larger universe, such as the judgmental lists from which the SCCS and HRAF PFS were drawn.

Recently Murdock, Wilson & Frederick (33) analyzed the theories of illness from around the world using the SCCS. As part of the analysis they organized the larger sample into Murdock's six impressionistic world areas so as to provide analyses by regions. This procedure would allow them to determine if the same relations were replicated in each area. In so doing they discovered, though did not anticipate, that theories of illness not only segregated by region (e.g. witchcraft in Africa and the Circum-Mediterranean, spirit aggression in East Asia and the Insular Pacific) but also "tend strongly to remain constant among the societies belonging to any particular linguistic family" (33). This reviewer is surprised that such results were not anticipated. Franz Boas, Alfred Kroeber, Stanislaw Klimek, and especially Harold Driver produced a stream of elegant comparative studies that made these exact points time and again about the effects of ecological similarity, geographical propinquity, intercultural contacts, and genetic language similarity on American Indian societies, while over a decade ago Jorgensen (22) and Driver & Schuessler (17), with the aid of multivariate techniques, made the same points about worldwide samples of societies.

A decade ago Murdock & White (32) anticipated differences among the distributions of types of variables—such as social organization and technology—in their initial analysis of the SCCS. More recently Smith & Crano (41) have produced an elegant analysis of 863 societies on 63 variables from the *Ethnographic Atlas* that uncovered intraregional similarities and interregional differences in the distributions of variables among societies. Moreover, in controlling for distances between societies while measuring similarities and differences on several types of variables, such as those dealing with purely subsistence economic factors, they demonstrated that interneighbor association decreased steadily over distance. That is, the greater the number of societies that separated any pair of societies in the sample, the less the similarity of the subsistence economy variables of that pair. On the other hand, political organization and the nature of family organization did not behave in the same fashion with respect to distance as did the economic and kinship organization variables. They show that all variables are not monotonic with respect to distances between societies, but that distributions seem to be determined by the nature of the variables. Moreover, one can infer various cultural processes from the differences that they uncovered.

Smith & Crano (41) have provided a clear-headed analysis that helps to explicate, for worldwide samples, the interdependencies of functional entailment and diffusion relative to different kinds of trait content. They were able to do so because their sample was large enough to measure similarities among neighbors, and, of course, because they were sufficiently adroit to follow the leads of Driver, Murdock, and White, and others, and investigate differences among sets of variables.

Nevertheless, there can be little doubt about the importance of the "discoveries" made by Murdock's team, even if those discoveries had been made previously on worldwide samples, because they point to the very question that Galton asked Tylor about the independence of his sample units, hence the applicability of the probability values and the validity of the explanations that Tylor offered for the transformation of the maternal stage to the maternal-paternal stage to the paternal stage of culture. Murdock et al (33), upon discovering that regional and language similarity correlations obtain in the data (interdependencies), argue that the SCCS is much better than the HRAF PFS because the former is not only "more accurate but more representative of the universe [it] samples." It is undoubtedly true that the SCCS gives a better picture of regional and linguistic variations than does the HRAF PFS, primarily because it is stratified to do so. But Smith and Crano, in using a much larger sample of societies from the *Ethnographic Atlas,* are able to say more about interdependencies because they cannot only control for trait associations among neighbors, but they can also restore the ethnographic context of a region by dealing with many societies within a continuous geographic locale (see the section below on "Ethnographic Understanding"). In an earlier study this reviewer showed that even when using a so-called probability sample of only 89 societies drawn from a worldwide sample, regional correlations could be demonstrated (22). The early study was a testimony to the powerful nature of propinquity (ecological similarity and borrowing) and language relatedness (inheritance from mother cultures). Regional differences must be explained. Unless there are explicit means to analyze those differences, and Smith & Crano (41) offer some excellent suggestions toward that goal, evolutionary explanations, historical explanations, ecological explanations, or functional explanations that are asserted to account for culture in general, or all societies throughout the world, are unwarranted. Yet it would defy common sense to argue that strong interdependencies do not obtain within regions.

Because high-speed computers allow us to analyze enormous data sets, it is an appropriate time to derive regions (culture areas) through correlation analyses of cultural inventories for the over 1300 societies in the *Ethnographic Atlas* and then to analyze the relations among the hundreds of societies that are classified in each region. By arriving at strata, or culture areas, in this fashion, the effects of history and ecology can be assessed rather than dismissed when attempting to understand the regularities in cultural relations.

Synchrony and Timeless Correlation

Much of the work to achieve samples of societies very little influenced by interdependencies among those societies is a result of Galton's challenge to Tylor, on the one hand, and common sense on the other. If researchers are attempting to demonstrate causal regularities in cultural evolution or functions, it behooves them to separate parallel developments from shared history. Because the incidence of cultural attributes is not randomly distributed with respect to geography, and because cultural attributes such as kin avoidance customs, matrilineal descent customs, and barter practices occur in nonrandom areal distributions, some scholars have attempted to separate independent inventions from historical acquisitions by employing statistical tests of a variety of types. An extensive literature has developed around these attempts to solve Galton's unsolvable problem (e.g. 13, 36, 39, 43, 44). Headlong attacks at Galton's Problem have produced a lot of headaches and no recognizable dents in the wall.

The problem of sample independence cannot be solved by drawing a probability sample from a judgmental sample, nor can it be solved by stratifying the universe of societies known to the researcher on the basis of his or her impressions, although the latter technique, employed in a formal fashion by Murdock, a less formal fashion by Carneiro (3, 4), and even more informal fashions by scholars such as White (50), Service (40), and Harris (21) has been standard procedure in anthropology since the nineteenth century.

To probe more deeply into the question of valid inferences from cross-cultural comparisons, we must recognize that in addition to the problem of sample independence, Tylor's data, as has been true of the data employed in practically all worldwide comparative studies since Tylor's time, were drawn from the "ethnographic present." The ethnographic present refers roughly to a timeless period just prior to European contact. The ethnographic present for North American Indians, for instance, would be the early seventeenth century for most societies along the eastern seaboard, but the late eighteenth century for most societies along the Pacific coast.

The ethnographic present, then, assumes *synchrony,* that is, that all data culled from all societies, whether in seventeenth century North America or sixteenth century Africa, are drawn from a single timeless period immediately prior to European contact and subsequent influence. "Sychronic" refers to a period in which time is held constant by disregarding the temporal and succeeding events of documented history. For Tylor and all other scholars who, on the basis of correlations that obtain among synchronic data, have inferred temporal sequences such as the transformation of kinship organizations from simpler forms to more complex forms, the temporal inferences have been based on timeless correlations. At best the inference of a causal sequence from a string of first-order correlations for which time is not controlled is a non sequitur. Timeless correlations that obtain among variables allow researchers to describe "what is" (or "what was" during the ethnographic present), but they do not allow the researcher to postdict either "how things came to be," or "why things had to develop (in the inevitable sense) as they did." Inasmuch as worldwide cross-cultural research by and large seeks to provide causal explanations, such explanations, when based on synchronic correlations derived from interdependent sample units, are non sequiturs.

Causal Inferences

Worldwide cross-cultural analyses of synchronic data have not included explicit means to test rival causal hypotheses that account for diffusion, secondary development, and the like. Nevertheless, worldwide cross-cultural analysts seek to validate unique, panhuman, and pancultural hypotheses. In the words of Ember (19), a cross-culturalist commenting on a recent wrestling match over Galton's Problem, "we should exorcise our preoccupation with Galton's Problem . . . because to pursue diffusionist explanations detracts from our more important task, the pursuit of causal explanations." This suggestion muddies the waters. An account that explains how, when, and why something was borrowed or inherited is, of course, a causal explanation, so the opposition of cause and diffusion is erroneous. Yet, as is also true of functional or evolutionary explanations adduced by cross-cultural scholars, diffusion explanations can be validated only when data are available for many societies in various forms of contact and when those data cover at least three levels of time—prior conditions, transitional conditions, and post conditions.

As Driver (6–8), Jorgensen (22, 24), and White (48) have pointed out, causal inferences from autocorrelations obtained among synchronic data in the absence of autocorrelational controls for space, time, language related-ness, and environmental similarities and differences are not warranted. This general rule holds for causal explanations of any and all kinds. How, for instance, can one discriminate among independent cases of the development of avunculocality in which in-law avoidances were developed at a later date, when the only evidence available to the researcher is the presence of both customs in some societies in the ethnographic present? And how are these cases compared with societies in which in-law avoidances occurred but avunculocality did not, and vice versa (22)? As White (48) has written, where residence or in-law avoidances or residence and avoidance practices have spread by diffusion, it becomes problematical to tell whether a correla-tion between the variables resulted from functional adaptation (the adapta-tion of two or more societies to the same general conditions), codiffusion of functionally linked variables (the diffusion of a set of variables from one society to others sharing similar cultural and environmental conditions), codiffusion due to functional linkage with still other factors (the diffusion of particular residence and avoidance practices in conjunction with, say, particular ownership and inheritance customs), and accidental overlap in the areas of diffusion of the two variables. On the other hand, when histori-cal causation is inferred from synchronic data, one asks why similarities of variable inventories as measured by correlations among societies in the same geographic region should be interpreted as being determined by borrowing or inheritance?

Recently two strategies have been advanced to distinguish different kinds of relations from synchronic data. In the first, Driver (8) has demonstrated by means of correlations which control for propinquity, language relations, and posited sequences of variables in a lag hypothesis that there are regulari-ties in diffusion (secondary developments where borrowing or inheritance operate in certain regional contexts to spread certain variables in associa-tion) as well as regularities in independent invention or causal-functional sequences of variables in which no change in the external environment is assumed (primary developments). In the former, one society (recipient) is acted upon by others (donors) in its regional environment, while in the latter, the interaction is not assumed.

Ember's (19) comment, cited above, is but one snip of evidence that the importance of the distinction between primary and secondary developments is not recognized by worldwide cross-culturalists. Indeed, cross-culturalists are no less immune than their more impressionistic colleagues (21, 40, 50) from making unwarranted claims about cultural regularities. Worldwide cross-culturalists "still appear to be content with correlations as evidence of uniform causality, in spite of numerous objections about the validity of causal inferences from correlational data" (48).

The second strategy, a "constraint theory" evaluated by "entailment analysis," was developed by White, Burton & Brudner (49) in a worldwide cross-cultural analysis of the sexual division of labor. Entailment analysis is a technique that operates on many variables at the same time in order to produce a structure of relations among the attributes under consideration. The constraint theory that White, Burton & Brudner (49) employ is different from the causal hypotheses that dominate worldwide cross-cultural inquiry. In the latter, first-order correlations (the relation between, say, "A" womens' contributions to housebuilding and "B" womens' contributions to wild plant collecting) are interpreted as causal relations so that A causes B. Usually several first-order correlations are concatenated, without the benefit of multivariate analysis, into a causal string supported chiefly by narrative.

White, Burton & Brudner (49), on the other hand, dichotomize their variables (each variable is divided into two attributes), tally the frequencies in each cell of the four cell tables, and derive "entailograms" by observing the pattern of zero entries throughout the joint-occurrence tables. The entailograms are graphic representations of the structures that obtain among attributes. Entailograms can show directions of relations, including branchings and convergences. The methodology being worked out by White, Burton & Brudner seeks universal and unvarying relations among phenomena. The cells with zero frequencies in their four cell tables provide clues to unvarying relations. Inasmuch as everything ethnographic known to this reviewer varies in time and space, it is likely that entailment analysis and constraint theory, unless they are addressed to very trivial relations, will prove more successful in the analysis of relations among regional phenomena than worldwide phenomena. Nevertheless, entailment analysis, because it uncovers directions of relations and allows for branching and convergences, goes beyond factor analysis (e.g. 17) and seriation cluster analysis (e.g. 22) as an analytic device useful for explaining relations among worldwide samples of societies.

CONTINUOUS AREA CROSS-CULTURAL ANALYSIS

Tylor's late nineteenth century attempt to demonstrate pancultural laws of cultural evolution through statistical comparisons was largely responsible for prompting Franz Boas, the famous American anthropologist of German birth and education, to compare ethnographic data statistically. But Boas's interests, generated from his first-hand field research experiences, his expertise in the psychophysics of perception, and his interest in Neo-Kantian explanations, were different from Tylor's, so the explanations he sought led him to use different kinds of samples and different forms of data than those employed by Tylor. From Boas's (2) comparative study of mythology on a continuous area sample of North American societies (adjacent Northwest Coast and Plateau tribes with one eastern Canadian society and one Plains society as controls), a second type of formal cross-cultural analysis was stimulated—continuous area comparisons—and took shape over the succeeding 80 years, even though Boas, like Tylor, made formal (statistical) cross-cultural comparisons only once in his career.

Boas was skeptical of pancultural hypotheses. He first sought to account for similarities and differences among cultures in the same region, and then between regions, before moving on to explain the universe of world cultures. Moreover, he was always interested not only in how cultural features originated, but how and why they diffused, and why societies in contact with one another were not only selective in the features that they shared, but used those features in different ways. He concluded that formal comparative analysis would not allow him to answer the questions he asked, so he abandoned the undertaking.

In brief, in continuous area studies, as they have evolved since Boas's time, samples can take many forms and sizes. In general, they are composed of all societies for which there is adequate ethnographic reporting from the same region, such as the Northwest Coast of North America, all of western North America, the entire North American continent north of Panama, the entire African continent, and so forth. The strengths of continuous area samples, whether as small as a culture area or as large as a hemisphere, are many. But problems in interpretation from synchronic data beset continuous area studies just as they do their worldwide cousins. Nevertheless, controls can be exercised for geographic propinquity, environmental barriers, environmental similarities and differences, and language relatedness that, when used in various partialing techniques, shed light on the plausibility of various explanations about origins, diffusions, and the conditions that favor both.

In the earliest manifestations of continuous area cross-cultural studies, especially in the works of Boas, Kroeber, and Kroeber's students (9), societies rather than variables were the sampling units. Moreover, the researchers had, for the most part, conducted the comparative primary field research on which the comparative secondary studies were based. In making comparisons, each society was analyzed for its cultural features, then each pair of societies was compared in order to determine the similarities and differ-

ences between them. A coefficient of association or correlation was calculated for each pair, and these coefficients were ordered by inspection in a
matrix so as to place most similar tribes close together and separate them
from those with which they were least similar. The ordering of societies in
the matrix could then be matched with the languages spoken by the societies
in order to determine the relations between language similarity and cultural
similarity, and the ordering could also be matched with the locations of the
societies in geographic space to gain rough impressions about the relations
between cultural similarity and geographic propinquity. The ordering of the
culture similarity matrices represents the earliest use of multivariate techniques in comparative ethnology (see Tables 2, 3).

When tribal inventories or language inventories or the like are compared,
the analysis is called Q-mode in statistical parlance. So the earliest continuous area studies were conducted in Q-mode.

Kroeber had a career-long fascination with historical explanations. In his
comparative analyses he always recognized that environment exercised a
mediating effect on culture, but he also argued that similarities among
cultures in the same and adjacent regions were due to historical factors of
borrowing or inheritance. Moreover, as a good comparative linguist and
comparative environmentalist, Kroeber was able to advance compelling,
though impressionistic, explanations of cultural similarities and differences.
Kroeber's penchant for postdicting historical relations among tribes by
comparing intertribal relations statistically was every bit as strong as the
penchant of worldwide cross-culturalists working in the R-mode to postdict
all significant correlations among variables as if each occurrence of the
relation was independent of every other occurrence. Students of both
schools operated from explicit assumptions about the meaning of the correlations that they obtained, both employed "causal explanations," but both
were quite reckless.

In an early paper, Driver (6), who was trained by Kroeber, recognized
that reliance on Q-mode analysis and historical explanations from synchronic data was challengable because the method assumed near total
dependencies of adjacent societies sharing similar traits. It left no room for
assessment of functions, independencies, and interdependencies. Yet Driver

Table 2   Q-Mode table of cultural variables in northwest California tribes[a]

		Yuork	Absent
Hupa	Present	705	167
	Absent	183	809
			$\phi = .62$

[a] From Kroeber (27).

also saw the folly in the worldwide cross-culturalist assumption of independence of sampling units. Judgmental samples ("hop, skip, and jump") provided no real controls for interdependence. Moreover, they obscured the question of independence because interdependencies had been so obscured. If Kroeber erred on the side of historical assertions, Tylor and his followers erred on the side of assertions about independent inventions or causal-functional entailments.

Major breakthroughs in comparative methodology and conceptualization of explanations came from the joining of Q-mode and R-mode analyses in continuous area studies and in comparing language data and human biological data, however crude, with the cultural data. Klimek (26), a Pole who was interested in Kroeber's comparative research, analyzed Kroeber's California Indian data employing a double clustering technique in which correlations among tribes (Q-mode) were ordered in one matrix and correlations among the variables (R-mode) were ordered in a second matrix. He then went a step further and ordered California tribes along one dimension of a matrix and their cultural variables along a second dimension of the same matrix. The result was several crude scalograms that grouped tribes together on the basis of shared variables and grouped variables together on the basis of the tribes that shared them (Table 4). His measures of language and physical type sought to correlate these phenomena with cultural phenomena into "strata."

Klimek's interpretations of "strata" were even less cautious than Kroeber's interpretations because Klimek called his strata "historical facts," and he interpreted migrations and diffusion from these strata. From his strata Klimek went so far as to pin the origin of particular variables with particular groups of societies, say the California Penutian-speakers, at particular points in prehistory. Whereas Klimek made contributions of considerable value to cross-cultural methodology, his interpretations left much to be desired in that he did not attempt to account for parallel developments or any of the other processes by which societies might be similar or different.

Table 3 Q-Mode matrix of intertribal relationships in northwest California[a]

	Tolowa	Yurok	Karok	Hupa	Chilula
Yurok	.44				
Karok	.36	.52			
Hupa	.43	.62	.89		
Chilula	.41	.43	.39	.54	
Wiyot	.35	.41	.31	.32	.32

[a] From Kroeber (27).

Table 4 Partial scalogram of tribes and variables from northwest and southeast California[a]

Cultural traits	Tribes					
	Karok	Yurok	Wiyot	Mohave	Yuma	Chemehuevi
Flat hat	+	+	+			
Alnus decor	+	+	+			
Overlay twine	+	+	+			
Pottery paddle				+	+	+
U-Ladder cradle				+	+	+
Twined bags				+	+	+

[a] Excerpted from Klimek (26)

Driver (62), building on Klimek's methods but discarding Klimek's inter-pretations, began reshaping continuous area research methods and explana-tions in his study of girls' puberty rights in western North America. Driver used Q-mode, R-mode, and scalogram matrices and exercised crude con-trols for language relations and for physiological factors associated with pubescence and first menses as well. His explanation sought to integrate evolutionary, historical, ecological, and psychological explanations to ac-count for the origins and distributions of girls' puberty rights.

In 1956 Driver (7) returned to the question of explaining the relations among kinship institutions originally tackled by Tylor (1), and subsequently by Murdock (29) and many others, yet he did so working with a continu-ously distributed sample of variables drawn from 280 native North Ameri-can societies located north of Panama. His sample included societies from the tropics through the Arctic. Driver (8) elaborated on this research in 1966 when he explicitly tested for the effects of language similarity and geographic propinquity on the social organization customs of America's native societies. It was here that he invented the technique for differentiat-ing donor and borrower societies, primary and secondary developments. In 1975 he went on to publish a massive analysis in both Q-mode and R-mode of 280 North American societies and 392 culture traits which were distrib-uted among them (14). He used Jorgensen's nonmetric trees program to classify the societies into hierarchical culture areas so as to obtain a strictly inductive culture stratification scheme, and he also tested the relations between language similarity, as measured by lexicostatistical percentages, and culture similarities within North American Indian language families.

Ethnographic Understanding

Since Boas's time it has been apparent that research among societies from a continuous area allows the researcher to be more deeply grounded in the ethnographies of the societies in their samples, whether or not those researchers conducted the primary field research, or some part of that research, on which the comparative analysis is based.

Typically, continuous area studies, whether of large samples (8) or small samples (23), analyze large numbers of variables covering the major categories of culture such as technology, economic organization, social organization, political organization, and religion-ceremonialism. In order to rate variables on all of these topics, much of the ethnographic literature on every society is read, and each variable is usually distributed on a map so that the researcher can see at a glance, say, the postnuptial residence practices of every society in the sample. It is then possible to compare distributions of two or more variables by inspection simply by looking at several maps. Visual impressions can then be checked against the correlations that are obtained among variables, but visual impressions also help sensitize the researcher to local and regional ethnography and often uncover relations that the researcher did not anticipate.

Recent continuous area studies have demonstrated that the regional approach allows the researchers to employ ethnographic knowledge to a considerably greater extent than is possible in worldwide comparisons. Donald Callaway's analysis of the relations between subsistence resources and raiding patterns in western North America (submitted for publication), the analysis of technology on the Northwest Coast of North America by Donald & Mertton (5), Driver's analyses of North American Indian economic organizations, social organizations, and technologies (7, 8, 14), and Jorgensen's analyses of environments, languages, and cultures in aboriginal western North America (25) are examples of the way in which researchers, perforce immersed in the ethnographies of a region by the nature of the questions that they ask, the samples that they have selected, and the wide range of variables they analyze, become familiar with those societies, the environments in which they operate, the languages spoken, the histories of the region, and the relations among tribes. This knowledge makes it possible to gain sufficiently good impressions of how things fit together to be able to identify ethnographic variables, such as sodalities and their powers, that may be crucial to an analysis of political organization, religious organization, or the relations between the two, and that may be overlooked or not understood in a worldwide study where few variables are analyzed.

Ethnographic context, of course, merges with inferential historical context as well. Regularities can be inferred from synchronic distributions, with the help of linguistic information, that allow the researcher to avoid the errors of interpreting all significant cross-cultural correlations as evidence of direct evolutionary or causal-functional associations. For instance, if Omaha-type cousin terms and patrilineal descent are widely distributed among societies that speak languages classified as belonging to the California Penutian family, the researcher asks whether it is likely that there was one or several inventions of the relation and can test several hypotheses in order to isolate the factors that might account for the relation. Furthermore, if the same two variables occur among societies that neighbor the California Penutians, one can exercise further controls to test for inheritance, diffusion, secondary developments, and functional entailments.

In general, knowledge of language relation is not nearly sufficient to ferret out the probable sources of regularities. Knowledge of trade, raiding, the circulation of religious specialists, marriage, and ceremonial attendance between and among societies, as well as migrations of societies, in conjunction with language data helps the researcher distinguish some plausible instances of diffusion while also distinguishing overlapping diffusions of traits. But more importantly, regularities in diffusion as a secondary development, such as the diffusion from Mexico to what is now the southwestern United States of maize, beans, squash, rectangular housing, and pottery making, and the subsequent growth of populations throughout southwestern North America, can be interpreted neither as fortuity nor as a remarkable series of independent inventions. Rather, the researcher can assess the importance of stable, predictable, storable, concentrated resources to elaborations and differences in other aspects of culture, while distinguishing differences among southwestern societies on the basis of farming techniques, economic organization, and the like. Then the cultural variation can be compared with language variation (is inheritance as measured by language a factor that explains cultural variations?), environmental variation (is environment a factor that explains variation?), and so forth (see Jorgensen's forthcoming paper in one of the *Southwest* volumes, edited by Alfonso Ortiz, of the *Handbook of North American Indians* edited by William Sturtevant).

Language and Culture

In 1969 Jorgensen (23) published the first formal comparative analysis of the relations between language and culture among the members of a single language family. By controlling for contact intervals between each pair of societies in the sample (Salish languages and cultures distributed over a continuous area on the Northwest Coast and Plateau of western North America), it was demonstrated that the greater the number of societies (or languages) that were situated between any pair of societies, regardless of the geographic distances involved, the lower the average similarity of culture or language between that pair. This topological approach to comparative analysis demonstrated montonic relations of language and culture when controlling for contact intervals, and also demonstrated that although relations for language and culture were monotonic when controlling for contact intervals between Salish-speaking societies on the coast and in the Plateau, societies from these regions were less similar to one another in language and culture than they were to societies within their own environmental areas. Thus, propinquity and environment influenced similarities in language and culture in the same direction and those relations were monotonic. When the relative effects of inheritance were assessed by correlation ratios of language and culture, the variation in language accounted for more variation in culture than vice versa, yet this measure was conflated with propinquity because the fewer the language communities separating two languages, the more similar those languages. The interdependencies stemmed from contacts, inheritances, and adaptations to rather similar environments.

Dyen & Aberle (18), in analyzing the Athapaskan language and kinship system, looked closely at the kinship terminological patterns in order to reconstruct one aspect of proto-Athapaskan culture, its kinship system, and to account for the changes that occurred through innovation and borrowings throughout the system. The Athapaskan language family is distributed in three discontinuous patches in western North America, so the analysis of distributions of terms, while controlling for innovations, has allowed them to ferret out some of the probable historical retentions in one aspect of Athapaskan culture. This study points the way toward other possible reconstructions of cultural phenomena with protolanguages and will help in the analysis of culture in general.

Culture Area Stratification

Driver et al (15) conducted a Q-mode analysis of Murdock's *Ethnographic Atlas* data for 273 North American societies so as to produce a useful set of strata, or culture areas, from which further comparative studies could draw objective, continent-wide samples. They also sought to produce the first inductively derived culture area scheme for any continent in the world. The strata they determined from the *Ethnographic Atlas* data by way of this inductive technique did not match well with any of the intuitive culture area schemes of North America. The strata that emerged were more similar to Steward's concept of "culture types" (42) in which societies are clustered on the basis of features that are presumed to be functionally related, such as aspects of social organization, rather than the broader domains of culture, including technology, religion, and so forth. The strata that were obtained from the *Ethnographic Atlas* were discontinuous in distribution.

Soon thereafter Driver & Coffin (14) used the same inductive technique to analyze part of the Driver-Massey (16) sample for all of North America in the Q-mode. This analysis, three-fourths based on material culture and economic organization and only one-fourth based on social organization, produced several strata, each of which formed a continuous geographic unit. The strata closely matched the major intuitive culture area schemes that have been created over the years. The Driver & Coffin (14) ordering demonstrated the importance of material culture in shaping intuitive culture area schemes, but also suggested that geographic propinquity, environment, technology, and economic organization were closely related.

The strata produced from Murdock's sample and from the Driver-Massey sample will be useful for subsequent sampling because of the differences they suggest about the relations that obtain among different realms of culture. The former will allow researchers to test for the factors, perhaps environmental and economic, that cause widely separated societies that are classified in the same culture type, such as "Fishers" from eastern Canada, the Plateau, and the Northwest Coast, to be similar. The latter will aid researchers who wish to control for propinquity in rating samples so as better to investigate the interdependencies that obtain within and between areas.

The interesting thing about the results from the two inductively obtained culture classification schemes for North America is the difference between classifications based on different data categories. Murdock & White (32) provided evidence that some types of phenomena might have diffused more readily than others and that the differences should be accounted for in cross-cultural research. Future research can only profit from these analyses and from that of Smith & Crano (41), who demonstrated that when *Ethnographic Atlas* data were subdivided into several strata, such as (*a*) economic and some social organization variables, (*b*) kinship organization and some gaming variables, and (*c*) political organization and family extendedness variables, that the three behaved quite differently with respect to interneighbor associations over distance. Associations were highest among neighbors and diminished least as a function of distance for economy (set *a*), and yielded moderate association among neighbors with no clear pattern of correlations when controlling for distances for political organization and family extendedness (set *b*). The kinship organization variables took an intermediary position.

Recently Jorgensen (25) derived a culture area taxonomy (strata) for 172 western North American Indian societies on the basis of 292 variables (1577 attributes). The variables covered eight major topics of culture, ranging from about 30 to 45 variables per topic. They were (*a*) technology, (*b*) subsistence economy, (*c*) economic organization, (*d*) settlement pattern and demography, (*e*) social and kinship organization, (*f*) political organization, (*g*) ceremonialism, and (*h*) spirits and shamanism. Using the cultural categories in the *Outline of Cultural Materials* (31) to test the representativeness of the Jorgensen-Driver sample, it proved to be the largest and most balanced list of cultural variables ever used in comparative cultural inquiry.

Six culture areas that fitted rather well with the major intuitive schemes for western North America were produced when all the data were used. When each of the eight cultural categories were analyzed separately and the matrix for each was compared with the others, technology, subsistence economy, and economic organization variables produced highly similar orderings (matrix coefficients averaged about .700) and orderings that replicated the solution for the total variable sample. The probable interplay among environment, economic adaptations, and diffusion in producing similar orderings was unmistakable and worthy of much more extended analysis. Moreover, the highest average correlations for all cultural topics were with the three technology-economy sets. The intertopic correlations for all eight topics were high and positive, but the sets on spirits-shamanism and political organization correlated less well with the others. The social and kinship organization and ceremonialism sets took intermediary positions.

Working independently of Smith and Crano, Jorgensen speculated that the shamanism and political organization sphere of culture throughout the world were more subject to local variation and were more independent than technology, economy, or the social and ceremonial variables. The strata for synchronic cultural data from both the *Ethnographic Atlas* and the Jorgensen-Driver sample suggest excellent possibilities for more refined analyses of the interdependent factors of the relations among cultural, linguistic, and environmental phenomena.

More particularistic variables, perhaps area-specific variable definitions, will be required to analyze sub-Saharan Africa, say, in the same way that western North America is now being analyzed. But expansion of the *Ethnographic Atlas* to account for regional variation with sufficiently specific traits will allow scholars to infer probable borrowings, inheritances, secondary developments, functional entailments, and the like. More importantly, in this reviewer's estimation, cross-regional and cross-continental comparisons can then be offered to account for the regularities in worldwide cultural phenomena. In the future, perhaps the far distant future, the generalizations that emerge can be tested on diachronic data sets and the forms and causes of interdependencies will become more clear to us.

Literature Cited

1. Bidney, D. 1953. *Theoretical Anthropology.* New York: Columbia Univ. Press
2. Boas, F. 1894. *Indianische Sagen von der Nord-Pacicishen Kuste Amerikas.* Berlin: Asher
3. Carneiro, R. 1968. Ascertaining, testing, and interpreting sequences of cultural development. *Southwest. J. Anthropol.* 24:354–74
4. Carneiro, R. 1970. Scale analysis, evolutionary sequences, and the rating of cultures. *Handbook of Method in Cultural Anthropology,* ed. R. Naroll, R. Cohen, pp. 834–71. Garden City: Nat. Hist. Press
5. Donald, L., Mertton, J. 1975. Technology on the Northwest Coast. *Behav. Sci. Res.* 10:73–100
6. Driver, H. E. 1939. Introduction. *Culture Element Distributions X: Northwest California,* pp. 297–306. *Anthropol. Rec.* 1:6. Berkeley: Univ. California Press
6a. Driver, H. E. 1942. *Culture Element Distributions XVI: Girls' Puberty Rites in Western North America,* pp. 21–90. *Anthropol. Rec.* 6:2. Berkeley: Univ. California Press
7. Driver, H. E. 1956. An integration of functional, evolutionary, and historical theory by means of correlations. *Indiana Univ. Publ. Anthropol. Ling.* 12:1–28
8. Driver, H. E. 1966. Geographical-historical versus psycho-functional explanations of kin avoidances. *Curr. Anthropol.* 7:131–48
9. Driver, H. E. 1970. Statistical studies of continuous geographical distributions. See Ref. 4, pp. 620–39
10. Driver, H. E. 1973. Cross-cultural studies. *Handbook of Social and Cultural Anthropology,* ed. J. J. Honigmann, pp. 327–68. Chicago: Rand McNally
11. Driver, H. E. 1973. Cultural diffusion. *Main Currents of Anthropological Theory,* ed. R. Naroll, pp. 157–84. New York: Appleton-Century-Crofts
12. Driver, H. E. 1974. Diffusion and evolution. *Comparative Studies by Harold E. Driver and Essays in His Honor,* ed. J. G. Jorgensen, pp. 60–63. New Haven: HRAF Press
13. Driver, H. E., Chaney, R. P. 1970. Cross-cultural sampling and Galton's Problem. See Ref. 4, pp. 990–1003
14. Driver, H. E., Coffin, J. L. 1975. Classification and development of North American Indian cultures: a statistical analysis of the Driver-Massey sample. *Trans. Am. Philos. Soc.* 65 (3):1–120
15. Driver, H. E., Kenny, J. A., Hudson, H. C., Engle, O. M. 1972. Statistical classification of North American Indian ethnic units. *Ethnology* 11: 311–39
16. Driver, H. E., Massey, W. C. 1957. Comparative studies of North American Indians. *Trans. Am. Philos. Soc.* 47 (2):165–456
17. Driver, H. E., Schuessler, K. F. 1967. Correlational analysis of Murdock's 1957 ethnographic sample. *Am. Anthropol.* 69:332–52
18. Dyen, I., Aberle, D. F. 1974. *Lexical Reconstruction. The Case of the Proto-Athapaskan Kinship System.* London: Cambridge Univ. Press
19. Ember, M. 1978. Comment on Strauss and Orans. *Behav. Sci. Res.* 13:25–26
20. Harris, M. 1968. *The Rise of Anthropological Theory.* New York: Crowell
21. Harris, M. 1978. *Cannibals and Kings.* New York: Random House
22. Jorgensen, J. G. 1966. Geographical clusterings and functional explanations of in-law avoidances: an analysis of comparative method. *Curr. Anthropol.* 7:161–69
23. Jorgensen, J. G. 1969. Salish language and culture. *Lang. Sci. Monogr. 3.* Bloomington/The Hague: Indiana Univ. and Mouton
24. Jorgensen, J. G. 1974. On continuous area and world wide studies in formal comparative ethnology. See Ref. 12, pp. 195–203
25. Jorgensen, J. G. 1979. *Western Indians. Comparative Environments, Languages, and Cultures of 172 Western American Indian Societies.* San Francisco: Freeman
26. Klimek, S. 1935. Culture element distributions I: the structure of California Indian society. *Univ. Calif. Publ. Am. Archeol. Ethnol.* 37:1–70
27. Kroeber, A. L. 1939. Local ethnographic and methodological inferences. See Ref. 6, pp. 425–30
28. Lagace, R. O. 1978. *Sixty Cultures.* New Haven: HRAF Press. 507 pp.
29. Murdock, G. P. 1949. *Social Structure.* New York: Macmillan
30. Murdock, G. P. 1967. *Ethnographic Atlas: A Summary.* Pittsburgh: Univ. Pittsburgh Press. 125 pp.
31. Murdock, G. P. et al. 1971. *Outline of Cultural Materials.* New Haven: HRAF Press. 4th rev. ed. 207 pp.
32. Murdock, G. P., White, D. R. 1969.

Standard cross-cultural sample. *Ethnology* 8:329–69

33. Murdock, G. P., Wilson, S. F., Frederick, V. 1978. World distribution of theories of illness. *Ethnology* 17:449–70
34. Naroll, R. 1967. The proposed HRAF probability sample. *Behav. Sci. Notes* 2:70–80
35. Naroll, R. 1970. What have we learned from cross-cultural surveys? *Am. Anthropol.* 72:1227–88
36. Naroll, R. 1970. Galton's problem. See Ref. 4, pp. 974–89
37. Naroll, R. 1970. Cross-cultural sampling. See Ref. 4, pp. 620–39
38. Naroll, R., Michik, G. L., Naroll, F. 1974. Hologeistic theory testing. See Ref. 12, pp. 121–48
39. Schaefer, J. M. 1971. Sampling methods, functional associations and Galton's Problem. *Behav. Sci. Notes,* 6:229–57
40. Service, E. R. 1962. *Primitive Social Organization: An Evolutionary Perspective.* New York: Harper & Row
41. Smith, F. J., Crano, W. D. 1977. Patterns of cultural diffusion: analyses of trait associations across societies by content and geographical proximity. *Behav. Sci. Res.* 12:145–67

42. Steward, J. H. 1955. *Theory and Culture Change.* Urbana: Univ. Illinois Press
43. Strauss, D. J., Orans, M. 1978. Residence and descent is hyperdiffusional? *Behav. Sci. Res.* 13:1–23
44. Strauss, D. J., Orans, M. 1975. Mighty sifts: a critical appraisal of solutions to Galton's problem, and a partial solution. *Curr. Anthropol.* 16:573–94
45. Tylor, E. B. 1871. *Primitive Culture.* London: Murray
46. Tylor, E. B. 1889. On a method of investigating the development of institutions: applied to laws of marriage and descent. *J. R. Anthropol. Inst.* 18:245–72
47. Udy, S. H. Jr. 1973. Cross-cultural analysis: Methods and scope. *Ann. Rev. Anthropol.* 2:253–70
48. White, D. R. 1975. Process, statistics and anthropological theory: an appreciation of Harold Driver. *Rev. Anthropol.* 2:295–314
49. White, D. R., Burton, M. L., Brudner, L. A. 1977. Entailment theory and method: a cross-cultural analysis of the sexual division of labor. *Behav. Sci. Res.* 12:1–24
50. White, L. A. 1959. *The Evolution of Culture.* New York: McGraw-Hill

Ann. Rev. Anthropol. 1979. 8:333–52
Copyright © 1979 by Annual Reviews Inc. All rights reserved

RECENT FINDS
AND INTERPRETATIONS
OF MIOCENE HOMINOIDS

♦9636

David Pilbeam

Department of Anthropology and of Geology and Geophysics, Yale University,
New Haven, Connecticut 06520

> "I often think it odd that it should be so dull, for a great deal of it must be invention."
> Catherine Morland on History, in *Northanger Abbey,* quoted by E. H. Carr in *What is history?*

INTRODUCTION

The Miocene Epoch, which began almost 23 m.y. (million years) ago and lasted until around 5 m.y. ago, was a period of great change (8). It was the time during which the foundations—climatic, geographic, floral, and faunal—of the modern world were laid. At its beginning, the world of the Miocene was an archaic one, both geologically and biologically. But by the dawn of the succeeding Pliocene, animals and habitats had become recognizably modern in aspect. And by 4 m.y. ago, species undoubtedly related to us, but still quite different, had appeared, while the ancestors of the great apes probably lived as their descendants do today. Although much remained to be achieved, by this time most of the major evolutionary changes had occurred for the hominoids. In this review, I will discuss these changes along with recent developments and discoveries that concern the evolution of apes and humans.

GEOLOGICAL BACKGROUND

The world did indeed look different 20 m.y. ago than it does today (10): continents were in unfamiliar positions, their interconnections were differ-

333

0084-6570/79/1015-0333$01.00

ent; climates were warmer and less seasonal; forests and woodlands were more abundant and grasslands were less widespread; the fauna were commensurately archaic, many groups now dominant having either not started or barely begun their adaptive radiations. Africa and Arabia were part of a single block which was partially divided by a seaway running from the north and separated from the Eurasian land mass by an east-west seaway, the Tethys (which connected the Atlantic and Indian oceans). Northward drift of this Afro-Arabian block resulted first in the constriction and then in the eventual closing of the Tethys as it collided with Eurasia. The major point of land contact was between Arabia and central Eurasia, although it is possible that there were occasional brief connections at the western edges of the continents. Other important geological changes which were associated with the continental collisions of Afro-Arabia, and also with the earlier and continuing joining of India and Eurasia, occurred at this time. These changes included the building of major mountain systems. The Himalayas, Tauros, Zagros, and various European Alpine mountain chains are a few of those upthrust during the Miocene. In addition, whole areas of land were elevated, and major rifts in the earth's surface began to form.

These events and many others contributed to significant changes in world climate (9, 18, 28); in particular, to a cooling which began around the middle of the Miocene, some 15 million years ago. This change in climate is well documented by the analysis of marine invertebrates preserved on the ocean floors and recovered in deep sea cores. The land record, mainly in the form of plants and animals, is more difficult to interpret, being more regional and considerably more fragmentary. However, a good deal of support is emerging from this record for the view that from middle Miocene time on, world climates became cooler and more seasonal. This was probably correlated with habitat changes, such as significant reductions in the area of tropical and subtropical forest and expansion of nonforest habitats such as woodland and savannah. Several mammalian groups exploited these changes by radiating into the new habitats; in particular, cursorial forms increased greatly in diversity, as did grazers and browser-grazers. Thus bovids, elephants, various rodents and pigs, and new kinds of carnivores that preyed upon the new herbivores all became more abundant, exploiting opportunities created by the new habitats (30). Some hominoids probably also participated in these important events.

THE END OF THE STORY

Most living species of higher primates (hominoids and monkeys) are forest forms, and the bulk of them are arboreal (26). All the New World ceboids are arboreal animals; except for a few smaller species that take insects as important parts of their diets, most of the larger ceboids are fruit and leaf eaters. Among Old World cercopithecoid monkeys, the bulk of present species are also arboreal forest types. However, a few forms exploit more open country (geladas, baboons, patas, vervets, some macaques); and there is increasing fossil evidence to suggest that these represent the end products of what was, in later Miocene, Pliocene, and Pleistocene times, a more substantial open country adaptive radiation (17).

There are three families of hominoids: the Hylobatidae, the Pongidae, and the Hominidae. This review will concentrate on the last two, the "large hominoids." Four species of pongid live today (26): *Pongo pygmaeus,* the orangutan which is now confined to Borneo and Sumatra; *Pan troglodytes* and *Pan paniscus,* the common chimpanzee and the pygmy chimpanzee or bonobo; and *Gorilla gorilla,* all of which live in western and central equatorial Africa. The pongids are species from tropical forests and dense woodlands which utilize trees for much of their daily activity and frequently use the ground too—particularly the African apes. None is as terrestrial as the baboon. The single living species of hominid, *Homo sapiens,* is found today in a great variety of habitats. However, at least until late Pliocene times (ca 2 m.y. ago), hominids were apparently restricted to tropical and subtropical open or nonforested habitats.

The orangutan, which is the most arboreal pongid (although large males spend considerable amounts of time out of the trees), is a large (males about 70 kg, females about 35 kg), slow-climbing but acrobatic species. The African apes, which vary in size (gorilla males 140 kg, females 70 kg; chimpanzee males 50 kg, females 40 kg; bonobos, somewhat smaller than chimpanzees), are all quadrupedal knuckle-walkers, at home in the trees and on the ground (32). Postcranially, all pongids are basically similar, although the knuckle-walkers differ from the orangutan in a number of minor though relatively important features, particularly of the forelimb. All pongids are principally herbivores, eating a wide variety of fruits, leaves, shoots, flowers, and stems, together with varying amounts of insects and vertebrates. They are all sexually dimorphic in the canine-premolar parts of the dentition. However, while the African apes have relatively small cheek teeth with thin enamel, the orangutans have larger teeth with thicker enamel (20), less prominent cusps, and a more molarized or cuspidate postcanine lower tooth (dP_3 and P_3). The orangutan face is also deeper and less projecting than those of the African apes.

Apart from numerous isolated Pleistocene orangutan teeth, definite evidence of fossil pongid ancestors is unknown. However, I assume that the pongids had evolved essentially to their modern form by the early Pliocene, 4 or 5 m.y. ago, and that they were then distributed approximately as they are today: in the African and east Asian tropical and subtropical rain forests, perhaps extending into woodland habitats. At that same time, at least one species of undoubted hominid was living in east and northeast Africa (24, 25). This species, which probably lived in open rather than forested habitats, was characterized by a variety of features quite different from those of the pongids, including well-developed adaptations to bipedal locomotion in the vertebral column, pelvis, and hindlimb; forelimb-hindlimb proportions somewhere between those of humans and pygmy chimpanzees; forelimbs (joints, wrist- and hand-bones) morphologically different from those of both apes and humans; brains a little larger (perhaps 20–30%) than those of apes of similar body size, and perhaps internally reorganized; a reorganized dentition, with relatively large and thick-enameled cheek teeth, molarized dP_3 and P_3, small, rather incisor-like, and moderately sexually dimorphic canines that barely projected yet still interlocked, and relatively large upper central incisors.

Whence came these late Neogene hominoids? We have a slowly expanding picture of Miocene hominoids which shows "archaic" species in the earlier parts of the epoch being replaced by somewhat less archaic forms in the middle Miocene. It is possible that at least one of these currently known apes is ancestral to the Pliocene forms. But it is also possible that none of them are, in which case the ancestry of large hominoids remains unknown.

HISTORY OF STUDY

In interpreting the evolutionary history of the large hominoids, we face two basic problems: (1.) the living hominoids are of low diversity compared to species in the Miocene, where the fossil record hints at a quite extensive adaptive radiation; (2.) at the same time, our knowledge of the fossil record is sparse and heavily skewed toward representation of jaws and teeth. In fact, the hominoids are one of the poorest represented of fossil mammal groups, relative to their apparent past diversity (30). This is a paradoxical problem to which I shall return.

The first Miocene large hominoid was discovered in France and was described in 1856 as *Dryopithecus fontani* (43). During the second half of the nineteenth century and the first few decades of the twentieth, a modest sample of hominoid specimens was added from other parts of Europe and from south Asia (Indo-Pakistan). Virtually all specimens were isolated teeth or (usually fragmentary) jaws. Nevertheless, various attempts were made to integrate the fossils into schemes of hominoid evolution, usually by placing extinct species on or close to lineages leading to modern forms [for example, see (23)].

During the 1920s and 1930s, fossil hominoids were recovered at a steady rate from south Asia, and, beginning in the 1930s, from east Africa (Kenya). By the early 1960s, the total sample of fossil hominoids included several hundred specimens, the bulk of them from Kenya, for which a large number of generic and specific names had been coined. Most workers placed the fossils in a subfamily of Pongidae, the Dryopithecinae. Dryopithecines were often described as "broadly" ancestral to the living pongids and hominids, though exact ancestry was not specified. Many were seen as extinct side branches. A more detailed summary of the history of the study is contained in Simons & Pilbeam (43), Pilbeam (33), and Andrews (1).

In the early 1960s, Simons and I performed a taxonomic revision of the dryopithecines which involved rigorous wielding of Occam's razor (43). The result was a greatly reduced number of Miocene hominoid genera and species and a much clearer set of evolutionary pathways. The bulk of the material was placed in seven species of *Dryopithecus,* which were clustered into three subgenera. These subgenera had mostly geographic significance, (*Dryopithecus*) and (*Sivapithecus*) species being virtually restricted to Europe and Asia respectively, with (*Proconsul*) exclusively African. The genus *Dryopithecus* was viewed as the most probable source of the living pongids.

Subsequently, I made a more concrete suggestion (33) that *D.* (*P.*) *major* and *D.* (*P.*) *africanus* were specifically ancestral to gorilla and chimpanzee; and that *D.* (*S.*) *sivalensis* (including then *D.* (*S.*) *indicus*) was ancestral to the orangutan. All were classified, along with the few remaining *Dryopithecus* species, in Pongidae. Also included in Dryopithecinae was an enigmatic form, *Gigantopithecus blacki,* from the Chinese Pleistocene. In 1969 (33), Simons described a second Miocene species, *G. bilaspurensis,* from India. This I considered (34) to be an intermediate form between *D.* (*S.*) *indicus* and *G. blacki.*

Finally, Simons and I (43) separated *Ramapithecus* from the rest of the dryopithecines, placing it in Hominidae as a definite ancestor of *Australopithecus* and *Homo. Ramapithecus* was known only from a small number of jaw fragments and teeth, which permitted a good deal of interpretive freedom. Arcade shape, dental proportions, and inferred implemental and positional behavior were all reconstructed by us as quite "human." Figure 1 summarizes the phylogenetic scheme as I would have seen it in the late 1960s. Such a system was fairly influential in shaping thinking and research, both for those who agreed and those who disagreed with the scheme (35).

Briefly, the phylogeny shown is clear-cut, simple (early hominoids are of low diversity like living ones), and dichotomous (fossil forms are subdivided between two families, Pongidae and Hominidae, as are the extant forms). What does not show in the diagram, but what we perceived and considered

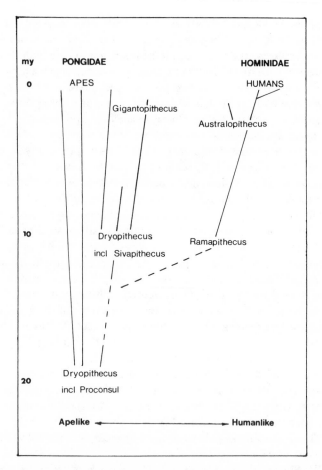

Figure 1 Diagrammatic representation of earlier ideas of hominoid evolution; the scheme is very simple and clear-cut.

important, was the relative modernity of the fossils. Thus, *Ramapithecus* was thought quite advanced, while *Dryopithecus (Proconsul) major* and *D. (P.) africanus* were seen as rather like modern pongids.

This simple scheme was by no means unanimously accepted. First of all, it was criticized on comparative anatomical grounds by those who thought that modern hominoids shared too many anatomical features to be derived from a common ancestor that was as primitive looking as the putative ancestral candidates (47). Furthermore, alternative interpretations of the various fossils, both the supposed hominid *Ramapithecus* and the supposedly rather modern dryopithecines, suggested that *Ramapithecus* and *Dryopithecus* species were better seen as primitive forms, quite like each other and rather different from any later species (19). Finally, the pattern of biochemical similarities and differences for a number of proteins suggested to some workers that the close similarity of humans to the apes, especially the African apes, indicated a more recent common ancestry, between 4 and 7 m.y., rather than the 14 m.y. plus advocated by many paleoanthropologists (38).

A great deal of heated debate has occurred over the past 10 years or so concerning Miocene hominoids and hominid origins. As an often active participant, I must admit that sometimes the "facts" have been used in the way a drunk uses a lamp-post: for support rather than illumination. The last decade has seen a number of significant changes both in the nature of the arguments and the available evidence. I believe we are now in a period of uncertainty concerning Miocene hominoids and hominid origins. This contrasts with the preceding period, during which much seemed so clear-cut and obvious. It is possible that we shall emerge from uncertainty soon, but only if we find certain kinds of evidence. Meanwhile, we can say with some confidence what did *not* happen; however, concerning what *did* happen, there remain several plausible positive alternatives, among which it is hard to choose (35). These alternatives will be discussed later. Clearly, though, the Miocene hominoids hold the key to the story of human origins.

NEWER PERSPECTIVES

Briefly, some of the changes of the past 5 or 10 years can be summarized as follows. Compared to preceding periods, we have many more Miocene fossils, distributed over broader geographic areas and time periods. Several excellent descriptions of some of this material are now available (1, 16), and accounts are being prepared for most major collections. Many of the descriptions include data important for "functional" reconstructions; that is, those that would help us understand what kind of animal an extinct species might have been (e.g. habitat preference, feeding and positional behaviors, etc).

What could be called "contextual" data are greatly improved too. We have a much clearer understanding of geochronology. This has grown out of better radiometric age determinations and more comprehensive analyses of past fauna. However, the degree of resolution in dating is still a good deal lower than for the late Cenozoic, and this should not be forgotten. For example, the spread throughout the Old World of the New World three-toed horse genus *Hipparion* is an important stratigraphic event and one that has been considered geologically instantaneous (8); a great deal of weight has been attached to it. However, the "event" may have been spread over a million years or more (B. MacFadden, personal communication 1978).

"Accuracy" in the Miocene is, and for some time to come will continue to be, a good deal less than for the Pleistocene. This will affect the kinds of questions that can be reasonably considered.

Similarly, progress has been made in understanding how much, and how little, can be said about habitats of the past. We know signficantly more about general earth climates during the Cenozoic, thanks largely to increasingly active research on the oceans and their history. Taphonomy, the science of bone deposition and recovery, has contributed enormously to interpreting fossil assemblages (7). We now realize how difficult it is to reconstruct backwards from a recovered fossil assemblage to an original living community, and how much information is inevitably lost in the process. However, we are certainly making progress with both temporal and paleoecological frameworks. What is perhaps not fully realized is the extent to which the record is, and probably will remain, incomplete.

At any rate, the hominoids of the Miocene seem to have been more abundant and also less "modern" than many of us had thought. Until a few years ago relatively simple schemes that viewed past hominoids as foreshadows of living ones functioned very well as organizing paradigms. However, the diversity of earlier hominoids was clearly greater than was previously believed. And we now see that the hominoids themselves were rather different from anything living today. Consequently, classification of past forms on the basis of present day distinctions between, say, pongids and hominids may not be very useful. Interconnections among fossil species and between them and present species are increasingly difficult to draw. Concern with phylogeny and phylogenetic classification is perhaps on the wane at the moment, and is being replaced by a more immediate concern with reconstructing the world of the past as it was at each stage in time.

Another development in the past 10 years is the galvanizing effect of comparative biochemistry on paleontologists and primate anatomists (38, 39). At the very least, it now seems established that the African apes are more closely related, in terms of common ancestry, to hominids than is the orangutan. Although the point is disputed by some comparative anatomists, a majority do seem to agree with this branching sequence. A number of workers have attempted to "reconstruct" from living species the common ancestors of all large hominoids, and of just African apes and hominids, without much agreement. Debate seems to focus on several issues. Was the hominid-African ape common ancestor a small knuckle-walking quadruped like the pygmy chimpanzee? For large hominoids, which is the primitive condition: knuckle-walking or orangutan-style quadrumanism? Or neither? Are African apes, with small, thin-enameled cheek teeth dentally primitive, or was the ancestral condition more like that of the larger-toothed, thicker-enameled orangutan? Using just the very limited number of living large hominoid species, is it possible to say *anything* very sensible about past evolutionary stages?

In addition to raising questions about ancestral conditions, comparative biochemistry has also contributed to the debate on divergence dates, with some proponents arguing that rates of molecular evolution are (stochastically) constant enough to permit the use of phenetic distance comparisons to estimate the time of lineage origins (38, 39). One scheme sees all hominoids radiating since the middle Miocene, 12 m.y. ago, with proto-orangutans diverging in the late Miocene and the African pongids and hominids in the Pliocene, 3 to 5 m.y. ago. Such a temporal framework can be "fleshed out" in a number of ways, with protohominids originating either in African forests or in Asia before crossing the open habitats of Eurasia en route to Africa.

In my opinion, the hominoid fossil record is still too poor for it to be used reliably in evaluating the various hypothetical evolutionary schemes based on comparative studies of living hominoids, either anatomical or biochemical. Until recently, implicit expectations of what the fossil record should tell us, based on ideas derived from studies on the living, have biased many attempts at analysis. Probably this will continue to be the case.

THE FOSSIL RECORD

Overview

The oldest hominoids are found in north Africa in Oligocene times, at least 30 to 35 m.y. ago (40). By the end of the Oligocene and into the early Miocene, less primitive hominoids are found in some abundance in Uganda and Kenya (remains attributable to at least 300 individuals) in deposits between about 23 and 17 m.y. old (1). Our knowledge of African geography and habitats at this time is very limited, and our sampling of what was probably a more extensive hominoid fauna is also sparse. Seven hominoid species have been sampled in a quite small area. All are relatively primitive forms that are best classified in a group distinct from living apes, the Dryopithecidae (35, 36).

Dryopithecids are known in Africa up until at least 14 m.y. ago. They are also found in West and central Europe in the middle Miocene, where the oldest is at least 13 or 14 m.y. old (the linkup of the African plate with Eurasia occurred around 17 m.y. ago). Dryopithecids, which disappear around 8 or 9 m.y. ago, are found with fauna that are of predominantly forest aspect, although it is important to remember that classifications of present or past habitats into a few categories such as "forest," "woodland,"

and "savannah" are likely to be oversimplifications. Dryopithecid anatomy is variable, but suggests adaptations paralleling those seen in living Old World monkeys.

During the middle Miocene, a somewhat different set of hominoids appears. These forms, classified by me (35, 36) recently in another hominoid family, the Ramapithecidae, are found at least as early as 14 m.y. and virtually disappear from the record by about 8 m.y. ago. Anatomically, the ramapithecids are similar in many ways to dryopithecids. However, they differ in several features, including one that seems to me quite important: enamel thickness. Also, they are found in generally different areas from dryopithecids; although habitat types undoubtedly overlapped those of dryopithecids, it is likely that they inhabited more open ("woodland") habitats. I believe that, as a group, the ramapithecids stand to the dryopithecids as the living baboons and woodland macaques do to their more forest adapted fellow cercopithecines. That is, they were more omnivorous and less arboreal.

Though they differ morphologically from dryopithecids, pongids, and hominids, the ramapithecids are themselves a morphologically heterogeneous group. Geographically they are widespread throughout the Old World, in central Europe, south Asia, and east Africa. This is especially true during the period prior to the emergence of undoubted hominids. The full diversity of the ramapithecids is probably still underestimated. But the available material suggests that they are vitally important to an understanding of hominid origins. The first hominid to be well known, *Australopithecus afarensis,* has an age range from about 3.75 to 3.00 m.y. [earlier hominid specimens may be known back to almost 7 m.y. (24)].

Plausible Schemes

There are three schemes of Miocene hominoid evolution that I find relatively plausible (35, 36, 38, 49). According to the first, the ramapithecids were derived from one of the early Miocene dryopithecids, as were the pongids. A ramapithecid, *Ramapithecus* or a similar form, gave rise to hominids around 6 to 8 m.y. ago. This would put the last common ancestor of hominids and African apes 14 m.y. ago or more. According to the second scheme, the dryopithecids gave rise to ramapithecids. A middle Miocene radiation of the ramapithecids, beginning around 14 m.y. ago, produced lineages leading on the one hand to the orangutan (perhaps represented in the Miocene by a form not unlike *Sivapithecus*) and on the other to the rest of the large hominoids, which in turn underwent a radiation. This second radiation of large hominoids, which included the African apes and hominids, occurred before about 6 or 7 m.y. According to this scheme, the last common ancestor of the chimpanzees, gorilla, and humans would resemble about equally *Pan paniscus, Australopithecus afarensis,* and *Ramapithecus.* Finally, it is possible to reconstruct a third phylogenetic scheme that derives hominids from a species essentially indistinguishable from a chimpanzee.

Having briefly described the types of hominoids present during the Miocene, and their possible evolutionary relationships, I will now review the Miocene fossils and their contexts. This review will be followed by a few thoughts on what the fossils tell us about human evolution, and on the way that human evolution has been studied.

New Material

DRYOPITHECIDS The earliest Miocene hominoids come from east Africa, from geographically tiny areas of Kenya and Uganda (41). The first specimens were described in 1933, and discoveries of Miocene hominoids in east Africa are still being made. The early Miocene sites fall within the time period 23 to 17 m.y., although published dates suggest that the bulk of the material clusters around 19 and 20 m.y. Geological, paleobotanical, and paleontological evidence suggests that habitats were mainly forested, although there was almost certainly a good deal of variation present (5); it is probably best to imagine areas of both closed and open canopy, with heavy undergrowth in the more open areas.

As noted earlier, remains of 300 individuals representing at least 7 hominoid species have been recovered from 10 sites in Kenya and Uganda, the bulk coming from 4 sites. These species range in size from that of a small gibbon to that of a large male chimpanzee (a few kilograms to over 50 kg). Most of the species are well known dentally; very little cranial material is preserved, with the exception of one species; postcranial remains are becoming better known, with the recent discovery and recognition of some new material (1, 33, 41).

Recently the early Miocene hominoids were reclassified in their original genera (1, 11, 36, 41), *Proconsul* (five species) and *Limnopithecus* (one species), though the variation currently subsumed under *Proconsul* is probably equivalent to that found in several living genera of New World or Old World monkeys.

Cranially these species do not closely resemble any of the living Old World higher primates, nor are they particularly "ape-like" (14). But in many features one of them, *Proconsul africanus,* is rather like cercopithecoid monkeys or lesser apes and is best seen as "primitive." *P. major* differs from *P. africanus* and resembles gorilla in a few characters which may well be convergent. A partial endocast of *P. africanus* resembles that of a modern gibbon in most features (37). Estimates of body size are hard to make accurately for fossils, but *P. africanus* probably had a relative brain size somewhat smaller than apes and closer to baboons (22).

Species of *Proconsul* and *Limnopithecus* differ dentally from later hominoids and are best regarded as primitive. Occlusal enamel may be the same thickness or slightly thicker than in living pongids; molar cingula are prominent. The canine-premolar complex shows apparently strong sexual dimorphism, as in later apes. Incisors, although not as large as in most living pongids, are nonetheless of respectable size. Overall dental proportions resemble those found in living omnivorous or frugivorous monkeys; studies of one aspect of occlusal anatomy support the idea that all but one species were frugivores (27).

Postcranial remains are generally rather scrappy, although quite a large number of specimens (several dozens) is now known. As with the cranial and dental systems, these early Miocene species seem to differ from living apes and also from monkeys in the overall combination of postcranial features (13, 31, 48). The material is badly in need of comprehensive restudy, but the closest analogs seem to be quadrupedal, nonknuckle walking, arboreal forms, perhaps capable of some arm-swinging. The position of particular species along an arboreal-terrestrial axis is unclear, although in habitat preference it is likely that, with increasing body size, species were more ground-living.

Overall, this group is best seen as ecologically analogous to the cercopithecines (5), from the mostly arboreal species of *Cercopithecus,* through intermediates such as *Macaca,* to more terrestrial forms like *Papio.* It now seems clear that previous attempts to link some of these early Miocene species to extant apes were unwarranted.

Geological and faunal evidence suggests that around 17 m.y. ago contact between Afro-Arabia and Eurasia was established, permitting interchange of many animal groups (8). The development of a permanent (?) east Antarctic ice-sheet (28) and shifts in oceanic and atmospheric circulation patterns consequent upon continental movements and mountain building affected climates; they became cooler and probably more seasonal. Habitats seem also to have changed, with the total amount of forest being reduced relative to more open habitats such as woodland.

Around this time, a variety of mammalian groups evolved, taking advantage of these ecological changes, exploiting terrestrial habitats by evolving adaptations to rapid running, and by eating the tougher vegetation of woodland and grassland (30). The more open country "browsers" such as bovids, suids, elephantids, and other herbivores became more diverse, as did certain groups of rodents. Several species of *Proconsul* and *Limnopithecus* are found at two Kenyan sites, Maboko and Fort Ternan, dated at around

14 m.y. At both localities these species are associated with a mammal fauna that is basically different from earlier Miocene fauna, and which probably reflects the intercontinental faunal exchange beginning around 17 m.y. ago. Palecocological information suggests, in the case of Fort Ternan, open habitats. At Maboko, many monkeys are associated with hominoids, marking the first abundant appearance of cercopithecoids in the fossil record (6, 45).

It is difficult to specify exactly when large hominoids appeared in Eurasia: it seems to be less than 17 m.y., but how much less is unclear. This uncertainty is due to the very small number of good radiometric age determinations. Though many correlations and age estimates have been published, they are based on faunal comparisons. Consequently, the estimates involve a large number of often problematic assumptions and, in some cases, are not accurate to less than a couple of million years.

The oldest Eurasian hominoids occur in Turkey (4), Saudi Arabia (2), and possibly central Europe (Czechoslovakia) (4), and subsequently are found in west Europe (Spain, France) (15, 43), east Europe (Greece) (16), south Asia (Pakistan, India) (36), and east Asia (China) (43), in deposits that may be as young as 8 or 9 m.y. Migration out of Africa was probably via Arabia-Turkey-Iran, although another link at the western end of the Mediterranean might have existed briefly (8). Europe was itself subdivided by a major inland sea, the Paratethys, during the middle Miocene (~17 to ~10 m.y.). This sea became a chain of lakes in the later Miocene and probably presented a barrier to faunal migration (44). There is, in fact, considerable faunal and floral evidence to suggest that the habitats and animal communities of west central Europe were different from those of east Europe and west Asia.

Hominoids from the western part of Eurasia represent at least two species of *Dryopithecus,* and possibly two genera (15, 43). The probable age limits of this group are 13 to 9 m.y. Apart from a couple of postcranial fragments, the material consists only of dentitions which show dimorphic canines, small to moderate incisors, and relatively small cheek teeth with thin enamel. In these and other features, *Dryopithecus* species resemble the *Proconsul* and *Limnopithecus* species more closely than they do other hominoids. However, many of the features of resemblance may well be primitive retentions, and may therefore tell us nothing about evolutionary relationships.

Like the earlier and contemporary species in Africa, the western European hominoids are best seen as primitive forest or woodland apes, as quadrupedal arboreal forms which probably (especially the larger ones) came to the ground, and as herbivorous feeders of relatively soft foods of a kind eaten by the living apes. For the moment, the European and African species discussed so far can be classified together in the Dryopithecidae. Species of this family, which are not found after about 9 m.y. ago, disappear from Europe and east Africa when climates and habitats are thought to have moved farther toward cooler, more seasonal, less forested conditions.

RAMAPITHECIDS As I noted previously, at least by middle Miocene times, 14 or more m.y. ago, substantial parts of the Old World were covered by open, nonforest habitats, particularly in the central portions, i.e. east Europe, west Asia, north Africa. No doubt an oversimplified paleoecological model would have this central nonforest area expanding at the expense of forests during middle and late Miocene times. There is some sense in seeing these nonforest habitats as ranging from woodland to savannah, with somewhat different animal communities characterizing the varying habitat types. The hominoids of the middle and late Miocene that remain to be discussed seem to occur mainly with woodland habitats; in areas where savannahs occurred, or at later times in situations where savannahs locally replaced woodlands, these hominoids are absent.

The large hominoids found in such woodland habitats during the middle and late Miocene, between 14 or more and 8 or 9 m.y. ago, have previously been classified collectively or separately in Dryopithecinae or Hominidae (43); in particular, *Ramapithecus* has been the center of a great deal of debate concerning its possible hominid status. I have proposed alternatively that a number of the middle and late Miocene genera be classified together in Ramapithecidae (35, 36), in an attempt both to draw attention to morphological features shared by the group which differentiate it from others and to focus discussion on adaptation and biology rather than phylogeny. At the moment I think it better to speculate on what kinds of animals *Ramapithecus* or *Sivapithecus* were rather than on what their descendants might have been.

Ramapithecids were a rather diverse group of animals ranging in body size from that of a medium sized baboon to that of a female gorilla (about 20 to 70 kg). The most widely distributed ramapithecid genera are *Ramapithecus* and *Sivapithecus*. These species are known from Kenya, Turkey, possibly Greece, India, Pakistan, and China, and range in age from at least 14 to 8 m.y. (3–6, 16, 35, 36, 43). The taxonomy of this group is in a rather confused state, which newer material from Pakistan will hopefully help clarify. Isolated teeth of *Ramapithecus* and *Sivapithecus* are very difficult to distinguish except on the basis of size; *Ramapithecus* teeth are smaller. It is possible that only one very dimorphic species is being sampled, but that seems unlikely for a number of reasons, including differences in enamel histology [which are of uncertain value (21, 46)]. What seems more probable is that both *Ramapithecus* and *Sivapithecus* are quite dimorphic dentally, and that the size ranges of the two forms overlap, perhaps substantially. *Ramapithecus* may show less canine dimorphism than *Sivapithecus*, though more than the Pliocene hominid *Australopithecus afarensis*. Another feature of the canines in *Sivapithecus* is their characteristic wear: even those that are large and projecting become worn down from the tip during life and so project relatively less than they would unworn. This phenomenon is also found in some other ramapithecids (35). For those species where we have some indication of body size, it seems likely that cheek teeth (molars and premolars) were relatively larger than in pongids, cercopithecoid monkeys, and dryopithecines; also, enamel thickness was greater in ramapithecids than in the other groups. These two features, relative cheek teeth size and enamel thickness, are probably linked. Some ramapithecids probably had less dimorphic canines than pongids or dryopithecids, and male canines may have been lower crowned, showing the characteristic wear mentioned before. Incisors were variable, but probably not particularly small relative to body size (35).

A handful of ramapithecid postcranial remains has been recovered during recent work in Pakistan, attributable to *Ramapithecus, Sivapithecus,* and to a third form *Gigantopithecus bilaspurensis* (but no *definitely* associated postcranial and cranial material has been found). Though these remains are unfortunately fragmentary, they suggest that all the ramapithecids were smaller than previously expected: *Ramapithecus* ~20 kg, *Sivapithecus* ~40 kg, and *Gigantopithecus* ~70 kg. The last may have moved rather like *Gorilla,* the two former were probably more arboreal. *Ramapithecus* was almost certainly not an (obligate) biped (35, 36; see Figure 2).

In addition, at least two other ramapithecids are known from Greece and Hungary; precise ages are unclear, but 9 to 11 m.y. is the most probable range. *Ouranopithecus macedoniensis* has been found in northern Greece (16); a similar form, *Bodvapithecus altipalatus* comes from Hungary (29). Both are known only from jaws and teeth. Several excellent specimens (representing at least 10 individuals) of *O. macedoniensis* come from a single locality near Salonika. According to de Bonis, the smaller specimens with small canines are females, and the bigger ones with large canines are males. The cheek teeth of *O. macedoniensis* have thick occlusal enamel and resemble those of Hominidae (smaller *Australopithecus* species) rather closely. Anterior lower premolars, although not bicuspid, are quite molarized. No postcranial remains are known, but I think it quite likely that, as with some other ramapithecids, *O. macedoniensis* had relatively large cheek teeth. If small and large specimens are indeed different sexes of one species, and are reasonably representative of the species range of variation, this extinct hominid exhibited greater dimorphism in its posterior dentition than do highly dimorphic living primates. For example, if female

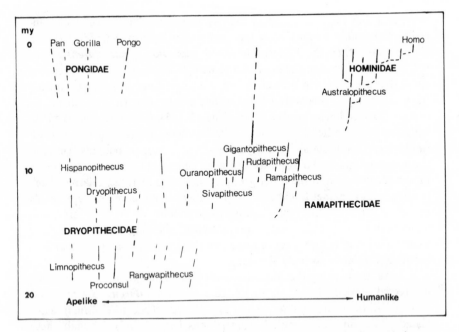

Figure 2 Distribution of currently recognized large hominoid genera in time and along a subjective "ape-human" continuum, without attempting to add hypothetical evolutionary relationships.

average cheek tooth breadths are expressed as a percentage of male average breadth, they fall between 92% and 95% in samples of gorillas and baboons (which are among the most sexually dimorphic living species); in *O. macedoniensis,* the values average around 87%. On the other hand, its anterior teeth—canines and incisors—are no more dimorphic than in many living primates.

Bodvapithecus altipalatus (29) is a poorly known large form from Hungary which resembles *O. macedoniensis.* Though both are broadly similar to species of *Sivapithecus,* they are, in my opinion, best placed in separate genera. *Rudapithecus hungaricus,* also from Hungary (29), is smaller than the others. It has moderate sized incisors and canines. Postcranial remains from Rudabanya, which have yet to be fully described, could represent *R. hungaricus, B. altipalatus,* both, or neither. Until associations are settled it is impossible to make firm statements about relative tooth size.

As I mentioned earlier, the ramapithecids are grouped together on the basis of certain common dental features. However, it is quite possible that these features may not have arisen only once, in a common ancestor, but may instead represent separate parallel evolutionary events; in which case, the family would not be maximally monophyletic. (A similar stricture may apply to the dryopithecids.) These dental changes—thick enamel, some changes in occlusal morphology, molarized premolars, perhaps reduced canines—may be associated with shifts in habitat preference, from more to less forested, which may have occurred several times. Presumably diet is involved in the dental shifts, although at present one can only speculate about the changes in a very general way.

The most frequently discussed ramapithecid, *Ramapithecus*, has figured widely in speculation about human evolution. As it has become slightly better known (4, 6, 36), questions concerning its precise role have arisen. With newer material, the question seems even more problematical. It is now possible that *Ramapithecus punjabicus*, known from Pakistan (35, 36) and India around 9 m.y. ago, was, like *Ouranopithecus*, markedly size dimorphic, perhaps to the same extent as *O. macedoniensis*. Canines may also have been even more dimorphic than those of early hominids like *Australopithecus afarensis* (24, 25). Relative to body size, cheek teeth seem to have been large, and consequently more like hominids than pongids or dryopithecids; occlusal morphology, however, was still dryopithecid-like or intermediate between dryopithecids and hominids (12). Canines were larger relative to body size than in hominids, even in females, as were incisors. Incisor proportions seem to have resembled those of the more omnivorous macaques or baboons. As I noted, the few fragmentary possible *Ramapithecus* postcranials come from a small, arboreally adapted hominoid which was not an obligate biped (35).

This conception of *Ramapithecus* is unlike earlier ones in that it does not paint *Ramapithecus* species as being very much like later hominids. It has the added advantage that it is equally acceptable to those who would or would not have it as a hominid ancestor! As with the other Miocene hominoids, we do not have any convenient living analogs of this intriguing and enigmatic species.

At the very end of the Miocene, hominids appear in the fossil record (24). In Kenya, an isolated lower molar and lower jaw fragment with one molar come from Lukeino and Lothagam, respectively, in deposits between 6 and 7 m.y. old. They resemble later hominids, in particular *Australopithecus afarensis* (25), although it is perhaps best not to assign them yet to that species. *A. afarensis* is represented by excellent Pliocene samples from Ethiopia and Tanzania. It is a small-brained, bipedal form, which is markedly sexually dimorphic if large and small specimens are correctly attributed to males and females. The dentition shows some presumably primitive features of the canine-premolar complex; canines are not very dimorphic in size and apparently not in morphology. Cheek tooth size dimorphism is, as in the ramapithecids mentioned earlier, greater than for living forms, if large (?male) and small (?female) specimens are compared.

The evolutionary transition to Hominidae presumably occurred in the late Miocene, at least in Africa. Whether or not it also occurred in Asia and (less likely) in Europe remains to be seen. Late Miocene times saw a great deal of faunal continental interchange and evolution (30), though we know this only from "before" and "after" data.

CONCLUSIONS

As I have emphasized, in order to make future confident statements about hominoid evolution we shall need quite specific kinds of information about dental, cranial, and postcranial associations. Our current relatively clear picture of hominid (Pliocene and Pleistocene) evolution is a function only of the recent recovery of quite complete material; even entire dentitions may yield at best ambivalent information. Our knowledge of Miocene forms is very much less complete, so we should be cautious. We must avoid simple, clear-cut schemes which sort fossils into "hominids" and "pongids"; and we must be cautious about drawing conclusions regarding "primitive" or "derived" characters too.

However, some points can be made. Early and middle Miocene hominoids such as *Proconsul* and *Dryopithecus* seem to have been in many ways distinctly different from all later hominoids. They were probably predominantly frugivorous or omnivorous species, mainly arboreal forms living in mostly forested habitats. One or more of the known forms, or, more likely, as yet unknown species, gave rise to the ramapithecids during middle Miocene times around 14 to 16 m.y. ago. Ramapithecids were found in woodland habitats until almost the end of the Miocene. (One probably lingered on into the Pleistocene.) These species perhaps spanned both arboreal and terrestrial niches and were probably on average more omnivorous than dryopithecids.

Until quite recently, it has been assumed by many of us that living apes were derived from dryopithecids rather than ramapithecids, on the grounds that features of the ramapithecid dentition were derived or specialized relative to what is seen in pongids and dryopithecids. However, it has recently been suggested as an alternative that a ramapithecid could be the common ancestor of all living pongids and hominids, or of both living African apes and hominids (36, 49). Such a possibility, it seems to me, is worth exploring. With the fossil record still open to a variety of interpretations, there remains a possibility that hominoid branching sequences and timings may eventually mesh a little better than previously with estimates derived from comparative biochemistry. If nothing else, and perhaps the only thing that is certain, the next decade will provide many surprises.

ACKNOWLEDGMENTS

Bonnie Lipschutz contributed much to the completion of this paper.

Literature Cited

1. Andrews, P. J. 1978. A revision of the Miocene Hominoidea of East Africa. *Bull. Br. Mus. Nat. Hist. Geol. Ser.* 30(2):85–224
2. Andrews, P. J., Hamilton, W. R., Whybrow, P. J. 1978. Dryopithecines from the Miocene of Saudi Arabia. *Nature* 274:249–50
3. Andrews, P. J., Tekkaya, I. 1976. *Ramapithecus* in Kenya and Turkey. In *Les Plus Anciens Hominides,* ed. P. V. Tobias, Y. Coppens, pp. 7–25. Paris: CNRS. 464 pp.
4. Andrews, P. J., Tobien, H. 1977. New Miocene locality in Turkey with evidence on the origin of *Ramapithecus* and *Sivapithecus. Nature* 268:699–701
5. Andrews, P. J., Van Couvering, J. A. H. 1975. Palaeo-environments in the East African Miocene. In *Approaches to Primate paleobiology,* ed. F. S. Szalay, pp. 62–103. Basel: Karger
6. Andrews, P. J., Walker, A. 1976. The primate and other fauna from Fort Ternan, Kenya. In *Human Origins,* ed. G. Ll. Isaac, E. R. McCown, pp. 279–304. California: Staples. 591 pp.
7. Behrensmeyer, A. K., Hill, A. P. 1979. *Fossils in the Making.* In press.
8. Berggren, W. A., Van Couvering, J. A. 1974. The late Neogene. *Palaeogeogr. Palaeoclimatol. Palaeoecol.* 16(1/2):1–216
9. Buchardt, B. 1978. Oxygen isotope palaeotemperatures from the Tertiary period in the North Sea area. *Nature* 275:121–23
10. Butzer, K. W. 1977. Environment, culture, and human evolution. *Am. Sci.* 65:572–84
11. Clark, W. E. Le G., Leakey, L. S. B. 1951. The Miocene Hominoidea of East Africa. *Fossil Mammals of Africa. Br. Mus. Nat. Hist.* 1:1–117
12. Corruccini, R. S. 1975. *A metrical study of crown component variation in the hominoid dentition.* PhD thesis. Univ. California, Berkeley, Calif. 104 pp.
13. Corruccini, R. S., Ciochon, R. L., McHenry, H. M. 1976. The postcranium of Miocene hominiods: were dryopithecenes merely "dental apes"? *Primates* 17:205–23
14. Corruccini, R. S., Henderson, A. M. 1978. Palato-facial comparison of *Dryopithecus (Proconsul)* with extant catarrhines. *Primates* 19:35–44
15. Crusafont-Pairo, M., Golpe-Posse, J. M. 1973. New pongids from the Miocene of Valles Penedes Basin (Catalonia, Spain). *J. Hum. Evol.* 2:17–23
16. de Bonis, L., Melentis, J. 1977. Les primates hominoides du Vallesien de Macedoine (Grece). Etude de la machoire inferieure. *Geobios* 10:849–85
17. Delson, E. 1975. Paleoecology and zoogeography of the Old World monkeys. In *Primate Functional Morphology and Evolution,* ed. R. Tuttle, pp. 37–64. The Hague: Mouton. 583 pp.
18. Douglas, R. G., Savin, S. M. 1973. Oxygen and carbon isotope analyses of Cretaceous and Tertiary Foraminifera from the Central North Pacific. In *Initial Reports of the Deep Sea Drilling Project Vol. 17,* ed. P. H. Roth, J. R. Herring, pp. 591–605. Washington: Natl. Sci. Found.
19. Frayer, D. W. 1974. A reappraisal of *Ramapithecus. Yearb. Phys. Anthropol.* 18:19–30
20. Gantt, D. G. 1977. *Enamel of primate teeth: its thickness and structure with reference to functional and phyletic implications.* PhD thesis. Washington Univ., St. Louis, Mo. 403 pp.
21. Gantt, D. G., Pilbeam, D., Steward, G. P. 1977. Hominoid enamel prism patterns. *Science* 198:1155–57
22. Gingerich, P. D. 1977. Correlation of tooth size and body size in living hominoid primates, with a note on relative brain size in *Aegyptopithecus* and *Proconsul. Am. J. Phys. Anthropol.* 47:395–98
23. Gregory, W. K. 1916. Studies on the evolution of the primates. *Bull. Am. Mus. Nat. Hist.* 35:239–355
24. Howell, F. C. 1978. Hominidae. In *Evolution of African Mammals,* ed. V. J. Maglio, H. B. S. Cooke, pp. 154–248. Cambridge, Mass: Harvard, 641 pp.
25. Johanson, D. C., White, T. D., Coppens, Y. 1978. A new species of the genus *Australopithecus* (Primates: Hominidae) from the Pliocene of Eastern Africa. *Kirtlandia* 28:1–14
26. Jolly, A. 1972. *The Evolution of Primate Behavior.* New York: Macmillan. 397 pp.

27. Kay, R. F. 1977. Diets of early Miocene African hominoids. *Nature* 368:628–30
28. Kennett, J. P. 1977. Cenozoic evolution of Antarctic glaciation, the Circum-Antarctic Ocean, and their impact on global paleoceanography. *J. Geophys. Res.* 82:3843–60
29. Kretzoi, M. 1975. New ramapithecines and *Pliopithecus* from the Lower Pliocene of Rudabanya in north-eastern Hungary. *Nature* 257:578–81
30. Maglio, V. J., Cooke, H. B. S. 1978. *Evolution of African Mammals.* Cambridge, Mass: Harvard. 641 pp.
31. Morbeck, M. E. 1975. *Dryopithecus africanus* forelimb. *J. Hum. Evol.* 4: 39–46
32. Napier, J. R., Napier, P. H. 1967. *A Handbook of Living Primates.* London: Academic. 456 pp.
33. Pilbeam, D. R. 1969. Tertiary Pongidae of East Africa: evolutionary relationships and taxonomy. *Bull. Peabody Mus. Nat. Hist. Yale Univ.* 31:1–185
34. Pilbeam, D. R. 1970. *Gigantopithecus* and the origins of Hominidae. *Nature* 225:516–19
35. Pilbeam, D. R. 1979. Major trends in human evolution. In *Current Argument on Early Man,* ed. L.-K. Königsson. New York: Pergamon. In press
36. Pilbeam, D. R., Meyer, G. E., Badgley, C., Rose, M. D., Pickford, M. H., Behrensmeyer, A. K., Shah, S. M. I. 1977. New hominoid primates from the Siwaliks of Pakistan and their bearing on hominoid evolution. *Nature* 270: 689–95
37. Radinsky, L. 1974. The fossil evidence of anthropoid brain evolution. *Am. J. Phys. Anthropol.* 41:15–28
38. Sarich, V. M. 1973. Just how old is the hominid line? *Yearb. Phys. Anthropol.* 17:98–112
39. Sarich, V. M., Cronin, J. E. 1976. Molecular systematics of the primates. In *Molecular Anthropology,* ed. M. Goodman, R. E. Tashian, pp. 141–70. New York: Plenum. 466 pp.
40. Simons, E. L. 1972. *Primate Evolution.* New York: Macmillan. 322 pp.
41. Simons, E. L., Andrews, P., Pilbeam, D. R. 1978. Cenozoic apes. In *Evolution of African Mammals,* ed. V. J. Maglio, H. B. S. Cooke, pp. 120–46. Cambridge, Mass: Harvard. 641 pp.
42. Simons, E. L., Chopra, S. R. K. 1969. *Gigantopithecus* (Pongidae, Hominoidea) a new species from North India. *Postilla Peabody Mus. Yale Univ.* 138:1–18
43. Simons, E. L., Pilbeam, D. R. 1965. Preliminary revision of the Dryopithecinae (Pongidae, Anthropoidea). *Folia Primatol.* 3:81–152
44. Steininger, F., Rögl, F., Martini, E. 1976. Current Oligocene/Miocene biostratigraphic concept of the Central Paratethys (Middle Europe). *Newsl. Stratigr.* 4:174–202
45. Van Couvering, J. A. H., Van Couvering, J. A. 1976. Early Miocene mammal fossils from East Africa: aspects of geology faunistics and paleo-ecology. See Ref. 6, pp. 155–96
46. Vrba, E. S., Grine, F. E. 1978. Australopithecine enamel prism patterns. *Science* 202:890–92
47. Washburn, S. L. 1968. *The Study of Human Evolution.* Eugene: Univ. Oregon Press. 48 pp.
48. Wood, B. A. 1973. Locomotor affinities of *Hominoid* tali from Kenya. *Nature* 246:45–46
49. Zihlman, A. L., Cronin, J. E., Cramer, D. L., Sarich, V. M. 1978. Pygmy chimpanzee as a possible prototype for the common ancestor of humans, chimpanzees and gorillas. *Nature* 275:744–46

Ann. Rev. Anthropol. 1979. 8:353–71

LANGUAGE CHANGE—   ◆9637
A LEXICAL PERSPECTIVE

William S-Y. Wang[1]

Osmania University, Hyderabad, India

Within the Western tradition, the study of language change began with the *I,E.* famous observation of William Jones in a lecture delivered on February 2, *hypothesis* 1786.[2] After some detailed comparisons of the classic languages of Europe, Greek and Latin, with far-flung languages like Persian and Sanskrit, he suggested that (*a*) the similarities among them were too strong to be attributed to chance—consequently they must be due to "some common source"; and (*b*) this parent language, "perhaps, no longer exists." Considering the year, which was decades before biologists came to parallel observations concerning speciation of organisms, this was a remarkable pair of insights, which centuries of historical studies on language were to build upon. Although this observation has been called the "Indo-European hypothesis" because of the languages referred to, its implications were, of course, equally applicable to all languages.

Before Jones, discussions on language history were mostly mired in philosophical and theological speculations. The small amount of empirical work that had been done was largely unfruitful. It was vitiated by the misconception that one language could have evolved from another language contem-

[1]On leave from the University of California at Berkeley, 1978–1979. I wish to thank the Guggenheim Foundation for their support, Osmania University for their hospitality, and, in particular, Bh. Krishnamurti and M. Hashimoto for much stimulation and helpful comments.

[2]In footnote 7 of their important paper, Weinreich, Labov & Herzog (51) trace discussions of language change to Dante and Tolomei in the early sixteenth century. However, we should surely learn more about non-Western traditions (e.g. Chinese, Indian, Semitic) before accepting their claim that "For obvious reasons, awareness and discussion of language change developed first in the Romance world."

0084-6570/79/1015-0353$01.00

poraneous with it. (A very similar mistake was made in the middle of the nineteenth century in evolutionary discussions, when many misunderstood Darwin to claim that man evolved from the living apes.) The Indo-European hypothesis turned the study of language change into a serious field, where pieces of objective data could be cumulatively gathered and finer and finer theories could be constructed on the basis of these data.

This is indeed what took place. In the ensuing decades, a tremendous amount of empirical work was done on the Indo-European languages by a series of outstanding scholars, starting with names like Rask, Bopp, and Grimm. A very readable account of their accomplishments is available in Pedersen's brief survey (37). In Lehmann's anthology (28), one can read the English translations of some of the original contributions.

The regularity hypo-

After almost a century of gathering data and reconstructing the linguistic past, a movement took place that continues to influence diachronic thinking to this day. This movement has been vividly recounted in Hockett's presidential address to the Linguistic Society of America. The major figures of this movement called themselves "neogrammarians", and Hockett (17) labeled the central product of this movement "the regularity hypothesis."

A classic piece of scholarship from this movement is Karl Verner's study of the so-called Grimm's Law (45)—an exemplary work for its lucidity and boldness. The data here have to do with the "exceptional" voicing of certain Indo-European plosives as these are found in Germanic. In successfully explaining away these exceptions, Verner showed more clearly than ever before (*a*) the distinction between a conditioned change and an unconditioned change, and (*b*) the critical importance of taking in account as possible conditioning factors not only the segmental context, but the *suprasegmental* context as well. Although point (*a*) was not new with Verner (Grassman had used this distinction in an earlier investigation of the same data), point (*b*), with its innovative conception of two types of accent, was definitely an original contribution. But even more significant than these two points was the boldness of his victory proclamation: "There must . . . exist a rule for the irregularities; the task is to find this rule" (45, p. 36).

The use of the word "law" has not been consistent. Discoveries of the sort Grimm made among a specified set of languages, e.g. Indo-European and Germanic, are better termed "correspondences" since they refer to particular events. Phonetic formulas which recur in a variety of correspondences across time, space, and genetic groups can rightly be called "laws," with the implication that their recurrence has a basis in the mechanisms of speech production and perception. Linguistic laws, unlike physical laws, are not predictive, though they are explanatory to varying degrees. In this respect, they are like evolutionary laws in biology, as explained, for example, by Luria:

The modern theory of evolution, like all historical theories, is explanatory rather than predictive. To miss this point is a mistake that theoreticians of history have often made. Prediction would require not only a knowledge of the main force—natural selection—but also a prescience of all future environmental conditions, as well as of future balances between the quasi-deterministic effects of the law of great numbers and the purely probabilistic role of genetic drift (31, p. 23).

With a few obvious substitutions of terms, this statement has a perfect fit for linguistic laws.

Encouraged by a series of successes like that of Verner, the neogrammarians stated their doctrine, its clearest wording offered by two leaders of the neogrammarian movement, Osthoff and Brugmann (35):

> . . . every sound change, inasmuch as it occurs mechanically, takes place according to laws that admit no exception. That is, the direction of the sound shift is always the same for all the members of a linguistic community except where a split into dialects occur, and all the words in which the sound subjected to the change appears in the same relationship are affected by the change without exception.

This neogrammarian doctrine, formulated most forcefully in the 1870s, *Except-ions* has been accepted in various forms by virtually all major groups of historical linguists since that time. There were critics, of course, most notably Hugo Schuchardt (41), who pointed out internal paradoxes in the doctrine itself and also referred to large bodies of exceptions from dialect studies. As a more recent example, Malkiel (33) pointed out that in Bloomfield's influential book, *Language,* the chapters on the comparative method and on dialect geography depicted views of sound change that are mutually contradictory. Elsewhere he remarks, as do many other scholars of change, that exceptions are "embarrassingly numerous" (34). But by and large those challenges were not heeded, and the doctrine passed down across the generations through Saussure, the structuralists, and the generativists, in one form or another. Lucid analyses of this historical development have been provided by Weinreich, Labov & Herzog (51), and by Chen (5).

Basically there are two related sources of difficulty with the neogrammarian conception of language change: the isolation of language from its social context, and the exclusive assumption of phonetic gradualness. The first difficulty is reflected in Hermann Paul's influential neogrammarian text, *Prinzipien der Sprachgeschichte* of 1880 (36). As has been pointed out by Weinreich et al (51), "the price of such isolation was the creation of an irreconcilable opposition between the individual and society." The difficulty became greater in Saussure's writings, where there is an increased tendency to retreat to the language of the isolated individual, and where furthermore, such language is supposed to be "homogeneous." The ultimate retreat along this line of reasoning is the "monastic" model advocated by Chomsky, "the ideal speaker-listener, in a completely homogeneous speech-community . . .", which is to my mind the *reductio ad absurdum* of such isolationism.

This characterization of "monastic," which comes from Labov, is particularly apt for describing the withdrawal symtoms of the kind of puristic linguistics that weaves grand designs of "logical structure" that somehow manages to remain untainted by work either in the field or in the laboratory. Little wonder that this sort of pursuit has drawn embarrassing criticisms from other fields, such as that from Wilson (53), that linguistics appears to be more concerned with "celebrating personal visions" than serious empirical work. These criticisms, however, are unfair to linguistics-at-large. Responsible, cumulative, empirical work has been and continues to be carried out in many sectors, adding to the long-term heritage of the field. Such work typically has less popular appeal and is less likely to be noticed by people from other fields.

Time and again it has been shown that completely homogeneous speech communities have no more reality than the ideal speaker-listener. [An early demonstration of this was the study of Gauchat in 1905 (13).] To advocate that the primary concern of linguistic theory is with those two illusions is to seduce linguistics onto the path of sterility. It is like trying to understand chess by watching the movements of some single piece in isolation, without regard to its relation and interaction with all the other pieces. More than any others, Weinreich et al (51) exposed the difficulty of the neogrammarian position and at the same time provided a strong foundation for cumulative empirical research. This foundation has been built upon by a host of scholars who show that orderly heterogeneity not only exists in every language,[3] but that it can be elegantly treated by techniques developed for describing variation. Although the bulk of this research grew out of investigations on English, the techniques should prove even more fruitful when applied to settings which are typically much more multilingual, which is the case with the majority of speech communities in the world today.

In this chapter, however, I will be concerned more with the other major source of difficulty that has been passed down from the neogrammarians, the exclusive assumption of phonetic gradualness. Osthoff & Brugmann (35) conceive of the manner of the change as being "mechanical," and it is by virtue of this fact that "all the words . . . are affected by the change

---

[3]The orderly heterogeneity that must be there by the very nature of linguistic development has not escaped the sharp observations of scholars looking at language from the outside, as it were. Consider this suggestive metaphor by L. Wittgenstein, brought to my attention by B. Abbot: "Our language can be seen as an ancient city: a maze of little streets and squares, of old and new houses, and of houses with additions from various periods; and this surrounded by a multitude of new buroughs with straight regular streets and uniform houses" (*Philosophical Investigations* I:18).

without exception." In other words, the regularity is guaranteed by the mechanical nature of sound change—it is not an independent fact to be discovered and verified, but a consequence of the nature of the process itself. The faith in this mechanical process is what prompts Bloomfield, for instance, to put the matter in two crisp words: "phonemes change," i.e. not morphemes or words or other possible units.

But what *is* the nature of this mechanical process? This was not elucidated by the neogrammarians themselves. Later scholars proposed various metaphors toward an explanation. Jespersen, for one, compares shifts in phonetic values with random errors that one observes when sawing logs, estimating the length of the next log on the basis of the one just sawed off. The picture that Hockett offers is one where numerous phonetic events scatter into a statistical distribution, much as the hits and misses are scattered on a target board; the statistical modes of these distributions gradually shift in time by small, imperceptible increments. Although such metaphors of random events do not entail a directionality per se, presumably these authors would accept some hypothesis of least effort, such as that proposed by Paul as well as many others, so that the fluctuations are cumulative rather than mutually cancelling.

In the Osthoff-Brugmann passage quoted earlier, we can discern two parameters of a sound change—lexical and phonetic. To build regularity into the process, the neogrammarian assumption is that all relevant words change at once—that is, in a lexically abrupt fashion. Yet we all know that sound changes do not take place overnight. So graduality along the phonetic parameter is an inevitable consequence of assuming lexical abruptness. Furthermore, many writers of the neogrammarian persuasion appear to believe that this combination of lexical abruptness and phonetic gradualness is *the* process of sound change. Within the perspective advanced in this paper, however, I will argue that there must be other processes as well for implementing sound change.

I first encountered difficulty with such a conception of sound change when I was trying to understand a peculiar development in Chaozhou Chinese,[4] where the short high tone became the short low tone during the same period that the short low tone became the short high tone. Since such a phenomenon is of great theoretical interest, though they are rarely reported in the literature, I suggested the term "flip-flop" to call attention to them (47). The logical difficulty with the situation is that if X is gradually shifting toward Y during the same period of time that Y is gradually shifting toward X, then surely X and Y would merge phonetically. To get around

---

[4]This is by no means an aberration of some isolated community; similar phenomena can be observed in numerous dialects of the South Min group.

this difficulty, I suggested that a sound change of this type must be implemented in a lexically gradual fashion, diffusing across the lexicon by several words at a time (47). In a later paper, I called this process "lexical diffusion" (48).

Lexical diffusion —

The logic is the same in metathesis and in flip-flops, which can be viewed as syntagmatic and paradigmatic versions of the same type of development. It simply makes no phonetic sense to say that a cluster like /ks/ gradually shifted to /sk/ through a series of imperceptible increments. Neither is it plausible to believe in a gradual continuum between members of well-attested changes, such as m > n or t > k, since altogether different articulators are involved (48).

A more general way of seeing the difficulty is the absence of intermediate forms, a situation not unlike that discussed by evolutionary biologists (e.g. 15). If there is indeed the kind of constant massive shifting along continua that phonetic gradualness assumes, then there should be evidence for this everywhere in the living language of the world. Since all living languages are always undergoing change, we should be able to observe many intermediate forms as the various sounds shift from one prototype to another. For an ubiquitous change like t > č, for example, phonetic gradualness would predict that one can easily gather data from the living languages to document the infinite continuum between the t and the č. Yet such data are strikingly rare in the literature; for many types of change, such as those involving articulatory discontinuities exemplified in the preceding paragraph, they may not be obtainable at all.

Quantal theory —

To get around the problem of articulatory discontinuities, one may entertain the hope that perhaps the gradualness can be found in the acoustic signal instead. But this hope would be short-lived when we consider in greater detail the complex relationship between articulation and acoustics, along the line suggested by Stevens (43, 43a). By modeling the vocal tract electronically and mathematically, Stevens has found that the articulatory-acoustic relations can best be understood as relatively discrete "quanta." These quanta are schematized in Figure 1.

In the diagram, regions I and III show areas where relatively large differences in articulatory configuration have negligible acoustic consequences, that is, they correspond to minor differences in the speech signal. We would hear the same sound in I and III, even though they involve a large range of different articulations. On the other hand, region II shows areas where relatively small differences in articulation have major acoustic consequences corresponding to large changes in the acoustic parameter. The inference to be made from this quantal theory is that the prototypical speech sounds are constructed in regions like I and III, the quanta, which would permit the speaker a larger range of imprecision in his articulation with

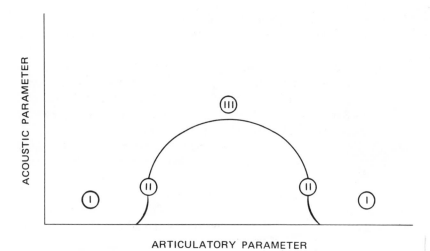

Figure 1   Schematized relation between an acoustic parameter of speech and a parameter that describes some aspect of articulation. Regions I and III show phonetic areas where relatively large articulary movements have negligible acoustic consequences, whereas region II shows the converse. Taken from Stevens (43).

a minimum distortion on the intended acoustics. Such a theory would predict, then, that the actual acoustic space populated by the sounds of human language does not have uniform density, but is made of clusters of stable regions. Although it would be a tremendous task to verify this theory in detail, the evidence that Stevens has presented on selected examples is quite persuasive. [However, see the criticisms of Ladefoged (27a).] If we accept these quanta, the hope that phonetic gradualness is to be found in acoustics rather than articulation would be considerably dimmed.

Having considered the discontinuities in the articulatory and the acoustic, one might still wish to pursue phonetic gradualness into the one remaining domain, the perceptual, since again the acoustic-perceptual relations are anything but straightforward. Is the perceptual space made up of multidimensionally gradual continua? Again, recent results on categorical perception suggest that the perceptual space is like that which Stevens proposes for acoustic space, quantal rather than smooth (30). Furthermore, the perceptual boundaries for these quanta, for some linguistic features at least, appear to be located at consistent places and detectable even in very young infants, suggesting such boundaries may have a genetic basis (10). Establishing discontinuities in all three phonetic domains—articulatory, acoustic, and perceptual—does not conclusively rule out the possibility that there may be a very few types of change that are phonetically gradual, namely those for which the space is smooth in all three domains. But we are justified in concluding that phonetic gradualness cannot be the exclusive process for sound change.

In the above paragraphs I have only given a brief outline of the arguments surrounding phonetic gradualness; more detailed reviews of this problem, including the opinions of a variety of scholars (e.g. Wheeler, Sturtevant, Sommerfelt, Sapir, Martinet, Greenberg, Halle, etc), have been presented by Chen (5) and Wang (48). To take just one example, we find Sweet (44), under the influence of Paul and Sievers (p. xii), writing confidently that ". . . all sound change is gradual: there are no sudden leaps in the phonetic history of a language" (44, p. 15).

It appears that an analogous problem was discussed much earlier in biology, as seen in this prescient remark from Thomas Huxley to Charles Darwin, made on the day before publication of the *Origin of Species* "You have loaded yourself with an unnecessary difficulty in adopting *Natura non facit saltum* so unreservedly" (15, p. 115). With the benefit of hindsight, the same remark might very well be made to the neogrammarians.

These two sources of difficulty in the dominant doctrine, namely the isolation of the individual from his social context, and the assumption of exclusive phonetic gradualness, are of course importantly related. If indeed the sounds undergoing change shift by minute *imperceptible* increments, it is difficult to see how the various members can calibrate against each other and keep the speech community "homogeneous," since no one presumably can hear these increments. If, on the other hand, the change were to be lexically gradual, an inevitable consequence of admitting phonetic abruptness, then the changed words are clearly observable from speaker to speaker in a community characterized by "orderly heterogeneity." Those words are part of each speaker's linguistic personality, which can be imitated or avoided, much like many other cultural traits, depending on a host of other linguistic and extralinguistic factors. Alexander Pope must have had some such scenario in mind when he wrote:

> In words, as fashions, the same rule will hold
> Alike fantastic, if too new or old.
> Be not the first by whom the new are tried
> Nor yet the last to lay the old aside.

In the remainder of this paper, my concern will be with two related tasks. First, I will present some detailed results which show the reality of lexical diffusion as it is observed in a variety of languages. In doing this, it will be seen that certain methods of working with large quantities of data are more likely to lead to fruitful results.

With the proof of lexical diffusion and exchanging of the neogrammarian monolithic path of phonetic gradualness for one that has multiple paths, new areas of research become available that prompt even deeper questions on the nature of language change. What is the relation between a particular type of sound change (say, final obstruent devoicing vs vowel raising) on the one hand and the process of change on the other, i.e. phonetic gradualness, lexical diffusion, and statistical variation in the sense of Labov? (These paths, it should be emphasized, are not mutually exclusive.) How are these different processes related to central linguistic issues like language acquisition, dialect borrowing, the comparative method, and techniques of genetic subgrouping? My second task here will be to pursue these new questions for diachronic linguistics in a preliminary way in the hope of eventually sharpening them enough so that useful hypotheses can be formulated on them.

In sharp contrast with the case of phonetic gradualness, where intermediate forms are all but easy to come by, intermediate forms for lexical diffusion are everywhere, provided we recognize them for what they are. One of the clearest statements of this issue is that by Vogt (46, p. 367):

> At any moment, between the initiation and conclusion of these changes, we have a state characterized by the presence of more or less free variants, so that the speakers have the choice between alternative expressions. In each case the choice will be determined by an interplay of factors, some linguistic, some esthetic and social, an interplay so complex that most often the choice will appear as being due to pure chance.... What therefore in a history of linguistic system appears as a change will in a synchronic description appear as a more or less free variation between forms of expression, equally admissible within the system.

Although such synchronic variation has been widely observed in literature, discussions of it have been largely within the context of dialect borrowing. Scholars like B. Wheeler, for example, specifically rejected synchronic variation as evidence for system-internal change because of their acceptance of phonetic gradualness. The following quote is a good example of how expectation determines perception: "It is to be noticed that the operation of the laws of sound is unconscious and gradual, so that the old form cannot, except through mixing of dialects, survive alongside the new (52)."

Freed from the illusions of homogeneous speech communities with ready-made geographical and social boundaries, the concept of dialect turns out to be both subtle and complex. Many linguists have too easily resorted to the facile escape clause of "dialect mixture" without adequate verification. For the present purposes, I see no reason why synchronic variation cannot be a mechanism in the implementation of sound change, whether the actuation was from inside or outside the linguistic system undergoing change.

In Table 1, a schematized version of lexical diffusion via synchronic variation is given. For any W_i, the notation $\overline{W}_i$ represents the changed counterpart of that particular word. So a typical change involves three stages: u (unchanged), v (synchronic variation) and c (changed). In the table, W_1 is the most advanced word, having already reached the last stage, i.e. the c stage. W_2 and W_3 are in the v stage, while W_4 and W_5 are still in the u stage. Although it is obviously important to know whether a change is actuated internally or externally, phonetically or conceptually, the implementation by such a process of lexical diffusion should be the same.

Once we recognize the critical role that synchronic variation plays in lexical diffusion, then such evidence is indeed easily found in every living language. Here is an example from American speech.

There is an ongoing change of vowel laxing that is diffusing across the lexicon, where /ūw/ in monosyllables is becoming /ŭ/. Usually in such cases, one can detect subregularities. So the words which end in /k/ have mostly reached the c-stage: book, nook, rook, hook, shook, cook, brook, took, look, etc. On the other hand, those in which the vowel is morpheme-final remain in the u-stage, (since English phonotactics does not permit final /ŭ/), even when it is not word final: whose, zoos, twos, shoes, mooed, wooed, cooed, etc. Perhaps it is the model of words like "zoos" that keeps another group in the u-class: ooze, choose, lose, loose, booze, goose, noose, etc. Similarly, the words which end in /l/ have conservatively remained in the u-stage: tool, pool, spool, drool, etc.

If the above were the sum total of the relevant data, then lexical diffusion is no more than the specification of regular sound change in terms of very fine classes, where each class is uniquely defined by a condition, either phonological or morphosyntactic. However, the point is that typically the data are more complex, and that words leak through the boundaries of these definable classes, forming groups which are too idiosyncratic to justify setting up new classes, and stretch across the stages of change. So for the words ending in /t/, we have all three stages of the change in the words

Table 1 Lexical diffusion via synchronic variation

Words \ Stages	u	v	c
W_1			$\overline{W}_1$
W_2		$W_2 \sim \overline{W}_2$	
W_3		$W_3 \sim \overline{W}_3$	
W_4	W_4		
W_5	W_5		

u-stage: boot, loot; v-stage: soot, root; c-stage: foot. Words ending in labials largely exhibit the first two stages of change—u-stage: boom, loom, gloom, groom, spoof; v-stage: roof, room, broom, coop; though for many speakers there is the c-stage: hoof. Words ending in /d/ show the u-stage: food, mood, versus the c-stage: hood, wood, stood, good. (The word "good," incidentally, appears to be involved in a later stage change from /ŭ/ to /ʌ/, where it is in the v-stage, while words like "blood" and "flood" have already reached the c-stage).

The above data are given to illustrate the complex dynamics of the diffusion process; they are far from complete. (One should also consider, for example, the large class of words spelled with "u" or "w," e.g. flute, dune, rouge, newt, etc. Is it the spelling or the palatal onglide that is keeping them from joining this laxing?). Although not every American speaker will agree with each pronunciation reported here, the data do give a time-slice of the change in progress. The variation across speakers is something we should expect within an "orderly heterogeneity."

A more fine-grained study of lexical diffusion has been reported by Bauer (4) for the Cantonese spoken in Hongkong. In this language there is a change that has been going on over several decades in which the final velar nasal is becoming alveolar, a trend that goes against the general development of final nasals as observed by Chen and Wang (7, p. 267). Again there are subregularities. For Bauer's informant, the words which have low vowels are the most advanced; they have reached the c-stage. At the other end, the words with high vowels are all in the u-stage. So the process of alveolarization is obviously operating on the velar nasal in a way that is conditioned by the height of the preceding vowel. At present it is the mid-vowel words that exhibit the greatest synchronic variation. Whereas words with the vowel /ɛ/ have all changed, many words with the vowels /œ/ and /ɔ/ are pronounced with either nasal, with the conservative velar occurring in more formal contexts.

In another study of lexical diffusion, Janson (21) noted that Swedish words were losing word-final /d/ as early as the fourteenth century in their pronunciation, though not in their spelling. The point of special interest here is that the words that can undergo optional d-deletion are now much *fewer* than a half-century ago, as determined by earlier descriptions. In Stockholm speech the deletion used to be possible for more words across more grammatical categories. Since the "d" has been kept in the orthography, the reversal of this change probably came as a result of the rapid rise in literacy in Sweden in recent decades. In a few cases, furthermore, single words have bifurcated and the bifurcation is probably made permanent by the new spellings. "Träd" now means "tree", with the "d" spelled, while "trä" means "wood"; "skuld" means "dept", while "skull" means "sake."

Typically in historical work, linguists have not paid much attention to the influence that orthography may have on changes in the spoken language. That this has not been a source of difficulty is probably due to the fact that although writing has existed for many thousands of years, the frequent use of written language has been restricted to a very small percentage of people during almost all of these millenia. With the dramatic rise in literacy in the world, however, over recent decades, it is likely that orthography will figure more and more prominently in language change, as will some other cultural innovations (e.g. mass communication and transportation devices) as these become increasingly available and widespread.

In all cases of lexical diffusion, we find leaders and laggers among the words, which raises the issue of what determines these schedules. As Vogt (46) remarked, they appear to result from an interplay of factors so complex that "most often the choice will appear as being due to pure chance." Yet it seems that slowly some of these factors are being sorted out. One such factor is frequency.

The notion that more frequent words will change earlier has been around for a while, though the tools for its verification were not available. At times the notion has been misused. A century ago, Scherer tried to apply this notion to certain apparent exceptions in Germanic, but as Verner correctly criticized (45, p. 37), his interpretation of the frequencies of the exceptional words was very vulnerable. Indeed tools like frequency dictionaries for even living languages need to be used with care in the light of various problems of statistical sampling; *a fortiori* intuitive guesses on old languages of the kind Scherer made cannot be convincing.

With judicious care, however, frequency data like those for English provided by Kucera & Francis (25) can be used to good advantage. Such is the case of Hooper's (18) study of schwa deletion in sequences like -*a*ry, -*e*ry, -*o*ry, and -*u*ry. As Janson (21) did with the d-deletion in Swedish, she relied upon introspective judgments of subjects for phonetic data. She presented them with a list of 112 "schwa" words and asked them to classify each word into one of three categories.

There are subregularities here that Hooper duly factored out before correlating the phonetic data with the frequency data. The deletion is blocked, as one might expect, if a sequence results that is not permitted by English phonotactics, as with the vowel laxing discussed earlier. The three varieties of this subregularity, Hooper observes, are when the schwa is preceded by (*a*) a flap (e.g. watery), (*b*) certain consonant clusters (e.g. burglary), or (*c*) affricates (e.g. forgery).

The result of this study is a very good correlation between the phonetic data and the frequency data. The higher the frequency of the word, according to the count by Kucera and Francis, the greater its likelihood of losing its schwa, according to the tabulation of subjects' responses. From this result it would seem that when everything else is equal (which unfortunately is rarely the case), the leading words in a sound change are the most frequent ones.

An important aspect of Hooper's study is that she extended her study to cases of analogical change. In these cases, there has never been any doubt that the process of implementation is via lexical diffusion. In the cases of phonological change that we have recounted, the words undergoing the stages of change are scattered irregularly over the various grammatical categories, making it more difficult for the analyst to observe the fact that the c-stage words are the models and the v-stage words provide the bridge for the change. In contrast, since analogical change typically takes place within paradigms of specific morphological classes, it has always been easy to observe lexical diffusion at work here with its stage by stage progression. Some strong verbs to illustrate the progression are given in Table 2.

A striking difference emerges when we compare these analogical data with the earlier cases in terms of frequency. In Table 2, the leading words are the least frequent ones, whereas the most frequent words are the laggers, a fact that Hooper was able to verify against the Kucera and Francis count. An early prediction of this relationship, which Hooper attributes to Paul around 1886, is thus now confirmed through the availability of the necessary tool.

In the context of the contrasting tendencies between these two types of change, the question naturally arises whether these tendencies can be traced to differences in how the changes are actuated. In discussing this question, Hooper suggests that analogy is actuated in the learning process, whether by child or adult. The less frequent words would be changed earlier (i.e. more vulnerable to overgeneralization by the learner), because it is less likely that the learner has encountered the unchanged form. In phonological changes, on the other hand, which are frequently phonetic reductions, the actuation is probably to be sought in the two-step process of reduced pronunciations in casual or rapid speech by the user and of acquiring the

Table 2 Analogical change by lexical diffusion

u	v	c
kept	crept ~ creeped	bided
left	leapt ~ leaped	reaped
slept	dove ~ dived	seethed
rose	dreamt ~ dreamed	mowed
lost		seeped
knew		

reduced form by the learner. Even though the articulatory gestures in the frequent and infrequent words may be quite comparable in their full forms, the speaker is more likely to reduce the more frequent forms because of their familiarity to the hearer. These are promising ideas that merit further investigations.

Among the languages of the world, only relatively few are associated with sizeable historical documentation. In cases where this exists, we have the opportunity of tracing an individual change through the centuries and arrive at an approximate "chronological profile" for that change. The study by Sherman (42) is aimed at providing such a profile for the development of diatones in English.

Diatones are noun-verb pairs where the stress falls on the first syllable for the noun but the second (or third) syllable for the verb, e.g. address, permit, subject, contract, etc. Evidence from early dictionaries show that such words used to have the stress on the noninitial syllable for both nouns and verbs. For words longer than two syllables, the picture is somewhat more complicated. Note, however, that in words like "delegate," the last syllable is different both in stress and vowel quality depending on whether it is used as a noun or verb, showing an aftereffect of the stress shift.

The stress shift onto the first syllable to mark nouns is a change that started 400 years ago. For example, a word like "affix" was stressed on the second syllable for both noun and verb in 1612, as well as in Samuel Johnson's dictionary of 1755. In 1775, however, it was first entered in John Ash's *New Dictionary of the English Language* as having initial stress when used as a noun. This was, in short, how "affix" became diatonic and how a new diatone entered the lexicon. By referring to some 30 dictionaries and grammars published over these four centuries, Sherman was able to construct a chronological profile of this change. The change apparently is still in progress: of the 1315 disyllabic candidates for this change, where the noun and the verb are homographs, only some 150 have become diatones. See Figure 2.

Many other examples for lexical diffusion can now be given for a variety of languages. When the first cases of lexical diffusion were presented from Chinese data, there was the suspicion that this was an atypical phenomenon that was restricted in its occurrence to languages of the Chinese type, either due to the nonalphabetic orthography or to the noninflectional morphology. This suspicion can no longer be maintained, of course, now that lexical diffusion has been reported for a wide range of languages besides Chinese and English, including Canadian French (9), Dravidian (23), Dutch (14), German (3, 40), Nitinat (12), Swedish (21, 38), and Tibetan (32). It appears to be a basic process of change for all languages that exhibit "orderly heterogeneity," which means, more simply, all human languages.

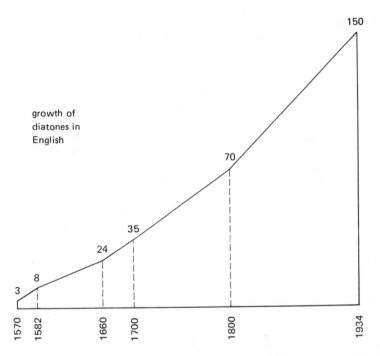

Figure 2 Increase in number of disyllabic diatonic N-V homographs in a chronological profile [based on Sherman (42)].

Several other significant issues arise within the perspective of lexical diffusion, some of which are discussed by Chen & Wang (7). Due to page limitations, I will allude to them only briefly here.

Given the gradualness of the diffusion process across the lexicon, there is no a priori reason to expect the process to complete itself. In particular, the process will be *prevented* from completion when during the course of the diffusion one or more changes compete against it for some of the same words. Some instances of such competing changes have been observed (6, 39) and provide interesting data for examining the dynamic relations of interacting processes along the time dimension.

Another basic issue is the relation of lexical diffusion with processes of language acquisition. Such a relation has been hinted at in my earlier recapitulation of Hooper's results on word frequency and schedule of change. How a child learns a behavior as intricate as language must of course be an extremely complex process, composed of numerous different strategies at various stages. Furthermore, we should not underestimate the considerable differences that must exist from child to child, much as there are such differences across mature individuals. Nonetheless, some very clear data are available from Chinese (19) and from English (11) which show that the acquisition is word-by-word rather than phoneme-by-phoneme, and that there are ontogenetic analogs in the 3-stage progression, i.e. from wrong pronunciations through variable pronunciations to right pronunciations.

Yet another issue of fundamental importance to our understanding of language change is the following. Can we take advantage of the diversity of the lexicon as it undergoes diffusion to arrive at finer genetic subgroupings of the languages or dialects undergoing change? Traditionally such groupings were primarily based on categorical changes—two dialects either share a change or they do not, one single bit of information. But if we take words as units, in cases of lexical diffusion, where for each dialect some words have changed and others have not, then clearly we have access to many more bits of information on which to base the subgrouping.

An early attempt to formulate this idea was made by Hsieh (20), in which a set of Wu dialects were grouped by criteria made available by lexical diffusion on one tone change. The results were encouraging in that they corresponded well with the subgroupings that scholars have made on the basis of other linguistic criteria. More powerful methods have now been developed by Bh. Krishnamurti (23), working with Dravidian languages. By supporting his methods with extensive computer programs and using the valuable *Dravidian Etymological Dictionary* as a point of departure, Krishnamurti has been able to make much more fine-grained comparisons than Hsieh did. Even though the comparisons were made on just a handful of changes, these methods have proved to be successful. With these powerful methods developed and available, the relations within and among the languages of the world can now be investigated with much greater objectivity and precision.

Use of genetic trees in ling.

However, in studying these relations, it is critical to bear in mind the intrinsic limitation that tree diagrams impose. The use of trees is based on analogy with biological speciation [see (42a) for a historical sketch of Darwin's influence on Schleicher]. The vital difference is that whereas species by definition do not interbreed and can transmit features only vertically, languages in contrast typically transmit horizontally as well. Furthermore, the manner of this transmission probably varies with different patterns of population movement, with very interesting consequences on the language histories, as seen in the recent comparison of Indo-European with Sino-Tibetan by Hashimoto (16a).

Conclusions

To conclude, from the studies discussed cursorily in this chapter, several trends in research method can be discerned which depart from the style of earlier scholarship. One has to do with the much larger empirical data base that we can now draw upon, which was not available even a few decades ago. This data base has been enriched both horizontally, in terms of the range of languages and dialects, and also vertically, by the recent availability of more etymological dictionaries and more reliable reconstruction (43b). This method has been especially valuable in the work on Chinese and Dravidian.

Another trend is working in teams. The larger problems in linguistics simply are beyond the scope of single scholars working in isolation—not unlike the situation in other "harder" sciences. Their solution requires the collaboration of a coordinated team of investigators working in a symbiotic environment, each member contributing his own piece of expertise. In the cases of the quantitative work with the Chinese dialects and with the Dravidian languages, some of the expertise required came from outside linguistics proper, namely from statistics and data-processing by computer. Interdisciplinary work is no longer an accidental luxury; for many problems in linguistics such a mode of research is indispensable and must be consciously cultivated.

Lastly, note that current technology has been an important part of several of the studies I discussed. Without the computer to process immense bodies of linguistic data, or without the instruments of experimental phonetics to quantify speech sounds, many of the arguments recapitulated here would lose much of their force.

In providing this discussion of language change with a historical perspective, and in putting some earlier problems in relief, my intention has been to trace the stimuli which led to the present lexical perspective, not to detract from the solid contributions that the neogrammarians have made. Current researches on language change, in many ways, are building on the achievements of our predecessors. Indeed, reading Verner's paper must rank among one of the most exciting experiences for many a budding linguist, as it surely did for me.

Occasionally, one hears the lament from younger scholars who despair that "the truth of today inevitably turns into the mistake of tomorrow."[6] Not so! A more accurate account is rather "the truth of today will be the 'special case' of tomorrow," when, hopefully, our perspective will be widened still more. The neogrammarian conception of language change will probably continue to be part of the truth. With the benefit of richer data and more powerful methods, our perspective on language change has been enlarged. We see that, given the remarkable complexity of language, which we are always too prone to underestimate, changes occur along other paths as well. Hopefully, this wider perspective will provide a more realistic foundation upon which deeper questions concerning language change and language relations can be raised and explored.

[6]Such a distinction was made in a discussion between two biologists, as recounted by Konrad Lorenz in his preface to the reprinting of Darwin's *The Expression of Emotion in Man and Animals.*

Literature Cited

1. Allen, A. 1978. *Lexical diffusion of a derivational morpheme.* Presented at Ling. Soc. Am. Winter Meet.
2. Baldi, P., Werth, R. N., eds. 1978. *Readings in Historical Phonology.* Pennsylvania State Univ. Press
3. Barrack, C. 1976. Lexical diffusion and the High German consonant shift. *Lingua* 40:151–75
4. Bauer, R. 1979. Alveolarization in Cantonese: a case of lexical diffusion. *J. Chin. Ling.* 7:132–41
5. Chen, M. 1972. The time dimension: contribution toward a theory of sound change. *Found. Lang.* 8:457 (Ref. 50)
6. Chen, M., Hsieh, H. I. 1971. The time variable in phonological change. *J. Ling.* 7:1–13
7. Chen, M., Wang, W. S-Y. 1975. Sound change: actuation and implementation. *Language* 51:255–81
8. Cheng, C. C., Wang, W. S-Y. 1972. Tone change in Chaozhon Chinese: a study in lexical diffusion. *Papers in Linguistics in Honor of Henry and Renee Kahane,* ed. B. Kachru et al, pp. 99–113. Univ. Illinois Press (Ref. 50)
9. Dumas, D. 1978. *Phonological Change in Canadian French.* PhD thesis. Univ. Quebec, Quebec, Canada
10. Eimas, P. D., et al. 1971. Speech perception in infants. *Science* 171:303–6
11. Ferguson, C., Farwell, C. B. 1975. Words and sounds in early language acquisition. *Language* 51:419–39 (Ref. 50)
12. Gamble, G. 1977. Nootkan glottalized resonants in Nitinat: a case of lexical diffusion. See Ref. 50
13. Gauchat, L. 1905. L' Unité phonétique dans le patois d' une commune. *Festschr. Heinreich Morf. Halle*
14. Gerritsen, M., Jensen, F. 1978. Word frequency and lexical diffusion in dialect borrowing and phonological change. *Dutch Studies IV, Studies in Dutch Phonology.* Amsterdam
15. Gould, S. J., Eldredge, N. 1977. Punctuated equilibria: the tempo and mode of evolution reconsidered. *Paleobiology* 3:115–51
16. Hashimoto, M. 1972. The linguistic mechanism of flip-flop. *Unicorn* 10:1–19. Princeton Chinese Linguistics Project
16a. Hashimoto, M. 1978. *Language Typology and Geography* (in Japanese). Tokyo: Kōbundō
17. Hockett, C. F. 1965. Sound change. *Language* 41:185–205
18. Hooper, J. 1977. Word frequency in lexical diffusion and the source of morphophonological change. In *Current Progress in Historical Linguistics,* ed. W. Christie, pp. 95–105. Amsterdam
19. Hsieh, H. I. 1972. Lexical diffusion: evidence from child language acquisition. *Glossa* 6:89–104 (Ref. 50)
20. Hsieh, H. I. 1973. A new method of dialect subgrouping. *J. Chin. Ling.* 1:64–92 (Ref. 50)
21. Janson, T. 1977. Reversed lexical diffusion and lexical split: loss of -d in Stockholm (Ref. 50)
22. Krishnamurti, Bh. 1977. Sound change: shared innovation vs. diffusion. *Phonologica,* pp. 205–11
23. Krishnamurti, Bh. 1978. Areal and lexical diffusion of sound change: evidence from Dravidian. *Language* 54:1–20
24. Krishnamurti, Bh., Moses, L., Danforth, D. 1979. Unchanged cognates as a criterion for linguistic subgrouping. Unpublished manuscript
25. Kucera, H., Francis, N. 1967. *Computational Analysis of Present-day American English.* Brown Univ. Press
26. Labov, W. 1972. *Sociolinguistic Patterns.* Univ. Pennsylvania Press
27. Labov, W. 1974. On the use of the present to explain the past. *Proc. 11th Int. Congr. Ling.,* pp. 825–51 (Ref. 2)
27a. Ladefoged, P. 1978. Review of P. Lieberman, *Speech Physiology and Acoustic Phonetics. Language* 54:920–22
28. Lehmann, W. P., ed. 1967. *A Reader in 19th Century Historical Indo-European Linguistics.* Indiana Univ. Press
29. Lehmann, W. P., Malkiel, Y., eds. 1968. *Directions for Historical Linguistics.* Univ. Texas Press
30. Liberman, A. M. 1974. The specialization of the language hemisphere. *The Neurosciences: Third Study Program.* Cambridge: MIT Press
31. Luria, S. E. 1973. *Life—the Unfinished Experiment.* New York
32. Lyovin, A. 1977. Sound change, homophony, and lexical diffusion. See Ref. 50
33. Malkiel, Y. 1967. Each word has a history of its own. *Glossa* 1:137–49
34. Malkiel, Y. 1968. The inflectional paradigm as an occasional determinant of sound change. See Ref. 29
35. Ostoff, C. H., Brugmann, K. 1878. Morphologische Untersuchungen auf dem Gebiete der Indogermanischen Sprachen. English transl. in Ref. 28
36. Paul, H. 1880. *Prinzipien der Sprachgeschichte.* 5th ed., 1920

37. Pedersen, H. 1935. *The Discovery of Language.* Reprinted by Indiana Univ. Press

38. Ralph, B. 1974. *Orderly Profusion.* Goteborg

39. Ramarao, C. 1978. Rule chase. *Indian Ling.* 39:183–88

40. Robinson, O. W. 1977. Rule reordering and lexical diffusion. See Ref. 50

41. Schuchardt, H. 1885. *Uber der Lautgesetze: gegen die Junggrammatiker.* Berlin

42. Sherman, D. 1973. Noun-verb stress alternation: an example of the lexical diffusion of sound change in English. POLA Rep. 17:46–82. Berkeley

42a. Stam, J. H. 1976. *Inquiries into the Origin of Language.* New York: Harper & Row

43. Stevens, K. N. 1972. The quantal nature of speech. In *Human Communication: A Unified View,* ed. E. E. David, P. B. Denes, pp. 51–66. New York: McGraw-Hill

43a. Stevens, K. N. 1978. The speech signal. In *Speech and Language in the Laboratory, School, and Clinic,* ed. J. F. Kavanagh, W. Strange, pp. 3–28. Cambridge: MIT Press

43b. Streeter, M. L. 1972. DOC 1971: a Chinese dialect dictionary on computer. *Computers and Humanities* 6:259–70 (Ref. 50)

44. Sweet, H. 1888. *History of English Sounds.* Oxford Univ. Press

45. Verner, K. 1877. Eine Ausnahme der ersten Lautverschiebung. English transl. In Refs. 2, 28

46. Vogt, H. 1954. Contact of languages. *Word* 10:365–74

47. Wang, W. S-Y. 1967. Phonological features of tone. *Int. J. Am. Ling.* 33:93–105

48. Wang, W. S-Y. 1969. Competing changes as a cause of residue. *Language* 45:9–25 (Ref. 2)

49. Wang, W. S-Y. 1976. Language change. *Ann. NY Acad. Sci.* 280:61–72

50. Wang, W. S-Y., ed. 1977. *The Lexicon in Phonological Change.* The Hague: Mouton

51. Weinreich, U., Labov, W., Herzog, M. I. 1968. Empirical foundations for a theory of language change. See Ref. 29

52. Wheeler, B. I. 1887. *Analogy and the Scope of its Application in Language.* Cornell Univ. Press

53. Wilson, E. O. 1978. *Sociobiology.* Harvard Univ. Press

Ann. Rev. Anthropol. 1979. 8:373–91

NEUROLINGUISTICS ◆9638

John T. Lamendella

Linguistics Program, San Jose State University, San Jose, California 95192

INTRODUCTION

The field of neurolinguistics is one of the many new "hyphenated" disci- *NL* plines established within the past several years, and as such it draws from an interlocking network of related subfields in linguistics, psychology, and the biomedical and neurological sciences. Broadly viewed, its subject matter is "language and brain," and while many of the issues which occupy investigators in this field have been of longstanding concern, the particular blend of goals, methods, and theoretical orientations which provide some degree of coherence to the field are a quite recent development.

One view of neurolinguistics sees it closely allied with the field of linguistics, but in spite of early efforts to outline a unified theoretical framework which merged linguistic theory and neurological facts (e.g. 93, 101), a tight association with linguistic theory has not been sustained. Focusing on language disorders as its principal object of study (with a strong secondary interest in brain lateralization), neurolinguistics proper has actually developed more as a branch of *neurology* than as a branch of linguisitics (see 60, 64). This divergence has perhaps been due in part to a tendency to gravitate toward the already well-established research interests of clinical neurologists and in part to the waning in importance within linguistics of *transformational grammar* (cf 21), and the subsequent absence of one generally accepted theoretical framework within linguistics.

In this country, the initial involvement of theoretical linguistics with biological (and specifically neurological) concerns may to some extent be traced to the work of the late Eric Lenneberg (see 61) which, in conjunction with the "nativist" orientation of transformational theory, turned many linguists' attention away from the preoccupation with overt speech behavior toward the biological bases of our species' capacity to acquire and use language. This shift in emphasis simultaneously contributed to the emer-

373

0084-6570/79/1015-0373$01.00

gence of psycholinguistics as a more or less independent branch of linguistics and psychology emphasizing the study of child language acquisition (see 1). More recently, there has been a partial marriage of psycholinguistic and neurolinguistic concerns revolving around the investigation of congenital language disorders in children (see 9, 62, 68, 82).

As may be seen from the review of neurolinguistic research findings presented by Dingwall & Whitaker (30) in Volume 3 of this series, the range of neurolinguistic interests is quite broad and far-reaching in its implications for that constellation of multidisciplinary concerns which encompass human communication, culture, and cognition (see also 96–99, 102). In this review, I will not attempt to provide a comprehensive (much less exhaustive) survey of neurolinguistics. Rather than a systematic description of empirical findings, I will present a brief personal assessment of the theoretical state of the field as I see it, focusing on certain fundamental issues relevant to the way the field is viewed by both potential users in other disciplines and by investigators in the field.

ORIENTATIONS TO THE FIELD

In confronting neurolinguistic research, the person with little or no background in brain studies may feel oppressed by a morass of exotic Latin names for a seemingly endless array of anatomical structures and physiological processes. The many technical terms derived from specific research paradigms can daunt all but the most persistent linguist or anthropologist. Even worse, perhaps, is the unpleasant extent to which even those articles written for users in other fields may presuppose a good deal of substantive background knowledge, knowledge which as often as not is absent. This problem arises not (only) from a lack of effort on the part of a given author, but from the impossibility of treating a highly specialized research topic while at the same time providing an adequate review of basic material for the general reader. The problem is of sufficient magnitude that it is difficult for many users in the social and behavioral sciences to "tap into" the primary literature of the field in order to monitor relevant findings. Needless to say, there is no easy solution to this problem beyond believing that a nonspecialist user first needs to assess the degree to which neurolinguistic evidence and explanations are relevant to his/her proper concerns, and, to that degree, be willing to devote time and effort toward acquiring necessary background knowledge. The level of neurological acumen among social and behavioral scientists, and even for the humanities, has already grown considerably. As more and more students take courses in basic neuroscience as an auxiliary component of their graduate programs, the problem of limited access to primary research findings in neurolinguistics should diminish.

Non-neurolinguists concerned with language, mind, and culture can be roughly divided into three categories: those who feel that neurological evidence on language and the brain is relevant to their interests, those who feel that it is not relevant, and those who aren't sure one way or the other. The manifestations of these beliefs range from outright hostility, through indifference, to rabid enthusiasm. Because the attitudes of potential users of neurolinguistic evidence bear directly on the assessment of the state of the field with regard to its potential contribution to other fields, let us consider in turn four hypothetical stances which reflect divergent attitudes toward the significance of neurolinguistic research findings:

Attitudes towards NL

1. *Knowledge gained from studies of the brain, while perhaps interesting in its own right, will ultimately prove irrelevant to understanding human cognitive behavior since the principles upon which human cognition are based are of a fundamentally different existential order from the principles upon which brain activity is based.*

Although most nonphilosophers have been prone to forget the fact, twentieth century science operates from highly specific (but usually implicit) philosophical assumptions about the nature of knowledge (i.e. *epistomological* assumptions) and the ultimate nature of being (i.e. *ontological* assumptions). For the most part, the neurosciences have embodied a version of *naive realism* which blithely assumes that the scientific investigator is simply an "objective observer" who attempts to describe reality as it is in the absolute. However, from the viewpoint of the modern physicist, the concrete objects of our ordinary perception fade away into mostly empty space and probabilistic energy patterns of uncertain status whose properties depend in crucial way on the observational criteria brought to bear by a particular observer. The abstract theoretical constructs of a field such as neurolinguistics have even less claim to any kind of absolute reality. Naive realism ignores the substantive role of the scientific observer who, by choosing the parameters of observation, and by selective juggling of figure/ground relationships, as well as by the very act of observation itself, virtually creates the "objects" to be described. Counterintuitive though it may seem to the "natural attitude," both concrete objects and theoretical objects exist only as culturally conditioned consensual constructs arising via transactions between observers and the properties adhering in the universe [see Bunge (17) for discussion of the philosophical impact in the natural sciences of relativistic notions concerning the nature of objects in the universe].

Consensual agreement based on our manner of viewing the "evidence" cannot in itself guarantee the absolute correctness of our conclusion that the brain is "responsible" for human language and cognition. Most neuroscientists consider cognitive processes to *be* brain processes, or at most an alternative characterization of the same absolute reality [cf the "identity hypothesis" in philosophy; see Feigl (31)], and the position reflected by Statement 1 is therefore perfunctorily dismissed. However, a philosophical issue at the heart of neurolinguistic explanation is the age-old question of the relationship between *mind* and *body* (or *mind* and *brain*). In studies of brain and language, this issue has more often been embedded in the "locationist" versus "diffusionist" controversy. Some investigators attempt to localize particular cognitive functions in brain "centers" (or in "areas" or "regions" of brain tissue), and other investigators resist the identification of particular brain tissue as having responsibility for particular functions [for a historical treatment of this issue in relation to brain studies more generally, see (22, 23; see also 5, 12, 64, 72)].

It is beyond argument that a great many empirical correlations between brain activity and overt behavior have been identified. Damage to the brain results in particular sorts of linguistic and cognitive deficits. However, the strength of the intercorrelations between damage to a particular brain region and the specific behavioral impairments in speech performance concomitant to this damage is not quite high enough to force an otherwise doubtful person to agree that the brain tissue in question is "responsible" for carrying out that behavior, as against merely being some kind of "precondition" for normal behavior, or just one component in some larger system. We would be in a position to summarily dismiss Statement 1 as false if and only if we had available some well-worked-out formal metatheoretical framework in terms of which we could understand the nature of mind and its relationship to the brain and body. The popular wisdom in the field that human language and cognition are the product of brain processes is actually not an incontrovertible empirical fact or an unarguable philosophical conclusion; even if this consensus is correct (and I believe it is), it is hardly clear what it means. Our belief at this point has more the status of a working hypothesis than a proven fact. Until an adequate metatheoretical foundation is established for the neurosciences, we can only affirm our conviction that in some presently unknown fashion, brain processes are responsible for the acquisition and utilization of the linguistic structures which are manifested in overt speech behavior.

2. *Nothing significant is now known about the functioning of the brain, and it will be several hundred years before our understanding of brain processes approaches a level which is adequate for explaining human communication, cognition, and culture.*

This position, more common than might be supposed (if mutterings at conferences are to be believed), is also to some extent within the bounds of legitimate difference of opinion, even given the large volume of facts uncovered since the middle of the nineteenth century about the associations between covert brain activity, i.e. *microbehavior* and publicly observable *macrobehavior*. On the other hand, I suspect that few linguists would propose that neurolinguistics can safely ignore theoretical developments in linguistics simply because our current understanding of human language is woefully inadequate. The key word in Statement 2 is "significant," since converting *"facts"* of behavior into *"evidence"* about functional organization is at best a tricky business, and, depending on what one is interested in, it may be true that neurolinguistics has little or nothing to contribute at this point in time.

It might be difficult to completely satisfy the descriptive linguist who belligerently asks: "OK, you tell me, based on neurolinguistic evidence, what it is that I must believe about the basic structure of language that I didn't already know from other sources?" However, linguists with a more "open" attitude should not fail to see the many ways in which neurolinguistic data bear directly on attempts to test and confirm specific linguistic hypotheses at all levels of language structure (see 86; see also 10, 19, 80, 83–85, 91, 95). If neurolinguistics seems less relevant to fundamental aspects of linguistic theory than one would hope, the reason is less likely to be an inadequate level of understanding of brain processes than the relatively low level of interest most theoretical linguists have thus far shown in applying neurolinguistic and psycholinguistic data to the development of linguistic theory.

Clinical neurologists and neuropsychologists have their own empirical and theoretical axes to grind, and, more often than not, possess little understanding of, or interest in theoretical linguistics. If, as a field, linguistics merely waits for neurolinguistic insights into language structure to develop on their own, the field may indeed wait several hundred years. However, a certain amount of optimism is in order since increasing numbers of linguists have been carrying out neurolinguistic research and, if they can resist the temptation to become aphasiologists or neuropsychologists instead of linguists, the not too distant future might produce insights into language which could satisfy all but the most recalcitrant believer in Statement 2. For example, Schnitzer (86) has made a promising start toward the development of a dynamic neurolinguistic theory of language based on *stratificational grammar* (cf 52) and, along the way, presents a quite satisfying way of viewing the troublesome "competence/performance" distinction in neurolinguistic terms.

Cultural anthropologists may be understandably skeptical about the immediate relevance of neurolinguistic findings for ethnographic description, but even in this seemingly distant interest, many lines of connection are discernible. For example, questions about individual and group variability in cognitive mode and style could profit from consideration of the literature on laterality in brain processing. This research has identified complexes of specialized linguistic and cognitive functions that seem to be carried out preferentially (or exclusively) in relation to one cerebral hemisphere rather than the other, or both (see 25, 27, 28, 35, 44, 50, 87). Linguistic and other sorts of symbolic information processing in neural systems have clear and direct relevance to attempts to investigate cultural symbolism and symbolic behavior [for discussion of symbolic and other semiotic functions in brain systems, see Lamendella (56); cf also (32, 58)].

The recently developed concern among neurolinguists and others in male/female differences in brain anatomy and cognitive processing bears directly on gender differences, sex roles, and sex-stereotyped behavior across different cultures (see 34, 51, 66, 75, 104). This same body of research incorporates a strong concern for other ethnographically significant variables such as social class, occupation, age, and family history (see 14, 15, 36). Although it is generally assumed that all genetic subpopulations within our species have the "same" neural equipment, with brain organization differing only at the individual level, it is certainly worth determining whether the correlation of population genetics with asymmetries of brain anatomy [see Galaburda et al (33) for a general review] and with language processing in lateralized brain systems can add to our understanding of the specific combinations of biological and cultural factors contributing to individual and group variability at various levels of functional organization.

Physical and biological anthropologists concerned with cross-species comparisons in anatomy and behavior, and with human evolution and prehistory, perhaps do not need to be convinced of the relevance of neurolinguistic findings to these interests [see, for example, Laughlin & D'Aquili (59) for a general theoretical approach to brain systems from within anthropology]. For example, close ties already exist in relation to the recent investigations into the origins of speech and language over the course of hominid evolution [see Dingwall (29) for a comprehensive review of current research into the evolution of human communication; for a compendium of such research, see Harnad et al (45)].

As anthropologists might suspect, cross-cultural verification of neurolinguistic findings is all but absent, with the result that anthropologists have a good deal to contribute to neurolinguistic research, rather than only being in the position of potential users. The basis for the investigation of cross-cultural variables in language and brain research has begun to develop around the investigation of aphasic disorders in monolingual speakers of languages other than the standard Indo-European languages, in bilinguals, and in polyglots (for review see 3, 73).

Given the centrality of language in human cognition and culture, it would be foolhardy for psychologists or anthropologists to decide in advance to totally ignore findings in neurolinguistics on the supposition that nothing of significance is known about brain organization. My purpose here has not been to convince someone who believes Statement 2 that it is false, but only to temper the quality of such a conviction with the realization that neurolinguistic findings are ignored at the expense of being able to profit from whatever degree of significance these findings do have for a given research concern. Such evidence can minimally provide constraints on the sorts of theoretical positions held, since hypotheses in some other discipline which are contravened by known neurological facts should be modified to bring them in line with the total body of evidence available.

3. *While a few details remain to be clarified, our ability to explain the manner in which neural systems operate is essentially complete, and it only remains to apply this understanding to the explanation of communication, cognition, and culture.*

I think it is safe to say that this view is patently false. There is a sizable body of knowledge currently in existence which identifies significant empirical correlations between research variables from brain studies and research variables in the study of overt macrobehavior. Nevertheless, there has been a notable lack of theoretical understanding of the functional implications of these facts or the causal factors which underlie the observed correlations. No means exist at this time for incorporating these facts into a comprehensive, formal account of cognitive information processing in neural systems. It is not clear to me, for example, that our theoretical understanding of the functional basis in the brain for language disorders has progressed to any amazing degree beyond that possessed by the founders of nineteenth century neurology of language [for example, J. Hughlings Jackson; see (90)].

We do know a good deal more about the symptomological character of specific disorders, their pathological bases, and their correlations with other behaviors. Many highly revealing case studies exist, but apart from the identification of damage to particular cortical (and subcortical) regions as correlating with particular sorts of behaviors and behavioral deficits, neither the anatomical, physiological, nor functional organization of the responsible brain systems has been explained in a way which goes much beyond Hughlings Jackson's insightful understanding of a century ago. It is important to be able to point to the brain sites where speech functions are "represented," but it would be of much greater theoretical significance to have some idea of how speech functions are represented in these sites. To know that a given functional activity correlates with the activity of one cerebral hemisphere rather than the other (or both) is interesting, but to be content with this level of knowledge is to be satisfied with too little.

Many investigators would perhaps agree with such sentiments, but would be quick to point out that the goal of comprehensive theory construction can only be approached when our "data base" becomes adequate. With only a few exceptions [N. Geschwind, for example; see (37)], mid-twentieth century neurolinguistic investigators have not been overly concerned with a functional understanding of language processing in brain systems, as against a consuming preoccupation with the gathering of additional data on behavioral manifestations of functional processing, analyzing and organizing these data to draw quite restricted conclusions at a shallow theoretical depth. Naturally, these conclusions are strictly bound to the specific observational parameters and analytical methods employed in a particular study, and are therefore difficult to relate systematically to other similar studies and impossible to generalize to the species at large. Also troublesome are the many methodological problems which make problematic the justification of even limited inferences from many empirical studies (e.g. 24, 42, 76, 79). No less real when they go unnoticed are the prodigious leaps of faith which often occur between the "Results" section and the "Conclusions" section of empirical reports, a popular place to magically transform operationally defined technical terms back into ordinary English words with their attendant vague connotations. Responsible researchers in the field oblige themselves to restrict conclusions to the level supported by the evidence, often with the result that the meaning and significance of these findings remain obscure to anyone outside that sub-branch of the field.

An examination of the literature in neurolinguistics does not reveal a single example of a formal model which presents an explicit processual characterization of the flow of information in neuropsychological systems. This stands in contrast to the many sorts of formal models presented within information-processing psychology concerning language, thought, and memory (e.g. 4, 11, 41, 78, 81). The mutual lack of interest between neurolinguistics and this branch of cognitive psychology persists to the detriment of both disciplines.

The non-neurolinguist who attempts to extrapolate to the general understanding which is legitimately supported by current findings in neurolinguistics is likely to run up against a great many atomistic clusterings of unrelatable facts and a painful absence of any overall formal theoretical framework that systematically supports interpretations of these facts.[1] Pos-

---

[1]Let me stress that these comments should not be taken as an antiempirical stance, but only a plea of recognition of the nature and limitations of empirical data as only one component (albeit a necessary component) in the derivation of comprehensive theoretical understanding in any discipline. I also do not mean to pick out neurolinguistics as especially remiss in failing to give theory its due, since such comments could be directed at many other disciplines as well. The pendulum of scientific fashion and fad will perhaps swing back toward abstract theorizing at some point, leaving armchair neurolinguists needing to be reminded that theories require data for their validation.

iting theoretical explanations which are not immediately verifiable in terms of existing evidence runs counter to the spirit of the times, and the value of unverified theoretical formulations (which are nevertheless congruent with all available evidence) in guiding and structuring empirical research is all but ignored. This is unfortunate since, in principle, empirical facts "underdetermine" theoretical hypotheses; that is, no matter how many facts are amassed, they can at best disconfirm incorrect hypotheses, but can never *prove* the correctness of any given theoretical formulation. There are always an indeterminate number of contradictory alternative hypotheses consistent with the same body of data and possessing the same predictive power.

One accommodation to this fact of scientific life might be an attempt to formulate the abstract properties of the range of possible models consistent with a given body of evidence, on the supposition that it is this set of properties which best represents the understanding actually supported by the evidence. The more prevalent accommodation within major segments of psychology and the neurosciences has been a lowering of research goals to remain satisfied with the accumulation of additional facts and shallow theoretical inferences, and no systematic means to determine the level of theoretical understanding which actually obtains. The present tendency to overvalue particularistic empirical findings to the exclusion of global theoretical explanation is self-defeating and futile in the long run.

Laments about the current "spirit" of the field aside, it is perhaps the case that for some people, both positions 2 and 3 reflect the implicit belief that at the point when our understanding of the brain becomes "adequate," the majority of theoretical problems in the social and behavioral sciences will somehow be resolved, or at least resolvable. Such a belief in fact follows from the *reductionist* assumptions which have been at the foundation of twentieth century American science: i.e. the highly dubious notion that psychology somehow reduces to neurology, neurology reduces to biology, biology reduces to chemistry, and chemistry reduces to physics (and thus that the physicist will have the final word on all theoretical issues in science).

A more plausible (nonreductionist) approach would recognize that whatever the "ultimate" nature of reality, the universe may validly be seen as organized into a hierarchically ordered gradient of *levels,* each level characterized by properties and processes that adhere to it alone and are not possessed by the next level down in the hierarchy [cf arguments pro and con presented by Ayala & Dobzhansky (6); cf also (8)]. Thus, for example, *molecules* are not simply conglomerates of atoms, but holistic gestalts with unique properties not explicable (or even directly observable) at the atomic level. Similarly, *cells* are not merely aggregates of molecules, but higher level unities with properties that arise from the organization of cellular components. In short, both molecules and cells are *systems.* Systems cannot be understood if one relies exclusively on a study of their parts individually. A system is precisely an organization of parts in which the *functional relations* between parts are determined by the relationship of each part to the whole, and thus invisible to a level-specific approach. Systems have an intrinsic organization which establishes their existence at a level above their constituent parts. Any attempt to describe a system that does not begin with coherent hypotheses about the general nature of the system will leave the investigator in roughly the same position as the proverbial blind sages who each derived a different (wrong) understanding of the nature of elephants.

In the nonreductionist view espoused here, cognitive systems do not reduce to brain processes, but are "lifts" off of brain activity, higher level functional unities greater than the sum of their neuroanatomical and neuro-physiological parts. A strong entailment of nonreductionist views is the belief that even were our understanding of brain processes adequate, there is no sense in which the goals of linguistics, psychology, or anthropology would ipso facto have been achieved.

Some of those people in other disciplines who overenthusiastically accept tentative neurolinguistic findings as the entire story may do so because there is always the temptation to assume that it is only in one's own field that complexities abound, and that contributory fields contain only simple, un-controversial answers. Some of those who globally and incorrectly reject the significance of neurological evidence might be reacting against the need to master yet another body of knowledge which, in the end, may or may not pay dividends in the currency of increased understanding of one's own special interests. Whatever the actual reasons why the beliefs reflected in Statements 2 and 3 are held, to my mind neither is true as stated, and I think that many people in the field might argue for a fourth position:

4. *At the present time, a good deal is understood about the nature of brain functioning, but a good deal remains unknown. Neurolinguistic evidence should take its place along with evidence from other frameworks in contribut-ing to the best understanding of communication, cognition, and culture which we can derive at this stage of the field's development.*

The sheer volume of empirical findings, and the breadth of research interests which have developed in neurolinguistics since the 1960s, is quite impressive. Recent technological advances have placed powerful research tools in the hands of the neurolinguist; of particular note is *computerized tomography* (CT Scan), a radiographic technique which allows the quick and easy localization of brain lesions and thus, in conjunction with diagnos-tic testing, an excellent basis for correlating neural pathology and behav-ioral symptomology (see 69). Also of great value are the many new experimental techniques which have opened the door to the study of neuro-linguistic processing in *normal* individuals, thereby providing an important check on conclusions possibly limited to, or confounded by *disordered* brain functioning. Examples of research techniques applicable to speech and language processing in normal individuals are: (*a*) *dichotic listening* (see 7, 88, 89); (*b*) *EEG research* (see 18, 26, 63); (*c*) *conjugate lateral eye movements* (see 43, 94); (*d*) *delayed auditory feedback* (see 13) and (*e*) *visual half-field research* (see 46, 103).

Potential users of neurolinguistic research findings would hopefully not operate from fixed beliefs established in advance of serious consideration of the available evidence and determination of the actual relevance particular findings have to their specific interests. Neurolinguistic evidence should be taken into account where appropriate, without overreacting either in the direction of falsely upgrading or downgrading the degree of understanding which exists in the field or the potential of this domain of evidence to provide explanations in other disciplines. Neurolinguists themselves might pause in thier empirical pursuits long enough to assess the most appropriate theoretical goals for the field and the most productive empirical means to achieve those ends.

FUNCTIONAL ORGANIZATION OF HUMAN COMMUNICATION SYSTEMS

One approach to neurolinguistics sees its special concern to be the *formal levels description and explanation of the functional organization and operation of hierarchy neural information-processing systems for speech and language.* As discussed by Hughlings Jackson, a pervasive characteristic of the nervous system is its organization into a *levels hierarchy,* each level of anatomy being correlatable with particular sorts of physiological activity and functional roles. Of course, there are many criteria by which one can decompose the nervous system into a levels hierarchy; e.g. one can construct a hierarchical view according to the manner in which the brain evolved, the manner in which it matures during child development, or the functional organization that underlies normal or pathological behavior. All three perspectives are derivable from inferences based on correlations between overt macrobehavior and covert microbehavior, and all three overlap considerably. Many valuable generalizations can be made about brain organization from all three simultaneously [see, for example, Milner (67); for further discussion, see Lamendella (54–56)]. For example, it is generally the case that the lower a structure or function lies in its neural hierarchy, the earlier it arose in the evolution of species, i.e. *phylogenetically,* and the earlier it tends to become operational in the maturation of the individual, i.e. *ontogenetically.*

Thus, low level spinal reflexes are phylogenetically old and develop early in the ontogeny of the nervous system. Cognitive functions are correlated with higher levels of anatomy and physiology, are phylogenetically newer, and arise later in ontogeny [see (53) for discussion of possible relations between the evolution of language in our species and maturational stages in child language acquisition; cf (40)].

The lower a functional system lies in its neural hierarchy, the more fully it tends to be specified in the genetic material (i.e. the more "innate" it tends to be), and the less it needs particular environmental experience and learning for normal development to occur. The higher a system is, the less genetically determined it tends to be, the more individual experience and cultural norms play a role in development, and the wider the range of individual differences which may be observed in adult behavior. For example, the spinal level knee jerk reflex does not have to be learned and is highly consistent in our species. Cognitive and linguistic systems require a protracted period of acquisition and exhibit a good deal of individual variation in developmental schedule and range of possible "normal" behavior patterns exhibited.

Although they involve structures and functions across a large number of levels and a variety of functional domains, especially in relation to speech perception and speech production functions, neurofunctional systems for speech and language depend in some essential way on the physiological activity and anatomical structures at the highest levels of *cortical* organization.[2] We might say that speech and language are "represented" in these cortical structures, if we remember the highly abstract, vague meaning this term has outside of a formal model of functional representation in neural systems. Additionally, a good deal of evidence has been presented that speech functions also involve a variety of *subcortical* structures, particularly the *thalamus,* a forebrain complex which participates in a large number of functional domains and for which lateralized speech activity has been inferred (cf 70, 71; see also 65).

The attempt to determine the manner in which behavioral impairments concomitant to brain lesions may usefully be grouped into distinct syndromes with regular symptomological manifestations has remained one of the major foci of clinically oriented neurolinguistic research. However, the nonspecialist who happens to read two different treatments of language disorders might wonder if it is the same body of evidence at issue. One

[2]Cortical structures in the brain are marked by cells arranged in more or less distinct layers (Latin *cortex* "bark, rind") and there exist a great many different types of cortex. The most complex and highest level cortical structures are the varieties of six-layered *neocortex* (*Isocortex*) of the cerebral hemispheres.

treatment may make no mention at all of "language areas" in the brain and lump all aphasic syndromes into a small number of general categories. A second treatment may identify several specific brain regions as "language areas" and provide a long list of distinct aphasic syndromes, each character-ized by a set of criterial symptoms. These differences reflect continuing disagreement in the field on the "locationist versus diffusionist" controversy and the extent to which classificatory schemata based on behavioral symp-tomology can justifiably be viewed as supporting the existence of distinct aphasic syndromes with stable characteristics across large numbers of aphasic patients [for nontechnical reviews of language disorders, see (39, 100)]. Whatever they call them, clinical investigators are in basic agreement on the two major categories of aphasic disorders: *expressive disorders* result-ing most often from anterior lesions in secondary motor cortex of the cerebral hemispheres, and *receptive disorders* resulting most often from posterior lesions in secondary sensory regions.

Disagreement also exists over the extent to which the two most generally recognized "language areas" of the "dominant" hemisphere, *Broca's area* in the frontal lobes and *Wernicke's area* within the tempero-parietal region, exist as coherent functional entities tied to specific regions of cortex. Con-troversy remains on the extent to which these areas are specifically linguistic in character versus a manifestation of more general motor or sensory pro-cessing systems (cf 49, 74). No consensus has been reached on whether Broca's and Wernicke's areas are true "language" areas or only lower level "speech" areas.

Confounding such a determination is the existence of a continuum from automatic to propositional speech modes, the former involving utterances which are less meaningful, memorized, or more frequent (e.g. expletives, songs, social formulas), and the latter involving expressions which are meaningful, productive, or novel. [For a review of this issue, see Van Lancker (92); for discussion of this issue in relation to second language acquisition, see Lamendella (57).] For many aphasic patients, automated speech behaviors may persist in the face of the virtual loss of propositional speech and no evidence of any internal mental experience. With global loss of speech comprehension and speech formulation capabilities, some patients may retain the capacity to carry out certain low level grammatical opera-tions during the compulsive echoing of utterances presented to them [see H. Whitaker (95) for an extremely interesting case study with important implications for linguistic theory].

Those few neurolinguistic investigators who have dealt with the issue at all have been very cautious when drawing conclusions about the conscious experience of aphasic patients based on their internal reports. However, if appropriate controls were exercised, the internal reports of aphasics could provide an important basis for understanding many aspects of human consciousness and thought, particularly in relation to the role that inner speech plays in our interior mental experience. Interpersonal communication functions are the most visible (or audible) aspect of language. Intrapersonal cognitive coding functions in thought, memory, problem solving, etc are at least as important in the overall adaptation of the human species. In spite of obvious methodological difficulties, neurolinguistic evidence from aphasics and other neurologically impaired individuals has a potentially strong part to play in the investigation of human consciousness and its realization in brain systems (see 16, 35, 38). This issue relates directly to the question of automatic versus propositional speech modes in that the latter involves "volitional" and "conscious" elements lacking in the former. The extent to which aphasic disorders involve only the "disruption" of speech performance versus the "loss" of language capabilities is scarcely approachable apart from a broad theoretical framework which attempts to account for consciousness and thought.

Theoretical linguists could not be content to merely identify a "phonological" level of language structure and not go on to derive a theory of the organization of phonological structures. Theoretical neurolinguists should not be content to identify a *"motor speech region"* (Broca's area) or a *"Sensory speech region"* (Wernicke's area) without having as a high priority the description of the organization of speech functions and subfunctions which accounts for the capacity of these areas to process speech. Whether our concern is the understanding of functional organization for neurologically impaired individuals or normal individuals, some major portion of the field's energies should be devoted to a formal theory of neurolinguistic organization in brain systems.

The levels of language structure with which linguists are familiar obviously relate to functional hierarchies of neurolinguistic systems (cf 86), and the bulk of neurolinguistic research has thus far been carried out with reference to the lateralized neocortical systems involved in specifically linguistic behavior. However, our species utilizes many different types of *nonverbal* communication systems, most of them residing at lower levels than language, but some of them symbolic systems seemingly on a par with language (e.g. 47, 48, 56). Any general neurolinguistic theory which attempted to account for language behavior would hopefully recognize the need to place language within the context of the entire range of communication functions in neural systems across various levels of brain organization.

The single most important non-neocortical, nonlinguistic neurofunctional system involved in human communication is the *limbic system,* based on a complex of cortical and subcortical forebrain structures located in the "center" portion of the brain (see 54, 77). The limbic system is part of our mammalian heritage and the basis for fundamental aspects of our appetitite, emotional, social, and communicative behavior.[3] We continue to share many types of nonverbal social communication functions with other mammals and primates based on appetitive and affective level limbic activity. Up to some point in hominid evolution, it was the limbic system which was responsible for communication in a social context. The neocortical systems for speech and language identifiable in *Homo sapiens* represent overlays on these limbic functions, incorporating them into a higher level gestalt that includes verbal and nonverbal functions simultaneously. Up to some point in human ontogeny, it is the limbic system which is the principal basis for the child's communicative interactions. As adults, multimodal limbic gesture complexes continue to play an important role in constructing and interpreting the total "message" which is being communicated by speech utterances.

Our understanding of neurological disorders and their implications for speech and language organization in neocortical systems is made more difficult because superseded lower level functional systems are not eliminated when higher systems become operational in ontogenetic development, but only become subject to inhibitory influences as they are incorporated into higher level metasystems. If a higher level metasystem is disrupted due to a brain lesion, a new functional organization emerges which may find lower level systems playing different and/or augmented roles in the new behavioral patterns which result. The breakdown of cognitive and linguistic capacities which occurs in senility is not haphazard, and seems to exhibit interesting similarities (and differences) with the manner in which these functional capacities arose during the maturational process (cf 2, 20). Thus, it is not only for a broader perspective that lower level nonverbal communication systems should be taken into account by neurolinguists, but because disruption of speech and language systems in neurological disorders cannot be fully understood apart from them. Since evidence from neurological disorders will most likely remain our principal source of data concerning speech and language systems in the brain, it becomes even more important to develop coherent views of language that recognize it as only one form of human communication.

SUMMARY

The task facing the field of neurolinguistics is a difficult one; i.e. the development of an adequate formal theory of the organization and operation of neurofunctional systems for speech and language. Too exclusive a focus on

---

[3]In the only humorous remark ever publicly uttered by a neuropsychologist, Karl Pribram has characterized the limbic system as having responsibility for the "Four F's": fear, flight, feeding, and reproduction.

any one facet of this enterprise, whether on empirical facts or abstract theory, leads to an imbalance that will surely impede progress in our understanding of language and brain. Since language processing is comprehensible only in light of cognitive information processing more generally, any adequate theory of speech and language must at the same time incorporate a theory of human cognition. Since the acquisition of language capabilities is highly subject to environmental modification, it would be serious mistake to ignore cultural and individual variables in interpreting neurolinguistic findings. Since speech and language are only part of human communication, they must ultimately be considered in light of the entire hierarchy of communication systems characteristic of our species. In developing an adequate formal theory of language and brain, three distinct but integrated perspectives will have to be managed simultaneously: overt *speech and language behavior,* covert *neuroanatomy and neurophysiology,* and the *functional organization of speech and language systems* viewed as a contingent reality.

In this review, I have provided a personal perspective on the field of neurolinguistics that addresses a two-sided concern: attitudes of investigators in other disciplines toward the potential utilization of neurolinguistic research findings, and attitudes of neurolinguists themselves toward the nature and goals of the field. I have stressed the need for a formal theory of neurolinguistic systems in terms of which empirical findings may best be interpreted and understood. For other purposes, I could just as easily have stressed the many exciting insights into language and brain which have been developed within the field. Overall, I think it is safe to say that a good deal is presently understood about the nature of brain functioning in relation to speech and language, but a good deal remains unknown. Neurolinguistic evidence should take its place along with evidence from other frameworks in contributing to the best theoretical understanding of communication, cognition, and culture which we can derive at this stage of the field's development.

Literature Cited

1. Abrahamsen, A. A. 1977. *Child Language: An Interdisciplinary Guide to Theory and Research.* Baltimore: Univ. Park Press
2. Ajuriaguerra, J. de, Tissot, R. 1975. Some aspects of language in various forms of senile dementia (comparisons with language in childhood). See Ref. 62, 1:323–39
3. Albert, M. L., Obler, L. K. 1978. *The Bilingual Brain.* New York: Academic
4. Anderson, J. R. 1976. *Language, Memory, and Thought.* New York: Wiley
5. Anderson, R. M. 1974. Wholistic and particulate approaches in neuropsychology. In *Cognition and the Symbolic Process,* ed. W. B. Weimer, D. S. Palermo, pp. 389–96. Hillsdale, NJ: Erlbaum
6. Ayala, F. J., Dobzhansky, T., eds. 1974. *Studies in the Philosophy of Biology.* Berkeley: Univ. California Press
7. Berlin, C. I. 1977. Hemispheric asymmetry in auditory tasks. See Ref. 44, pp. 303–23
8. Bertalanffy, L. von. 1968. *General Systems Theory.* New York: Braziller

9. Bloom, L., Lahey, M., eds. 1978. *Language Development and Language Disorders.* New York: Wiley
10. Blumstein, S. E. 1973. *A Phonological Investigation of Aphasic Speech.* The Hague: Mouton
11. Bobrow, D. G., Collins, A., eds. 1975. *Representation and Understanding.* New York: Academic
12. Bogen, J. E., Bogen, G. M. 1976. Wernicke's region—Where is it? See Ref. 45, pp. 833–43
13. Boller, F., Vrtunski, P. B., Kim, Y., Mack, J. L. 1978. Delayed auditory feedback and aphasia. *Cortex* 14(2): 212–26
14. Borowy, T., Goebel, R. 1976. Cerebral lateralization of speech: the effects of age, sex, race, and socioeconomic class. *Neuropsychologia* 14(3):363–70
15. Briggs, G. G., Nebes, R. D. 1976. The effects of handedness, family history and sex on the performance of a dichotic listening task. *Neuropsychologia* 14(1):129–33
16. Brown, J. W. 1977. *Mind, Brain, and Consciousness.* New York: Academic
17. Bunge, M. 1959. *Metascientific Queries.* Springfield, Ill: Thomas
18. Callaway, E. 1975. *Brain Electrical Potentials and Individual Psychological Differences.* New York: Grune & Stratton
19. Caplan, D., Holmes, J. M., Marshall, J. C. 1974. Word classes and hemispheric specialization. *Neuropsychologia* 12:331–37
20. Caramazza, A., Zurif, E. B., eds. 1978. *Language Acquistion and Language Breakdown: Parallels and Divergencies.* Baltimore: Johns Hopkins
21. Chomsky, N. 1965. *Aspects of the Theory of Syntax.* Cambridge, Mass: MIT Press
22. Clarke, E., Dewhurst, K. 1972. *An Illustrated History of Brain Function.* Berkeley: Univ. California Press
23. Clarke, E., O'Malley, C. D. 1968. *The Human Brain and Spinal Cord: An Historical Study Illustrated by Writings from Antiquity to the Twentieth Century.* Berkeley: Univ. California Press
24. Colbourn, C. J. 1978. Can laterality be measured? *Neuropsychologia* 16(3): 283–89
25. Corballis, M., Beale, I. L. 1976. *The Psychology of Left and Right.* New York: Halsted
26. Desmedt, J. E. 1977. *Language and Hemispheric Specialization in Man: Event-related Cerebral Potentials, Progress in Clinical Neurophysiology,* Vol. 3. Basel: Karger
27. Dimond, S. J., Beaumont, J. G., eds. 1974. *Hemispheric Function in the Human Brain.* New York: Wiley
28. Dimond, S. J., Blizard, D. A., eds. 1977. *Evolution and Lateralization of the Brain, Annals of the NYAS,* Vol. 229. New York Acad. Sci.
29. Dingwall, W. O. 1979. The evolution of human communication systems. See Ref. 99, Vol. 4
30. Dingwall, W. O., Whitaker, H. A. 1974. Neurolinguistics. *Ann. Rev. Anthropol.* 3:323–56
31. Feigl, H. 1967. *The 'Mental' and the 'Physical.'* Minneapolis: Univ. Minnesota Press
32. Gainotti, G., Lemmo, M. A. 1976. Comprehension of symbolic gestures in aphasia. *Brain Lang.* 3:451–60
33. Galaburda, A. M., LeMay, M., Kemper, T. L., Geschwind, N. 1978. Right-left asymmetries in the brain. *Science* 199:852–56
34. Gannett-Conrad, C. L. 1978. *Sex and the single brain: A neurolinguistic perspective on language and literature.* Presented at World Congr. Sociol., Uppsala, Sweden
35. Gazzaniga, M. S., LeDoux, J. E. 1978. *The Integrated Mind.* New York: Plenum
36. Geffner, D. S., Dorman, M. F. 1976. Hemispheric specialization for speech perception in four-year-old children from low and middle socioeconomic classes. *Cortex* 12(1):71–73
37. Geschwind, N. 1974. *Selected Papers on Language and the Brain.* Boston: Reidel
38. Globus, G. G., Maxwell, G., Savodnik, I., eds. 1976. *Consciousness and the Brain.* New York: Plenum
39. Goodglass, H., Geschwind, N. 1976. Language disorders (aphasia). In *Language and Speech,* ed. E. C. Carterette, M. P. Friedman. *Handbook of Perception* 7:390–428. New York: Academic
40. Gould, S. J. 1977. *Ontogeny and Phylogeny.* Cambridge, Mass: Harvard Univ. Press.
41. Gregg, L. W., ed. 1974. *Knowledge and Cognition.* New York: Wiley
42. Grözinger, B., Kornhuber, H. H., Kriebel, J. 1975. Methodological problems in the investigation of cerebral potentials preceding speech: determining the onset and suppressing artefacts caused by speech. *Neuropsychologia* 13:263–70
43. Gur, Raquel, Gur, Reuben 1977. Corre-

lates of conjugate lateral eye movements in man. See Ref. 44, pp. 261–81

44. Harnad, S. R., Doty, R. W., Goldstein, L., Jaynes, J., Krauthamer, G., eds. 1977. *Lateralization in the Nervous System.* New York: Academic

45. Harnad, S. R., Steklis, H. D., Lancaster, J., eds. 1976. *Origins and Evolution of Language and Speech, Annals of the NYAS,* Vol. 280. New York Acad. Sci.

46. Holmes, J. M., Marshall, J. C. 1974. Word perception in the visual half fields: Some relations between laterality measures and overall accuracy. *ICRS* 2:1552 (Research on: Eye, Neurobiology, & Neurophysiology; Psychology)

47. Key, M. R. 1975. *Paralanguage and Kinesics.* Metuchen, NJ: Scarecrow Press

48. Key, M. R., Preziosi, D., eds. 1980. *Nonverbal Communication: Current Research.* In preparation

49. Kimura, D., Archibald, Y. 1974. Motor functions of the left hemisphere. *Brain* 97(II):337–50

50. Kinsbourne, M., ed. 1978. *Hemispheric Asymmetries of Function.* Cambridge: Cambridge Univ. Press

51. Lake, D. A., Bryden, M. P. 1976. Handedness and sex differences in hemispheric asymmetry. *Brain Lang.* 3:266–82.

52. Lamb, S. M. 1966. *Outline of Stratificational Grammar.* Washington DC: Georgetown Univ. Press

53. Lamendella, J. T. 1976. Relations between the ontogeny and phylogeny of language: A neorecapitulationist view. See Ref. 45. pp. 396–412

54. Lamendella, J. T. 1977. The limbic system in human communication. See Ref. 98, pp. 157–222

55. Lamendella, J. T. 1977. General principles of neurofunctional organization and their manifestation in primary and nonprimary language acquisition. *Lang. Learn.* 27:155–96

56. Lamendella, J. T. 1979. The neurofunctional foundations of symbolic communication. In *Symbol as Sense,* ed. M. Foster, S. Brandes. In press

57. Lamendella, J. T. 1979. Neurofunctional basis of pattern practice. *TESOL Q.* 13(1). In press

58. Laughlin, C. D. 1979. The evolution of brain and symbol. See Ref. 56

59. Laughlin, C. D., D'Aquili, E. G. 1974. *Biogenetic Structuralism.* New York: Columbia Univ. Press

60. Lebrun, Y. 1976. Neurolinguistic models of language and speech. See Ref. 96, pp. 1–30

61. Lenneberg, E. H. 1967. *Biological Foundations of Language.* New York: Wiley

62. Lenneberg, E. H., Lenneberg, E., eds. 1975. *Foundations of Language Development: A Multidisciplinary Approach,* Vols. 1, 2. New York: Academic

63. Levy, R. S. 1977. The question of electrophysiological asymmetries preceding speech. See Ref. 98, pp. 287–318

64. Luria, A. R. 1974. Language and brain: Towards the basic problems of neurolinguistics. *Brain Lang.* 1(1):1–14

65. Luria, A. R. 1977. On quasi-aphasic speech disturbances in lesions of the deep structures of the brain. *Brain Lang.* 4(3)432–59

66. McGlone, J. 1978. Sex differences in functional brain asymmetry. *Cortex* 14(1):122–28

67. Milner, E. 1967. *Human Neural and Behavioral Development: A Relational Inquiry.* Springfield, Ill: Thomas

68. Morehead, D. M., Morehead, A. E., eds. 1977. *Normal and Deficient Child Language.* Baltimore: Univ. Park Press

69. Naeser, M. A., Hayward, R. W. 1978. Lesion localization in aphasia with cranial computed tomography and the Boston Diagnostic Aphasia Exam. *Neurology* 28(6):545–51

70. Ojemann, G. A., ed. 1975. The thalamus and language. *Brain Lang.* 2:1–120

71. Ojemann, G. A. 1976. Subcortical language mechanisms. See Ref. 96, pp. 103–38

72. Ojemann, G. A., Whitaker, H. A. 1978. Language localization and variability. *Brain Lang.* 6(2):239–60

73. Paradis, M. 1977. Bilingualism and aphasia. See Ref. 98, pp. 65–121

74. Poeck, K., Huber, W. 1977. To what extent is language a sequential activity? *Neuropsychologia* 15:359–63

75. Ray, W. J., Morrell, M., Frediani, A. W., Tucker, D. 1976. Sex differences and lateral specialization of hemispheric functioning. *Neuropsychologia* 14(3):391–94

76. Richardson, J. T. E. 1976. How to measure laterality? *Neuropsychologia* 14: 135–36

77. Robinson, B. W. 1976. Limbic influences on human speech. See Ref. 45, pp. 761–71

78. Rumelhart, D. E. 1977. *Introduction to Human Information Processing.* New York: Wiley

79. Satz, P. 1977. Laterality tests: An inferential problem. *Cortex* 13(2):208–12

80. Schachter, J. 1976. Some semantic prerequisites for a model of language. *Brain Lang.* 3(2):292–304

81. Schank, R. C., Colby, K. M., eds. 1973. *Computer Models of Thought and Language.* San Francisco: Freeman

82. Schiefelbusch, R. L., Lloyd, L. L., eds. 1974. *Language Perspectives—Acquisition, Retardation, and Intervention.* Baltimore: Univ. Park Press

83. Schnitzer, M. L. 1972. *Generative Phonology—Evidence from Aphasia.* University Park: Pennsylvania State Univ. Press

84. Schnitzer, M. L. 1974. Aphasiological evidence for five linguistic hypotheses. *Language* 50:300–16

85. Schnitzer, M. L. 1976. The role of phonology in linguistic communication: some neurolinguistic considerations. See Ref. 96, pp. 139–60

86. Schnitzer, M. L. 1978. Towards a neurolinguistic theory of language. *Brain Lang.* 6(3):342–61

87. Segalowitz, S. J., Gruber, U. A. 1977. *Language Development and Neurological Theory.* New York: Academic

88. Studdert-Kennedy, M., ed. 1974. *Brain and Language* 1(4) (Dichotic Studies I)

89. Studdert-Kennedy, M., ed. 1975. *Brain and Language* 2(2) (Dichotic Studies II)

90. Taylor, J., ed. 1932. *Selected Writings of John Hughlings Jackson.* London: Hodder & Stoughton

91. Traill, A. 1970. Transformational grammar and the case of a Ndebele speaking aphasic. *J. S. Afr. Logopedic Soc.* 17:48–66

92. Van Lancker, D. 1975. *Heterogeneity in Language and Speech: Neurolinguistic Studies.* UCLA Work. Pap. Phonetics #29

93. Weigl, E., Bierwisch, M. 1970. Neuropsychology and linguistics: topics of common research. *Found. Lang.* 6:1–18

94. Weiten, W., Etaugh, C. 1974. Lateral eye-movement as a function of cognitive mode, question sequence, and sex of subject. *Percept. Mot. Skills* 38(2): 439–44

95. Whitaker, H. 1976. A case of the isolation of the language function. See Ref. 97, pp. 1–58

96. Whitaker, H., Whitaker, H. A., eds. 1976. *Studies in Neurolinguistics,* Vol. 1. New York: Academic

97. Whitaker, H., Whitaker, H. A., eds. 1976. *Studies in Neurolinguistics.* Vol. 2. New York: Academic

98. Whitaker, H., Whitaker, H. A., eds. 1977. *Studies in Neurolinguistics,* Vol. 3. New York: Academic

99. Whitaker, H., Whitaker, H. A., eds. 1979. *Studies in Neurolinguistics,* Vol. 4. New York: Academic. In press

100. Whitaker, H., Whitaker, H. A. 1976. Language disorders. In *A Survey of Applied Linguistics,* ed. R. Wardhaugh, D. Brown, pp. 250–74. Ann Arbor: Univ. Michigan Press

101. Whitaker, H. A. 1970. A model for neurolinguistics. *Occas. Pap. 10,* Lang. Cent., Univ. Essex, Colchester

102. Whitaker, H. A. 1976. Neurobiology of language. See Ref. 39, pp. 121–44

103. White, M. J. 1972. Hemispheric asymmetries in tachistoscopic information-processing. *Br. J. Psychol.* 63:497–508

104. Witelson, S. F. 1976. Sex and the single hemisphere: specialization of the right hemisphere for spatial processing. *Science* 193:425–27

Ann. Rev. Anthropol. 1979. 8:393–415
Copyright © 1979 by Annual Reviews Inc. All rights reserved

ECONOMY, SOCIETY, AND   ◆9639
MYTH IN ABORIGINAL AUSTRALIA

Aram A. Yengoyan

Department of Anthropology, University of Michigan,
Ann Arbor, Michigan 48109

INTRODUCTION

Throughout the anthropological world, the study of the Aboriginal population of Australia has always had a central and pivotal position. Many of our theories have been generated from the ethnography of this unique culture, and theories developed outside of the Aboriginal context have had to be tested against that corpus of ethnographic detail. Yet the interest in Aboriginals has gone much beyond strictly anthropological concerns. Early philosophical treatises, the Western conception of man in nature, the whole idea of man's evolution, and the very nature of our inquiries into the notion of "primitiveness" have dealt with the problem of defining who the Aboriginals are, what they mean, and what they tell us about ourselves. From the days of Rousseau onward, the question of human nature has been critical to our understanding of the anthropological message. It is no wonder that Burridge (9, p. 150) can state that "Insights of this kind, pushing ourselves into otherness and incorporating otherness into ourselves, are the very stuff of anthropology." For if anthropology is the understanding or even the appropriation of the other, then the Aboriginal in Australia is in some sense the "ideal other."

If cultural distance is conceived of as the other extreme from Western culture, surely a cultural system which has complex cosmologies, superincision, subincision, tooth evulsion, body scarification, denial of physiological paternity, mythic time, totemism, and elaborate marriage systems, all of which are combined in various ways in each culture, would emerge as the prime candidate for the "ideal other."

The aim of this essay is to discuss recent developments in the social anthropology of Aboriginal Australian culture. Given the vast amount of

393

literature, both past and present, it is virtually impossible to do full justice to the problem. Not only have scores of volumes been written on the subject, but also the use of Aboriginal ethnographic data in theory is so widespread that it would be foolish to try to unravel and appraise all that has transpired. In approaching this survey, I will start with a brief overview of the historical dimension of the study of Aboriginals. The second part of the essay will enumerate a number of aspects in which critical work and theoretical argumentation have brought forth renewed interest in old problems. It covers four general topics which are as follows: Economy and Local Organization; Population, Kinship, and Social Organization; Religion, Myth, and Symbolism; Aboriginals in the Context of Australian Society. The last section of the essay will discuss some general ethnographic and theoretical issues as they relate to anthropological interpretation.

HISTORICAL DIMENSION

Aboriginal Australian societies have always had a privileged position in anthropological theory and ethnography, and in all likelihood this will continue in the future. One could write virtually the entire history of anthropological thought in terms of Aboriginal Australia, for there is no anthropological theory or interpretation which has not dealt with the ethnography of these cultures. From the earliest beginnings of anthropological inquiry in the middle of the nineteenth century, questions of cultural evolutionism and social organization have been critically dealt with by Morgan, Tylor, Lubbock, and Marx, using the Aboriginal ethnography as reported through early travel accounts, and later in the works of Spencer and Gillen, R. H. Mathews, Carl Strehlow, and numerous early observers.

With the beginning of this century, anthropological and sociological understanding of the Aboriginal materials was focused on the general nature of society and the relationship of the family to the surrounding culture. By the early 1930s the systematic and comparative study of human societies had entered what might be called the classic phase of British social anthropology. Durkheim (10), soon followed by Malinowski (41) and Radcliffe-Brown (61), concluded that the evidence of Aboriginal societies must be the critical test for any understanding of how societies worked and that this rich body of ethnographic information could be the basis for a truly comparative science. Through the 1930s, aspects of Aboriginal kinship and social organization were discussed not only by British social anthropologists, but also by Kroeber (33), Lowie (37), and Goldenweiser (16), who were fully involved trying to relate this corpus of information to general anthropological concerns. It was also during the 1920s and 1930s that new fieldwork was initiated among Aboriginals, and this in turn led to revised interpretations of social organization as well as to the emergence of interest in mythology, religion, cosmology, and psychology. The works of Elkin (11–13), based on his field studies in the Western Desert and the Kimberleys, added new insight to our understanding of totemism, religion, and kinship. Warner (92) wrote *A Black Civilization,* based on work among the Murngin and other eastern Arnhem Land societies, and the insight and controversies over the "Murngin case" are still central to current debates. Stanner (78) worked among the Murinbata, and soon after, his most original and creative insight into Aboriginal religion was published. It was also during this period that Róheim (64, 65) did fieldwork in Australia and published a number of works which still have a strong fascination for students of comparative psychology and Freudian theory. All of the aforementioned fieldworkers and theorists contributed fundamental information and insight to the study of Aboriginal Australian cultures, and no student of this field can ignore their classic works.

While most of the above works are critical both to the theory and ethnography, another tradition also existed which stressed ethnographic observation and description while keeping theoretical interests secondary. Tindale did fieldwork from the early 1920s to the 1960s and published a voluminous number of papers based on data from Groote Eylandt to northern Queensland as well as on work done in the Western Desert and among half-castes in Tasmania. The most general statement by Tindale (88) was recently published. Strehlow continued his father's interest in the Aranda and has done fieldwork among the Aranda for over 40 years. Mountford, who worked primarily in the Western Desert as well as in northern Arnhem Land for 30 years, recently published his most comprehensive statement on his work (51). Ronald and Catherine Berndt (4–6) have worked for nearly 40 years among various societies in Arnhem Land as well as in western and southern Australia, and their publications range from descriptive accounts to theoretical statements. Their recent work on love songs (3) is the first of its kind and one which will introduce a new dimension to the problem of emotionality among Aboriginal Australians.

By the late 1950s and early 1960s, some scholars were stating that no further ethnographic fieldwork could be done and that a phase of "salvage ethnography" must ensue. It was assumed that since the impact of change was so widespread and dominant, none of the Aboriginal societies could be considered "pristine"; once the tribal way of life had changed through contact and assimilation, the "real basis" of society could no longer be described. The study of economic organization, modes of hunting, gathering, and fishing, and the ascertainment of the structure of local group composition could no longer be accomplished due to depopulation, contact, and the appropriation of lands and resources by the dominant European society. There is no doubt that most cultural factors which we call "economic and material culture" can no longer be studied adequately. Yet it must be stressed that Aboriginal society, where it has been able to make the transition without serious population disturbance and economic disloca- tion, can be studied. Current widespread interest in myth, religion, symbol- ism, kinship and social organization, and problems of structuralism all indicate that the viability of these societies is high and a continuity of cultural form is intact.

During the late 1950s and after, some of the most critical and insightful ethnography appeared in the works of Meggitt (43, 46), the Berndts (4–6), L. R. Hiatt (27, 30), Pilling (24), who followed up early investigations done by Hart (22–24); Goodale (17, 18), Reay (62, 63), Beckett (1, 2), and Falkenberg (14). Since this body of work appeared, another generation of fieldworkers has studied Aboriginal cultures, and some of their findings will be discussed in this essay. It is clear that the viability of anthropological investigations is strong and that many problems, both in terms of the Aboriginal context per se and anthropological theory in general, will con- tinue to be pursued.

CONTEMPORARY ISSUES

Since the early 1960s, new data and a rethinking of anthropological theories have brought forth a florescence of work on the Australian Aboriginal. Much of the impetus for this work came with the establishment of the Australian Institute of Aboriginal Studies, which represented the first time the Australian government had directly involved itself in funding research on Aboriginal cultures.

Anthropological interest during the last 20 years has hovered around Aboriginal economy and cultural adaptation to the structure of cosmologies and belief systems.

Economy and Local Organization

Of all aspects of Aboriginal society, economic pursuits and the socioeco- nomic units involved with subsistence are the most difficult to deal with. In part this is due to the early, shattering effects of the colonial experience on Aboriginal life, but even when the cultures were not totally disrupted, economic and population factors deriving from the impact of colonialism have continuously brought about demographic displacement and a marked decline in traditional modes of economic life. Except for the pioneering work of Mountford and his ethnographic team in Arnhem Land (50) and Worsley's (93) study of food utilization among the inhabitants of Groote Eylandt, most of the work on economic production and consumption has been done by archaeologists. Gould's (19) studies in the Western Desert are among the most recent work in this vein, and his accounts have been supplemented by the work of Betty Hiatt (25) and Rhys Jones (32), who have attempted to ascertain through archaeological investigation the basic features of economic production among the Aboriginals of Tasmania.

Although work is limited, a number of critical factors have emerged. Almost all recent work and reanalysis indicate that the basis of Aboriginal economy in both the interior desert areas and in the tropical coastal areas of Arnhem Land and Queensland was the gathering and collecting of vegetable foods which formed the bulk of the day-to-day diet. Meggitt (44) concludes that 70 to 80 percent of the diet was composed of vegetable foods and that the majority of these foods were provided through the labor of women. Although hunting was the dominant cultural concern and the principal work of males, the overall contribution of meat through hunting was minimal and highly variable in terms of daily consumption.

The vegetal basis of Aboriginal diets not only represents another aspect of environmental constraints, but also indicates that there must have been basic regional differences as to the kinds of flora which were exploited. Seeds and seed-grinding technologies were only critical in the more arid areas of central and interior Australia; consequently, the wide spectrum of floral species in the coastal and interior coastal localities of continental Australia indicates that an increasing variability existed in terms of consumption patterns. The utilization of roots, fruits, and nuts among most tropical and semitemperate hunters and gatherers indicate that dietary variability should relate to the question of speciation and the density of different species in these particular environmental confines.

If vegetable matter provided the bulk of the diet, the importance of game and fishing activities must be understood in terms of the whole dietary complex. The hunting of large macropods throughout the continent, the stress on marine life exploitation in various regions, and the elaboration of specific technologies all indicate that microenvironmental adaptation should be basic to understanding how Aboriginal populations supported themselves. Within virtually any type of ecological niche, archaeologists have found different assemblages of tools which must have been used toward the exploitation of divergent sources of food. This regionalism was most marked and has been thoroughly discussed by Lawrence (34), but despite this, one can still characterize a basic form of exploitation that was common to peoples throughout the continent. Generalized tool kits which could compensate for variations in collecting, gathering, hunting, fishing, and trapping were common and indicate a unity of human activities which we may refer to as Aboriginal subsistence techniques and economy.

Over the past 20 years, the question of local organization among Aboriginals has drawn much attention and, as would be expected, much controversy. From Radcliffe-Brown (61) and later Steward (82), the idea of the patrilineal, patrilocal, and exogamous band or horde became the common framework for describing the structure and composition of local organization. In the 1960s, this view was challenged by Meggitt (43) and Hiatt (26, 28), and in turn the classic position was defended by Stanner (76) and Birdsell (7). Meggitt and Hiatt speculated that the horde as defined by Radcliffe-Brown probably never existed in terms of the formal properties which Radcliffe-Brown attributed to it. Furthermore, they stated that even if we had complete data, the composition of hordes was so variable that any claims for the specific existence of a particular kind of social organization, let alone for the universality of such social organization, must be considered carefully. Nevertheless, Meggitt and Hiatt held that communities ranging from 200 to 300 individuals might have been the basis of local organization from which small task groups moved over the terrain.

In response to these suggestions, Stanner (76) established the concepts of estate and range. Estates pertain to sacred localities which are the ancestral home of clans and totemic units. Such localities are sacred and in theory are only accessible to individuals who have a claim through descent and who are members of particular clans and totemic units. The range is composed of the areas which members of different totemic or clan groups could enter and cross for purposes of economic exploitation. Under normal circumstances the individuals of a particular estate formed a core group based on membership in the same patrilineal descent group. The range was composed of the specific resources around the estates which these descent groups normally exploited. The border areas of different ranges intersected, and it can be demonstrated that such boundaries were not rigid over time. Thus, bands from different patrilineal descent groups would mutually exploit adjacent areas as long as they avoided sacred and ancestral sites. Interspersed between ranges and estates were areas which different local groups exploited without reference to differential title and rights.

At this stage in our inquiry, it is nearly impossible to reconstruct the pristine pattern, and in all probability the pristine situation never existed. Rather, it is quite possible that variance in structure and composition of local groups was fundamental due to regional and microenvironmental differences. Since household structure and composition and rules of residence are known to be the most adaptive aspects of social organization as it relates to economic imperatives, we should expect such variation. The stability of local group structure not only must be seen to derive from environmental and economic forces, but also must be interpreted as an expression of totemic and religious philosophies which are imperatives for all Aboriginal cultures. Aboriginal philosophy as manifest in myth, cosmology, and totemism has a number of critical axioms that should be stressed as they refer to the question of local groups. One of the underlying themes in Aboriginal thought is the continuous collapsing of the natural into the supernatural and the supernatural into the natural. In fact, virtually everything in the supernatural sphere of life has a natural counterpart, and vice versa. It could therefore be argued with much justification that the natural/supernatural distinction, which is so basic in Western thought, has no relevance in Aboriginal culture and only divides the continuity of cultural form into arbitrary and meaningless categories and contrasts. In understanding what this means, it must be noted that for most Aboriginal cultures the terrain as expressed through locality, residence, and livelihood is not only a territorial phenomenon, but also a spiritual force which relates to the whole question of existence and being. Thus, the structuring of local groups must be interpreted as a source of emotional sustenance based on totemic ideologies. These ideologies and their corresponding emotional expressions form the "real" basis of what locality is as a structural process and what continuity means. Once this is established then the processes of group composition, intergroup affiliations, and residential changes must be viewed as means through which individuals and groups cope with problems of economic production, consumption, and distribution. It is no wonder that virtually every ethnographer has found discrepancies between structure and composition. The structure has its source in totemic and religious imperatives, while the composition represents the interaction of this structure and economic imperatives.

The totemic basis of land and spatial mobility meant that the very source of existence, be it spiritual or emotional, was nearly always expressed through ties to the soil. This emotional attachment to land is well expressed by Strehlow (84, p. 145) when he states, "Their supernatural beings were not living in the sky, far beyond human reach: the immortals were dwelling in their very midst, and had done so from all eternity." Yet it must be realized that this tight link between the supernatural and the natural did not create a "straightjacket" which limited and curtailed spatial mobility. Local groups were interconnected with one another through bonds of kinship, through common ties based on section and subsection categories, and through mutual bonds based on ritual groups. Social organization did possess adequate flexibility through which individuals and groups could move from local group to local group, or from poor refuge areas to environmentally better endowed areas during conditions of drought. Since drought is the basic rule throughout most of central Australia, local groups had to maintain ties which could be activated during periods of stress. In my own fieldwork among the Pitjantjatjara, the number of cases in which individuals and groups moved beyond the normal confines of the Mann-Musgrave-Petermann Ranges was so great that one could only conclude that the adherence to strict boundaries by local groups was basically the exception.

Over the past years, a number of writers such as Strehlow (83–85) and Yengoyan (94–100) have discussed the processes by which population dispersion and resource deployment occurred.

Another means of establishing how local groups related to their own totemic localities while being able to move out and cover hundreds of miles of territory is through an understanding of what constitutes geographic knowledge. Again among the Pitjantjatjara it was noted that geographic knowledge in terms of one's particular totemic sites was based on a detailed acquaintance with particular events in the mythic history of that site. Thus, not only knowledge was limited to qualitative categories which yielded particular cases, but also the detailed variance was critical and always transmitted. Once individuals moved to adjacent areas and localities away from their own totemic sites, detailed geographic knowledge became primarily qualitative in that the possible existence of vegetable foods was determined by general principles from which one could predict what kinds of yields would occur. These microshifts in how geographical knowledge is maintained, transmitted, and utilized are in part an expression of social and spatial distance from particular totemic sites. Microdifferences indicate the degree of experience and knowledge which one possesses as one moves from locality to locality.

Seasonality in economic and cultural factors occurs among those tribes which occupy coastal areas as well as some of the interior coastal vicinities. Throughout the coastal areas, almost all tribal units are characterized by changes in economic activity, types of foods consumed and variations in settlement patterns as these factors relate to climatic change. The shifts in settlement and economy in Cape York are well described by Thomson (87); and throughout Australia, Lawrence (34) has documented the various seasonal adjustments made by the riverine tribes of southeast Australia as well as by marine groups of New South Wales.

While seasonality is critical on the fringes of the continent, the interior desert areas are minimally affected by seasonal shifts. The most important geographical difference in the center is the contrast between the mountain ranges, spinifex areas, and the intervening deserts. Faunal and floral differences between these environmental areas were expressed in the ways in which Aboriginals adapted to each context. The desert groups have a more limited floral and faunal base to exploit, and the means of exploitation also differ from those groups which survive on the ranges. Nets and traps, which are utilized by the Aranda through the collective efforts of a number of individuals, were absent among the desert groups which almost always hunted on a more individual basis.

Theoretically, the question of economy and local organization should be understood in terms of certain structural tendencies which characterize Aboriginal society. Maddock (39) has stressed the idea that Aboriginal society operates within two basic modes. One is the push toward "universality" in which ties and networks are continuously regenerated and extended outward. This is accomplished through the major means of exchange (e.g. marital, ritual, and economic). The universalistic tendency not only interconnects local groups but also expands ties beyond tribal boundaries. Mutualism and hospitality as an expression of universalistic tendencies are not only economic imperatives through which population survival and mobility occur, but are also definite religious impulses which maintain the expansive quality of Aboriginal culture. Strehlow (84) notes that hospitality was extended to less fortunate groups throughout central Australia, not simply as an act of charity, but also as the fulfillment of an obligation which rested on tradition. The obligatory basis of hospitality is revealed by the trackings of mythic ancestral beings as they meandered over thousands of miles in central Australia. Mythic trails crossed over many local areas and provided linkages in which all groups articulated with one another.

While universalism occurs through many forms, the second tendency is particularism, a feature which is promulgated through principles of exclusion. Estates, totemic sites, and virtually all aspects of the sacred are maintained either through total exclusion of outsiders or through exchanges in which outsiders assist in maintaining these sites while being unable to participate in ritual activities. The basis of particularism is primarily in the religious domain, but its implications are far-reaching.

Recently Turner (91) characterized Aboriginal society and its modes of production as a "production group diversity system" in which structurally differentiated and diverse production groups are created through the operation of principles of lineality and exclusion, as these are expressed in the patrilineal clan and various types of marriage arrangements. Ties linking estates together for resource exploitation are an expression of the tendency toward outward expansion, but the centrifugal forces are simultaneously counterbalanced by patrilineality and adherence to ancestral sacred localities which maintain a centripetal focus which continously work back towards the center. Turner's analysis, which he later compares to the Cree as another alternative, is most insightful in terms of eliciting the forms of structural contradictions which permeate Aboriginal society as it adapts to situations of economic survival and population dispersal. Contradictions are statements of how a highly structured society maintains its coherence while at the same time promoting organizational variability in the quest for human survival.

Population, Kinship, and Social Organization

Whatever else Aboriginal society is known for, kinship has always dominated our attention. The formal foundations of Aboriginal Australian kinship were delineated by Radcliffe-Brown, who based his theoretical findings on the solid foundations of numerous predecessors. In stressing rules and structural principles, Radcliffe-Brown established a number of formal properties which still underwrite the study of Aboriginal kinship systems, and from these properties a series of types (i.e. Aranda, Kariera, etc) were set forth as a means of organizing the body of enthnographic data on kinship and as a way of systemizing the problems of transformations from one type to another. Formalistic accounts stress structural discreteness, thus relegating the influence of nonkinship cultural features to a secondary position which in many cases justified their exclusion from theoretical considerations. Furthermore, the early interpretations stress descent as a primary kinship process, but later work by Lévi-Strauss (36) balanced the theoretical argumentation in favor of alliance theories in which marriage bonds not only determine the discrete elements within societies but also generate the total social structure. During the past 20 years, the debate between alliance theorists and descent theorists has utilized the Australian data in attempting to develop their respective arguments. Thus not only have the Murngin gained a place in ethnographic history, but now the Wik Monkan of Cape York are also part of another lengthy theoretical debate (see 42, 57, 70, 87).

Over the past 20 years of work on kinship, at least three themes have emerged. The first is the dominant concern with developing descriptions and analytic schemes for devising formal sets of rules for studying and understanding kinship, both as sets of categories and as behavioral attributes. A second concern involves the relationship between kinship and the whole of Aboriginal culture. Here the aim is not only to comprehend kinship as a system unto itself, but also to understand kinship as part of the larger system of symbolic coherence and cosmological axioms. The last theme is concerned with questions of how kinship and social structure are constrained by ecological and demographic parameters.

The analysis of kinship as sets of formal rules which generate the whole social system is best exemplified in the recent work of Scheffler (71). Given the initial assumption that relations based on genealogical connections and classifications are universal throughout Australia, it is claimed that kin classifications are not only universal but are the very basis of social structure. This position has been hotly debated over the past 50 years, not only within the Aboriginal context, but also in the larger domain of kinship studies, the relationship of kinship to social structure and behavior. There is no need to discuss the various points of view here, but it should be noted that the underlying assumption of kinship as genealogical connections has always been pivotal in our understanding of how kinship works in Aboriginal society. Radcliffe-Brown stressed this position in his early work, and Scheffler has advanced our understanding of the implications of Radcliffe-Brown's contention. Furthermore, if kinship as genealogical connection is the basis of social structure, then the existence of marriage systems, section categories, moieties, etc can be generated from the structure and operation of kinship. This is not to say that other features of Aboriginal social structure are to be understood as epiphenomena which are superfluous to kinship. Basically sections, moieties, semimoieties, etc are indices or summary expressions of kinship relations. In each case, kinship is categorized by different lines, some of which might be considered as primarily social, others as religious, ritualistic, or totemistic in nature. The polysemic aspect of kinship terms, categories, and usage provides the basis upon which the social structure articulates and reproduces itself. Scheffler (71, pp. 523–24) notes that whereas Radcliffe-Brown dealt with the patrilineal clan and lines of descent as partly separate from kinship and genealogy, while arguing that the patrilineal band was the basis of social structure, in reality local groups and descent are structurally derived and dependent on culturally defined kinship categories as they are extended throughout the whole of society.

Yet kinship as a system is culturally animated through cosmological axioms and arrangements of symbolic coherence which provide emotional sustenance to members of every Aboriginal society. In a brilliant reanalysis of his Walbiri material, Meggitt (48) demonstrates the intricate connections between Walbiri kin categories and relations and the impact of the dreamtime experience on social life. Throughout Walbiri culture, the initial separation of all life and substance into the noumenal, which is equated to the sacred and maleness, and the phenomenal, which is associated with the profane and femaleness, provides a series of links which interconnect moieties to sections/subsections and eventually to age grades, female ceremonies, and male cult lodges. If kinship is the dominant vehicle of social expression, then the basis and meaning of this expression rests in the realm of cosmology and ontology. Causation emanates from the Dreamtime, gradually working itself through the kinship system, and is materially expressed in the differential utilization of land, resources, and native geographical categories. Meggitt's analysis is supported by other interpretations such as Strehlow's accounts of the Aranda, Hiatt's understanding of the Gidjingali, and Maddock's (38–40) description of the Dalabon. Scheffler (71, p. 524) also stresses that there are no critical differences between his interpretation and Meggitt's analysis of cosmological coherence and kinship. In all of the recent writings on Aboriginal kinship, one readily notes a growing interest in relating questions of structural formalism to questions of meaning and symbolic understanding. The works of Peterson (58, 59), Shapiro (72, 73), and Turner (90) especially indicate this growing tendency.

While kinship systems and social organization are based on formal properties of categorization, descent, and marriage, the full comprehension of kin group composition and marriage rates depends on ecological and demographic variables which are embedded in the system of rules and behavior. Throughout Aboriginal Australia, the realm of behavior and its relationship to structural rules has always been of interest to social anthropologists. Durkheim, Radcliffe-Brown, and Lévi-Strauss all assumed that rules and behavior were isomorphic and that there was always a close fit between the two. Other interpretations have stressed that behavior is the basis of rules, thus implying that changes in behavior should reflect changes in structural rules. Finally, another interpretation has it that behavior is an expression of rules which are paramount. Therefore behavior which deviates from either verbalized or nonverbalized rules is always recast to approximate the rule. Of these three positions, the latter interpretation most often characterizes the structure and workings of Aboriginal society. Since rules, whether they concern marriage, kinship, ritual, or totemic beliefs, are based on cosmological and ontological axioms as established in the Dreamtime, such principles are taken as cultural givens and are neither questioned nor debated as to their pristine status.

How rules work "on the ground" is another question. Every Aboriginal society recognizes the possibility that things will not work along ideal lines, and this realization necessitates mechanisms by which behavioral fluctuations and variations can be recast back onto structure. One case will be given to demonstrate the force and domination of rules. Among the Pitjantjatjara of the Western Desert, marriages which deviate from the rule do occur either as unions which are in complete violation of the rule or as unions which might be considered as optional. Some of these unions are simply left as is; but in most cases after a marriage is consummated, genealogical changes occur which have the effect of producing "correct" marriages. In such cases, the kinship category of a person in the second ascending generation is changed to make the marriage "come out right." But in no case is the rule ever changed to accommodate to behavior.

Demographic constraints have been related to marriage systems, and, in general, the conclusion is that constraints do not determine the presence or absence of a rule. Nevertheless, they do have a marked impact on the statistical frequency in which marriages of different degrees of correctness occur. The works of Rose (66), Reay (62, 63), Goodale (17, 18), Meggitt (43, 45, 47), and Yengoyan (95, 97, 98) have demonstrated that population size, differentials in age of marriage, infanticide rates, and imbalances in the sex ratio have a critical impact on the determination of how these rules are behaviorally expressed. The fluctuations in marriage rates over time within any society must be related to demographic imbalances and spatial factors which render behavioral variability.

Religion, Myth, and Symbolism

If kinship has been the most fertile area of interest to social anthropologists, religion has probably been the most difficult aspect or feature of Aboriginal culture to understand and interpret. In part, this is due to the limited nature of the ethnographic accounts, but also this lack of anthropological comprehension results from the perennial confusion in Western thought as to what religion means and how it is to be dealt with. As Stanner (77) points out, even Spencer and Gillen, after describing numerous Aranda ceremonies, beliefs, and cosmological features, seldom use the term religion in referring to the richness of the data and its interpretation. Durkheim conceived of these rites and belief systems as "expressing the religious principle," but probably not as being religion in any European sense. By the 1920s and 1930s, the empirical foundations for the study of Aboriginal religion emerged from the works of Elkin, Warner, Strehlow, and Thomson. Over the next decades, the accounts of Stanner, Ronald Berndt, Catherine Berndt, and McConnel through the 1940s and onward contributed to the data and interpretation. By the 1960s, Meggitt, Hiatt, and Munn added another dimension to anthropological interpretation and contributed new insights to the ethnographic corpus.

Over the past 50 years, the work of Stanner (74–80) stands out as among the most insightful and perceptive, in regards both to his understanding of native categories of thought and to what this thought means in terms of belief, rites, and behavior. Stanner's (77) article on religion, totemism, and symbolism is probably the single most important piece written on the general features and problems involved in studying Aboriginal religion and thought, while his lengthy monograph *On Aboriginal Religion* is a must for any student of religion. In stressing the vitality of Aboriginal religion, Stanner emphatically supports the position that the eternal aspect of the Aboriginal religion as expressed through the Dreaming is central in combining all aspects of Aboriginal religion together as a unified thought process. Questions of eschatology, aetiology, and ontology are not only interrelated, but the very force which they have on society must be seen as an expression of the ultimate causative influences of the Dreamtime during which thought, mind, and culture work themselves onto the sphere of life. It is this oneness of thought, belief, and expression through time and space which makes Western theological and scientific contrasts and distinctions irrelevant and inappropriate to the Aboriginal context. Christian theology is predicated on contrastive modes of thought as can be seen in its preoccupation with questions of damnation and salvation, and in the dichotomy between the spiritual/ideal/mental and the material; moreover, the sacred and profane distinction, though useful for understanding, is another form of contrast based on the Western model. Throughout Aboriginal religion, statements of spiritual meaning and content arise out of the Dreaming, an experience which all Aboriginals inherit (but cannot disinherit). This experience not only is the basis of emotional sustenance, but it provides the major vehicle by which morality is regenerated through time.

Not only does morality result from the Dreaming, but virtually all behavior is an expression of a well-developed sense of moral conduct which provides the basis for all human imperatives. The sacred quality of the moral is never debated nor is it compromised in the rigors of everyday life. The code of morality is based on myth and liturgy, two areas which embrace almost every aspect of Aboriginal society. In fact, the isomorphic fit between the natural and supernatural means that all nature is coded and charged by the sacred, while the sacred is everywhere within the physical landscape. Myths and mythic trackings cross over numerous tribal boundaries and over thousands of miles, and every particular form and feature of the terrain has a well-developed "story" behind it.

On the level of interpersonal behavior, the moral basis of conduct governs almost every sphere of life. In Western thought, we have always made a clear-cut division between behavior and morality which underwrites behavior, and this split serves as an expression of emerging secularism and individualism. In Aboriginal society, every individual is responsible for his/her behavior, since behavior is the enactment of the moral.

Myth is the basis of religion as well as the central feature of the symbolic system. Not only does myth permeate all aspects of Aboriginal culture and society, but myth provides the ontological characteristics which give meaning to human action. Through ethnographic analysis and theoretical discussions, Hiatt (31) has stressed that purely functional accounts and interpretations of myth and ritual are limiting and prevent our grasping the full impact of myth on Aboriginal society. Since functionalism commonly interprets myth and ritual as counterparts of one another, it fails to explain the Aboriginal context in which most myths are riteless and most rites are mythless. Stanner (78, 79) noted this and recognized that the dynamic quality of Aboriginal religion rested primarily in its ability to relate differences in one cultural sphere to those in another. Thus, myth and ritual provide different messages, and it becomes critical to understand how these messages constrain each other.

Beyond this, a purely functional approach to myth as a charter which underwrites society is simply not very powerful. As Hiatt (31) notes, the negative element in Aboriginal rites and myths, whether it is represented as the deceiver or the antagonist, is commonly the one who survives and comes out ahead. Therefore, it is clear that while functional analysis may be of some utility, it cannot establish what myth and rites mean to the participants. The structure of myth may have a logic, and probably does, but purely structural and/or functional interpretations, which advance the notion of promoting social solidarity or in the classic Lévi-Straussian binary oppositions, tell us almost nothing of particular ontologies which underscore the mythic and ritual drama.

In invoking the ontological quality of mythic substance, we must return to the thought-provoking work of Stanner (78) and his interpretation of Murinbata realities. For the Murinbata, Stanner (78, p. 37) notes that life is seen as "a joyous thing with maggots at the centre." Life is construed as good and benevolent, but each course and twist in life has numerous painful sufferings which must be understood and endured by each individual. This is the underlying cultural message, a philosophy of life which is mirrored in the myths and rites of the Murinbata. It is this philosophy of life which provides emotional meaning to individuals, and at the same time it is this quality which animates myth and rituals. The brilliance of this interpretation is the basis of Hiatt's (30, 31) recent attempt to relate questions of ontogeny to models of ontology. In developing this broad perspective, Hiatt (30, 31) notes that the Freudian complex of separation anxiety, as understood by Róheim, might provide the coherence in which myth could demarcate the significant linkage for understanding human ontogenies.

Just as questions of ontogeny must be related to ontological processes, symbolic inquiries also represent another means of understanding how ontologies are constructed and what they mean. Again Stanner (77) has set forth the basic issue concerning symbolism in arguing that Aboriginal symbols are expressions and conceptualizations which are inferable and partly perceivable in the religion while not being in themselves "religion." In this sense, symbolic equations are a means of trying to comprehend the basic metaphysical qualities of religion. Religion as the internal ontological core is expressed in many ways, most of which occur through symbolic thought as manifest in ritual, music, drama, art, and above all in language. Building on this foundation, the work of Nancy Munn (52, 53) brilliantly reveals the basic vehicles which Aboriginals work through in generating and fully animating the very essence of what religion is and how religious experiences take place. According to Munn, the mechanisms by which inner subjectivity is externalized and objectified onto the social plane and the geographic landscape is best exemplified by subject-object transformations in myth and in the meaning of graphic designs as part of Walbiri iconography.

The centrality of ontological forces expressed in Aboriginal culture is best exemplified in the corpus of Aranda ethnography. Strehlow (86) has noted the Aboriginal perception of the timeless quality of life, a life that was unfolded once and for all time. The most conclusive statement pertaining to these eternal features is Strehlow's (86, p. 658): "There were no prophecies; no changes were envisaged for the future. The work of the totemic ancestors was believed to have been done for all time." Not only is culture encoded through time, but the dominance of ontological features, such as the close emotional tie to land and the basic male/female dichotomy, is central to a philosophy of life which penetrates as myth, ritual, kinship, and behavior.

The male/female opposition underwrites most Aboriginal cultures and is continuously expressed in various cultural forms. Meggitt (43, 48), Munn (52, 53), and Peterson (58, 59) have demarcated the various ways in which this male/female opposition permeates Walbiri culture, while Hiatt (30) and Hamilton (21) have discussed the centrality of male dominance among the Gidjingali. Yengoyan (101) has discussed the symbolic contrast of male/female throughout Australia as it relates to categorization of nature and culture. The emotional basis of male to female as part of family and group dynamics has been minimally stressed, but recent work by R. M. Berndt (3) and Myers (54–56) should add new understanding to these problems.

Throughout this chapter, the importance of totemic behavior has been stressed as it relates to religion through time and to the emotional qualities which tie humans to one another and to their surroundings. Totemism as a general category has been rightfully criticized by Stanner (77) for both theoretical and parochial reasons. Therefore, in addressing this old issue, Stanner attempts to clarify what "totemism" has meant within anthropological history and theory. In turn, Stanner focuses on the importance of "totems" to the ontological understanding of continuity which is maintained through associations of events in the past and generated into the present and future. The totem is the expression of the social as it works back onto eternal time. In whatever form the totem occurs and whatever it accomplishes, the point is that totems are real. They do have a very basic existence to humans, since virtually everything is perceived as having totemic significance.

The reason why the actual existence of totems must be stressed is that recent interpretations by Lévi-Strauss (35) argue that totemism or "so-called totemism" is at worst an illusion or at best a null category. Whatever the case, the structural position interprets totemism as an expression of something else, and thus reality is seen to exist only at a more generalized level of categorization. Although the structural interpretation might possess an intellectual appeal, it debases, distorts, and bankrupts the most vital force in Aboriginal religion. On this point, the cogent analysis of the totemic argument by Hiatt (29) and Meggitt (48) must be read in conjunction with the structuralist interpretation. It is clear from the ethnographic evidence that in no way can one dismiss totems and totemism in Aboriginal Australia as an "illusion."

Aboriginals in the Context of Australian Society

Since the initial contact period in the late eighteenth century, the European impact on Aboriginal culture can only be described as devastating. From an estimated population of 250,000 to 300,000 at time of contact, the number of Aboriginals declined to nearly 40,000 by the late 1930s. The historical events and processes of nearly 200 years of contact are replete with cases in which Aboriginals were exterminated by direct physical violence or through the effects of endemic disease and famine which spread throughout the continent soon after the arrival of Europeans. By the 1860s, the last of the Aboriginal Tasmanians had died. At the beginning of this century, the coastal and interior coastal groups of Victoria, New South Wales, South Australia, Queensland, and West Australia were in various phases of cultural decay.

Throughout central Australia, Arnhem Land, and northern Queensland, most of the Aboriginal societies maintained their traditional way of life even though the hunting and gathering economy was no longer practiced as the sole means of support. By the 1950s, societies which were able to resist the initial onslaught brought about by population decline responded in different ways (and in general this led to the survival of their culture). Walbiri population increased to 1700 by the early 1970s and the Pitjantjatjara population increased to about 800. While various stages of physical and cultural dislocation occurred in Arnhem Land, most of the region's societies have survived. And throughout the Western Desert, many Aboriginal societies survived and have maintained their cultural vitality.

Documentation of contact and change between Aboriginal and European society is ample, but relatively few broad interpretive accounts exist which highlight the policies and adaptations that occurred over 200 years of contact. The best interpretation of the historical process is Rowley's (67–69) three-volume study of policy and practice during the colonial and national periods of Australian political growth. Rowley not only discusses the colonial policies which intensified the destruction of Aboriginal society, but also points out how issues of racism, land rights, wages and unemployment, and relative deprivation characterize the plight of Aboriginals in the 1970s. While racism in one form or another underwrites the basic attitudes that whites maintain toward Aboriginals, most of its forms take expression through issues pertaining to economic opportunity. The best example of this mixture of racism and differential economic access is the cattle industry of northern Australia, where report after report indicates that Aboriginals are not only underpaid to a marked degree, but also suffer chronic unemployment, underemployment, and deliberate social and personal abuse (81).

While Australian policy has varied from complete integration to cultural assimilation to social accommodation to "cushioning the dying pillow," none of these policies have alleviated the current socioeconomic condition of the Aboriginals. The literature on this subject is vast, whether it explores State-level policy or the national policy emanating from Canberra.

On the local level, a number of accounts indicate different responses and patterns of interaction through which local Aboriginal communities have maintained their cultural viability. Tomkinson (89) demonstrates how the Mandjildjara of Jigalong, West Australia, overcame the forces of Apostolic Christianity, not by accommodating to Christian themes, but through the maintenance of their own religion whose basic axioms are simply not represented in Christianity. It should be noted that among the Mandjildjara rates of religious conversion to various Christian denominations are quite low and that, in general, Christian dogma has had minimal impact on those Aboriginal societies whose cultural traditions have not been eroded. The Walbiri and Pitjantjatjara also demonstrate this general pattern. In contrast, the Aranda succumbed to Christianity after nearly 100 years of missionary activities. Yet Strehlow notes that Christianity per se was never ideologically acceptable to the Aranda; rather, the economic consequences of conversion were important inducements to at least "hear out" Christianity.

Writing about the corner area of New South Wales, Beckett (1, 2) has demonstrated how half-caste communities evolve in the context of white society. Beckett notes that after many decades of contact and change, kinship is still the basic idiom which governs behavior and mobility. Any type of success and monetary accumulation among local individuals is siphoned off through the dynamics of kinship.

Besides the historical dimension, a number of insightful works have appeared recently, pertaining to urban Aborigines (15), health and medicine (49), education and employment (8), and the relationship between legal norms and the growth of political consciousness. Whatever the arguments are, the role of Aboriginals within the political economy of Australia is marginal at best and nonexistent at worst. Yet over the past decade, issues of Aboriginal land claims, rights of access to traditional territorial sites, and a greater interest in self-rule and political consciousness are slowly emerging. The winds of change are now openly expressed among Aboriginals as well as among some segments of the dominant society. But it might be too little, too late.

CONCLUSION

Understanding the Aboriginal Australian has always been a central interest in anthropology, both in terms of theory construction or in the utilization of Aboriginal ethnography for comparative purposes. In some directions, the Aboriginal does typify human societies, and they are comparable to other cultures based on the hunting-gathering-fishing mode of production. At the same time, Aboriginal culture in terms of its general features as well as particular historical adaptations is highly unique in regards to its overelaboration of most aspects of culture. Although anthropological explanations of the Aboriginal ethnographic corpus has had varying degrees of success, overall our attempts and concerns might profit by relating social anthropological inquiries with other forms of explanation and understanding.

One of the most fruitful areas of inquiry is to ascertain how language and culture are expressions of Aboriginal epistemology and ontology. If myth is the dominant religious focus, then we should postulate a relationship between particular grammatical structures and myth. As stated earlier, Aboriginal culture is eternally possessed by each individual, and myth is daily expression of the eternal. The language of myth requires grammatical structures which continuously maintain myth as a living thing that is not relegated to the secular past. Among many central Australian cultures myth is expressed in the imperfective tense or aspect. The imperfective is a statement of ongoing action and events which never reach a finality. In the eaglehawk myths, eaglehawk was falling off a branch but never fell off, a condition indicating the continuity of action. It is this continuity of action which emerges into the present and the future and combines all time and thought into a single coherence. Language structures provide one of the essential imperatives which express the oneness of life.

The implications of the relationship of linguistic structure on the sacred have a far-reaching effect beyond the Australian case. It would be of interest to determine if the imperfective is commonly the language of myth, especially if myth is the central focus of epistemology. A recent reanalysis of narrative and tense in the Old Testament seems to indicate that the imperfective was also the basic vehicle in conveying the impact of the original message (60). After generations of translations of the Old Testament, the original language structure has been much modified and distorted.

It is a tribute that the Aboriginal in Australia has maintained the richness of language, cultural content, and formal structures through decades of change. The internal complexity of structure and content, the elaboration of oppositions and inversions, and the perseverance of the society in times of change and cultural decay must be understood as testimonials to the existence of a highly creative cultural form. It is this total cultural form and structure which continuously baffles the attempts of anthropologists to understand what it *really is* and what it *really means.* Yet we are no better or worse than other disciplines. Virtually all Aboriginals who possess the eternal through their totems would take delight in refuting Tillich's statement that "there are no societies which possess the eternal."

And, of course, Aboriginals also take pleasure in knowing that the creativity and originality of cultural substance and form are truly the working of the eternal. Hale (20, p. 482), after finally understanding some of the principles of ritual associations in *tjiliwiri,* remarked to a Walbiri man: "You certainly have something here!" The Walbiri adult replied: "Indeed we have!"

ACKNOWLEDGMENTS

I wish to thank Alton L. Becker, Robbins Burling, David Edwards, Ken George, Kenneth Hale, and William Kelleher for discussing various issues with me and for reading parts of this essay. These people have always been a source of stimulation and provocation. I extend special thanks to the Rackham School of Graduate Studies at the University of Michigan for providing spatial assistance, and to Jan Opdyke for suffering through the typing of my numerous drafts.

Literature Cited

1. Beckett, J. R. 1958. Marginal men: A study of two half-caste Aborigines. *Oceania* 29:91–108
2. Beckett, J. R. 1965. Kinship, mobility and community among part-Aborigines in rural Australia. *Int. J. Comp. Sociol.* 6:7–23
3. Berndt, R. M. 1978. *Love Songs of Arnhem Land.* Chicago: Univ. Chicago Press. 244 pp.
4. Berndt, R. M., Berndt, C. H. 1945. *A preliminary report of field work in the Ooldea Region, western South Australia.* Sydney: Oceania Bound Offprint. 343 pp.
5. Berndt, R. M., Berndt, C. H. 1964. *The World of the First Australians: An Introduction to the Traditional Life of the Australian Aborigines.* Sydney: Smith. 509 pp.
6. Berndt, R. M., Berndt, C. H. 1970. *Man, Land and Myth in North Australia: The Gunwinggu People.* Sydney: Smith. 262 pp.
7. Birdsell, J. B. 1970. Local group composition among the Australian Aborigines: A critique of the evidence from fieldwork conducted since 1930. *Curr. Anthropol.* 11:115–42
8. Broom, L., Jones, F. L. 1973. *A Blanket a Year.* Canberra: Aust. Natl. Univ. Press. 98 pp.
9. Burridge, K. 1973. *Encountering Aborigines: Anthropology and the Australian Aboriginal.* New York: Pergamon. 260 pp.
10. Durkheim, E. 1915. *The Elementary Forms of the Religious Life: A Study in Religious Sociology.* London: Allen & Unwin. 507 pp.
11. Elkin, A. P. 1938. *Studies in Australian Totemism.* Oceania Monogr. No. 2. Sydney. 209 pp.
12. Elkin, A. P. 1938–1940. Kinship in South Australia. *Oceania* 8:419–52, 9:41–78, 10:198–234, 10:295–399, 10:369–89
13. Elkin, A. P. 1964. *The Australian Aborigines: How to Understand Them.* Sydney: Angus & Robertson. 393 pp.
14. Falkenberg, J. 1962. *Kin and Totem: Group Relations of Australian Aborigines in the Port Keats District.* Oslo: Oslo Univ. Press. 271 pp.

15. Gale, F. 1972. *Urban Aborigines*. Canberra: Aust. Natl. Univ. Press. 283 pp.
16. Goldenweiser, A. 1922. *Early Civilization: An Introduction to Anthropology*. New York: Knopf. 428 pp.
17. Goodale, J. C. 1962. Marriage contracts among the Tiwi. *Ethnology* 1:452–66
18. Goodale, J. C. 1971. *Tiwi Wives: A Study of the Women of Melville Island, North Australia*. Seattle: Univ. Washington Press. 368 pp.
19. Gould, R. A. 1969. Subsistence behaviour among the Western Desert Aborigines of Australia. *Oceania* 39:253–74
20. Hale, K. L. 1971. A note on the Walbiri tradition of antonymy. In *Semantics: An Interdisciplinary Reader in Philosophy, Linguistics and Psychology*, ed. D. D. Steinberg, L. A. Jakobovits, pp. 472–82. New York: Cambridge Univ. Press. 603 pp.
21. Hamilton, A. 1968. *Aboriginal models of male–female relationships*. Unpublished manuscript. Dep. Anthropol., Univ. Sydney
22. Hart, C. W. M. 1930. The Tiwi of Melville and Bathurst Islands. *Oceania* 1:167–80
23. Hart, C. W. M. 1954. The sons of Turimpi. *Am. Anthropol.* 56:242–61
24. Hart, C. W. M., Pilling, A. R. 1960. *The Tiwi of North Australia*. New York: Holt, Rinehart & Winston. 118 pp.
25. Hiatt, B. 1967. The food quest and the economy of the Tasmanian Aborigines. *Oceania* 38:99–133, 190–219
26. Hiatt, L. R. 1962. Local organization among the Australian Aborigines. *Oceania* 32:267–86
27. Hiatt, L. R. 1965. *Kinship and Conflict: A Study of the Aboriginal Community in Northern Arnhem Land*. Canberra: Aust. Natl. Univ. Press. 162 pp.
28. Hiatt, L. R. 1966. The lost horde. *Oceania* 37:81–92
29. Hiatt, L. R. 1969. Totemism tomorrow: The future of an illusion. *Mankind* 7:83–93
30. Hiatt, L. R. 1971. Secret pseudo-procreation rites among the Australian Aborigines. In *Anthropology in Oceania: Essays presented to Ian Hogbin*, ed. L. R. Hiatt, C. Jayawardena, pp. 77–88. San Francisco: Chandler. 290 pp.
31. Hiatt, L. R. 1975. Introduction. In *Australian Aboriginal Mythology: Essays in Honour of W. E. H. Stanner*, ed. L. R. Hiatt, pp. 1–23. Canberra: Aust. Inst. Aboriginal Stud. 213 pp.
32. Jones, R. 1971. The demography of hunters and farmers in Tasmania. In *Aboriginal Man and Environment in Australia*, ed. D. J. Mulvaney, J. Golson, pp. 271–87. Canberra: Aust. Natl. Univ. Press. 389 pp.
33. Kroeber, A. L. 1938. Basic and secondary patterns of social structure. *J. R. Anthropol. Inst.* 68:299–309
34. Lawrence, R. 1968. *Aboriginal Habitat and Economy*. Occas. Pap. No. 6, Dep. Geogr. Canberra: Aust. Natl. Univ. 290 pp.
35. Lévi-Strauss, C. 1962. *Totemism*. Boston: Beacon. 116 pp.
36. Lévi-Strauss, C. 1969. *The Elementary Structures of Kinship*. Boston: Beacon. 541 pp.
37. Lowie, R. 1920. *Primitive Society*. New York: Liveright. 463 pp.
38. Maddock, K. 1970. Myths of the acquisition of fire in Northern and Eastern Australia. In *Australian Aboriginal Anthropology*, ed. R. M. Berndt, pp. 174–99. Perth: Univ. Western Australia Press. 341 pp.
39. Maddock, K. 1972. *The Australian Aborigines: A Portrait of Their Society*. London: Penguin Press. 210 pp.
40. Maddock, K. 1975. *The Emu Anomaly*. See Ref. 31, pp. 102–22
41. Malinowski, B. 1913. *The Family Among the Australian Aborigines*. London: Hodder. 322 pp. (Reprinted with an introduction by J. A. Barnes. New York: Schoken Books, 1963).
42. McKnight, D. 1971. Some problems concerning the Wik-mungkan. In *Rethinking Kinship and Marriage*, ed. R. Needham, pp. 145–80. London: Tavistock. 276 pp.
43. Meggitt, M. J. 1962. *Desert People: A Study of the Walbiri Aborigines of Central Australia*. Sydney: Angus & Robertson. 348 pp.
44. Meggitt, M. J. 1964. Aboriginal food-gatherers of tropical Australia. *Proc. and Papers 9th Tech. Meet. I.U.C.N., Nairobi, Kenya*, pp. 30–37. Morges (Vaud), Switzerland: Int. Union Conserv. Nat. Natl. Resour.
45. Meggitt, M. J. 1965. Marriage among the Walbiri of Central Australia: A statistical examination. In *Aboriginal Man in Australia: Essays of Honour of Emeritus Professor A. P. Elkin*, ed. R. M. Berndt, C. H. Berndt, pp. 146–66. Sydney: Angus & Robertson. 491 pp.
46. Meggitt, M. J. 1967. *Gadjari Among the Walbiri Aborigines of Central Australia*. Oceania Monogr. No. 14. Sydney: Sydney Univ. Press. 129 pp.
47. Meggitt, M. J. 1968. Marriage classes and demography in Central Australia. In *Man the Hunter*, ed. R. B. Lee, I.

DeVore, pp. 176–84. Chicago: Aldine. 415 pp.

48. Meggitt, M. J. 1972. Understanding Australian Aboriginal society: kinship systems or cultural categories? In *Kinship Studies in the Morgan Centennial Year,* ed. P. Reining, pp. 64–87. Washington DC: Anthropol. Soc. Washington. 190 pp.

49. Moodie, P. M. 1973. *Aboriginal Health.* Canberra: Aust. Natl. Univ. Press. 307 pp.

50. Mountford, C. P., ed. 1960 *Records of the American–Australian Scientific Expedition to Arnhem Land, Vol. 2, Anthropology and Nutrition.* Melbourne: Melbourne Univ. Press. 297 pp.

51. Mountford, C. P. 1976. *Nomads of the Australian Desert.* Adelaide: Rigby. 628 pp.

52. Munn, N. D. 1970. The transformation of subjects into objects in Walbiri and Pitjantjatjara myth. See Ref. 39, pp. 142–63

53. Munn, N. D. 1973. *Walbiri Iconography: Graphic Representation and Cultural Symbolism in a Central Australian Society.* Ithaca: Cornell Univ. Press. 234 pp.

54. Myers, F. R. 1976. *"To have and to hold": A study of persistence and change in Pintupi social life.* PhD thesis. Bryn Mawr Coll. Bryn Mawr, Pa. 578 pp.

55. Myers, F. R. n.d. *Emotions and the self: A theory of personhood and political order among Pintupi Aborigines.* Unpublished paper

56. Myers, F. R. n.d. *Ideology and experience: The cultural basis of politics in Pintupi life.* Unpublished paper

57. Needham, R. 1962. Genealogy and category in Wikmunkan society. *Ethnology* 1:223–64

58. Peterson, N. 1969. Secular and ritual links: Two basic and opposed principles of Australian social organization as illustrated by Walbiri ethnography. *Mankind* 7:27–35

59. Peterson, N. 1970. Totemism yesterday: Sentiment and local organization among the Australian Aborigines. *Man (n.s.)* 7:12–32

60. Price, R. 1978. *A Palpable God: Thirty Stories Translated from the Bible with an Essay on the Origins and Life of Narrative.* New York: Atheneum. 195 pp.

61. Radcliffe-Brown, A. R. 1931. *The Social Organization of Australian Tribes.* Oceania Monogr. No. 1.Sydney: Sydney Univ. Press. 124 pp.

62. Reay, M. 1962. Subsections at Borroloola. *Oceania* 33:90–115

63. Reay, M., ed. 1964. *Aborigines Now.* Sydney: Angus & Robertson. 175 pp.

64. Róheim, G. 1945. *The Eternal Ones of the Dream.* New York: Int. Univ. Press. 270 pp.

65. Róheim, G. 1974. *Children of the Desert.* New York: Harper & Row. 262 pp.

66. Rose, F. G. G. 1960. *Classification of Kin, Age Structure and Marriage Amongst the Groote Eylandt Aborigines: A Study in Method and a Theory of Australian Kinship.* New York: Pergamon. 572 pp.

67. Rowley, C. D. 1970. *The Destruction of Aboriginal Society.* Canberra: Aust. Natl. Univ. Press. 430 pp.

68. Rowley, C. D. 1971. *Outcasts in White Australia.* Canberra: Aust. Natl. Univ. Press. 472 pp.

69. Rowley, C. D. 1971. *The Remote Aborigines.* Canberra: Aust. Natl. Univ. Press. 379 pp.

70. Scheffler, H. W. 1972. Afterword. In *Kinship and Behaviour in North Queensland: A Preliminary Account of Kinship and Social Organization on Cape York Peninsula,* by D. F. Thomson, pp. 37–52. Canberra: Aust. Inst. Aboriginal Stud. 59 pp.

71. Scheffler, H. W. 1978. *Australian Kin Classification.* New York: Cambridge Univ. Press. 569 pp.

72. Shapiro, W. 1968. The exchange of sister's daughter's daughters in northeast Arnhem Land. *Southwest. J. Anthropol.* 24:346–53

73. Shapiro, W. 1970. Local exogamy and the wife's mother in Aboriginal Australia. See Ref. 39, pp. 51–69

74. Stanner, W. E. H. 1936. Murinbata kinship and totemism. *Oceania* 7:186–216

75. Stanner, W. E. H. 1958. The dreaming. In *Reader in Comparative Religion,* ed. W. A. Lessa, E. Z. Vogt, pp. 513–23. New York: Harper & Row. 656 pp.

76. Stanner, W. E. H. 1965. Aboriginal territorial organization: Estate, range, domain and regime. *Oceania* 36:1–26

77. Stanner, W. E. H. 1965. Religion, totemism and symbolism. See Ref. 45, pp. 207–37

78. Stanner, W. E. H. 1966. *On Aboriginal Religion.* Oceania Monogr. No. 11. Sydney: Sydney Univ. Press. 171 pp.

79. Stanner, W. E. H. 1967. Reflections on Durkheim and Aboriginal religion. In *Social Organization: Essays Presented to Raymond Firth,* ed. M. Freedman, pp. 217–40. London: Cass. 300 pp.

80. Stanner, W. E. H. 1969. *After the Dreaming: Black and White Australi-*

ans. Sydney: Aust. Broadcast. Comm. 63 pp.

81. Stevens, F. 1974. *Aborigines in the Northern Territory Cattle Industry.* Canberra: Aust. Natl. Univ. 226 pp.

82. Steward, J. H. 1955. *Theory of Culture Change: The Methodology of Multilinear Evolution.* Urbana: Univ. Illinois Press. 244 pp. (Note: The three articles on band organization in this volume were first published as a single article in 1936.)

83. Strehlow, T. G. H. 1947. *Aranda Traditions.* Melbourne: Melbourne Univ. Press. 181 pp.

84. Strehlow, T. G. H. 1965. Culture, social structure, and environment in Aboriginal Central Australia. See Ref. 45, pp. 121–45

85. Strehlow, T. G. H. 1970. Geography and the totemic landscape in Central Australia: A functional study. See. Ref. 39, pp. 92–140

86. Strehlow, T. G. H. 1971. *Songs of Central Australia.* Sydney: Angus & Robertson. 775 pp.

87. Thomson, D. F. 1972. See Ref. 70, pp. 3–36

88. Tindale, N. B. 1974. *Aboriginal Tribes of Australia: Their Terrain, Environmental Controls, Distribution, Limits and Proper Names.* Berkeley: Univ. California Press. Two vols. 404 pp.

89. Tomkinson, R. 1974. *The Jigalong Mob: Aboriginal Victors of the Desert Crusade.* Menlo Park: Cummings. 166 pp.

90. Turner, D. H. 1974. *Tradition and Transformation: A Study of Aborigines in the Groote Eylandt Area, Northern Australia.* Canberra: Aust. Inst. Aboriginal Stud. 224 pp.

91. Turner, D. H. 1978. *Dialectics in tradition: Myth and social structure in two hunter-gatherer societies.* Occas. Pap. No. 36, R. Anthropol. Inst. 46 pp.

92. Warner, W. L. 1958. *A Black Civilization: A Study of an Australian Tribe.* New York: Harper. 618 pp. (First edition 1937)

93. Worsley, P. M. 1961. The utilization of food resources by an Australian Aboriginal tribe. *Acta Ethnogr.* 10: 153–90

94. Yengoyan, A. A. 1967. A comparison of certain marriage features between the Pitjandjara and other groups of the Western Desert with the northern groups, also some comments on the red ochre ceremonies. *J. Anthropol. Soc. S. Aust.* 5:16–19

95. Yengoyan, A. A. 1968. Demographic and ecological influences on Aboriginal Australian marriage sections. See Ref. 47, pp. 185–99

96. Yengoyan, A. A. 1968. Australian section systems—demographic components and interactional similarities with the Kung Bushmen. *Proc. Int. Congr. Anthropol. Ethnol. Sci., 8th, Tokyo* 3: 256–60

97. Yengoyan, A. A. 1970. Demographic factors in Pitjandjara social organization. See Ref. 39, pp. 70–91

98. Yengoyan, A. A. 1972. Biological and demographic components in Aboriginal Australian socio-economic organization. *Oceania* 43:85–95

99. Yengoyan, A. A. 1972. Ritual and exchange in Aboriginal Australia: An adaptive interpretation of male initiation rites. In *Social Exchange and Interaction,* ed. E. N. Wilmsen, pp. 5–9. Anthropol. Pap. No. 46, Univ. Michigan Mus. Anthropol. 147 pp.

100. Yengoyan, A. A. 1976. Structure, event and ecology in Aboriginal Australia: A comparative viewpoint. In *Tribes and Boundaries in Australia,* ed. N. Peterson, pp. 121–32. Canberra: Aust. Inst. Aboriginal Stud. 250 pp.

101. Yengoyan, A. A. 1978. Copulation, conception and deception in Aboriginal Australia. *Rev. Anthropol.* 5:107–15

Ann. Rev. Anthropol. 1979. 8:417–30

PHYSICAL ANTHROPOLOGY IN AUSTRALIA TODAY

♦9640

Joseph B. Birdsell

Emeritus Professor of Anthropology, University of California, Los Angeles, California 90024

INTRODUCTION

For more than a century, Aboriginal Australia has provided anthropologists with a rich field for their inquiries. Isolated, a continent inhabited only by hunter and gatherer peoples at the time of contact with Europeans, it presented a unique kind of laboratory for the testing of evolutionary hypotheses. Many of these hypotheses involve the origins of human culture and society, and time has proved most of them to have been poorly formulated. But interest in the Aborigines continues apace professionally, even though in most areas they are now passing to extinction both culturally and biologically.

Research on the Aborigines has flourished in the last decade or so as never before. Linguists have comprehensively surveyed the languages spoken in the continent. Prehistorians have pushed the occupancy of man in Australia well back into the Pleistocene, to some 40,000 years ago. Human fossils are being recovered systematically at an increasing rate with support from workers in geomorphology, paleoclimatology, and chronometric dating.

Human geneticists have surveyed the remaining Aboriginal population intensively, using an ever-expanding number of genetic markers. The development of computer software has revivified interest in the cranial remains which are being reexamined on a multivariate basis. Anthropometric research on the living Aborigine has declined in recent years, owing to the ethnic sensitivity of the subjects and their generally declining numbers.

0084-6570/79/1015-0417$01.00

The number of professional workers interested in the Australian Aborigines as models for human evolution has increased dramatically in recent years, both within Australia and among foreign scholars. The establishment of new state universities has provided new researchers in departments of genetics and schools of medicine. Unfortunately, two of the earlier students of physical anthropology of the Aborigines, both anatomists, have recently passed away. Professor N. G. W. MacIntosh (28) of the University of Sydney and Professor Andrew A. Abbie (1) of the University of Adelaide in the past have stated their views about the origins of the natives with such vigor that their positions will be remembered into the future.

THE PARTITION OF VARIABILITY

The pursuit of biological anthropology in Aboriginal Australia revolves primarily about two areas of inquiry: (*a*) the origin of the Aborigines and (*b*) the operation of microevolutionary processes in the very special environment of Australia, of a people with uniformly simple technology and social organization. An attempt to partition biological variability of human populations into logical compartments in present-day terms is shown in Table 1.

This partition of human variability is subject to both revision and dispute, but it strikes a fair preliminary balance. Perhaps the most important message from the table is that cranial studies, although indispensable for probing prehistory, cover only about one-third of the recognizable variability of a human population. Multivariate craniometric studies, now coming into such vogue, deal with but one-fifth of the total population variability. This may explain why they remain primarily taxonomic in nature and seldom come to grips with evolutionary processes and issues.

Studies of living subjects can and usually do investigate the entire postcranial body as well as the head and face. The use of measurements and

Table 1 Total population variability

A. Cranial variability	1. Metrical and indicial	20%
	2. Morphological	15%
(Postcranial variability seldom considered in recent materials)		
B. Living subjects	1. Metrical and indicial variability of the head and body	25%
	2. Morphological variability of the head and body	15%
C. Dental variability		10%
D. Biochemical variability		15%
		100%

morphological observation on the living are estimated to provide a coverage of more than one-third of the total variability evident in a population. Body variability is of course important in the study of human adaptability.

Dental variation is both real and important. Ultimately it should both illuminate the distant Asiatic origins of the Aborigines and help in the unraveling of microevolution on the continent. But since the classic study of Campbell (102), little research has been done until recent years. The long-continuing study at Yuendumu in the Northern Territory by Barrett & Brown (see 4) gives longitudinal information on a single desert population. The recent work by Hanihara (15) reexamines the dental characters of the regionally limited series of crania in Australian museums. To date there has been little investigation of spatial variation of dental characters in Australia.

Today biochemical variability may be estimated as contributing about 15 percent to the total found in a population. But its boundaries are expanding rapidly as new genetic markers are being identified, so its share of the total will increase in the future. These marker traits are genetically simple and so are particularly responsive to such random microevolutionary processes as intergenerational drift and founder effect. Selection certainly operates upon them in a variety of ways, unidentified at this time. Genetic characters seem more useful as indicators of microevolutionary change than for the determination of long-term biological relationships. This was dramatically disclosed in the 1974 symposium on "The Origin of the Australians," which will be discussed later.

A METHODOLOGICAL VOGUE

It is one of the scientific vogues these days to use the computer to calculate various forms of "genetic distance" between series of populations. The methods are statistically complex and varied in form, but all fail in terms of expressing evolutionary significance. At best these statistical devices are measuring differences between populations and not biological relationships. Each fails to take into account those evolutionary processes which are constantly working on all populations. The matter will be discussed in more detail below.

Basic to much confusion in evolutionary biology is the idea that "likeness equates with relationship." In long-term evolution, where parallel and convergent evolution can be checked against an extensive record, similarity in analogous structures is used as a measure of relationship. But even within a genus, and certainly within a species, the degree of likeness does not uniformly express lineal relationships. This is true whether one is dealing with gene markers, metrical measurements and indices, or morphological characters. Biomathematicians playing their own games have in general ignored the impact of evolutionary processes or have used such simple assumptions as to be totally unrealistic (3). To assume, as have Cavalli-Sforza and Edwards (in a series of papers), that evolution has proceeded mainly through random genetic drift and so to ignore both the effects of selection and migration does not lend confidence in either their measures of "genetic distance" or the family trees constructed using them. To consider, as have Morton and his coworkers (302), that all populations have a common ancestry, with evolution proceeding through descent, and ignoring other evolutionary processes, lends no confidence to their constructs. As pointed out by Balakrishnan (2), measures of "genetic distance" need have no biological meaning. This makes them dubious instruments for unraveling either biological relationships or processes of evolution. That they contain further contentious statistical assumptions is beside the point.

FOSSIL MAN IN AUSTRALIA

Only a decade ago time depth for man's occupancy of Australia was limited to about 6000 years. This seemingly short time span gave consolation to those who believed that the continent had been peopled by a single wave of relatively homogeneous people. Today cultural time depth approaches 40,000 years, and the fossil remains of man himself are nearly 30,000 years old, as in the case of Mungo III. Well-directed searches for the remains of ancestral Australians have been so successful that their numbers recovered now rival those of modern man in Europe both in quantity and in evolutionary significance.

The two major regions which provide this paleoanthropological wealth are Kow Swamp, on the Victorian side of the middle Murray River, and the Willandra Lakes district of western New South Wales. The Kow Swamp series of finds, with dates ranging around 10,000 years ago, are the results of the intensive work of A. G. Thorne (37, 38). Working out of the Australian National University in Canberra, this energetic anatomist has uncovered some 40 burials at the Kow Swamp site. They include a number of fairly complete crania, eight of which yield a reasonable number of measurements, and serve to define the local population.

This fossil group of Australians differs significantly from recent inhabitants in southeastern Australia. In common with other Pleistocene forms of modern man, they are large and robust. Their archaic features include unusually sloping foreheads, heavy brow ridges, big faces, and a massive anterior mandible. Their teeth are larger generally than those of recent Aborigines. All in all, they might be considered to represent suitable ancestors for the living southeastern Australians, perhaps showing archaic anatomical flourishes reminiscent of the last of the Javanese Pleistocene forms, *Homo soloensis.*

The view of Australian prehistory sketched above is rudely shattered by a series of fossil finds from the Willandra Lakes region which date from 15,000 to 20,000 years earlier. In this district a series of shallow freshwater lakes came into existence about 44,000 years ago and continued until 18,000 years ago. Around their shores early Australians left their burials, tools, the ashes of their fires, and the remains of their meals, including fish and shellfish.

Mungo I, the first of the fossils discovered at Lake Mungo, has been chronometrically dated to about 25,000 B.P. The burial, which had been cremated, represents a very delicate female. Enough of the vault has been restored to indicate how widely she deviates anatomically from the Kow Swamp population which lived some 15,000 years later. A further series of burials has been recovered from the Willandra Lakes' shores, but they have not yet been published in sufficient detail except to note that they, too, in both male and female sexes are said to represent the lightly built kind of people indicated by the first burial.

As things now stand in this rapidly changing scene, there seem to be two ancestral populations, the earliest one from the Willandra Lakes dating from about 25,000 years ago, and then a subsequent one from Kow Swamp about 10,000 years old. The latter is notably robust and archaic appearing. This sequence is an unexpected one, and to date Thorne has provided no easy solution. Certainly these finds indicate considerable heterogeneity of population in time. The Mungo I is somewhat reminiscent of the skull from Niah in North Borneo, which certainly is to be classified as Negritoid in derivation. The evidence in a preliminary fashion seems to indicate a sequence of biologically differing populations migrating into Australia in Terminal Pleistocene times. Prehistory offers little consolation to those who claim homogeneity for the living Aborigines.

Some of the fossil remains discovered earlier can be fitted into the new pattern. The undated Cohuna skull, long a problem in Australian prehistory because of its archaic anatomy, can now confidently be assigned to the Kow Swamp series. Appropriately, it was found nearby. On the other hand, the Keilor cranium from southern Victoria, a little older than 10,000 years, is very unlike its near contemporaries at Kow Swamp. Keilor is a big skull, but it is rather gracile and shares none of the archaic features found in the Kow Swamp population.

So in spite of the rich new materials, problems of Australian prehistory proliferate at the human level. The gracile population is uncomfortably early. The archaic peoples from Kow Swamp are much later in time, and apparent contemporaneity with such dissimilar forms as Keilor is not helpful. The future of paleoanthropology in Australia should be full of exciting new discoveries and problems to be solved.

ON THE ORIGIN OF THE AUSTRALIANS

An appropriate summary of the state of physical anthropology in Australia was provided by an international symposium held in 1974 in Canberra, Australia (8). Its 26 invited papers, solicited from an international field of scientists, were devoted to the topic "The Origin of the Australians." The two-day session was organized by R. L. Kirk, a serologist of world stature, and A. G. Thorne, an anatomist in whose fortunate hands rest most of the Pleistocene hominid finds from the continent. In spite of high expectations, no lasting contributions were made toward solving the origin of the Australians. It was almost as though the Aborigines had no ancestors.

Seventeen of the papers delivered are pertinent to this discussion. Among those devoted to the Pleistocene background of the origin of the Aborigines several stood out. Chappell (11) summarized the late Quaternary paleogeography of the Australian-East Indonesian region in a useful fashion. Bowler (8) gave a superb reconstruction of the late Pleistocene environments in Australia. The Hopes (16) offered the interesting suggestion that during the terminal glaciation in New Guinea, man could have occupied the boundary zone between the shrubby tree-fern grasslands and the alpine heaths. There is some archaeological evidence to substantiate this hypothesis.

During a session devoted to early man in Australia, Jacob (22) reviewed the Pleistocene finds from Java and presented his own taxonomic scheme for the pithecanthropines of that island. He distinguished gracile forms from robust ones, discounting that they may represent age or sex differences, and believes them to overlap contemporaneously in time. He doubted that the pithecanthropines ever migrated to Australasia, but thought it likely that some of their genes might have been inherited by the earliest migrants to the further region. Thorne (37) provided data on morphological contrasts between the Kow Swamp and Mungo types of Pleistocene Australians. Microevolution has produced significant morphological change within the continent over the last 10,000 years, but this does not explain the origin of the divergent populations. Thorne recognized that important problems remain unsolved. Bowler & Thorne (9) documented the discovery and excavation of the fossil hominid known as Lake Mungo III. The fully articulated burial was extended, represented a short, gracile male, and the dating was placed between 28,000 and 30,000 B.P. These were all very useful papers and served to indicate the great progress made in Australian prehistory and paleoanthropology.

The papers on morphological variation contained considerable variety. Howells (17–19) presented another version of his multivariate analysis of Oceanic crania. He concluded that the Australians stand separately from the others, that they are not related to any of the present populations of Asia, and he indicated no origins. He identified the Tasmanians as Melanesians, but did not solve the difficulty this presents to his scheme. Howells concedes that the Tasmanian ancestors came overland from continental Australia, but does not reconcile this with his steadfast belief that the Australian Aborigines represent a single homogeneous population. Giles (14) used a discriminant function analysis on more than a thousand crania from Australia. He found that the cranial series from Arnhem Land can be distinguished from those of other parts of the eastern portion of the continent. This same finding was made by Morant (29), Hrdlicka (21), Wagner (40), using metrical data, and by Fenner (13) using morphological data. All of these authors, on the basis of simple univariate analysis and massive cranial series, anticipated Giles' conclusion. Giles himself gives no extracontinental relationships for the Australians and so does not contribute to the solution of their origins. Indeed, the complex multivariate methods used by Howells and Giles do not appear to justify the analytical complexity they introduced.

In an interesting paper on Aboriginal paleophysiology, MacFarlane (27) suggested that the persistence of high rates of water use in desert Aborigines indicates an ultimate wet tropical region of origin. Presumably Southeast Asia might be a candidate. Brown (10) reported on the striking change in phenotypic dimensions among Aboriginal children born at Yuendumu in the Northern Territory. Compared to their parental generation, they show large increases in stature and other body attributes such as head size. While his paper does not bear upon origins, it strikingly suggests that at least in this locale dietary differences may have resulted in dramatic phenotypic changes in size.

Dermatoglyphic data are considered in two papers. Prokopec & Sedivy (33), using a substantial series of dermatoglyphs from Arnhem Land, find no other populations with similar characteristics. The closest comparisons seem to lie with Asiatic pygmies and Micronesians, but the differences revealed are more important than the likenesses. Parsons & White (32), using both dermatoglyphic materials and certain nonmetrical cranial traits, concluded that microevolutionary variation had been important in Australian populations, both before and after their arrival on that continent. But they offer no opinions as to the origins of the Aborigines.

It might have been anticipated that patterns of variability in the rich store of genetic markers available these days would disclose biological relationships between the Australians and living Asiatic populations. But a series of four authoritiative papers dash this hope. Lie-Injo (25), using nearly half a hundred genetic markers including blood groups, enzymes, and serum proteins as well as others, finds the Australian Aboriginal groups clearly separated from all Southeast Asiatic populations. The latter included Negritoes, Senoi, and a variety of Mongoloids. There were even greater differences in terms of populations from India and China. In short, he found nothing to indicate Australian origins in Southeastern Asia using this wide panel of genetic markers.

Simmons (36), after 35 years of working with blood group genes, regretted that they failed to provide any clues as to the origin of the Aborigines. Kirk (23, 24), having spent 15 years diligently searching for specific genetic markers that might link the Australians with Asiatic populations, finally concluded that an array of 100 or more genetic markers might be needed to do so. In view of Lie-Injo's failure with nearly 50 genetic markers to do so, Kirk's optimism may not be justified. Time depth and microevolution seem to have blurred relationships too effectively to be traced in this fashion. Omato & Misawa (31), using another formidable battery of gene markers, conclude that the Ainu show greater genetic similarities to the Mongoloid groups surrounding them than they do to other populations. By these data they reveal no affinities with either Australians or Europeans. Sanghvi (34), in a paper devoted primarily to the analysis of allelic variation, compares data from Australia with ten tribal populations from western India. He finds no particular genetic similarity between these two blocs of populations.

Several factors help to explain the failure of the Canberra symposium to find any traces of the origins of the Australians. The depth of time now involved in their antiquity, which is documented to 40,000 years ago in Australia and may stretch twice as far back, is important in blurring traces of relationship with populations in Asia. Microevolution has proceeded both among the relict groups on the mainland and in Australia itself. It is likely that simple genetic markers have been the most altered in this span of time.

Certainly the equation that "likeness equals relationship" is a rickety basis for the elaborate methodological approaches being used these days. Until the processes of microevolution have been successfully dissected and their consequences become quasi-predictable, ancient taxonomic relationships will remain badly blurred. The Australians have origins but the methods used recently have not recovered evidence for them.

The character of research upon the Australians has been something of a handicap. Most workers have limited themselves to the materials from restricted regions, usually those easily accessible. They have tended to operate within the narrow limits of a specialized approach, be it craniometry, population genetics, or the study of the living. Each area has its own contributions to make, but these must be synthesized in the end for Australian origins to be determined.

The Aborigines themselves pose problems in regional sampling. The 1200 crania housed in the museums of the world disproportionately come from the eastern and southern coastal regions and the adjacent Murray and Darling drainages. About 150 crania have been derived from northwestern Arnhem Land. The rest of this vast continent is virtually unrepresented in cranial collections.

Living Aborigines regrettably are greatly reduced in numbers. After the establishment of permanent white contact, Tindale (39) demonstrated that full-blooded Aborigines declined at the rate of 50 percent per generation save in a few isolated or protected areas. Since most investigators preferred to work with the "wild" natives of the Northern Territory, this meant that with few exceptions the living subjects in Queensland, New South Wales, Victoria, South Australia, and Western Australia have been ignored. Only Birdsell and Tindale, during two separate periods of field work each lasting 2 years, concentrated in those unworked areas.

As strange as it may sound, simple numerical and statistical errors have in at least two cases distorted the picture of Aboriginal origins. MacIntosh (28) measured 41 male Aboriginals in southwest Arnhem Land. Their mean stature was 167.4 cm, a very ordinary value for the continent. But he was much impressed that individuals in this series varied from short to tall stature. MacIntosh concluded that his group represented all the populations of Australia and so claims for regional population differences must be in error. He fatally failed to distinguish between intragroup variation and intergroup variation. In fact, regional populations of male Aborigines range in stature from the very short mean of 155 cm to a tall 174 cm.

Howells & Warner (20), in an early analysis of 240 male Arnhem Landers, provided a kind of baseline against which to judge later results. Howells believed that his data revealed the Australian Aborigines as a homogeneous continental population. Unfortunately, his published work includes a very simple error that seems to have gone unrecognized. In calculating the cephalo-facial index, he divided skull breadth by face breadth, giving regional subgroups a range of 93 to 101 percent. These values were concordant with those published for the rest of Australia. Had he calculated the index correctly, that is, divided facial breadth by cranial breadth, the cephalo-facial index would have ranged from 99 to 105 percent. These values are exceptional for Australia and for all but a few other human populations. This single variable separates the Arnhem Landers from all other Australians and would have changed Howells' decision about the origins of the Australians had he recognized it. Unfortunately, this simple numerical mistake has not yet been corrected in print.

ON THE HETEROGENEITY OF THE ABORIGINES

There are no satisfactory rules to follow in evaluating the original homogeneity or heterogeneity of a continental population such as the Australians. Routine statistical tests of significance applied to regionally different populations need have little biological meaning. Decisions must be based upon criteria originating in evolutionary biology, as we will see later. For the present, the following straws are in the wind of professional opinion. Researchers dealing with genetic markers primarily sampled in the northern half of the continent (12, 30, 35) are much impressed with the variability revealed. Rather uniformly they tend to view the Australians as heterogeneous in their origins, but they are reluctant and unable to point to specific Asiatic populations as ancestors. The enriched record of fossil man in Australia indicates very considerable differences between earlier and later population strata. To most observers the differences would be too great to be submerged in the normal range of variation of a single population element. On the other hand, workers with interests limited to craniometry, while recognizing regional differences within the continent, have no evolutionary criteria by which to test their meaning. Accordingly, they still tend to feel that the Australians were originally a homogeneous population upon which microevolution has produced patterns of regional differentiation. Few workers dealing with living Aborigines have surveyed widely enough to form strong impressions.

Birdsell (5) has seen no reason to change his original view that the Australians are trihybrid in origin in which successive waves of immigrants were drawn from Negritoid populations in Southeast Asia, Ainoid strata from East Asia, and Veddoids from peninsular India. Although his views were first published many years ago, it is of interest that none of the proponents of Aboriginal homogeneity ever bothered to visit the still living populations of southeast Australia and the Cairns rain forests of northeast Queensland to confirm through their own experience the existence there of suggestive relict populations.

The great time depth now available in Australia, approaching 40,000 years on the mainland and 18,000 years on now insular Tasmania (7), has changed the scale of the problem. Given that these are minimum estimates, it becomes very difficult to maintain that over this time span the ports of exit in Southeast Asia were continuously populated by the same types of peoples. Certainly much happened on that continent during the Upper Pleistocene, and population shifts and pressures must have been considerable. This single factor of increasing time depth is sufficient to alter the odds notably in favor of heterogeneity for the ancestors of the present Australians.

THE ANALYSIS OF CLINES

Clines are biological gradients in space whose complex sloping surfaces reflect past evolutionary events. An individual clinal surface, representing a single trait, usually shows complex systems of curves looking much like those on a weather map (which is in itself a cline). The primary significance in clinal distributions lies not in the pattern, but rather in the gradient of the slopes of the surfaces. A method of analysis has already been published by Birdsell (6).

The data are now sufficiently rich to create clinal maps of much of Australia in terms of its Aboriginal biology. When the writer's ongoing analysis is complete, the results should be of importance both to the problem of Australian origins and the identification and measurement of microevolutionary processes. Generally the clinal structures for different traits show little or no linkage, that is, they are not organized so that the patterns of gradients, or peaks and sinks, are concordant. This led to the statement by Livingston (26) that "clines are chaos." In a very broad way the proposition holds for data on the Australians.

The unlinked character of clines allows for the formulation of a hypothesis for the origin of the Australian. If it should prove that in areas marginal in terms of distance from the point of entry across the northern shores of Australia, or patterned in terms of topography or flora, clines repeatedly define steep slopes in terms of characters in a linked fashion, these will reflect ancient population residues on the continent. Random events in evolution can be predicted to show a haphazard pattern rather than consistent clinal gradients. The data useful for such an analysis include cranial characters, those derived from the living Aborigines, and of course genetic markers. Care must be taken to distinguish between the consequences of microevolution since man has arrived in Australia and the pattern of biological variation introduced by migrating waves of peoples. It is not too early to say that the approach has promise.

The clinal approach to Aboriginal data has the even more important prospect of displaying spatial variation in such a fashion as to allow some estimation of the types of evolutionary processes ongoing on the continent,

and perhaps even their duration and intensity. Certainly some understanding of the forces of evolution which produce differentiation in human
populations is a more important goal than merely understanding the origins
of the Aborigines. In a broad way, clinal variation on the continent tends
to be oriented in north-south axes. This may be interpreted either as indicating selective processes varying with the environment or as residues left by
incoming waves of populations over long periods of time. But there are ways
in which the two different factors can be distinguished. In addition, when
data are distributed in terms of tribal units, that is, effective breeding
populations, it becomes apparent that random factors in evolution such as
intergenerational drift, and possibly more importantly founder effect, have
quite dramatically altered gene frequencies on the local scene. Thus there
appear series of peaks and sinks in some of the clinal surfaces. It should be
noted that the heterogeneous sampling of Aborigines on white settlements,
be they missions or working stations, degrade the real differences between
tribes and so suppress much of this kind of information. The prospects are
exciting for this type of analysis, and Australia is a continent where biology
offers this approach.

However that may be, it is apparent that both the data of paleoanthropology and the results of clinal analysis must in final terms be concordant with each other. With the continuing recovery of Pleistocene fossils in
Australia, it seems certain that population differences will become more
apparent at various places and at various stages of time. The affinities of
these ancient populations should be recognizable in the residuals detected
by the method of clinal analysis. The fossil record uniquely works directly
with time differences in population. It has produced the Pleistocene population at Kow Swamp, which would not have been predicted from any data
on living Aborigines. On the other hand, it is unlikely that the fossil record
will ever be sufficient to define clinal gradients in time over the whole of
Australia. The two approaches are supplementary.

CONCLUSIONS

As a continent exclusively occupied by hunters and gatherers, Australia in
Aboriginal times represented a unique natural laboratory. Time depth has
now been established as about 40,000 years of human occupancy, and may
be much greater. This is ample for the operation of microevolutionary
forces on a culturally homogeneous continental population. This is the real
goal in studying the Australians, but progress has barely commenced, even
though most of the data are in hand. Important results can be expected for
the future.

An interesting but secondary goal is to unravel the population origins of the people who migrated to Australia. Many workers in various subfields have presented hypotheses on this issue. Today the craniometrists, in spite of computers and statistically sophisticated approaches, still tend to believe that the Australians represent a single population of homogeneous origins. Workers dealing with genetic markers, on the other hand, seem convinced of heterogeneity among the Aborigines, but in no case do their data point to Asiatic populations as likely ancestors. Noise in evolutionary processes and great time depth suffice to explain this failure. Workers dealing with living Aborigines have seldom sampled widely enough to evaluate the real continental variability present. The analysis of clines holds the promise of investigating in terms of biological evolution instead of routine statistical restraints. It can be used to detect the residuals of characters left by ancient populations differing in biology, and more importantly to identify micro-evolutionary processes in action, and perhaps even to estimate their intensity and duration. When combined with the great enrichment of the fossil record on the continent, these diverse approaches offer an exciting series of developments in the future.

Literature Cited

1. Abbie, A. A. 1969. *The Original Australians.* London: Muller
2. Balakrishnan, V. 1972. Comments on "The Theory and Estimation of Genetic Distance," by M. Nei. In *Genetic Structure of Populations,* ed. N. E. Morton. Honolulu: Univ. Hawaii Press
3. Balakrishnan, V., Sanghvi, L. D., Kirk, R. L. 1973. *Genetic Diversity Among Australian Aborigines.* Aust. Aboriginal Stud., Res. Reg. Stud., No. 3. Canberra: Aust. Inst. Aboriginal Stud.
4. Barrett, M. J., Brown, T. 1971. Increase in average height of Australian Aborigines. *Med. J. Aust.* 2:1169–72
5. Birdsell, J. B. 1967. Preliminary data on the trihybrid origin of the Australian Aborigines. *Arch. Phys. Anthropol. Oceania* 2 (2):100–55
6. Birdsell, J. B. 1972. The problem of evolution in human races: Classification or clines. *Soc. Biol.* 19:136–62
7. Bowdler, S. 1974. Pleistocene date for man in Tasmania. *Nature* 252:697–98
8. Bowler, J. M. 1976. Recent developments in reconstructing Late Quaternary environments in Australia. In *The Origin of the Australians,* ed. R. L. Kirk, A. G. Thorne, pp. 55–77. Canberra: Hum. Biol. Ser. 6, Aust. Inst. Aboriginal Stud.
9. Bowler, J. M., Thorne, A. G. 1976. Human remains from Lake Mungo: Discovery and excavation of Lake Mungo III. See Ref. 8, pp. 127–38
10. Brown, T. 1976. Head size increases in Australian Aborigines: An example of skeletal plasticity. See Ref. 8, pp. 195–209
10a. Campbell, T. D. 1925. *Dentition and Palate of the Australian Aborigines.* Publications under Keith Sheridan Found. No. 1, Univ. Adelaide
11. Chappell, J. M. A. 1976. Aspects of Late Quaternary paleogeography on the Australian-East Indonesian region. See Ref. 8, pp. 11–22
12. Curtain, C. C., van Loghen, E., Schanfield, M. S. 1976. Immunoglobulin markers as indicators of population affinities in Australia and the Western Pacific. See Ref. 8, pp. 347–64
13. Fenner, F. J. 1939. The Australian Aboriginal skull: its non-metrical morphological characters. *Trans. R. Soc. S. Aust.* 63 (2):248–306
14. Giles, E. 1976. Cranial variation in Australia and neighbouring areas. See Ref. 8, pp. 161–72
15. Hanihara, K. 1976. *Statistical and comparative studies of the Australian dentition.* Bull. 11, Univ. Tokyo Museum

16. Hope, J. H., Hope, G. S. 1976. Palaeo-environments for man in New Guinea. See Ref. 8, pp. 29–54

17. Howells, W. W. 1973. Cranial variation in man: A study by multivariate analysis. *Peabody Mus. Pap.* 67

18. Howells, W. W. 1973. *The Pacific Islanders.* London: Weidenfeld & Nicolson

19. Howells, W. W. 1976. Metrical analysis in the problem of Australian origins. See Ref. 8, pp. 141–60

20. Howells, W. W., Warner, W. L. 1937. Anthropometry of the natives of Arnhem Land and the Australian race problem. *Pap. Peabody Mus. Archaeol. Ethnol. Harv. Univ.* 16 (1):1–97

21. Hrdlicka, A. 1923. Catalogue of the human crania in the United States National Museum collections: Australians, Tasmanians, South African Bushmen, Hottentots and Negroes. Washington DC:GPO

22. Jacob, T. 1976. Early populations in the Indonesian region. See Ref. 8, pp. 81–93

23. Kirk, R. L. 1965. The distribution of genetic markers in Australian Aborigines. *Occas. Pap. Aboriginal Stud.* 4. Canberra:Aust. Inst. Aboriginal Stud.

24. Kirk, R. L. 1976. Serum protein and enzyme markers as indicators of population affinities in Australia and the Western Pacific. See Ref. 8, pp. 329–46

25. Lie-Injo, L. E. 1976. Genetic relationships of several Aboriginal groups in South East Asia. See Ref. 8. pp. 277–306

26. Livingston, F. B. 1962. On the non-existence of human races. *Curr. Anthropol.* 3:279–83

27. MacFarlane, W. V. 1976. Aboriginal palaeophysiology. See Ref. 8, pp. 183–94

28. MacIntosh, N. W. G. 1952. Stature in some aboriginal tribes in SouthWest Arnhem Land. *Oceania* 2:208–15

29. Morant, G. M. 1927. A study of the Australian and Tasmanian skulls based on previously published measurements. *Biometrika* 19:417–40

30. Morrison, J. 1967. The biracial origin of the Australian Aborigines. *Med. J. Aust.* 2:1054–56

30a. Morton, N. E., Keats, B. 1976. Human microdifferentiation in the Western Pacific. See Ref. 8, pp. 379–99

31. Omoto, K., Misawa, S. 1976. The genetic relations of the Ainu. See Ref. 8, pp. 365–76

32. Parsons, P. A., White, N. G. 1976. Variability of anthropometric traits in Australian Aboriginals and adjacent populations. See Ref. 8, pp. 227–43

33. Prokopec, M., Sedivy, V. 1976. Australian Aboriginals and the outer world: dermatoglyphical evidence. See Ref. 8, pp. 215–26

34. Sanghvi, L. D. 1976. Comparative genetic studies between some groups of Australian Aboriginals and certain tribal peoples of India. See Ref. 8, pp. 401–14

35. Schanfield, M. S. 1977. Population affinities of the Australian Aborigines as reflected by the genetic markers of immunoglobulins. *J. Hum. Evol.* 6 (4):341–52

36. Simmons, R. T. 1976. The biological origin of the Australian Aborigines. An examination of blood group genes and gene frequencies for possible evidence in populations from Australia to Eurasia. See Ref. 8, pp. 307–28

37. Thorne, A. G. 1976. Morphological contrasts in Pleistocene Australians. See Ref. 8, pp. 95–112

38. Thorne, A. G., Wilson, S. R. 1977. Pleistocene and recent Australians: a multivariate comparison. *J. Hum. Evol.* 6 (4):393–402

39. Tindale, N. B. 1941. Survey of the half-caste problem in South Australia. *Proc. R. Geogr. Soc. Aust. SA Branch Adelaide* 1940–41:66–161

40. Wagner, K. 1937. The craniology of the Oceanic races. *Skr. Nor. Vidensk. Akad. Oslo 1:* Mat.-Naturv. K1. (2):1–193

Ann. Rev. Anthropol. 1979. 8:431–43

THE NATURE
AND DEVELOPMENT
OF AUSTRALIAN LANGUAGES

◆9641

R. M. W. Dixon

Department of Linguistics, SGS, Australian National University, P.O. Box 4, Canberra, A.C.T., 2600, Australia

INTRODUCTION

The first Australian word list was taken down in 1770 by Captain James Cook (12) and Sir Joseph Banks (3) during their six weeks on shore in northeast Queensland repairing the *Endeavour* after it had been damaged on the Great Barrier Reef. The 180 Guugu Yimidhirr words included /kaɲurru/, transcribed as "kangaroo," the most notable loan word from an Australian language into English. In 1820 Captain P. P. King (43) revisited the Endeavour River and replicated most of Cook's list, except that he obtained *menuah* for "kangaroo," suggesting perhaps that Cook had made a mistake with his term; in fact, King had been given /minha/, a generic term meaning "edible animal." Roth (53) and Haviland (34) have pointed out that /kaɲurru/ is a bone fide Guugu Yimidhirr word.

When Governor Arthur Phillip brought the first convict party to Sydney Cove in 1788, he was greatly surprised to find that none of the words recorded by Cook were recognized by the local Aborigines. Then, in April 1791, Phillip explored to the Hawkesbury River, 40 miles to the northwest of Sydney, and found a different language spoken there (51); this gave the first clue that there must in fact be many different languages spoken in Australia. The next advance in Australian linguistics was due to the explorer Captain George Grey (28). In 1841 he pointed out the similarities in form and meaning between lexical items, and also pronouns, in languages from different parts of the continent and suggested, in effect, that the many different languages of Australia comprised a single family.

Most later workers have implicitly followed Grey in ascribing a genetic unity to the 200 or so distinct languages of Australia. Yet attempts at proof

431

0084-6570/79/1015-0431$01.00

of this genetic connection—in terms of reconstruction of aspects of the proto-language and the regular changes by which modern systems have developed—have seriously commenced only within the last dozen years. There was until recently a dearth of sound descriptive studies of Australian languages on which to base a comparative study. There were a handful of useful missionary grammars in the nineteenth century (e.g. 46, 54, 58, 59) but, apart from the work of Capell, virtually nothing was done from 1920 until 1955. Following Capell's 1956 monograph, *A New Approach to Australian Linguistics* (6), an increasing number of professional linguists have been working intensively in the Australian field (e.g. 2, 5, 9, 14, 17–19, 22–24, 27, 31, 39, 41, 45, 55, 61).

Capell (6) distinguished two major classes of Australian languages: those in an area in the western and central far north use prefixes as well as suffixes and are fairly different from one another; languages over the rest of the continent use only suffixes and share many lexical and grammatical forms. A lexicostatistical classification (49) was attempted in the early 1960s, recognizing 29 "phylic families." Most nonprefixing languages, covering 90% of the continent, were said to comprise the "Pama-Nyungan family" (after the words for "man" at its northeastern and southwestern extremes); the other 28 families covered Capell's prefixing type and a few nonprefixing languages adjacent to the prefixing block. The data on which the lexicostatistic classification was based, and even the percentage figures themselves, have not been made available; the classification has little to commend it.

Recent comparative work (21) indicates that almost all mainland Australian languages do belong to a single genetic family. The criterial evidence is a set of monosyllabic verb roots which can be reconstructed for proto-Australian (pA) and have reflexes in almost every modern language, of both prefixing and nonprefixing types. There are just two languages—Tiwi (50) and Djingili (11)—which lack verb cognates; we cannot at present be certain that these do belong in the Australian family.

It appears that pA had an agglutinative structure. Nouns and pronouns inflected for case and verbs for tense. The languages in a northern block have developed bound pronominal and other types of prefix, and have undergone various phonological changes so that words cannot now be clearly segmented into morphemes; these prefixing languages have developed into an inflectional (or fusional) type. Since information about subject and object noun phrases is cross-referenced in the verb, there is little need for ergative and accusative inflections (marking transitive subject and object respectively) and these have generally been lost in prefixing languages.

Over the rest of the continent there has been a tendency toward augmenting the case systems, maintaining a basically agglutinative profile. Free-form pronouns have developed into enclitics which can be attached to the end of the verb, or of the first word in the sentence, in some nonprefixing languages; this has probably been a relatively recent development.

There is no evidence on which to date proto-Australian. It could well have been spoken by the first men to enter the continent 40,000 or more years ago; or it could, equally well, have been considerably later. But if it were spoken only 10,000 years ago (and it is likely to be at least this old), it was twice as far away in the past as, for instance, proto-Indo-European. There has been much movement of tribes in Australia as water incidence and other geographical features have shifted. Constant interchange between tribes has led to the diffusion of physical, cultural, and also linguistic traits.

Although we can show that almost all Australian languages are genetically related and can establish many low-level subgroups containing from two to seven or eight languages (e.g. 29, 33, 47), no detailed work has yet been done on the possibility of higher-level subgrouping in terms of shared innovations during the development from pA. Indeed, in Australia it is particularly hard to separate similarities that are evidence of genetic relationship from areal features that have been borrowed from one language to another across a geographically defined region of the continent (see 37).

PHONOLOGY

Most Australian languages have remarkably similar sets of consonant and vowel phonemes and also phonotactic structures (49). There are generally no fricatives or sibilants, and voicing is not phonologically contrastive for stops. There can be from four to seven stops, with a nasal corresponding to each, and from one to four laterals. All languages have two semivowels and almost all show two rhotics—an apico-alveolar trill /rr/ and an apico-postalveolar (semiretroflex) continuant /r/.

The maximal system is shown by Yanyuwa (44; see Table 1), spoken just south of the Gulf of Carpentaria (we employ a standard practical orthography with digraphs *rd, dh, ny, rr*, etc).

Table 1 Maximal phonological system shown by Yanyuwa

Active articulator	Tongue tip (apico-)		Tongue blade (lamino-)		Back of tongue (dorso-)		Labial
Passive articulator	Alveolar	Postalveolar	Dental	Palatal	Palatal	Velar	
Stop	d	rd	dh	j	gy	g	b
Nasal	n	rn	nh	ny	ŋy	ŋ	m
Lateral	l	rl	lh	ly			
Rhotic	rr	r					
Semivowel			y		w		

Comparative evidence points to proto-Australian having had a smaller consonant inventory (21):

	Apical	Laminal	Dorsal	Labial
Stop	d	j	g	b
Nasal	n	ny	ŋ	m
Lateral	l	(ly?)		
Rhotic	rr, r			
Semivowel		y		w

Some languages preserve essentially this system; others have split apical and/or laminal and/or dorsal into two phonemically contrastive series. It is likely that in pA the laminal stop and nasal (articulated with the blade of the tongue) had lamino-palatal pronunciation (blade against the hard palate) before *i* and lamino-dental (blade against the teeth) before *a* and *u*. Some modern languages preserve this allophonic distribution, but others have innovated *dh, nh* before *i* and/or *j, ny* before *a* and *u,* so that there are now two laminal stop and two laminal nasal phonemes. Similarly, the apical stop and nasal (involving the tip of the tongue) originally had a postalveolar (retroflex) articulation after *u,* but apico-alveolar articulation elsewhere. Again, some modern languages preserve this pattern, but others now have a phonemic contrast between /d/, /n/ and /rd/, /rn/, all occurring after all vowels. It is significant—providing support for this hypothesis of historical evolution—that in most modern languages with a laminal contrast this is neutralized in word-final position; and an apical contrast, where it occurs at medial and final positions, is generally neutralized word-initially.

Two laminal series are found along the west and southwest coasts and over the eastern half of the continent, except for a strip on the central east coast. Two apical series are found in almost all languages outside Queensland and New South Wales [maps of distribution are in (21).] The third split, of dorsal stop and nasal into dorso-palatal /gy/, /ŋy/ and dorso-velar /g/, /ŋ/, has been reported very recently for Yanyuwa and two or three neighboring languages (11, 26). All other Australian languages have a single dorso-velar stop /g/ and nasal /ŋ/; all have bilabial /b/ and /m/.

There is generally a lateral in each apical and laminal stop-nasal series for languages west of the Gulf of Carpentaria (although some of these languages have only two or three laterals, where more would be expected); languages east of the Gulf have a single lateral, /l/. Almost all languages have two rhotics (irrespective of whether there are one or two apical stop/nasal series). Just three or four have a single rhotic, while a number have three distinct rhotic phonemes—trilled /rr/, continuant /r/, and either flap /ɾ/ or voiceless trill /r̥r̥/. The glottal stop occurs in a few northern languages, the result of recent phonological changes.

There is strong evidence that pA had both monosyllabic and polysyllabic roots (and probably also words). In the basic syllable structure $C_1V(C_2)$, C_1 could be a stop, nasal, semivowel, or r, while C_2 was restricted to nasal, lateral, rr, or y. In many modern languages all words (and in some, all roots too) must have at least two syllables; the basic word structure is $C_1V(C_2)C_3V(C_4)$ with different possibilities at each of four consonantal positions. This move away from monosyllabic roots and words has led to the augmentation of many lexical roots and restructuring of grammatical paradigms.

A system of three vowels /a, i, u/ is likely for pA. This is retained in most modern languages although five-vowel systems have developed in the northern prefixing area. A contrast between long and short vowels applied in pA for at least the first, stressed, syllable of a word; this has been retained in some modern languages from all parts of the continent, but long and short vowels have fallen together in other modern tongues.

Stress generally falls on the first, third, fifth, ... syllables of a word. Australian languages are almost all syllable-timed (like French and Italian); indeed, preference for a regular stressed-unstressed rhythmic pattern may have been at least partly responsible for the development of the requirement in many modern languages that each word should consist of (at least) two syllables.

Unusual phonological systems are found in a minority of languages from widely separated areas—the center, the New England highlands (in New South Wales), and parts of Cape York Peninsula, in northeast Queensland. Similar changes have applied, quite independently, in all these areas. Basically, an initial consonant and often also the following vowel have been lost, creating monosyllabic words and exposing medial consonant clusters, e.g. *bamba* > *mba*. Allophonic variants in medial consonants and vowels, that were conditioned by some part of the initial syllable, have become phonemically contrastive, due to loss of the conditioning environment. In this way fricative phonemes, prestopped nasals and laterals, and more extensive vowel systems have evolved in these limited areas (13, 29, 33, 40).

NOUNS

Each noun phrase (NP) typically bears a case inflection indicating its function in the sentence in which it occurs (one inflection is absolutive, which in most languages has zero realization). In many languages the case inflection goes onto every word in the NP; the words from a phrase may then be scattered through the sentence (word order is remarkably free in most Australian languages). In a few languages the case inflection can be added just to the last word in an NP.

Four nominal cases can be reconstructed for pA (21): absolutive, with zero realization, for intransitive subject (S) and transitive object (O) functions; ergative, *-lu~-du,* for transitive subject (A) function; general locative *-la~-da;* and dative-genitive *-gu.* Increments could probably be added to some of these inflections; a form like *-ŋuru* may have produced an ablative form when added to the general locative and causal when added to ergative.

Most prefixing languages have dropped the ergative inflection since information about which NP is subject is coded in the verb; a few retain an ergative case which is used sparingly, only when ambiguity might otherwise result (20, 61, 62). Nonprefixing languages have generally augmented the pA case system; most now have between six and eight nominal inflections. They may distinguish allative ("going *to the camp*"), dative ("showed it *to mother*"), purposive ("went out *for wallabies*"), ablative ("coming *from the river*"), causal ("tired *from a walk*"), aversive ("hiding *for fear of the policeman*") and the like (4). Instrumental ("hit him *with a stick*") coincides in realization with ergative in most languages and with locative ("sit *on the stone*") in others; no explanation has yet been given for this distribution (18).

There are a fair number of derivational suffixes which come between noun root and inflection—intensifiers, dual/plural markers, "with," and "without." An alienable possessor is marked by genitive, which behaves like a derivational suffix, taking the full range of case inflections, e.g. in "Mother's dog bit me," "dog" will bear ergative case marking, and "mother" will have the genitive suffix followed by ergative inflection.

PRONOUNS

In most Australian languages pronouns have one case form (nominative) for transitive subject (A) and intransitive subject (S) and another case form (accusative) for transitive object (O). This is in marked contrast with the absolutive (S,O)–ergative (A) system of inflection on nouns and adjectives. Most other nominal case inflections apply fairly regularly to pronouns.

The commonest pronoun system in Australia shows singular, dual, and plural distinctions for first and second person pronouns. There are a few languages that also have a trial number (e.g. 38) and also a few with just singular and nonsingular, lacking a dual (14, 32). About half the languages with a sg/du/pl system distinguish between inclusive and exclusive for first person dual and plural. A rather different type of pronoun system is found in some northern languages, from both prefixing and nonprefixing regions (e.g. 45, 50, 55). This is based on four "minimal" pronouns, exploiting the possible combinations of "+/–speaker" and "+/–addressee"; and four augumented forms, adding additional referents to the minimal specifications. Thus in Umpila, northeast Queensland (data from G. N. O'Grady):

Minimal	*Augmented*
ŋayu "I"	*ŋana* "I and one or more others (not including you)"
ŋali "you and I"	*ŋambula* "You and I and one or more others"
ŋanu~ŋunu "you(sg)"	*ŋuʔula* "you and one or more others (not including I)"
nhulu "he/she"	*bula* "they (two or more)"

Comparative evidence suggests that pA may have had a minimal/augmented system. Some languages have kept this semantic arrangement, but most have restructured it into sg/du/pl. The original "you and I" minimal form, *ŋali,* has become first person dual inclusive in languages which show an inclusive/exclusive distinction; it is simply first person dual in languages that lack this distinction (and *ŋali* is the first person nonsingular pronoun in Bandjalang from eastern New South Wales, one of the languages which lacks a dual number, 14).

Monosyllabic roots can be reconstructed for singular pronouns: 1 sg **ŋay,* and 2 sg **ŋin* (*>nyin*). The roots may have been used unsuffixed for S function; ergative *-ju~-du* marked A and accusative *-nya* marked O function. When monosyllabic forms were eliminated, *ŋaju* and *ŋindu* were extended to cover S as well as A function in many languages, giving rise to the modern nominative(SA)-accusative(O) pronoun paradigms (21).

Bound pronomical prefixes and enclitics are all nominative-accusative in type. Where bound pronominals must obligatorily be included in any sentence, free-form pronouns become less frequent, being used mainly for emphasis. In Walbiri, originally nominative-accusative free forms gave rise to nominative-accusative bound clitics; the absolutive-ergative declension of nominals was then extended to free-form pronouns—the original 1 sg SA form *ŋaju* is now taken as the basic stem, to which the nominal ergative inflection is added to mark A function, and so on (31).

Some languages have a straightforward third person in the pronoun paradigm, but in many languages there is instead a system of demonstratives "this," "that," etc, indicating distance from speaker, visibility, and so on (e.g. 17, 24). These demonstratives inflect like first and second person pronouns in some languages; in others they follow the pattern of nominal declension. There is usually an array of interrogative/indefinite forms, "who/someone," "what/something," "where/somewhere," etc; some languages also have interrogative verbs "do what/do how" (17).

VERBS

Each verb in an Australian language is either strictly transitive—occurring in a sentence with A and O NPs—or else strictly intransitive—occurring just with a core NP in S function (peripheral NPs—in dative, locative, causal, etc cases—can co-occur with either type of verb). There is typically a range of derivational affixes for forming transitive stems from intransitive roots, reflexives and reciprocals (derived intransitive stems) from transitive roots, and so on. There are also derivational suffixes for forming transitive and intransitive verbal stems from noun and adjective roots.

Australian languages typically have a rich set of verbal inflections, although both forms and meanings differ a good deal from language to language. They can sometimes mark perfect aspect, past tense, present tense, irrealis (something that might happen), as well as various subordinate clause types. The most pervasive verbal inflection is purposive -*gu* (probably cognate with nominal dative -*gu*); on a main clause verb it indicates desire or necessity ("I *should go*"), while in a subordinate clause it marks a consequential activity ("I went *to spear wallabies*") (6, 22).

There are typically a number of distinct conjugations; each verbal stem takes the set of inflectional allomorphs associated with the conjugation to which it belongs. Conjugational membership correlates with—but does not coincide with—transitivity classes; 80% of the members of one conjugation will be transitive, 80% of those in another will be intransitive, etc. Languages in the west, and a few isolated languages in the east, have between four and six conjugations (24, 27, 35, 41, 48, 60). In some languages the conjugations are of approximately equal size while in others there will be just two open conjugations—one predominantly transitive and one predominantly intransitive—and two to four small closed classes with just a handful of members, most of them monosyllabic. Many eastern languages have only two conjugations in all while those in the center lack conjugational distinctions, each inflection having the same form with all verbal stems; in languages of these types all verbal roots have at least two syllables.

Many verbal forms can be analyzed in terms of STEM+CONJUGATION-MARKER+INFLECTION, e.g. participial forms from Dyirbal (northeast Queensland). However, the most frequently used forms may not be segmentable in this way, as in Dyirbal present-past:

root	*nyina-* "sit"	*baga-* "spear, pierce"
participial	*nyina+y+muŋa*	*baga+l+muŋa*
present-past	*nyina+nyu*	*baga+n*

The two Dyirbal conjugations have markers *-y-* and *-l-*; where there are more conjugations the markers can include *-ŋ-*, *-m-*, *-n-*, *-rr-* and zero, there being clear correspondences between conjugation classes, their markers and memberships, across different languages (21).

Detailed comparison of modern systems suggests that pA verbs had a simple agglutinative structure, affixes being added directly to roots, which could end in a vowel or in *-y, -l, -rr, -ŋ, -m* or *-n*. In the development from pA, phonological changes have obscured this structure—the original root-final segment may have been dropped before certain inflections but be retained before others (these segments are the modern conjugation markers). Or root-final and suffix-initial consonants may have blended into a single segment. Thus Dyirbal present-past relates to pA past tense *-nyu* by the changes *nyinay+nyu > nyinanyu; *bagal+nyu > baganu > bagan* (17).

Proto-Australian had a score or more monosyllabic verbal roots— *nyaa-ŋ* "see," *bu-m* "hit," *nyii-n* "sit," and so on. Some languages retain these, but all inflections to them are syllabic so that all verbal words have at least two syllables. In other languages they have been assigned new disyllabic roots—an original root-plus-inflection becomes the new root. Thus imperative form *nyii+n+a* "sit!" is the basis for the modern Dyirbal root *nyina-* (Dyirbal is one of the many languages that have lost the pA contrast between long and short vowels). A newly formed root is assigned to that open conjugational class associated with its transitivity value, *nyina-* going into the *-y-* class in Dyirbal. This illustrates one of the several factors leading to loss of some conjugational classes (Dyirbal lacks the *-n-*class, to which *nyii-* originally belonged).

Nonprefixing languages in the east can, like Dyirbal, have many hundreds of monosyllabic verb roots. But many in the west have only 50–100 roots to which verbal inflections can be added, with many compound verb stems being based on these (48). Most prefixing languages go one step beyond this, with from 5 to 50 inflecting roots and a rich array of compound forms (8). There are many reflexes of pA monosyllabic roots among these small sets of verb roots in modern prefixing languages; as noted earlier, this provides the major evidence for genetic connection between languages of the prefixing and nonprefixing types.

SYNTAX

Since syntactic function is marked by case inflections and/or cross-referencing elements in the verb, word order can be quite free in Australian languages. Most languages have underlying orders AOV, SV, and noun-adjective within an NP, but there can be unlimited variation from these patterns.

Most Australian languages (especially those outside the prefixing area) have one of a number of types of syntactic devices for indicating coreferentiality of NPs within complex sentence constructions. A number of languages in South Australia and an adjacent portion of Western Australia show switch-reference marking (2, 24, 27, 60); the verb of a subordinate clause bears one inflection if it has the same subject as the main clause and a different inflection if their subjects differ. (Switch-reference marking is an areal feature applying to all the languages in a certain region, whether they are or are not closely related genetically.)

Some languages require that there be an NP common to main and subordinate clauses in a complex sentence, which must be in S or O function in each clause. There then has to be a grammatical derivation (=transformation) for placing an underlying A NP in surface S function. This is referred to as the "antipassive" derivation—deep A NP becomes surface S, deep O is marked by an oblique case (dative, locative, or instrumental, in different languages) and the verb bears an antipassive derivational suffix (17–21). In two small areas of the continent there has been a change in grammatical type. The antipassive construction has been adopted as the unmarked transitive construction, the antipassive verbal marking being dropped. There is then nominative(SA)-accusative (O) case inflection on nouns, as well as on pronouns, the accusative inflection corresponding to dative, locative, or instrumental, in other languages which still preserve absolutive(SO)-ergative(A) marking (based on unpublished papers by T. J. Klokeid and P. McConvell).

SPEECH AND SONG STYLES

Perhaps every Australian language has a special speech style which must be used in the presence of a taboo relative (for a male, his mother-in-law, etc). Sometimes the avoidance style involves just a few score special lexical forms; but in a group of eastern tribes there is a complete second vocabulary, no lexical form being common to avoidance and everyday styles (there is in fact a many-to-one correspondence between everyday and avoidance lexemes). Avoidance and everyday styles have identical phonology, and the only grammatical difference is distinct pronouns in some dialects of the Western Desert language. [See (7, 56) for general surveys and (16, 36) for particular case studies.]

Some tribes have, in addition, secret languages that are confined to initiated males. Damin, of the Lardil tribe, has a quite different phonology from

Lardil, involving glottalic egressive, pulmonic ingressive, velaric egressive, and velaric ingressive (click) sounds (10, 30).

Little work has been done on everyday speech styles—recitative, political harague, and the like. The language of songs, with its different phonological, grammatical, and lexical possibilities, is just beginning to receive detailed study (1, 25, 42, 57).

TASMANIAN, AND RELATIONSHIP BETWEEN AUSTRALIAN AND OTHER LANGUAGE FAMILIES

At the end of the last century, Tasmanians were believed to be unAustralian in physical type, culture, and language. Anthropologists have now reassessed the physical and cultural evidence, and it is generally believed that the Tasmanians were a group of Australian Aborigines, isolated when their island was cut off by the rising sea level about 12,000 years ago. There is very little linguistic information available on Tasmanian languages, almost all of it poorly transcribed word lists (52). Few lexical or grammatical cognates can be found with mainland languages, but philological reconstitution does suggest that Tasmanian phonology could have conformed to the regular Australian pattern—apical, laminal, dorsal, and labial stops with probably a nasal corresponding to each, two rhotics, a lateral, two semivowels, and probably just three vowels (15). All we can conclude is that there is no evidence that the Tasmanian languages were not in some way related to Australian.

Links have been suggested between Australian and all manner of other language families, but none stand up under close examination. There are considerable typological similarities to the Dravidian family in south India, but intensive search has failed to reveal any systematically related cognate forms. Australia and New Guinea were connected as one land mass until 9000 years ago, but no genetic links have yet been uncovered with any of the 700 or so non-Austronesian languages of New Guinea.

Literature Cited

1. Alpher, B. J. 1976. Phonological peculiarities of Yir-Yoront song words. In *Languages of Cape York,* ed. P. Sutton, pp. 78–83. Canberra: Aust. Inst. Aboriginal Stud. (AIAS)
2. Austin, P. K. 1978. *A grammar of the Diyari language of north-east South Australia.* PhD thesis. Australian National Univ., Canberra, Aust. To be published by Cambridge Univ. Press
3. Banks, J. 1962. *The Endeavour Journal,* ed. J. C. Beaglehole. Sydney
4. Blake, B. J. 1977. *Case Marking in Australian Languages.* Canberra: AIAS
5. Blake, B. J. 1979. *A Grammar of Kalkatungu.* Canberra: Pacific Ling.
6. Capell, A. 1956. *A New Approach to Australian Linguistics.* Sydney: Oceania ling. monogr.
7. Capell, A. 1962. Language and social distinction in Aboriginal Australia. *Mankind* 5:514–22
8. Capell, A. et al. 1976. Simple and compound verbs: conjugation by auxiliaries

in Australian verbal systems. See Ref. 18 pp. 615–740

9. Capell, A., Hinch, H. 1970. *Maung Grammar, Texts and Vocabulary.* The Hague: Mouton

10. Catford, J. C. 1977. *Fundamental Problems in Phonetics.* Edinburgh Univ. Press

11. Chadwick, N. 1975. *A Descriptive Study of the Djingili Language.* Canberra: AIAS

12. Cook, J. 1955. *The Voyage of the Endeavour, 1768–71,* ed. J. C. Beaglehole. Cambridge Univ. Press

13. Crowley, T. 1976. Phonological change in New England. See Ref. 18, pp. 19–50

14. Crowley, T. 1978. *The Middle Clarence Dialects of Bandjalang.* Canberra: AIAS

15. Crowley, T., Dixon, R. M. W. 1980. Tasmanian. See Ref. 22, Vol. 2

16. Dixon, R. M. W. 1971. A method of semantic description. In *Semantics, an Interdisciplinary Reader in Philosophy, Linguistics and Psychology,* ed. D. D. Steinberg, L. A. Jakobovits, pp. 436–71. Cambridge Univ. Press

17. Dixon, R. M. W. 1972. *The Dyirbal Language of North Queensland.* Cambridge Univ. Press

18. Dixon, R. M. W., ed. 1976. *Grammatical Categories in Australian Languages.* Canberra: AIAS

19. Dixon, R. M. W. 1977. *A Grammar of Yidiny.* Cambridge Univ. Press

20. Dixon, R. M. W. 1979. Ergativity. *Language* 55. In press

21. Dixon, R. M. W. 1980. *The Languages of Australia.* Cambridge Univ. Press

22. Dixon, R. M. W., Blake, B. J., eds. 1979. *Handbook of Australian Languages,* Vol 1. Canberra: Aust. Natl. Univ. Press. (Further volumes in preparation)

23. Donaldson, T. J. 1977. *A description of Ngiyamba:, the language of the Waŋa:ybuwan people of central western New South Wales.* PhD thesis. Australian National Univ., Canberra, Aust. To be published by Cambridge Univ. Press

24. Douglas, W. H. 1964. *An Introduction to the Western Desert Language.* Sydney: Oceania ling. monog. Rev. ed.

25. Elkin, A. P., Jones, T. A. 1957. *Arnhem Land Music (North Australia).* Sydney: Oceania monogr.

26. Furby, C. E. 1974. Garawa phonology. In *Papers in Australian Linguistics* No 7, pp. 1–11. Canberra: Pacific Ling.

27. Glass, A., Hackett, D. 1970. *Pitjantjatjara Grammar—A Tagmemic View of the Ngaanyatjara (Warburton Ranges) Dialect.* Canberra: AIAS

28. Grey, G. 1841. *Journal of Two Expeditions of Discovery.* London 2 vols.

29. Hale, K. L. 1964. Classification of the Northern Paman languages, Cape York Peninsula, Australia: a research report. *Oceanic Ling.* 3:248–65

30. Hale, K. L. 1973. Deep-surface canonical disparities in relation to analysis and change: An Australian example. In *Current Trends in Linguistics, Vol. 11— Diachronic, Areal and Typological linguistics,* ed. T. A. Sebeok, 401–58. The Hague: Mouton

31. Hale, K. L. 1973. Person marking in Walbiri. In *A Festschrift for Morris Halle,* ed. S. R. Anderson, P. Kiparsky, pp. 308–44. New York: Holt, Rinehart & Winston

32. Hale, K. L. 1976. Tʸaˑ pukay. In *Languages of Cape York,* ed. P. Sutton, pp. 236–42. Canberra: AIAS

33. Hale, K. L. 1976. Phonological development in particular Northern Paman languages. See Ref. 32, pp. 7–40

34. Haviland, J. B. 1974. A last look at Cook's Guugu Yimidhirr wordlist. *Oceania* 44:216–32

35. Haviland, J. B. 1979. Guugu Yimidhirr. See Ref. 22, pp. 27–180

36. Haviland, J. B. 1979. How to talk to your brother-in-law in Guugu Yimidhirr. In *Languages and Their Speakers,* ed. T. Shopen, pp. 161–239. Cambridge, Mass: Winthrop

37. Heath, J. 1978. *Linguistic Diffusion in Arnhem Land.* Canberra: AIAS

38. Hercus, L. A. 1966. Some aspects of the form and use of the trial number in Victorian languages and in Arabana. *Mankind* 6:335–37

39. Hercus, L. A. 1969. *The Languages of Victoria: A Late Survey,* 2 parts. Canberra: AIAS

40. Hercus, L. A. 1972. The prestopped nasal and lateral consonants of Arabana-Waŋaŋuru. *Anthropol. Ling.* 14:293–305

41. Hudson, J. 1978. *The Core of Walmatjari Grammar.* Canberra: AIAS

42. Keen, I. 1977. Ambiguity in Yolngu religious language. *Canberra Anthropol.* 1:33–50

43. King, P. P. 1827. *Narrative of a Survey of the Intertropical and Western Coasts of Australia.* London: Murray. 2 vols.

44. Kirton, J., Charlie, B. 1979. Seven articulatory positions in Yanyuwa consonants. *Papers in Australian Linguistics,* No. 11. Canberra: Pacific Ling.

45. McKay, G. R. 1975. *Rembarnga, a language of central Arnhem Land*. PhD thesis. Australian National Univ., Canberra, Aust.
46. Meyer, H. A. E. 1843. *Vocabulary of the Language Spoken by the Aborigines of the Southern and Eastern Portions of the Settled Districts of South Australia . . . preceded by a grammar*. Adelaide
47. O'Grady, G. N. 1966. Proto-Ngayarda phonology. *Oceanic Ling.* 5:71–130
48. O'Grady, G. N. 1970. Nyangumarda conjugations. In *Pacific Linguistics Studies in Honour of Arthur Capell*, ed. S. A. Wurm, D. C. Laycock, pp. 845–64. Canberra: Pacific Ling.
49. O'Grady, G. N., Voegelin, C. F., Voegelin, F. M. 1966. *Languages of the World: Indo-Pacific Fascicle 6. Anthropol. Ling.* 8 (2)
50. Osborne, C. R. 1974. *The Tiwi Language*. Canberra: AIAS
51. Phillip, A. 1791. Letter to Sir J. Banks, 3 Dec. 1791. In *Banks' Papers*, Vol. 18—Botanical and Horticultural 1789–98, pp. 41–43. (Manuscripts in Mitchell Library, Sydney)
52. Plomley, N. J. B. 1976. *A World-list of the Tasmanian Aboriginal Languages*. Launceston
53. Roth, W. E. 1898. The word 'Kangaroo'. Letter to the editor of *The Australasian*, 2 July 1898, p. 33
54. Schürmann, C. W. 1844. *A Vocabulary of the Parnkalla Language [and] Grammatical Notes*. Adelaide: Dehane
55. Sharpe, M. C. 1972. *Alawa Phonology and Grammar*. Canberra: AIAS
56. Sommer, B. A. 1976. Sociolinguistic issues in Australian language research: a review. In *Australia Talks: Essays on the Sociology of Australian Immigrant and Aboriginal Languages*, ed. M. Clyne, pp. 229–44. Canberra: Pacific Ling.
57. Strehlow, T. G. H. 1971. *Songs of Central Australia*. Sydney: Angus & Robertson
58. Teichelmann, C. G., Schürmann, C. W. 1840. *Outlines of a Grammar . . . of the Aboriginal Language of . . . Adelaide*. Adelaide
59. Threlkeld, L. E. 1834. *An Australian Grammar*. Sydney
60. Trudinger, R. M. 1943. Grammar of the Pitjantjatjara dialect, central Australia. *Oceania* 13:205–23
61. Walsh, M. J. 1976. *The Murinypata language of north-west Australia*. PhD thesis, Australian National Univ., Canberra, Aust.
62. Walsh, M. J. 1976. Ergative locative and instrumental case inflections: Murinypata. See Ref. 18, pp. 405–8

Ann. Rev. Anthropol. 1979. 8:445–66
Copyright © 1979 by Annual Reviews Inc. All rights reserved

THE FIFTH CONTINENT: PROBLEMS CONCERNING THE HUMAN COLONIZATION OF AUSTRALIA

♦9642

Rhys Jones

Department of Prehistory, Research School of Pacific Studies,
The Australian National University, Canberra, Australia

The last 15 years have seen a revolution in Australian prehistory. In 1961, the oldest acceptable date for human occupation in Australia was 8700 BP (122, 123), several scholars being convinced that man had only a post-Pleistocene antiquity here [Abbie in (115, pp. 82–83)], and Grahame Clark in his Olympian review of world prehistory (23, p. 243) could find no convincing evidence for any site older than after "Neothermal times." In 1962, John Mulvaney obtained a 10,000-year-old date from Kenniff Cave in south Queensland, followed soon by a sequence thought in 1964 to extend back to some 16,000 years (the basal date for this site is now established at some 19,000 years ago). By 1968, carbon dates of just over 20,000 years had been obtained from four Australian sites, with six others showing terminal Pleistocene occupation of the highlands of eastern Australia and New Guinea (60). By 1973, there were 26 sites older than 10,000 years (62, 63, 102), and this figure has now been increased to over 35 (Figure 1), even if we restrict whole complexes of sites such as those on the lower Willandra or lower Darling river and lake systems to single entities. Several hundred archaeological sites have now had some scientific investigation mostly with radiocarbon chronologies established.

The rapid development of Australian archaeological research since the early 1960s can be followed by reading a series of reviews (15, 24, 29, 30, 39, 40, 55, 59, 60, 85, 88, 89, 94, 96–99, 104, 118, 123) to assessments of the contemporary situation as interpreted by many authors (1, 9–11, 25, 27,

445

0084-6570/79/1015-0445$01.00

34, 41, 42, 46, 52, 62–64, 66, 70–72, 80, 82, 100, 102, 119, 126, 132). The situation in New Guinea as it related to Australian prehistory has also been reviewed (2, 3, 18, 19, 53, 72). Although completed site reports unfortunately have been slow in their transmogrification from the theses in which so many were originally written, the scope of excavated data is well illustrated by reports on Kenniff Cave, Queensland (104), Lake Burrill, NSW (78), Seelands and other sites in northern NSW (87), Seton rock shelter on

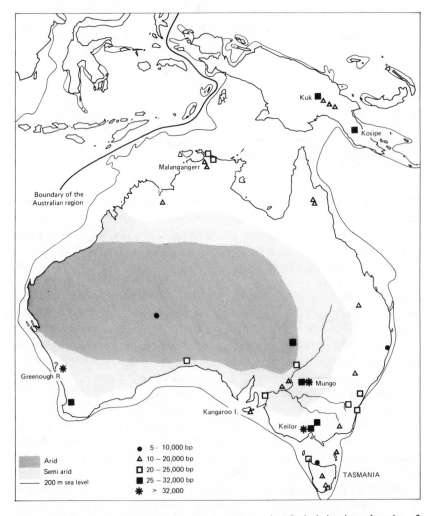

Figure 1   Map showing the basal dates for the oldest archaeological sites in each region of Greater Australia.

Kangaroo Island (54), Puntutjarpa, central Australia (43), and Kafiavana and other sites in the New Guinea Highlands (130, 131). Recently a mass of new information and of theoretical debate has been made available with the publication of several books of collected essays (4, 32, 44, 47, 49, 58, 76, 103, 106, 112, 125, 128, 134) which altogether contain some 150 chapters of direct relevance to current Australian archaeological research. It is likely that the broad outlines of Australian prehistory over the past 25,000–30,000 years are already known and that the theoretical problems that will engage Australian prehistorians over the next 25 years have already been established. The days of "cowboy archaeology" may be coming to a close.

At this stage of research one set of interrelated issues dominate all others —that is to find out when man first arrived in Australia, who he was, what was the nature of his economic adaptation to the new ecological conditions which he was to find there, and conversely what was his own impact on the environment. In this brief review I can deal with only a few aspects of these problems.

SEA JOURNEYS ACROSS WALLACEA

Australia once formed part of old Gondwanaland, but unlike its sister plates of southern Africa or India, it has not yet impinged upon a northern continent, and so is separated from oriental Asia by tectonically uplifted island arcs and a series of immensely deep oceanic troughs never exposed by glacial period low sea levels (20). A superficial look at an atlas shows Australia merely as the largest island in a massive archipelago stretching 8000 km to the southeast of Asia [(4) frontispiece], but the structure of the continental shelves together with the biological distributional data reveal a fundamental bilateral symmetry to this kaleidoscope of land and sea recognized since the days of A. R. Wallace. Greater Australia consists of Australia, New Guinea, Aru, Tasmania, Kangaroo Island, and many smaller islands of both the Sahul and Bassian shelves, all joined together to form a single land mass with a sea level drop of more than 65 meters as occurred during the last and probably previous ice ages (9, 20, 62). To the northwest, the continental islands of Asia such as Java, Sumatra, and Borneo, rising from the floor of Sundaland, would equally be a part of the Asian landmass at such times. Simpson, in a deceptively simple paper (113), has redefined the intermediate zone not as a distinct region or as a series of biogeographic lines of faunal balance, but simply as a zone of truly oceanic islands subject to well-known laws of faunal colonization and of extinction (26, 83).

The fossil record shows that in ancient times of all the placental land mammals of Asia, only mice and rats managed to cross through this entire archipelago to reach the continent of marsupials. However, other animals, notably the elephant-like Stegodons, crossed water straits to the islands of the Sunda Arc, Flores and Timor, where their fossils are found in gravels which may date to the middle or early upper Pleistocene (50, 113). Stone tools have also been found eroding from these gravels and from old Tjabenge industry sites on Sulawesi, showing that men had already managed to cross some substantial water barriers by this time (35, 36, 45, 102, pp. 144–47). There still remained the final water crossing to Australia which even during low sea periods was never less than about 80 to 100 km wide (9). The colonization of the Wallacean islands and of Australia itself is probably the oldest evidence that we have in the world of the ability of man to cross substantial bodies of water, and it is almost certain that at least the final stages of this process to Australia itself would have involved the use of some kind of watercraft.

PERFORMANCE OF MODERN TASMANIAN AND AUSTRALIAN ABORIGINAL WATERCRAFT

Ethnographic and archaeological studies on the performances of Tasmanian Aboriginal watercraft, which were basically canoe-shaped floats made from bundles of bark, give us an insight as to the limited capacity of such simple craft safely to traverse sea crossings of only a few kilometers width (9, 65, 67). There was an inverse relationship between the width of water to be crossed to Tasmanian offshore islands and the intensity of their economic use; so that islands up to 2 or 3 kilometers offshore were regularly visited on a seasonal basis by entire bands of people, but those requiring a voyage of 5 and up to 8 km were visited only for especially rich resources such as seals during good weather and probably by specialist hunting parties only (67). Archaeological evidence shows that Banks Strait, 20 km wide and with strong cross currents, between northeast Tasmania and the rich islands of the Furneaux Group was too formidable a barrier to be crossed even over the time period of 10,000 years that it has been in existence (67, pp. 358–61).

A similar situation may have pertained with the 16 km of water separating the South Australian mainland from the large Kangaroo Island, which was unoccupied by Aborigines at the time of European contact and probably for the previous 2000 years at least. The few archaeological sites on it dating to post-Pleistocene times may be the remains of a tiny stranded population which persisted there for several thousand years before becoming extinct; or they may be the result of extremely infrequent cross-water colonizations, say of the order of a few per millenium, the difficulties of the crossing being too great for any systematic visiting or the establishment of a successful founding population (67, pp. 341–55; 79, 80, 114). In the nineteenth century, a captured Aboriginal woman did manage to swim from the island to the mainland to escape from her sealer persecutors, showing that *in extremis* people will do things which under normal circumstances are not attempted (117). On the Gulf of Carpentaria on the northern side of the continent, fugitive bands of Kaiadilt people on Bentinct Island, using simple rafts of dry mangrove wood, suffered an average mortality rate of 50% on two trips involving a total of 34 people making sea journeys of 13 km to another small island (124).

Given such simple watercraft, it is likely that there was an exponential inverse relationship between the probability of a disaster-free trip and cross-water distance (67, p. 330), journeys of over 15–20 km having a low probability of success. Nevertheless, reference to G. G. Simpson's dictum concerning the biological colonization of oceanic islands by the "sweepstake route" shows that situations involving even the smallest chances can end in success if they are repeated often enough. For a successful colonization there must be fertile members of both sexes, and McArthur et al (86) have shown by computer modeling experiments that the chances of survival over several generations of such tiny founding populations are greatly enhanced as the numbers of the founders are increased from two or three up to half a dozen or so, and of course such groups are highly exposed to the risks of accident.

In terms of plant foods, shell fish, and fish, the recipient coastline itself would have been sufficiently familiar to colonists from the shorelines of southeast Asia who presumably would also know how to tap sources of undersurface water on coastal dunes during the dry season (40, 91, 92). If such colonists had not managed to carry fire with them and if they did not know how to make it, as was the case with both the Tasmanians and the Andamanese (21, pp. 25, 65–66; 107, pp. 11–12), then opportunities to obtain fire from dry season lightning storms may not have come for many years, causing massive stress on the capacity of such a group to survive because many of the plant foods need some cooking to remove slight toxins (72, 93).

We thus have a scenario of peoples foraging on the shorelines of the southeastern part of Asia, and with some capacity to ride on water with rafts or other primitive craft, slowly and stochastically gaining access to the islands of Wallacea and eventually Australia by random processes outlined above (8, 9). The chances of success for any particular voyage would have been extremely low, and it is also likely that there had been many unsuccessful landfalls on the Australian or New Guinean coast which did not lead to viable founding populations. Man in Java at ca 2 million years ago, in the Wallacean islands of Flores, Timor, Sulawesi, and the Phillipines at say middle or early Upper Pleistocene times, and his arrival in Australia in only the late Pleistocene, gives a time scale against which these colonizing processes operated. White & O'Connell (132, pp. 22–24), asserting that late Pleistocene watercraft in the region must have been more sophisticated than any used ethnographically by Australian Aborigines,[1] reject the model outlined here. However, they give no coherent arguments as to why this hypothesis is falsified by the data we have available, and on the grounds of parsimony it must stand.

PALAEOCLIMATIC CONSIDERATIONS

Australia is the world's driest continent, with over 75% of its surface area under a regime where potential annual evaporation exceeds precipitation (14, p. 360). Recent geomorphological and pollen analytical research has demonstrated great changes in climate during the late Pleistocene period, especially as they affected the semiarid zone fringing the desert core (13, 14, 74, 114, 128). A key site is the now dry Lake Mungo on the Willandra Creek in the dry region of western New South Wales (Figure 1), where a local depositional sequence has been set up spanning the past 120,000 years, the most recent third of which being exceptionally well supported by over a hundred radiometric determinations (6, 12, 13, 17, 52).

A dune deposit called the Mungo Unit was formed when the lake was full of water 15 meters deep, so that sand was blown from its beach by westerly winds to form an immense crescentic shaped flanking sand dune, called a lunette, up to 30 meters thick on its eastern shore. This lake-full stage lasted from 45,000 to 25,000 years ago and involved lakes of a total surface area of 1000 km² on the Willandra Creek system alone (13, 14). It was succeeded by a drying phase of oscillating lake levels of gradually increasing salinity, some of which allowed the formation of smaller clay dunes until about 17,000 years ago when the lake was dry as it has been ever since. This "Mungo Lacustral Phase" is now recognized from fossil geomorphic features in the ephemeral stream and playa lake systems along the entire eastern flank of the desert core from Coopers Creek to the lower Murray as well as in the subtropical north and southwestern Australia (13, 14, 74).

It was followed by a short period of intense aridity and of strong wind activity which, especially between 16,000 and 18,000 BP, reactivated the great anticlockwise continental dune system of the desert heartland and caused some mobile dunes to be formed even in the southeastern tablelands and northeastern Tasmania where they are now totally vegetated (13, 14).

---

[1]Excepting the dugout "lippa lippa" of the Arnhemland coast, which is a recent introduction from Macassan visitors and which needs iron tools to manufacture, and the outriggers of Cape York derived from Melanesia.

This aridity correlated in time with the height of the last Glacial period and it was caused by a combination of cold winters and strong hot summer winds from the desert, especially in the lee region of southeastern Australia. Such intensification of the atmospheric circulation pattern was a function of the equator-ward expansion of the polar ice sheets, and in the middle latitudes of the Globe, it caused such a phase of dust that layers of dust particles have been found in deep sea cores far out in the middle of the oceans (14, 109, 110).

Stratified beneath the Mungo Unit at Lake Mungo is another heavily weathered dune soil, the Gol Gol Unit, again indicating a lake-full phase and believed on radiometric and palaeomagnetic grounds to date prior to the penultimate Glaciation of the order of 120,000–140,000 years ago, suggesting that these climatic changes were probably cyclical, associated with the various Glacial periods, several of which have now been recorded in extremely old pollen curves in eastern Australia (12–14, 75, 114). Ice sheets themselves were restricted to small areas of the southeastern highlands, Tasmania, and the tops of the New Guinea mountains (14, 53, 60, 74).

THE ANTIQUITY OF MAN IN AUSTRALIA

Lake Mungo

The oldest well-published carbon date from an archaeological site in Australia is one of 32,750 ± 1250 BP (ANU 331) obtained from freshwater mussel shells (*Velesunio ambiguus*) from a small midden in the upper part of the Mungo Unit lunette at the site of Lake Mungo itself (6, 12, 15; Figure 1). There are some 10 other published charcoal and shell dates ranging from 25,000 to 31,000 years BP from hearths and middens found in situ at this and neighboring sites, all attesting to human occupation of the sandy shores of the then full lake (6, 12, 13, 17, 52, 102, pp. 147–52).

The original archaeological discoveries made in 1969 at this site consisted of stone tools such as horse-hoof cores, steep-edged and notched scrapers, ochre, hearths, shell middens and faunal remains from camp debris, together with the cremated bones of a young woman, all from the upper part of the Mungo Unit and dated to between 25,000 and 30,000 years ago (15, 16, 62). The foraging economy of these people straddled the ecotone between water and land. Freshwater mussels were collected from the lake shore muds in large quantities to form discrete middens, and fish including perch (*Plectroplites ambiguus*) and Murray cod (*Maccullochella macquariensis*) up to 15 kg in weight were caught. From the back scrubs came emu eggs and a variety of small marsupials of species such as rat kangaroos and wallabies (e.g. *Bettongia lesueur, Lagorchestes leporides*) which survived in this area until the nineteenth century (15, pp. 47–56). Such a broad spectrum foraging focused on the edges of wetlands is characteristic of the Aboriginal economic response as recorded ethnographically (11, 63, 72, 91–93), and the Mungo site provides evidence for intensive lacustrine exploitation as old as anywhere in the world [cf the situation in Africa, Clark in (47)]. Apart from the absence of seed grinding dishes which appear in the sequence only some 15,000 years ago, there is a broad continuity of economic response in this region right through from ca 25,000 years ago to ethnographic times (1) (H. Allen, unpublished PhD thesis, Australian National University 1972, p. 351).

During the past 6 years, the Mungo and related sites have been subject to a major multidisciplinary archaeological study, though only few results have yet been published (13, p. 59; 90; 101; 102, p. 153; 111). On the Mungo lunette itself, excavations into lower Mungo Unit deposits below the level of the finds described above revealed some stone artifacts within it down to its base associated with high lake beach gravels (101; 102, p. 153) "conservatively estimated at a good forty thousand years or more," though no further details have as yet been forthcoming. Below 32,000 BP the artifacts were flakes (D. J. Mulvaney, personal communication). Bowler refers to a thin in situ midden lens of freshwater mussel shells associated with finely divided charcoal in a nearby dune section dated to between 34,000 and 37,000 BP (N 1665), and concludes that "man's presence in western New South Wales at least by 35,000 years BP seems assured" (13, p. 59). Accepting this, and indeed a probable antiquity down to at least early Mungo Phase times, one might also speculate whether or not the relative paucity of remains both absolutely and in terms of range of cultural manifestations before ca 30,000, as opposed to those pertaining afterwards between 25,000 and 30,000 years ago, document an initial sparse occupation followed by an intensive use of the lakeshore edges some 10,000 years later.

Keilor

A very different site, but one which has been in the literature since the middle 1940s, is the terrace sequence of the Maribyrnong River at Keilor just north of Melbourne. The Keilor terrace silts, which contain stone tools and the well-known human cranium (33, 85, 97), date back to some 18,000 BP. These lie unconformably on an alluvial clay deposit called the "D clay" by Gallus (31). Despite diagnostic problems concerning the human or natural origins of some of the stone objects in this deposit (31; 102, pp. 146–47), at least some indisputable struck flakes of human origin have been found in situ in this "D clay" (13, p. 62; 31; personal observation at a field demonstration by A. Gallus and J. M. Bowler, 1971). The date of this deposit has been excellently reviewed by Bowler (13, pp. 62–64), who argues on both radiometric and pedogenetic grounds that conservatively it must be between 25,000 and 36,000 years old, with basal levels possibly extending back to 45,000 years ago. Excavations are now in progress to test whether or not tools can be found in situ at these or older levels where Gallus has also claimed stone tools in situ (31).

Greenough and Murchiston Rivers

On the other side of the continent, stone tools including flakes and crude choppers have been found in situ in a heavily weathered alluvial deposit on the banks of the Greenough River in Western Australia (135). Called the "Older Fill," this contains bands of partly silicified calcrete, and probably reflects the same geomorphic events as the "Murchiston cement" from the nearby Murchiston River, from which Merrilees reported a stone tool as long ago as 1968 (94), and which has also been receiving recent scientific attention by Lofgren and Clark. On geomorphological grounds, Wyrwoll and Dortch believe that this "Older Fill" is of comparable antiquity to deposits from a nearby coastal alluvial sequence dated to somewhat more than 37,000 years. While systematic direct dating work needs to be done at these sites, a prima facie case is being built up suggesting an antiquity at least of the same order as the Keilor and Mungo situations discussed above, though the investigators themselves consider much higher ages to be possible.

Thus archaeologically we can demonstrate man's presence in the southern part of Greater Australia in the time period 35,000–45,000 years ago with every expectation of older dates being obtained with continuing research, so that even conservative opinion is now talking in terms of a 50,000 year antiquity for man on the continent (46; 102, p. 128; 132; 133, p. 272). The maximum limits have also been discussed by Bowler (13, pp. 64–66), who points out that despite recent intensive search by several workers, no remains have ever been found either from Gol-Gol lacustrine phase lake dunes nor from the widespread Last Interglacial high sea beach systems of the east coast dated to ca 120,000 years ago, both being prime potential locations for foraging man. One might conclude that the archaeological evidence so far supports an entry of man into Australia of the order of 50,000 years ago.

FILLING OF THE CONTINENT

The evidence for man's presence before 32,000 BP seems to be sparse and is so far restricted to large lakesides or rivers close to the then presumed coast, giving some support to Bowdler's model (11) that the economic adaptation of the very first men in Australia may have been restricted to the coastline or analogous situations. Following such an argument, the Mungo Lacustrine Phase would have given major access to the reactivated river and lake systems which ringed the arid heart.

In contrast to this, the situation after 30,000 and especially between 20,000 and 27,000 BP shows not only a great intensification of use of the lake shores and river banks of, for example, the Murray-Darling system, but also the presence of man in many rock shelters, caves, and open sites throughout much of the geographical spread of the continent (62). Figure 1 indicates sites with basal dates of this time range in the tropical savanna of northern Australia, down the spine of the Great Dividing Range, on the eastern coastline, on some of the open plains and isolated lake country of southeastern Australia, and in the tip of southwestern Australia (1, 5, 11, 15, 27, 28, 34, 46, 54, 60, 62, 63, 66, 78–80, 82, 83, 87, 90, 98, 102, 104, 108, 132). In many cases these traces may actually have represented the first substantial presence of man in these areas, as suggested by Hughes & Lampert (56), who pointed to major erosional features such as fire-induced hill slope instability and great acceleration of rock shelter wall erosion associated with the earliest archaeological evidence in these sites.

Perhaps of special interest are the data from the other islands of Greater Australia. To the north in the highlands of New Guinea, embedded beneath volcanic ash dated to ca 26,500 BP, the open Kosipe site has stone tools including large bifacially flaked pieces with oppositely placed indentations which are called "waisted blades" (2, 19, 39, 131). These together with a hearth and burnt stones at the base of the Kuk Swamp site (4, pp. 612–30; Jack Golson, personal communication) show that man had penetrated to over 1500 meters above sea level before the height of the last glaciation (53). There is also ample evidence for Late Pleistocene occupation of these high-land valleys in limestone caves and rock shelters such as Kafiavana, Kiowa, Yuku (2, 3, 18, 19, 130), and the exceptionally interesting Nombe, where waisted blades have been found at the base in the same layer as bones of *Protemnodon* sp., an extinct kangaroo-like "giant marsupial," though the primary stratigraphic association of these finds needs further work (95). This region in early post-Glacial times saw the establishment of a horticul-tural system involving large-scale drainage works in the floor of the swamps probably for the cultivation of taro. The earliest phase of drainage in the Kuk Swamp is well dated to 9000 BP (4, pp. 612–17), when New Guinea still formed the tropical northern belt of the Greater Australian continent (72).

To the south, the Bassian Plain was exposed by an eustatically lowered sea level at about 24,000 years BP (20, 67), giving a dry road to Tasmania, some 250 km to the south of the present Australian mainland. A date of 22,750 ± 420 BP (ANU 1498) from Cave Bay Cave (11) on what is today Hunter Island just northwest of Tasmania showed that man was quick to take this opportunity of extending his range to the mountainous peninsula which at about that time supported an ice sheet on its central plateau (14, 51, 60).

Beginners Luck Cave in a high mountain valley in the southwest has stone tools in a deposit dated to ca 20,000 BP showing that men could at least seasonally exploit this country which pollen analysis indicates was then under cold steppe herbfield vegetation (37, 38, 51, 67). Tools have also been found on what are now islands in the Bass Strait such as the Kent and Furneaux Groups (67, 73, 105, 123) and King Island (personal observation) in deposits believed on geomorphological grounds to date from the time when they formed hills rising out of the cold plain. Kangaroo Island also has carbon-dated sites back to 17,000 BP (54, 79, 80), but surface collections of the typologically archaic Kartan industry indicate a much higher antiquity for occupation of this place either as a part of the continent or during one of its several phases as an island over the past 50,000 and more years (20, 79, 80, 123).

Thus every major ecological zone of Greater Australia had some human occupation at least by 20,000–25,000 years ago with the exception of the true desert core. Here the oldest date so far is one of 10,000 BP from the Puntutjarpa site in the Warburton Ranges west of Alice Springs (41–43), but much more exploratory work needs to be done in the vast arid region of central Australia before we can posit an absence of man during the previous 15 millenia. Bowdler's view that man was not able to exploit the Australian landscape away from the coast or major rivers until terminal Pleistocene times (11, p. 234) is not supported by the site distributional evidence, though she is right in stressing that the highest human populations in the period under review were related to the richest lacustrine and coastal resources as indeed they have been throughout Australia's prehistory until modern times (8; 63, pp. 22–3; 91–93). What the effects were of the full Glacial period arid phase on these people as their lakes dried up around the desert fringe is the subject of current research (1, 11, 42, 46, 81, 90, 101). Whether or not such environmental pressures might have led to an intensification of the use of dry land vegetable foods, especially the grinding of grass seeds, have major implications for general theories about the origins of agriculture [(1, 11, 42, 133) Tindale in (134)].

STONE TOOL TECHNOLOGIES

Concerning the stone tools presumed to be older than about 32,000 BP, very little has been published. From the descriptions we have, they seem to consist of flakes, some large and with edge retouch, together possibly in some cases with roughly flaked choppers (31, 101, 135; personal observation at Keilor).

However, in contrast to this, where collections are large enough for meaningful analysis, stone tools at Pleistocene sites more recent than about 30,000 years ago are similar enough to be seen as belonging to a single technological complex called the "Australian Core Tool and Scraper Tradition" (15, 46, 62, 68, 79, 80, 82; 102, pp. 172–97). As its name implies, it is dominated by large horse-hoof shaped or in some cases pebble core tools and by scrapers mostly with steep step-flaked edges and with notches. An element increasingly being recognized in some assemblages are small thumbnail shaped scrapers often made from quartz (80), which also provides the raw material for bipolar flaked pieces, possibly little cores for tiny quartz flakes.

The common origin of both New Guinea industries and those of Pleistocene Australia is indicated not only by the general similarity of the scraper forms, now augmented by metrical studies, but also by the presence in both regions of the distinctive waisted blades (2, 3, 19, 39, 46, 62, 80). These are found from the earliest levels of the New Guinea highland sites as noted previously (2, 18, 39, 130, 131) and also, among other places in Australia, on Kangaroo Island, 3500 km on the southern side of the continent (80). Here they form an integral part of the Kartan industry of large horse-hoof cores and pebble choppers, believed by some to be the ancestral industry from which the Australian Core Tool and Scraper Tradition developed (79; 80; 82; 102, pp. 181–84; 123). Such a wide distribution of a specialized tool type suggests rapid dispersal of a technological idea, and it is possible that the earliest phase of this tradition was quickly and widely established across the Australian continent approximately 30,000 years ago. Identical waisted tools, together with core tools and scrapers reminiscent of the oldest Australian ones, have also been found in Late Pleistocene contexts in Southeast Asia, such as at Sai Yok in Thailand, thus suggesting a potential historical source from which these technological ideas were brought to the southern continent (39, 46, 80, 127). In the New Guinea sites, there also seems to be a gradation from purely flaked waisted tools to those having ground edges, and in several sites in the tropical north of Australia, such as at Malangangerr near Arnhemland (Figure 1), small edge-ground hatchet heads with waists or grooves around their middles have been dated back to ca 23,000 years BP, the oldest dates in the world for edge-ground axes [(39; 102, pp. 192–93); White in (103)], though it is likely that similar tools of comparable antiquity will also be found in Southeast Asia [(39, 45) Hayden in (4); Jack Golson, personal communication].

Within the assemblages of the Australian Core Tool and Scraper Tradition, seen over a period of some 25,000 years and on a continent-wide scale, there was a very slow developmental pattern. As time proceeded there was a gradual diminution in the total size of tools, though the worked edges themselves tended to remain more constant (46, 80, 82). Parallel with this there was a shift from the oldest industries such as the Kartan from Kangaroo Island where core tools dominated with few scrapers (79, 80), through the Mungo assemblage of 26,000 years BP (15), to Late and Post-

Pleistocene assemblages with few core tools and mostly scrapers (28, 80, 82; H. Allen, personal communication). Within the scrapers themselves there was a parallel trend from rougher steep-edged ones to those with finer round edges, noses, etc (68, 82). These reflect a process toward greater efficiency which can be measured in terms of the average length of working edge per unit weight of tool, which over a period of a thousand human generations increased crudely by a factor of eight times from 0.5 mm/g to 4 mm/g (82).

Such a process in mid-Recent times was augmented and probably accelerated by the appearance of new suites of what are loosely referred to as "small tools" (27; 41; 42; 68; 102, pp. 210–37; 132) which were added onto the old stone technology. These small tools consisted variously of backed microliths, adze flakes, unifacial and bifacial points etc, which were differentially distributed across the continent but which all reflected the same technological advances—namely a transformation in the methods of hafting of the stone bits to their wooden handles (104). Whereas it is likely that the "tula" and other mounted adzes of the central parts of Australia were an internal development within Australia, perhaps starting some 10,000 years ago (27, 41–43, 80, 132), other technologies such as the backed microliths which appear at about 4000 years ago right across the southern part of the continent but not in the north may have been influenced from outside by cultural processes which are beyond the scope of this paper (40). The dingo also appeared on the mainland at about this time showing that at least some important cultural contacts were still coming to Australia during Mid-Recent times [see (132) for a contrary view].

Tasmania was cut off from these new developments by the Post-Glacial rising sea some 12,000 years ago. The Tasmanian Aborigines preserved in isolation over a period of 500 generations until modern times the technological ideas of late Pleistocene Australia affected both by the ecological needs of their southern latitudes and by the effects of isolation (59, 60, 67–71, 73). When met by the French explorers of the late eighteenth century, the Tasmanians had the simplest technology in the world (68).

FROM TECHNOLOGY TO CULTURE

Bone tools such as stout awls and spatulae made from kangaroo and wallaby fibulae have been found from about 20,000 years ago in several sites such as Devil's Lair in the extreme southwest of Australia and Cave Bay Cave in Tasmania (Figure 1) (11, 27, 28). A bone bipoint, possibly the tip of a barbed spear head, is presumed to be more than 25,000 years old from the Mungo site, whereas bone beads and a fine bone needle date from late Pleistocene levels at Devils Lair (27; 102, pp. 151, 158). The peat of Wyrie Swamp in South Australia revealed seven wooden boomerangs, a barbed wooden spear head, and several hardwood double-pointed objects possibly detachable spear tips, all dated to about 10,000 years ago, together with typical stone scrapers of the period—showing that advanced ideas about projectiles were fully recognized by these Pleistocene Aboriginal ancestors (R. Luebbers, personal communication).

The Mungo 1 girl was cremated at 26,000 years ago, her bones smashed and put into a small pit (15). The coeval Mungo 3 man was buried on his side and covered with red ochre powder (16). The Nitchie man of at least 8000 years ago had a magnificent necklace of scores of drilled teeth of *Sarcophilus harrisii,* the Tasmanian Devil, now extinct on the mainland (85; 102, p. 199). There are pieces of ochre at most sites, those at Mungo going back to at least 32,000 years ago (15; 102, p. 152). Complex patterns of circles, other geometric designs, and the tracks of birds and animals were pecked and abraded onto rock slabs in hundreds of sites, most of which are heavily weathered through age. Claims that this art style had a Pleistocene antiquity because of its similarity with that found in Tasmania, and thus the implications of a common artistic heritage older than Bass Strait (e.g. 102, pp. 279–82; 125), have been confirmed by the Early Man Site in Cape York, where a large panel of such art is older than the 14,000-year-old carbon-dated deposit which covers it [Rosenfeld in (49; 125)].

In total darkness, 30 meters below the surface of the Nullarbor Plain at Koonalda Cave, are great panels of latticework designs on the soft limestone walls, scratched by people who left their torches behind, the charcoal from which having been dated to about 22,000 years ago [Gallus in (102, pp. 156–57)].

In terms of art, personal decoration, and ideas about the mysteries of death, the Aborigines 20,000–30,000 years ago in Australia showed the same concern about things of the mind and of the soul (62; 66; 102, pp. 279–82) as did their contemporaries on the other side of Asia.

ONE PEOPLE OR TWO

Behind these archaeological data lies a thorny question which has been perceived for a long time but which has still not been resolved. Are the cultural remains the product of one group of colonists or of several (7, 9, 55, 84, 85, 118, 119)? The Mungo 1 and Mungo 3 crania, both excellently dated to between 25,000 and almost 30,000 years old (16, 17), are gracile and of modern sapient morphology, with rounded foreheads and delicate skeletal features. They represent some of the oldest evidence of modern *Homo sapiens* in the world.

In contrast to this is another group of fossil skulls whose morphological primitivity [in the evolutionary sense (133)] was noticed since the days of the announcement of the Talgai skull in 1914, and of which Macintosh (84,

p. 59), following Weidenreich (129, p. 83), said that "the mark of ancient Java is on all of them." This morphological group has been brought into focus by the fossil assemblage at Kow Swamp, consisting of some 60 individuals of both sexes and excellently radiocarbon dated to as recently as 10,000 to 15,000 years (120). For such a young date, these skulls exhibit extraordinarily archaic features, especially in the frontal region. They are large and robust, with flat receding foreheads, thick vaults, and heavy supraorbital ridges which in some cases approximate to a torus. In some specimens, the standard measurement of the frontal curvature index is even flatter in this respect than the holotype Javan erectus specimens. The face is prognathous and the mandibles large with exceedingly large teeth (118, 120, 121).

Using multivariate techniques, Thorne & Wilson (121) have shown that all these Pleistocene hominid remains lie outside the range of contemporary Australian skeletal forms of the appropriate sex and that they fall neatly into two groups, one more gracile than any modern Australians and the other more rugged and primitive in a morphological sense (119, p. 189). In order to explain this, some authors have resorted to a notion of extreme morphological plasticity among late Pleistocene populations in southeast Australia, but it is strange that only the two extremes of such a putative wide range have been found and not the forms in the middle. Wright (133) proposed that the Kow Swamp forms with their prognathism and large tooth size may have evolved out of Mungo-like ancestors due to extreme selection processes associated with eating foods with a high grit content such as roots and grass seeds in the dusty, sandy environment of the Australian plains, as opposed to the allegorical diet of "rain-washed fruits" in the forests of the ancestral southeast Asian homeland, a view with which White & O'Connell (132) concur. Such selective pressures are posited as having been relaxed due to technological inventions such as seed-grinding stones or netting methods for fish etc in the terminal Pleistocene period, thus resulting in the modern Aborigines of the same region being more "modern" again than their Kow Swamp forebears (133). However, the time available from 26,000 to 15,000 years ago seems too short for such drastic changes (46), especially when we bear in mind that the physical differences involved are greater than those found anywhere within the variation of the entire human species today. All of the traits displayed in the Kow Swamp series, such as flat foreheads, have not been demonstrated to be related to the same selection processes which putatively produced prognathism and large teeth etc. If man had been in Australia at least 15,000 years before the time of the Mungo population, why had these selection pressures not already operated on the Mungo ancestors, since they lived in precisely the same sandy environment as the Kow Swamp people?

Of all the alternative explanations that Thorne outlines for these two fossil groups in Australia (119, p. 193), I feel that the data point to the inescapable conclusion that there were two races of man in late Pleistocene Australia (31, 46, 84, 118) and that the Aborigines at least of mainland Australia were the result of some degree of hybridization between the two. At the present state of research, it might seem that the gracile Mungo people were the first colonists and that the Kow Swamp people came later, thus supporting part of Birdsell's theory as proposed in 1949 (7). However, this would go against the general trend of human evolution as viewed elsewhere in the world where rugged forms have always been succeeded by gracile ones. Taking a world view also points to the strong implication that if man was in Australia at 50,000 or more years ago, he would have to have been of an archaic sapiens form, since nowhere do we find modern sapiens man older than about 40,000 years BP. Thus the Kow Swamp forms may represent a relic population (118), giving a hint of the morphology of the putative first Australians.

A HYPOTHESIS

Bringing together the various strands of the argument, I am now in a position to propose a hypothesis for the human colonization of Australia, although many elements have been stated or are implicit in the work of several other authors (e.g. 30, 31, 46, 118, 123). Greater Australia was colonized by man probably of the order of 50,000 years ago (or even more), the process itself occurring through random journeys on primitive watercraft. The first men were archaic sapiens standing in relation to their Javanese erectus forebears in roughly the same evolutionary position as the Neanderthals did to the western erectines or Mapa man did to Pekin man. These first Australian colonists had limited technological capabilities compared to modern hunters and gatherers and so may have had a much lower population density than that observed ethnographically, or they were limited to the easier foraging areas around the wetland edges or both. Their stone tools may have consisted of roughly retouched flakes and possibly flaked choppers. They could use fire and began to set in motion vast ecological changes in the floral composition of the Australian landscape (22, 45, 48, 57, 60, 61, 63, 75, 81, 114, 116). In the long run, such changes affected many species of marsupial and other fauna, placing suites of animals at risk to future environmental changes. However, the arrival of these archaic men did not cause a massive phase of extinction as posited by me previously (60, 63).

About 30,000 years ago, modern *Homo sapiens* of a gracile form arrived in Australia, possibly across somewhat wider water crossings than the first

men, but with watercraft no more sophisticated than those seen ethnographically in Australia. These modern men quickly spread through the
continent (8) and either replaced their predecessors or were able to occupy
land not used by them. Objections that hunters cannot move through land
already occupied by other hunting societies (77, 132) do not apply here
because we are dealing with two sets of people with considerable differences
in their cultural capacities. After all, modern sapiens Cro Magnon man
managed to inherit Europe from its previous Neanderthal owners during
almost exactly the same time period, an episode which I think reflects the
same fundamental evolutionary process as the Australian one 10,000 km
away on the other side of Asia. The new Mungo people had a broad
spectrum economy capable of exploiting the inland wetlands possibly with
additional food sources such as large fish, but they also had the technology
to occupy new lands, such as the savanna plains and slopes and even the
high montane valleys of New Guinea. Their stone technology was the
foundational phase of the Australian Core Tool and Scraper Tradition and
included waisted blades. Possibly the Kartan industry is an example of it.
Bone tools were also made. They practiced cremation and other complex
burial customs, used ochre, and expressed their artistic feelings on the faces
of rocks.

There was some intermarriage between the two groups of peoples, which
resulted in a population ancestral to the modern Australian Aborigines. In
some environments, especially the riverine one of the middle Murray, the
older group must have had a high enough population density to survive with
less genetic input from outside than elsewhere until at least late Glacial
times (118), when its morphological range is exemplified by the Kow
Swamp population. Even afterwards the modern Aborigines of this region
held within them a greater proportion of genes of the older group than any
others, which is why Birdsell chose the name "Murrayan" to exemplify
what he thought was a second wave of people of "rugged" morphology (7,
9).

An awkward problem for theories of Australian origins has always been
that of the Tasmanian Aborigines. Locked away on their island on the
southward side of the relatively rugged Aborigines of the mainland, their
own morphology was more rounded and gracile (7, 55)—indeed much
closer to the Mungo form than the Kow Swamp one. A solution for this
problem may be one of sheer coincidence that at about the time that bands
of the putative gracile and modern group reached the southeastern coast of
Australia, the sea level was dropping, giving land access to Tasmania for
the first time for some 30,000 years, and thus allowing the new immigrants
to reach a part of the continent not already occupied to some extent by a
previous population. The Tasmanian Aborigines may have held within their

genetic pool a closer approximation of the biological heritage of the putative second group than their cousins on the mainland, who gradually through intermarriage absorbed some of the genes of the first group. Perhaps similar processes may have been at work on some Melanesian islands such as New Britain, which has always required a cross-water access, yet whose modern population seems closer morphologically to the Tasmanians than either do to the intervening Australians, yet all are of one group compared to the other races of modern man (55). Did the second Mungo-like group represent the first colonists on this island sometime around 20,000–25,000 years ago, and are the waisted blades recovered there as surface finds legacies of such an act of Pleistocene colonization (39)?

This filling of the continent by modern man occupied many more ecological spaces than had probably been the case with the archaic first group. There is a consistent pattern that the first appearance of stone tools in many sites dated to between 18,000 and 26,000 years ago lie immediately over deposits devoid of man and his works but containing many bones of the "giant marsupials" (5, 15, 28, 34, 38, 52, 54, 90, 94, 95). These constituted the extinct third of the late Pleistocene marsupial fauna, whose demise must have been a catastrophic phase of faunal pauperation sometime between 25,000–30,000 and 18,000–20,000 years ago. The relative roles of climate and of man in this extinction process are the subject of intense current debate beyond the scope of this paper [(5, 11, 34, 38, 46, 52, 54, 60, 63, 90, 94, 132); Calaby in (76)], but I am left with a feeling that man, his fire-induced vegetational and erosional changes, and even his direct predation placed an additional stress on the marsupial fauna, which made the arid phase of the height of the last Glacial Period so much more devastating than all the others throughout the Pleistocene which had allowed the marsupials to proliferate and to radiate. Only twice in human history were entire continents, Australia and the Americas, colonized suddenly. Recent archaeological research is now placing these events into the broader perspective of the physical and cultural evolution of modern man.

Literature Cited

1. Allen, H. 1974. The Bagundjii of the Darling Basin: cereal gatherers in an uncertain environment. *World Archaeol.* 5:309–22
2. Allen, J. 1972. The first decade in New Guinea archaeology. *Antiquity* 46: 180–90
3. Allen, J. 1977. The hunting Neolithic: adaptations to the food quest in prehistoric Papua New Guinea. In *Hunters, Gatherers and First Farmers Beyond Europe,* ed. J. V. S. Megaw, pp. 167–88. Leicester: Leicester Univ. Press
4. Allen, J., Golson, J., Jones, R., eds. 1977. *Sunda and Sahul: Prehistoric Studies in Southeast Asia, Melanesia and Australia.* London: Academic
5. Balme, J., Merrilees, D., Porter, J. K. 1978. Late Quaternary mammal remains, spanning about 30,000 years from excavations in Devil's Lair, Western Australia. *J. R. Soc. West. Aust.* 61:33–65
6. Barbetti, M., Allen, H. 1972. Prehistoric man at Lake Mungo, Australia by 32,000 years BP. *Nature* 240:46–48

7. Birdsell, J. B. 1949. The racial origin of the extinct Tasmanians. *Rec. Queen Victoria Mus. Launceston* 2:105–22
8. Birdsell, J. B. 1957. Some population problems involving Pleistocene man. *Cold Spring Harbor Symp. Quant. Biol.* 22:47–69
9. Birdsell, J. B. 1977. The recalibration of a paradigm for the first peopling of Greater Australia. See Ref. 4, pp. 113–67
10. Bordes, F. 1976. Coup d'oeil sur la préhistoire Australienne. *Bull. Soc. Prehist. Fr.* 73:170–78
11. Bowdler, S. 1977. The coastal colonisation of Australia. See Ref. 4, pp. 205–46
12. Bowler, J. M. 1971. Pleistocene salinities and climatic change: evidence from lakes and lunettes in southeastern Australia. See Ref. 103, pp. 47–65
13. Bowler, J. M. 1976. Recent developments in reconstructing late Quaternary environments in Australia. See Ref. 76, pp. 55–77
14. Bowler, J. M., Hope, G. S., Jennings, J. N., Singh, G., Walker, D. 1976. Late Quaternary climates of Australia and New Guinea. *Quat. Res.* 6:359–94
15. Bowler, J. M., Jones, R., Allen, H., Thorne, A. G. 1970. Pleistocene human remains from Australia: a living site and human cremation from Lake Mungo, western New South Wales. *World Archeol.* 2:39–60
16. Bowler, J. M., Thorne, A. G. 1976. Human remains from Lake Mungo: discovery and excavation of Lake Mungo III. See Ref. 76, pp. 127–38
17. Bowler, J. M., Thorne, A. G., Polach, H. A. 1972. Pleistocene man in Australia: age and significance of the Mungo skeleton. *Nature* 240:48–50
18. Bulmer, S. 1975. Settlement and economy in prehistoric Papua New Guinea: a review of the archaeological evidence. *J. Soc. Oceanists* 31(44):7–75
19. Bulmer, S. 1977. Waisted blades and axes: a fundamental interpretation of some early stone tools from Papua New Guinea. See Ref. 143, pp. 40–59
20. Chappell, J., Thom, B. S. 1977. Sea levels and coasts. See Ref. 4, pp. 275–91
21. Cipriani, L. 1966. *The Andaman Islanders.* New York: Praeger
22. Clark, G. 1952. *Prehistoric Europe: the Economic Basis.* Cambridge: Cambridge Univ. Press
23. Clark, G. 1961. *World Prehistory, an Outline.* Cambridge: Cambridge Univ. Press
24. Clark, G. 1968. Australian stone age. In *Liber Iosepho Kostrzewski Octogenario a*

25. Clark, G. 1978. *World Prehistory: a New Outline.* Cambridge: Cambridge Univ. Press
26. Diamond, J. M. 1972. Biogeographic kinetics: estimation of relaxation times for avifaunas of southwest Pacific islands. *Proc. Natl. Acad. Sci. USA* 69:3199–3203
27. Dortch, C. E. 1977. Early and late stone industrial phases in western Australia. See Ref. 143, pp. 104–32
28. Flood, J. 1974. Pleistocene man at Clogg's Cave: his tool kit and environment. *Mankind* 9:175–88
29. Gallus, A. 1968. New discoveries in Australian prehistory. See Ref. 24, pp. 636–38
30. Gallus, A. 1970. Expanding horizons in Australian prehistory. *Twentieth Century* (Spring) 25:66–75. Melbourne
31. Gallus, A. 1971/1972. Excavations at Keilor. *The Artefact* (Newsl. Archaeol. Soc. Victoria) 24:1–12; 27:9–19
32. Garanger, J., ed. 1979. *La Préhistoire de l'Océanie.* Paris: Cent. Natl. Rech. Sci. In press
33. Gill, E. D. 1966. Provenance and age of the Keilor cranium: oldest known human skeletal remains in Australia. *Curr. Anthropol.* 7:581–84
34. Gillespie, R., Horton, D. R., Ladd, P., Macumber, P. G., Rich, T. H., Thorne, R., Wright, R. V. S. 1978. Lancefield Swamp and the extinction of the Australian megafauna. *Science* 200: 1045–48
35. Glover, I. C. 1973. Island Southeast Asia and the settlement of Australia. In *Archaeological Theory and Practice,* ed. D. E. Strong, pp. 105–29. London: Seminar
36. Glover, I. C., Glover, E. A. 1970. Pleistocene flake tools from Timor and Flores. *Mankind* 7:188–90
37. Goede, A., Murray, P. 1977. Pleistocene man in south central Tasmania: evidence from a cave site in the Florentine Valley. *Mankind* 11:2–10
38. Goede, A., Murray, P., Harmon, R. 1978. Pleistocene man and megafauna in Tasmania: dated evidence from cave sites. *The Artefact* 3:139–49
39. Golson, J. 1971. Both sides of the Wallace Line: Australia, New Guinea and Asian prehistory. *Archaeol. Phys. Anthropol. Oceania* 6:124–44
40. Golson, J. 1971. The remarkable history of Indo-Pacific man: missing chapters from every world prehistory. Fifth

David Rivett Mem. Lect. *Search* 3: 13–21

41. Gould, R. A. 1973. *Australian Archaeology in Ecological and Ethnographic Perspective.* Warner Modular Publ. 7: 1–33

42. Gould, R. A. 1977. Puntutjarpa Rockshelter and the Australian Desert Culture. *Anthropol. Pap. Am. Mus. Nat. Hist.* 54(1):1–187

43. Gould, R. A. 1978. The anthropology of human residues. *Am. Anthropol.* 80:815–35

44. Gould, R. A., ed. 1978. *Explorations in Ethnoarchaeology.* Santa Fe: School Am. Res.; Albuquerque: Univ. New Mexico Press

45. Hallam, S. J. 1975. *Fire and Hearth.* Canberra: Aust. Inst. Aborig. Stud.

46. Hallam, S. J. 1977. The relevance of Old World Archaeology to the first entry of man into new worlds: colonization seen from the Antipodes. *Quat. Res.* 8: 124–48

47. Harris, D., Weiner, J. 1979. *Human Ecology in the Tropical Savanna.* London: Academic. In press

48. Haynes, C. D. 1978. Land, trees and man: (Gunret, gundulk, dja bining). *Commonw. For. Rev.* 57:99–106

49. Henderson, K. R., ed. 1978. *From Earlier Fleets: Hemisphere an Aboriginal Anthology.* Canberra: Aust. Gov. Publ. Serv.

50. Hooijer, D. A. 1967. Indo-Australian insular elephants. *Genetica* 38:143–62

51. Hope, G. S. 1978. The late Pleistocene and Holocene vegetational history of Hunter Island, north-western Tasmania. *Aust. J. Bot.* 26:493–514

52. Hope, J. H. 1978. Pleistocene mammal extinctions: the problem of Mungo and Menindee, New South Wales. *Alcheringa* 2:65–82

53. Hope, J. H., Hope, G. S. 1976. Palaeoenvironments for man in New Guinea. See Ref. 76, pp. 29–54

54. Hope, J. H., Lampert, R. J., Edmondson, E., Smith, M. J., Van Tets, G. F. 1977. Late Pleistocene faunal remains from Seton rock shelter, Kangaroo Island, South Australia. *J. Biogeogr.* 4: 363–85

55. Howells, W. 1973. *The Pacific Islanders.* New York: Scribner

56. Hughes, P. J., Lampert, R. J. 1977. Occupation disturbance and types of archaeological deposit. *J. Archaeol. Sci.* 4:135–40

57. Jackson, W. D. 1965. Vegetation. In *Atlas of Tasmania,* ed. J. L. Davies, pp.

30–35. Hobart: Tasmanian Gov. Publ. Serv.

58. Johnson, I., ed. 1979. *Proc. 1st Kioloa Prehist. Conf.* Canberra: Aust. Natl. Univ. In press

59. Jones, R. 1966. A speculative archaeological sequence from northwest Tasmania. *Rec. Queen Victoria Mus. Launceston* 25:1–12

60. Jones, R. 1968. The geographical background to the arrival of man in Australia and Tasmania. *Archaeol. Phys. Anthropol. Oceania* 3:186–215

61. Jones, R. 1969. Fire stick farming. *Aust. Nat. Hist.* 16:224–28

62. Jones, R. 1973. Emerging picture of Pleistocene Australians. *Nature* 246: 275–81

63. Jones, R. 1975. The neolithic palaeolithic and the hunting gardeners: man and land in the Antipodes. In *Quaternary Studies,* ed. R. P. Suggate, M. Cresswell, pp. 21–34. Wellington: R. Soc. N.Z.

64. Jones, R. 1976. Greater Australia; research into the Palaeoecology of early man, 1974–75. *Early Man News* 1:2–61. NQUA Commission into the Palaeoecology of Early Man. Tubingen

65. Jones, R. 1976. Tasmania: aquatic machines and offshore islands. See Ref. 112, pp. 235–63

66. Jones, R. 1977. Australia felix: the discovery of a Pleistocene prehistory. *J. Hum. Evol.* 6:353–61

67. Jones, R. 1977. Man as an element of a continental fauna: the case of the sundering of the Bassian Bridge. See Ref. 4, pp. 317–86

68. Jones, R. 1977. The Tasmanian paradox. See Ref. 143, pp. 189–204

69. Jones, R. 1978. Why did the Tasmanians stop eating fish? See Ref. 44, pp. 11–47

70. Jones, R. 1979. Un Île comme miroir d'un continent; la place unique de la Tasmanie dans la préhistoire de l'Australie. See Ref. 32

71. Jones, R. 1979. Bytes and calories: towards a history of the Australian islands. *Inaugural Wentworth Lecture.* Canberra: Aust. Inst. Aborig. Stud. In press

72. Jones, R. 1979. Can't finish him up; hunters in the Australian tropical savanna. See Ref. 47

73. Jones, R., Lampert, R. J. 1978. A note on the discovery of stone tools on Erith Island, the Kent Group, Bass Strait. *Aust. Archaeol.* 8:146–49

74. Kalma, J. D., Nix, H. A. 1972. Climate as a dominant control in the biogeogra-

phy of northern Australia and New Guinea. See Ref. 128, pp. 61–91

75. Kershaw, A. P. 1974. A long continuous pollen sequence from north-eastern Australia. *Nature* 251:222–23

76. Kirk, R. L., Thorne, A. G., eds. 1976. *The Origin of the Australians.* Canberra: Aust. Inst. Aborig. Stud.

77. Kranz, G. S. 1976. On the non-migration of hunting peoples. *Northwest. Anthropol. Res. Notes* 10:209–16

78. Lampert, R. J. 1971. *Burrill Lake and Currarong. Terra Australis 1.* Canberra: Aust. Natl. Univ.

79. Lampert, R. J. 1977. Kangaroo Island and the antiquity of Australians. See Ref. 143, pp. 213–18

80. Lampert, R. J. 1979. Variation in Australia's Pleistocene industries. See Ref. 32

81. Latz, P. K., Griffin, G. F. 1978. Changes in Aboriginal land management in relation to fire and to food plants in central Australia. In *The Nutrition of Aborigines in Relation to the Ecosystem of Central Australia,* ed. B. S. Hetzel, H. J. Frith, pp. 77–85. Melbourne: Commonw. Sci. Ind. Res. Organ.

82. Lorblanchet, M., Jones, R. 1979. Les premieres fouilles à Dampier (Australie de l'ouest) et leur place dans l'ensemble Australien. See Ref. 32

83. MacArthur, R. H., Wilson, O. E. 1967. *The Theory of Island Biogeography.* Princeton: Princeton Univ. Press

84. Macintosh, N. W. G. 1965. The physical aspect of man in Australia. See Ref. 86, pp. 29–70

85. Macintosh, N. W. G. 1967. Fossil man in Australia. *Aust. J. Sci.* 30:86–98

86. McArthur, N., Saunders, I. W., Tweedie, R. L. 1976. Small population isolates: a micro-simulation study. *J. Polynesian Soc.* 85:307–26

87. McBryde, I. 1974. *Aboriginal Prehistory in New England.* Sydney: Sydney University Press

88. McCarthy, F. D. 1958. Culture succession in southeastern Australia. *Mankind* 5:177–90

89. McCarthy, F. D. 1965. The Aboriginal past. In *Aboriginal Man in Australia,* ed. R. M. Berndt, C. H. Berndt, pp. 71–100. Sydney: Angus & Robertson

90. McIntyre, M. L., Hope, J. H. (n.d.) Procoptodon fossils from the Willandra lakes, western New South Wales. *The Artefact* 3:117–32

91. Meehan, B. 1977. Hunters by the seashore. *J. Hum. Evol.* 6:363–70

92. Meehan, B. 1977. Man does not live by calories alone: the role of shellfish in a coastal cuisine. See Ref. 4, pp. 493–531

93. Meehan, B. 1979. *Shell Bed to Shell Midden.* Canberra: Aust. Inst. Aborig. Stud. In press

94. Merrilees, D. 1968. Man the destroyer: late Quaternary changes in the Australian marsupial fauna. *J. R. Soc. West. Aust.* 51:1–24

95. Mountain, M. J. 1979. The rescue of the ancestors in Papua New Guinea. *Bull. Inst. Archaeol. London.* In press

96. Mulvaney, D. J. 1961. The stone age of Australia. *Proc. Prehist. Soc.* 27:56–107

97. Mulvaney, D. J. 1964. The Pleistocene colonization of Australia. *Antiquity* 38:263–67

98. Mulvaney, D. J. 1969. *The Prehistory of Australia.* London: Thames & Hudson. 1st ed.

99. Mulvaney, D. J. 1971. Discovering man's place in nature. *Proc. Aust. Acad. Hum.* 2:47–58

100. Mulvaney, D. J. 1971. Discovering from Antipodean perspectives. *Proc. Prehist. Soc.* 37:228–52

101. Mulvaney, D. J. 1974. The Lake Mungo Project, 17 Aug.–1 Sept. 1973. *Aust. Inst. Aborig. Stud. Newsl.* (new ser.) 1:21–22

102. Mulvaney, D. J. 1975. *The Prehistory of Australia.* Melbourne: Penguin. 2nd ed.

103. Mulvaney, D. J., Golson, J., eds. 1971. *Aboriginal Man and Environment in Australia.* Canberra: Aust. Natl. Univ. Press

104. Mulvaney, D. J., Joyce, E. B. 1965. Archaeological and geomorphological investigations on Mt. Moffet Station, Queensland. *Proc. Prehist. Soc.* 31:147–212

105. Orchiston, D. W., Glenie, R. C. 1978. Residual holocene populations in Bassiania: Aboriginal man at Palana, northern Flinders Island. *Aust. Archaeol.* 8:127–41

106. Peterson, N., ed. 1976. *Tribes and Boundaries in Australia.* Canberra: Aust. Inst. Aborig. Stud.

107. Plomley, N. J. B. 1962. A list of Tasmanian Aboriginal material in collections in Europe. *Rec. Queen Victoria Mus. Launceston,* No. 15

108. Pretty, G. L. 1977. The cultural chronology of Roonka Flat. See Ref. 143, pp. 218–31

109. Rognon, P., Williams, M. A. J. 1977. Late Quaternary climatic changes in Australia and North Africa: a preliminary interpretation. *Palaeogeogr. Palaeoclimatol. Palaeoecol.* 21:85–327

110. Shackleton, N. J., Opdyke, N. D. 1973. Oxygen isotope and paleomagnetic stratigraphy of equatorial Pacific core V28-238: oxygen isotope temperature and ice cream volumes on a 10^5 and 10^6 year scale. *Quat. Res.* 3:39–55

111. Shawcross, W. 1975. Thirty thousand years and more. *Hemisphere* 19:26–31. Reprinted in *From Earlier Fleets,* ed. K. R. Henderson, pp. 4–9. Canberra: Aust. Gov. Publ. Serv.

112. Sieveking, G. de G., Longworth, I. H., Wilson, K. E., Eds. 1976. *Problems in Economic and Social Archaeology.* London: Duckworth

113. Simpson, G. G. 1977. Too many lines; the limits of the Oriental and Australian zoogeographic regions. *Proc. Am. Philos. Soc.* 121:107–20

114. Singh, G., Kershaw, A. P., Clark, R. L. 1979. Quaternary vegetation and fire history in Australia. In *Fire and Australian Biota,* ed. A. M. Gill, R. A. Groves, I. R. Noble. Canberra: Aust. Acad. Sci. In press

115. Stanner, W. E. H., Sheils, H., eds. 1963. *Australian Aboriginal Studies: A Symposium of Papers Presented at the 1961 Research Conference.* Melbourne: Oxford Univ. Press

116. Stocker, G. C. 1971. The age of charcoal from old jungle fowl nests and vegetation change on Melville Island. *Search* 2:28–30

117. Taplin, G. 1878. *The Narrinyeri.* Adelaide: Wigg. 2nd ed.

118. Thorne, A. G. 1971. Mungo and Kow Swamp: morphological variation in Pleistocene Australians. *Mankind* 8:85–89

119. Thorne, A. G. 1977. Separation or reconciliation? Biological clues to the development of Australian society. See Ref. 4, pp. 187–204

120. Thorne, A. G., Macumber, P. G. 1972. Discoveries of late Pleistocene man at Kow Swamp, Australia. *Nature* 238:316–19

121. Thorne, A. G., Wilson, S. R. 1977. Pleistocene and recent Australians: a multivariate comparison. *J. Hum. Evol.* 6:393–402

122. Tindale, N. B. 1937. Relationship of the extinct Kangaroo Island culture with cultures of Australian Tasmania and Malaya. *Rec. South Aust. Mus.* 6:39–60

123. Tindale, N. B. 1957. Culture succession in south-eastern Australia from late Pleistocene to the present. *Rec. South Aust. Mus.* 13:1–49

124. Tindale, N. B. 1962. Some population changes among the Kaiadilt people of Bentinck Island, Queensland. *Rec. South Aust. Mus.* 14:297–336

125. Ucko, P. J., ed. 1978. *Form in Indigenous Art: Schematisation in the Art of Australia and Prehistoric Europe.* Canberra: Aust. Inst. Aborig. Stud.

126. Urry, J. 1978. Old questions: new answers? Some thoughts on the origin and antiquity of man in Australia. *Aborig. Hist.* 2:149–66. In press

127. Van Heekeren, H. R., Knuth, E. 1967. *Archaeological Excavations in Thailand, Vol. 1. Sai Yok: Stone Age Settlements in the Kanchanaburi Province.* Copenhagen: Munksgaard

128. Walker, D., ed. 1972. *Bridge and Barrier: The Natural and Cultural History of Torres Strait.* Canberra: Aust. Natl. Univ.

129. Weidenreich, F. 1946. *Apes, Giants and Man.* Chicago: Univ. Chicago Press

130. White, J. P. 1972. *Ol Tumbuna. Terra Australis 2.* Canberra: Aust. Natl. Univ.

131. White, J. P., Crook, K. A. W., Ruxton, B. P. 1970. Kosipe: a late Pleistocene site in the Papuan Highlands. *Proc. Prehist. Soc.* 36:152–70

132. White, J. P., O'Connell, J. F. 1979. Australian prehistory: new aspects of antiquity. *Science* 203:21–28

133. Wright, R. V. S. 1976. Evolutionary process and semantics: Australian prehistoric tooth size as a local adjustment. See Ref. 76, pp. 265–74

134. Wright, R. V. S., ed. 1977. *Stone Tools as Cultural Markers: Change, Evolution and Complexity.* Canberra: Aust. Inst. Aborig. Stud.

135. Wyrwoll, K-H., Dortch, C. E. 1978. Stone artifacts and an associated Diprotodontid mandible from the Greenough River, Western Australia. *Search* 9:411–13

Ann. Rev. Anthropol. 1979. 8:467–502

RECENT DEVELOPMENTS IN SOUTH ASIAN PREHISTORY AND PROTOHISTORY

♦9643

Jerome Jacobson

Department of Anthropology, City College, City University of New York,
New York, NY 10031

INTRODUCTION

Five years ago, the dean of Indian prehistory, H. D. Sankalia, wrote, "... in a sense Indian prehistory is where the European was in 1860" (180, p. 13). If that was an excessively critical assessment of the state of the art in 1974, it certainly cannot be applied to Indian prehistory—or protohistory —in 1979. Today there are few world areas of comparable size where knowledge of the ancient past is growing so rapidly and over so broad a geographical and chronological spectrum.

Far from being similar to European prehistory of 1860, Indian prehistoric and protohistoric research incorporates some of the latest advances in archaeological science. Questions that until recently could hardly be asked —about absolute chronologies, ancient environments, and human adaptations—are today finding answers.

Some of the salient developments within the past few years that are summarized in this paper include: the first excavation of a site in which every major stage of the Paleolithic and Mesolithic are represented (Bhimbetka, Madhya Pradesh); excavation of open-air habitation sites of the Lower Paleolithic; the emergence of a blade-and-burin complex of Late Pleistocene age with associated bone implements and the earliest art of India; discovery of what may be the first human skull of Pleistocene date known from South Asia; the first excavation of Mesolithic dwellings and an extensive Mesolithic cemetery; evidence for animal domestication dating

467

0084-6570/79/1015-0467$01.00

possibly to the sixth and definitely to the fifth millennium, and for plant cultivation possibly to the sixth; and linguistic research that has led to virtual agreement on the language of the Harappan script.

These findings have been made with little stated theoretical underpinning, however. Indian archaeology today is characterized by scientific methods without *the scientific method*, descriptions of environments and traits without systems theory, and reconstruction of culture history without regard to culture process. These features, and even the presence of a few voices pleading for and experimenting with new approaches to the problems of understanding the past, give the observer an impression not of Europe of 1860 but of United States archaeology of 1960, as a parallel of Indian archaeology in 1979.

This paper briefly discusses some concepts, methods, and overall results in Indian archaeology. It then reviews some recent findings pertaining to major cultural stages in most of mainland South Asia—India, Pakistan, and some of Afghanistan. Rather than a detailed summary, the paper presents some significant current developments, partly updating syntheses by Allchin & Allchin (11), Fairservis (56), and Sankalia (180, 182); see also a recent overview by Jain (87).

In the limited space available here, usually only one or two of the more recent sources for each topic are cited, and coverage of much substantial research is regretfully omitted. To some extent, inclusions and omissions reflect the degree to which recent research has affected previously held concepts of India's past.

Within the Republic of India, archaeological research has been conducted almost entirely by Indian archaeologists from an increasing number of universities with archaeological programs, from the Archaeological Survey of India and its many branches and regional circles, and from the archaeological departments in some of the state governments. The pattern is similar in Pakistan, but the proportion of foreign archaeological field projects there has been higher; in Afghanistan it has been higher still.

APPROACHES AND METHODS

Indian archaeology has tended to utilize two frames of reference: a geological one to cover the Paleolithic and the Mesolithic, and an historical particularistic approach for later cultural stages. Concepts of the nature of culture, or of culture change, however, have often remained essentially unstated, generally uninformed by anthropological theory, and beyond the concern of most workers in the field.

Today there are signs of change. Recently, S. P. Gupta (72, pp. viii-ix) listed the following trends in what he regards as the present period of transition in Indian archaeology: multidisciplinary research, the questioning of diffusionary theories, and growing concern with problems of social structure, economic process, settlement pattern, colonization, urbanization, and metallurgy. While these developments are certainly welcome, they still engage the attention of relatively few archaeologists; in part, perhaps, because too few have heeded Gupta's earlier warning that unless Indian archaeologists redirected their energies toward hypothesis testing and processual analysis, they would become "drop-outs from the main stream" of world archaeology (70, p. 361). Long before Gupta's plea, Malik had for years urged the injection of anthropological theory into archaeological research (117), and had produced a model of cultural evolution in South Asia (118). Now Agrawal and Chakrabarti have added their voices to Malik's in calling for orientation toward broad cultural issues and for a "social archaeology" rather than concern with only "problems of sequence and chronology" (2, p. 3).

Sankalia, the most productive prehistorian ever to have worked in South Asia, seems to have mixed feelings about the recent "new" approaches to archaeology in the United States and Britain. In his 1977 volume, *New Archaeology: Its Scope and Application to India* (183), he accepts the value of some specific techniques currently advocated in the West, e.g. tight contextual controls, on-site analysis and feedback, and certain statistical procedures. However, he finds practical difficulties in the horizontal excavation of deeply buried sites urged by the "New Archaeologists," and he emphasizes the limitations of the archaeological record in reconstructing ancient cultures. More importantly, he tends to ignore or minimize some of the basic assumptions of recent Anglo-American archaeology—the concepts of cultural evolution, cultural process, and systemics—and fails to indicate where these would be applicable in South Asia. Additional insight into Sankalia's theoretical stance is revealed in an earlier paper (181) on the same theme, in which he wrote ". . . in the name of science and technology, we should not . . . look for things which were never contemplated by a prehistoric man."

This statement reveals an emic approach [i.e. orientation toward the subject's view of his culture (78)] that stops far short of the goals and accomplishments of recent systemic and processual archaeology. Certainly, significant trends in evolving man-environment relationships can be seen archaeologically that may not have been obvious to a "prehistoric man" participating in them.

Culture process and systems theory notwithstanding, Sankalia has organized and vigorously advocated (181) multidisciplinary field research for obtaining paleoenvironmental data to help reconstruct ancient adaptations. Further, many archaeologists he has trained at Deccan College, Pune (formerly Poona), tend to follow his explicitly environmental approach (131, 134, 142, 153, 156, 163).

Environmental orientation has also characterized the work of many of the foreign archaeologists who have conducted research in South Asia in recent years, including, most notably, Fairservis in Pakistan (55, 56) and Bridget Allchin, primarily in India (12).

In recent years, Fairservis at Allahdino (57, 81) and Dales at Balakot (40a) have conducted extended excavations into Harappan components. These projects are utilizing sophisticated sampling techniques and statistical analyses to determine more precisely the nature of the Harappan adaptation. Recently a number of former students and field assistants of Fairservis, or of his former student Possehl, have utilized some of the insights of ecological studies and culture systems theory in understanding early South Asian culture process (58, 59, 81, 82, 160). One of the most ambitious and explicit applications of systems theory to South Asian archaeology is Shaffer's (189) revised and published dissertation on his work in Afghani Baluchistan. His analysis of culture change there replaces with systemic, processual interpretations the diffusionary and migratory models usually applied to studies of that area. At the very least, such investigations provide a relief from the usual archaeological report on South Asia in which a change in pottery type is automatically equated with the arrival of a different "people."

RECENT RESEARCH EMPHASES AND SOME GENERAL RESULTS

The general lack of concern with anthropological theory, however, has not slowed the development of sophisticated analytical methods that have produced important research results in recent years. Some of the most significant findings have come in chronological and paleoenvironmental studies. Radiocarbon dates have been obtained for all major cultural stages with the exception of the Lower Paleolithic [Table 1; see also (5, 119, 165)]. For the Paleolithic sequence, recent field investigations of paleoenvironments have centered on western India (9), but field research has been wide-ranging, including studies of Himalayan glaciations (101), riverine geomorphology (156, 162, 163), sedimentology (97, 103), paleobotany (20, 21), desert activity (12), miliolite formation (10, 120), pedology (174), and sea level fluctuations (4, 69, 186). Together these investigations, and many others too numerous to cite, have provided the most detailed views yet available of the successive geological changes and climatic regimes that affected the subcontinent during the Quaternary. Some of these ancient climates have been tentatively correlated with cultural stages and are referred to in the appropriate sections below.

Table 1 Chronology of South Asian prehistory and protohistory

Cultural development	Approximate date of inception, B.C.	Comment on chronology
Historic urbanization	600	

Historic and archaeological evidence for kingdoms and fortified towns (222, pp. 48–49; 71, p. 56).

Iron in peninsular India	1,100	

A conservative chronology based partly on ^{14}C readings from Eran, Madhya Pradesh; iron production may date to 1300 B.C. in Central India, coincident with end of Malwa Chalcolithic culture [see text and (133, p. 119)] ; in South India by 1,000 B.C., with reservations (5, pp. 144–45); widespread by mid-first millennium B.C. (22).

Post-Harappan farming villages	1,700	

Harappan cities disappear although many traits persist in northern and western India; regional Chalcolithic traditions (7, p. 373).

Mature Harappan civilization	2,600	

Cities; seals with writing, standardization across vast area. For chronology, see Harappan civilization section.

Chalcolithic	4,500	

Villages with copper artifacts, wheel-made pottery; chronology based on uncalibrated radiocarbon date P-2148 on uppermost level of Period I at Rana Ghundai, Baluchistan (74, p. x), suspiciously early compared with analogous levels of other sites in Baluchistan and Indus valley; where calibrated, earliest ^{14}C readings (at Damb Sadaat and Amri) extend to only ca 3,600 (180, pp. 564–65).[a] At Mundigak, Afganistan, a calibrated date for early Chalcolithic provides a 67% confidence reading to ca 3,800 (189, p. 96). A bronze-using culture in northern Afganistan dates to about the 6th millennium (53, pp. 44–45, 75).

Ceramic Neolithic	5,000?	

Dated to about 7,000 ^{14}C years in northern Afghanistan (53). Evident but undated in Pakistan (Gumla, Sarai Khola, Jalilpur) (40, p. 70). Possibly in this time range in Gangetic plain [(74, p. 272); see section on Domestication, etc.]

Aceramic Neolithic	6,000	

Dated to about 10,200 ^{14}C years in northern Afghanistan (53, p. 77) and *estimated* by Gupta at "6th or 7th millennium B.C., if not earlier" at Mehrgarh, Baluchistan (74, p. 268).

Mesolithic	8,000	

Based on questionable ^{14}C date from Sarai Nahar Rai, and on geological data from the arid zone of western India (see Mesolithic section).

Upper Paleolithic	>23,000	

Based on ^{14}C dates of ca 23,800 from Deoghat, Belan Valley, Uttar Pradesh [PRL 86; (129, p. 63)] and another, of about 25,000 ^{14}C years, on ostrich egg shell fragment from Patne, Maharashtra [GRN 7200; (173)] . These readings thought to be up to 5000 (Maharashtra) to 8000 (U.P.) years younger than earliest Upper Paleolithic deposit at those sites.

Middle Paleolithic	>38,000	

Based on 9 samples from 6 river gravels in Central and western India (8, p. 5).

Lower Paleolithic	120,000–300,000 B.P.	

Based on late Middle Pleistocene chronology suggested as maximum age of stone tools in Kashmir, perhaps oldest known from South Asia. *Most* other Lower Paleolithic materials date from Upper Pleistocene (96). Absolute age of late Middle Pleistocene derived from de Lumley (46, Figure 3).

---

[a] The MASCA calibration is a formula whereby radiocarbon years are converted into calendrical years by adjusting for apparent discrepancies in the ^{14}C "clock" (128). This calibration, however, is not accepted as universally valid or even warranted by some experts (7, pp. 371–72).

One result of multidisciplinary research in the Himalayan area has been rejection of the classic Pleistocene glacial sequence proposed by de Terra & Paterson (50), in the absence of evidence for glaciation below 2500 m (100) and in light of new insights into the nature of the Pleistocene glacial cycles (30). While a severely cold glacial phase is recognized in the Himalayan zone for the early Middle Pleistocene (100), subsequent climate both there and in peninsular India (163) "since the arrival of Acheulian man . . ." ameliorated and remained semiarid with changes "of degree only and not of kind" (96, 163).

The known beginnings of art in India have been pushed back 20,000 years or more within the last few years with the discoveries of Upper Paleolithic sculpture, engraving, and possibly painting (see section below on Upper Paleolithic). The greatest effort in studying the early art of South Asia has been devoted to the paintings in at least 23 rock shelter regions in Central and South India (27, 68, 122, 166). Most intensive analysis in recent years has focused on Bhimbetka and the adjacent Central Vindhyan hills in Madhya Pradesh (124a, 132a), where more than 500 painted rock shelters have been counted (123), one of the richest lodes of rock art anywhere, and, by one count, equal to all the other known painted shelters in India (27, p. 1) [but less than 10 percent of Wakankar's recent estimate of at least 6000 known painted shelters (218, p. 6)]. In addition to paintings, rock engravings have been found at Bhimbetka and elsewhere in Madhya Pradesh (218, p. 9), and engravings and "bruisings" are known from South India (13, pp. 11–17; 184, p. 88).

Analyses of palimpsests, historic inscriptions, and parallels with Chalcolithic pottery designs have led to the dating of many of the paintings to the Mesolithic and possibly earlier. The thousands of pictographs already analyzed have permitted cultural reconstructions of the Mesolithic in details unavailable from other archaeological sources. Some of these and other recent developments in the study of the early art of India have been recently synthesized by Sankalia (184).

Leshnik (111), Nagaraja Rao (149), and Nagar (146) pioneered in recent ethnoarchaeological research in India, with studies of present-day villages in Madhya Pradesh and Rajasthan as aids in understanding house types, ceramic remains, and other material and social aspects of prehistoric farming villages. Within the past few years, numerous scholars have made ethnographic observations of wild plant use to help reconstruct prehistoric plant exploitation patterns (127, 143, 147, 148, 164, 187, 215). Murty & Sontheimer (145) have studied South Indian shepherd nomads as models for interpreting prehistoric pastoralism. Current megalithic practices are under investigation for clues toward understanding the behaviors surrounding ancient funerary monuments (90, 198). A chair in ethnoarcheology has been established at Deccan College, Pune (180, p. 87).

"Linguistic Archaeology," or the application of historical linguistics to archaeological problems, has made recent contributions to South Asian studies (203). In addition to the attempts by several scholars to decipher the Indus script, Southworth has investigated problems in earliest contacts between speakers of Indo-Aryan and Dravidian languages (202), origins of domesticated cereals in India (201), and the nature of the migration of Indo-Aryan speakers into the subcontinent (204). The substantive results of some of this work are covered below in the review of various archaeological periods.

The investigation of ancient settlement or habitation patterns has attracted growing research interest. Most of these researches have focused on the patterning of dwelling units and other features in Neolithic and Chalcolithic communities for clues to demographic and social parameters (51; 180, pp. 516–19), while other studies include the mapping of the distribution and dimensions of Acheulian occurrences (85, 153) and of Iron Age and Early Historic sites (109).

Technological and statistical studies of stone tools have been undertaken in recent years (81, 89, 98, 154, 155, 168). One result of research by Jayaswal was the revelation of a surprisingly close technological relationship between Lower and Middle Paleolithic assemblages (89a). Earlier, Sankalia had drawn numerous behavioral inferences from a study of the stone tools from a Chalcolithic component (176).

Technical studies of ancient materials have determined their composition and production, including copper (79), bronze (1), iron (24), and ceramics (80, 138).

Data on ancient burial practices in South Asia have been synthesized in major works (69a, 199), although considerable scope remains for application of recent methods of sociological interpretation of funerary evidence (e.g. 205a). While reports of human skeletal finds from the Pleistocene remain unconfirmed (see Upper Paleolithic section), the interpretation of human osteology from Mesolithic and later prehistoric and protohistoric complexes has added important dimensions to the understanding of early human populations in South Asia (103a) and will be summarized in next year's *Annual Review of Anthropology* (104a).

The study of the relationship of ancient South Asian cultures with those of surrounding areas also has seen increased interest, generated especially by recent excavations in Iran (43, 44, 110), the Persian Gulf zone (25), and Central Asia, including northern Afghanistan [see (74) for bibliography]. Sites in those regions have revealed indications of culture contact with South Asia; major syntheses of these connections have been published recently (19, 74) and are mentioned in appropriate sections below.

Perhaps a word on nomenclature may be helpful here. Although the title of this paper mentions both prehistory and protohistory, the latter term has been ambiguous in South Asian contexts. It is used by Sankalia (180, pp. 7–8, 15) to include all cultural developments from farming villages of about 4000 B.C. to the beginning of decipherable writing at about 300 B.C. Others prefer to restrict its use to the cultures without writing that are described in traditional texts (11, p. 27), and still others simply divide South Asian culture history into prehistoric and historic periods, at 300 B.C. (62, pp. 510–11). It would seem most consistent with generally accepted definitions of protohistory (42a, p. 8) to include under that heading all cultures in South Asia from the time of the earliest known pre-Harappan pottery marks of roughly 3000 B.C. (uncorrected), which are genetically related to the Indus script (107a, pp. 14–15), until the beginning of known early historic writing about 300 B.C.

On another terminological note, the various "lithic" stages referred to below have replaced the formerly used Early-Middle-Late Stone Age designations to accommodate the newly discovered blade-and-burin complex of India as "Upper Paleolithic" (180). These newly adopted terms have the advantage of being previously established in the archaeological literature, and they represent a relative sequence as well as an absolute chronology which to some extent mirror those of European prehistory, to which the terms were originally applied. In important respects, however, many of the South Asian artifacts bear stronger resemblances to counterparts in Africa than in Europe, and thus the new application of European nomenclature to South Asian assemblages can be misleading.

The outlines of Indian culture history are probably familiar to the reader, or if not, can be readily grasped when it is understood that the broad evolutionary sequence follows that of Europe, Africa, and West Asia. That is, the Paleolithic is a Pleistocene foraging adaptation that reveals stone tool kits of increasing efficiency in technology and function. A succeeding Mesolithic stage is characterized by new exploitation patterns, microlithic implements, and more permanent settlements, followed by a period in which farming villages appear. Urbanization occurs first in the Indus Valley in what is today Pakistan. The earliest cities disappear by about 1700 B.C. After an apparent gap of more than a thousand years, cities reappear in the Ganges valley at the dawn of the historic period as by-products of a vigorous Iron Age.

LOWER PALEOLITHIC

When did people first inhabit South Asia? Probably not before the late Middle Pleistocene, according to the latest estimate. This comparatively late chronology—especially so when compared with the much earlier evidence for man's presence in Africa—is based on a detailed reexamination and analysis of the geology of the Vale of Kashmir (96, 101). [At one time, Sankalia had suggested a Lower Pleistocene date for Lower Paleolithic tools he found there (177).] Joshi believes that the tools in Kashmir probably antedate any other signs of human habitation in South Asia (100).

Other comparably early signs of human occupation come from elsewhere in the Himalayan area of both India and Pakistan. For almost 40 years many of these finds had been tied to the Himalayan glacial sequence proposed by de Terra & Paterson (50). But that interpretation of Himalayan geology is now rejected by Joshi on two counts: first, careful reexamination of Himalayan valleys indicates the absence of glaciation below 2500 m elevation, and the presence of strong tectonic activity during the Pleistocene (100), and second, recent syntheses of the Pleistocene have shown that the classic four-glaciation Alpine sequence is an oversimplification of what may have been some 10 major Pleistocene glacial advances, at least in the higher latitudes (29, 46).

In general, the earliest man-made tools in the Himalayas appear to be dominated by the pebble-chopper tradition linked by Movius to early stone tool industries of East Asia (135). In some of the Himalayan foothill and piedmont zones, these pebble-chopper assemblages with associated flake tools tend to concentrate at higher altitudes than finds of the Acheulian biface tradition (133). This has led Mohapatra (133) to support Movius's postulate of an independent cultural adaptation—the Soan—to a demanding ecozone. The rare Acheulian hand ax assemblage in that zone, according to Mohapatra, represents an unsuccessful attempt at habitation by human groups of another cultural tradition.

In peninsular India, Pebble choppers have been seen as part of the Acheulian industries (94). Now, however, Wakankar has claimed the discovery of at least four sites in Madhya Pradesh in which assemblages with pebble choppers and without bifaces lie stratigraphically below those with Acheulian tools (49, 219). He has found this evidence not only at riverbank localities, but also in two of the Bhimbetka rock shelters, in at least one of which the pebble-chopper and biface layers were separated by a sterile soil. Unstratified sites with pebble choppers and no bifaces are also recently reported from Madhya Pradesh (18), the west coast of the peninsula (96), and Rajasthan (12, p. 307).

Whether or not these sites are verified as manifestations of a pre-biface tradition in India, it remains apparent that no technological evolution produced the Acheulian complex on the subcontinent. The Acheulian hand axes, cleavers, and associated implements, however, show close enough typological parallels with East African counterparts to suggest a cultural link between the two. Allchin, Goudie & Hegde propose a possible migration route from Africa to western India "possibly via parts of the continental shelf now submerged by rising sea levels" (12, p. 308).

Once having appeared in India, however, the hand-ax makers (or hand-ax making) spread into virtually every area and ecozone of the peninsula, apparently following the same nomadic foraging pursuits thought to characterize their adaptations elsewhere. Although most of the stone tools have been collected from riverbanks and beds, recent fieldwork has uncovered Acheulian evidence from two rock shelter groups, Bhimbetka and Adamgarh, across the Narmada River from each other in Madhya Pradesh (95, 132), and from buried (38, 39, 152) and surface (84, 86) habitation sites. In Karnataka, Paddayya has excavated what appears to have been an Acheulian boulder-lined dwelling (152). These and other recent explorations indicate that previous assumptions that Acheulian groups preferred locales along main waterways (56, p. 74) must be revised, since heavy site concentrations have been found far from the nearest rivers (84).

Nowhere in India has stratigraphic evidence been found of an evolution of Acheulian tool technology or typology. Unstratified collections do hint of a developmental sequence, however, and recently Misra divided the bifacial assemblages into two groups (132, p. 166). One he equates with the East African Middle Acheulian; the other, typologically more evolved, resembles the French Mousterian of Acheulian tradition. A possibly less advanced manifestation of the biface tradition identified as Early Abbevillean has been found in the Narmada valley, but its chronological position is unclear (18).

MIDDLE PALEOLITHIC

The Middle Paleolithic is dominated by small tools: mainly points, borers, and scrapers made on flat flakes, cores, or nodules; it has few bifaces, and is the first stage of the Indian Paleolithic for which radiocarbon readings are available. The chronological range is between an undetermined date more than 40,000 to about 11,000 radiocarbon years ago—later Upper Pleistocene—on nine samples from six river gravel sites in Central and Western India (8, p. 5).

The Middle Paleolithic apparently represents the continuation of a foraging adaptation, but except for some faunal associations that show little differentiation from those of the Acheulian (21; 153, p. 104), relatively little is known about this stage. The flakes and cores of this tradition have a somewhat more limited known geographic distribution than the Acheulian finds, but they have been collected from every major area of India and from at least one site in Pakistan (180, p. 197).

Components of this complex are found stratified in river gravels below those containing tools of the blade-and-burin tradition (180, p. 144). They also are found above Acheulian levels in riverine contexts (180, pp. 143–206) and in a Bhimbetka rock shelter (132, p. 39). Rajaguru (163) points out, however, that the Acheulian and Middle Paleolithic tools occur in the same geological deposits in three major river valleys of peninsular India.

Indigenous origins of Indian Middle Paleolithic tool-making traditions are suggested by the evidence from one of the Bhimbetka caves, which revealed "clear evidence for the evolution of Middle Paleolithic" from the lower, Acheulian assemblage [V. N. Misra, letter, May 11, 1979; (131a, p. 14)]. Moreover, Middle Paleolithic assemblages from Central India have revealed striking technological parallels with Indian Acheulian material from the same area (89a). Viewed from western India, however, the Indian Middle Paleolithic seems linked to similar traditions beyond the subcontinent in the West Asian Mousterian and in the Levallois-Mousterian of Afghanistan (182, p. 197). These links are technological, including "the extensive use of flakes struck from prepared cores, and the methods of preparing the cores ..." (12, p. 314). However, the Middle Paleolithic collections have

a distinctive overall South Asian character which distinguishes them as a group in addition to their regional characteristics which differentiate them from one another within the group. . . . The Middle Palaeolithic was a time of diversifications and regional specialization throughout the old world, and it is to be expected that in South Asia . . . there should be variant forms of it in each environmental region (12, p. 315).

Within the Indian Middle Paleolithic, Allchin, Goudie & Hegde (12, p. 315) identify three such variant forms or regional industries associated respectively with 1. Central India and the Deccan, 2. Southern and Central Rajasthan, and 3. the Indus plains. Distinctions among these are based on techno-typological parameters, including a greater affinity of those in Rajasthan with the Asiatic Mousterian (12, p. 310). All three are distinct from the Upper and Final Soan industries of the sub-Himalayan Punjab (159, pp. 71–88), which also are characterized by a preponderance of relatively small flake tools, but in which pebble tools, reminiscent of the Early Soan, persist.

A gradual evolution in stone tool types of the peninsular Middle Paleolithic has been seen stratigraphically only at Bhimbetka (V. N. Misra, personal communication), although western Rajasthan has yielded a possible evolutionary sequence in surface sites (12, p. 317).

Most of the Middle Paleolithic materials have been gathered from redeposited river gravels, but tools and debitage also have been found associated with outcrop veins of silecious rocks in Madhya Pradesh (180, p. 147) and Karnataka (151, pp. 23–67). These factory sites reflect a trademark of the Indian Middle Paleolithic: the preference for silecious rock—mainly chert and jasper—over the quartzites and basalts favored by the

Acheulian tool makers. Sankalia suggests that this change may have come about, in part, "because the sources of the earlier material—such as the river gravels—were submerged or became inaccessible" (182, p. 59).

Research in Rajasthan, Gujarat, and Maharashtra in recent years seems to indicate a wetter climatic setting than that of the present for Middle Paleolithic occupation. Perhaps the most dramatic evidence has come from the present desert and arid zone of Rajasthan, Gujarat, and Sind. Allchin, Goudie & Hegde (12, p. 309) found a deeply weathered paleosol there that apparently stabilized dunes formed during an arid phase which intervened between the Lower and Middle Paleolithic occupations of the area. Thick gravel deposits of this period offer additional evidence of wetter conditions (131, p. 49). This is reflected throughout much of peninsular India, where tools of this stage are typically associated with a second, "middle," gravel in river bank sections (180, p. 147).

UPPER PALEOLITHIC

A blade-and-burin complex of somewhat limited distribution on the subcontinent is the most recent prehistoric stage to emerge from Indian archaeological research and was installed as the Upper Paleolithic in Sankalia's 1974 synthesis (180, pp. 207–30). Sankalia so named this stage because of its chronological position in the terminal Pleistocene starting more than 20,000 years ago, its stratigraphic situation between Middle Paleolithic and Mesolithic deposits, and its technotypological resemblance to European industries of the same time period.

Sankalia admits, however, that the Indian blade-and-burin industries include both European-like and non-European-like assemblages, and that even the former differ from European industries in having far fewer tool types and a higher proportion of scrapers (180, p. 230). Moreover, Desmond Clark (personal communication) has declared that at least one of the Indian blade-and-burin assemblages he examined has strong resemblances to the South African Howieson's Poort culture of that area's Middle Stone Age.

Evidence for a blade-and-burin complex had been found in India during the nineteenth century (28). Its position remained uncertain, however, until the 1970s, when discoveries of stratified sites, art, and bone tools, and radiocarbon chronology provided the data for postulating this stage. [This discussion of the Upper Paleolithic is based primarily on Murty (144) unless otherwise noted; the most complete published source on this stage of Indian prehistory at this writing is Sankalia (180, pp. 207–30).]

Although sites containing evidence of this complex are far fewer than those of earlier and later cultural affinities, Murty's site list covers a wide variety of ecozones, including desert and forested hills. None are yet known, however, from such large states as Punjab, Haryana, West Bengal, Orissa, and Kerala. Most Upper Paleolithic artifacts have been found in surface scatters or in stratified riverbank sections, but they recently have been discovered in sand dunes in northwestern India (12), in stratified deposits from at least two shelters in the Bhimbetka group (219), and in Muchchatla Chintamanu Gavi cave in Andhra Pradesh.

In the desert and arid regions of Rajasthan and Gujarat, Allchin, Goudie & Hegde (12, pp. 321–22) see the early appearance of the Upper Paleolithic during the final millennia of the same wet phase that characterized the Middle Paleolithic, but through most of its course, the blade-and-burin complex persisted during a period of greater aridity than today. These scholars bracket that dry phase between perhaps 20,000 and 10,000 B.P., citing dune associations and other evidence from their own fieldwork as well as sedimentological, eustatic, and ocean core data from Pakistan and from elsewhere in Gujarat.

Citing recent geomorphological and sedimentological studies in peninsular river valleys, Rajaguru also sees a (slightly) drier climate for the terminal Pleistocene of 20,000 to 10,000 B.P. (163), and Wakankar recognizes a similar situation in the Vindhyan hill region of Central India (217, p. 23; 219).

Only two direct radiocarbon dates are available (6), but paleontology and geomorphology do not contradict a bracket of at least 23,000 (99, pp. 90–91) to 10,000 B.P. for this stage (but see Table 1).

Murty's discoveries of blade-and-burin sites in Andhra Pradesh were among the first in recent years [along with those of Reddy (169), also in Andhra, and Ghosh (63) in Bihar] to call attention to this previously neglected segment of Indian prehistory (139). Murty now distinguishes three technotypological groups within this stage, all of which include blades and burins: he names these groups flake-blade, blade tool, and blade and burin. The distinctions between the groups are made on the basis of the presence or absence of backed blades and the proportion of burins and other tools made on blades vs flakes. Scrapers, points, borers, burins, and various backed blade types are typical, and rare choppers, tanged and shouldered points, anvils, and bored stones are also found. Tools were fashioned typically of quartzite or of silecious rock such as chert, jasper, or chalcedony. On average, the size of the tools is intermediate between those of Middle Paleolithic and Mesolithic.

Bone tools now appear for the first time in the Indian sequence. Confirming nineteenth century reports of bone tools associated with Pleistocene fauna (60, 113, 114), a recent excavation in the Muchchatla Chintamanu Gavi cave of Andhra Pradesh yielded a similar association as well as an assemblage of Upper Paleolithic stone tools (141, 142). The bone tools are described as scrapers, perforators, chisels, scoops, shouldered points, barbs, and spatulas.

Of potentially greater interest is Wakankar's discovery of most of a human skull from the base of what he describes as an Upper Paleolithic layer of one of the Bhimbetka caves (218, p. 8). If substantiated, this find would constitute the earliest known human physical remains found in South Asia [except for unconfirmed nineteenth century discoveries (104, p. 102)]. Sporadic reports of discoveries of human bones in Pleistocene contexts appear from time to time in the Indian press (e.g. 16), but thus far none has been published in a scientific journal or otherwise authenticated. [For a detailed discussion of early human remains in South Asia, see (103, 103a, 104, 104a, 140).]

The earliest recognizable art and ornamentation first appear in this segment of the Indian prehistoric record. The most striking example is the bone figurine found by G. R. Sharma's team in the Belan Valley of the Gangetic basin, associated with an Upper Paleolithic complex dated to about 19,700 radiocarbon years (184, pp. 7–8). Sankalia has examined the specimen and describes it as:

> about 8 cm. high, between 1.5 cm. and 2.5 cm. broad, and about one cm. in thickness. The face is featureless, a triangular formation, the trunk stick-like with a pointed, triangular portion for the legs and probably the extremity broken. The pendant breasts, and the broad loins definitely indicate that this is a female figurine (184, p. 8.).

Three ostrich egg shell fragments engraved with one or two outlined bands of cross-hatching were found in a river section at the site of Patne, in Maharashtra, in the youngest two of five Upper Paleolithic layers. Ostrich egg shell also was used in the production of three of four beads found in the same layers, the other being of estuarine shell (172, 173). Wakankar also has found etched eggshell fragments in a similar cultural context at a site near Bhopal, Madhya Pradesh (218, p. 9). He further suggests that Upper Paleolithic artists may have produced some of the earliest paintings, including those of ostrich, in the Central Indian rock shelters (218, pp. 6, 7, 9). Some of the paintings were executed in the same shade of green as obtained from a rubbed fragment of *terre verte* (glauconite) found in an excavation layer dominated by blades and burins in one of the Bhimbetka caves. Wakankar admits, however, that distinctions between Upper Paleolithic paintings, if they do exist in those shelters, and Mesolithic ones are still unclear.

MESOLITHIC

The term "Mesolithic" may have been first applied to microlithic tool collections from India as early as the 1860s (26, p. 314; 83), but it is only within recent years that cultural and chronological dimensions of this stage have begun to be clarified.

As in other areas of the Old World, the Mesolithic in India constitutes the adaptations of human populations to post-Pleistocene environments, prior to the advent of sedentary farming villages. These adaptations are marked in India as elsewhere by the predominance of microlithic implements, notably backed bladelets of various forms. The Indian Mesolithic differs from that of some other areas, however, in its relative scarcity of large sedentary sites and of substantial evidence for the exploitation of aquatic resources. Nevertheless, the large number of sites and implements relating to a span of time more brief than those of previous prehistoric stages testify to the apparent success of the Mesolithic adaptation in South Asia.

An exception to the general pattern of relatively small, thinly occupied Mesolithic sites divorced from aquatic association is the recent discovery of what appears to be a full-fledged Mesolithic village on the bank of an oxbow lake formed by an old channel of the Ganges, in southern Uttar Pradesh state (192). The site, Sarai Nahar Rai, has provided the earliest radiocarbon date yet determined for a Mesolithic component in India, ca 10,300 radiocarbon years (193). Although this date was derived from unburned bone, an unreliable indicator, this chronology is supported by geological dating of this stage in western India (12, p. 326).

A date of about 7500 radiocarbon years has been obtained from shells associated with a Mesolithic component of the Adamgarh rock shelter group in Central India (5, p. 61), but the excavator has expressed doubts about its interpretation (R. V. Joshi, personal communication). The earliest unchallenged ^{14}C date on the Indian Mesolithic is one of approximately 4500 B.C., uncorrected, at the Bagor site in Rajasthan (5, p. 61).

Sarai Nahar Rai and Bagor provide some of the oldest evidence for man-made dwellings on the subcontinent, Sarai Nahar Rai revealing post molds indicating a beehive-type pole structure (194), and Bagor showing floors of schist slabs used as paving in some dwellings and apparently arranged to brace walls around a circular earthen surface in others (130, p. 104).

Other Mesolithic sites are known from open-air stations in widely varying environments and from numerous rock shelters, mainly in western and Central India. [Sankalia (180, pp. 231–78) provides a detailed summary of the Indian Mesolithic.]

Technologically, the microliths of this stage apparently owe much to their Upper Paleolithic predecessors, but the picture is complicated by (a) distinctive industries along the Tamilian coast (224a) and in Kerala (164a) that share more with apparently coeval microlithic traditions in Sri Lanka, and (b) highly evolved microliths in Central India that may have borrowed sophisticated techniques of bladelet production from stoneknappers in early farm villages (83).

Indeed, the so-called "Mesolithic" adaptation itself apparently tended to include pastoralism as well as hunting, since bones of domesticated herd animals have been found in most major Mesolithic components (see section below on Domestication and Early Villages).

The Mesolithic deposits of Sarai Nahar Rai revealed the largest number of human burials excavated in a prehistoric Indian site prior to the Indus civilization. The 35 Sarai Nahar Rai skeletons represent an extraordinarily tall group according to preliminary measurements. A microlith was found imbedded in a rib of one individual, and two other skeletons were associated with microliths that may have been lodged in soft tissue (192); these microlith contexts are unique for pre-urban South Asia.

A wide variety of game animals is represented in the relatively few excavated sites of this stage in which organic material was preserved. As yet no direct evidence for plant food has been found.

Art enjoyed a florescence during the Mesolithic in the form of numerous rock shelter paintings and engravings. These have provided rich cultural details of a stage until recently known only from its stone tools (27, 124, 218). Bone sections engraved in geometric patterns also have been discovered recently in Mesolithic contexts at Bhimbetka (218, pp. 9, 14).

DOMESTICATION AND EARLY VILLAGES

Until recently, domestication had been viewed as an adaptation introduced relatively late to South Asia from regions to the west and east (e.g. 220, p. 91). Although diffusion and migration are still seen as significant in the origins of domestication in India, more attention is turning to indigenous contributions to this process. Further, the beginnings of herding and cultivation in this region now seem older than formerly believed.

For many years, the earliest known evidence for the taming of animals in South Asia consisted of the sheep, goat, and cattle bones in the lowest levels of the Kile Gul Mohammad site at Quetta, Baluchistan (54), excavated by Rose Lilien Solecki (personal communication). The inception of this phase of seminomadic settlement had been estimated, based partly on radiocarbon dating, at about 4000 B.C. (56, p. 138). In peninsular India, no tangible evidence of domestication dating before about 2300 B.C. had been available (14, p. 318).

Recent excavations in the Mesolithic site of Bagor in Rajasthan, however, have yielded firm radiocarbon determinations for a herding economy by about 4500 B.C. (5, p. 61), MASCA corrected to more than 4800 B.C. (see footnote a, Table 1).

Additional archaeological clues from peninsular India suggest an even greater antiquity for animal domestication. One is the evidence for recurrent fire in the desert savannah of Rajasthan, starting about 10,000 years ago. Vishnu-Mittre, a paleobotanist, interprets this as indication of "Mesolithic man . . . burning . . . perennial stiff and injurious grasses . . . to induce lush growth of fresh ones for his domesticated animals," a practice he reports continues today in that region (215).

Wild sheep or goat bones in the previously mentioned Mesolithic site of Sarai Nahar Rai, dated to more than 10,000 radiocarbon years (193), are the earliest known in India and may signify at least a preadaptation toward domestication. A radiocarbon date of about 7400 radiocarbon years for a Mesolithic deposit with herd animals at Adamgarh in Madhya Pradesh apparently supports a long chronology for domestication, but because it was made on shell, and in a pottery-bearing deposit, the date is suspect (95, pp. 44, 82).

The study of faunal remains from archaeological sites is still in its infancy in India, but strong if inconclusive indications are that humped cattle (*Bos indicus*), buffalo [*Bos (Bubalus) bubalis*], and pig (*Sus scrofa cristatus*) were domesticated in South Asia from local wild populations (14, 66, 67). That the same could hold true for sheep and/or goat (14, p. 319) is a possibility strengthened by the Sarai Nahar Rai data.

Until recently, the earliest radiocarbon dates for domesticated plants in South Asia were for the cereals found in late fourth millennium Afghanistan (15, p. 323) and at sites of the Indus civilization of perhaps mid-third millennium (102). Recently, however, potsherds with impressions of rice were excavated by G. R. Sharma from a Neolithic component at Koldihawa (or Koldihwa or Koldihevah) in the Belan valley 80 km southeast of Allahabad, an extension of the Gangetic plain of Uttar Pradesh (129, p. 109). Electron microscopic study of the Koldihawa impressions shows that both domesticated and wild species of rice were present (214, 215).

The Neolithic level of Koldihawa has been dated to older than 4500 B.C. If this date is confirmed, it would provide evidence for what could be the world's oldest known domesticated rice (64). The dating is based on a ^{14}C reading on charcoal from an overlying Chalcolithic deposit of about 6500 radiocarbon years (before present). Typologically, however, the Chalcolithic assemblage conforms with components in that region which have been securely dated to the second millennium B.C. (129, pp. 113–17). Clearly, firmer dating is needed for this site of such potential significance to Indian culture history.

Another early hint of change in man-plant associations has been provided by pollen profiles from Rajasthan which reveal the appearance of what Singh identified as Cerealia species starting about 9300 radiocarbon years ago (197). However, Vishnu-Mittre has pointed out that distinguishing Cerealia from other grass pollens by size, as Singh did, is not reliable (215).

From his observations of wild plant collection and manipulation by present tribal populations and by others in marginal subsistence situations, Vishnu-Mittre has reconstructed a detailed developmental sequence of people-plant relationships in India that ranges from acquaintance through intensive exploitation to cultivation (215). He concludes, in part, that "long before conventional cereals were brought under cultivation . . . early man had subsisted [on] unconventional cereals . . ." including certain millets (*Panicum miliare, Pennisetum orientale*) and Job's tears (*Coix lacryma jobi*).

Mehra & Arora (127) have indicated how early Indian cultivators eventually utilized indigenous, West Asian, and African cultigens to develop a viable farming economy. In addition to rice, the indigenous group included a dwarf wheat (*Triticum vulgare*), horse gram (*Dolichos biflorus*), green gram (*Phaseolus radiatus*), and black gram (*Phaseolus mungo*). Among the West Asian contributions were field peas (*Pisum arvense*), wheat (*Triticum compactum* and *T. vulgare*), barley (*Hordeum vulgare*), lentil (*Lens culinaris*) and grass pea (*Lathyrus sativus*). The Indian finger millet known as *ragi* (*Eleusine coracana*) is said to have been developed from an African species, *Eleusine africana* (208, p. 18). Bulrush millet (*Pennisetum typhoides*) also is believed to have an African origin (11, p. 266).

As mentioned above, the archaeological contexts for the earliest signs of domestication in South Asia have been termed "Mesolithic" in some areas. In other regions, however, similar components have been designated "Aceramic Neolithic" (74, pp. 30–31). Sites of both categories have yielded microliths or other stone blade implements and ground stone tools and/or domesticated animal bones.

The period of aceramic Neolithic settlements in which the earliest signs of domestication have been detected date to at least the beginning of the fifth millennium in Baluchistan. This date is derived by adding a MASCA correction factor to Fairservis's estimate of the inception of the lowest cultural deposit at Kile Ghul Mohammad (4000 B.C.), which in turn was based on an uncorrected ^{14}C reading from the upper part of the deposit (56, p. 138). Gupta suggests that an early village level at the recently discovered Baluchistan site of Mehrgarh (88) began in the sixth or seventh millennium B.C., "if not earlier" (74, p. 268), but he offers no evidence to support this early chronology. Other aceramic Neolithic components in Baluchistan have been found at the sites of Gumla (41) and Rana Ghundai (170).

Egalitarian social and settlement systems that probably characterized the aceramic Neolithic also are most likely represented in the subsequent early "Ceramic Neolithic." Farming, herding, and foraging provided the subsistence base for this incipient village farming adaptation. Fleetingly represented at a few sites in Pakistan (74, pp. 33–36) and possibly of considerable antiquity in the Belan River valley of the Gangetic plain at sites such as Koldihawa (above), Mahagara, and Panchoh (129, pp. 57–58), the early Ceramic Neolithic is characterized by high proportions of unpainted, handmade pottery, and by bone implements and polished and chipped stone tools [(74, pp. 33–34) quoting (136, 137)]. Gupta estimates that this phase may date to the sixth or fifth millennia. He sees no stylistic connections between the Pakistan sites—Sarai Kohla and Jalilpur in the Punjab, and possibly Mehrgarh in Baluchistan—and other regions (74, p. 272). The material culture of the Belan sites, however, shows strong resemblances to Neolithic complexes of Assam (195) and areas of eastern Asia (129, pp. 113–15).

Settlements proliferated and copper objects and the potter's wheel appeared during a succeeding phase ["C" of Dales (40, pp. 70–71)] recognized in southern Afghanistan and northern Baluchistan. While peninsular India —with the possible exception of the south central Gangetic basin—maintained its Mesolithic-pastoral adaptation, apparently the "borderlands" in the west of the subcontinent erupted into a Chalcolithic age of more complex villages. These show stylistic connections with widely separated regions on and around the Iranian plateau (74, pp. 273–82). In the Indus plain, Chalcolithic farming villages eventually gave rise to the world's third oldest civilization by the middle of the third millennium (to be discussed in the next section).

During the florescence of that Indus civilization, itself composed primarily of villages, and following its disintegration, small farming communities began to emerge in many areas of the subcontinent previously peopled by nomadic foragers and/or pastoralists. Regional groups of these early peninsular settlements shared common material traits and styles of pottery decoration, which indicate cultural affinities with each other and, in some instances, suggest connections with other regions within and sometimes beyond South Asia. Such outside affiliations are generally accepted for village farming cultures in some of the northern extremities of the subcontinent, e.g. Assam with China and Southeast Asia (180, pp. 297–98; see also 195), Kashmir with China (14, p. 160), Baluchistan with Central Asia (19, pp. 14–36), but have been disputed for others, notably the relationship of Central Indian Chalcolithic complexes with Iran [e.g. Chakrabarti (34) opposed vs Sankalia (178) in favor]. Nevertheless, the regional stylistic distinctions within South Asia provide the first substantial preview of the cultural and linguistic diversity that still characterizes the Indian subcontinent.

The regional village traditions of the late third and second millennia are known by various "Neolithic" or "Chalcolithic" designations and include the "Late Harappan" (52) and Ochre Coloured Pottery (196) complexes of northern India. Only some of these regional traditions, especially the last two, show stylistic affinities with the Harappan civilization. But testimony to the dynamics of these village cultures is seen in the remains of defensive structures and in signs of status differentiation and craft specialization, especially as revealed at the current excavation of many years' duration at Inamgaon, Maharashtra (180, pp. 478–84). Eventually, with the introduction of iron, some of these villages developed into the early political and urban centers of Iron Age India.

HARAPPAN CIVILIZATION

In a brief overview of Indian prehistory and protohistory, only a few highlights of the extensive recent research on Harappan topics can be mentioned. [For a fuller treatment, see (3, pp. 9–215; 105; 108a; 161a; 191).]

Harappan or Indus civilization studies may be topically divided into questions of origin, nature, and decline, all of which remain intriguingly obscure.

Even the chronology of the Harappan civilization is uncertain. On one hand, radiocarbon dates uncorrected for dendrochronological calibration indicate a span of the mature civilization from 2300–1700 B.C. Agrawal & Kusumgar (7, pp. 371–73) prefer this range because uncorrected ^{14}C dates using the 5730 year half-life provide closer approximations of known calendar dates than do the corrected or calibrated dates. On the other hand, finds of Mature Harappan materials in Early Dynastic IIIa levels of Mesopotamian cities extend the range back to 2500–2600 B.C (35, p. 90). This would push the *inception* of the Mature Harappan closer to the MASCA calibrated date of 2750 B.C. (5, p. 71). It would also agree with Mandal's calculation of a starting date of at least 2500 (uncorrected), based on readings from deposits with Mature Harappan sherds at the site of Damb Sadaat, Baluchistan (119, p. 77).

The origins of the civilization first known from the cities of Harappa and Mohenjodaro remain unclear, although surveys and excavations have brought to light many antecedent cultures. Scattered across almost as vast an area as the full civilization, the pre- or Early Harappan Chalcolithic settlements each incorporated one or more traits which as a complex and in more elaborate form were to characterize the Mature Harappan. These include intensive agriculture, fortifications, metallurgy, community planning, standardized brick sizes, some Harappan pottery and bead styles, toy carts, terra cotta "cakes" (votive objects?), long-distance trade for luxuries, and even the beginnings of a script (108, pp. 94–95). But precisely how these villages or small towns of various regional traditions coalesced into a culturally more uniform, more elaborate civilization with cities, standardized town planning, etched seals with a single writing system, and a uniform standard of weights, measures, and even proportions, remains uncertain. Gupta suggested recently that the need for organized response to flood disasters could have produced the administrative mechanism that resulted in the regularities of form seen in the archaeological record (73). Lal credits the stimulus of "large-scale trade and commerce," but does not explain their origins (108, p. 95). Earlier, Fairservis had proposed a more complex model in which three elements played significant roles: the environmental potential of the Indus plain, the "social readiness" of the populations in the borderlands, and the stimuli of Mesopotamian urbanization (56, pp. 222–39).

As to the nature of the Indus civilization, doubts have been raised recently about previous suggestions (e.g. 220, pp. 97–98) that priest-kings ruling a monolithic empire from twin capitals dictated standardized modes of production throughout the realm. Fairservis, for example, noting the apparent lack of military emphasis or imposing palaces, suggested that without a strong military, this "more villagelike than citylike" civilization was unified by a common religious tradition rather than a strong central government (56, p. 299). Malik (118, pp. 99–110) and Service (188, pp. 238–46) carry this point to its logical if extreme conclusion: the Indus civilization may have been a "chiefdom" rather than a state-level society.

Recent discoveries cast doubt on that inference on three counts: settlement stratification, social stratification, and militarism. The size range of Harappan settlements (36) would seem to satisfy Wright & Johnson's criterion of a four-tiered community size pattern for state systems, which are characterized by three-tiered administrative hierarchies [(223, pp. 267–71), but see critique in (224, p. 20)]. In that context, Fairservis's reconstruction of Harappan political organization, based on his admittedly experimental "model of decipherment" of the Indus script—a model strongly but superficially criticized by Mahadevan (116)—indicates a three-tiered administrative system with an overall ruler, regional governors, and subregional chieftains (57, p. 126). Also, Gupta interprets the remains of certain buildings on the citadels of three Harappan centers as possibly representative of structures "primarily for political and administrative purposes" (71, p. 60).

The three known major administrative centers of the Indus civilization —Mohenjodaro, Harappa, and Kalibangan—may now have been joined by a fourth. A site described as one square kilometer in area—and thus possibly the largest Harappan site known—was discovered early in 1979 at Dhoraji, near the center of the Saurashtrian peninsula of Gujarat (77).

The seals and sealings of the Harappans may represent "administrative artifacts" (223, p. 271), also indicative of a state, while the standardization of weights, measures, writing system, and pottery styles provide evidence for a viable, long-range communication network considered characteristic of state societies by Wright and Johnson.

In advancing the nonstate theory of Harappan political organization, Malik, Service, and Fairservis all refer to the peaceful nature of the civilization, its lack of military accoutrements, and the powerful role of religion as a unifying force. Recent excavations, however, have indicated the major investments in energy expended by the Harappans in constructing massive defensive fortifications at both Indus valley sites and those in outlying areas (91, p. 36), as well as signs of violent destruction of pre-Harappan settlements (31; 41, p. 167; 106). Sankalia states that ". . . this civilization was not non-violent, but had taken enough precautions to safeguard its cities by putting up fortifications through the length and breadth [of] its cultural empire" (181). Mate disagrees and postulates that the walls were built for internal security of the citadel rather than external defense (121).

Indications of social stratification by employment and access to material comforts are known from Harappa (56, p. 299) and now are hinted at Kalibangan (108, p. 86). Although Fried (61, pp. 185–226) has suggested that a stage of cultural evolution characterized by social stratification probably existed fleetingly just prior to state formation in "pristine"—i.e. locally developed—civilizations, most cultural evolutionists consider stratification to be associated exclusively with state-level societies. "Civilized society," wrote Sanders & Price, "is above all stratified society" (175, p. 227). By civilized society, these authors meant a society characterized by state-level political organization (175, pp. 44–45).

As to the unifying role of religion, recent fieldwork has revealed apparent divergences in religious practices among the various Harappan areas. Female figurines, thought to be votive, were typical finds of the more northerly sites but were absent from the sites in Rajasthan and Gujarat. Conversely, fire altars, absent from sites in Pakistan, were a prominent feature in western India. Noting these variations, Thapar describes Harappan religion as "an amalgam of various regional beliefs and practices" (206, p. 269). In general, evidence of religious orientation is weaker for the Harappan than for other early civilizations, thereby bringing into question the degree to which religion was a significant unifying mechanism for the full civilization.

The relationships between the Indus valley civilization and cultures to the north and west of it have come under intensive study (19, 40, 210), spurred by excavations in Iran, Afghanistan, and Soviet Central Asia. Numerous similarities in cultural form and content have been noted, but interpretations of these parallels have been varied. Earlier analyses cited migration and diffusion from the west—ultimately Mesopotamia—as significant factors in the developments of domestication in the Indian borderlands and urbanization in the Indus plain (56, p. 223; 221, pp. 23, 25). Lately these analyses have been questioned by Chakrabarti (34) and Gupta [(74, pp. 294–96) following (110)], who see the Indus and the borderlands as part of a large cultural "interaction sphere" in and around the Iranian plateau which shared and exchanged traits through trade and similar mechanisms. Gupta stresses the indigenous contributions as well, in the form of both early domestication and village communities (74, p. 270) and urbanism (73), in addition to secondary diffusion (rather than direct diffusion) from the north and west (74, p. 28).

Perhaps the most dramatic recent development in Harappan research has been the discovery of a group of seven Mature Harappan sites in far northern Afghanistan, hundreds of kilometers from the nearest known Harappan site in Pakistan (74, p. 294). Dales points out the proximity of these sites to the source area for lapis lazuli, a luxury item traded into the Indus valley (40, p. 78).

Major international research efforts in recent years have been directed toward deciphering the Indus script. Despite differences in approach and interpretation among leading Indian, Russian, Finnish, and American scholars concentrating on the problem, many now seem agreed that the language was an early Dravidian tongue (e.g. 57, 115, 158, 225), and thereby probably closely related to proto-Elamite (125, 126). Rao, however, still maintains that the script represents Sanskrit (167). With the exception of Fairservis, there is also a consensus that the direction of writing was primarily from right to left. There is less agreement on other points, however. Even the basic form of the script, which has now been subject to sophisticated computer-aided analysis, is thought by Mahadevan to represent words (116), by Fairservis, syllables (57, p. 30), by Parpola, both (157, pp. 174–75), and by Rao to represent, in part, alphabetical letters (167, p. 329).

No new theories have emerged to explain the rather sudden disappearance of the civilization. Floods, invasions, aridity, overgrazing, and deforestation had been mooted previously (221, pp. 126–34). Recent support for the aridity theory from palynology (198) has now been challenged by Vishnu-Mittre [(212, 213) quoted in (207, p. 68)].

Changing, however, is the perception of what seemed to be a cultural gap between the end of the Indus civilization and the emergence of Iron Age cities of the Gangetic plain more than a thousand years later. That apparent blank is being filled as the pace of survey and excavation accelerates, especially in the northwestern Gangetic area. In that zone rich in the traditional history of early India, so-called "Late Harappan" communities seem to persist at least until the beginning of the first millennium B.C. (52). These settlements are distinguished by many ceramic and other artifactual attributes first recognized in components of the Indus civilization. But introduction of new pottery styles and the absence of cities and of many of the relatively uniform features of architecture and town planning are typical. Also absent are such characteristic Harappan artifacts as triangular terra cotta cakes, inscribed seals, and large fired-brick structures and features;

imported precious gems and metals are also fewer (52, p. 130). These sites perhaps represent "the end of a state and continuity of a tradition" (161).

The chronology of this phase, seen across much of the eastern and southern peripheries of the former civilization, ranges from about 1700 to 1000 B.C. (52).

ARCHAEOLOGY AND TRADITIONAL LITERATURE

With the decline of the Harappan civilization and the proliferation of regional ceramic traditions in northern and peninsular India comes the puzzle of correlating archaeological evidence with the traditional sacred accounts of Indian protohistory. Scholary efforts in that direction continue unabated (e.g. 17, 75, 179), but connections between "myth" and "reality" remain tenuous and controversial. For every posited correlation between textual allusion and archaeological fact, there have been countercorrelations.

As Sankalia indicates, reasonable but at least partially conflicting correlations equate the Vedic Aryans with pre-Harappan settlements (185, p. 83), the Harappan civilization (p. 84), sites of the Ochre Coloured Pottery tradition (p. 84), the Gandhara Grave culture (42), the Black-and-Redware ceramic tradition (209), the western Indian Chalcolithic (216, pp. 49–52), the Painted Gray Ware ceramic tradition (107), and the Northern Black Polished Ware horizon (37, p. 70). Moreover, correlations have been posited between various regional Chalcolithic ceramic traditions and specific tribes and extended kin groups mentioned in traditional accounts (209; 216, pp. 49–52), although Thapar warns that the evidence for such associations is far from conclusive (209, pp. 97–98).

Other scholars suggest that between the difficulties of separating fact from fancy, original version from later redaction of the texts, and of associating archaeological artifact with epic poetic license, the whole exercise should be at least temporarily abandoned (93). An outsider might be tempted to agree and wish for a greater emphasis on questions regarding the nature of changing human adaptations in South Asia and less concern with proofs of the existence of one or another dynasty through pottery types. It must be recognized, however, that archaeology derives support from the society at large and will typically reflect the concerns and interests of that sponsorship. Westerners need only be reminded of the popularity of Biblical archaeology to understand this.

One of the long-standing questions concerning the association of archaeology and traditional literature has centered on the Painted Gray Ware pottery of Northern India (211). Lal had discovered this ceramic style at sites which he linked with the "early Aryans" of the Vedic texts (107). Radiocarbon dating at first seemed to refute the connection: historic consensus dated the early Vedic period to roughly the second half of the second millennium B.C. (222, p. 25), but the dependable PGW dates clustered at 800–350 B.C. (5, p. 132). The beginning of the phase with PGW, however, was then tentatively extrapolated back to 1000 B.C. (119, p. 166), and MASCA calibration (footnote a, Table 1) would add another 100 years to its antiquity. J. P. Joshi's excavations in Haryana and Punjab (92) now have extended the advent of PGW to between 1300–1600 B.C. (109), strengthening that tradition's claim to Rig Vedic association and filling a long-standing "gap" between Harappan and PGW in North India, with components in which type artifacts of both Late Harappan and PGW are associated.

What is perhaps more surprising is the discovery of a PGW site approaching the dimensions of a small urban center at Bhukari in northern Haryana (23, p. 66). If substantiated by excavation, this find would require a reassessment of the current view, which recognizes a gap of at least a millennium between the disappearance of the cities of the Indus civilization by about 1700 B.C. and next emergence of urbanism in South Asia (71).

Some recent linguistic analysis (204) provides new support for an old theory which postulated a two-wave movement of Indo-Aryan speakers into the subcontinent. According to that reconstruction, "pre-Vedic" groups first fanned out into the areas now occupied by speakers of various Indo-Aryan languages (65). Sometime later, it is suggested, speakers of languages that evolved into the northern and central Indo-Aryan tongues (Western Hindi, Panjabi, Pahari, Lahnda) entered the subcontinent. It may be worth noting that the Chalcolithic cultures of the second and late third millennia B.C. all fall within the present-day Indo-Aryan linguistic zone.

This linguistic analysis lends some support to Sankalia's thesis, based mainly on ceramic parallels, that the Chalcolithic settlements represent a "colonization" of the peninsula by pre-Vedic Indo-Aryan speakers from Iran (178). This diffusionist approach has been strongly criticized on a number of grounds, including an apparent geographic gap between Iran and the Indian peninsula where the shared traits do not occur (34).

One obstacle to the understanding of Indian culture history during the Vedic Age had been the tendency to assume that the Rig Vedic Aryans represented the first wave of Indo-Aryan speakers to enter the subcontinent. But the Vedic texts provide no hint of a movement into India from the west (185, p. 76), suggesting that by the time the hymns were compiled, starting about 1500 B.C., any tradition of migration or other forms of movement into India—hundreds of years earlier?—had been obliterated. This would still leave unanswered Chakrabarti's objection to schemes of this type, which do not account for the absence of a series of archaeological deposits, west to east, testifying to the putative movement into India of the earliest Indo-Aryan speakers (34).

IRON AGE

Iron metallurgy was long thought to have been introduced into India from Western Asia, but Chakrabarti has synthesized data from geology, ancient literature, ethnography, and archaeology to indicate the possibility that this significant technological advance may have been developed independently in South Asia (33). Shaffer cites additional evidence to support this interpretation (190) and sees "a wide range of functional artifacts . . . being manufactured" of iron in India toward the end of the second millennium B.C. A recent review of the evidence from the site of Ahar in Rajasthan would place the beginning of iron smelting in peninsular India at least as early as the first half of the thirteenth century B.C. (171), perhaps a century or more before iron technology had spread from Asia Minor to Mesopotamia. Although the disturbed nature of the iron-bearing levels of that site raises serious doubts concerning the accuracy of Sahi's (171) interpretation (V. N. Misra, personal communication), radiocarbon readings on iron-associated material from Eran, in Madhya Pradesh, also extend to about 1300 B.C. (33, p. 119). This date neatly coincides with the end of the Malwa Chalcolithic culture, but Chakrabarti nevertheless prefers a more conservative estimate of 1100 B.C. for the beginnings of iron technology in Central India (33, p. 119).

At least five archaeological contexts are now recognized as constituting the Early Iron Age of South Asia (as distinguished from the Iron Age per se, which includes the Early Historic period, outside the scope of this review) (33). These are the Gandhara Grave Culture of the Swat Valley, northern Pakistan (74, pp. 206–17; cf 40b, 204a), the site of Pirak in the Kachhi plain of Pakistani Baluchistan (31a, 87a), the Painted Gray Ware horizon (211) and post-Chalcolithic Black-and-Redware phases of North, Eastern, and Central India (22), and the Megalithic complexes of Central (33, p. 119) and South India (47).

Some of these archaeological complexes are known primarily from burials and others only from narrow vertical excavations. It is difficult, then, to generalize about an Early Iron Age extant from the first half of the first millennium B.C. in those far-flung locations and disparate cultural settings. But it is clear that while iron implements and weapons played a part in the "second urbanization" of India about the mid-first millennium B.C. (32, p. 30), iron seems to make its first appearance in South Asia in nonurban settings: as either an addition to an established Neolithic or Chalcolithic culture in socially unstratified villages (Gandhara, PGW, Black-and-Redware), or as part of the technology of relatively small and at least partly mobile equestrian groups (Megalithic).

Although recent excavations in the Belan valley of the Gangetic plain (129, pp. 107–21) indicate that farming could be successful in heavily wooded ecozones prior to the introduction of iron tools for forest clearance, the expansion of agriculture facilitated by such implements apparently provided the additional "techno-environmental efficiency" (78a, pp. 233–60) that led to the urbanization and civilization of the entire subcontinent.

Early Megalithic sites provide further indications of the considerable antiquity of iron production in India. [This brief abstract of megalith research in South Asia is based on Deo (48); other recent sources include (47, 76, 112, 205).] Indian megaliths include a wide variety of stone monuments, mostly archaeological burial features which typically contain iron weapons and implements and a characteristic red-and-black pottery. Concentrated in South India, they are also found in many other areas of the subcontinent. The Megalithic complex was once known exclusively from its cairns, stone circles, alignments, dolmens, cist graves, and other monuments, but it has been associated recently with a growing number of excavated village sites. The chronology of Iron Age megaliths has been extended recently by typology and radiocarbon cross-dating to about 1000 B.C. (150). Some reservations about this date have been expressed, partly because it exceeds by about 350 years the next two oldest dated southern Megalithic sites (5, pp. 144–45). However, the recent discovery of megaliths with Chalcolithic artifacts in Central India would seem to suggest a greater antiquity for this monument-building trait than previously recognized (200).

The addition of iron to the technology of peninsular settlements in North and Central India seems to have been associated with an intensification of urbanization and warfare, traits evidenced in some of the earlier, Chalcolithic, levels. Chakrabarti attributes this second urbanization to "a local agricultural base, an organized trading activity, and a centralised political power-structure," and indicates that each of the four known major centers (Rajagriha, Varanasi, Kausambi, Ujjayini) "lay on a well-defined early historic trade route from the middle Gangetic Valley to the Deccan" (32, pp. 30–31). These major centers were fortified by about 600 B.C.; the defensive wall of Ujjayini at the dawn of Indian history encompassed about double the area of any Harappan city (22, p. 197; 36).

CONCLUSION

Much of the framework of Indian prehistory and protohistory would now seem established: a chronology has been outlined, major cultural stages delineated, and some aspects of past lifeways reconstructed. These accomplishments have been made with the aid of sophisticated advances in chronology, earth sciences, paleontology, and paleobotany, among other disciplines. Archaeologists working in South Asia have begun to tap the potentials of settlement and burial analyses and of ethnoarchaeology and prehistoric art in the investigation of ancient cultures.

The Paleolithic is coming into sharper focus as actual habitation sites are being investigated, climates reconstructed, and technologies analyzed and compared with greater precision. An Upper Paleolithic has been recognized, complete with India's earliest known art and possibly with human remains. Also for the first time, the outlines of regional cultural traditions across much of the subcontinent can be discerned starting as early as the Middle Paleolithic but coming into sharp focus with the emergence of regional ceramic styles.

The advent of domestication is undergoing review as new finds suggest earlier beginnings for, and more indigenous contributions to, this major change in man-resource relationships. Cultural connections with areas beyond South Asia are being discovered and critically examined in order to understand their nature more precisely. Major efforts in cracking the Harappan script have brought about a wide, although not universal, consensus that the language is Dravidian, which would now seem to connect the civilization, linguistically at least, with an early language of Iran. Growing evidence for what is interpreted here as militarism, strong indications of complex settlement stratification, and other cited data seem to indicate that the Indus civilization was a political state, contrary to the views of some scholars.

While correlating archaeological fact with traditional Indian literature is seen by some as an exercise in culture historical futility, it continues apace and, with some aid from recent "linguistic archaeology," provides a tantalizing bridge between prehistory and history.

Archaeology has been said to involve three major objectives: the reconstruction of culture history, detailing of past lifeways, and explanation of culture process (45, p. 115). Much of South Asian culture history has been reconstructed, at least in outline, and investigation of past ways of life is well under way. South Asian archaeology can now move on to the explanatory stage of research and thereby provide a fuller understanding of South Asia's ancient past.

ACKNOWLEDGMENTS

Many of the scholars whose work is cited here have been helpful in providing research materials for this review. Space does not permit naming them individually, but I wish to express my gratitude to them collectively. The faculty and students of the Departments of Archaeology, Deccan College and Poona University, Pune, were especially generous with reprints and unpublished data. Dr. V. N. Misra, Department of Archaeology, Poona University, and Dr. Kenneth A. R. Kennedy, Department of Anthropology, Cornell University, read a draft of this review and made helpful suggestions, for which I am very grateful.

The writer's four trips to India since 1964 have provided first-hand knowledge of Indian archaeological research; for those opportunities, thanks are due to the American Institute of Indian Studies, the Faculty Research Award Program of the City University of New York, and the Smithsonian Institution. I also wish to thank Dr. Doranne Jacobson for her invaluable editorial assistance in the preparation of this paper.

Literature Cited

1. Agrawal, D. P. 1971. *The Copper Bronze Age in India.* New Delhi: Munshiram Manoharlal. 270 pp.
2. Agrawal, D. P., Chakrabarti, D. K. 1979. Archaeology in India: a professional assessment. See Ref. 3, pp. 389–92
3. Agrawal, D. P., Chakrabarti, D. K., eds. 1979. *Essays in Indian Protohistory.* Delhi: B. R. 392 pp.
4. Agrawal, D. P., Guzder, S. J. 1974. Quaternary studies on the western coast of India: preliminary observations. *Palaeobotanist* (1972) 21(2):216–22
5. Agrawal, D. P., Kusumgar, S. 1974. *Prehistoric Chronology and Radiocarbon Dating in India.* New Delhi: Munshiram Manoharlal. 170 pp.
6. Agrawal, D. P., Kusumgar, S. 1975. Tata Institute radiocarbon date list 11. *Radiocarbon* 17(2):219–25
7. Agrawal, D. P., Kusumgar, S. 1979. Radiocarbon chronology of Indian protohistoric cultures. See Ref. 3, pp. 371–86
8. Agrawal, D. P., Kusumgar, S., Pant, R. K. 1975. Radiocarbon and Indian archaeology. *Phys. News* 6(4):1–10
9. Agrawal, D. P., Pande, B. M., eds. 1977. *Ecology and Archaeology of Western India.* Delhi: Concept. 255 pp.
10. Agrawal, D. P., Rajaguru, S. N., Roy, B. 1978. SEM and other studies on the Saurashtra miliolite rocks. *Sediment. Geol.* 20:41–47
11. Allchin, B., Allchin, R. 1968. *The Birth of Indian Civilization: India and Pakistan Before 500 B.C.* Baltimore: Penguin. 365 pp.
12. Allchin, B., Goudie, A., Hegde, K. 1978. *The Prehistory and Palaeogeography of the Great Indian Desert.* London: Academic. 370 pp.
13. Allchin, F. R. 1960. Piklihal excavations. *Archaeol. Ser.* 1. Hyderabad: Gov. Andhra Pradesh. 154 pp.
14. Allchin, F. R. 1969. Early domestic animals in India and Pakistan. In *The Domestication and Exploitation of Plants and Animals,* ed. P. J. Ucko, G. W.

Dimbleby, pp. 317–22. Chicago: Aldine. 581 pp.
15. Allchin, F. R. 1969. Early cultivated plants in India and Pakistan. See Ref. 14, pp. 323–30
16. Ancient Skull Found. 1978. *Indian Express,* Sept. 19
17. Archaeology and Tradition: Theme Papers (special section). 1978. *Purātattva* (1975–1976) 8:63–122
18. Armand, J. 1978. *On the emergence of the Handaxe Culture in Asia; with special reference to India.* presented at Symp. Recent Adv. Indo-Pac. Prehist., Pune
19. Asthana, S. 1976. *History and Archaeology of India's Contacts with Other Countries; From Earliest Times to 300 B.C.* Delhi: B. R. 175 pp.
20. Badam, G. L. 1976. *Quaternary palaeontology of the Central Narmada Valley and its implications in the prehistoric studies.* Presented at Colloq. Geol. Surv. India. Hyderabad
21. Badam, G. L. 1977. Significance of palaeontological studies in the Indian Pleistocene deposits. *Archaeol. Stud.* 2:71–82
22. Banerjee, N. R. 1965. *The Iron Age in India.* Delhi: Munshiram Manoharlal. 264 pp.
23. Bhan, S., Shaffer, J. G. 1978. New discoveries in northern Haryana. *Man Environ.* 2:59–68
24. Bharadwaj, H. C. 1973. Aspects of early technology in India. See Ref. 62, pp. 391–400
25. Bibby, G. 1958. The ancient Indian style seals from Bahrain. *Antiquity* 32:242–46
26. Binford, L. R. 1968. Post-Pleistocene adaptations. In *New Perspectives in Archeology,* ed. S. R. Binford, L. R. Binford, pp. 313–41. Chicago: Aldine. 373 pp.
27. Brooks, R. R. R., Wakankar, V. S. 1976. *Stone Age Painting in India.* New Haven: Yale Univ. 116 pp.
28. Brown, J. A. 1889. On some highly specialized forms of stone implements

found in Asia, North Africa and Europe. *J. R. Anthropol. Inst.* 18(2): 134–39

29. Butzer, K. W. 1971. *Environment and Archeology: An Ecological Approach to Prehistory.* Chicago: Aldine. 703 pp.

30. Butzer, K. W. 1976. Pleistocene climates. *Geoscience and Man* 13:27–43

31. Casal, J. M. 1961. *Fouilles De Mundigak, Memoires de la Délégation Archéologique Française en Afghanistan,* T. 17. Paris: Libr. Klincksieck. Vol. 1, 260 pp.; Vol. 2, plates

31a. Casal, J. M. 1973. Excavations at Pirak, West Pakistan. In *South Asian Archaeology: Papers from the First International Conference of South Asian Archaeologists Held in the University of Cambridge,* ed. N. Hammond, pp. 171–79. London: Duckworth. 320 pp.

32. Chakrabarti, D. K. 1972–1973. Concept of urban revolution and the Indian context. *Purātattva* 6:27–36B

33. Chakrabarti, D. K. 1976. The beginning of iron in India. *Antiquity* 50:114–24

34. Chakrabarti, D. K. 1977. India and West Asia: an alternative approach. *Man Environ.* 1:25–38

35. Chakrabarti, D. K. 1978. The Nippur Indus seal and Indus chronology. *Man Environ.* 2:88–90

36. Chakrabarti, D. K. 1979. Size of the Harappan settlements. See Ref. 3, pp. 205–15

37. Chattopadhyaya, B. D. 1978. Indian archaeology and the Epic Tradition. *Purātattva* (1975–1976) 8:67–72

38. Corvinus, G. 1970. The Acheulian workshop at Chirki on the Pravara River, Maharashtra. *Indian Antiq.* 4:13–22

39. Corvinus-Karve, G. 1969. Stratigraphy and geological background of an Acheulian site at Chirki-on-Pravara, India. *Anthropos* 63/64:921–40

40. Dales, G. F. 1976. Shifting trade patterns between the Iranian Plateau and the Indus Valley in the third millennium. B.C. *Proc. Colloq. Int. Cent. Nat. Rech. Sci. No. 567, Le Plateau Iranien et l'Asie Centrale des Origines a la Conquete Islamique,* Paris, pp. 67–78

40a. Dales, G. F. 1979. The Balakot Project: summary of four years of excavations in Pakistan. *Man Environ.* 3:45–54

40b. Dani, A. H. 1967. Timargarha and Gandhara Grave Culture. *Anc. Pakistan* 3:1–407

41. Dani, A. H. 1970–1971. Excavations in the Gomal Valley. *Anc. Pakistan* 5:1–177

42. Dani, A. H. 1976. Comment. See Ref. 75, pp. 61–67

42a. Daniel, G. 1950. *A Hundred Years of Archaeology.* London: Duckworth. 343 pp.

43. de Cardi, B. 1967. The Bampur Sequence in the 3rd millennium B.C. *Antiquity* 41:33–41

44. de Cardi, B. 1970. Excavations at Bampur: a third millennium settlement in Persian Baluchistan, 1966. *Anthropol. Pap. Am. Mus. Nat. Hist.* 51:232–355

45. Deetz, J. F. 1970. Archeology as a social science. *Current Directions in Anthropology;* a special issue., ed. A. Fischer. *Bull. Am. Anthropol. Assoc.* 3(3, 2):115–25

46. de Lumley, H. 1975. Cultural evolution in France in its paleoecological setting during the Middle Pleistocene. In *After the Australopithecines; Stratigraphy, Ecology, and Culture Change in the Middle Pleistocene,* ed. K. W. Butzer, G. L1. Isaac, pp. 745–808. The Hague: Mouton

47. Deo, S. B. 1973. *Problem of South Indian Megaliths.* Dharwar: Kannada Res. Inst., Karnatak Univ. 72 pp.

48. Deo, S. B. 1978. *Megalithic problem: A review.* presented at Symp. Recent Adv. Indo-Pac. Prehist., Pune

49. Deshpande, M. N., ed. 1975. *Indian Archaeology 1971–72—A Review.* New Delhi: Archaeol. Surv. India, Gov. India. 139 pp.

50. de Terra, H., Paterson, T. T. 1939. *Studies on the Ice Age of India and Associated Human Cultures.* Carnegie Inst. Wash. Publ. No. 493, Washington, 354 pp.

51. Dhavalikar, M. K. 1977. Inamgaon: the pattern of settlement. *Man Environ.* 1:46–51

52. Dikshit, K. N. 1979. The Late Harappan cultures in India. See Ref. 3, pp. 123–33

53. Dupree, L. 1972. Prehistoric research in Afghanistan (1959–1966). *Trans. Am. Philos. Soc.* 62(4):1–84

54. Fairservis, W. A. Jr. 1956. Excavations in the Quetta Valley, West Pakistan. *Anthropol. Pap. Am. Mus. Nat. Hist.* 45(2):169–402

55. Fairservis, W. A. Jr. 1967. The origin, character, and decline of an early civilization. *Am. Mus. Novit.* No. 2302. New York: Am. Mus. Nat. Hist. 48 pp.

56. Fairservis, W. A. Jr. 1974. *The Roots of Ancient India.* Chicago: Univ. Chicago Press. 480 pp. 2nd ed.

57. Fairservis, W. A. Jr. 1977. Excavations at the Harappan site of Allahdino: the

graffiti; a model in the decipherment of the Harappan script. *Pap. Allahdino Exped. 3,* New York

58. Fentress, M. A. 1978. *Winter rains and summer floods: ecological incentives and the intensification of Harappan food production.* Presented at Symp. Recent Adv. Indo-Pac. Prehist., Pune

59. Flam, L. 1976. Settlement, subsistence and population: a dynamic approach to the development of the Indus Valley civilization. See Ref. 82, pp. 76–93

60. Foote, R. B. 1885. Notes on the results of Mr. R. B. Foote's further excavations in the Billa Surgam Caves. *Rec. Geol. Surv. India* 28(4):227–35

61. Fried, M. H. 1967. *The Evolution of Political Society: An Essay in Political Anthropology.* New York: Random House. 270 pp.

62. Ghosh, A. 1973. The terms "Prehistory" and "Protohistory." In *Radiocarbon and Indian Archaeology,* ed. D. P. Agrawal, A. Ghosh, pp. 510–11. Bombay: Tata Inst. Fundam. Res. 526 pp.

63. Ghosh, A. K. 1970. The Palaeolithic cultures of Singhbhum. *Trans. Am. Philos. Soc.* 60(1):1–68

64. Glover, I. 1978. *Some problems relating to the domestication of rice in Asia.* Presented at Symp. Recent Adv. Indo-Pac. Prehist., Pune

65. Grierson, G. A. 1927. *Linguistic Survey of India.* Calcutta: GPO, India. 11 vols.

66. Grigson, C. 1978. The craniology and relationships of four species of *Bos,* IV. The Relationship between *Bos primigenius* Boj. and *Bos taurus* L. and its implications for the phylogeny of the domestic breeds. *J. Archaeol. Sci.* 5:123–52

67. Grigson, C. 1978. *Bos indicus and Bos namadicus and the problem of autochthonous domestication in India.* Presented at Symp. Recent Adv. Indo-Pac. Prehist., Pune

68. Gupta, J. 1967. *Prehistoric Art of India* (in Hindi). Delhi: National. 609 pp.

69. Gupta, S. K. 1977. Holocene silting in the Little Rann of Kutch. See Ref. 9, pp. 201–5

69a. Gupta, S. P. 1972. *Disposal of the Dead and Physical Types in Ancient India.* Delhi: Oriental Publ. 346 pp.

70. Gupta, S. P. 1973. An introduction to models and model-making. See Ref. 62, pp. 359–65

71. Gupta, S. P. 1974. Two urbanizations in India: a side study in their social structure. *Purātattva* 7:53–60

72. Gupta, S. P. 1976. Forward. See Ref. 19, pp. vii-ix

73. Gupta, S. P. 1978. Origin of the form of Harappan culture: a new proposition. *Purātattva* (1975–1976) 8:141–46

74. Gupta, S. P. 1979. *Archaeology of Soviet Central Asia and the Indian Borderlands,* Vol. 2. Delhi: B. R. 344 pp.

75. Gupta, S. P., Ramachandran, K. S., eds. 1976. *Mahābhārata: Myth and Reality: Differing Views.* Delhi: Agam Prakashan. 264 pp.

76. Gururaja Rao, B. K. 1972. *Megalithic Culture in South India.* Mysore: Prasaranga, Univ. Mysore. 390 pp.

77. Harappan site discovered. 1979. *M. P. Chronicle,* Feb. 2. Bhopal

78. Harris, M. 1968. *The Rise of Anthropological Theory: A History of Theories of Culture.* New York: Crowell. 806 pp.

78a. Harris, M. 1975. *Culture, People, Nature: an Introduction to General Anthropology.* New York: Crowell. 694 pp. 2nd ed.

79. Hegde, K. T. M. 1973. Early stages of metallurgy in India. See Ref. 62, pp. 401–5

80. Hegde, K. T. M. 1978. Analysis of ancient Indian deluxe wares. *Proc. Int. Symp. Archaeometry, 18th.* Bonn: Rheinisches Landesmuseum

81. Hoffman, M. A., Cleland, J. H. 1977. Excavations at the Harappan site of Allahdino: The lithic industry at Allahdino; a metric and quantitative analysis of an Harappan activity system. *Pap. Allahdino Exped.* 2. New York. 150 pp.

82. Hoffman, M. A., Shaffer, J. G. 1976. The Harappan settlement at Allahdino and related surface sites—1973 season. In *Ecological Backgrounds of South Asian Prehistory,* ed. K. A. R. Kennedy, G. L. Possehl, pp. 94–117. Cornell Univ. South Asia Occas. Pap. Theses 4. 236 pp.

83. Jacobson, J. 1970. *Microlithic contexts in the Vindhyan Hills of Central India.* PhD thesis. Columbia Univ., New York, NY. 487 pp.

84. Jacobson, J. 1975. Early Stone Age habitation sites in eastern Malwa. *Proc. Am. Philos. Soc.* 119:280–97

85. Jacobson, J. 1976. Evidence for prehistoric habitation patterns in eastern Malwa. See Ref. 82, pp. 1–6

86. Jacobson, J. 1978. *Acheulian surface sites in Central India.* Presented at Symp. Recent Adv. Indo-Pac. Prehist., Pune

87. Jain, K. C. 1979. *Prehistory and Protohistory of India.* New Delhi: Agam Kala Prakashan. 367 pp.

87a. Jarrige, J. F., Enault, J. F. 1973. Recent excavations (French) in Pakistan. See Ref. 62, pp. 163–72

88. Jarrige, J. F., Lechevallier, M. 1977. Excavations at Mehrgarh, Baluchistan: their significance in the prehistorical context of the Indo-Pakistani borderlands. *Abstr. Int. Conf. South Asian Archaeol., 4th, Naples,* pp. 46–48

89. Jayaswal, V. 1978. *Palaeohistory of India: A Study of the Prepared Core Technique.* Delhi: Agam Kala Prakashan. 243 pp.

89a. Jayaswal, V. 1979. Old Stone Age of Central India: a technological study. *Man Environ.* 3:19–26

90. John, K. J. 1978. *Megalithic culture of Kerala.* Presented at Symp. Recent Adv. Indo-Pac. Prehist., Pune

91. Joshi, J. P. 1974. Surkotada: a chronological assessment. *Purātattva* 7:34–38

92. Joshi, J. P. 1978. Interlocking of Late Harappa Culture and Painted Grey Ware Culture in the light of recent excavations. *Man Environ.* 2:98–101

93. Joshi, M. C. 1978. Archaeology and Indian tradition: some observations. *Purātattva* (1975–1976) 8:98–102

94. Joshi, R. V. 1965. Comment on "Is Soan a separate culture?" by K. V. Soundara Rajan. In *Indian Prehistory: 1964,* ed. V. N. Misra, M. S. Mate, pp. 5–6. Poona: Deccan Coll. Postgrad. Res. Inst. 266 pp.

95. Joshi, R. V. 1978. *Stone Age Cultures of Central India: Report on the Excavations of Rock Shelters at Adamgarh, Madhya Pradesh.* Poona: Deccan Coll. Postgrad. Res. Inst. 96 pp.

96. Joshi, R. V. 1978. *Some problems concerning Lower Palaeolithic cultures of India.* Presented at Symp. Recent Adv. Indo-Pac. Prehist., Pune

97. Joshi, R. V., Marathe, A. R. 1974. Stone Age sediments from the Kan River (Tapti Basin), Dhulia District—a sedimentological study. *Bull. Deccan Coll. Res. Inst.* 34(1–4):40–51

98. Joshi, R. V., Marathe, A. R. 1978. *Comparative study of the metrical data on handaxes and its cultural interpretation.* Presented at Symp. Recent Adv. Indo-Pac. Prehist., Pune

99. Joshi, R. V., Pappu, R. S. 1979. Bhokar: an Upper Palaeolithic factory site from Central Godavari Basin. *Man Environ.* 3:86–91

100. Joshi, R. V., Rajaguru, S. N., Badam, G. L., Khanna, P. C. 1978. Environment and culture of Early Man in northwest India—a reappraisal. *J. Geol. Soc. India* 19(2):83–86

101. Joshi, R. V., Rajaguru, S. N., Pappu, R. S., Bopardikar, B. P. 1974. Quaternary glaciation and palaeolithic sites in the Liddar Valley (Jammu-Kashmir). *World Archaeol.* 5(3):369–79

102. Kajale, M. D. 1974. Appendix I: Antiquity of grains. See Ref. 180, pp. 560–63

103. Kajale, M. D., Badam, G. L., Rajaguru, S. N. 1976. Late Quaternary history of the Ghod Valley, Maharashtra. *Geophytology* 6(1):122–32

103a. Kennedy, K. A. R. 1972. The physical anthropology of prehistoric South Asians. *Anthropologist* 17:1–13

104. Kennedy, K. A. R. 1977. Fossil man in India: the "missing link" in our knowledge of human evolution in Asia. *NSS Bull.* 39:99–103

104a. Kennedy, K. A. R. 1980. Physical anthropology of prehistoric and protohistoric South Asia. *Ann. Rev. Anthropol.* 9. In press

105. Khan, A. N., ed. 1975. *International Symposium on Moenjodaro, Moenjodaro, 1973.* Karachi: Nat. Book Found. 187 pp.

106. Khan, F. A. 1965. Excavations at Kot Diji. *Pakistan Archaeol.* 2:11–86

107. Lal, B. B. 1954–1955. Excavations at Hastinapura and other explorations in the Upper Ganga and Sutlej Basins 1950–52. *Anc. India* 10–11:5–152

107a. Lal, B. B. 1975. The Indus script: some observations based on archaeology. *J. R. Asiat. Soc.* 1975(2):14–177

108. Lal, B. B. 1979. Kalibangan and Indus civilization. See Ref. 3, pp. 65–97

108a. Lal, B. B., Malik, S. C., eds. 1979. *Indus Valley Civilization: Problems and Issues.* Simla: Indian Inst. Adv. Study. In press

109. Lal, M. 1978. *Settlement pattern of Painted Gray Ware Culture in Ganga Valley.* Presented at Symp. Recent Adv. Indo-Pac. Prehist., Pune

110. Lamberg-Karlovsky, C. C., Tosi, M. 1973. Shahr-i-Sokhta and Tepe Yahya: tracks on the earliest history of the Iranian Plateau. *East and West* 23 (1–2):21–57

111. Leshnik, L. S. 1964. *Sociological interpretation in archaeology.* PhD thesis. Univ. Chicago, Chicago, Ill. 287 pp.

112. Leshnik, L. S. 1974. *South Indian "Megalithic" Burials: The Pandukal Complex.* Wiesbaden: Steiner. 309 pp.

113. Lydekker, R. 1886. Preliminary note on the mammalia of Karnul Caves. *Records Geol. Surv. India* 19(2)120–22

114. Lydekker, R. 1886. The fauna of Kur-

nool Caves. *Palaeontol. Indica* Ser. X:4(2):22–58

115. Mahadevan, I. 1970. Dravidian parallels in proto-Indian script. *J. Tamil Stud.* 2(1):1–120

116. Mahadevan, I. 1978. *Recent advances in the study of the Indus script.* Presented at Int. Congr. Anthropol. Ethnol. Sci., 10th, New Delhi

117. Malik, S. C. 1968. Archaeology as a source in writing socio-cultural and socio-economic history. *East. Anthropol.* 21(3):291–304

118. Malik, S. C. 1969. *Indian Civilization: the Formative Period.* Simla: Indian Inst. Adv. Study. 204 pp.

119. Mandal, D. 1972. *Radiocarbon Dates and Indian Archaeology.* Allahabad: Vaishali. 273 pp.

120. Marathe, A. R., Rajaguru, S. N., Lele, V. S. 1977. On the problem of the origin and age of the miliolite rocks of the Hiran valley, Saurashtra, Western India. *Sediment. Geol.* 19:197–215

121. Mate, M. S. 1970. Harappan fortifications—a study. *Indian Antiq.* (Special issue on Studies in Indian Archaeology) 4(1–4):75–84

122. Mathpal, Y. 1976. Rock art of India. *J. Indian Hist.* 54:29–51

123. Mathpal, Y. 1977. Prehistoric art of Bhimbetka. In *Bhimbetka: Prehistoric Man and His Art in Central India,* ed. V. N. Misra, Y. Mathpal, M. Nagar, pp. 17–26. Pune: Bhimbetka Souvenir Comm., Deccan Coll. 26 pp.

124. Mathpal, Y. 1978. *Hunter-gatherer way of life as depicted in Mesolithic rock paintings of Central India.* Presented at Symp. Recent Adv. Indo-Pac. Prehist., Pune

124a. Mathpal, Y. 1978. *Prehistoric rock paintings of Bhimbetka, Central India.* PhD thesis. Poona Univ., Pune

125. McAlpin, D. W. 1974. Toward Proto-Elamo-Dravidian. *Language* 50(1):89–101

126. McAlpin, D. W. 1975. Elamite and Dravidian: further evidence of relationship. *Curr. Anthropol.* 16(1):105–15

127. Mehra, K. L., Arora, R. K. 1978. *Considerations on domestication of plants in India.* Presented at Symp. Recent Adv. Indo-Pac. Prehist., Pune

128. Michael, H. N., Ralph, E. K. 1970. Correction factors applied to Egyptian radiocarbon dates from era before Christ. In *Radiocarbon Variations and Absolute Chronology; Proc. Nobel Symp., 12th, Uppsala, Sweden,* ed. I. U. Olsson, pp. 109–20. New York: Wiley Interscience. 652 pp.

129. Misra, V. N. 1977. *Some Aspects of Indian Archaeology.* Allahabad: Prabhat Prakashan. 121 pp.

130. Misra, V. N. 1973. Bagor—a Late Mesolithic settlement in North-West India. *World Archaeol.* 5(1):92–110

131. Misra, V. N. 1977. Prehistory and palaeoenvironment of Rajasthan. See Ref. 9, pp. 31–54

131a. Misra, V. N. 1977. Prehistoric culture sequence of Bhimbetka. See Ref. 123, pp. 10–16

132. Misra, V. N. 1978. The Acheulian industry of rock shelter IIIF-23 at Bhimbetka, Central India—a preliminary study. *Bull. Indo-Pac. Prehist. Assoc.* 1:130–71

132a. Misra, V. N., Mathpal, Y. 1979. Rock art of Bhimbetka region, Central India. *Man Environ.* 3:27–33

133. Mohapatra, G. C. 1975. Acheulian element in Soan culture area. *J. Archaeol. Soc. Nippon* 60(4):4–18

134. Mohapatra, G. C. 1976. *Geo-tectonic developments, Sub-Himalayan lithic complex and post-Siwalik sediments.* Presented at Union Int. Sci. Prehist. Protohist. 9th, Nice

135. Movius, H. L. Jr. 1949. The Lower Palaeolithic cultures of southern and eastern Asia. *Trans. Am. Philos. Soc.* 38(4)(1948):329–420

136. Mughal, M. R. 1972. Explorations in northern Baluchistan 1972: new evidence and fresh interpretation. *Proc. Ann. Symp. Archaeol. Res. Iran* (Iran. Cent. Archaeol. Res., Tehran), pp. 276–86

137. Mughal, M. R. 1974. New evidence of the Early Harappan Culture from Jalilpur, Pakistan. *Archaeology* 27(2):106–13

138. Mujumdar, G. G. 1973. Technical studies in ancient ceramics. See Ref. 62, pp. 446–51

139. Murty, M. L. K. 1969. Blade and burin industries near Renigunta. *Proc. Prehist. Soc.* 1968:83–101

140. Murty, M. L. K. 1974. Twenty-five years of research on human osteological remains from prehistoric sites in India. *Bull. Deccan Coll. Res. Inst.* 34(1–4):116–33

141. Murty, M. L. K. 1974. A late Pleistocene cave site in southern India. *Proc. Philos. Soc.* 118(2):196–230

142. Murty, M. L. K. 1975. Late Pleistocene fauna of Kurnool Caves, South India. In *Archaeozoological Studies,* ed. A. T. Clason, pp. 132–38. Amsterdam: North-Holland. 477 pp.

143. Murty, M. L. K. 1978. *Use of plant foods by some hunter-gatherer communities on the southeast coast of India: its possible relevance to prehistory.* Presented at Symp. Recent Adv. Indo-Pac. Prehist., Pune

144. Murty, M. L. K. 1979. Recent research on the Upper Palaeolithic phase in India. *J. Field Archaeol.* 6: In press

145. Murty, M. L. K., Sontheimer, G. D. 1979. Prehistoric background to pastoralism in the Southern Deccan in the light of oral traditions and cultures of some pastoral communities. *Anthropos.* In press

146. Nagar, M. 1967. *The Ahar culture: an archaeological and ethnographic study.* PhD thesis. Poona Univ., Poona

147. Nagar, M. 1975. Role of ethnographic evidence in the reconstruction of archaeological data. *East. Anthropol.* 29(1):13–22

148. Nagar, M. 1978. *The use of wild plant foods by tribal communities in Central India: with special reference to Bastar and Bhimbetka area.* Presented at Symp. Recent Adv. Indo-Pac. Prehist., Pune

149. Nagaraja Rao, M. S. 1965. Survival of certain Neolithic elements among the Boyas of Tekkalakota. *Anthropos* 60: 480–86

150. Nagaraja Rao, M. S. 1978. *Earliest Iron-Age graves from Karnataka.* Presented at Symp. Recent Adv. Indo-Pac. Prehist., Pune

151. Paddayya, K. 1968. *Pre- and protohistoric investigations in Shorapur Doab.* PhD thesis, Poona Univ., Poona

152. Paddayya, K. 1977. An Acheulian occupation site at Hunsgi, peninsular India: a summary of the results of two seasons of excavation (1975–76). *World Archaeol.* 8(3):344–55

153. Paddayya, K. 1978. New research designs and field techniques in the palaeolithic archaeology of India. *World Archaeol.* 10(1):94–110

154. Pant, P. C., Jayaswal, V. 1968–1971. A study of prepared core technique in Palaeolithic industries of Nagarjunakonda. *Bharati, Bull. Dep. Ancient Indian Hist. Culture, Archaeol., Banaras Hindu Univ.* 12–14:344–70

155. Pant, R. K. 1973. Mechanics of crested-guided-ridge and related technology. See Ref. 62, pp. 452–61

156. Pappu, R. S. 1978. *Geomorphic setting of Acheulian sites in peninsular India.* Presented at Symp. Recent Adv. Indo-Pac. Prehist., Pune

157. Parpola, A. 1979. The problem of the Indus script. See Ref. 3, pp. 163–86

158. Parpola, A., Koskenniemi, S., Parpola, S., Aalto, P. 1969. Decipherment of the proto-Dravidian inscriptions of the Indus civilization. Copenhagen, *SIAS Spec. Publ. 1*

159. Paterson, T. T., Drummond, H. J. H. 1962. *Soan: The Palaeolithic of Pakistan.* Karachi: Dep. Archaeol., Gov. Pakistan (Mem. Dep. Archaeol. Pakistan No. 2), 171 pp.

160. Possehl, G. L. 1973. An approach to surface collecting. See Ref. 62, pp. 462–75

161. Possehl, G. L. 1977. The end of a state and continuity of a tradition: a discussion of the Late Harappan. In *Realm and Region in Traditional India,* pp. 234–54. Duke Univ. Monogr. 14

161a. Possehl, G. L., ed. 1979. *Ancient Cities of the Indus.* Durham: Carolina Academic. 470 pp.

162. Rajaguru, S. N. 1973. Late Pleistocene climatic changes in western India. See Ref. 62, pp. 80–87

163. Rajaguru, S. N. 1978. *On the problem of Acheulian chronology in western and southern India.* Presented at Symp. Recent Adv. Indo-Pac. Prehist., Pune

164. Rajaguru, S. N., Kajale, M. D. 1978. Palaeoenvironmental studies. See Ref. 153, pp. 102–4

164a. Rajendran, P. 1978. *Mesolithic culture of North Kerala.* Presented at Symp. Recent Adv. Indo-Pac. Prehist., Pune

165. Ramachandran, K. S. 1975. Radiocarbon dates of archaeological sites in India. *Archaeol. Ser.* 42. Hyderabad: Gov. Andhra Pradesh. 146 pp.

166. Raman, K. V. 1978. Rock paintings in Tamil Nadu. *Times of India,* Dec. 24, p. 8

167. Rao, S. R. 1973. The Indus script—methodology and language. See Ref. 62, pp. 323–40

168. Ray, R. 1974. *Blade-bladelet industries in eastern India: an integrated study on culture area.* Presented at Semin. Indian Prehist. Protohist., Poona

169. Reddy, K. T. 1970. Vemula industry in the Cuddapah basin. *Indian Antiq.* 4(1–4):227–34

170. Ross, E. J. 1946. A Chalcolithic site in northern Baluchistan. *J. Near East. Stud.* 5(4):291–315

171. Sahi, M. D. N. 1979. Iron at Ahar. See Ref. 3, pp. 365–68

172. Sali, S. A. 1974. Upper Palaeolithic research since Independence. *Bull. Deccan Coll. Res. Inst.* 34(1–4):147–60

173. Sali, S. A. 1978. *The Upper Palaeolithic culture at Patne, District Jalgaon, Maharashtra.* Presented at Symp. Recent Adv. Indo-Pac. Prehist., Pune

174. Salim, M. 1979. Soil analysis from the Middle Stone Age sites in northern Pakistan. *Man Environ.* 3:1–6

175. Sanders, W. T., Price, B. J. 1968. *Mesoamerica: The Evolution of a Civilization.* New York: Random House. 264 pp.

176. Sankalia, H. D. 1967. The socio-economic significance of the lithic blade industry of Navdatoli, Madhya Pradesh. *Curr. Anthropol.* 8:262–68

177. Sankalia, H. D. 1971. New evidence for Early Man in Kashmir. *Curr. Anthropol.* 12:538–61

178. Sankalia, H. D. 1973. Prehistoric colonization in India. *World Archaeol.* 5(1): 86–91

179. Sankalia, H. D. 1973. *Ramayana: Myth or Reality?* New Delhi: People's. 86 pp.

180. Sankalia, H. D. 1974. *Prehistory and Protohistory of India and Pakistan.* Poona: Deccan Coll. 592 pp.

181. Sankalia, H. D. 1974. *The role of archaeology in India (in the past, at present and in future).* Presented at Semin. Indian Prehist. Protohist., Poona

182. Sankalia, H. D. 1977. *Prehistory of India.* New Delhi: Munshiram Manoharlal. 211 pp.

183. Sankalia, H. D. 1977. *New Archaeology; its Scope and Application to India.* Lucknow: Ethnographic & Folk Culture Soc. 122 pp.

184. Sankalia, H. D. 1978. *Pre-Historic Art in India.* New Delhi: Vikas. 110 pp.

185. Sankalia, H. D. 1978. Prehistoric colonization in India: archaeological and literary evidence. *Purātattva* (1975–1976) 8:72–86

186. Sarma, A. V. N. 1976. Upper Pleistocene and Holocene ecology of east central South India. See Ref. 82, pp. 179–90

187. Saxena, S. K. 1979. Plant foods of western Rajasthan. *Man Environ.* 3: 34–43

188. Service, E. R. 1975. *Origins of the State and Civilization; the Process of Cultural Evolution.* New York: Norton. 361 pp.

189. Shaffer, J. G. 1978. *Prehistoric Baluchistan.* Delhi: B. R. 195 pp.

190. Shaffer, J. G. 1978. *Bronze Age iron from Afghanistan: its implications for South Asian protohistory.* Presented at Wisconsin Conf. South Asia, 7th, Madison

191. Shaffer, J. G. 1979. The Indus Civiliza-

tion: new evidence from Pakistan. See Ref. 3, pp. 17–29

192. Sharma, G. R. 1973. Mesolithic lake cultures in the Ganga Valley. *Proc. Prehist. Soc.* 39:129–46

193. Sharma, G. R. 1975. Seasonal migrations and Mesolithic lake cultures of the Ganga Valley. In *K. C. Chattopadhyaya Memorial Volume,* pp. 15–20. Allahabad: Dep. Anc. Hist. Cult. Archaeol. Allahabad Univ. 175 pp.

194. Sharma, G. R. 1978. *Holocene prehistory in the central Gangetic plain.* Presented at Symp. Recent Adv. Indo-Pac. Prehist., Pune

195. Sharma, T. C. 1966. *Prehistoric archaeology of Assam (a study of Neolithic cultures).* PhD thesis. London Univ., London, England

196. Sharma, Y. D., ed. 1971–1972. OCP and NBP: 1971; Proceedings of the seminar held by the Indian Archaeological Society on the 11th May, 1971, at the National Museum, New Delhi, on Ochre-Coloured Ware and Northern Black Polished Ware. *Purātattva* 5:1–100

197. Singh, G. 1971. The Indus Valley Culture seen in the context of post-glacial climatic and ecological studies in northwest India. *Arch. Phys. Anthropol. Oceania* 6(2):177–89

198. Singh, O. K. 1978. *Live Megalithic culture in Manipur.* Presented at Symp. Recent Adv. Indo-Pac. Prehist., Pune

199. Singh, P. 1970. *Burial Practices in Ancient India.* Varanasi: Prithivi Prakashan. 204 pp.

200. Singh, P. 1978. *Megalithic remains in the Vindhyas.* Presented at Symp. Recent Adv. Indo-Pac. Prehist., Pune

201. Southworth, F. C. 1976. Cereals in South Asian prehistory: a look at the linguistic evidence. See Ref. 82, pp. 52–73

202. Southworth, F. C. 1976. *Lexical evidence for early Indo-Aryan/Dravidian contacts.* Presented at Univ. Mich. Conf. Aryan & Non-Aryan in India, Ann Arbor

203. Southworth, F. C. 1977. *South Asia and linguistic archaeology.* Presented at Ann. Meet. Am. Anthropol. Assoc., 76th, Houston

204. Southworth, F. C. 1978. *Grierson revisited: the "inner" and "outer" groups of Indo-Aryan.* Presented at Int. Congr. Anthropol. Ethnol. Sci., 10th, New Delhi

204a. Stacul, G., Silvi Antonini, C. 1972. The protohistoric graveyards of Swāt (Pakistan). *Istituto italiano per il Medio* ed Estremo Oriente. Centro studi e scavi archeologici in Asia. Reports and Memoirs 7. 536 pp.

205. Sundara, A. 1975. The Early Chamber Tombs of South India; a Study of the Megalithic Monuments of North Karnataka. Delhi: Univ. Publishers. 259 pp.

205a. Tainter, J. A. 1975. Social inference and mortuary practices: an experiment in numerical classification. World Archaeol. 7(1):1–15

206. Thapar, B. K. 1973. Synthesis of the multiple data as obtained from Kalibangan. See Ref. 62, pp. 264–71

207. Thapar, B. K. 1977. Climate during the period of the Indus civilization: evidence from Kalibangan. See Ref. 9, pp. 67–73

208. Thapar, B. K. 1978. Early farming communities in India. J. Hum. Evol. 7:11–22

209. Tapar, R. 1978. Puranic lineages and archaeological cultures. Purātattva (1975–1976) 8:86–98

210. Tosi, M. 1977. The protourban societies of eastern Iran and the Indus civilization. Abstr. Int. Conf. South Asian Archaeol., 4th, Naples, pp. 106–9

211. Tripathi, V. 1976. The Painted Grey Ware: an Iron Age Culture of Northern India. Delhi: Concept. 150 pp.

212. Vishnu-Mittre. 1974. Plant remains and climate from the Late Harappan and other Chalcolithic cultures of India—a study in inter-relationships. Geophytology 4(1):46–53

213. Vishnu-Mittre. 1975. Problems and prospects of palaeobotanical approach towards the investigation of the history of the Rajasthan desert. Proc. Problems of Deserts in India, Jaipur

214. Vishnu-Mittre. 1977. Discussion on local and introduced crops. In The Early History of Agriculture: a Joint Symposium of the Royal Society and the Brit-

ish Academy, organizer J. Hutchinson et al, pp. 129–41. Oxford Univ. Press. 213 pp.

215. Vishnu-Mittre. 1978. The use of wild plants and the process of domestication in the Indian subcontinent. Presented at Symp. Recent Adv. Indo-Pac. Prehist., Pune

216. Wakankar, V. S. 1967. Kayatha excavation number. Vikram, J. Vikram Univ., Ujjain

217. Wakankar, V. S. 1975. Bhimbetka—the prehistoric paradise. Prachya Pratibha 3(2):7–29

218. Wakankar, V. S. 1978. The Dawn of Indian Art. Ujjain: Vishnu Bhatnagar for Bharati Kala Bhawan. 24 pp.

219. Wakankar, V. S. 1978. Stone Age industries of Bhimbetka and its relation with rock paintings. Presented at Symp. Recent Adv. Indo-Pac. Prehist., Pune

220. Wheeler, M. 1959. Early India and Pakistan. London: Thames & Hudson. 241 pp.

221. Wheeler, M. 1968. The Indus Civilization. Cambridge Univ. Press. 144 pp. 3rd ed.

222. Wolpert, S. 1977. A New History of India. New York: Oxford. 471 pp.

223. Wright, H. T., Johnson, G. A. 1975. Population, exchange, and early state formation in southwestern Iran. Am. Anthropol. 77(2):267–89

224. Yoffee, N. 1979. The decline and rise of Mesopotamian civilization: an ethnoarchaeological perspective on the evolution of social complexity. Am. Antiq. 44(1):5–35

224a. Zeuner, F. E., Allchin, B. 1956. The microlithic sites of Tinnevelly District, Madras State. Anc. India 12:4–20

225. Zide, A. R. K., Zvelebil, K. V., eds. 1976. The Soviet Decipherment of the Indus Valley Script. The Hague: Mouton. 142 pp.

Ann. Rev. Anthropol. 1979. 8:503–41

STRUCTURALISM

♦9644

David Kronenfeld[1]

Department of Anthropology, University of California,
Riverside, California 92521

Henry W. Decker

Department of Literatures and Languages (French), University of California,
Riverside, California 92521

INTRODUCTION

"It is a problem to account for the renown of a theoretician who is unimpressive as an analyst and whose theories, which are seldom original, are regularly refuted by the facts" (68, p. 145).

This essay is directed toward the solution of Francis Korn's problem, for her judgments of the master's work are similar to ones we have made (133), but such judgments seem to be irrelevant to those attributes of Lévi-Strauss's work which have made him one of anthropology's dominant figures. If his importance stems neither from the power of his particular theories nor from the insightfulness of his analyses, then a consideration of his role in anthropology must turn elsewhere.

Like Leach (79, p. 37), we "shall assume that structuralism in Social Anthropology refers to the Social Anthropology of Lévi-Strauss and work which derives more or less directly from that source" (see also 20, p. 468). We first explore the Saussurean and Jakobsonian antecedents of Lévi-Straussean structuralism; we next relate these linguistic antecedents to other of Lévi-Strauss's important intellectual sources, and then move into a general discussion of his intellectual position. We conclude with discus-

[1]We wish to thank James Armstrong, Alan Beals, B. N. Colby, Hugh Gladwin, David James, Judy Z. Kronenfeld, Jacqueline Lindenfeld, Theda Shapiro, and Lynn Thomas for their generous and helpful comments on earlier drafts of this paper. We are grateful to the Academic Senate of the University of California at Riverside for the assistance provided by an Intramural Research Grant to David B. Kronenfeld.

0084-6570/79/1015-0503$01.00

sions of selected aspects of his analysis of kinship, of the theoretical aims of his analysis of myth, and of his actual implementation of his program for the analysis of myth.

Reviews in this series do not normally focus on the work of a single individual, but, as we shall see, apart from the work of Lévi-Strauss and explications, critiques, and celebrations of his work, little else might properly be called structuralist anthropology. Examples are (1, 36–39, 58, 73, 105, 126, 128, 134). Outside of anthropology there does exist a structuralism apart from Lévi-Strauss to which we occasionally allude, but which we have not space to consider systematically (129, pp. 207–8, 210; 135). Our decision concerning what to cover results in part from consideration of what other recent reviews have covered, in part from our sense of where the greatest problems of clarification and explication lie, and in part from the inevitable limits of our own knowledge.

Discussions of French structuralism inevitably become deeply enmeshed in considerations of Marxism. The connection is real, but is not as crucial to anthropological structuralism as it is to French structuralism in general. The issue is peripheral to our focus, and beyond our expertise. In our opinion, Jameson's (63) remains the best general treatment of this issue that we have seen, while Friedman (45) has provided by far the best discussion of the relationship between Marxism and anthropological structuralism (cf 3, p. 463–64; 11).

The discipline of folklore studies represents a universe all its own. Maranda (103) covers anthropological structuralism from this folklore perspective; Dundes (40) provides a more recent overview of structuralist work in folklore studies.

Jameson (63, p. 9) and others (e.g. 28, p.3) are right when they insist that Piaget's use of the structuralist label is very different from that of the Saussure/Lévi-Strauss/French-literary-critic axis. On the other hand, it is also true that Piaget's work itself offers the best available insight into how synchronic mental structures evolve in the individual, adapt to changing environments, and interact with history. Insofar as structures represent something like sets of codes and insofar as structuralists are concerned with the historical development of these codes (cf 63, pp. 193–94, 211–14), they would be well advised to attend seriously to Piaget's general theory of cognitive functioning [cf comments by Rayfield (119) in his review of Sperber (131)], and to the similar but more specifically linguistic work of Greenberg (52). The work of art historian E. H. Gombrich (50) is also relevant.

In recent years a number of general reviews of the structuralist movement have appeared. These tend to start with Saussure, carry through Jakobson to Lévi-Strauss, and then go on to consider attempted applications of structuralism in the arts and in politics. The best of these are by Jameson (63) and Culler (28). Both are subtle, sophisticated, and insightful. Culler provides much the better explication of the linguistic concepts and theory from which structuralism derives, and attends more to how such concepts might be employed in literary criticism. Culler concludes that since the particular analyses of the structuralists are logically weak and only partially consistent with their linguistic model, their theory itself can only be taken metaphorically. Jameson, on the other hand, even while being aware of the great weaknesses in their actual applications of that theory, takes their theoretical assertions more seriously and does a better job of explicating them from an inside, if Marxist, point of view. Hawkes (56) covers much the same territory as Culler in a much more superficial manner, while Pettit (114) comes up with an interpretation of his own that simply misconstrues the material (cf 122). Piaget (115) also misconstrues much of the structuralist enterprise, but in a much more creative and instructive manner; in many respects Piaget (115) describes what structuralism *should have been.* Gardner (47) provides discussions of Piaget and Lévi-Strauss.

There are a number of edited collections on the subject. The earliest is the now dated volume of Ehrmann's (43). Macksey & Donato's (102) work represents a symposium at Johns Hopkins that emphasized literary issues. Lane (71) provides a rich and full coverage of the Saussure-Prague-Lévi-Strauss axis as well as articles by Barthes and by Godelier and a useful introduction. The Robey book (121) represents a more recent lecture series in Oxford that seems in many ways to be the best of these collections; it contains specially written pieces by Lyons, Culler, Leach, Eco, Todorov, Mepham, and Gandy.

SAUSSURE

Lévi-Strauss has modeled his structural anthropology on modern structural linguistics. The key figure in the definition of the nature and task of structural linguistics, and the person who first spoke of the central role for linguistics in a broader science of signs—semiology—was de Saussure (cf 2, p. xxx; 91, p. 59). Saussure's influence on structuralism is not only direct —via linguistics—but also indirect via the notions that he shared with Durkheim (cf 107) about the role of language as the social phenomenon par excellence and about the special nature of such social phenomena. Before taking up his post in Geneva, Saussure had taught in Paris (while Durkheim was elaborating his theory of society), and his student Meillet was a member of the *Année sociologique* group. Thus Saussure's insights were embodied in the French sociological school to which Lévi-Strauss is heir.

In recent years the explication of Saussure's thought has become a major industry (see 67). Engler (44) has published a "critical edition" comparing the *Cours* line by line with the student notes in parallel columns; this supercedes Godel's work (49). De Mauro has published an extensively annotated Italian translation of the *Cours* that clears up a great many questions and ambiguities in the original text; this edition has been translated into French (33), and hopefully it will not be long until it is translated into English. Culler has written an excellent book on Saussure in the Modern Masters series (29).

We thus begin our account of structuralism with a consideration of key Saussurean concepts which enter heavily into structuralist discussions, and about which there is much confusion both within and without the movement. We consider how Saussure actually applied each concept in his discussion of language and how he would have applied the concept in question to those wider semiological issues now addressed by modern structuralists. The first and perhaps most crucial of these conceptual problems concerns what Saussure meant when he referred to the *arbitrary* nature of linguistic phenomena. This problem can best be elucidated by systematically examining the major senses in which the concept has been used by Saussure and others.

1. The strongest sense would be "absolutely arbitrary." In this sense signifiers would have no predictable relationships to their signifieds (functional, logical, social, historical . . .); they would be randomly connected. This absolute sense is far removed from Saussure's usage (34, pp. 68–69), but is one a number of his critics have imputed to him (e.g. 7, p. 126); it is also the sense which a number of French literary lights have taken to apply to various classes of nonlinguistic (or extralinguistic) signs (cf 28, Chap. 10).

2. The next sense is Saussure's "radically arbitrary" (34, pp. 113, 131), by which he means that there is no intrinsic connection between the signifier and the signified (that is, there is no way that a stranger to English who heard the word "tree" could guess that it referred to the willow outside our window). Saussure does not rule out *social* motivation; in fact, with Durkheim (41, pp. 2–8), he insists on social motivation as the *only* motivation for linguistic signs (34, pp. 76–77, 113). Language is a collective representation; a person learns it from the community and is not free to change it, but since the community is only made up of other persons who have similarly learned it, the sign has no source outside the community.

3. In other places (p. 112) Saussure, without using the word, refers to another kind of arbitrariness: the arbitrary segmentation of one's internal representation of some external natural continuum. This is the sense in which the referents of the word "sheep" form an arbitrary set and need not be equivalent to the set formed by the referents of the French word "mouton" (pp. 115–16). It is in this sense that language may be said to arbitrarily

categorize the external world. This relationship between concept and referent and between sound image and physical sound is one that Jakobson has misconstrued as an identity (62, p. 280)—perhaps in part because of confusions in Bally & Sechehaye's compilation—most blatantly on p. 68 (34) [see de Mauro's notes to this passage (33, pp. 442–45) and cf (44, pp. 149–52)]. Such a view (that of Saussure) does not deny the reality of the external world, the connectedness that exists among its parts, nor [*contra* Singer (129, p. 217)] the systematic relationship of linguistic concepts ("signifieds") to the world; it only asserts the arbitrariness of the cuts by which continuous (natural) phenomena are grouped into discrete (conceptual) categories (34, pp. 114–17). A similar arbitrariness is asserted for the relationship between the phonic continuum of potential speech sounds and the phonemic categories by which the continuum is represented in the "signifier" as a "sound image" (pp. 117–19). Important here is the fact that Sassure's assertions regarding this particular kind of arbitrariness are quite modest and consistent with recent work (10, 51). This is contrary to the kind of language-creates-reality view that prevails in much recent structuralism.

4. Another sense of partial "arbitrariness" or partial motivation (34, p. 68) is what might be called "natural conventions." The choice of the symbolic means by which some information is to be represented may be arbitrary in the sense of not being necessary, while the values of the attribute that are selected to represent alternative states may be more strongly motivated; that is, there is no intrinsic reason for the ancient Egyptians to have chosen to represent social importance via size in paintings and sculpture, but once that decision is made there are strong reasons or motivations for using "large" to represent "important" and "small" for "unimportant" (cf 50, pp. 135–36). Symbolic associations, for instance, of blood with body and semen with bone might best be seen in this light, as opposed to the purer arbitrariness of many structuralist accounts and the purer motivatedness asserted by many symbolic accounts (cf 79, p. 46). Saussure did not have a theory of "symbols," but did explicitly contrast symbols with signs on the basis of the symbols' more motivated relationship between signifier and signified. Saussure's projected science of "semiology" was to embrace both (p. 68), and thus one may infer that Saussure had no intention of asserting any *necessity* to the arbitrariness of the signifier-signified relationship for semiological systems in general.

5. At the extreme motivated end of our continuum would be relationships such as that between the picture of peas on the can and the peas inside, or Leach's indexical one between smoke and fire (81, p. 12).

Our next conceptual problem concerns the famous oppositions: *langue/ parole,* synchrony/diachrony, and syntagmatic/paradigmatic. Various authors have erroneously treated these as if they referred to the *same kind* of distinction; in some cases the distinctions themselves have been conflated or confounded with one another.

Langue refers to a particular code (or organized *system* of knowledge); it is equivalent to Chomsky's *competence* [with the reservation that Chomsky defines as intrinsic to this system certain syntactic operations (23, pp. 59–60; 24, pp. 4, 23) that Saussure did not know existed]. *Parole* refers to the actual act of speech or *performance* in which the system of *langue* is brought to bear along with various other systems (which Saussure doesn't name, but which presumably include social class markers, situation markers, etc), various communicative intents, and chance factors. The contrast between *langue* and *parole,* then, is not a symmetric one between one system and another, but is an asymmetric one between a system in isolation and the concrete situation in which that system interacts with other systems and is instantiated. The asymmetry explains why various calls for a theory of *parole* comparable to a theory of *langue* (e.g. 17) are misguided; the rules of *langue* are the axioms which generate a system, while the "rules" of *parole* are the devices by which the products of different systems are combined with each other and adapted to whatever situational constraints exist.

The contrast between diachrony and synchrony thus refers to *langue* and not *parole* [contra (96) p. 27]. Diachrony does not refer to time ordering per se [contra (63) p. 126; (81) pp. 44–45)], but refers to changes in *langue* (that is, in the code or the set of rules) over time. Saussure knew that a single sentence has a temporal ordering, but that was not the kind of temporal ordering that he meant by diachronic change, (cf 62, p. 227). In his famous chess analogy (34, pp. 88–89; cf 52, pp. 57–58; see also 2, pp. xxxvi–xxxviii) the history of a given language is represented by the game; a given configuration of the board represents a sychronic state of the language (*langue,* a functioning system); time per se is not represented at all by diachrony, but rather diachrony represents successive changes in state. The rules of the game would be the panchronic rules of language, as opposed to *a* language (34, p. 95).

It should also be pointed out that Saussure was aware that the synchronic stasis between moves was a fictional construct abstracted from a continuing process of change (34, pp. 101–2) which was only approximated (52, p. 347). This working fiction could only be avoided after the distinction between *langue* and *parole,* and the process by which regularities in *parole* gradually came to be incorporated as changes in *langue,* were well understood (cf 53). That a language over time represented a succession of frozen states and that changes between states were instantaneous (as in the chess analogy) was the major aspect of Saussure's *Course* that troubled Meillet in his review of the *Course* (107).

The contrast between paradigmatic and syntagmatic has sometimes been confounded with that between synchronic and diachronic (e.g. 63, pp. 37–38; 81, pp. 26–27). Leach's error stems from (*a*) his confusion of diachrony with *any* kind of temporally ordered event as opposed to changes in the system of rules or relations (63, p. 126) and (*b*) his confusion of syntagmatic with sequential and paradigmatic with contemporaneous. Syntagmatic relations, according to Saussure, are relations of co-occurrence. Natural (spoken) language is linear, and hence the only kinds of co-occurrence relations possible are sequential ones; but in other less strictly linear forms of linguistic expression (e.g. the deaf language) those same relations may be both contemporaneous (i.e. spatially juxtaposed) and sequential. Generalizing Saussure's concepts to semiological systems in general, syntagmatic relations include both Leach's contemporaneity or harmony and his sequentiality or melody (81, pp. 15, 43). Paradigmatic relations, for Saussure, are the relations which obtain among alternative possible fillers of some position in a syntagmatic chain and among the alternative forms that some particular filler might take in alternative positions (34, pp. 125–26, 128–31). Such relations in language can be phonological (spot vs. spit), morphological (run vs. ran), syntactic (brought vs. had brought) semantic (hit the ball vs. catch the ball), or other (e.g. sociolinguistic; yes ma'am vs yeah). For semiological systems in general, paradigmatic relations are those which we isolate when we ask "X as opposed to what?" For structuralism, these relations are important because they represent all the nonpresent associations (or planes of contrast) which the use of some particular form raises or potentially can raise; it is through this aspect of the systematicity (cf 34, pp. 113–17) of language that a change in one place (e.g. the addition of "pork" to English along side of "pig") affects the whole system of a language (the meaning of "pig" in opposition to "pork" is notably different from the meaning of "pig" in opposition to "cow," "sheep," etc; the meaning of syntagmatic units that include "pig" is also thereby affected.)

Saussure's work relates in various ways to that of other thinkers. A few instances are worth pointing to because they represent areas of confusion about structuralism. Saussure's initial work in structural linguistics was significantly developed, amplified, and integrated with that of the Kazan school by Troubetzkoy, Jakobson, and others in the Prague school (62, pp. 394–428, 527–38). Jakobson, during the 1940s in New York, introduced Lévi-Strauss to structural linguistics in general and to Saussure's work in particular [as well as to Boas (cf 60, p. 190)]. Given Lévi-Strauss's Jakobsonian sources, it is worth noting two important ways in which Prague school structuralism differed from Saussurean. First, the Prague theorists placed much less emphasis on the sign itself (the unit of signifier/signified) or on relations among signs, and instead concentrated on the contrastive and sequential (paradigmatic and syntagmatic) relations of signifier to signifier, and on the basic elements—distinctive features that tend to be binary —out of which signifiers are built (cf 62, p. 718). Jakobson (62, pp. 280–84) himself maintains that one must look at the whole sign ("*signum*") including both its signifier ("*signans*") and signified ("*signatum*"). However, his very discussion illustrates the problem; he treats the signified (a la Peirce) as if it were itself the (external to the mind) object being referred to and not a mental concept relating to that object. Such a view, besides being too simplistic, deprives the signified of any linguistic interest and thereby necessarily reduces the study of the sign to the study of its signifier (cf 62, pp. 267–68).

Second, this focus on the relationship of Saussure's "sound image" to external sounds led them to think in terms of less arbitrary and more motivated linguistic phenomena than had Saussure (62, p. 717). Additionally, the threat represented by archaic theories of the naturalness of linguistic signs was less significant than it had been when Saussure did his work, and therefore they had less reason to make a point of stressing the arbitrary nature of linguistic phenomena. However, it is worth stressing that even for Saussure, different aspects of the sign were arbitrary in different ways, and it was only the relationship between signifier and signified that he called "radically arbitrary." As we shall see, these two points of Saussure-Prague contrast are significant because Lévi-Strauss initially adopted a Praguean view of semiological structures and initially placed considerable emphasis on motivated relations between signifier and signified. This retains a Praguean resonance, even though Saussure himself would have considered such "symbols" to be motivated.

The question of motivations necessarily leads us to Saussure's relationship to Durkheim. The kinds of linguistic motivations that Jakobson has considered are essentially ones that operate on an individual, while Saussure was at one with Durkheim concerning the *collective* and *passive* nature of the sign. Language was, for Durkheim, the example par excellence of a collective representation (41, pp. 2–8; cf 96, p. 84; 106, pp. 1–2). In Saussure's formulations it was a human creation that no single human could change. The individual, and active pressures operating on the individual, enter into *parole*—which is a concept that Doroszewski (35) and others (cf 135) have considered as a device by which Saussure meant to link Durkheimian-type theories to theories of individual motivation (even if Saussure did *not* explain how *parole* became *langue*).

Langue was a collective phenomenon that only existed in the shared understandings that enabled communication to take place; it was passive in the sense that only the regularities and rules by which understanding was enabled were part of *langue* itself—individual intentions and the active process by which messages were actually constructed belonged instead to *parole*. Saussure's strong assertion of the collective, social nature of language was basic to his conception of the science of linguistics (2, p. xxxiv), though not to his more general science of semiology, which would have to encompass individual as well as collective representations.

For Saussure, language was furthermore a collective *mental* phenomenon. The mental nature of Saussure's sign absolutely prevents it from being the kind of simplistic dyadic concept that Singer (129, pp. 216–17) among others (9) considers it to be. Singer opposes the supposedly dyadic Saussurian sign to the triadic one of Peirce and subsequent derivative positivist philosophers. For Singer's Peirce (cf 130), the "sign" is only the linguistic token; the "object" is the external (to the sign) thing (with its associations, implications, etc) referred to, while the "interpretant" is the response of the person in whose mind the sign is linked to its object and who interprets the implications of the sign's use (129, pp. 216–17, 220, 224). For Saussure the sign is a unit embodying the union of a signifier—a (mental) sound image —and a signified—a (mental) concept representing (possibly) some external reality. Seen thus narrowly, the Saussurean unit appears dyadic, but we must remember that the signifier and signified are both mental units and only exist within a set of minds (cf 2, p. xxxiii). If the signifier and signified are the first two elements of the Saussurean sign, then the mind (whose constructs they are), the external sounds represented by the sound image, and the external objects referred to by the concept represent the other three essential elements of the individual sign. Within this individual "pentadic" unit there are three relationships that can be investigated more or less independently: 1. the relationship of sound to sound-image (signifier); 2. the relationship of signifier to signified; and 3. the relationship of concept (signified) to external referent. At one step further removed are 4. the relations of signs to one another, the syntagmatic relations by which signs are combined with one another to make larger linguistic units; 5. the paradigmatic relations of contrast that exist among alternative signs and sets of signs; and 6. the relationship between the representation of signs or other linguistic phenomena in different minds. This latter relationship is by definition constrained for signs in *langue,* but is more fully investigatable in *parole* and among other semiological phenomena such as symbols. Finally, a Saussurean view of the function of sign systems requires a consideration of the syntagmatic relations existing between concepts entailed in a sign system and other pragmatic concepts and a similar consideration of paradigmatic relations among alternative sign systems and among alternative pragmatic possibilities.

Saussure's conception of the role of mind in language seems richer than the interpreted nomenclature of Peirce's that Singer presents (cf 33, p. 439),

and its clear distinguishing of the cognitive structures by which we conceptualize the external world from any structure automatically inherent in that
world seems more in accord with the findings of modern cognitive psychology (cf 18, 108, 116, 127). To Saussure, the function of language does
depend on our knowledge of the external world, but it also depends on the
organization which we impose on that world with language [cf (34), the
banks of the river on p. 112; also pp. 115–17]. The active organizing role
of the mind in Saussure's *parole* accords better with our creative use of sign
systems than does Singer/Peirce's more passive "interpretant"; *langue* provides the passively received codes out of which such creations can be
constructed.

The unconscious nature of linguistic phenomena is what has protected
such phenomena from manipulation by particular individuals and has made
them lawful phenomena which could be studied in isolation from the specifics of individual motivations, intentions, and explanations. It is this unconscious nature of linguistic phenomena which precludes folk theories of
them from having any privileged position. Saussure, Boas, and Sapir all
recognized this, though Jakobson's discussion (60, pp. 189–90) implies that
it was Boas who brought its importance for language-like anthropological
phenomena home to Lévi-Strauss. Rossi (123, p. 21) misses the point when
he mistakes such an enabling assumption for a "fundamental hypothesis"
of Lévi-Strauss.

Some structuralist writers have tried to link the Saussurean notion of
opposition (cf "value") in language—in which one element only acquires or
signals meaning in contradistinction to some other element with which it
contrasts—with the Hegelian (and Marxist) opposition between opposed
elements out of which comes a new synthesis (cf 63, pp. 22–24; 80, pp. 5–6).
As Culler (28, pp. 14–16) and others have noted, the Saussurean opposition
refers to a static condition, a set of existent differences which can be used
toward some (not necessarily intrinsic) end, and which exists within a
system of other such differences, while the Hegelian opposition is an active
contending of contradictory elements which necessarily pushes toward a
new (intrinsically related) system in which those elements no longer exist,
and which tends to absorb all other elements in itself. Saussurean structuralism provides neither a demonstration of the reasonableness of the Marxist
dialectic nor a mechanism by which that dialectic might be implemented
(83, pp. 120–21).

Saussure described a linguistics that dealt directly and firmly with meaning. The central topic of linguistics for him was the sign, a unit that was
from one perspective a sound image and from another a concept. Linguistics
dealt first of all with the relationship between signifier and signified—with
semantics. Derivatively one studied the paradigmatic relations by which

signs contrasted with one another and the syntagmatic patterns by which they were concatenated; in the *Course* [(34) pp. 122–31—especially 126, 130] it is clear that syntagmatic and paradigmatic relations refer as much to conceptual relations as to grammatical relations.

Saussure's science of signs was not intended as the mere study of the forms of signs and the combinatorial properties of these signs abstracted from their meanings and their communicative functions—as it has become in most modern linguistics. The Americans, after Bloomfield, explicitly eschewed meaning. Jakobson and other Prague linguists dealt only with the structure of form (that is, of signifiers) and ignored the structure of content (signifieds) even though they sometimes talked about meaning; their distinctive feature analysis dealt with the elements out of which signifiers were built and had nothing to do with signifieds; other grammatical units, parallels, and the like were described and were asserted to carry meaning, but no theory of meaning was ever provided. Transformational linguists have presented themselves as mentalists, but their contributions have all dealt with the structure of signifiers—that is, with relations among forms. They have developed a new and powerful syntactic theory out of a Bloomfieldian base, specific philosophic disagreements notwithstanding (cf 61, p. 143), and have married it to a Praguean phonology. Semantic representations have been mentioned, but relegated to a background position (cf 101, p. 34); the only attempt within the orthodox school to deal with semantics has been Katz & Fodor's (65) unsubtle and inadequate stab; generative semanticists have given semantics a more crucial role, but have provided no explication of semantics itself [cf Jakobson's characterization of Boas (61, p. 142) in this connection].

Of the post-Saussurean schools of linguistics that have had any appreciable effect on anthropology (this excludes London and Copenhagen) none has dealt with the aspect of language that is most central to its development and function—meaning. Jakobsen's concern with the function of language (62, pp. 522–26) stopped short of this final step. It is as if they were trying to describe the form of a ship without any mention of the fact that it was designed to float, and without any consideration of the factors that enable the ship to float or that affect its seaworthiness.

LÉVI-STRAUSS

Lévi-Strauss has returned to a genuinely Saussurean concern with meaning (cf 93; 96, p. 169), but from a roundabout route—since he learned his linguistics, including apparently all that he knew about Saussure, from Jakobson (cf 94, p. xxvi) and so understood "structural linguistics" and the Saussurean framework to refer to the binary-feature, componential analysis of Jakobsonian phonology (cf 80, p. 23; 123, p. 27). Jakobson's phonological thrust was unfortunate because, even within the Saussurean paradigm, phonemes were merely the particular material out of which the signifier face of the sign happened to be built—that is, phonemes were not intrinsic to signs per se (34, p. 10), and thus represented an unlikely basis for the generalization of specifically linguistic insights out to a general science of signs (cf 2, p. xlix; 34, p. 11). The special contribution of Prague phonology concerned the substantive nature of phonology itself and not the formal properties of sign systems (cf 25, p. 65). The generalizable aspects of linguistics were more likely to concern the relations of signs to one another and the relations of signifieds to the external world of phenomena.

Particularly Jakobsonian are: Lévi-Strauss's early insistence that all oppositions must be binary; his (implicit) view that linguistic analysis pertains to the structure of the signifier, rather than to the structure of the sign as Saussure had it; his attention to relatively motivated kinds of symbolic systems; and his emphasis on the importance of systems of contrast in structural analysis, as opposed to Saussure's more balanced emphasis on the role of syntagmatic structures as well, and as opposed to more recent linguistic concern with the hierarchical organization of language.

Lévi-Strauss first tried to come up with Jakobsonian analyses of cultural materials (89, pp. 41–49, 73, 144–60, 222, 226, 286; cf 60), including affect relations in kinship and mythology; he seems to have been perhaps a bit naive in the simplicity and directness with which he named a couple of dimensions, rated sets of phenomena on them with pluses and minuses; found that some possible patterns of signs existed in his corpus while some did not; explained why it was so; and called that an analysis (cf 2, pp. lii–liv). Even apart from questions of replicability and validity, such analyses told one very little; it appears to have been only subsequently, as he began to explore the logic of his proffered explanations, that he came to realize that his concern in these studies was with the symbolic systems and the process through which cultural meanings were worked out [that is, with species that are "*bonnes à penser*" (90; cf 93, pp. 11–12; cf 80, pp. 31–39) and not with the mere identification of a tale's major issue]. With analyses such as that of Asdiwal, and with *Savage Thought,* he begins to show a more explicit concern with the content of the various cultural codes and with the ways in which these codes are linked together and ordered so as to encompass a cultural problem. He is back to a Saussurean concern with how meaning is expressed within (cultural) sign systems, but because of his Jakobsonian lens he does not realize that Saussure, too, was concerned with meaning (and not just form alone) and so he is unable to build on the theoretical bases that Saussure has laid, and he is unable to benefit from the rigor with which Saussure approached linguistic problems. He feels he has to give up on the formalism and rigor of linguistics in order to talk about cultural meanings (93, p. 7). He inherits Durkheim's concern with collective representations, but without Saussure's and Whitney's (137) linguistic model for how these cultural codes come to be implemented in messages of individuals. The relatively strong Jakobsonian concern with linguistic substance (as opposed to the more purely formal views of Saussure and later Hjelmslev), and its attendant de-emphasis of the importance of the *langue/parole* contrast leave Lévi-Strauss with theoretical machinery that is inadequate for the task that he sets himself. While he aims at a science of meaning, he is forced, in part by his linguistic naivete, to discovery by insightful guess and proof by "if I see it the it must be there for other human minds as well" type assertions. By not being nearly as clear as Saussure was about what he expected of an account, he leaves himself no theoretical basis for telling a valid one from an invalid one, and exposes himself to the attacks of looseness of execution which have so often obscured the importance of his analytic aims.

Many (e.g. 42, p. 375; 80, p. 66) claim that Lévi-Strauss's method of myth analysis is based directly on that of Propp (118). As Lévi-Strauss himself points out, such claims are deeply in error (88). Propp's analyses deal with the syntactic form of tales—that is, with the permissible orderings of classes of elements. Lévi-Strauss explicitly eschews any concern with the sequential ordering or story lines of tales, but instead addresses the constraints on content—that is, the relations of contrast and co-occurrence that obtain among various tale elements. Beidelman's (8, p. 220) claim that Lévi-Strauss minimizes "the significance of content in order to discern form and structure", while explicable in terms of Beidelman's conception of content, seems quite far off the mark. We have often been told by linguistically knowledgeable folklorists (and have ourselves told others) that the true implementation of the methods of structural linguistics for the study of folk literature is that of Propp rather than that of Lévi-Strauss. If one understands structural linguistics to be the study of the combinatorial properties of form classes (as it seems to have been for most post-Saussurean linguistics), then these arguments are clearly correct. And, of course, if one is concerned with the formal rigor of the analysis, then Propp's work seems much the better model. But Propp does not offer us anything about the specific meanings of folktales. If we return to Saussure's concern with *how* language has meaning, we find that Lévi-Strauss does have many of the right concerns and does ask many of the right questions. His aims and methods seem closer than Propp's to Saussure's original conception of structural linguistics. The issues that he raises are crucial for structural linguistics itself; what now is needed are methods for dealing with those issues.

Lévi-Strauss does not talk much about it, but his meetings in New York with Jakobson and Boas (cf 123 p. 25–26) point to another important strand in his development. His initial attempts to apply linguistic insights to the study of social organization seem to owe nothing to North America beyond a few ethnographic examples. Boas might have suggested to Lévi-Strauss the relevance of linguistics to the study of culture, but such was already implicit in Durkheim's discussion of the role of language as a collective representation and in the role of Meillet in the *Année sociologique,* and thus may have come to Lévi-Strauss in other ways. It does appear that Lévi-Strauss became familiar with Northwest Coast cultures and ethnography through the work of Boas (cf 60, p. 190). But more importantly, he seems to have gotten from Boas the notion that important insights into culture could come from the study of folklore (96, pp. 63–64), as well as some intuitive sense of how structural patterns might work themselves out in the folk forms of a culture (cf 13; 14, pp. 403–6, 421, 429, 433–34, 485, 488). He went beyond Boas's particular forms of analysis and claims about the results of analysis (as indeed have almost all of Boas's students in linguistics and in anthropology), but he does seem to have been influenced by Boas in his conception of the nature of the enterprise—especially in his un-British and un-French concern with the specifics of cultural content (perhaps it was, if belatedly, Boas who freed him from his Jakobsonian focus on forms?) (cf 8, p. 220).

Lévi-Strauss's early romances with cybernetics and information theory came from the fact that they reinforced the binary thrust and the view of formal structures that he got from Jakobson. Additionally, in the notions of feedback loops and anticipation of the moves of others that these new fields (including game theory) explicitly recognized, he found a mechanism by which collective mental structures could arise and operate, and thus he found reassurance that the collective mental structures that he wanted to study were in the realm of science and not of mysticism. The idea of collective mental structures derives both from Saussure (via Jakobson) and from Durkheim (via French sociology). The question of how and where such mental structures could exist (and of what one meant by emergent properties) has been of particular concern to students of Durkheim's work, and has been consigned to mysticism by many of Durkheim's critics. Lévi-Strauss understood that the work of Wiener and of Shannon and Weaver provided the general answer to those questions, and had no particular concern with the specifics by which Durkheim's assertions might be accounted for. Thus cybernetics and game theory were important to the emergence of Lévi-Straussean structuralism, but played no specific role within it.

Lévi-Strauss himself cited geology as the final formative influence upon his notion of structuralism. It was geology that showed him how a jumbled synchronic mass could contain origins, history, and synchronic structural relations all at once, and thus geology that showed him how particular cultural products might be unraveled (91, pp. 60–62). In that discussion, however, he neglects to point out that the jumbled mass of rock reveals history only *because* some past geologist has patiently worked out the stratigraphy elsewhere (in places where the rock was not so jumbled), and that relations of synchrony can only be extracted in the light of this historical information. Geology seems to have been a productive metaphor for him; it is a shame that he did not carry it further.

Studies of Lévi-Strauss's work are found in (4, 15, 47). Leach provides an interesting and useful introduction to Lévi-Strauss's work in his Modern Masters volume (80). Leach's text (81) contains many interesting examples, but is theoretically simple-minded; much of the technical discussion, especially of Saussure, is just plain wrong. Ardener's introduction to ASA 10 (2) remains the best discussion available of the Saussurean and structural linguistic background to Lévi-Straussean anthropology. The best recent overview of work on myth in the Lévi-Straussean framework that we have seen is that of Carroll (20). Commentaries on Lévi-Strauss's kinship work include (6) and (54). Edited volumes focusing on the work of Lévi-Strauss include Rossi's useful collection (124) and Hayes & Hayes' more pop coverage of Lévi-Strauss from a variety of perspectives (57). LaPointe & LaPointe (72) provide a general and extensive bibliography of Lévi-Strauss's own work and of works about him.

Lévi-Strauss: Kinship

Lévi-Strauss's work on kinship is relatively old and has already been reviewed extensively in a variety of places (16, 32, 59, 109), and so will not require much discussion here. There are, however, a very few points that still merit some attention. The first has to do with the way in which Lévi-Strauss's theoretical statements concerning marriage systems are to be taken. Following the original publication of *Elementary Structures,* Rodney Needham tried to make the theoretical assertions of that work available to English-speaking anthropology. In so doing he (laudably) tried to clarify some of the more enigmatic assertions of the master—and thereby got into a storm of controversy.

Lévi-Strauss offers his particular discussion as a theory of elementary (vs complex) kinship structures. The questions concern what is meant by elementary structures and wherein such structures exist. Needham maintained that elementary structures were ones that had prescriptive marriage systems while complex structures were ones with preferential marriage systems. Needham implied that this prescriptiveness or preferentiality inhered in native conceptions of their system (as opposed to statistical summaries of any actual behavior of the people in question), as expressed in their assertions about marriage choices and in the relationship of these assertions to their terminologically recognized classes of kin. Prescriptive systems were ones in which the indicated kind of marriage was obligatory while preferential systems were ones in which it was optional.

Lounsbury, in his review of *Structure and Sentiment,* demonstrated problems of both logic and empirical application with Needham's form of the contrast. He suggested instead that the preferential/prescribed contrast had to do with one's *right* (rather than obligation) to contract a marriage and with the consequences in folk law of such a marriage (100, pp. 1307–8).

Boon & Schneider (16) erroneously treat Lévi-Strauss's kinship work as if it represented a functionalist theory. A concern with the effects of social forms and with the relative selective advantages for a society of one form vs another hardly constitutes the kind of functional prerequisites argument or the kind of teleological goal orientation that one normally associates with functionalist theories. One also remains doubtful about their assertion of the similarity of Lévi-Strauss's work on myth to Schneider's on kinship.

Lévi-Strauss himself used the occasion of the emergence of the English translation of *Elementary Structures* to publicly and strongly deny Needham's assimilation of prescriptive/preferential to elementary/complex. Since he did so in his preface to an edition for the theoretical accuracy of the translation of which he had just taken special responsibility, Needham understandably felt somewhat chagrined. Needham has since disassociated himself from structuralism, while Ardener (3, p. 455) has maintained that if Needham's interpretation was indeed an emendation (instead of merely a clarification), it was one that Lévi-Strauss would have been well advised to accept (cf 80, p. 4). Others have professed confusion, complaining that Lévi-Strauss's disavowal of Needham leaves everything as confused as it was before Needham entered on the scene.

Korn (68) shows convincingly that Lévi-Strauss does indeed have many of his facts wrong, that the various criteria he adduces for the linkage of systems to societies are often inconsistent with one another, and that statements he makes about theoretical entities contradict one another. That is, Korn does for *Elementary Structures* what others (133) have done for an example of Lévi-Strauss's myth analysis; she has shown that, taken literally, Lévi-Strauss's analyses are ill defined, self-contradictory, and empirically sloppy (cf 104). What she has not done is show what the conception was that accounted for the almost revolutionary impact of Lévi-Strauss's work on kinship.

It seems possible that Lévi-Strauss, in writing *Elementary Structures,* might not have been altogether specific in his own mind about what he meant by prescriptive or preferential, nor about the sense in which some particular society was to be considered to have an elementary structure or a complex one. But as the arguments developed, he may have become aware of the pitfalls of one or another interpretation. He did know that he meant his work to speak to the development of society generally, and not just to details involving a few unusual societies (94, p. xxxi). Having read Lounsbury's review of Needham (94, p. xxxii) and understood the weaknesses of Needham's interpretation, he may have decided that he must have meant something else. If his attention to the issue of just what he did mean was late in coming, the genesis of what he decided to claim he meant was already clear in other works of his that date from the same general period as *Elementary Structures* (89, pp. 229–287, 298, 311–12).

In spite of claims to the contrary, the new preface to *Elementary Structures* does make the issue clear enough. In talking about elementary or complex structures in terms of marriage rules, Lévi-Strauss is not referring to the actual pattern one observes of actual marriages (94, p. xxxii; cf 45, p. 453); he is aware that by this distinction demographic factors would preclude the existence of societies with elementary structures (94, p. xxx). He also is not referring to the explicit rules which natives espouse (94, pp. xxxii–xxxiii), an interpretation which would lead naturally to Needham's distinction between preference and prescription. Basically he is talking about the effects of different kinds of marriage rules on models of societies with different kinds of descent groups. His analysis is of these models, not of the actual social facts of the societies that they represent. The models are simplified axiomatic systems and the relations that he is most concerned with are logical deductions from these axioms. [Caws (21) provides a nice discussion of the issues involved in various kinds of models.] He goes on to maintain, though, that to the degree that any particular society embraces these axioms the consequences of the axioms to that degree apply to that society (94, pp. xxxiii–xxxv). Different societies can take these axioms into account in different ways. Some will have explicit rules that embody the axioms and will thus have some kind of conceptual dependency on the deduced relations (94, pp. xxxii–xxxiv) even if they don't clearly or unambiguously follow the rules. Others will more or less inadvertantly tend to marry in patterns that to some degree match one of the models; to this degree they will reap the predicted structural effects. In other words, Lévi-Strauss's kinship models can be implemented either mechanically or statistically, either conceptually or behaviorally, and either prescriptively or preferentially, but his models are not defined as or bound up in any of these particular implementations. For him the distinction between prescription and preference has to do with the natives' degree of self-consciousness concerning their following of the model.

Social anthropology has been bedeviled by an inability to conceive of a theory as anything but a one-to-one relationship between theory and a body of data. For social anthropology a theory could only be valid if it had been directly induced from a given body of data, and if one could totally deduce that data from it. This is precisely the kind of behaviorist notion for which Chomsky (22, pp. 49–60) has so soundly castigated Bloomfieldian linguistics. Like the Bloomfieldians, the classic Radcliffe-Brownians (e.g. Fortes) tried to induce their theories from behavioral data. Needham, in rebellion against the Radcliffe-Brownian orthodoxy, turned from such data to native rules and normative statements. But Needham treats these rules and normative statements in the same manner that Fortes treated behavioral data; he tries to induce his theoretical statements about some group directly from their rules and norms, and he still sees his theory as being in a one-to-one relationship with his natives' "behavior"—only he substitutes conceptual behavior for observed actions [cf Friedman's (45, p. 452) characterization of Needham and Maybury-Lewis as "empiricist" even if "mentalist," and Bloch's (12, p. 363) contrast of Lévi-Strauss's concern with underlying structure with Maybury-Lewis's more empiricist concerns].

Lévi-Strauss, if sloppy and careless [to a degree, even by his own admission (94, p. xxvii)], and if too quick to push a strained metaphor too far (cf references to puzzles and cams, tale elements on cards, binary oppositions, linguistics and whatnot), does understand that a theory, to be useful, should go beyond accounting for the facts at hand (though it should indeed account for them); it should go on to generate a wide range of additional propositions which may themselves be empirically evaluated. The attraction that his work on kinship holds for so many anthropologists seems not to lie in the particular ethnographic cases which he may or may not have explicated. The attraction seems rather to lie in the very rich set of formal implications that he was able to demonstrate (or claimed to be able to demonstrate) for a set of abstract kinship patterns which he had distilled from a variety of specific cases and models that anthropologists had already been discussing. His theories represent conceptions and understandings that to some degree at least he brought to the data rather than abstracted from it; his fame rests not on the sociological or ethnological accuracy of his theories but on his demonstration of the kind of powerful and general theories that one might look for and that might eventually be brought to bear on ethnographic data. He reintroduced the kind of theoretical scope that had been lost since Morgan in the descriptive particularism of the Radcliffe-Brownians, in the linguistic particularism of much American work on kinship, and in the statistical induction of Murdock—even if actual *empirical* assertions are hard to come by in his work.

Having briefly looked at the kinship problem, we might now consider what it is about Lévi-Strauss's work on kinship that is structuralist or Saussurean.

He *is* dealing with formal concepts and relations rather than with actual substantive units and marriages—that is, with an abstracted pattern rather than with any simple summation of what people in any particular culture do or say. This is the aspect of his work which seems most successfully to have eluded Needham's and Korn's attention (at least as an overt aim as opposed to an inadvertent by-product of sloppy work). He *is* talking about formal structures.

Like structural linguists, Lévi-Strauss has abstracted out frozen and complete synchronic states from the inconsistencies and flux that occur in any actual system as a result of normal and constant diachronic change. He provides a formal analysis of the attributes of such synchronic states that allows a consideration of which states are possible immediate precursors or followers of which others.

However, his work on kinship contrasts with the Saussurean model in other ways. He is concerned with *evolutionary* relations among states— which is perhaps a reasonable object of investigation for the study of social structure, but which in linguistics proved to be a distraction of which structuralists found they had to rid themselves. This concern of Lévi-Strauss with primitive systems and basic oppositions is, of course, highly reminiscent of Jakobson's work on the emergence of phonemic contrasts.

Lévi-Strauss especially contrasts here with Saussure, as well as with his own later work on mythology, in his concern with logical (or mathematical) structures or systems as opposed to mental ones. His kinship structures, unlike Saussure's *langue* or Lévi-Strauss's own mythemes, are not mental representations, collective or otherwise. Whether this concern with logical (vs mental) structures was the result of his brush with cybernetics, or of some misunderstanding of the linguistic enterprise, or simply of some intuitive sense of where the significant problems lay, it contrasted sharply with his overt role-models in structural linguistics as well as (in an identical manner) with his French forebears in the *Année sociologique.*

A final red herring: Lévi-Strauss's attempt to assimilate the exchange of women to the exchange of words—as another kind of "communication"— was an ill-considered overextension of a bad metaphor at best. The metaphor (or analogy) represented a first, too literal stab at generalizing the linguistic mode. Communication is between people and relies on mental structures (at least in the sense he means); his disembodied logical structures do not communicate and do not constitute any kind of a cultural sign system. Lévi-Strauss's work on kinship really, if unsurprisingly, owes more to Durkheim's and Mauss's discussion of the role of exchange in producing solidarity than to any other obvious outside source (cf 2, p. liv; 45, p. 452).

Myth

As we have already said, Lévi-Strauss's work on folklore/mythology is quite different from his work on kinship (cf 16). He does deal here with mental structures that permit communication; he does here utilize a very Saussurean conception of the problems and of the goal of analysis—perhaps more so than he realizes.

There appear to be two central concerns that characterize structuralist anthropology—at least as represented by structuralist analyses of myth: (*a*) there is a concern with the nature of the shared understandings in a culture that constitute the "codes" by means of which particular cultural messages are constructed; and (*b*) there is a concern with the intellectual process by which contradictions (or deep problems) within systems of cultural values or norms are transformed, via these cultural codes, into more tractable forms that allow the contradictions to be encompassed and/or the problems to be resolved.

The first characteristic is exhibited in Lévi-Strauss's analysis of the Asdiwal tale when he considers that the presence in the tale of "a single rotten hawberry" represents the minimal presence of vegetable food vs the "maximal" absence of animal food from the sea and animal food from the land (87, pp. 36–39; cf 133, p. 165). In the Saussurean paradigm, and by and large in its Praguean offshoot, signs only acquire value through the combination of their syntagmatic associations with their paradigmatic contrasts. In any given syntagmatic situation a particular item represents a choice among sets of alternatives, and the presence of one item implies the absence of these contrasting alternatives. An "item" can be a unit of any level of the linguistic hierarchy, a word, phrase, clause, sentence, thematic element, setting, and so forth. The meaning of an assertion, such as that in the Asdiwal tale, hinges on the attributes by which the given item differs from those over which it was chosen. The attributes are identified by contrasting the given element with what else it might have been, and by considering what elements out of that set normally would be expected to go into that syntagmatic slot.

So Lévi-Strauss asserts that the hawberry is an example of vegetable food. As such it contrasts with animal food, which in this context is not an undifferentiated class, but instead is composed of two major subclasses: animal food from the sea and animal food from the land. The typical kind of animal food from the sea is fish and the typical kind of animal food from the land is meat. Since the tale is concerned with social relations among humans, the assertions made in the tale about food must concern social relations among the people who provide these various kinds of food; and so we have women (the providers of vegetable food) in their own place, isolated both from the men who provide fish and from the men who provide meat.

The connections outlined above are not implausible; it would be strange to have the hawberry specifically mentioned in the tale unless its presence was meant to convey something (cf 127)—and so we do need to know what its presence might bring to mind to a Tshimshian. However, the answer to that question is not as obvious as Lévi-Strauss would have it. How do we know that the berry referred to a food type instead of, say, a meal part— why could it not, even within Lévi-Strauss's framework, be dessert vs a main course (implying in the tale that the women have the luxury of independence from their men, but only at the price of foregoing the basic support provided by those men), or why could it not be one particular kind of berry vs some other [implying association with some particular commu- nity—in the manner of *Pensee sauvage* (92)], or one particular class of vegetable food vs another (say, fruit vs starchy staple, signifying relations of relative importance among social groups). Even if one takes the hawberry as exemplifying vegetable food itself, one then wonders why animal food does not constitute a similarly undifferentiated class (perhaps implying men vs women), why "animal food from the sea" does not refer to sea lions (implying meat, hunters and so forth), why "animal food from the land" does not refer to fish caught in spawning season in streams (implying different categories of people in a different set of relations from those considered in Lévi-Strauss's interpretation), and so forth. The problem, then, does not lie in Lévi-Strauss's intention, but rather in the methods by which that intention is realized.

This treament of structuralism as being about the systems of under- standings or "codes" which enable cultural communication to take place also characterizes structuralist French literary critic Roland Barthes' most anthropological work, *Mythologies* (7). Barthes' stress on history in that work represents a concern with the experiences which produce the (passive —cf Saussure) understandings that constitute the codes. In terms of the communicative import of cultural forms and objects, it is not, to Barthes, their current functions which are important, but rather the functions that they have had in the (experiential—and hence relatively recent) past and that have defined the understandings and expectations of their current users.

Barthes emphasizes the social motivation of the cultural signs that he analyzes as if he were contradicting Saussure's claims concerning the arbi- trariness of the sign (7, p. 126). He fails to appreciate that Saussure referred only to the lack of any natural relationship between the substance of the *signifier* and the substance of the *signified;* social motivation, formed by the facts of history but acting at any given moment as a timeless system, was precisely what Saussure (and Durkheim) felt to be the very basis of language. Barthes' position is perfectly consistent with Saussure's. We are not worrying about the fact that the Saussurean paradigm does allow for "motivated" signs—ie. symbols—since the signs that Barthes treats are genuine ("unmotivated" in Saussure's sense). Barthes' avowed concern with speech (vs language) does not represent the inversion of Saussure that he claims; rather, we should see him (and other structuralists) as exploring the other, nonlinguistic, codes that along with language itself are brought to bear in any specific speech act. Let us set aside Barthes' analysis of his own analysis —which errs in other ways as well as in those we have mentioned (cf 2, p. xi)—and attend to what it is that makes his work of interest to anthropologists.

Barthes is interested in the cultural information transmitted by the use of certain kinds of items or materials; his various "neologisms" represent the cultural codes which enable the transmission. Thus, to use an example closer to home, if a friend suggests going out for a "hamburger," the friend is not simply saying "let's go eat." The friend is picking a certain kind of food, "fast food" vs other possibilities, e.g. haute cuisine, family restaurant, foreign restaurant, food at home, etc. The kind of food does not just entail a style of cooking, but has other direct entailments including speed, cost, and so forth. A style such as "fast food" additionally has another more general set of associations; these associations include a social class, a lack of aesthetic culinary discriminations, and a lack of individuality (of the meal and of its consumer). That last set of associations brings to mind a class of machine-like proletarians who have been tricked into preferring the cheap, fast glop that it is most efficient to feed them; such socio-political implications of the choice of one set of products over another explain why Barthes sees such products as political statements (and, as a Marxist, condemns most of these political statements).

The implications of the choice of one code over another need not be political, but Barthes has made an important contribution by emphasizing how such choices among alternative codes (whether in life itself or in stories about life, including myths) do transmit information. In a folktale, for instance, it is not just the message implied by the sequence of events that has meaning; the choice of which categories of objects and events to include itself conveys information. This kind of information seems to be the basis (even if only implicitly) for structuralist discussions of meaning within some work where the discussions ignore story line, plot, and the detail of particular story elements. Besides the paradigmatic relations of items to one another within a code, Barthes has shown us that the codes themselves exist in a paradigmatic relationship to one another.

Barthes does not consider the significance of one message vs another within a given code. That is, he does not consider what meaning is conveyed by the choice of a hamburger instead of a hot dog, or of onion rings instead of fries. Lévi-Strauss similarly ignores such messages in his Oedipus analysis, but does seem to be attending to them implicitly in his Asdiwal one.

An understanding of the paradigmatic meaning implied by the choice of one code over another allows us to see what kind of meaning Lévi-Strauss has in mind in his analysis of the Oedipus tale, and to see how he could talk of a structuralist analysis of folktales while ignoring all the advances in the analysis of syntagmatic structures produced by modern linguistics and by linguistically derived work in folklore such as that of Propp.

In stating that "it is in the last resort immaterial whether in this book the thought processes of the South American Indians take shape through the medium of my thought, or whether mine take place through the medium of theirs" (93, p. 13), Lévi-Strauss appears to be asserting that many codes can lie behind any one message, and that any code which one human mind can find in a message is there for any other human mind to find (cf 91, p. 59). This seems to be a reasonable claim. In kinship studies where a claim such as this has been rigorously explored, it does appear that the search for a single "psychologically real" analysis has been misguided. It appears that any reasonably parsimonious analysis of any part of English kinship terminology that any anthropologist has been able to come up with will actually be used at one time or another by any native speaker of English (48). In other words, any *conceivable* analysis is a true one—at least within some broad limits. If this is true, then the analyst of a native folktale deals with whichever codes she or he finds most approachable.

Lévi-Strauss has not himself done any intensive fieldwork anywhere, and knows no particular culture really well (cf 80, p. 12), but he has an extensive familiarity with a large set of similar texts from a great variety and span of cultures. Consequently, it is natural enough for him to turn to reasonably universal codes in his explications. He necessarily analyzes the universal codes that all humans understand because these are the only ones to which he has access.

On the other hand, French anthropologists of his students' generation are going out into the field and conducting intensive field studies [(e.g. 27, 31, 84, 99, 113, 131); but see also the Panoffs' discussion (112) of the problems of doing fieldwork within the French academic framework]. They lack his encyclopedic knowledge of the forms that various tales take in different cultures, and so they cannot duplicate his analyses. However, they make up for this lack with their intensive knowledge of their field cultures, and so they tend to come up with particular codes that inhere more particularistically in their specific cultures.

In structural analysis, the primary sense in which every version of a tale is equivalent to every other (cf 89, pp. 216–17) might seem to be that which depends on native judgments of whether two stories are or are not the "same" story. The same/different test is the classical device in structural linguistics for separating out the regularities of *langue* from the incidental details of any particular act of *parole*. Even in linguistics such a device requires a fair understanding by one's informants of what one is after—and thus of the various linguistic levels at which the question of "same or different" could be answered. In folklore the question becomes even harder because there are many more senses in which "it" may or may not be the "same story," as the variety of forms that Lévi-Strauss provides in *Mythologiques* (93, 95, 97, 98) makes clear. One may have the same incident with different characters; an incident in one tale may in another become the whole tale; the major story outline may be the same while all the details are changed; and so forth. And remember the linguistic test depends on having an informant at hand who has a "native" command of all of the items being compared. In Lévi-Strauss's Oedipus analysis, the variants involved span in excess of 2000 years; he himself *is* a "native informant"—but only for the latest synchronic state. To a "native" now, all versions look to be the same, but who knows how these variants would have seemed to Sophocles. The fact that all versions are (*now*) called "the Oedipus tale" makes Lévi-Strauss's judgment seem less subjective, but no less specific in its temporal perspective. The complete set of versions only constitutes a single synchronic system now, at the end of the diachronic chain, and yet the meat of Lévi-Strauss's analysis (the concepts and meanings he uses) belongs to the beginning of the chain. The problem that temporally vitiates his Oedipus analysis has the same effect spatially on his *Mythologiques;* the tales are more or less contemporaneous but collectively belong to no single "native." There exists no one who has the privileged position from which to call them all "the same"; the linguistic analogy—the analytic basis for separating the invariants of *langue* (or code) from the ephemera of *parole* (or message) —has broken down. What we, or Lévi-Strauss, are left with are the myriad ways in which tales resemble one another—and the problem that Tale A may resemble B in one respect but not in some other respect, wherein instead it resembles C. Two tales which are each separately "similar" to some third tale may not be similar to each other in any *direct* sense; *indirect* bases of similarity (based on the separate knowledge of the two direct similarities) represent no synchronic *system,* but instead depend on the accidents of one's previous personal experience of particular tales. He can't be using "communicative content" as his basis for such similarity judgments because such content is the very goal of his analysis.

And so one must conclude that in his analyses of folk tales Lévi-Strauss is dealing with the codes from which the tales are constituted rather than the messages which the tales represent. He cannot be dealing with the totality of codes implicit in the tales, but only with selected universal ones, and these codes must be directly inferable from the specific message elements that we (and he) attend to when we recognize some particular text as a version of some particular story (say, the Oedipus tale). These facts allow us finally to understand his claim that every version of the tale is equivalent to every other one (cf 95, pp. 565, 567) and his feeling that he need not worry about different meanings of different texts (even different texts produced in different cultures). The claim refers only to the codes, and not to messages expressed in the codes; the claim does not refer to all the codes entailed by the texts, but only to the consistently present codes that he chooses to attend to. In this sense the claim is a reasonable one, and fairly hard to argue with; it is also a bit less impressive than it first sounds.

In a typical analysis, Lévi-Strauss identifies a code and then identifies the focal concern of the tale with the implicit meaning which underlies that code. If we accept his implicit claim that any code which within reason an analyst can find is there for natives as well, then we have to recognize that much of the criticism of Lévi-Strauss's analyses of folk tales (including our own) has been slightly off the mark. The typical criticism amounts to asking how we know that the indicated codes are indeed entailed by the tale. However, if all possible codes are automatically present, then that becomes a meaningless question. Even if a great many codes can be used in a given tale and entailed by it, and even if each code can refer back to any of several underlying implicit meanings, it does not seem obvious that all of those meanings can at the same time be the central or focal concern of the tale —the "what it is about" (cf 93, p. 347). The question that critics should be asking instead of "How do we know that this code is truly entailed by the tale?" is "How do we know that this particular underlying meaning (represented by this particular code) is one that is at *issue* in this tale?" (cf 28, p. 53) This is the question that Codère (26) so charmingly—if also so devastatingly—raises; this proper question concerns the focus (or foci) of the tale, not its contents.

No criteria are anywhere discussed for making this determination. Discussions of tale topics concern the way the tale handles supposedly focal problems, not how these are identified.

Our second central characteristic of structural anthropology is the dialectical process by which deep problems with, or contradictions within, systems of cultural values or norms are supposedly transformed into more tractable forms that allow the contradictions to be encompassed or the problems to be solved (89, p. 240). This process is built on the focal codes which we have just been discussing. It consists of taking the relatively abstract contrasts entailed by the initial code in which the problem is stated, finding other codes which entail similar contrasts, transforming the problem statement into whichever of these other codes allows the problem to be simplified and encompassed, and then solving (or dealing with) this transformed version of the problem. It is the abstract entailed contrasts, which one keeps constant throughout the process, that represent the structure which is preserved under the transformations, and that ensure that the solution to the final (transformed) version of the problem is felt or seen to refer to the initial version. This is the process by which, according to Lévi-Strauss, the Oedipus tale deals with the contradiction between one ancestry and two parents, and by which the Asdiwal tale deals with the inability of a new couple to live at once with both the bride's parents and the groom's parents.

In the insoluble problems which Lévi-Strauss considers, the goal of analysis is not to explain how natives solve their problems, but rather to explain how they encompass them and make them manageable (cf 80, p. 71, 95). The process is one of successive narrowings, in which a basic opposition is transformed into an equivalent opposition between two elements that are both on one side of the original opposition. The antinomy between the two remains, but is now brought within a common framework; in the transformation, other attributes that might have been central to the original opposition can be lost, and such loss becomes a device for asserting the inessentiality of those attributes for the original opposition. In a sense the transformation becomes a way of asserting that the opposed elements are really the same, but the assertion can never be allowed to stand because then the story would cease to speak to the insolubility of the original opposition. And so the opposition reemerges—if in a reduced form—and the transformation/reduction process then may be recursively applied to the new reduced opposition.

One might take a literary example [adapted from (69), cf (70)] which has the advantage of involving both cultural and historical material that is much better known and understood than is the case with most anthropological examples. Several of Leach's examples of a different kind of analysis (e.g. 74, 75, 77, 82) seem to have been selected for similar reasons. Pastoral literature of the English Renaissance is concerned, in part, with the opposition between nobles and peasants. The nobility and would-be nobility (the endowers of the literature) appreciate the benefits of being rich (including both power and poetry) but espouse a moral code that emphasizes the virtues (and heavenly rewards) of poverty. Their problem is to reap the virtues of being both rich and poor at the same time. Their solution is to transform the insoluble opposition between rich and poor into a less extreme one between kinds of poor by seeking an analogy for themselves within the third estate; they pick the poor side of the original opposition because that is where virtue lies. They pick the shepherd as their analog because of his classical associations with poetry and the other arts and because of his Christian associations with meekness and the acceptance of God's bounty (vs the grubbing and instrumental nature of ploughmen). The nobility shows that they, represented by shepherds, are just like peasants, represented by farmers, but for a slight difference in occupation. However, the position of the nobility depends on the *intrinsic* differences between those fit to rule and those not, and so even as nobles merge themselves into the third estate they must reassert their distinctions lest they lose the rationale for their position. And so, within the third estate, shepherds are distinguished from ploughmen by their courtly skills and protective prowess; the opposition remains, if on a smaller scale. Within the realm of shepherds the contrast sometimes again is transformed—into a contrast between noble shepherds who play panpipes and write of love and cloddish working shepherds who talk funny and smell of sheep. The successive transformations allow the opposition to be reduced from a global one between estates to a very local one between kinds of shepherds; however, the initial distinction continues to exist because of the intrinsic contradictions within the aims of the nobility, whose literature this is.

The process of successive narrowing of oppositions shown in Lévi-Strauss's work is somewhat reminiscent of the dialectical process described by Hegel (and Marx)—thesis, antithesis, and synthesis (cf 80, pp. 6–7). However, there are differences. In Lévi-Strauss the opposed elements seem coevally present; there is no evidence that the one develops as a reaction to (or outgrowth of) the other. In Lévi-Strauss the movement in the process is illusory: no synthesis is ever reached and nothing intrinsic is ever changed; there is only an increasingly restricted restatement of the problem. In short, Lévi-Strauss provides us with a way of thinking about cultural problems; he does not (in his myth analysis) provide any model for how cultural forms change (a la Marx) nor for how the ideas that shape our comprehension of the physical world might change. His concern is with the sign systems by which thought is expressed and with the ways in which these are used (93, pp. 13, 14); as such his work clearly belongs in Saussure's universe rather than in Marx's—however strange an inhabitant of that universe it may occasionally seem.

As was the case with the codes themselves, these structuralist claims about mythological handling of problems do not strike us as inherently implausible, even if they do seem somewhat less inevitable than do the claims about the codes. But again there remains the problem of passing from plausibility to probability or certainty. Given that in the kind of code system that we are dealing with, one tale may exemplify at the same time a large number of codes, it seems unlikely that every underlying contrast of every relevant code represents a basic problem with which people in the culture at hand are trying to wrestle. But unless such is the case, we need some criteria for deciding which codes pertain to basic problems and which do not; and we need some criteria for deciding which of the several deep contrasts entailed by any particular code are relevant and which are not. Such criteria (or procedures) are precisely what Lévi-Strauss does not give us. This problem is central, not just for structuralist analysis, but for symbolic anthropology as well—where, instead of providing criteria (or procedures) for recognizing the concerns that are inherent in some particular system or work, many practitioners have come up with a universal set of symbols and concerns that they impose on whatever work they consider. The aims and general assumptions of the structuralists seem to us to be reasonable and preferable to those of other symbolic schools; what is needed are the methods and standards which will enable these aims and assumptions to be validly implemented in actual analyses.

A paradox seems to confront many readers of Lévi-Strauss's myth analyses: on the one hand they find the texture of the analyses very convincing and very satisfying, but on the other hand they find that his oft asserted method remains forever out of reach and that many of his particular deductive claims seem either weak or nonexistent (cf 80, p. 13; 104). His theory is often considered brilliant while his control of the ethnographic materials required to evaluate it is found wanting.

This little piece of academic mythology seems to have things backwards. Lévi-Strauss is thoroughly familiar with the mythology and folklore, the published ethnography, and the pre-Western ecology of New World cultures (even if he is often careless and selective in his use of this material). What he lacks is any *theory* about how particular myths operate or what they accomplish. We are aware that this claim flies in the face of most Lévi-Strauss criticism, and that it apparently contradicts the explication of his theory that we have just provided, but consider the following arguments.

We first distinguish among three analytic levels: (meta-) theories about mythology (including what it does, how it works, and so forth); theories about the operations of particular bodies of folk or mythic material; and characterizations of the patterns of similarity and interrelatedness that one finds in some particular body of folk or mythic material. Lévi-Strauss's introduction to *The Raw and the Cooked,* his concluding chapters to *L'Homme nu,* and various articles constitute the first kind of metatheory; it is this theory about theories of myth which strikes us as eminently reasonable. It is this metatheory which we have just attempted to explicate and show the usefulness of. Even so, we have complained about his execution, by which we refer not to his grasp of the facts but to the particular theories which he claims account for the specific body of ethnographic material he is treating. This actual, concrete theory is missing in his work. He constantly talks as if he has such a theory, speaking of formal analysis

(93, p. 108), of isomorphisms (pp. 97–98), of transformations (pp. 2, 108, 118), of inversions, of demonstrations (p. 105), of proof (p. 138), and so forth, but he never lays out any set of formal concepts or propositions from which anything could actually be deduced. When he goes through the set of items that are supposed to make up a deductive argument (e.g. 93, pp. 96, 101, 105, 108), the specific connections or logic are never explained; the actual structure of his arguments is really one of free association rather than of logical deduction or inference. He does not explain what a transformation is (93, p. 108, 118; 95, p. 449)—i.e. how we might recognize one that he had not shown us. Nor does he tell us what it accomplishes—are the items thus related to be considered equivalent to each other (in general, in some particular context, or in conjunction with some other pair, and to what end) or are they supposed to perform similar functions in contrasting situations.

At the third analytic level, which amounts simply to some kind of ordered recapitulation of the data itself, his work is, as is his metatheoretic discussion, quite good. But here, we would like to suggest, the basis for his success lies not in his theories, nor even in his analytic ability, but instead in the very nature of such a large and dense body of regional mythic material as he has chosen to examine. The connections that he makes among the various tales are indeed in the tales themselves, as is the complexity, heterogeneity, and convolutedness exhibited by the set of connections taken together; the richness of the connections that he makes is thus further impressive testimony in favor of the breadth and intensity of his control of the relevant data. Tales in such a group constantly echo one another in a great variety of ways, but never consistently over a large set; the tales contain ethnographic and ecological minutiae which continually tempt one to try to tie them to particular cultures and places, and yet at the same time a single tale will be collected over a span of 1000 miles, 100 years, and several levels of technological development. The analytic problem is not to find connections among such tales; the problem is to find some basis for throwing out most of the connections that suggest themselves, and for thereby identifying some single (small) set of interrelated connections on which to focus one's initial analysis. Lévi-Strauss has found threads which allow him to organize and present the tales in a kind of intuitively sensible manner; he has allowed us to see at least some of the patterns which inhere in the set of tales, but he has not to any great degree analyzed for us the variables or attributes which produce those patterns, and he has not in any sense produced specific theories from which those patterns can be deduced.

The usual characterization of Lévi-Strauss's work is doubly inverted, for not only does Lévi-Strauss's work possess the inverse of those attributes which are claimed for it, but the implicit contrast to Lévi-Strauss's work —that of anthropologists such as Leach—tends also to possess the inverse of those attributes which are implicitly ascribed to it. That is, even though Leach's own structuralist analyses (74–77; 80, pp. 16–20) tend to include relatively clear and reasonable theories, they often are found, upon careful examination, to be based on faulty data and incorrect facts (cf 19, 46, 55, 111). For the earliest of these critiques, that of Pamment, Leach has with some justice rejoined that aspects of his argument were misrepresented (78); however, one must also note that many of Pamment's criticisms were left unchallenged. Leach appears not yet to have had the time to respond to the later critiques, but we also suspect that he will have trouble doing so.

Leach himself notes Lévi-Strauss's reservations concerning his Genesis analysis (71, p. 251), and refers to two reasons: "deformation" by biblical editors who imposed their own interpretative schemas on the raw folk material, and a lack of adequate ethnographic context. Leach makes light of both problems, but misconstrues their force. Lévi-Strauss's approach depends on having multiple examples of the same tales in hand in order to sift out the underlying constant elements of the "code" from the ephemera of each particular telling. The problem is not, as Leach would have it, whether the unconscious structures will be expressed, but rather with the analyst's ability to identify them. A single work by a single author allows no such sifting. Even if one manages to find repeated elements, they are still part of the same single telling. Similarly, it is not *ethnographic* context which is at issue (in which case Leach's reference to the sketchy nature of our knowledge of Tsimshian and Bororo culture would represent a telling riposte to Lévi-Strauss), but the comparative context provided by other versions of the same tale; again, the context is needed to allow the necessary sifting. We find Leach's analyses stimulating, insightful, and thought-provoking; in many respects we prefer them to those of Lévi-Strauss—our point is only that they are indeed only imperfect examples of the Lévi-Straussean method.

Leach's method contrasts in other ways with that of Lévi-Strauss. He, like most of the rest of us, endeavors to examine in a very careful way a small and finite body of material (cf 82)—while Lévi-Strauss has chosen in a thorough, but less systematic, manner to encounter a very large and open body of material. The characteristic strengths and weaknesses of the work of each seem to derive in part from these basic choices; not only is it a question of how much care one can afford to take with each connection (which concern, taken alone, would make Leach's work preferable), but it is also a question of how likely one's analysis is to actually meet and take account of all the ethnographic difficulties which might be raised in criticism of it. Perhaps Lévi-Strauss is right when in one of his more revealing moments he admits that it is still too soon for us to have a true science of mythology (cf 93, p. 31; 95, pp. 567–70). A continuation of such candor would have contributed greatly to the development of such a science, for it would have caused him to eschew the technical jargon which he uses constantly to connote the explicitness of theory, precision of statement, and logic of deduction which form the basis of science even while these particular characteristics are in fact absent from his work. The strength of his work lies in the richness and breadth of his encounter with mythic material, it does not lie in a formal rigor that he only aspires to.

There are two further specific problems that trouble us in Lévi-Strauss's analytic discussions. In *Mythologiques* his analysis consists of finding "transformational" relations ("inversions", "isomorphisms", etc) that first place individual tales into "transformational groups" and that in turn place these groups in higher level groups. His analytic goals seem to be to show that all possible variants occur and that superficially disparate tales are in fact ultimately the same tale. The point behind such demonstrations is unclear. If the ultimate aim is to demonstrate historical contact (cf 95, p. 319), then he is certainly going about it the long way around. If the aim is to show how a specific tale is adapted to particular social, political, or environmental conditions [cf (95) p. 319, where he speaks in terms reminiscent of the *Annales* school of history], then the volumes are a failure since their lack of any systematic presentation of the relevant social, political, or environmental conditions makes it impossible for the reader to see any such patterns of adaptation. The mere fact of some sort of "ecological" relation seems hardly worth any demonstration at all since that is the traditional null assumption of anthropology; the *lack* of any sort of "ecological" relationship would be quite worthy of demonstration—but no such demonstration is made and none is intended. If the aim is to show that the human mind will, given enough time and scope, work out and produce all the various combinatorial possibilities that some particular corpus of materials enable, then the demonstration, again, is a failure. Such a demonstration would require some clear definition of the various elements which are to be combined and of the putative rules of combination; the demonstration would then require some kind of systematic comparison of the actual corpus of tales with such a deduced set of possibilities—neither the systematic definitions nor the systematic comparisons are in fact provided.

In *Mythologiques* he has found it necessary to abridge many of the tales and to only minimally characterize the contents of others (cf 93, p. 6; 95, p. 565). Such truncations and restatements of the basic data, however necessitated by the economic constraints of publication, do raise questions in the reader's mind concerning the degree to which he may have tailored his presentation of the basic data to accord with his analytic aims (133). The problem would have been considerably eased if he had used traditional literary devices for distinguishing summary statements from literal quotes and for indicating omissions of text and so forth.

At a number of points Lévi-Strauss writes as if there is some kind of intrinsic order or progression to the events that he is considering (e.g. 93, p. 99; 95, p. 407). Thus, he finds "rules that enable us to transform a given scene into a different one ... " and claims "This procedure would be decisively confirmed if it were possible to repeat the process, but in the opposite direction ... " (93, p. 99). If his analysis is correct, then all the relations that he finds in any tale from the series are equally present in all of them—even if in some cases in forms less apprehendable than in others (cf 2, 3, 93). The "direction" of his transformational movement, then, has only to do with his voyage of discovery, and has no significance as a developmental sequence within the body of tales themselves: if the connections he speaks of are present in the tales at all, then they are there synchronically and should be as traceable from one starting point as another. On the other hand, if the connections do *not* inhere in the tales but are only his analytic creation, then his reverse voyage would again prove nothing— since what he created in one direction he could as easily create in the other.

Lévi-Strauss claims that he is doing science [even if there is confusion on this issue (cf 117, 125, 132, 138)] and that the proof is that his theory is capable of predicting as yet undiscovered phenomena—much in the manner in which astronomers predicted the existence of the planet Neptune (95, p. 504). Astronomers, however, had precisely observed phenomena and precise theories which allowed them to make explicit logical deductions from those phenomena. Lévi-Strauss gives us neither the precise aspect of his phenomena nor the logic by which the deduction is to be made. In place of a deductive chain he lists a chain of free associations that link his phenomenon with what he claims to have deduced. He then asserts the deduction and goes on to say, "ethnography confirms this *a priori* demand of formal analysis" (101, p. 108). He then describes some perfectly reasonable textual evidence from a new tale—which he claims to have predicted (93, p. 108). One cannot help thinking that he knew the new tale was there *before* he made his deductions, and that his "deductions" were contrived to predict a known outcome. He admits (93, pp. 1–4) that he knew how the book was going to come out when he wrote it, but claims that it does in fact recreate his actual voyage of discovery "as far as [is] possible" (93, p. 2). His proof then is no proof because he provides no deductive apparatus and only "predicts" the existence of *known* Neptunes.

This same reservation applies more generally to the decisive confirmation of his theories which he speaks of at the end of *L'Homme nu*. He has found on the Northwest Coast the explanation of problems in his initial Bororo myth and has shown the unity of these two traditions. He begins his "journey" with the Bororo myth, and in the first volume can only see in his mind the second volume and "the outline of yet a third"—though he can foresee that his journey will lead "to the furthermost regions of North America" (93, pp. 1–3). He writes as if we are with him on the trip, and as if he himself does not know what is coming next until his method reveals it to him. But in fact we know that he is traversing familiar territory—even if with new concerns in mind—and in a familiar order. We know that in 1934–1939 he was in Brazil and encountered the Bororo among others. His accounts (89, 91) suggest a primary concern then with their social organization, their physical culture, and their art. His interest in structural linguistics (cf 85) and in mythology/folklore seems to date from the early 1940s when in New York he encountered Jakobson and joined Jakobson in conversations with Boas (96, p. 63). He starts doing his own myth analysis in 1955 with his analysis of the Oedipus story (86), and in 1958 had already begun his consideration of Northwest Coast tales. Thus he was at least somewhat familiar with Northwest Coast tales even before he began examining Brazilian material for his work on social organization, and he had already analyzed a variety of North American tales before he began the "journey" described in *The Raw and the Cooked*. By the time he came to the end of *l'Homme nu* and found familiar mythic structures on the Northwest Coast he can hardly have been surprised by the find, and can hardly have been required to depend on his "method" to lead him to those structures.

CONCLUSION

Our examination of the literature has convinced us that structuralist analysis has been little done in American and British anthropology. Most of what one sees are either works of Lévi-Strauss himself or discussions of his work. The chief virtue of his work has been that he has reopened the study of meaning as a legitimate anthropological aim. The reason why even the most devastating critiques leave his followers unfazed is that it is only the aim that they take from him, along with some very general transformation machinery. Since he has no criteria for success, no actual theory, and no method, attacks on his execution are, to his followers, irrelevant.

Rather than constituting a school in Anglo-American anthropology, structuralism has served as a charter for breaking loose from structural functionalism and for examining symbolic systems without the particularism and detail of ethnoscience or the technological/materialistic emphasis associated with Leslie White and Marvin Harris. In a less direct way it has rejuvenated such theoretical orientations as Kroeberian ethnology, culture and personality, and folklore motif analysis.

Our survey of articles in *L'Homme,* the journal founded and edited by Lévi-Strauss and his colleagues in France, suggests that structuralist anthropology is almost as rare in France as it is in England and America.

Obviously work there is much influenced by Lévi-Strauss; but each piece seems also equally influenced by diverse other interests. The situation suggests that, rather than some particularly structuralist school developing in France, post-Lévi-Straussean French anthropology is part of the same eclectic mainstream that includes the bulk of North American, British, and other European anthropology.

Among recent works that seem fairly structuralist (e.g. 5, 64, 136) it is interesting to note that in many cases the majority of the basic citations are not to British (or American) symbolic anthropology but to American ethnoscience or cognitive anthropology (e.g. Goodenough, Lounsbury, Conklin, Frake, Romney, and Buchler and Selby). We seem almost to have a system of asymmetrical alliance in which Americans look to Britain for their basic sources while the British look to France and the French look to America. The circle becomes something more of a spiral when we realize that the Americans at the beginning of the chain seem rather deeply at war with those at the end. Thus Beidelman, in support of Needham (109), calls Lévi-Strauss's (94) acceptance of some fairly straightforward demonstrations of Lounsbury's (100) "perverse" (8, p. 220) and goes on to refer naively to Lounsbury's "antisociological notions about the linguistic determination of kinship structures". Lounsbury's concern with *how* social facts actually and precisely have their terminological effects is considered in some quarters to be essential to good sociological analysis.

The major beneficiary in the United States of structural anthropology has been the emerging field of symbolic anthropology (cf 135). The reasons for structuralism's role as godparent to symbolic anthropology rather than as parent to its own children seem worthy of some brief consideration. They seem primarily to be that 1. unlike American cognitive anthropology, symbolic anthropology has been concerned with meaning, and not just the forms of meaning; and 2. unlike Lévi-Strauss in his own work, symbolic anthropology does provide criteria for success and a method (cf 30).

In essence, structuralist anthropology proved to be too hard to do. The rules of analysis were presented as linguistically derived and automatic, without any awareness that the rules for linguistic analysis itself are far from automatic, and without specifying analytic procedures for reproducing existing structuralist analysis. Analyses were presented as being true or valid without any criteria being provided for assessing their validity; alternative and contrasting analyses of the same phenomena were asserted to be true at the same time without any theoretical rationale being given for how such alternatives could coexist, even though such a rationale does exist. Structuralist analyses were genuinely concerned with the implications of particular sets of cultural axioms, but they provided no basis for differentiating relevant axioms from irrelevant ones, no methods for finding a culture's axioms, and no basis for making assumptions about such axioms based on universal premises, for according to their linguistic model, such absolute content relations did not exist.

The analytic aim of the structuralists—the explication of the semiotic systems of culture—is reasonable and important, as also is their Saussurean-derived assumption that a priori assumptions about the communicative content of "signifieds" in semiotic systems cannot be made from the substantive nature of their "signifiers." We note with approval their assertion that the description and analysis of such systems lay in the domain of science (cf 96, p. 323) and were not to be simply the products of inspired intuition or intersubjective sensitivity. The problems were that they had no means of identifying the content of symbolic systems nor of demonstrating the validity of assertions about the content of such systems. The illustrative but only metaphoric adoption of the actual linguistic methods [e.g. by Barthes and Levi-Strauss, cf (28) Chap. 2] did not solve the problem, but rather came to be seen as evidence of the failure of any kind of inductive approach to symbolic content. This apparent failure has caused students of symbolic anthropology in the US to turn to a more deductive approach. Our feeling is that would-be students of structural anthropology have given up too easily and too soon.

Literature Cited

1. Ardener, E. 1970. Witchcraft and the continuity of belief. In *Witchcraft: Confessions and Accusations,* ed. M. Douglas. ASA Monogr. 9, pp. 141–60. London: Tavistock. 387 pp.
2. Ardener, E. 1971. Introductory essay. In *Social Anthropology and Language,* ed. E. Ardener. ASA Monogr. 10, pp. ix–cii. London: Tavistock. cii + 318 pp.
3. Ardener, E. 1971. The new anthropology and its critics. *Man* 6:449–67
4. Babcock, C. R. 1976. *Lévi-Strauss: Structuralism and Sociological Theory.* New York: Holmes & Meier. 125 pp.
5. Bare, J. 1974. La Terminologie de parenté sakalover du nord (Madagascar): règles sémantiques, règles sociologiques. *L'Homme* 14:5–42
6. Barnes, J. A. 1971. *Three Styles in the Study of Kinship.* London: Tavistock. 318 pp.
7. Barthes, R. 1972. *Mythologies.* London: Cape. 158 pp.
8. Beidelman, T. O. 1971. Public relations officer of the mind. A review of *Lévi-Strauss* by E. R. Leach. *Anthropos* 66:217–22
9. Benveniste, E. 1971. *Problems in General Linguistics.* Coral Gables, Fla: Univ. Miami Press. 317 pp.
10. Berlin, B., Kay, P. 1969. *Basic Color Terms.* Berkeley: Univ. Calif. Press. 178 pp.
11. Bloch, M., ed. 1975. *Marxist Analyses and Social Anthropology.* ASA Commonw. Stud. No. 2. New York: Wiley (Halstead). 240 pp.
12. Bloch, M. 1975. Review of Lévi-Strauss: Anthropologie Structurale Deux. *Man* 10:323–35
13. Boas, F. 1908. Decorative designs of Alaskan needle cases: A study in the history of conventional designs, based on materials in the U. S. National Museum. *Proc. US Natl. Mus.* 34:321–44. Reprinted in Ref. 14
14. Boas, F. 1940. *Race, Language and Culture.* New York: Free Press. 647 pp.
15. Boon, J. A. 1972. *From Symbolism to Structuralism: Lévi-Strauss in a Literary Tradition.* New York: Harper & Row. 250 pp.
16. Boon, J. A., Schneider, D. M. 1974. Kinship vis-á-vis myth: contrasts in Lévi-Strauss' approaches to cross-cultural comparison. *Am. Anthropol.* 76: 799–817

17. Bourdieu, P. 1977. *Outline of a Theory of Practice*. Cambridge: Cambridge Univ. Press. 248 pp.
18. Bruner, J., Goodnow, J. J., Austin, G. A. 1956. *A Study of Thinking*. New York: Wiley. 330 pp.
19. Carroll, M. P. 1977. Leach, genesis, and structural analysis: a critical evaluation. *Am. Ethnol.* 4:663–77
20. Carroll, M. P. 1978. The savage bind: Lévi-Strauss' myth analysis and anglophone social science. *Pac. Soc. Rev.* 21:467–85
21. Caws, P. 1974. Operational, representational and explanatory models. *Am. Anthropol.* 76:1–10
22. Chomsky, N. 1957. *Syntactic Structures*. The Hague: Mouton. 116 pp.
23. Chomsky, N. 1964. Current issues in linguistic theory. In *The Structure of Language: Readings in Philosophy of Language*, ed. J. Fodor, J. Katz, pp. 50–118. Englewood Cliffs, NJ: Prentice-Hall. 612 pp.
24. Chomsky, N. 1965. *Aspects of the Theory of Syntax*. Cambridge: MIT Press. 251 pp.
25. Chomsky, N. 1968. *Language and Mind*. New York: Harcourt, Brace & World. 88 pp.
26. Codère, H. 1974. La Geste du Chien d' Asdiwal: the story of Mac. *Am. Anthropol.* 76:42–46
27. Coyaud, M. 1977. Fêtes japonaises: un essai d'analyse sémiotique. *L'Homme* 17:91–105
28. Culler, J. 1975. *Structuralist Poetics*. Ithaca: Cornell Univ. Press. 301 pp.
29. Culler, J. 1976. *Ferdinard de Saussure*. New York: Penguin. 140 pp.
30. David, K. 1973. Until marriage do us part: a cultural account of Jaffna Tamil categories for kinsmen. *Man* 8:521–35
31. deHeusch, L. 1972. *Le Roi Ivre ou Origines de l'Etat: Mythes et Rites Bantous*. Paris: Gallimard. 313 pp.
32. de Josselin de Jong, J. P. B. 1952. *Lévi-Strauss' Theory of Kinship and Marriage*. Leiden: Rijksmuseum voor Volkenkunde. Mededelingen #10. 59 pp.
33. de Mauro, T., ed. 1973. *F. de Saussure, Cours de linguistique generale*. Paris: Payot. 510 pp.
34. de Saussure, F. 1959. *Course in General Linguistics*. Transl. W. Baskin. New York: McGraw-Hill. 240 pp.
35. Doroszewski, W. 1933. Quelques remarques sur les rapports de la sociologie et de la linguistique: Durkheim et F. de Saussure. *J. Psychol.* 30:82–91
36. Douglass, M. 1966. *Purity and Danger.*

London: Routledge & Kegan Paul. 188 pp.
37. Douglass, M. 1970. *Natural Symbols*. New York: Vintage. 219 pp.
38. Dumont, L. 1971. *Introduction à deux théories d'anthropologie sociale: groupes de filiation et alliance de marriage* (Les textes sociologiques 6). The Hague: Mouton. 139 pp.
39. Dumont, L. 1975. *Dravidien et Kariera: l'alliance de marriage dans l'Inde du Sud, et en Australie*. The Hague: Mouton. 148 pp.
40. Dundes, A. 1976. Structuralism and folklore. *Stud. Fenn.* 20: 75–93
41. Durkheim, E. 1938. *The Rules of the Sociological Method*. Glencoe, Ill: Free Press. 146 pp.
42. Edmundson, M. S. 1973. Review of Lévi-Strauss's *Mythologiques: L'Homme nu*, 1971. *Am. Anthropol.* 75:374–78
43. Ehrmann, J., ed. 1966. *Structuralism*. Yale French Studies No. 36–37. Republished 1971. New York: Doubleday Anchor. 264 pp.
44. Engler, R., ed. 1967. *Ferdinand de Saussure, Cours de linguistique générale: edition critique*. Wiesbaden: Harrassowitz. 146 pp.
45. Friedman, J. 1974. Marxism, structuralism and vulgar materialism. *Man* 9:444–69
46. Gamst, F. C. 1975. Rethinking Leach's structural analysis of color and instructional categories in traffic control signals. *Am. Ethnol.* 2:271–96
47. Gardner, H. 1972. *The Quest for Mind: Piaget, Lévi-Strauss and the Structuralist Movement*. New York: Random House. 276 pp.
48. Gladwin, H. 1972. *Semantics, Schemata, and Kinship*. Presented at Math. Soc. Sci. Board Adv. Res. Semin., Formal Analysis of Kinship, Riverside, Calif.
49. Godel, R. 1957. *Les sources manuscrites du Cours de linguistique generale de F. de Saussure*. Geneve: Droz. 282 pp.
50. Gombrich, E. H. 1960. *Art and Illusion: A Study in the Psychology of Pictoral Representation*. Bollinger Ser. Princeton: Princeton Univ. Press. 466 pp.
51. Greenberg, J. H. 1966. *Language Universals*. The Hague: Mouton. 89 pp.
52. Greenberg, J. H. 1970. *Is language like a chess game?* Distinguished Lecture, Am. Anthropol. Assoc., 69th, San Diego. In *Bull. Am. Anthropol. Assoc.* 4:53–67
53. Greenberg, J. H. 1978. Diachrony, synchrony and language universals. In *Uni-*

versals of Human Language, ed. J. Greenberg, pp. 61–72. Stanford: Stanford Univ. Press. 286 pp.

54. Hage, P. 1976. The atom of kinship as a directed graph. Man 11:558–68

55. Halverson, J. 1976. Animal categories and terms of abuse. Man 11:505–16

56. Hawkes, T. 1977. Structuralism and Semiotics. Berkeley: Univ. Calif. Press. 192 pp.

57. Hayes, E. N., Hayes, T., eds. 1970. Claude Lévi-Strauss: The Anthropologist as Hero. Cambridge, Mass: MIT Press. 264 pp.

58. Hershman, P. 1974. Hair, sex and dirt. Man 9:274–98

59. Homans, G., Schneider, D. 1955. Marriage, Authority and Final Causes. Glencoe, Ill: Free Press. 64 pp.

60. Jakobson, R. 1944. Franz Boas' approach to language. Int. J. Am. Ling. 10:188–95

61. Jakobson, R. 1959. Boas' view of grammatical meaning. In The Anthropology of Franz Boas, ed. W. R. Goldschmidt, pp. 139–45. Am. Anthropol. Assoc. Mem. #89. 165 pp.

62. Jakobson, R. 1971. Selected Writings: Word and Language. The Hague: Mouton. 752 pp.

63. Jameson, F. 1972. The Prison House of Language: A Critical Account of Structuralism and Russian Formalism. Princeton: Princeton Univ. Press. 230 pp.

64. Juillerat, B. 1977. Terminologie de parenté Iafar (Nonvelle-Guinee): étude formelle d'un système dakota-iroquois. L'Homme 17:5–34

65. Katz, J. J., Fodor, J. A. 1964. The structure of a semantic theory. See Ref. 23, pp. 479–518

66. Kearney, M. 1963. Lévi-Strauss and his critics. Unpublished paper, Univ. Calif., Berkeley

67. Koerner, E. F. K. 1972. Bibliographia Saussureana 1870–1980. Metuchen, NJ: Scarecrow Press. 406 pp.

68. Korn, F. 1973. Elementary Structures Reconsidered: Lévi-Strauss on Kinship. Berkeley: Univ. Calif. Press. 168 pp.

69. Kronenfeld, J. Z. 1977. Blinking the needle's eye: a speculative theory of pastoral. Presented in departmental talks series, English Dep., Purdue Univ.

70. Kronenfeld, J. Z. 1978. Social rank and the pastoral ideals of As You Like It. Shakespeare Q. 29:333–48

71. Lane, M., ed. 1972. Introduction to Structuralism. New York: Basic Books. 456 pp.

72. Lapointe, F., Lapointe, C. 1977. Lévi-Strauss and His Critics: an International Bibliography of Criticism (1950–1976). New York: Garland. 219 pp.

73. Lave, J. 1977. Eastern Timbira moiety systems in time and space: A complex structure. Proc. 42nd Int. Congr. Americanists, Vol. 3

74. Leach, E. 1961. Lévi-Strauss in the Garden of Eden: an examination of some recent developments in the analysis of myth. Trans. NY Acad. Sci. 2:386–96

75. Leach, E. 1962. Genesis as myth. Discovery 3:30–35

76. Leach, E. 1964. Anthropological aspects of language: animal categories and verbal abuse. In New Directions in the Study of Language, ed. E. H. Lenneberg, pp. 23–64. Cambridge: MIT Press. 194 pp.

77. Leach, E. 1966. The legitimacy of Solomon: some structural aspects of Old Testament history. Eur. J. Sociol. 7:58–101. Reprinted in Ref. 71

78. Leach, E. 1973. Solomon's succession. Man 8:303–4

79. Leach, E. 1973. Structuralism in social anthropology. See Ref. 121, pp. 37–56

80. Leach, E. 1976. Claude Lévi-Strauss. New York: Viking. 142 pp.

81. Leach, E. 1976. Culture and Communication. The Logic by which Symbols are Connected: an Introduction to the Use of Structuralist Analysis in Social Anthropology. New York: Cambridge Univ. Press. 105 pp.

82. Leach, E. 1977. Michelangelo's genesis: structuralist comments on the paintings on the Sistine Chapel ceiling. Times Lit. Suppl. 3914:311–13

83. Leacock, E. B. 1978. Structuralism and dialectics. Rev. Anthropol. 5:117–28. Review of Ref. 94

84. Levi, J. 1977. Le Mythe de l'âge d'or et les théories de l'evolution en Chine ancienne. L'Homme 17:73–103

85. Lévi-Strauss, C. 1945. L'analyse structurale en linguistique et en anthropologie. WORD, J. Ling. Circle NY 1:1–21

86. Lévi-Strauss, C. 1955. The structural study of myth. J. Am. Folklore 68:428–42

87. Lévi-Strauss, C. 1960. La Geste d'Asdiwal. Transl., reprinted in The Structural Study of Myth and Totemism, ed. E. Leach, pp. 1–48. London: Tavistock; New York: Praeger. 185 pp. Reprinted in Ref. 96

88. Lévi-Strauss, C. 1960. La structure et la forme Réflections sur un ouvrage de Vlademir Propp. Cah. Inst. Sci. (economique appliquee n. 9) Ser. M, 7:3–36. Reprinted as L'analyse morphologique

des contes russes. *Int. J. Slavic Ling.
Poetics* 3:122–49

89. Lévi-Strauss, C. 1963. *Structural Anthropology,* Transl. C. Jacobson, R. G. Schoeph. New York: Basic Books. 410 pp.

90. Lévi-Strauss, C. 1963. *Totemism.* Transl. R. Needham. Boston: Beacon. 116 pp.

91. Lévi-Strauss, C. 1964. *Tristes Tropiques: An Anthropological Study of Primitive Societies in Brazil.* Transl. from French by J. Russell. New York: Atheneum. 404 pp.

92. Lévi-Strauss, C. 1966. *The Savage Mind.* Transl. anonymous. Chicago: Univ. Chicago Press. 290 pp.

93. Lévi-Strauss, C. 1969. *The Raw and the Cooked: Introduction to a Science of Mythology,* Vol. 1. Transl. J. Weightman, D. Weightman. New York: Harper & Row. 387 pp.

94. Lévi-Strauss, C. 1969. *The Elementary Structures of Kinship.* Transl. J. H. Ball, J. R. Von Sturmer; ed. R. Needham. London: Eyre & Spottiswood. xlii + 541 pp.

95. Lévi-Strauss, C. 1971. *Mythologiques (IV): L'Homme nu.* Paris: Plon. 688 pp.

96. Lévi-Strauss, C. 1973. *Anthropologie structurale deux.* Paris: Plon. 450 pp. Transl. as *Structural Anthropology II,* M. Layton (1976). London: Penguin. 383 pp.

97. Lévi-Strauss, C. 1973. *From Honey to Ashes: Introduction to a Science of Mythology,* Vol. 2. Transl. J. Weightman, D. Weightman. New York: Harper & Row. 512 pp.

98. Lévi-Strauss, C. 1978. *Origin of Table Manners: Introduction to a Science of Mythology,* Vol. 3. Transl. J. Weightman, D. Weightman. New York: Harper & Row. 551 pp.

99. Lizot, J. 1976. *Le cercle des feux: faits et dits des Indiens Yanomani.* Paris: Editions du Seuil. 248 pp.

100. Lounsbury, F. G. 1962. Review of Ref. 109. *Am. Anthropol.* 64:1302–10

101. Lyons, J. 1970. *Noam Chomsky.* New York: Viking. 143 pp.

102. Macksey, R., Donato, E. 1972. *The Languages of Criticism and the Sciences of Man: The Structuralist Controversy.* Baltimore: Johns Hopkins Univ. Press. 367 pp.

103. Maranda, P. 1972. Structuralism in cultural anthropology. *Ann. Rev. Anthropol.* 1:329–48

104. Maybury-Lewis, D. 1969. Review of Lévi-Strauss's *Du Miel aux Cendres. Am. Anthropol.* 71:114–21

105. McKnight, D. 1973. Sexual symbolism of food among the Wik-Mungkan. *Man* 8:194–209

106. Meillet, A. 1904–1905. Comment les mots changent de sens. *Annee Sociol.* 9:1–38

107. Meillet, A. 1916. *Review of Saussure: Cours de Linguistique Generale. Bull. Soc. Ling. Paris* 64:32–36

108. Miller, G. A., Galanter, E., Pribram, K. 1969. *Plans and the Structure of Behavior.* New York: Holt, Rinehart & Winston. 226 pp.

109. Needham, R. 1962. *Structure and Sentiment: A Test Case in Social Anthropology.* Chicago: Univ. Chicago Press. 135 pp.

110. Needham, R. 1975. The Tarau case continued: mathematics or mimetics. *Ethnos* 40:25–45

111. Pamment, M. 1972. The succession of Solomon: a reply to Edmund Leach's essay 'The legitimacy of Solomon.' *Man* 7:635–43

112. Panoff, M., Panoff, F. 1968. *L'ethnologue et son ombre.* Paris: Payot. 193 pp.

113. Perrin, M. 1976. *Le chemin des Indiens morts: mythes et symboles goajiro.* Paris: Payot. 268 pp.

114. Pettit, P. 1977. *The Concept of Structuralism.* Berkeley: Univ. Calif. Press. 117 pp.

115. Piaget, J. 1971. *Structuralism.* Transl., ed. Chaninah Maschler. London: Routledge & Kegan Paul. 153 pp.

116. Piaget, J., Inhelder, B. 1969. *The Psychology of the Child.* Transl. H. Weaver. New York: Basic Books. 173 pp.

117. Prattis, J. I. 1972. Science, ideology, and false demons: a commentary on Lévi-Strauss critiques. *Am. Anthropol.* 74:1323–35

118. Propp, V. A. 1958. *Morphology of the Folktale.* Transl. L. Scott. Bloomington, Ind: Publ. Indiana Res. Cent. Anthropol, Folklore, Ling. 10. 134 pp.

119. Rayfield, J. R. 1976. Review of Sperber, 1974. *Am. Anthropol.* 78:397

120. Regnier, A. 1968. De la theorie des groupes a la pensee sauvage. *Homme Societe* 7:201–14

121. Robey, D., ed. 1973. *Structuralism: an Introduction.* Oxford: Clarendon. 154 pp.

122. Rosaldo, M. Z. 1977. Review of Ref. 114. *Am. Anthropol.* 79:703–4

123. Rossi, I. 1973. The unconscious in the anthropology of Claude Lévi-Strauss. *Am. Anthropol.* 75:20–48

124. Rossi, I., ed. 1974. *The Unconscious in*

Culture: The Structuralism of Claude Lévi-Strauss in Perspective. New York: Dutton. 487 pp.

125. Rossi, I. 1977. Reply to Cohen. Am. Anthropol. 79:114–15

126. Sapir, J. D. 1977. Fecal animals: an example of complementary totemism. Man 12:1–21

127. Schank, R., Abelson, R. 1977. Scripts, Plans, Goals, and Understanding. Hillsdale, NJ: Erlbaum. 248 pp.

128. Shore, B. 1978. Ghosts and government: a structural analysis of alternative institutions for conflict management in Samoa. Man 13:175–99

129. Singer, M. 1978. For a semiotic anthropology. In Sight, Sound, and Sense, ed. T. A. Sebeok, pp. 202–31. Bloomington: Indiana Univ. Press. 289 pp.

130. Singer, M. 1978. Signs of the Self: an exploration in semiotic anthropology. Distinguished lecture, Ann. Meet. Am. Anthropol. Assoc., 77th, Los Angeles

131. Sperber, D. 1974. Le symbolisme en general. Paris: Hermann. 163 pp. Transl. as Rethinking Symbolism by A. L. Morton (1975). New York/

Cambridge: Cambridge Univ. Press. 153 pp.

132. Strenski, I. 1974. Falisfying deep structures. Man 9:571–84

133. Thomas, L. L., Kronenfeld, J. Z., Kronenfeld, D. B. 1976. Asdiwal crumbles: a critique of Lévi-Straussian myth analysis. Am. Ethnol. 3:147–74

134. Turner, T. S. n.d. Dialectical societies: variation and invariance in Ae and Bororo social structure. Unpublished manuscript

135. Umiker-Sebeok, D. J. 1977. Semiotics of culture: Great Britain and North America. Ann. Rev. Anthropol. 6:121–35

136. Wald, P. 1977. La Variabilité dans les terminologies de parenté comme critère d'adéquation de l'analyse. L'exemple de la terminologie consanguine francaise. L'Homme 17:23–70

137. Whitney, W. D. 1971. Whitney on Language: Selected Writings of William Dwight Whitney, ed. M. Silverstein. Cambridge: MIT Press. 360 pp.

138. Wilden, A. 1972. System and Structure: Essays in Communication and Exchange. London: Tavistock. 540 pp.

Ann. Rev. Anthropol. 1979. 8:543–78

LINEAR PROGRAMMING   ♦9645
MODELS IN ARCHAEOLOGY

Van A. Reidhead

Department of Sociology and Anthropology, University of Missouri,
St. Louis, Missouri 63121

INTRODUCTION

Since the 1950s archaeology has become increasingly concerned with the relationship between prehistoric populations and the production characteristics of their environments. Many popular modeling approaches such as systems theory, simulations, geographical location analysis, and site catchment analysis have gained prominence partly for their utility in the systematic analysis of man-environment relationships. Underlying many such approaches is the assumption that people select optimizing strategies in the allocation of resources.

During the years surrounding World War II, mathematicians (25; see also 56a, 58a) developed *linear programming* as a method for modeling optimal resource allocation systems. Economists recognized the applied and theoretical value of the new method and moved quickly to establish linear programming in the economic analysis of decision making (30–32, 64). The method also played an important role in the newly emerging field of operations research (52). In addition to economics and operations research, linear programming and closely related techniques are used in a wide variety of disciplines concerned with the analysis of resource allocation, including agricultural economics (37a) and most recently ecology (7, 97, 103a).

The purpose of this review is to examine the potential of linear programming applications in archaeology. To help the reader determine how his own interests match the content of this article, it is worth noting some of the areas in which linear programming can be usefully applied in archaeology. As a general rule, if a researcher is concerned with the use of natural or social resources by human populations, he *may* find linear programming useful. Linear programming has potential for the analysis of a wide variety of problems and can be adapted for use with a wide range of methodological

543

0084-6570/79/1015-0543$01.00

and theoretical frameworks which are common in archaeology today. Some of these include: approaches to carrying capacity; least effort analysis of settlement, subsistence, trade, and information flow; site catchment analysis, locational analysis, and other aspects of regional analysis; analysis of the impact of demographic, technological, and environmental change on resource use opportunities; systematic or stochastic simulations of economic and ecological systems; decision making under conditions of uncertainty. These and other approaches will be discussed within a linear programming context in the discussions which follow.

There are three primary objectives in the organization and selection of the sections which follow. The first is to introduce the reader to important methodological and theoretical problems and issues in linear programming analysis of archaeological phenomena. The second is to demonstrate how linear programming fits within the context of current research trends in archaeology. Third, for this review to be meaningful to most readers, it must serve as an introduction to linear programming. The discussions which follow begin with an introduction to basic concepts in linear programming analysis. A comprehension of this section does not require a mathematical background. Nevertheless, some readers may want to move ahead and return to this section later. The reviews of the social anthropology and archaeology studies which follow emphasize substantive findings, selected for their utility in achieving all of the primary objectives stated above, while the final sections focus primarily on the first and second objectives.

The reader need not have a mathematical background to digest this review. Similarly, one need not have a mathematical nor computer science background to effectively use linear programming. Linear programming packages have been developed along user-oriented lines and are readily accessible. At the same time, one need not approach the method as a "black box." The rudiments of linear programming can be learned quickly if a researcher perceives an advantage in doing so. Nevertheless, it *is not* the intent of this article to encourage archaeologists to embrace linear programming in an effort to upgrade their "methodological tool kits," without recognizing its limitations. Linear programming is applicable to a wide variety of anthropological problems, but it is not a panacea and should not be used without evaluation of appropriateness to specific research problems and objectives.

BASIC CONCEPTS

As the term states, linear programming encompasses a group of closely related techniques in which relationships between inputs and outputs are linear. The term *programming* is not synonymous with computer programming but refers to a planning process or program of activities. Linear programming allows the analysis of systems by decomposing them into a series of interrelated *activities* of production or allocation (58, p. 176). As Dantzig (25, p. 6) puts it: "Linear programming is concerned with describing the interrelationships of the components of a system." The *objective function* (goal) of the problem formulation is to determine how resources (e.g. labor, energy, raw materials, money, or even social involvement) can be allocated among competing *activities* in the best possible (*optimal*) way. The objective function of a problem is stated in terms of *maximizing* an output or *minimizing* an input. Examples might be maximizing nutrient production in an environment, as in carrying capacity problems, or minimizing labor costs, as in least-effort approaches to settlement and subsistence systems.

Like any modeling technique, linear programming is subject to basic assumptions. As the name implies, the most basic among these specify that the total mathematical model must be expressed in terms of linear relationships. For example, it is assumed that input-output relationships are linear. This issue is discussed by Dantzig (25) and Baumol (5), who recognize that most allocation problems in the real world are characterized by input-output relationships in which returns do not remain constant but rather decrease to scale. Nevertheless, both authors contend that many real situations can be generalized in linear form and still yield useful results. The linearity assumption is not as problematic as it seems at first, since techniques have been developed to accomodate many nonlinear relationships. These are discussed later.

As a general rule, a problem can be organized as a linear programming formulation when the researcher can: (*a*) state a real, assumed, or hypothesized goal (objective function) in the allocation of resources; (*b*) identify the resources available for achieving the goal; and (*c*) identify the constraints or limits to resource use.

Analysis of a programming problem may be conceptualized as progressing through three increasing levels of analysis: (*a*) identification of an objective function and problem formulation; (*b*) problem solution; and (*c*) postoptimality analysis. The remainder of this section is organized to explicate these levels of analysis.

Problem Formulation

To formulate a problem, the system must be stated in matrix form. This level of analysis can be achieved with minimal data. Because of the absence of quantified data, in his analysis of the Fur economy, Joy (58) constructed a matrix which totally lacked specific input-output coefficients, statements of resource availability, and the minimum requirements of production. In

spite of this, the matrix served to make explicit the interrelationships between the entire set of potential resource production activities and the
constraints of production, i.e. what the Fur "needed" to produce. His
matrix could be compared to the matrix of Table 1, if it contained no
quantitative statements. Table 1 is a sample formulation in which a fictitious
population must obtain ≥360 units of energy, ≥300 units of protein, and
≥8 units of hides to survive during some specified time period. To satisfy
these survival constraints, the population has access to a plant and an
animal resource with the input-output and availability characteristics specified in Table 1. As Joy clearly demonstrates through his nonquantitative
matrix analysis, even if the coefficients of Table 1 were totally lacking, an
insightful analysis is made possible by the explication of relationships between activities of production (plant and animal use) and the constraints
(energy, protein, and hides).

Joy (58, p. 180) argues that even without quantification the matrix analysis of programming formulations allows the analysis to advance further
than is possible using the diagramatic representation of flow formulations.
He argues that the chief advantage is that in matrix formulations it is
conceptually easy to trace the implications of postulated relationships
among variables. It forces one to explicitly conceptualize the nature of the
relationship between *activities* and *constraints,* and even in the absence of
quantified data one must ask "whether a coefficient is zero, positive, or
negative" (58, p. 180). For example, if the matrix of Table 1 lacked quantified coefficients, it would still be possible to identify that the value for hide
content in plants would be *zero,* while all other coefficients would be *positive.* For those interested in programming formulations, Joy's discussion is
essential reading.

A higher level of analysis is possible when matrices can be quantified, as
with the fictitious coefficients provided in Table 1. When a matrix is quantified, it is possible to complete the problem formulation by specifying an
objective function (minimize the cost of survival in Table 1) in matrix

Table 1   Formulation of a sample problem with a minimizing objective function

Nutrients and hides	Nutrients and hides per resource unit		Minimum requirements
	Plant x_1	Animal x_2	
Energy	30	25	≥360
Protein	10	25	≥300
Hides	—	1	≥ 8
Cost per unit of resource	30 man-hours	15 man-hours	minimum cost = ?
Resource availability	25 units	25 units	

algebra. One can then calculate an *optimal solution*. Such minimization problems can be generalized as follows (103, p. 78):

$$\text{minimize} \quad z = \sum_{j=1}^{n} c_j x_j \qquad\qquad 1.$$

$$\text{subject to} \quad \sum_{j=1}^{n} a_{ij} x_j = b_i; \text{ for } i = 1, 2, \ldots, m \ (b_i \geqslant 0) \qquad 2.$$

$$\text{and} \quad x_j \geqslant 0 \text{ for } j = 1, 2, \ldots, n, \qquad\qquad 3.$$

where z = the cost of production, c_j = the cost per unit of resource j, x_j = the quantity of j produced, a_{ij} = the amount of each constraint (in Table 1 the amount of nutrients or hides per unit of plant or animal) in j, and b_i = the amount of each constraint required in the problem. Table 2, containing symbolic notation, is provided to assist the reader in generalizing the formulation of a minimization problem to any suitable situation (see 61, 73). The columns (jth activities) and rows (ith constraints) in Table 2 are referred to as *column vectors* and *row vectors* respectively. By working between Tables 1 and 2 and Equations 1, 2, 3, the tables and the general problem formulation can be conceptualized regardless of the reader's mathematical background.

Two points are pertinent to the above formulations. First, all linear programming formulations contain *non-negativity constraints* $[x_j \geqslant 0$ (Equation 3)] which specify that resources cannot be allocated in negative quantity (5, pp. 75–76). Second, the generalized formulation of Table 2 can be used to illustrate maximizing or minimizing problems. In a maximization problem the b vector (Table 2) will specify the upper limits of production ($\leqslant b$), while in a minimization problem the b vector specifies the minimum acceptable level of production ($\geqslant b$).

Table 2 Generalized matrix for formulating linear programming problems

Constraints (i)	Constraints per unit of production activities (j)						Requirements
	1	2	3	4	5 $\ldots$ n		
1	a_{11}	a_{12}	a_{13}	a_{14}	a_{15}	a_{1n}	b_1
2	a_{21}	a_{22}	a_{23}	a_{24}	a_{25}	a_{2n}	b_2
3	a_{31}	a_{32}	a_{33}	a_{34}	a_{35}	a_{3n}	b_3
$\vdots$							
m	a_{m1}	a_{m2}	a_{m3}	a_{m4}	a_{m5}	a_{mn}	b_m
Costs	c_1	c_2	c_3	c_4	c_5	c_n	$z = \Sigma c_j x_j$

The reader should now have a reasonable understanding of problem formulations. The next step in the analysis is to produce an *optimal solution* by solving the problem of Table 1.

Problem Solution

The problem formulated in Table 1 can now be stated algebraically, and an optimal solution can be found by use of the *graphical method* (see Figure 1). The reader may need to work back and forth between Table 1, the legend of Figure 1, and the following problem statement to follow the solution process. The problem may be stated as follows:

Variables:

X_1 = plant   1.

X_2 = animal

Objective function:

minimize z (cost) $= 30X_1 + 15X_2$ 2.

where 30 man-hours = the cost per unit of X_1

and 15 man-hours = the cost per unit of X_2;

subject to constraints:

$30X_1 + 20X_2 \geqslant 360$ (energy requirement)   3.

$10X_1 + 25X_2 \geqslant 300$ (protein requirement)

$1X_2 \geqslant 8$ (hide requirement)

where 30 = number of units of energy available per unit of X_1

and 20 = number of units of energy available per unit of X_2,

with similar reasoning applying to protein and hides;

and nonnegativity constraints to avoid negative allocation:

$X_1 \geqslant 0$ 4.

$X_2 \geqslant 0$

and subject to maximum resource availability:

$X_1 \leqslant 25$ (cannot allocate more than 25 units of plants)   5.

$X_2 \leqslant 25$ (cannot allocate more than 25 units of meat).

This problem can now be solved graphically by plotting lines on a graph which indentify how *activities* can be allocated to achieve the minimum acceptable level of each constraint. To do this, the inequalities (Element 3) must be converted to equality form, as in the legend of Figure 1, to allow the constraints to be plotted on the graph.

With the constraints plotted, a solution can be found in Figure 1. The minimum requirement of each constraint can be achieved by the mix of resources prescribed at any point on the line plotted for that resource. Thus, the minimum energy requirement (360 units) can be filled by any combination of resources specified on line EE'. The same applies to protein (line PP') and hides (line HH'). Any point on or above and to the right of EE'

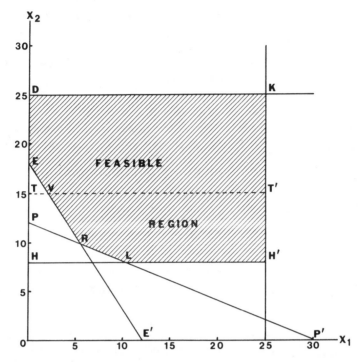

Figure 1   Graphical solution of a linear programming problem. Plotting constraints: Energy, $EE' = 30X_1 + 20X_2 = 360$; Protein, $PP' = 10X_1 + 25X_2 = 300$; Hides, $HH' = 1X_2 = 8$; nonnegativity constraints, $X_1 \geqslant 0$, $X_2 \geqslant 0$. Limits of production: plants, $X_1 \leqslant 25$; animals, $X_2 \leqslant 25$. Optimal solution: best activity mix $= E = 18X_2 = 270$ man-hours $=$ minimum labor cost.

satisfies the energy requirement. But since this same logic applies to each other line, one quickly sees that all constraints can be met only in the area of the *feasible region.* Production at any point in the feasible region will yield a *feasible solution,* one which satisfies all constraints. Although optimal solutions are sometimes found along straight line segments, an optimal solution will always be found at one of the corner points of the feasible solution (5, pp. 84–86; 52, pp. 1–41). The reader can check this for the sample problem by calculating the cost at points within the feasible region, along straight line segments (e.g. *ER*), and at the corner points. The optimal solution to the sample problem is found at point E where $z = 18X_2 = 270$ man-hours.

The graphical solution technique can only be used when solving extremely simple problems. As additional activities are added, the problem becomes multidimensional and other solution methods must be used. The *simplex method* developed by Dantzig was designed to solve such multidimensional problems. Figure 1 can be used to illustrate how the simplex method operates. The solution process consists of three steps. First, in the *initialization step* a *corner point* in the feasible region (say K) is selected and evaluated in comparison to both adjacent corner points (D and H'). This evaluation identifies D and H' as better solutions since at both points production costs are less than at K. Second, in the *iterative step* the procedure moves to one of the better corner points (say D). D is compared with K and E, revealing that E is a less costly solution. A second iteration is made moving to E where it is found that E is better than D and R. Third, when a better solution cannot be found at any adjacent *corner-point feasible solution,* the *stopping rule* identifies E as the optimal solution (52, pp. 31–51) and the problem is solved. In complex problems the solution is found through any of a variety of computer algorithms which move systematically from corner to corner using established pivoting rules which operate in successive iterative tableaus, beginning with the initial problem formulation (*initial tableau*) and proceeding to the optimal solution in the *final tableau* (see 105, pp. 85–102). However, linear programming analysis does not end with the identification of an optimal solution.

Postoptimality Analysis

Most linear programming algorithms produce data which make possible a level of analysis that is more useful than the optimal solution per se. *Postoptimality analysis* generally involves *sensitivity analysis* and the identification and analysis of *binding constraints* and *shadow prices.* Using Table 1 and Figure 1, it is possible to identify which of the constraints (nutrients and hides) are binding. To illustrate, production at point E (the optimal solution in Figure 1), will yield more than the minimum acceptable quantities of hides and protein, but only the minimum required 360 units of energy. Thus, energy is the *binding constraint* of the problem, i.e. unless specific decisions are made to provision energy, the minimum requirement may not be met or may be filled at an increased (nonoptimal) cost. Only at point E are all constraints satisfied at the lowest cost. For example, if the population chose to focus on protein production, the lowest cost strategy would be at P, resulting in an energy deficit and failure to satisfy all the survival constraints, i.e. a *nonfeasible solution.* Now assume an increase of 1 unit each in the minimum requirement of hides and protein. Under such conditions, how much would the cost of survival increase due to the higher protein and hide requirements? Answer: 0.00 man-hours, because hides and protein are already supplied in surplus. But an increase of 1 unit in the energy requirement will require a production adjustment and extra labor cost. One additional unit of energy would cost an additional 0.75 man-hours, as seen in Table 1; 20 units of energy using X_2 costs 15 man-hours.

Such marginal cost statements, i.e. an additional unit of energy would cost 0.75 man-hours, are provided in the output of most linear programming algorithms, making it possible to identify (a) binding constraints, (b) how changes in constraints will affect optimal decision making, and (c) how production costs will be affected by such changes.

Shadow prices identify how the structure of optimal decision making will be affected by changes in the costs and availability of resources. As such, they provide insights into optimal decision-making under conditions of technological, environmental, and market change. To illustrate, plant use (X_1) does not form part of the optimal strategy of Figure 1, because the use of plants in any quantity would increase survival costs above the minimum. Under such conditions, at what cost could plant use become part of the optimal solution? Since the binding constraint of the problem is energy, to answer this question one need only compare the efficiencies of energy production using plants and animals. Under the hypothetical technological conditions of the problem, 1 man-hour of labor produces 1.33 units of energy using animals and 1.00 units using plants (Table 1). From the data of Table 1, it can be seen that at a cost of 22.5 man-hours/unit of plants, the energy production efficiency of plants would equal that of animals (1 man-hour/1.33 units) and plants would form part of the optimal solution. In this problem, 22.5 man-hours is the shadow price of plants. This statistic, provided by most linear programming algorithms, makes it possible for one to assess the magnitude of technological change required for plants to achieve optimal value. Alternatively, if one observes that in spite of their high costs plants are currently used by the population, the shadow price helps assess at what cost in optimality the choice to use plants is made.

To identify the value of increasing the supply of high demand resources, shadow prices are also provided for resources whose total availability is projected for use by the model. To illustrate, assume that the maximum availability of animals in Figure 1 is 15 units as defined by the dotted line TT'. Under such conditions, the optimal allocation (now changed to point V) consists of 15 units of animals and 2 units of plants, costing 285 man-hours. If the supply of animals could be increased by 1 unit (from 15 to 16 units), the cost of production would decline to 277.5 man-hours, a saving of 7.5 man-hours. Thus, the shadow price of animals is 22.5 man-hours (15 + 7.5). From this the researcher can assess the impact, on optimal resource allocation, of environmental or market changes resulting in an increased animal supply. Alternatively, assuming a decrease in the supply of animals, one can project the magnitude of the resulting decline in production efficiency.

From the above one can readily identify the utility of postoptimality analysis in projecting the impact of change on optimal resource allocation. However, postoptimality data serve another function in *sensitivity analysis.*

Through the ranging of the model parameters (a_{ij}, b_i, c_j, see Table 2), postoptimal data help the researcher test the stability of his model and of the assumptions upon which it is based. To illustrate, from the above discussion it can be seen how changes in the constraints (nutrient and hide requirements, b_i parameters) will affect optimal allocation. Substantial increases in the hide and protein constraints would be required to yield a new optimal solution. But any change in the energy constraint will require an adjustment. Since the model is sensitive to changes in the energy requirement, any problems in the energy requirement estimate should be carefully scrutinized. In the case of shadow prices, one can identify the sensitivity of a model to changes in the costs of resources. For example, the cost of plants must decline by 7.5 man-hours before plants will enter the optimal strategy and restructure the model. Thus, using shadow prices one can assess the sensitivity of a model to specific changes in resource costs. Such data are important in evaluating the reliability of models and can lead to model improvements by identifying problem areas in input estimates. A number of specialized programming techniques can be used to increase the efficiency and sophistication of sensitivity analysis. These include *parametric programming,* the *dual simplex method,* and the *upper bound technique* (see 52, 103).

LINEAR PROGRAMMING IN ANTHROPOLOGY

Linear programming approaches have been used infrequently in social anthropology. Game theory, comprising some decision-making models which are closely related to linear programming (71), have been applied in anthropology since Barth's (3) analysis of Pathan organization and Davenport's (26) minimax model of Jamaican fishing strategies. Aspects of game theory in anthropology and related disciplines have been treated in some detail in an edited volume by Buchler & Nutini (12). It is significant that any $m \times n$ two-player zero-sum game can be converted to a linear programming problem and solved using the simplex or related algorithms (52, pp. 291–94; 105, pp. 134–35). Conversely, any linear programming problem can be converted to a game formulation (13). However, linear programming formulations need not be constrained by the same assumptions as game theory, as for example the assumption of the environment as a rational decision maker. The first application of linear programming to anthropological data was Heyer's (48) study of the constraints on crop production options among the Kamba of Kenya.

In 1967 Leonard Joy, an economist, demonstrated the general applicability of linear programming formulations to the kinds of production analyses often conducted by anthropologists (58) when he converted Barth's (4) flow model of economic spheres in Darfur to a programming matrix. Unfortunately, quantitative data were lacking and it was not possible for Joy and Barth to quantify the matrix and produce a solution. Even so, Joy's article is important reading. He lucidly illustrates the analytical power of formulating problems in programming form (whether or not solutions are possible), and he discusses possible applications of general theoretical interest in economic anthropology.

Hoffmann (54) used linear programming as a method to measure "cultural intensity" (quantitatively), as defined by Kroeber (65). He formulated a problem whose objective function was to minimize labor in the production of minimum acceptable levels of protein and energy for a Shipibo family. He found energy to be the binding constraint, with the protein requirement met in surplus.

Buchler & McKinlay (11) used a linear programming model to analyze the decision-making process underlying the selection of Mexican peasants for religious cargos. They used a maximizing objective function to analyze optimal assignment of individuals to specific cargos. Since they did not know precisely how the different characteristics of individuals were weighed (valued) by those making the selections, they assigned values arbitrarily, generated optimal solutions, and then compared these with empirically observed assignments. In successive formulations they systematically modified the weighted inputs until solutions were achieved which approximate ethnographic cases, with the expectation that these could have predictive value. Their modeling procedure is interesting as it constitutes a kind of experimentation process (52, p. 602) simulating input through repeated comparisons of modeled and empirical results.

Gladwin (39) discussed the implication of using linear programming to produce a risk-minimizing model of market decisions among Ghanaian fish traders. However, she chose to use a hierarchical tree model instead, because of the problems of using ordinal measures of risk to formulate a linear programming problem. Her paper is important for its discussion of decision-making models which can be used as alternatives to linear programming analysis.

Perhaps the most important use of a linear programming model in social anthropology is found in a recent study by Selby & Hendrix (92). They used the technique to assess the correlation between stated goals and actual behavior in the individual decision making of Indian villagers and urban migrants in Mexico. Their article warrants special consideration because of its importance in the discussion of archaeological problems which follows.

Selby and Hendrix questioned informants to identify what the informants wanted most out of life (goals), activity options for achieving goals, and the resources available for goal achievement. The relationships among goals, activities, and resources were scaled through an elaborate process of measurement and reliability checking. In relationships where the rates of return were not linear, but increased or decreased to scale, a composite linear equation was constructed to approximate the actual relationships, illustrating one method of modeling nonlinear relationships using linear programming techniques. The resulting data were used to formulate a linear programming problem whose objective function was to maximize leisure, personal betterment, quality of life style, security, self-respect, and respect of others. The optimal solution identified how the persons under study ought to allocate time, labor, and capital to best achieve their *stated* goals in life. Each model represented decision making for one year with successive runs made to simulate long-range optimality. Selby and Hendrix are explicit in declaring that their model is not intended to predict behavior, but rather to provide a framework within which the feelings of individuals about the articulation between stated goals and empirical activities can be evaluated. The model, when compared with empirical observations, is a test of rationality in goal fulfillment. In contrast to what might be expected, the optimal solutions specify that an individual should work hard for the first few years, raising his minima to acceptable standards, and then pursue a leisurely life with ample camaraderie and drinking until monetary security, personal betterment, etc begin to fall.

An earlier linear programming analysis by Granskog [(40) discussed in (92)], which modeled only material production, suggested that the Zapotec Indians of her study pursued suboptimizing strategies. However, when Selby and Hendrix expanded the formulation to include the full range of culturally defined goals, it was found that the model described not only how people should act, but how they do in fact behave. The models and associated behavior clearly identify that the rates of return for different activities are variable and nonlinear. The utility of returns from social security producing activities diminish when they cut too deeply into the need for leisure and respect, which are associated with social exchange relationships, and vice versa. One of the most important conclusions of the study is that the goals of individuals and groups are not obvious. It has been assumed that the major goal of the poor is security, but the findings suggest that achieving a "sense of independence" may be the highest priority (92, pp. 238–39). This is especially clear in view of the fact that models which incorporated only material production suggested that Zapotec behavior is not optimal, while the Selby & Hendrix model, incorporting cultural goals, when empirically evaluated, suggests behavior approximating optimal decision making. This underlies the long debated issue that the rationality and optimality of decisions can only be assessed when the full range of social and material goals are assessed (see 14, 86). The problem of goal determination is especially difficult when dealing with archaeological data.

LINEAR PROGRAMMING IN ARCHAEOLOGY

Perhaps the first to recognize the potential applicability of linear programming to archaeological problems was the late David L. Clark, who suggested possible applications as early as 1968 (17; see also 18). A 1974 paper used sample data to illustrate the utility of linear programming models in the archaeological study of nutrient acquisition (84). Since then there have been several studies dealing with substantive problems (29, 61, 62, 81–83). In addition, two doctoral theses are currently in progress (Arthur S. Keene, personal communication; James F. Kerrigan, personal communication). These studies are organized around one of two popular issues in contemporary archaeology: effort minimization in subsistence and settlement, or carrying capacity. All have used variations of the so-called diet problem (98, 104), of which the sample problem of Table 1 is also a variant. In this section, models focusing on effort minimization will be discussed first and carrying capacity second. A general discussion of theoretical and methodological problems associated with linear programming applications follows.

Approaches to Effort Minimization

The works of Keene (61, 62) and Reidhead (82, 83) approach the principle of effort minimization from different theoretical perspectives. Both researchers are concerned with the factors involved in food selection, but Keene's model assumes least effort (and least risk) in meeting basic survival needs as the primary goal of hunter-gatherer populations (61), while Reidhead presents this assumption as an hypothesis to be tested against archaeological data (82, 83). Thus, while the models they develop are comparable, their functions are different at some levels, Keene's serving a predictive function and Reidhead's an evaluative function. In the discussion which follows, their works are first introduced separately and are then integrated into a single discussion to highlight overlapping findings.

Reidhead's dissertation (81), now restructured and expanded (82), was the first attempt to formulate a comprehensive analysis of prehistoric decision making using linear programming models. He made quantitative reconstructions of food resource availability, nutrient composition and costs, and estimated human population densities and nutrient requirements as the basis for generating models of optimal (minimum cost) resource allocation in the prehistoric Ohio Valley. His objective was to test the labor minimization hypothesis in two contexts: first, against the behavior of a group (Late Woodland) whose subsistence was assumed to be based primarily in hunting-gathering, with some horticulture; and second, against a group of corn agricluturalists (Fort Ancient). Annual models for each cultural period were produced by generating seasonal models which incorporated storage capabilities, changing nutrient quality through time and changing seasonal resource availabilities. The seasonal resource models were interactive, with the output of one season formulating the input of the next in a subtractive fashion. While this approach incorporates aspects of *dynamic linear programming* [cf Throsby (101)], the model remains static, treating allocation for one year in which resource costs and availabilities are assumed to be long-term averages. However, Reidhead achieves insights into the dynamic process of change from hunter-gatherer/early horticultural to agricultural society by formulating discrete models for the two technological stages. Each model treated independently is static. However, when treated in sequence they control for changes in technology (corn agriculture and the bow and arrow), resource availability, and human population densities, thus providing an avenue for dynamic analysis. As will be discussed later, linear programming can be used to build models which are more truly dynamic.

Reidhead compared his models with empirical evidence of subsistence activities recovered from a site in southeastern Indiana. He rejected the least effort hypothesis in its strict interpretation, finding that some high cost foods were used with intensity, adding unnecessary costs to subsistence, while others such as fish, which would have significantly reduced labor costs, were not used intensively. While rejecting the hypothesis in strict terms, Reidhead argued that labor minimization was a major outcome of the use of most major resources, such as deer, and important plant resources, but he cautions against strict acceptance of the least effort assumption.

In two important studies, Keene (61, 62) produces the same basic kinds of reconstructions and estimates for a group of Netsilik Eskimo living northwest of Hudson Bay. Keene's models are used to analyze the subsistence economy of an ethnographic group. His objective, however, is to produce a model for archaeological application which can predict resource use and related settlement phenomena, including how these will change through time with new technologies, and environmental perturbations. As such, he is concerned with how such predictions may be verified in the archaeological record. To test the synchronic and diachronic predictive value of his model, Keene also applies a discrete modeling approach to achieve dynamic analysis. First, he formulated a Netsilik problem under prerifle conditions and second under postrifle conditions. His annual models are organized differently than Reidhead's, with varying production possibilities and resource values formulated for each month of the year. He also uses a different computational procedure and algorithm to produce his models. The full range of possibilities represented by all 12 months are formulated in a single composite problem. This is accomplished by treating each resource as a separate resource for each of the 12 seasons and solving for all seasons simultaneously in the same matrix (61). The matrix resulting from Keene's formulation is 12 (row vectors) X 145 (column vectors). After combining resources in some seasons, the final matrix is 12 X 85, for 1020 individual coefficients. He used the *revised simplex method* to process his models. This approach offers a more efficient algorithm than the original simplex method (used by Reidhead) for solving large problems (52, pp. 671–80). His models also vary from Reidhead's in the incorporation of a hide requirement, along with 11 basic nutrients, as a constraint.

The optimal solution of the prerifle model predicts the use of six major resources and a variety of other resources on a limited opportunistic and survival related basis. When the rifle is incorporated, the major resources drop to two. Although an explicit comparison is not made, the models seem to predict Netsilik behavior with reasonable accuracy. Another important aspect of the models is that they provide a framework for predicting the Netsilik settlement system and pattern, because the use of specific resources is predicated on identifiable seasonal movements.

This discussion has focused on the general objectives and structures of Keene's and Reidhead's work. Only those aspects of their findings which derive directly from the optimal solutions have been summarized, because the different approaches taken in their studies result in somewhat different implications (i.e. evaluative vs predictive) when the optimal solutions are compared with empirical data. However, both researchers had, as major goals of their studies, the illumination of the general economic relationships and the technological and environmental constraints which underly the production of an optimal solution to any optimization problem. The generation of optimal solutions alone can shed little light on such issues. It is postoptimal analysis with its rich marginal data and parameter ranging characteristics which provides insight into systemic relationships. In the analysis of such relationships, the general implications of Keene's and Reidhead's analyses are in many ways comparable.

Some of the most important findings of the Netsilik and Ohio Valley research relate to the postoptimal identification of binding constraints, i.e. those needs which are most difficult to fill. In the Netsilik model, calcium and hides emerged as the binding constraints. According to the model, these are the limiting requirements of survival. A successful adaptation to the Netsilik environment must include methods of acquiring resources which contribute significantly to these needs. Whether the human population consciously recognizes the critical limiting nature of these constraints or not, decisions must be made which specifically provision them or a stable adaptation cannot be achieved. By comparison, all other constraints will, under the conditions of the model, be filled in excess by meeting the minimum requirements for calcium and hides.

These findings provide some significant general insights. Keene (61, 62) criticizes anthropological studies of carrying capacity for their tendency to rely only on energy or at best on energy and protein models. He demonstrates that an energy or protein-energy model of Netsilik carrying capacity would severely overestimate the actual environmental-technological potential for an adapted population. This issue is underscored by Reidhead's findings that the major limiting nutrients in his hunter-gatherer incipient/ horticulture model were energy, ascorbic acid, vitamin A, and possibly calcium (see 82, 83). Under these conditions an energy model would fall short of adequate nutrient provision of some vitamins and minerals. Nevertheless the fact that energy is a major limiting nutrient could lead one to argue that an energy model would yield an adequate approximation. This would be especially attractive since protein is not a limiting nutrient in the model. An energy model could thus automatically provision the protein requirement as a by-product of energy production. Thus, for those interested only in energy and protein control, an energy model might suffice. However, to generalize this situation to others would be a mistake, as can be seen from the results of Reidhead's agricultural model. In the agriculture model, the limits on nutritional adaptation change, with quality protein emerging as a new limiting nutrient. An energy model of carrying capacity in the Middle Ohio under agricultural conditions would fail to provision adequate resources to meet the protein need and thus seriously overestimate carrying capacity. While an improvement, an energy-protein model would also fail to account for the limiting nature of vitamins and minerals and would still result in overestimations. Two points are important here. First, a nutrition model which works under one set of technological and environmental conditions may not apply when generalized to other situations. Only a multinutrient approach provides results which will be reliable across technological and environmental boundaries. Second, these findings identify the importance of the technological component in the determination of limiting resources or binding constraints in an environment. The environment is clearly not the only, nor necessarily the most important, determinant of limiting conditions in all situations. A change in technological efficiency can completely reverse existing conditions [see discussion of input-output and technology in (70)].

Keene's analysis of the marginal cost data (shadow prices) of his model provides an opportunity to examine some dynamic implications of his findings. As noted, the optimal solution to the Netsilik model specified that under prerifle conditions the optimal strategy would be to diversify resource use. This diversification would have included the limited use of even minor resources, as indicated by the shadow prices (marginal costs) of such resources. However, a close examination of predicted resource use levels, the upper limits of resource acquisition under prerifle technological conditions, and associated shadow prices suggests possible changes given the appropriate opportunity. The marginal values of two major resources, caribou and ringed seal (see 61, Table 3) were disproportionately high. This means that the value of these resources was such that if conditions changed, allowing their use in greater quantities but with reasonable efficiency, the most efficient strategy would be to rely on them to the near exclusion of others. Keene notes that greater quantities of caribou and ringed seal were available during prerifle times, but could only be acquired at great cost. The predictions of the prerifle shadow prices became reality with the introduction of the rifle. The optimal solution of the rifle model is dominated by caribou and ringed seal (62). Netsilik ethnography confirms this prediction. Within 10 years after the adoption of the rifle, seal production increased and pressure on caribou was such that their numbers declined dramatically (62). The insight provided by the shadow prices was borne out when Keene modeled the changing dynamics of the postrifle Netsilik situation and the empirical evidence confirms many of the predicted changes.

A comparable set of conditions characterizes Reidhead's analysis (82, 83). It will be remembered that in the hunter-gatherer/incipient horticulture (Late Woodland) model, energy was identified as a binding constraint. From this it is obvious that an opportunity to adopt a technology with improved energy returns would be attractive. This would hold even if labor minimization in subsistence was important, but not *the* primary goal of the group. Subsequently, when in dynamic analysis the agricultural (Fort Ancient) problem was formulated to include population, environmental, and technological changes (the bow and productive corn agriculture), corn was specified as one of the most important resources of the optimal solution precisely because of its utility in improving the labor input/energy output ratio. As a result of the improved efficiency of energy production with corn, protein emerges as one of the most severely limiting nutrients in the Fort Ancient model. This important result could not have been foreseen from the data inputs without massive trial and error coefficient manipulation [45 column vectors X 10 row vectors = 450 total coefficients (see 82, table 15)].

Several insights are made possible by the dynamic modeling of the Late Woodland-Fort Ancient transition. Perhaps the most interesting in light of contemporary emphasis among archaeologists on population pressure as the prime cause of the adoption of agriculture (9, 20, 21, 75, 96) is the finding that heavy corn use entered the model because it improved the efficiency of energy production (82, 83). While this finding is far from conclusive, it clearly identifies one of the possibilities which exists as an alternative to the widely accepted population pressure explanation of agriculture [see (83) for a detailed discussion; see also (23, 44, 45, 68)].

The comparative postoptimal analysis of the Late Woodland and Fort Ancient models also hold implications for the study of the etiology of nutritionally related disease. The high production of protein in the Late Woodland model (83, Figure 4) is characteristic of populations whose diet is provided primarily by hunting-gathering activities (33, 67, 106). This suggests that prior to the adoption of agriculture, the protein requirement may have existed as a totally hidden human need. In spite of its limiting nature in Reidhead's Fort Ancient model, the model also indicates that protein rich resources would have remained more abundant than the accompanying human need. That protein becomes a binding constraint of the model means that for the first time it is more costly than other nutrients. Reidhead (see 82) argues that under agricultural conditions human populations would have grown rapidly. But he suggests that initially, under such conditions, established food preferences and hide requirements would have resulted in protein surplus as before, thus continuing to obscure the existence of a need for protein. In the middle Ohio, he argues, the first recognition of a protein need may have been associated with the first widespread occurrence of protein malnutrition accompanying the dramatic population increase made possible with the adoption of corn agriculture (83). While such a situation may seem intuitively obvious to some, the generation of such results within the context of a model which lays clear the underlying relationships of such conditions is important (see 62, conclusions).

The discussions to this point demonstrate some of the potential for dynamic analysis using linear programming techniques. Both Keene and Reidhead use a *discrete event* approach for modeling systems whose subsistence and/or settlement parameters change through time. Using this approach, they achieved dynamic analysis by making systematic modifications in static problems. By so doing, they reduced continuous dynamic problems to two-phase static problems which systematically control for changes in the environment, technology, human population densities, etc. This approach provided a method for analyzing the impact of such changes on optimal decision making through time [see discussions of dynamic applications in (61)]. Discrete event models are compatible with archaeological data because archaeologists organize time sequence data in a comparable fashion, using periods, phases, etc to accomodate continuous phenomena in what is essentially a sequential static framework. There is, however, great potential for the analysis of dynamic systems using techniques which extend beyond these discrete event models. The techniques of *dynamic linear programming* (101), *recursive linear programming* (27), and stochastic approaches (103) make possible the systematic or stochastic modeling of continuous system modifications. Using such approaches, the researcher can produce dynamic models in which decisions in one period feed into the next. Thus, feedback from past decisions and from the environment play a role in formulating new decision problems in which the sequence of outcomes converges toward the optimum. As Day (27, pp. 334–35) points up, such approaches make it possible to ask a variety of questions of significance to the adaptation of systems through time, such as: Do equilibria exist? Are they stable? Do cycles occur? Are they stable? Can growth occur? Such analyses also make possible the analysis of short vs long-range decision making. For example, is short-range optimization compatible with long-range optimization and adaptation (see 83)? Dynamic analysis holds considerable potential beyond what has been accomplished by Keene and Reidhead.

Another substantive issue of interest in the researches of Keene and Reidhead relates to the conditions of use of resources which do not enter the optimal solutions of linear programming models. One of the conditions of linear programming models is that the number of resources specified for use in an optimal solution cannot surpass the number of constraints to the problem. Thus, the total number of resources specified for optimal use in Reidhead's models cannot exceed ten for each season, since his models have only ten constraints (ten nutrient requirements). This can result in a small number of optimal activities which do not fully represent the range of selections that would occur in a real situation (38, pp. 247–49). Other factors often compound this situation. For example, attempts to simplify a problem formulation by including few constraints would have an impact. Another important factor can be seen in the works of Keene and Reidhead. The difficulty of estimating variable costs of resources under different conditions led both researchers to estimate average costs (Reidhed) or equivalent manufactured coefficients (Keene). This simplification of reality fails to account for the fact that under some conditions reduced quantities of some resources can be taken at a fraction of the average costs. For example, mobile groups which rely heavily on hunting and/or gathering for subsistence regularly encounter low cost opportunities to take resources with high average costs. The ethnographic film *The Hunters* vividly illustrates this process. While searching for large game, the Bushmen hunters in the movie collect a turtle which crosses their path, take newly hatched birds from nests which they encounter, and spend a short interval killing and processing two porcupines which they chance onto. These are all examples of resources with high average procurement costs, but which compose part of the Bushmen diet because of chance-related opportunities to acquire them at little or no cost. However, the optimal solutions of average cost models cannot include the use of such resources, even under the conditions described. This requires a more sophisticated problem formulation. However, the shadow prices of resources not included in the optimal solution provide a basic insight into this problem.

The shadow price of each "nonoptimal" resource specifies the unit decrease in cost which would be required for that resource to become a part of the optimal basis. In the case of Bushmen porcupine acquisition, for example, the shadow price would specify that if the procurement cost could be reduced by X number of man-hours, porcupines would become a part of an optimal hunting strategy. Thus, according to the model, if a situational opportunity developed to take porcupines at the prescribed marginal cost reduction, they would be taken. Assuming that people are ordinarily not adverse to unexpected optimal opportunities, the shadow prices become predictions of the relative probabilities of acquiring resources with high average costs under low cost conditions. Predictions of the probabilities associated with different resources can be ranked, using a percentile coefficient which expresses the percentage reduction in average cost required for a resource to enter the optimal solution. Presumably, optimal opportunities to acquire a resource requiring a high percentage cost reduction, as with small birds, will come infrequently, while more regular use will be made of a resource requiring a smaller percentage reduction in cost, such as porcupine.

Aside from their predictive utility, the shadow price rankings provide insight into the conditions of use of the hodgepodge of minor and costly resources often found in archaeological middens. It would be extremely difficult to achieve a systematic evaluation and predictions of the use of such resources using nonformal methods. The ranking of all resources in relation to each other cannot, for example, be achieved by ranking costs alone. It can only be achieved by ranking resources in terms of their utility in achieving the objective function, a statement which requires analysis of the complex interrelationships between resource costs, composition, and the constraints of the system. The general nonfeasibility of such computations when dealing with large problems was the motivating force behind the development of linear programming.

Approaches to Carrying Capacity

As archaeologists have attempted to explain the demographic behavior of human groups, carrying capacity studies have become an important research area (16, 110). As noted, Keene (61) discusses some of the implications of linear programming applications to the study of carrying capacity. This issue was first discussed by Keene in an unpublished paper (60). Dickson (29) has recently developed a linear programming model of the population development potential for the sustaining area of Classic period Tikal in Guatemala.

To formulate the Tikal carrying capacity problem, Dickson estimated the size of the agricultural production area surrounding the center; the productivity per hectare of corn, root crops, and ramon nuts using different cultivation practices; the energy output of each crop; and the labor requirement per hectare of each crop. He used these data to formulate a succession of problems in order to estimate carrying capacity using different maize productivity estimates, varying fallow periods, and different combinations of crops. The problem formulation consisted of three activities: maize, root, and ramon production. The number of constraints varied from two to three, consisting of available upland under varying conditions, available lowland (swamp) under varying conditions, and a constraint on maize which specified that a percentage of total calorie production had to come from maize. However, the bounds of the constraints were varied depending upon the fallow system used and the percentage of maize calories required. The objective function of each formulation was to maximize caloric yields under varying conditions. From the maximum caloric yield of each problem, he could calculate the human carrying capacity at Tikal using different cultivation strategies.

Of the three potential crops, the input-output characteristics of maize are poorest and best for ramon nuts. Consequently, according to the model, under the most favorable cultivation conditions the maximum population for the 260 km^2 arable area surrounding Tikal would vary from 14,726 people using a 100% maize strategy to 85,516 people using the uplands (240 km^2) for ramon nut arboriculture and the lowlands (20 km^2) for root cropping (29, Tables 2, 3). Dickson estimates that of the 85,516 maximum population, 64,137 people could have lived within the 163 km^2 Tikal sustaining area, supported partly by the 130 km^2 cropland within the area. He suggests that the remaining 21,379 people may have worked an additional 130 km^2 surrounding area as a support base for the sustaining area. After obtaining these results from his modeling exercise, Dickson estimates that when the dietary potential of nonagricultural foods is considered, a 10% larger population could have been supported, raising the sustaining area population to 70,551, a substantial increase over published estimates (cf 46, p. 480; 47, p. 138; 89, p. 358).

Perhaps the most important result of Dickson's model is the suggestion that the high Tikal population densities, suggested first by the late Dennis E. Puleston (see 29), could only have been achieved through the intensive practice of ramon nut arboriculture. Following Culbert (24, pp. 106–10), Dickson suggests that the population of immediate Post-classic Tikal fell to about 10% of the Classic period zenith. A 10% reduction from his 70,551 maximum figure results in a density close to that attainable through a strategy based primarily on maize cultivation. This suggests that the motives behind ramon arboriculture, if indeed it was practiced, disappeared with the fall of Classic Tikal, resulting in the maize-oriented cultivation system which characterizes the ethnographic Maya.

Although discussed later, it is important to note here that Dickson's model, controlling only for the human energy requirement, probably overestimates the actual carrying capacity of Tikal for the reasons pointed out earlier.

ISSUES AND PROBLEMS

In recent years Zipf's (109) principle of least effort has become a prominent theoretical tool of archaeology, being used both as an assumption (1, 19, 56, 57, 87) and as an hypothesis (28, 34, 51, 76). Zipf argued that all human behavior is governed by the principle of least effort. His book was reviewed by Kluckhohn (63), who found its position simultaneously fertile, suggestive, mad, and irrelevant. In anthropology "Zipf's law" is criticized perhaps most cogently by Burling (14, pp. 815–17), who argues that the minimization of effort is theoretically inadequate, being too simplistic to allow alternative explanations of the complex ordering of human priorities. Limp (forthcoming doctoral thesis) argues further that least effort approaches are incapable of accounting for changes in the ordering of priorities which originate within a system, thus restructuring definitions of what people are trying to accomplish by minimizing effort. Archaeologists have revived Zipf's law primarily to explain the relatively constricted sphere of human behavior which comprises subsistence and settlement activities. This approach is problematic because it fails to accommodate the goal conflicts which may arise to militate against labor minimization in material resource allocation. The works of Selby & Hendrix (92) and Granskog (40) underline some aspects of this problem. Mexican Indians opt not to diversify their crops in the optimal fashion identified by Granskog's model, choosing instead to pursue the apparently nonoptimal strategy of heavy corn production. According to Selby & Hendrix (92), the subsistence optimum seems to be knowingly shunned in favor of culturally defined priorities. Interestingly, what appears to be nonoptimal when Zipf's law is applied to subsistence emerges as optimal decision making when cultural priorities, which militate against the biological minimum, are incorporated.

Optimizing approaches, including the labor minimizing approach, have been criticized by the archaeologists Sullivan & Schiffer (99), who argue for the primacy of satisficer models. The satisficer approach (93, 94) argues that imperfect knowledge leads people to establish satisfactory levels of achievement which fall short of optimal attainment. In this framework, decisions are explained as attempts to meet satisfactory levels of performance, nothing more. The satisficer approach has been criticized in the economic (6, 72), anthropological (78), and archaeological literature (57; Limp, forthcoming doctoral thesis). While the simple labor minimizing, or production maximizing, approach to subsistence production behavior cannot explain the decisions observed by Granskog, the problem is more severe with the satisficer approach, since the only way to model the observed suboptimal behavior is to arbitrarily constrain optimization (6, 57).

Such criticisms of the labor minimizing approach are critical to the present discussion because the approach is central to the works of Keene and Reidhead. Such issues may lead one to question the value of Keene's model and to dismiss Reidhead's test of the effort minimization hypothesis as trite.

Practitioners and theoreticians in economics and operations research recognize that approaches such as linear programming are too simplistic in their assumptions to describe reality in complex situations. But according to Gass (38, p. 247), such approaches provide a framework for evolving successively more realistic models by using the solutions of simple models to develop more realistic ones. This process led from Granskog's (40) initial model, which failed to describe Mexican Indian behavior accurately, to the Selby & Hendrix (92) expanded model, which provided a closer approximation of decision-making reality. This also is the approach of Keene (61, 62), whose goal is to develop an *initial approximation* which might serve as a building block to a predictive model. Nevertheless, his initial model based on the *assumption* that the primary goal of human behavior is to meet biological needs at lowest cost is insightful and predicts aspects of Netsilik subsistence-settlement behavior with reasonable accuracy. In spite of the success of minimum cost models such as Keene's, their results should be taken cautiously. Archaeologists are prone to accept the effort minimization assumption as the major determinant of human subsistence and settlement behavior when, in fact, it has been demonstrated that this is not universally so. Keene's model does have predictive value among a group of hunter-gatherers in the arctic, a region with relatively few resource and settlement options. Undoubtedly, the predictive value of Keene's *initial approximation* is enhanced by the fact that arctic subsistence options are relatively limited compared with many other human systems, thus giving the effort minimizing assumption a degree of credibility lacking in more complex systems.

The analytical value of effort minimizing models is not limited to those situations in which they are intended to predict. The utility of optimization techniques such as linear programming does not lie as much in their ability to describe what *is* as in indicating what *ought to be* (5, p. 73). Johnson (57, p. 480) has argued that minimizing and maximizing approaches are useful in providing a "theoretical baseline" against which behavior can be compared. This same point is often stressed by economists. According to Joy (58, p. 187):

It should be noted that no claim is being made to represent actual behavior. What we are interested in here is the analysis of alternatives implicit in the ecological, technological, economic, and social environment, and the way choices bear on one another.

This position underscores Reidhead's (82, 83) approach to the effort minimizing problem as a hypothesis to be tested against empirical data. His objective was to identify the nature of the fit between models and empirical data and to assess the decision-making implications of the observed similarities and deviations. Reidhead's models provided a theoretical standard against which subsistence decisions in the prehistoric Ohio Valley could be compared and evaluated. His results suggested that while effort minimization describes much of the subsistence behavior of the study groups, there are important deviations from the subsistence optimum. Most notable is the failure of the populations to utilize fish intensively, when it is apparently an optimal resource, and the decision to use hazel nuts with relative intensity, in spite of their high nonoptimal costs.

Reidhead's hypothesis tests have been rightly criticized (unpublished reviews) as weak tests, a problem relating to sample size, but especially to the difficulty of comparing archaeological data with formal models. In spite of test problems, the results seem strong in the case of fish and hazels. (The use of hazels in any quantity violates optimality according to the model.) These findings are important in light of the current popularity of Zipf's principle of least effort in archaeology, since they suggest that factors other than biological needs are also involved in resource allocation decisions. These findings underscore Fletcher's assertion that motives beyond a drive to minimize effort in the acquisition of resources determine human behavior. Consequently, he argues that "group behavior will be incompletely correlated with environmental conditions" (36, p. 140). Reidhead's findings support this position and suggest that contrary to Zipf's "law," as often used by archaeologists, subsistence behavior cannot generally be expected to achieve the biological optimum. Furthermore, the empirical findings of Selby & Hendrix (92) and Granskog (40) and the arguments of Fletcher affirm that such "suboptimal" behavior occurs as a result of cultural choices and not just because people control poor information about the outcome of decisions, as argued by adherents of the satisficer approach (93, 94, 99). Selby and Hendrix argue that human behavior more closely approaches an optimum when cultural needs are modeled in the same system with biological needs. In contrast to the materialist definition of economics adopted by archaeologists (see 78), this supports the position taken originally by Robbins (86) and later by other economists (2, 32, 58; 66, pp. 1181, 1189) and anthropologists (8; 14; 22, p. 79a; 39a; 78; 90; Limp, forthcoming doctoral thesis) that cultural values and choices cannot be divorced from material needs in a study of economic decision making.

The material economy approach of archaeologists is understandable given the limitations of archaeological data (Keene's and Reidhead's models control only for materially identifiable constraints). It is difficult for archaeologists to model culturally determined constraints. But archaeologists must be cautious in assuming that models of least effort in settlement and subsistence will describe actual behavior. The findings of Keene do indicate that least effort/least risk models may reasonably predict the patterning of archaeological data in some cases. But such findings should be generalized to other cultural situations with great caution. Far from disclaiming models which assume minimization or maximization, such as linear programming models, this discussion is intended to focus on the recognized usefulness of such models in providing standards for evaluating allocation decisions. Such approaches make possible the evaluation of actual decisions in light of possibilities. By evaluating archaeological data against optimal standards, such as biological optima, it is possible to gain insight into the decision-making process and into plausible alternative explanations of behavior whether or not the model used predicts the actual disposition of the data.

Whether evaluative or predictive, the usefulness of a model is largely dependent upon the quality of the assumptions and data which go into its construction. In linear programming models of archaeological situations, nothing is more problematic than estimating costs in the use of resources. Different approaches can be taken to the cost problem. Keene uses coefficients derived from animal population behavior [densities, weights, etc (see 91)] and human technology to serve as surrogates or manufactured costs in his models. Reidhead uses combinations of ethnohistorical, ethnographic, and experimental data to estimate average procurement costs in man-hours. Keene (62) argues that manufactured coefficients are generally more amenable to archaeological applications than direct cost estimates, because such coefficients can be derived quickly in any environment using standard techniques, while labor cost estimates must be laboriously estimated anew in significantly different situations. Keene's point is well taken. His manufactured coefficients are analogous to "rules of thumb" in decision making, the utility of which, in optimization theory, has been discussed by Baumol & Quandt (6). However, rules of thumb require evaluation and to this point manufactured coefficients in archaeological modeling have not been tested to determine if they will produce results comparable to those derived from actual costs or cost estimates. Research needs to be undertaken to evaluate manufactured coefficients by comparison with actual costs in the same research universe. Such research should be able to isolate the critical variables from animal production statistics which can be used to generate reliable results. Until such evaluative research is undertaken, neither the unknown problems nor the ultimate value of manufactured coefficients can be assessed.

At present, the extent to which Keene's manufactured coefficients are accurate representations of direct costs is not known. However, Reidhead's direct cost estimates are also problematic and will need to be subjected to critical analysis to determine the extent to which they are representative of actual costs. In agreement with Keene, manufactured coefficients are likely to yield useful results for a much smaller research investment than direct cost estimating, making them potentially more useful in general applications. However, to the extent that reasonable direct costs can be estimated by archaeologists, these will likely prove most insightful of actual economic relationships and, therefore, may be preferable when research time and goals permit the derivation. A body of comparative resource cost estimates from different environments reflecting different technologies would be of extreme value, though admittedly difficult to derive.

Even though the determination of cost coefficients is problematic in programming analyses, this author agrees with Carneiro (15, p. 66) and Joy (58, p. 180) that a reasoned estimate is better than nothing and can yield useful results. If, as Baumol & Quandt (6) contend, economic rules of thumb are some of the most useful tools in optimization modeling of contemporary systems, the same should be true when modeling prehistoric systems. Furthermore, Keene (personal communication 1979) argues that the research required to construct cost estimates forces a more detailed analysis of local ecology than is usually achieved. In turn, the insights gained from such research make it possible to develop more sophisticated assumptions and hypotheses of subsistence systems. Thus, from its foundation the quantitative model building process serves a useful heuristic role.

Whether one uses manufactured coefficients or direct cost estimates, the *sensitivity analysis* component of linear programming analysis makes it possible to assess problems inherent in cost coefficients. The value ranges provided by shadow prices allow one to identify the sensitivity of models to precise changes given different levels of error in the cost coefficients.

Linear programming methods can be used to build models which integrate complex sets of material production and social choice variables (32, 58, 92). It is possible to build models of staggering complexity. The degree of simplicity or complexity built into models becomes an important issue, as stated by Rapoport (79, p. 129):

> If abstraction and simplification are undertaken to increase control, and so presumably to facilitate analysis of the observations, an increase of "realism" must be paid for in greater difficulty of control and greater complexity of analysis. Where to draw the line so as to get the most from this tradeoff is always an important methodological question.

Keene incorporated hides as a survival requirement in the Netsilik models. Subsequently, postoptimal analysis identifies hides as a limiting requirement in the problem, thus underlying the importance of incorporating hides in the model. In an effort to simplify an already complex model, Reidhead omitted hides, choosing to concentrate instead on foods alone. The impact of this simplification must be considered when evaluating the results of the Ohio Valley models. Though the environments are radically different, the importance of hides in the Netsilik models is sufficient cause to argue for their inclusion in the Ohio Valley models.

In line with many carrying capacity studies in anthropology, Dickson chose to simplify the nutritional realities of the Tikal problem, controlling only for energy. Consequently, his population estimates may be much higher than the real situation would allow, as it is doubtful that energy would have been a limiting nutrient in a system with rich energy production potential from combinations of ramon nut, root, and maize cropping.

Finally, because of the limitations of archaeological data, archaeologists generally build models which assume only the production potential of material goods as having critical importance in subsistence and settlement systems. This material approach characterizes the models of Dickson, Keene, and Reidhead. Such approaches constitute an attempt by archaeologists to simplify the realities of decision making to render their models compatible with the limitations of archaeological data. In this regard the archaeological models discussed here are considerable simplifications of reality, failing to control for social and cultural constraints. Such control will ordinarily be difficult, and sometimes impossible, for archaeologists to achieve. However, some possibilities exist. Jochim's (56) emic model of hunter-gatherer subsistence and settlement decision making is suggestive. It incorporates such variables as culturally defined preference for fat in the diet. Even etic models can provide insight into emic aspects of decision making. For example, Reidhead's models are etic, describing a system as perceived by the researcher. However, the disregard of labor costs in the use of hazel nuts and in the disuse of fish among some people in the prehistoric Ohio Valley may be indicative of culturally defined preferences and is insightful of emic aspects of subsistence decisions. Of a different nature, Green (41) and Green & Munson (42) argue that warfare was an important constraint of the settlement system in the Mississippian Angel Phase of prehistoric southwestern Indiana, resulting in suboptimal use of the environment with respect to a biological optimum. Conditions such as these can be incorporated into archaeological models of optimization.

LINEAR PROGRAMMING AND CURRENT THEMES IN ARCHAEOLOGY

With the current archaeological interest in a wide variety of economically related topics, there are many potential areas in which analysis might be enhanced by the use of linear programming and related techniques. A few of these are discussed below.

In the past decade, site catchment analysis (50, 55, 102) and its variants (74, 95) have gained prominence for their utility in analyzing the the resource potential of individual settlement locations and settlement aggregates. As Johnson (57) notes, the concept of effort minimization is basic to such analyses. Within the context of site catchment analysis a few of the potential applications of linear programming are: (*a*) testing of specific hypotheses with respect to resource potential; (*b*) analysis of resource uncertainty on decision making; (*c*) analysis of carrying capacity; (*d*) assessment of the predictive value of different assumptions regarding empirical evidence of resource use; and (*e*) description of the full range of economic relationships within the system comprising the catchment territory. The Netsilik and Ohio Valley models discussed earlier are examples of linear programming approaches to variants of catchment analysis.

Catchment analysis has recently been criticized by Flannery (35a) and Foley (37) for being too qualitative. Foley calls for methods which can quantitatively integrate population energy requirements, available energy, energy costs, the effects of changing technology, and environmental changes within defined areas. The reader will note that this list is a near perfect repetition of the requirements for formulating and solving linear programming problems. Foley has called for the kinds of analyses for which linear programming methods are ideally suited. He further criticizes catchment analysis for its selection of arbitrarily defined territorial limits, an approach which prevents the analysis of varying resource acquisition efficiencies at different distances. He argues that resource acquisition efficiency varies with distance, depending upon different animal population characteristics such as home range. Thus, catchment size would vary from species to species, depending upon energy input-output relationships at different distances. Foley's proposal adds complexity and added realism to the archaeological analysis of resource use potential. Again, a variety of linear programming techniques are designed to analyze the full set of relationships which will exist within a system such as that outlined by Foley, including simultaneous or sequential analysis of variable resource costs at different distances. *Separable convex programming* (52), also called *separable programming* (103), has been developed to accommodate the problems which arise when costs vary at different production levels and over distance. *Recursive linear pro-*

gramming (27) is another technique which allows the analysis of variable distance systems. Recognizing the same problems as Foley, Limp (69; forthcoming doctoral thesis) has developed techniques which make possible the economic analysis of settlement location decisions as they relate to variable use ranges for different resources. Limp's methods are not linear programming based, but share many of the same formal characteristics and further incorporate various aspects of graphic spatial analysis.

The principle of least effort has been a common assumption and hypothesis of the Southwestern Anthropological Research Group [SARG (35, 43)] over the last several years. Linear programming is ideally suited to facilitate the kinds of analyses being pursued by this group. In discussing the research propositions of SARG, Hill (51) argues the importance of "critical resources" in determining site locations. As discussed by Hill, critical resources are synonymous with the binding constraints of an allocation problem. The binding constraints of a subsistence-settlement system may be difficult to identify in the absence of formal methods, such as linear programming, which make explicit the description of the full set of relationships within a system.

In recent years simulation techniques have been used to model a fairly wide range of archaeological problems. In some cases simulation programs have been developed to deal with problems which have a distinct decision-making character, as in the models of Thomas (100), Zimmerman (108) and Zubrow (110), which deal variously with allocation of resources under conditions of population change and environmental uncertainty. Most treatments of linear programing discuss standardized modeling approaches, but the method is also adaptable to problems requiring simulation. Both stochastic and systematic processes can be simulated (27; 103, pp. 667–85), providing insights into long range decision making and adaptation under conditions of uncertainty in resource availability and costs, changing technologies and population variation, etc. Zubrow (111) has criticized simulation approaches for their problem-specific nature, a characteristic which can sometimes render them incomprehensible to those not involved in their development. Since all linear programming applications are dependent upon closely related assumptions, and formulation and solution techniques are highly standardized, linear programming simulations can be expected to be understood easily by anyone dealing with any of the widely used techniques. Well-developed sensitivity analysis techniques should also make linear programming an attractive tool for simulating prehistoric behavior, because it is generally difficult to test simulation results (111).

Problems in which variable distance plays a critical role in population interaction, including trade and information flow, are common in archaeology (53, 77, 85, 88). Gravity models (107) have been suggested for use in the analysis of such systems (57). A linear programming technique known as the *transportation method* uses a specially derived algorithm to find optimal solutions to problems in which goods are distributed from alternative supply centers to alternative destinations at costs which vary with distance (52). Transportation models should prove useful in archaeological studies of trade and information systems in which goods and ideas are distributed from alternative sources to alternative destinations. Additionally, Day (27) has suggested the use of recursive linear programming in the analysis of gravity problems.

The literature of ecology and cultural ecology have had a significant impact on the way archaeologists approach resource allocation problems. Economic theory has had a more recent and as yet less pronounced impact. Among some archaeologists [e.g. Foley's (37, p. 169) criticism of Higgs & Jarman (49)] there is an apparent sense of incompatibility between ecological and economic theory. Interestingly, both ecologists (80) and economists (10) have argued the dependence of the two disciplines on interrelated principles and especially the use of economic methods in ecological analysis. Concepts such as "adaptation" are common parlance in economics (6, 93, 94). According to Fletcher (36, p. 139), there are two primary concerns in dealing with adaptation: (*a*) the capacity of populations to adjust, and (*b*) the specific policies pursued by a population to obtain resources from the environment. Both issues are central to ecological and economic approaches to human behavior. By now it should be clear that linear programming formulations, solutions, and postoptimal analysis provide a powerful tool for the study of adaptive processes. Fletcher (36, p. 140) further argues that contemporary archaeology tends to deal with the second issue while by-passing the first because it ascribes sensible and intelligent decision-making capabilities to the people archaeologists study. This assertion is underscored by the popular assumption that the groups studied by archaeologists were "less optimizing societies" (19, p. 24), a position which has gained axiomatic status but is only an untested hypothesis. Furthermore, such propositions will remain uncontested in the absence of modeling techniques which allow the evaluation of alternative adaptive/production strategies and the analysis of the implications of alternative courses of action.

Linear programming methods provide avenues for the analysis and explication of relationships of both ecological and economic importance. The models discussed in this review are first approximations to such analyses. Using more advanced programming techniques, it will be possible for archaeologists to go beyond the assumptions of Keene and Reidhead to model systems which more realistically accommodate actual conditions. For example, Reidhead's models assume average costs and assume that human populations will use no more animals than the annual recruitment rate.

These assumptions simplify the realities of scale and the possibility that populations may ignorantly or knowingly overuse resources and have to live with the consequences. The economists Baumol and Quandt (6, pp. 41–44; see also 39a, p. 195), discuss trial and error "learning" processes in which the decision maker gropes his way toward an optimum through trial and error feedback. This economic concept is synonymous with the adaptive concept of ecology, which asserts that in the face of changing (uncertain) conditions, organisms grope toward adaptive equilibrium or an optimum (59). Such processes can be simulated using advanced linear programming techniques such as *separable convex programming* and *recursive linear programming*. The results of such potential research would produce equal insight into economic and ecological relationships, yielding information on the interplay between the ecological stability of resource populations and the economic considerations of cost, in addition to the other insights automatically obtained through systematic postoptimality analysis.

CONCLUSION

This article is an attempt to introduce the reader to linear programming approaches in archaeology through detailed discussions of research and problems and through an examination of the potential role of linear programming methods within the framework of contemporary archaeological method and theory. The intent has not been to argue the adoption of another "sophisticated" mathematical method. Methods have no value beyond their potential for describing or explaining phenomena of specific interest to a discipline. Hopefully, no one reading this discussion would rush to learn the rudiments of linear programming because it has the appearance of a slick technique. However, the history of the method argues convincingly that linear programming has considerable potential for the analysis of systems for which the researcher can assume or hypothesize a goal(s) of human behavior and can specify the material or social resources available for seeking goal satisfaction.

The preceding sections have emphasized evaluative and predictive aspects of linear programming analysis. Keene (61), however, correctly asserts that the greatest returns come from the potential of linear programming models to yield heuristic insights. As many writers have asserted, the clear demonstration of the interrelationships among all the variables of an operating system and of precisely how all of these will be affected by specific changes in one or more of the variables or by the addition of new variables is the task of linear programming. It is the explication of these relationships which makes possible the production of shadow prices, identification of binding constraints, and the systematic approach to sensitivity analysis. These in turn yield heuristic insights which can be used to generate new assumptions, new hypotheses, and ultimately to build better models and achieve better explanations.

Linear programming is not the only optimization method used by economists and operations researchers which may be of value in the archaeological analysis of decision making. Nonlinear programming, dynamic programming, quadratic programming, and other methods are also available. Some of these, however, are accompanied by highly specific assumptions and functions, while others are fraught with operational problems. Some, such as nonlinear programming, have no general algorithms for identifying global optimization (i.e. a best solution to the total problem) and are, therefore, restricted to local optima (i.e. a best solution to only subsets of the total problem), with no method of finding how the local optimum relates to the global. Others, such as dynamic programming, have no canonical approach to problem formulation, making it necessary to develop a specific structure for each distinct problem. It is *not* argued that linear programming is the one right approach to decision-making analysis. Many other approaches may be appropriate for specific research problems (see 39), including the location methods of cultural geography which are becoming important in archaeology. As noted earlier, Limp (69; forthcoming doctoral thesis) has developed an optimization approach which combines the input-output specificity of economic analysis with the spatial and graphic specificity of geographic models.

Finally, linear programming is not without problems. Most important among these are the quality of available quantitative data and the problems of comparability of results with the archaeological record. These problems have led some to argue that such methods are not useful in archaeological analysis and should be left to those who study living people. They argue that such methods are too far ahead of archaeological data to be of use. It is true that archaeological data are problematic, but these problems will not be solved, nor their ultimate limitations fathomed, without challenging the data with methods and theories which demand better data. The use of more sophisticated methods and theories results in better data control and ultimately in more sophisticated explanations of data.

Acknowledgments

I am grateful for the input of Kenneth Ames, Boise State University; Thomas J. Green, Idaho Historical Society; Karen Ferrario and Thomas Hay, University of Missouri-St. Louis; and John Parisi, University of Kansas. I owe a special debt to Arthur S. Keene, Anthropology, University of Massachusetts; Hon-Shiang Lau, Operations Management, University of

Missouri-St. Louis; and W. Frederick Limp, Kansas Archaeological Survey. I am also indebted to D. Bruce Dickson, Texas A & M University, for allowing me to reference his research.

Literature Cited

1. Asch, N. B., Ford, R. I., Asch, D. L. 1972. Paleoethnobotany of the Koster site: the archaic horizons. *Ill. State Mus. Rep. Invest.* 24
2. Arrow, K. J. 1963. *Social Choice and Individual Values.* New York: Wiley. 124 pp.
3. Barth, F. 1959. Segmentary opposition and the theory of games: a study of Pathan organization. *J. R. Anthropol. Inst.* 89:5–21
4. Barth, F. 1967. Economic spheres in Darfur. In *Themes in Economic Anthropology,* ed. R. Firth, pp. 149–74. London: Tavistock. 292 pp.
5. Baumol, W. J. 1977. *Economic Theory and Operations Analysis.* Englewood Cliffs: Prentice-Hall. 695 pp. 4th ed.
6. Baumol, W. J., Quandt, R. E. 1964. Rules of thumb and optimally imperfect decisions. *Am. Econ. Rev.* 54 (2) Pt. 1:23–46
7. Belovsky, G. E. 1978. Diet optimization in a generalist herbivore. *Theor. Popul. Biol.* 14:105–34
8. Belshaw, C. 1967. Theoretical problems in economic anthropology. In *Social Organization: Essays Presented to Raymond Firth,* ed. M. Freedman, pp. 25–42. Chicago: Aldine. 300 pp.
9. Binford, L. R. 1968. Post-Pleistocene adaptations. In *New Perspectives in Archaeology,* ed. S. R. Binford, L. R. Binford, pp. 313–41. Chicago: Aldine. 373 pp.
10. Boulding, K. E. 1970. *Economics as a Science.* New York: McGraw-Hill. 157 pp.
11. Buchler, I. R., McKinlay, R. M. 1969. Decision processes in culture: a linear programming analysis. See Ref. 12, pp. 191–211
12. Buchler, I. R., Nutini, H. G., eds. 1969. *Game Theory in the Behavioral Sciences.* Pittsburgh: Univ. Pittsburgh Press. 268 pp.
13. Buchler, I. R., Nutini, H. G. 1969. Introduction. See Ref. 12, pp. 1–20
14. Burling, R. 1962. Maximization theories and the study of economic anthropology. *Am. Anthropol.* 64:802–21
15. Carneiro, R. L. 1972. From autonomous villages to the state: a numerical estimation. In *Population Growth: Anthropological Implications,* ed. B.

Spooner, pp. 64–77. Cambridge: MIT Press. 425 pp.
16. Casteel, R. W. 1972. Two static maximum population density models for hunters and gatherers: a first approximation. *World Archaeol.* 4:19–40
17. Clarke, D. L. 1968. *Analytical Archaeology.* London: Methuen. 684 pp.
18. Clarke, D. L. 1972. Models and paradigms in contemporary archaeology. In *Models in Archaeology,* ed. D. L. Clarke, pp. 1–60. London: Methuen. 1055 pp.
19. Clarke, D. L. 1977. Spatial information in archaeology. In *Spatial Archaeology,* ed. D. L. Clarke, pp. 1–32. London: Academic. 386 pp.
20. Cohen, M. N. 1975. Archaeological evidence for population pressure in pre-agricultural societies. *Am. Antiq.* 40:471–75
21. Cohen, M. N. 1977. *The Food Crisis in Prehistory: Overpopulation and the Origins of Agriculture.* New Haven: Yale Univ. Press. 341 pp.
22. Cook, S. 1970. Price and output variability in a peasant-artisan stoneworking industry in Oaxaca, Mexico: an analytical essay in economic anthropology. *Am. Anthropol.* 72:776–801
23. Cowgill, G. L. 1975. On causes and consequences of ancient and modern population changes. *Am. Anthropol.* 77:505–25
24. Culbert, T. P. 1974. *The Lost Civilization: The Story of the Classic Maya.* New York: Harper & Row. 123 pp.
25. Dantzig, G. B. 1963. *Linear Programming and Extensions.* Princeton: Princeton Univ. Press. 632 pp.
26. Davenport, W. 1960. Jamaican fishing: A game theory analysis. *Yale Univ. Publ. Anthropol* 59
27. Day, R. H. 1973. Recursive programming models: a brief introduction. In *Studies in Economic Planning Over Space and Time,* ed. G. G. Judge, T. Takayama, pp. 329–44. Amsterdam: North Holland. 727 pp.
28. Dean, J. S. 1978. An evaluation of the initial SARG research design. See Ref. 35, pp. 103–17
29. Dickson, D. B. 1978. *Ancient agriculture and population at Tikal, Guatemala: an application of linear program-*

ming to the simulation of an archaeological problem. Presented at Ann. Meet. Soc. Am. Archaeol., 43rd, Tucson

30. Dorfman, R. 1951. Application of Linear Programming to the Theory of the Firm. Berkeley: Univ. Calif. Press. 98 pp.

31. Dorfman, R. 1953. Mathematical, or "linear", programming: a nonmathematical exposition. Am. Econ. Rev. 43:797–825

32. Dorfman, R., Samuelson, P. A., Solow, R. M. 1958. Linear Programming and Economic Analysis. New York: McGraw-Hill. 527 pp.

33. Dunn, F. L. 1968. Epidemiological factors: health and disease in hunter-gatherers. In Man the Hunter, ed. R. B. Lee, I. DeVore, pp. 221–28. Chicago: Aldine. 415 pp.

34. Euler, R. C., Chandler, S. M. 1978. Aspects of prehistoric settlement patterns in Grand Canyon. See Ref. 35, pp. 73–86

35. Euler, R. C., Gumerman, G. J., eds. 1978. Investigations of the Southwestern Anthropological Research Group: an experiment in archaeological cooperation: Proceedings of the 1976 Conference. Flagstaff: Mus. North. Ariz. 186 pp.

35a. Flannery, K. V. 1976. Empirical determination of site catchments in Oaxaca and Tehuacan. See Ref. 77, pp. 103–17

36. Fletcher, R. 1977. Settlement studies (micro and semi-micro). See Ref. 19, pp. 47–162

37. Foley, R. 1977. Space and energy: a method for analyzing habitat value and utilization in relation to archaeological sites. See Ref. 19, pp. 163–87

37a. Found, W. C. 1971. A Theoretical Approach to Rural Land Use Patterns. London: Arnold. 190 pp.

38. Gass, S. I. 1969. Linear Programming Methods and Applications. New York: McGraw-Hill. 358 pp. 3rd ed.

39. Gladwin, C. H. 1975. A model of the supply of smoked fish from Cape Coast to Kamasi. In Formal Methods in Economic Anthropology, ed. S. Plattner, pp. 77–127. Spec. Publ. Am. Anthropol. Assoc. 4

39a. Gladwin, H. 1975. Looking for an aggregate additive model in data from a hierarchical decision process. See Ref. 39, pp. 159–96

40. Granskog, J. E. 1974. Efficiency in a Zapotec Indian agricultural village. PhD thesis. Univ. Texas, Austin, Tex. 222 pp.

41. Green, T. J. 1977. Economic relationships underlying Mississippian settlement patterns in southwestern Indiana and north-central Kentucky. PhD thesis. Indiana Univ., Bloomington, Ind. 367 pp.

42. Green, T. J., Munson, C. A. 1978. Mississippian settlement patterns in southwestern Indiana. In Mississippi Settlement Patterns, ed. B. D. Smith, pp. 293–330. New York: Academic

43. Gumerman, G. J. 1971. The distribution of prehistoric population aggregates. Prescott Coll. Anthropol. Rep. 1

44. Hassan, F. 1974. Population growth and cultural evolution. Rev. Anthropol. 1:205–12

45. Hassan, F. 1976. Diet, nutrition and agricultural origins in the Near East. In Origine de l'elevage et de la domestication, ed. E. S. Higgs, pp. 227–47. 9th Cong. UISPP, Colloq. 20, Nice

46. Haviland, W. A. 1969. A new population estimate for Tikal, Guatemala. Am. Antiq. 34:429–33

47. Haviland, W. A. 1972. Family size, prehistoric population estimates and the ancient Maya. Am. Antiq. 37:135–39

48. Heyer, J. 1966. Preliminary results of a linear programming analysis of peasant farms in Machakos District, Kenya. E. Afr. Inst. Soc. Res. Conf. Papers, Kampala

49. Higgs, E. S., Jarman, M. R. 1975. Paleoeconomy. In Paleoeconomy, ed. E. S. Higgs, pp. 1–7. London: Cambridge. 244 pp.

50. Higgs, E. S., Vita-Finzi, C. 1972. Prehistoric economics: a territorial approach. In Papers in Economic Prehistory, ed. E. S. Higgs, pp. 27–36. London: Cambridge. 219 pp.

51. Hill, J. N. 1971. Research propositions for consideration Southwestern Anthropological Research Group. See Ref. 43, pp. 55–82

52. Hillier, F. S., Lieberman, G. J. 1974. Operations Research. San Francisco: Holden-Day. 800 pp. 2nd ed.

53. Hodder, I. R., Orton, C. 1976. Spatial Analysis in Archaeology. London: Cambridge. 220 pp.

54. Hoffman, H. 1969. A linear programming approach to cultural intensity. See Ref. 12, pp. 179–90

55. Jarman, M. R. 1972. A territorial model for archaeology: a behavioral and geographic approach. See Ref. 18, pp. 705–33

56. Jochim, M. 1976. Hunter-gatherer Subsistence and Settlement: A Predictive Model. New York: Academic. 206 pp.

56a. Johansen, L. 1976. L. V. Kantorovich's contribution to economics. *Scand. J. Econ.* 78:61–80

57. Johnson, G. A. 1977. Aspects of regional analysis in archaeology. *Ann. Rev. Anthropol.* 6:479–508

58. Joy, L. 1967. An economic homologue of Barth's presentation of economic spheres in Darfur. See Ref. 4, pp. 175–89

58a. Kantorovich, L. V. 1939. *Mathematical methods in the organization and planning of production.* Leningrad: Leningrad State Univ. Press. 68 pp. Transl. *Manage. Sci. (1960)* 6:366–422

59. Katz, P. L. 1974. A long-term approach to foraging optimization. *Am. Nat.* 108: 758–82

60. Keene, A. S. 1977. *Economic optimization models and the study of hunter-gatherer subsistence settlement systems.* Presented at Ann. Meet. Soc. Am. Archaeol., 42nd, New Orleans

61. Keene, A. S. 1979. Economic optimization models and the study of hunter-gatherer subsistence settlement systems. In *Transformations: Mathematical Approaches to Culture Change,* ed. C. Renfrew, K. Cooke. London: Academic. In press

62. Keene, A. S. 1980. Nutrition and economy: models for the study of prehistoric diet. In *Techniques for the Study of Prehistoric Diet,* ed. R. Gilbert, J. Mielke, Oxford: Univ. Mississippi Press. In press

63. Kluckhohn, C. 1950. Review of *Human Behavior and the Principle of Least Effort,* G. K. Zipf. *Am. Anthropol.* 52: 268–70

64. Koopmans, T. C., ed. 1951. *Activity Analysis of Production and Allocation.* New York: Wiley. 404 pp.

65. Kroeber, A. L. 1939. *Cultural and Natural Areas of Native North America.* Berkeley: Univ. Calif. Press. 242 pp.

66. LeClair, E. E. Jr. 1962. Economic theory and economic anthropology. *Am. Anthropol.* 64:1179–1203

67. Lee, R. B. 1968. What hunters do for a living, or, how to make out on scarce resources. See Ref. 33, pp. 30–48

68. Limp, W. F. 1977. *The economics of agricultural dispersal.* Presented at Ann. Meet. Soc. Am. Archaeol., 42nd, New Orleans

69. Limp, W. F. 1978. *Optimization theory and subsistence change: implications for prehistoric settlement location analysis.* Presented at Ann. Meet. Soc. Am. Archaeol., 43rd, Tucson

70. Limp, W. F., Reidhead, V. A. 1979. An economic evaluation of the potential of fish utilization in riverine environments. *Am. Antiq.* 44:70–78

71. Luce, R. D., Raiffa, H. 1957. *Games and Decisions: Introduction and Critical Survey.* New York: Wiley. 509 pp.

72. Machlup, F. 1967. Theories of the firm: marginalist, behavioralist, managerial. *Am. Econ. Rev.* 57:1–33

73. Machol, R. E. 1976. *Elementary Systems Mathematics: Linear Programming for Business and the Social Sciences.* New York: McGraw-Hill. 267 pp.

74. Munson, P. J., Parmalee, P. W., Yarnell, R. A. 1971. Subsistence ecology of Scoville, a terminal Middle Woodland village. *Am. Antiq.* 36:410–31

75. Patterson, T. C. 1971. The emergence of food production in Central Peru. In *Prehistoric Agriculture,* ed. S. Struever, 181–207. New York: Natural History Press. 733 pp.

76. Plog, F., Hill, J. N. 1971. Explaining variability in the distribution of sites. See Ref. 43, pp. 7–36

77. Plog, S. 1976. Measurement of prehistoric interaction between communities. In *The Early Mesoamerican Village,* ed. K. V. Flannery, pp. 255–72. New York: Academic. 377 pp.

78. Prattis, J. I. 1973. Strategizing man. *Man* 8:46–58

79. Rapoport, A. 1969. Games as tools of psychological research. See Ref. 12, pp. 129–50

80. Rapport, D. J., Turner, J. E. 1977. Economic models in ecology. *Science* 195:367–73

81. Reidhead, V. A. 1976. *Optimization and food procurement at the Prehistoric Leonard Haag Site, Southeastern Indiana: a linear programming approach.* PhD thesis. Indiana Univ. Bloomington, Ind. 556 pp.

82. Reidhead, V. A. 1980. A linear programming model of prehistoric subsistence optimization: a southeastern Indiana example. *Indiana Hist. Soc. Prehist. Res. Ser.* In press

83. Reidhead, V. A. 1980. The economics of subsistence change: [a test of] an optimization model. In *Subsistence Change: Economic and Ecological Models in Prehistory,* ed. T. K. Earle, A. Christenson. New York: Academic. In press

84. Reidhead, V. A., Limp, W. F. 1974. *Nutritional maximization: a multifaceted nutritional approach to archaeological research.* Presented Ann. Meet. Am. Anthropol. Assoc., 73rd, Mexico City

85. Renfrew, C. 1977. Models for exchange and spatial distribution. In *Exchange Systems in Prehistory*, ed. T. K. Earle, J. E. Ericson, pp. 71–90. New York: Academic. 274 pp.

86. Robbins, L. 1932. *An Essay on the Nature and Significance of Economic Science*. London: Macmillan. 141 pp.

87. Roper, D. C. 1974. The distribution of Middle Woodland sites with the environment of the lower Sangamon River, Illinois. *Ill. State Mus. Rep. Invest. 30*

88. Runnels, C. 1977. *Economic Man in the Prehistoric Aegean: 8000 years of Andesite Exploitation*. Presented at Ann. Meet. Soc. Am. Archaeol., 42nd, New Orleans

89. Sanders, W. T. 1973. The cultural ecology of the lowland Maya: a reevaluation. In *The Classic Maya Collapse*, ed. T. P. Culbert, pp. 325–65. Albuquerque: Univ. New Mexico. 549 pp.

90. Schneider, H. K. 1974. *Economic Man: the Anthropology of Economics*. New York: Free Press, 278 pp.

91. Schoener, T. W. 1971. Theory of feeding strategies. *Ann. Rev. Ecol. Syst.* 2:369–404

92. Selby, H. A., Hendrix, G. G. 1976. Policy planning and poverty: notes on a Mexican case. In *Anthropology and the Public Interest: Fieldwork and Theory*, ed. P. R. Sanday, pp. 219–44. New York: Academic. 363 pp.

93. Simon, H. A. 1955. A behavioral model of rational choice. *Q. J. Econ.* 69:99–118

94. Simon, H. A. 1959. Theories of decision-making in economics and behavioral sciences. *Am. Econ. Rev.* 49:253–83

95. Smith, B. D. 1975. Middle Mississippi exploitation of animal populations. *Anthrol. Pap. Mus. Anthropol. Univ. Mich. 57*

96. Smith, E. L., Young, T. C. Jr. 1972. The evolution of early agriculture and culture in greater Mesopotamia: a trial model. See Ref. 15, pp. 1–59

97. Smith, J. M. 1978. Optimization theory in evolution. *Ann. Rev. Ecol. Syst.* 9:31–56

98. Stigler, G. J. 1945. The cost of subsistence. *J. Farm Econ.* 27:303–14

99. Sullivan, A. P., Schiffer, M. B. 1978. A critical examination of SARG. See Ref. 35, pp. 168–76

100. Thomas, D. H. 1973. An empirical test for Steward's model of Great Basin settlement patterns. *Am. Antiq.* 38:155–76

101. Throsby, C. D. 1962. Some notes on "dynamic" linear programming. *Rev. Mark. Agric. Econ.* 30:119–41

102. Vita-Finzi, C., Higgs, E. S. 1970. Prehistoric economy in the Mt. Carmel area of Palestine: Site catchment analysis. *Proc. Prehist. Soc.* 36:1–37

103. Wagner, H. M. 1975. *Principles of Operations Research*. Englewood Cliffs: Prentice-Hall. 1039 pp. 2nd ed.

103a. Walters, C. J., Hilborn, R. 1978. Ecological optimization and adaptive management. *Ann. Rev. Ecol. Syst.* 9:157–88

104. Waugh, F. V. 1951. The minimum-cost dairy feed: an application of linear programming. *J. Farm Econ.* 33:299–310

105. Whitehouse, G. E., Wechsler, B. L. 1976. *Applied Operations Research: A Survey*. New York: Wiley. 434 pp.

106. Woodburn, J. 1968. An introduction to Hadza ecology. See Ref. 33, pp. 49–55

107. Yeates, M. 1974. *An Introduction to Quantitative Analysis in Human Geography*. New York: McGraw-Hill. 299 pp.

108. Zimmerman, L. J. 1977. Prehistoric locational behavior: a computer simulation. *Off. State Archaeol. Univ. Iowa Rep. 10*

109. Zipf, G. K. 1949. *Human Behavior and the Principle of Least Effort*. Cambridge, Mass: Addison-Wesley. 573 pp.

110. Zubrow, E. B. W. 1975. *Prehistoric Carrying Capacity: A Model*. Menlo Park, Calif: Cummings. 143 pp.

111. Zubrow, E. B. W. 1976. Models and complexity in archaeological simulations. *Newsl. Comput. Archaeol.* 12:1–16

Ann. Rev. Anthropol. 1979. 8:579–600
Copyright © 1979 by Annual Reviews Inc. All rights reserved

BIOLOGICAL AND CULTURAL DIFFERENCES IN EARLY CHILD DEVELOPMENT

♦9646

Daniel G. Freedman and Marilyn M. DeBoer [1]

Committee on Human Development, University of Chicago, Chicago, Illinois 60637

Anthropology's interest in early child development was coincident with the efflorescence of psychoanalysis in the 1940s and 1950s. The psychoanalytic causal system relating early experience and personality differences held promise for explaining individual differences within populations as well as "ethological" (from Bateson's "ethos") differences between populations. But, as is evident from the culture and personality literature (5, 39, 72, 75, 83), this early promise has flagged considerably. Only John Whiting's creative use of the HRAF files has served to keep the area active, but even here dissatisfactions are rampant (4, 39, 78).

Inherent in practically all the work in "culture and personality" and the "new look" cognitive and perceptual work (e.g. 63) is the premise that all people are born with equal potential and that differing circumstances of rearing and environment produce the perceived differences; this premise has been called the "psychic unity of mankind." While almost all anthropologists have flirted with the notion of constitutional or genetic differences in temperament, certainly no one in recent years has either given it more than lip service or incorporated it systematically into a theoretical view of cultural differences. As we shall see below, one cannot reasonably turn one's back on what might be half the story and expect one's theory to stand up.

This review, which lays no claim to exhaustiveness, will consist of an overview of recent studies showing ethnic differences in newborn behavior in part one, followed by an even more selective review of the enormous

[1]We acknowledge with thanks the help of Mrs. Jean Hansen in editing and typing the manuscript.

579

0084-6570/79/1015-0579$01.00

sex-difference literature, one which concentrates on cross-cultural findings in social behavior. In both parts we will try to demonstrate that the biological and the cultural are inextricably intertwined—so much so that even the aim of "teasing apart" one from the other seems a thankless goal.

CROSS-CULTURAL DIFFERENCES IN BEHAVIOR IN EARLY INFANCY

In the last 10 years or so, a number of cross-cultural workers have begun to look at infant development in a more systematic way than had been done previously. While Mead, for example, had reported on Balinese rearing techniques as crucial for Balinese character, she gave details on but one Balinese child, Karba (7). By today's standards this would hardly be acceptable.

One of the foremost workers of this new genre was the late William Caudill, whose comparison of mother-infant interactions in Tokyo with a Caucasian group in Baltimore was the first carefully controlled study of infant rearing techniques in two cultures (16). Very much in the environmentalist tradition, Caudill attributed the lower levels of Japanese infant vocalizations, play, and spontaneous movements to congruent differences in maternal treatment. However, with our own publication of Chinese-Caucasian differences at *birth* (30), the possibilities of important inborn differences in the behavioral repertoire of a population received credence.

Since the differences noted at birth were not unlike the differences noted by Caudill at 3 months (the Chinese newborns were considerably easier to quiet, easier to habituate to various stimuli, and in general more placid), Caudill felt a response was necessary. He and Frost (15) then published a study of third generation Japanese mothers and their fourth generation infants. They found that indeed the fourth generation infants were vocalizing at almost the Baltimore Caucasian rates; however, the Japanese mothers were stimulating them at *twice* the Caucasian rates. Using the terminology of the geneticist, the same phenotype may be achieved via a variety of genetic and environmental interactions; in this case it is a reasonable surmise that extraordinary stimulation of Japanese infants yielded the norm achieved by Caucasian mothers with half the amount of vocalization. In several other respects, the fourth generation infants were still more like the Tokyo infants: they were less playful and sucked their fingers more than did the Baltimore group.

A further attempt to bridge the Freedman and Freedman studies of newborn Chinese and Caucasians and the Caudill studies of 3-month-olds was performed by Kuchner (52). Starting soon after birth, Kuchner found that two university-based groups (infants of first generation Chinese stu-

dents vs infants of students of European background) differed in the newborn period in approximately the same way as in the Freedman and
Freedman study. At 3 months of age her findings were nearly identical with
Caudill's. Oriental mothers interacted less with their infants, and their
infants were less playful, vocalized less, and smiled less. Her interpretation,
which seems close to the data, is that the Oriental infants were born with
less need for stimulation and that mothers accommodated appropriately. To
judge from the Caudill studies above, the mothers had not (as yet?) exchanged old country values, as had the third generation Japanese, in the
service of "Americanizing" their children.

There are comparable neonatal data from other culture areas.

Navajo and Hopi

Freedman (27), Nisselius (69) and J. S. Chisholm & R. H. Woodson (unpublished) have reported on Navajo newborn behavior. Both Freedman and
Nisselius used the Cambridge Neonatal Scales (11), while Chisholm and
Woodson used the related "Brazelton" Scale (10). Amerindian newborns
differ from Caucasian neonates much as do the Chinese infants. They are
more likely not to protest a cloth held over the nose, are generally less
irritable, are easier to quiet once they do get upset, and show a reduced
Moro response or startle reaction [Kluckhohn had already noted this in the
1940s (47, 48)]. In general, these infants are on the more placid side of a
placid-to-excitable continuum. While Chisholm found that differences in
maternal blood pressure in the first stage of labor are significantly associated
with 5% of the newborn variance in irritability, it would appear that the
only robust hypotheses would involve the known facts relating Athabaskans
(Navajo) and a common Asian genetic stock (e.g. 76).

An issue of interest here is the cradleboard, still used for some 30% of
Navajo infants. It had been hypothesized (39) that rearing on the cradleboard may be causal to the self-restraint and impassivity that most agree
typify Navajo personality (e.g. 76). The above findings would tend to turn
this logic around, at least in part, and suggest that infants predisposed to
relative inactivity and placidity would be more likely to accept extended
periods on a cradleboard. The work of Chisholm and Richards (unpublished) bears this out. Following its introduction early in the first month,
Navajo mothers did not thereafter impose the cradleboard, and if an infant
started to complain, he was invariably released. Most did not complain with
much persistence until after 6 months, when weaning from the board typically started, and by one year most were permanently off. A group of
Caucasian infants raised on cradleboards was also followed by Chisholm,
who reported many more infant complaints—and that all were completely
off the board before 6 months.

What is going on over these early months between infant and mother? A recent study by Callaghan (14) helps lend some perspective. In this, his master's thesis, Callaghan asked 19 Navajo, 20 Hopi, and 20 Anglo mothers of 3- to 6-month-olds to "get the attention of your baby." The ensuing interaction was videotaped and a frame-by-frame analysis performed, and behavioral acts were coded in detail. As might now be expected, Caucasian mothers vocalized at twice the Navajo rates, with the Hopi falling in between. Anglo mothers usually spoke to their infants in full sentences ("Come on, give us a big smile"); Hopi women made the culture-specific noises one makes only to babies and animals; while Navajo mothers, if they vocalized at all, made low-keyed whispering sounds. Caucasian mothers kept readjusting the infants' positions, while Navajos maintained a steady, preferred position. Again the Hopi fell in between. These differences were statistically significant, and the Navajo comparisons paralleled closely the Japanese-Caucasian differences found by Caudill and the Chinese-Caucasian differences found by Kuchner. In all these studies, Oriental mothers were less stimulating, Oriental babies less excitable. To judge by the amount of mutual gazing between mother and infants, all mothers (Anglo, Navajo, and Hopi) were equally successful. Caucasian infants, however, kept actively turning toward and away from their mothers as if regulating excessive input. By contrast, Navajo babies maintained significantly longer bouts of gazing toward and away. Like the Chinese and Japanese infants studied by Caudill and by Kuchner (15, 16, 52), the Navajo infants also were less motorically active, tending not to move their limbs as much.

It would appear that different styles of mother-infant coalitions were being set up, based both on maternal styles and infant predilections. It further appears that long-term values are already at work in these early encounters. For example, the tendency of Navajo mothers not to intrude into their baby's state fits with the stated Navajo value that "each child and each adult must decide for himself what road to take," or the frequent observation that a Navajo does not impose his or her will or ambition on another (e.g. 90)—a telling contrast with the average middle American's concern with and plans for his or her child's "success." As we have already noted, this does not deny the hypothetical possibility that an Anglo newborn can be Navajo-ized, or vice versa. However, different maternal strategies would obviously be required to achieve the new phenotype, as the Caudill and Frost data on third and fourth generation Japanese-Americans suggests (15).

As for the Hopi results, falling in between Anglo and Navajo in almost every instance, Hopi access to electricity, television, and mainstream influence exceeds that of the Navajo; but perhaps it is also worth reporting that interim results of an unpublished study by Freedman and Callaghan of

Hopi newborns (N = 23) suggest that while these newborns are not as excitable or irritable as are Anglo newborns, they are not as placid as were Navajo newborns born at the same hospital (USPH Hospital, Keams Canyon, Arizona) and over the same period of time.

This suggests either different prenatal influences or differing gene pools for the Hopi and Navajo, and at present there is no way to decide [see Boyd (9) on differences in Amerindian blood group frequencies].

Sub-Saharan Africa, Jamaica, and Afro-Americans

A great deal has been written about black African motor precocity, starting with the study of Geber & Dean (33, 34) on a series of Ugandan newborns. Using a nonquantified neurological examination, they reported that the Ugandan neonates gave many indications of precocity relative to European infants: they held up their heads better and seemed to have lost some reflexes at birth that disappear at 2 weeks among Europeans. Ainsworth (1) was similarly impressed that Ugandan (Bagandan) newborns were motorically advanced. One dissenting study (also from Uganda) was that of Warren & Parkin (85). In an apprently well-controlled study, they could not duplicate Geber's critical observations regarding the absence of a number of reflexes at birth although similar procedures were used.

Freedman's (27) study of Nigerian newborns, using the Cambridge Scales (11), yielded results similar to Parkin and Warren in that no generalized precocity was found. However, he did note considerably better head and neck control in the Hausa group when the newborns were pulled to a sitting position than was seen in Asian and Caucasian newborns. He also noted the frequent presence of lordosis (an erect back when in the sitting position) among the Hausa as opposed to the collapsed, rounded back (kyphosis) in both comparison groups, and, like most workers in Africa, he found precocious development limited to such motor behavior.

The work of Brazelton, Koslowski & Tronick (12) may serve to bridge some of the potentially contradictory evidence in the newborn period. Zambian infants tested soon after birth were slow compared to American whites, apparently because of the high incidence of maternal malnourishment; but by 10 days of age the Zambians scored substantially higher on items relating to social attentiveness. Freedman, in his Nigerian study, had eliminated obviously malnourished mothers from his sample, which clearly shaped the study's outcome.

Probably because of the "racist" implications of designating such precocity as genetic in origin (27), the very workers who first made these observations among newborns later began stressing maternal training as the cause for the continued precocity over the first year (1, 35). In a similar vein, Warren, upon examining and charting some 14 studies comparing African and European development in the first year, decided that nine studies which had found motor precocity among Africans were not well done, and that the two which had found no difference were, by contrast, to be trusted (84).

Super's initial work (79) was largely devoted to this issue, and in cross-sectional studies among several African groups he found that mothers practiced their infants in just those motor behaviors in which the infants exceeded European norms. However, no clear-cut inference about what caused what could be made from these data. Did the initial hints that the child is ready to sit come first, or did the mother's pleasure in having the child achieve this behavior come first? From our previous discussion it would seem reasonable to interpret these data as a two-way street: mothers tend to pick up on baby's talents and then bring them to fruition with special attention. Super originally interpreted his results with a strongly environmental bias, but now seems to have modified his view by acknowledging the possibility of infant readiness as a factor (80). Hopkins (40) discussed these very issues with regard to West Indian precocity and Konner (49) with regard to !Kung Bushmen precocity, each coming to the approximate conclusion that both experiential and constitutional factors are at work. Hopkins, noting the psychometric separation between temperament and motor behavior in his London-based West Indian sample, but not in the English sample, points out that for the Heinz Werner school of development this is a sign of greater West Indian maturity (earlier differentiation of systems). Marshall & Tanner (57), also working among black West Indians, found that bone age was relatively advanced at birth and throughout early infancy.

Kilbride & Kilbride (46), in yet another study of Baganda infants, also found precocity in several areas relative to the American Bayley norms. They chose to emphasize precocity in early sitting and attributed this particular advance to the observation that the Baganda make much of teaching this skill. The problems in the attribution of cause, however, are the same as in Super's study above. It is notable that an even more striking advance in smiling to and "socializing" with their own mirror image (1.9 to 3.2 months sooner than American infants) is merely mentioned in passing, presumably because it would be difficult to make a similar case for special training here.

The most complete review in this area is Hopkins' (41) tabulated summary of 46 comparative studies of psychomotor development involving black and white infants from Africa, the Caribbean, the United States, and England. Including most of the studies mentioned here, plus many more, Hopkins' summary indicates a clear and unmistakable trend in infants of sub-Saharan African heritage to demonstrate better head control and better visual pursuit at birth, and to reach such motor mileposts as sitting, standing, and walking sooner than do white infants.

In an earlier review of this area, Werner (87) pointed out that infants of urbanized-modernized Africans tended to be not quite as precocious as rural samples, although they were still more precocious than Europeans. A subsequent study by Liederman et al in Kenya (53), however, contradicted this "trend" in that Kikuyu infants of higher SES levels achieved motor milestones before a control of lower SES Kikuyus. Freedman (26) speculated that the higher mortality of low SES African infants may be a major selection factor in producing the differential precocity favoring lower SES when it occurs. Obviously this SES effect is complex and demands more careful, analytic examination than it has yet received.

It has been speculated that the black African gestation period may be longer and that the observed precocity is an artifact of "postmaturity." However, recent data from the collaborative study in the United States (32), indicate that with SES, maternal education, parity, smoking during pregnancy, and maternal age held constant, Afro-American mothers have a significantly *shorter* period of gestation than whites, indicating somewhat sped-up intrauterine development (twice as many Afro-Americans gave birth before 37 weeks of gestation). These are the most complete data yet presented on this issue, including some 12,000 births in each group, and they are in the same direction as several previous studies (80).

In this regard, Hallet (36) reported extremely short gestation periods for Ituri pygmies and extraordinarily quick development over the first year: social smiles by 1 month, sitting up and grasping before 3 months, walking by 6 months, and climbing trees and speaking some 150 words by 1 year! These data are so startling that they clearly demand verification. As far as we can gather, no one else working with the Ituri pgymies has even hinted at these rapid rates of development.

As to what the somewhat greater developmental rates among Afro-Americans might mean, a few words of caution are required. Dr. T. B. Brazelton, the noted pediatrician, reports (12) that in his Cambridge, Massachusetts, practice, middle class black women often ask for advice on how to slow down their motorically precocious youngsters, apparently believing that motoric precocity and "mental primitivity" are related. There is not a shred of evidence for this, and, as we shall see below, many "Caucasian" East Indian infants are also motorically precocious in the first year.

Bali

Mead & MacGregor (62), in their analysis of Bateson's still photographs, largely of parents and children of the highland village of Bajung Gedé, spoke of a "meandering tonus," possibly of biological origin, that best described the unusual limb positioning seen time and again in the photos. On a visit to Bali in 1972, D. G. Freedman and S. Strieby (unpublished) examined 35 newborns with the Cambridge Newborn Scales and were impressed that approximately one third of the neonates had unusually *pliable* limb tonus; that is, limb positions could be readily manipulated by the examiner without crisply "snapping back" to their original position as is common, say in US Caucasian populations. Yet the tonus could not be rated "low" according to the test criteria since a "soft" snap-back did occur. Given the instrument used, there was no ready way to transform these observations into scores, and it is hoped that further studies will be done at the hospital in Den Pasaar. Ideally, films or videotapes should be made of the examinations for later comparisons with control groups.

Another passing note about Bali. In Mead's analysis of Balinese temperament, she laid emphasis on observations that mothers tease their children to a point where "typical" Balinese nonresponsivity replaces the initial temper tantrums. No one has since demonstrated so straightforward a method of incorporating a group's ethos, so it is perhaps worth examining in a little detail.

Mead's major case history was Karba, the child of a neighbor a few houses from the Mead-Bateson hut. In their famous film of Karba we see the entire process. Karba's mother induces jealousy by borrowing a "lap baby," and Karba's unhappiness is seen to give way to an extremely moderated responsivity to others that Mead says typifies the Balinese. However, in the very film in which this point is documented, serious Karba may be seen playing with two smiling if not outgoing age mates. Further, when Freedman and Bateson visited Bajung Gedé in 1972, Karba was still sober-faced relative to his fellow villagers, and, interestingly, had long held the role of village priest. For our present purposes, the question to raise is this: was Karba an example of individual differences, a child who may indeed have reacted to teasing in the way described, but who did so in contradistinction to peers who handled comparable experiences in other ways? Everything we know about individual differences would support such a generality, and few working child psychologists would dare predict that a specific parental treatment would yield so specific an outcome (24, 68).

Australian Aboriginals

As reported by Freedman (27), a series of Australian Aboriginal newborns appeared to yield a configuration on the Cambridge Neonatal Scales not previously seen. While exhibiting extremely brisk responses (the highest scores on automatic walk and on swiping at a cloth over the nose), they were nevertheless extremely placid and unirritable. Head control was comparable to the one-month level in Caucasian infants, and they were remarkably coordinated when pulled to a sitting or standing position, exhibiting a total body coordination rare in Caucasians and Orientals. A current, as yet incomplete, study by Chisholm, important because both Caucasian and Aboriginal newborns were examined at the same hospital over the same period, should go far in either confirming or disconfirming these initial findings.

In the meantime, it is perhaps reasonable to speculate over the fact that the Aboriginal newborns seem "ready to travel" within hours of birth. Special means of transport were never developed (compared with African slings, European swaddling, North American cradleboards), nor is there a traditional lying-in period (often about 30 days in Japan, parts of Africa, among Amerindians, and Europeans). Since, especially in the Australian interior, staying on the move was an economic necessity, selective pressure for such infants must have been high.

Puerto Rico, Mexico, Guatemala, and the Issue of Early Stimulation

A study has appeared by C. G. Coll, C. Sepkoski and B. M. Lester (unpublished) comparing Puerto Rican newborns with black and white North American newborns, using the Brazelton scale (10). Puerto Rican babies had better orienting and following, were easier to console, and more capable of controlling their physiological responses to stress (fewer startles). An interesting methodological feature of this study—one that holds promise for future work in the area—was a "discriminant analysis" that permitted the correct classification of protocols in nine out of ten infants. As the authors point out,

> This approach to the study of cross-cultural differences is useful as it enables us to avoid extracting a series of significant but possibly redundant individual effects as in an item by item comparison. It also enables us to capture constellations of behavior that discriminate among the groups.

Brazelton et al (12a) examined newborn and young infants among the Zincanteco of Mexico and describe a similar picture. They were impressed with the smooth, nonjerky movements, relative to Caucasian infants, and spoke also of a quiet alertness in the very young infants. The latter, however, may have been an artifact of the very dim lighting in which Zincanteco are traditionally kept. (Newborns usually perform better on visual tasks in dim lighting.) Navajo-like noninterference with the infant was observed; that is, they were *not* stimulated in the Anglo fashion. Unfortunately, no figures nor quantitative comparisons with a control population are reported, but this study does serve to introduce the next, by Kagan & Klein (45).

Kagan and Klein, working with a group of Guatemalan *mestizo* children, also found decidedly "unstimulating" parents over the first year and, rather reasonably, attributed slow development compared to Caucasian norms to this fact. At the same time, testing of older, prepubertal children resulted in norms completely comparable to US norms, and Kagan made the obvious deduction that stimulation or nonstimulation in infancy probably does not affect later performance. This was a 180° turnaround for Kagan, who had long advocated intervention programs among infants of underachieving segments of the United States. That debate still rages, but the evidence at this juncture appears to favor Kagan's new position.

In general, data from the field of behavior genetics (e.g. 31) would support a cautious view toward the issue of "optimal" child rearing. Within one species, different varieties or breeds will yield different and even opposite phenotypes following exactly the same rearing procedures. In mice, for example, Bar Harbor Strain HS increases in weight, while DBA/2 decreases in weight, with exactly the same amounts of experimental "handling" in the first month of life (2, 43). Similarly, different breeds of dogs react to the same rearing procedures in quite different ways and with quite different behavioral results (25). In an analogous situation, infant identical twin pairs have been shown to develop similar interactional patterns with their parents, in contrast to same-sexed fraternal pairs who develop quite different interactional and interpersonal pathways (27).

That is to say, one's biological makeup is a factor in how objectively similar experiences are differentially incorporated, and now there is evidence that this probably occurs at the group level as well. While it is true that any sizable human group contains substantial genetic variability, the gene pool basis for certain intergroup differences in temperament and motor abilities appears to be an empirically demonstrated fact. It is clear, however, that this area demands much more data, and in the next few years present speculation will doubtless give way to discussion based on more facts.

It should be pointed out now that the argument that group differences at birth may be due to differences in the intrauterine environment and not to genes would appear to beg the question. Aside from the fact that there are no supporting data or even reasonable hypothetical mechanisms for passing on temperament and nonpathological motor differences via the placental barrier, one usually ends such an argument by necessarily posing an "innate" teacher. Freedman (29) discusses this issue at some length and concludes that these data can be dealt with only within a monistic framework. Such dichotomies as culture and biology, environment and heredity are there seen as abstract artificialities and of limited use in certain statistical procedures. When reified, these dichotomizations foster the fruitless debate that has, for example, characterized the recent feuding between sociobiologists and their detractors. For a cyberneticist view reaching essentially the same conclusions see Bateson (7a).

SEX DIFFERENCES

Sex is a biological distinction which frequently enters anthropological discussion (6, 19, 60, 61). Recently there have been a number of cross-cultural studies using systematic observations of children's behavior within naturalistic settings which include findings on sex differences. In the following section we shall begin by reviewing this cross-cultural research, which suggests that prepubertal boys and girls differ with respect to aggression, dominance, nurturance, and movement in space. We then discuss directions future research of these phenomena could take.

Aggression, Dominance, and Rough-and-Tumble Play

Cross-cultural studies of play among prepubertal children support the observation that boys and girls differ in amount of aggression, dominance-seeking, and rough-and-tumble play found in comparable studies of British and American children. An argument can be made that if boys and girls in very different cultures consistently exhibit the same behavioral differences, those differences seem likely to involve biological factors. Maccoby & Jacklin (56), for example, used this argument along with several other kinds of evidence to conclude that aggression has some biological basis.

Much of the work of the Whitings and their associates has been aimed at this question of universal sex differences across various cultures. In the six-culture study (89), the behavior of children in India, Kenya, Mexico, Okinawa, Taiwan, and the United States was recorded in paragraph form. These behavior records were later coded into acts and adverbial qualifiers which were then categorized into larger classes of behavior such as aggression, nurturance, etc. In all cultures except the Gusii (Kenya), where the differences seemed negligible, boys tended to be more aggressive than girls as measured by frequency of insults, assaults, and play fighting. When the boys and the girls of all six cultures were grouped (N = 120), boys were significantly more aggressive than girls. In this study, aggression decreased with age, leading the Whitings to the conclusion that aggression was probably not simply a result of learning. Dominance, defined as seeking attention (e.g. clowning or bragging) or seeking dominance (e.g. attempts to subordinate or command), was found to increase with age. By this definition, boys were more dominant than girls in the older age period (8–11), but not in the younger age period (3–7).

In a later unpublished paper, Whiting and Edwards report that sex differences in aggression and dominance were replicated when data from five more African cultures were combined with the original six-culture study. In this report the behavior was differentiated by whether the boys and girls were interacting with their mothers, other children, or infants. In contrast to the earlier study, aggression was not seen to decrease with age, and it tended to be more physical among the oldest boys. Also, the oldest boys were found to direct their dominant/aggressive behavior less toward mothers and infants and more toward peers than did the younger boys.

Omark, Omark & Edelman (70) independently observed similar male-female differences in Ethiopia, Switzerland, and the United States. The children (N = 950), who ranged in age from 4 to 10 years, were observed playing on school playgrounds during recess. The procedures used involved observing a target child and the three nearest children for 30 seconds. The following information was recorded: the three neighbors' distance from the target, and whether the target child or his/her neighbors were talking, imitating each other, fighting, or physically aggressive (e.g. hitting, punching or pulling down when not smiling). In all three cultures, boys were significantly more aggressive than girls. The children were also asked to rank their classmates on toughness. To make sure the word "tough" was understood, they were told a story about a child who successfully competed for money or candy thrown into a crowd. In all cultures, each classroom's hierarchical structure, based on perceptions of toughness, included more boys at the top and more girls near the bottom. Also, the boys were more in agreement about their hierarchy than were the girls, suggesting its greater salience for them.

Blurton Jones & Konner's study (8) comparing British and !Kung Bushmen children also replicated sex differences in aggression, but raises further questions. They compared 3- to 6-year-old !Kung Bushmen children (N = 23) in four villages and age-matched children in three London playgroups (N = 21). Considering frequency of acts, boys were more aggressive than girls in both cultures (although since boys had more social acts in total, the proportion of total acts that were aggressive did not differ for London boys and girls). Boys in both cultures also engaged in rough-and-tumble play more than girls. This difference was pronounced in the London sample, but it did not reach significance in the !Kung sample. A similar pattern held for sex differences in activity. London boys were significantly more active than London girls, and there was no difference between Bushmen boys and girls. Thus, we are left with a puzzle as to why there is less behavioral differentiation between !Kung Bushmen boys and girls or why there is greater differentiation in the London sample.

Nurturance and Cooperation

Evidence that girls are more nurturant than boys can be found in studies of young children in Western nursery schools (13, 59). The cross-cultural observations done by the Whitings and associates have also shown a tendency for girls aged 5 through 12 to be proportionately more nurturant (i.e. to offer help and emotional support). In the first reports (88, 89), there was a question whether the fact that girls were more often assigned to take care of younger children accounted for these results. However, the later unpublished analysis, which differentiated interaction partner, revealed that girls were more nurturant than boys when interacting with infants and with same-sex children of their own age or younger. Also, by age 5 daughters were more nurturant toward their mothers.

Whiting & Edwards (88) also reported that girls were significantly more compliant to their mothers' commands and suggestions in the assignment of tasks and attempts to regulate social behavior. They speculated that this tendency for girls to be more cooperative could be one reason mothers more often assigned girls economic and child care responsibilities.

Movement in Space and Proximity to Adults and Peers

A second theme which persists in the observational literature of human and other animals has to do with spatial movement and relations with conspecifics. Two subthemes, which may be related, can be distinguished: (*a*) greater male movement in space and (*b*) greater male proximity to peers and greater female proximity to adults.

Observing the play of 5- to 7-year-old children in eight cultures (Japanese, Balinese, Kikuyu, Punjabi, Ceylonese, Taiwanese, Australian aboriginal, and Navajo), Freedman (28) noted that boys in these cultures tended to run in larger groups, cover more physical space, and do more physical and unpredictable activities. In general, girls seemed to hold more conversations and to be involved in games with repeated movements.

A number of cross-cultural observations of distance away from home yield quite similar results. Girls have usually been found closer to home than boys (21, 65, 88). Whiting & Edwards (88) hypothesized that the sex difference in distance from home which they observed may have reflected socialization pressure and differential task assignment. They argued that the assignment of babysitting and domestic chores to girls, training imposed for future roles, kept girls closer to home. Although there usually are different expectations and tasks for boys and girls, it is quite likely that males and females bring different behavioral preferences or learning potentials to the situation. This issue was addressed by Draper (21), who took advantage of her opportunity to observe !Kung Bushmen children living in two different situations. Using spot observations of 77 !Kung Bushmen children, Draper found that both settled and unsettled boys were found farther from home than girls. In the unsettled group the children were usually playing, therefore differential task assignment did not account for the difference. In the settled group, where the adults were engaged in subsistence activities near the home for longer periods, girls were more often employed as child caretakers and errand runners. Draper argues that when needed, girls were asked to help more often because they were found within closer range to adults and home. Thus, proximity to adults and home was hypothesized to become the basis for greater differentiation.

Another study reported by Whiting and Edwards in the later unpublished report involved the use of spot observations of 5- to 7-year-olds in seven societies (three in Kenya, two in Guatemala, one in Peru, and one in the United States). In contrast to their previous findings, no sex differences were observed in the distance from home. In this study it may have been important to differentiate voluntary and assigned excursions from home, since the girls were more often found working (including distant errands and home tasks), and they participated in herding activities as often as the boys.

In general, these studies suggest that it is time to elaborate or consider alternatives to the socialization-by-differential-tasks explanation of sex differences in spatial movement. Are boys more attracted to areas away from the home or adults for their play? It is possible that the difference in spatial range reflects boys' interest in rowdy, aggressive play, which may be tolerated only at a distance from adults? Whiting and Edwards' unpublished data do seem to weaken the hypothesis that dependence is a likely cause of the sex differences in spatial range. Young boys were found to be more dependent (seek help or attention) with their mothers than young girls, and there were no sex differences at the older ages. With the finding that girls were more responsible, more compliant to demands, and more nurturant (offer food, care, help, or attention) toward their mothers, Whiting & Edwards (88) have recently revised their shaping-via-assigned-tasks explanation of sex differences:

> However, before concluding that mothers' differential behavior to girls and boys is the *cause* of sex differences in children's behavior, it would be necessary to rule out the possibility that the mothers' differential behavior is not wholly or simply the *result* of behavior that girls versus boys present to the mothers. Longitudinal study would be the method of choice to examine such a question. We believe, however, that the most likely state of affairs (at least with respect to these behaviors) is that boys and girls present somewhat different behaviors to parents but that these are magnified by socialization pressures. That is, girls may receive more task commands because they are more accepting of them, and boys may "elicit" more reprimands from mothers. Yet mothers may intensify these sex differences in the children through their social behavior.

In several of the cross-cultural studies reviewed, there was a greater tendency for boys to interact with other boys and for girls to interact with adults (8, 21, 89). There was also evidence of segregation by sex among the children (8, 70, 88). Blurton Jones and Konner found that males tended to choose males for playmates over females in their London sample, but not among the !Kung Bushmen children. They analyzed whether the subject was interacting with a boy or girl, given the number of proximate boys and girls. In London, sex segregation was largely due to the males' preference for males, while females seemed not to prefer one sex over the other. Since the Bushmen girls engaged in rough-and-tumble play more often than London girls, the authors suggested that perhaps the Bushmen girls were more attractive partners for play to the boys. This hypothesis seems promising because the presence of other young males has been found to stimulate activity and rough-and-tumble play in preschool boys more than in girls (13). However, Draper (21) suggested an alternative explanation for the lack of sex segregation found among !Kung Bushmen children. Since band size is usually only 35–40 people, there are rarely children of the same sex at the same ages. Thus among the Bushmen, clusters of children tend to be heterogeneous with respect to age and sex.

As a final note to our review of cross-cultural sex differences, it can be mentioned that the drawings of 5- to 7-year-old children in nine cultures seem to confirm the behavioral differences observed (28). When asked to draw whatever they wished, each sex drew more same-sex figures. Boys drew significantly more monsters and vehicles, while girls drew more flowers. Though cultural differences were evident, these sex differences remained. For example, in Bali where all children drew flowers, boys more often included vehicles also. Navajo and Kikuyu girls drew more vehicles than the boys in some cultures, but in each case the Kikuyu and Navajo boys drew significantly more vehicles than the girls. If we think of pictures as an expression of interest, it appears that boys' interests lie more in themes of violence and threat as represented by monsters and movement in space as seen in the vehicles.

Thus, we find some fairly robust differences between boys and girls in nurturance, motility, and in real and play forms of aggression. These areas would seem to be a good starting point for future work aimed at trying to understand the function of these phenomena and the developmental processes which lead to them. The distinction between function or adaptive significance (ultimate cause) and ontogeny (proximate causes) is worth making. Functional explanations are appropriate for considering evolved behavioral characteristics at the population level, but not at the individual level (3, 58). In other words, while there may be information encoded in the genome which results in behavioral differences between sexes, this does not mean that at the individual level, learning or context-specific experience is not necessary for the expression of sex differences.

Adaptive Function

From an evolutionary perspective the question of adaptive function arises. That is, given the ecological and social characteristics of the population, what selective advantages does a phenomenon have for those who possess it? Classical evolutionary reasoning leads to the premise that males and females differ in reproductive strategy due to their physiological differences. The offspring of animals who are better able to survive and reproduce will tend to inherit characteristics advantageous to reproductive success. Especially in mammalian species, males have greater gametic potential, and in most species relatively few males inseminate a large portion of females. In the Yanomamö, a polygynous human society (17), there is some 10 times more variance in males' number of offspring than in females, who cluster about the mean in number of offspring. This is not atypical, and physical and behavioral characteristics which increase a male's advantage in competition with other males for the opportunity to mate should be a strongly selected attribute. Evolutionary selection, then, is said to occur primarily through the mammalian male, and the higher variance in mortality, aggression, and mating within that sex is taken as evidence for this somewhat circular assertion.

In species where there is potential for injury and fatal results from fighting, various social systems operate which appear to control the effects of aggression. Two common means are territoriality and dominance hierarchies. When there are advantages for animals to live in groups or when space is limited, some system of dominant-subordinate relations tends to develop. Although some scientists believe that hierarchical systems in primate species may be situation-specific and more complex than presently formulated, the organization of power and dominance certainly holds considerable promise for unraveling the adaptive function of behavioral sex differences such as aggression and rough-and-tumble play.

Since the form of rough-and-tumble play resembles some aspects of agonistic behavior, it may be a precursor of or practice for skills used in more serious fighting or for intermale competition such as sports. Savin-Williams (74) found that athletic ability was correlated with the dominance rank of adolescents in summer camp. Weisfeld (85) found the same trend in early high school. That academic achievement proved of little predictive value in social ranking in this latter setting was impressive since the study was done in a university laboratory school populated largely by academically achieving children of university professors. However, achievement became more predictive of rank in the older, college-bound students. Using longitudinal data, Weisfeld also found that rank on "toughness" in early grade school boys, perhaps reflecting a tendency to fight or engage in rough-and-tumble play, was correlated with the boys' rank in being dominant, athletic, good-looking, leadership-oriented and desirable to girls in early high school. Thus, it appears that "toughness" has a lasting effect, and rough-and-tumble play could have adaptive value for attracting and learning how to attract females as well as impressing other males.

It is interesting that there are some cultural differences in the degree of sex differentiation. For example, Gusii boys and girls did not differ in amount of aggression (89), and !Kung Bushmen girls were less differentiated from boys with respect to activity and rough-and-tumble play (8). These findings raise the issue of how such cultural differences in sexual differentiation come about and why they are adaptive in the social and ecological conditions where they are found. Do situational factors account for the differences? Are there less treatment differences in these cultures? Are these populations inherently more androgynous? Are these traits adaptive in courtship and parenting practices, given the social and ecological context within which they operate?

How female social organization and competitive strategies differ from and complement that of males is first being addressed by behavioral scientists (71). Adolescent girls in a summer camp had dominant-submissive relationships, but the strong hierarchical form of organization found in the boys' groups was not evident (74). Cronin et al (18) report that girls were inhibited in cross-sex competitive games whether or not the boys were more skilled than they were. They suggest that young females of courtship age are "specialists" in appeasement behavior, a suggestion enhanced by a series of studies which demonstrate lower thresholds to social smiling among females. These studies range from the newborn period through adulthood and include data among Anglo, Afro-American, Navajo, Hopi, and Australian Aboriginals (29).

Ontogeny

A second research direction for which cross-cultural study may be very useful is the study of the ontogeny of sex differences. Although finding sex differences in widely different cultures implies that there is a biological contribution, we need not assume biological determinism. Innate and environmental factors simultaneously affect and are affected by each other in a dynamic open system. Our objective will be to identify the relevant variables in such a system and determine how they are interrelated within the developmental process. This is of special concern in the human species where the process of sexual differentiation is likely to be even more of an open system (37).

There is considerable evidence that at a critical period of embryological development testosterone has a permanent organizing effect on the developing organism. Testosterone is normally secreted by the testes of the male fetus, and acts to masculinize the reproductive tract and the nervous system. In the absence of testosterone these systems develop in the female pattern. This process is inferred from the changes in behavior observed in female animals experimentally masculinized and male animals who were castrated during their critical period of sexual development (38, 73, 91). For example, masculinized female rhesus monkeys whose mothers were administered androgens during the critical period in gestation developed male genitalia and their behavior included more aggression, threats, mounting, rough-and-tumble play and initiation of play than a control group of females (91).

In humans, the administration of progestin, which has androgenic action, to pregnant women had a masculinizing effect on their female offspring. Studies of such girls revealed that they tended to prefer playing with boys and playing outdoors more than did a control group (64) or their own sisters (23).

Thus, we suspect that the presence of androgens at a certain period of prenatal development may play an important part in the differentiation of physiological and neural structures which somehow interact with environmental factors to produce differences in sexual and aggressive behavior in later life. A number of speculations have been made along these lines (20, 22, 51, 77). The basic idea is that a behavioral sex difference or predisposition can either result in different outcomes given the same treatment or can induce different treatment. The different outcome or treatment can then have an amplifying effect on the original difference. For example, greater size and muscularity in male infants (81) may encourage treatment emphasizing physical play which then contributes to greater skill development in the physical area. Earlier and more vocalization in the female (42) may encourage more conversational play which could contribute to greater ability and use of communication skills. Other affiliative characteristics attributed to the female infant such as more smiling (27, 50) or greater interest in social stimuli (44, 55) are likely to have a similar result. Thus, parents' expectations, derived from previous experience with the child and from general cultural beliefs and expectations (wherever they come from) about sex differences and roles, could affect the degree to which behavior is attributed with meaning and responded to or neglected.

When an undesirable characteristic is distributed differently between the sexes as irritability seems to be in American infants (66, 67), a negative feedback system may operate. In these instances a difference would diminish with time because the parent learns ways to prevent or stop the undesired event, but even though the original difference may diminish, differential treatment is the result. A process such as this could explain why Moss (66) found that 3-month-old boys in his sample were more irritable, while Lewis (54) found no sex differences in irritability in infants of the same age. In Lewis's sample, mothers of boys held their babies more than mothers of girls, possibly to prevent crying or as a result of responding to crying. The understanding of such interactive processes is then a promising direction for research in the development of sex differences.

CONCLUSION

Our conclusion is that there is more to biology than genes, chromosomes, and physiology. When Rhesus macaque troops form intra- and intergroup dominance-submission hierarchies as on Cayo Santiago Island, that too is biology, and when comparable behavior is seen in human groups, it is difficult to shunt aside the notion of homology. For just as ethologists hold that the demonstration of what is innate or hereditary involves a *difference* between two populations in which environment has been held constant, so is it required that the "purely" cultural as "purely" learned rests on a demonstrated difference between two genetically similar populations. Since for anthropologists neither experiment is feasible, we are left with the essential inseparability of the biological and the cultural, the inherited and the acquired.

Seen as an epistemological problem, the solution to this recurrent conundrum would seem to be that culture and biology are not coequal poles of a dichotomy at all, but rather are two differing and noncomparable "logical types" (7a). In any event, the lesson of this review, if taken to heart, can cause a revolution in anthropology, the science par excellence of the "two cultures." The time for such questions as "Is it cultural or biological?" has passed, for these two are, to paraphrase Bateson (7a), a necessary unity.

Literature Cited

1. Ainsworth, M. 1967. *Infancy in Uganda.* New York: Academic
2. Ambrose, J. A., ed. 1969. *Stimulation in Early Infancy.* New York: Academic
3. Archer, J. 1976. Biological explanations of psychological sex differences. In *Exploring Sex Differences,* ed. B. Lloyd, J. Archer, pp. 241–66. New York: Academic
4. Barkow, J. H. 1967. The causal interpretation of correlation in cross-cultural studies. *Am. Anthropol.* 69:506–10
5. Barnouw, V. 1963. *Culture and Personality.* Homewood, Ill: Dorsey
6. Barry, H., Bacon, M. K., Child, I. L. 1957. A cross-cultural survey of some sex differences in socialization. *J. Abnorm. Soc. Psychol.* 55:327–32
7. Bateson, G., Mead, M. 1942. Karba's first years. Film: 16mm sound., New York Univ. Film Libr.
7a. Bateson, G. 1979. *Mind and Nature: A Necessary Unity.* New York: Dutton
8. Blurton Jones, N. B., Konner, M. 1973. Sex differences in behavior of London and Bushman children. In *Comparative Ecology and Behavior of Primates,* ed.

R. P. Michael, J. H. Crook, pp. 690–749. London: Academic
9. Boyd, W. C. 1950. *Genetics and the Races of Man.* Boston: Little, Brown
10. Brazelton, T. B. 1973. *Neonatal Behavioral Scale.* Philadelphia: Lippincott
11. Brazelton, T. B., Freedman, D. G. 1971. The Cambridge neonatal scales. In *Normal and Abnormal Development of Brain and Behavior,* ed. G. B. A. Stoelinga, J. J. van der Werften Bosch, pp. 104–32. Leiden: Leiden Univ. Press
12. Brazelton, T. B., Koslowski, B., Tronick, E. 1976. Neonatal behavior among urban Zambians and Americans. *J. Am. Acad. Child Psychiatry* 15:97–108
12a. Brazelton, T. B., Robey, J. S., Scholl, M. L. 1966. Infant development in the Zinacanteco Indians of Southern Mexico. *Pediatrics* 44:274–83
13. Brindley, C., Clark, P., Hutt, C., Robinson, I., Wethli, E. 1973. Sex differences in the activities and social interactions of nursery school children. See Ref. 8
14. Callaghan, J. W. 1977. *Anglo, Hopi and Navajo mothers' face-to-face interaction*

with their infants. MA thesis. Univ. Chicago, Chicago, Ill.

15. Caudill, W., Frost, L. 1975. A comparison of maternal care and infant behavior in Japanese-American, American and Japanese families. In *Influences on Human Development,* ed. U. Bronfenbrenner, J. A. Mahoney. Hinsdale, Ill: Dryden

16. Caudill, W., Weinstein, H. 1969. Maternal care and infant behavior in Japan and America. *Psychiatry* 32:12–43

17. Chagnon, N. A., Irons, W., eds. 1979. *Evolutionary Biology and Human Social Behavior: An Anthropological Perspective.* North Scituate, Mass: Duxbury

18. Cronin, C., Callaghan, J. W., Weisfeld, G. E. 1977. *Sex differences in competitive behavior in children.* Presented at Meet. Anim. Beh. Soc., Univ. Park, Pa.

19. D'Andrade, R. G. 1966. Sex differences and cultural institutions. In *The Development of Sex Differences,* ed. E. E. Maccoby. Stanford, Calif.: Stanford Univ. Press

20. Draper, P. 1974. Comparative studies of socialization. *Ann. Rev. Anthropol.* 3:263–77

21. Draper, P. 1975. Cultural pressure on sex differences. *Am. Ethnol.* (4):602–16

22. Draper, P. 1975. Sex differences in cognitive styles: socialization and constitutional variables. In *Council on Anthropology and Education Quarterly,* ed. B. Fogleman, A. S. Nihlen, Vol. 6

23. Ehrhardt, A. A., Baker, S. W. 1973. *Hormone aberrations and their implications for the understanding of normal sex differentiation.* Presented at Soc. Res. Child Dev., Philadelphia

24. Escalona, S. K. 1968. *The Roots of Individuality.* Chicago: Aldine

25. Freedman, D. G. 1958. Constitutional and environmental interactions in rearing of four breeds of dogs. *Science* 127:585–86

26. Freedman, D. G. 1971. Genetic influences on development of behavior. See Ref. 11

27. Freedman, D. G. 1974. *Human Infancy.* New York: Halsted Press, Wiley

28. Freedman, D. G. 1976. Infancy, biology and culture. In *Developmental Psychology,* ed. L. P. Lipsitt. New York: Halsted, Wiley

29. Freedman, D. G. 1979. *Human Sociobiology: A Holistic Approach.* New York: Free Press

30. Freedman, D. G., Freedman, N. C. 1969. Differences in behavior between Chinese-American and European-American newborns. *Nature* 224:1227

31. Fuller, J. L., Thompson, W. R. 1960. *Behavior Genetics.* New York: Wiley

32. Garn, S. M., Bailey, S. M. 1978. The genetics of the maturational process. In *Human Growth, Vol. 1: Principles and Prenatal Growth,* ed. F. Faulkner, J. M. Tanner. New York: Plenum

33. Geber, M. 1958. The psychomotor development of African children in the first year and the influence of maternal behavior. *J. Soc. Psychol.* 47:185–95

34. Geber, M., Dean, R. F. A. 1957. The state of development in newborn African children. *Lancet* 1:1216–19

35. Geber, M., Dean, R. F. A. 1958. Psychomotor development in African children: The effects of social class and the need for improved tests. *Bull. WHO* 18:471–76

36. Hallet, J. P. 1975. The Pygmies of the Ituri Forest. Film: 16mm sound, *Encyclopedia Britannica*

37. Hamburg, D. A. 1971. Recent research on hormonal factors relevant to human aggressiveness. *Int. Soc. Sci. J.* 23: 36–47

38. Harris, G. W. 1964. Sex hormones, brain development and brain function. *Endocrinology* 75:627–48

39. Honigmann, J. J. 1967. *Personality in Culture.* New York: Harper & Row

40. Hopkins, B. 1976. *Considerations of comparability of measures in cross-cultural studies of early infancy from a study in the development of black and white infants living in Britain.* Presented at Int. Assoc. Cross-cult. Psychol. Congr. 3rd, Tilburg

41. Hopkins, B. n.d. Tabulated summary of comparative studies of psychomotor development involving black and white infants. Groningen: The Netherlands. Special report, Dep. Dev. Neurol.

42. Hutt, C. 1972. *Males and Females.* Baltimore: Penguin

43. Jumonville, J. 1968. *Influence of genotype-treatment interaction in studies of emotionality in mice.* PhD thesis. Univ. Chicago, Chicago, Ill.

44. Kagan, J. 1971. *Change and Continuity in Infancy.* New York: Wiley

45. Kagan, J., Klein, R. E. 1975. Cross-cultural perspectives on early development. In *Life: The Continuous Process,* ed. F. Rebelsky. New York: Knopf

46. Kilbride, J. E., Kilbride, P. L. 1975. Sitting and smiling behavior of Baganda infants. *J. Cross-Cult. Psychol.* 6:88–107

47. Kluckhohn, C. 1962. *Culture and Behavior; Collected Essays.* New York: Free Press

48. Kluckhohn, C., Leighton, D. 1946. *The Navajo.* Cambridge, Mass: Harvard Univ. Press

49. Konner, M. 1977. Infancy among the Kalahari Desert San. In *Culture and Infancy,* ed. H. Leiderman. New York: Academic

50. Korner, A. 1969. Neonatal startles, smiles, erections and reflex sucks as related to state, sex and individuality. *Child Dev.* 40:1039–53

51. Korner, A. 1974. The effect of the infant's state, level of arousal, sex and ontogenetic state on the caregiver. In *The Effect of the Infant on its Caregiver,* ed. M. Lewis, L. A. Rosenblum, pp. 105–21. New York: Wiley

52. Kuchner, J. 1979. *Chinese- and European-Americans: A cross-cultural study of infants and mothers.* PhD thesis. Univ. Chicago, Chicago, Ill.

53. Leiderman, P. H., Babu, B., Kagia, J., Kraemer, H. C., Leiderman, G. F. 1973. African infant precocity and some social influences during the first year. *Nature* 242:247–49

54. Lewis, M. 1972. State as an infant-environment interaction: An analysis of mother-infant behavior as a function of sex. *Merrill-Palmer Q.* 18:95–121

55. Lewis, M., Kagan, J., Kalafat, J. 1966. Patterns of fixation in the young infant. *Child Dev.* 37:331–41

56. Maccoby, E. E., Jacklin, C. N. 1974. *The Psychology of Sex Differences.* Stanford, Calif: Stanford Univ. Press

57. Marshall, W. A., Tanner, J. M. 1970. Skeletal maturation of the hand and wrist in Jamaican children. *Hum. Biol.* 42:419

58. McClintock, M. K. 1979. Innate behavior is not innate: comment on Alice Rossi's "A biosocial perspective on parenting." *Signs.* In press

59. McGrew, W. C. 1972. Aspects of social development in nursery school children with emphasis on introduction to the group. In *Ethnological Studies of Child Behaviour,* ed. N. Blurton Jones. Cambridge: Cambridge Univ. Press

60. Mead, M. 1935. *Sex and Temperament in Three Primitive Societies.* New York: Morrow

61. Mead, M. 1949. *Male and Female.* New York: Morrow

62. Mead, M., MacGregor, F. C. 1951. *Growth and Culture.* New York: Putnam

63. Mischel, W. 1973. Towards a cognitive social learning reconceptualization of personality. *Psychol. Rev.* 80:252–83

64. Money, J., Ehrhardt, A. A. 1968. Prenatal hormone exposure: possible effects on behavior in man. In *Endocrinology and Human Behavior,* ed. R. Michael. London: Oxford Univ. Press

65. Monroe, R. L., Monroe, R. H. 1971. Effect of environmental experiences on spatial ability in an East African society. *J. Soc. Psychol.* 83:3–10

66. Moss, H. A. 1967. Sex, age and state as determinants of mother-infant interaction. *Merrill-Palmer Q.* 13:19–36

67. Moss, H. A. 1974. Early sex differences and mother-infant interaction. In *Sex Differences in Behavior,* ed. R. C. Friedman, R. M. Richart, R. L. Vande Wiele, pp. 149–63. New York: Wiley

68. Murphy, L. B. 1962. *The Widening World of Childhood.* New York: Basic Books

69. Nisselius, J. K. 1976. *Behavioral assessment of the Navajo newborn.* MA thesis. Univ. Utah, Salt Lake City, Utah

70. Omark, D. R., Omark, M., Edelman, M. 1975. Formation of dominance hierarchies in young children: action and perspective. In *Psychological Anthropology,* ed. T. Williams. The Hague: Mouton

71. Omark, D. R., Strayer, F., Freedman, D. G., eds. 1979. *Human Dominance Hierarchies.* New York: Garland

72. Orlansky, H. 1949. Infant care and personality. *Psychol. Bull.* 46:19–23

73. Phoenix, C. H., Goy, R. W., Resko, J. A. 1968. Psychosexual differentiation as a function of androgenic stimulation. In *Perspectives in Reproductive and Sexual Behavior,* ed. H. Diamond. Bloomington: Indiana Univ. Press

74. Savin-Williams, R. 1977. *Dominance-submission behaviors and hierarchies in young adolescents at a summer camp: predictors, styles, and sex differences.* PhD thesis. Univ. Chicago, Chicago, Ill.

75. Sewell, W. H. 1952. Infant training and the personality of the child. *Am. J. Sociol.* 58:150–59

76. Shafer, R. 1952. Athapaskan and Sino-Tibetan. *Int. J. Am. Ling.* 18:12–19

77. Sherman, J. A. 1967. Problems of sex differences in space perception and aspects of intellectual functioning. *Psychol. Rev.* 75:290–99

78. Shweder, R. A. 1979. Rethinking psychological anthropology. Part I. A critical examination of the classical postulates. *Ethos.* In press

79. Super, C. M. 1973. Patterns of infant care and motor development in Kenya. *Kenya Educ. Rev.* 1(1):64–69

80. Super, C. M. 1979. Behavioral development in infancy. In *Handbook of Cross-Cultural Human Development,* ed. R. L. Monroe, R. H. Monroe, B. B. Whiting. New York: Garland
81. Tanner, J. M. 1974. Variability of growth and maturity in newborn infants. See Ref. 51, pp. 77–103
82. Terman, L. M. et al. 1925. *Genetic Studies of Genius, Vol. 1: Mental and Physical Traits of a Thousand Gifted Children.* Stanford: Stanford Univ. Press
83. Wallace, A. F. C. 1970. *Culture and Personality.* New York: Random House
84. Warren, N. 1972. African infant precocity. *Psychol. Bull.* 78:353–67
85. Warren, N., Parkin, J. M. 1974. A neurological and behavioral comparison of African and European newborns in Uganda. *Child Dev.* 45:966–71
86. Weisfeld, G. E. 1978. *Determinants and behavioral correlates of dominance in adolescent boys.* PhD thesis. Univ. Chicago, Chicago, Ill.
87. Werner, E. E. 1972. Infants around the world: cross-cultural studies of psychomotor development from birth to two years. *J. Cross-Cult. Psychol.* 3:111–34
88. Whiting, B., Edwards, C. P. 1973. A cross-cultural analysis of sex differences in the behavior of children aged 3 to 11. *J. Soc. Psychol.* 91:171–88
89. Whiting, B. B., Whiting, J. W. M. 1975. *Children of Six Cultures: A Psycho-Cultural Analysis.* Cambridge, Mass: Harvard Univ. Press
90. Witherspoon, G. 1977. *Language and Art in the Navajo Universe.* Ann Arbor: Univ. Michigan Press
91. Young, W. C., Goy, R. W., Phoenix, C. H. 1964. Hormones and sexual behavior. *Science* 143:212–18

AUTHOR INDEX

SUBJECT INDEX

CUMULATIVE INDEXES

CONTRIBUTING AUTHORS, VOLUMES 4–8

CHAPTER TITLES, VOLUMES 4–8